RESEARCH HANDBOOK ON THE REGULATION OF MUTUAL FUNDS

RESEARCH HANDBOOKS IN CORPORATE LAW AND GOVERNANCE

Series Editor: Randall S. Thomas, *John S. Beasley II Professor of Law and Business, Vanderbilt University Law School, USA*

Elgar *Research Handbooks* are original reference works designed to provide a broad overview of research in a given field while at the same time creating a forum for more challenging, critical examination of complex and often under-explored issues within that field. Chapters by international teams of contributors are specially commissioned by editors who carefully balance breadth and depth. Often widely cited, individual chapters present expert scholarly analysis and offer a vital reference point for advanced research. Taken as a whole they achieve a wide-ranging picture of the state-of-the-art.

Making a major scholarly contribution to the field of corporate law and governance, the volumes in this series explore topics of current concern from a range of jurisdictions and perspectives, offering a comprehensive analysis that will inform researchers, practitioners and students alike. The *Research Handbooks* cover the fundamental aspects of corporate law, such as insolvency governance structures, as well as hot button areas such as executive compensation, insider trading, and directors' duties. The *Handbooks*, each edited by leading scholars in their respective fields, offer far-reaching examinations of current issues in corporate law and governance that are unrivalled in their blend of critical, substantive analysis, and in their synthesis of contemporary research.

Each *Handbook* stands alone as an invaluable source of reference for all scholars of corporate law, as well as for practicing lawyers who wish to engage with the discussion of ideas within the field. Whether used as an information resource on key topics or as a platform for advanced study, volumes in this series will become definitive scholarly reference works in the field.

Titles in this series include:

Research Handbook on Shareholder Power
Edited by Jennifer G. Hill and Randall S. Thomas

Research Handbook on Partnerships, LLCs and Alternative Forms of Business Organizations
Edited by Robert W. Hillman and Mark J. Loewenstein

Research Handbook on Mergers and Acquisitions
Edited by Claire A. Hill and Steven Davidoff Solomon

Research Handbook on the History of Corporate and Company Law
Edited by Harwell Wells

Research Handbook on Corporate Crime and Financial Misdealing
Edited by Jennifer Arlen

Research Handbook on Fiduciary Law
Edited by Gordon Smith and Andrew Gold

Research Handbook on the Regulation of Mutual Funds
Edited by William A. Birdthistle and John Morley

Research Handbook on the Regulation of Mutual Funds

Edited by

William A. Birdthistle
Chicago-Kent College of Law at Illinois Institute of Technology, USA

John Morley
Yale Law School, USA

RESEARCH HANDBOOKS IN CORPORATE LAW AND GOVERNANCE

Cheltenham, UK • Northampton, MA, USA

© The Author and Contributors Severally 2018

All rights reserved. No part of this publication may be reproduced, stored in a retrieval system or transmitted in any form or by any means, electronic, mechanical or photocopying, recording, or otherwise without the prior permission of the publisher.

Published by
Edward Elgar Publishing Limited
The Lypiatts
15 Lansdown Road
Cheltenham
Glos GL50 2JA
UK

Edward Elgar Publishing, Inc.
William Pratt House
9 Dewey Court
Northampton
Massachusetts 01060
USA

A catalogue record for this book
is available from the British Library

Library of Congress Control Number: 2018944056

This book is available electronically in the Elgaronline
Law subject collection
DOI 10.4337/9781784715052

ISBN 978 1 78471 504 5 (cased)
ISBN 978 1 78471 505 2 (eBook)

Typeset by Columns Design XML Ltd, Reading
Printed and bound by CPI Group (UK) Ltd, Croydon, CR0 4YY

Contents

List of contributors	vii
Introduction to the *Research Handbook on the Regulation of Monetary Funds* William A. Birdthistle and John Morley	1

PART I THE ROLE AND REGULATION OF INVESTMENT FUNDS

1	Why do investment funds have special securities regulation? *John Morley*	9
2	The rise and fall of the mutual fund brand *Mercer Bullard*	22
3	Fiduciary contours: perspectives on mutual funds and private funds *Deborah A. DeMott*	57
4	The fiduciary structure of investment management regulation *Arthur B. Laby*	79

PART II IDENTITY AND BEHAVIOR OF MUTUAL FUND INVESTORS

5	Who are mutual fund investors? *Alan Palmiter*	112
6	Protecting mutual fund investors: an inevitable eclecticism *Lyman P.Q. Johnson*	141
7	The past and present of mutual fund fee litigation under section 36(b) *Quinn Curtis*	164
8	Toward better mutual fund governance *Anita K. Krug*	185
9	Mutual fund compliance: key developments and their implications *James Fanto*	205

PART III THE BROADER RANGE OF INVESTMENT FUNDS

10	Tales from the dark side: money market funds and the shadow banking debate *Jill E. Fisch*	228
11	Exchange-traded funds: neither fish nor fowl *Eric D. Roiter*	247

12	Free funds: retirement savings as public infrastructure *William A. Birdthistle*	267
13	Confluence of mutual and hedge funds *Wulf A. Kaal*	278

PART IV INTERNATIONAL PERSPECTIVES ON INVESTMENT FUNDS

14	The anatomy of European investment fund law *Dirk A. Zetzsche*	302
15	Governance aspects of mutual funds in Ireland *Blanaid Clarke and Mark White*	360
16	Regulating collective retail investment funds in the United Kingdom with the objective of investor protection, and some implications *Iris H-Y Chiu*	382
17	Regulation of mutual funds in Australia *Pamela Hanrahan and Ian Ramsay*	414
Index		447

Contributors

William A. Birdthistle, Chicago-Kent College of Law, USA

Mercer Bullard, The University of Mississippi School of Law, USA

Iris H-Y Chiu, University College London Faculty of Laws, United Kingdom

Blanaid Clarke, Trinity College Dublin School of Law, Ireland

Quinn Curtis, University of Virginia School of Law, USA

Deborah A. DeMott, Duke University School of Law, USA

James Fanto, Brooklyn Law School, USA

Jill E. Fisch, University of Pennsylvania Law School, USA

Pamela Hanrahan, University of New South Wales Business School, Australia

Lyman P.Q. Johnson, Washington and Lee University School of Law and University of St. Thomas School of Law, USA

Wulf A. Kaal, University of St. Thomas School of Law, USA

Anita K. Krug, University of Washington School of Law, USA

Arthur B. Laby, Rutgers Law School, USA

John Morley, Yale Law School, USA

Alan Palmiter, Wake Forest University School of Law, USA

Ian Ramsay, Melbourne Law School, Australia

Eric D. Roiter, Boston University School of Law, USA

Mark White, McCann FitzGerald, Ireland

Dirk A. Zetzsche, Université du Luxembourg, Luxembourg

Introduction to the *Research Handbook on the Regulation of Mutual Funds*
William A. Birdthistle and John Morley

Mutual funds are the way Americans invest today. In legal theory, the platonic ideal of a corporate relationship may still be the one between shareholder and firm, but, increasingly, that fundamental dyad is being intermediated by an investment fund. Whereas institutional investors owned less than 10 percent of the stock of America's largest 1,000 public companies in the 1950s, now investment funds hold more than 50 percent of public equity.[1] Some of those holdings rest in the hands of hedge funds and private equity funds, whose exotic deals and outrageous fortunes capture the public imagination. But the most ubiquitous investment vehicles—particularly for ordinary American households—are mutual funds, which today hold $22 trillion in the United States and almost $50 trillion globally.[2] The assets of these funds have long been important to the funds' shareholders, of course, but in recent years the gravitational force of mutual funds has waxed sufficiently powerful to begin to shape the broader American economic landscape and the governance of companies in which mutual funds invest.

The rise of mutual funds owes much to the shift, over the past 40 years in the United States, from defined benefit pension plans to defined contribution accounts. Since Section 401(k) was added to the Internal Revenue Code in 1978, eponymous 401(k) accounts have grown to hold more than $5 trillion dollars.[3] And within those accounts, the leading investment choice on the menu has become the mutual fund. While the defined benefit pensions that dominated retirement savings in the mid-twentieth century are overseen by relatively small groups of professional asset managers, decision-making power over defined contribution accounts such as the 401(k) and 403(b) lies in the hands of ordinary American workers. And this great mass of workers has turned to the mutual fund industry to help them carry the burden of decision-making. As 57 million American households have come to hold mutual funds not just for retirement, but also for children's education and home down payments,[4] the strengths and weaknesses of these funds have become more deeply manifest in American society.

---

[1] The Conference Board, WHAT IS THE OPTIMAL BALANCE IN THE RELATIVE ROLES OF MANAGEMENT, DIRECTORS, AND INVESTORS IN THE GOVERNANCE OF PUBLIC CORPORATIONS? 9–10 (2014).

[2] Investment Company Institute, 2017 INVESTMENT COMPANY FACT BOOK i (2017) (hereinafter "ICI Fact Book"),

[3] Investment Company Institute, Frequently Asked Questions about 401(k) Plan Research, available at www.ici.org/policy/retirement/plan/401k/faqs_401k.

[4] See *supra* note 2, ICI FACT BOOK at i.

Mutual funds manage so much money that they are now critical investors in broad swathes of the US economy. To understand how the United States—and, indeed, the world—invests, one must understand mutual funds and their related investment vehicles. This *Handbook* covers several topics that fall into at least four major categories central to the legal regulation of mutual funds today.

1 FIDUCIARIES AND FEES

Every student of business law in the United States quickly comes to learn of the critical importance of fiduciary duties to American corporations. Crudely put, in exchange for broad and far-reaching powers to direct the management of corporations, their directors and officers (and occasionally controlling shareholders) owe shareholders duties of loyalty and care, and perhaps a few other duties depending on the particular jurisdiction. Like the structural scaffolding of constitutional law, the relative powers of these branches of corporate governance determine many of the most important questions in business law.

Mutual funds are, of course, businesses also. But because of their peculiar structure—in which investors are shareholders of a mutual fund, but not necessarily of the investment adviser managing the fund—it is not obvious what duties an investment adviser owes to the fund's investors. In 1970, Congress created further confusion by imposing a fiduciary duty specific to advisory fees through the addition of Section 36(b) to the Investment Company Act of 1940. That provision states that "the investment adviser of a registered investment company [mutual fund] shall be deemed to have a fiduciary duty with respect to the receipt of compensation of services." This grafting on of a relatively new and artificial duty raises many questions that directly affect the welfare of mutual fund shareholders. Perhaps none of those questions is more important than this one: to what extent are fund managers constrained from charging high fees to fund investors?

Inasmuch as fees are the most important determinant in the returns achieved by mutual funds and, accordingly, the success or failure of shareholders' investments, the scope of the Section 36(b) fiduciary duty in mutual funds—and the efficacy of litigation to vitiate that duty—are key legal issues for funds and their investors today.

2 INVESTOR SOPHISTICATION

Investors in mutual funds can be arranged along a spectrum that spans a gulf of experience, wealth, and knowledge, ranging from large institutions at one end to small individuals at the other. Many purchasers of fund shares may naturally fall between these extremes, and their place on the spectrum may determine how well they can protect themselves in a market full of complex terms and self-interested investment advisers. Understanding the capacity of different investors to protect themselves and to manage their investments is critical to regulating the mutual funds that cater to them.

The rise of research in behavioral finance, in particular, is being embraced by scholars of mutual funds to analyze the strengths, weaknesses, intuitions, and biases of investors and then to theorize about the extent to which those behavioral tendencies may contradict more traditional assumptions of classical legal economics built into our current regulatory edifice. Where existing assumptions may be outdated, revisions to our regulatory system may be prudent.

3 FUNDS AS INVESTORS

The reach of mutual funds—and their structural cousins, such as money market funds and exchange-traded funds—continues to grow as the American and international investing public continually seeks newer and better investing tools. As these new types of funds have grown, however, they have been increasingly affecting and at times displacing existing financial ecosystems.

The systemic importance of mutual funds became clear during a pivotal moment in the financial crisis of 2008, when a money market mutual fund, the Reserve Primary Fund, dramatically failed. That fund's breaking of the buck—its inability to return 100 cents on every dollar invested—triggered a run by investors to withdraw their money not only from that fund but from many other similar funds. That stampede of investors fleeing money market funds then threatened to starve American corporations of the ready loans in the market for commercial paper upon which they rely to meet critical needs, such as regular payroll.

Scholars are exploring how funds operate in the shadow banking world and how they may affect other participants in the financial sector. Perhaps the largest public policy issue influenced by mutual funds today is the extent to which Americans are saving effectively for their retirement. Federal legislators regularly consider—though rarely enact—programs such as the Thrift Savings Plan, which is a defined contribution plan for millions of federal employees. Recently, however, state legislators have taken a more active role in enacting plans to stimulate retirement saving among broader pools of Americans. This regulatory conflict and federalist foment among states and between states and the national government is an increasing focus of attention for observers who fear that workers may not have sufficient tools to save prudent amounts for their later years.

4 INTERNATIONAL EXPANSION AND INNOVATION

Finally, the landscape of investment funds has changed dramatically since the passage of the two defining pieces of federal legislation in 1940, in at least two prominent ways: via innovation, and via international expansion.

Investment advisers are continually experimenting with new ideas for the structure and investing approach of funds, perhaps none more notable than the introduction of exchange-traded funds ("ETFs") in 1993. ETFs, which are essentially mutual funds that can be traded continuously on stock exchanges (rather than just redeemed or purchased from the issuing fund once a day, as is the case with traditional mutual funds), have attracted massive new inflows from institutional investors such as hedge funds seeking

4 *Research handbook on the regulation of mutual funds*

short-term havens for assets that retain exposure to equity returns and individual investors seeking lower fees and possible tax benefits.

The growth of mutual funds has been a truly global phenomenon and deserves a broad international analysis. Though other countries may not share the regulatory history of the United States, with its outsized emphasis on 401(k) plans, many have seen a similar decline in the importance or centrality of pension or government savings plans. Into that vacuum have stepped mutual funds or, in foreign jurisdictions, broadly equivalent pooled investment vehicles.

Just as local conditions might have spurred the growth of mutual funds at different times, so too have local political economies and legal regimes created different regulatory preferences for the oversight of these funds. Increasingly, money is moving across international borders, and money managers are operating in different jurisdictions. Academics, public officials, and legal practitioners wishing to understand the global investing environment need an appreciation of the general manner in which the investing laws in countries differ. And for the largest and most influential fund economies—such as the United Kingdom, Ireland, Liechtenstein, and Australia—specific details on local legal regimes are particularly illuminating.

5 AN OVERVIEW OF CHAPTERS IN THIS *HANDBOOK*

This *Handbook* addresses these and several other issues concerning mutual funds. The contributors—who are leading scholars in the field of investment law and who come from a number of different countries—provide a current legal analysis of funds from a variety of perspectives and using an array of methodologies.

In Part I, we consider some fundamental and large questions governing the role and regulation of investment funds. John Morley opens the volume with an inquiry into why investment companies are regulated so differently from every other kind of company. The multitude of other companies across our diverse spectrum of business endeavors—from software design to clothing retail to food service, and so forth—are regulated by a generic body of securities regulations. Morley asks what exactly makes an investment company so different from every other kind of company that it alone deserves special securities regulation. He concludes that, whatever the historical rationales for investment company regulation, the most compelling rationale for investment company regulation today is an investment company's unique organizational structure. An investment fund almost always has a separate legal existence and a separate set of owners from the managers who control it. A fund investor thus relates to her managers in a radically different way from an investor in every other kind of company.

Mercer Bullard then explores the rise and fall of the mutual fund brand, beginning with the observation that growth in the mutual fund industry has stagnated relative to the industry's dramatic rise in the preceding two decades. Bullard suggests that both that stagnation and the previous growth may be attributable to government policies. Specifically, he identifies a suspension of the SEC's program of aggressive regulatory innovation and the agency's inaction in the face of threats to the mutual fund brand. Bullard calls for the Commission to reclaim its role as a regulatory entrepreneur by using its broad exemptive authority to stave off the prospect of the mutual fund brand stagnating and withering in the vacuum of SEC paralysis. This chapter evaluates the efficiency of mutual fund regulation from a market perspective by considering whether investor preferences for potential market substitutes for mutual funds (e.g., hedge funds, separate accounts, CITs, mini-accounts) provide insights into whether mutual fund regulation is responsive to such preferences.

Deborah DeMott also considers the effect of the highly prescriptive regulatory structure of the Investment Company Act of 1940, focusing her attention upon the contours of fiduciary duties in mutual funds. In her chapter, DeMott advances the point that assessment of the role and significance of fiduciary obligations regarding investment funds, both mutual and private, turns on their distinctive characteristics, including those prescribed by regulation. DeMott notes that the population of investment advisers now registered with the SEC includes many who advise at least one private fund, and their actions during the financial crisis suggest that advisers' practices call into question whether they are acting consistently with their fiduciary duties.

In his chapter, Arthur Laby also examines the fiduciary structure of investment management regulation. Specifically, he addresses the relationship between investment managers' fiduciary obligations and regulators' efforts to control the investment management industry through rules and enforcement actions that constitute the bulk of fund law. Laby argues that much of that body of law is a response by regulators to the uncertainties inherent in the fiduciary obligation. On a broad series of issues, Laby contends, regulators attempt to specify the precise fiduciary obligations of managers as they exercise their duties to clients.

In Part II, we turn our attention to the identity and behavior of investors in mutual funds and their sophistication relative to one another and to investment advisers. Alan Palmiter begins this exploration by attempting to compile an investor profile that describes who mutual fund investors are. He concludes that this portrait of investors, painted by academic and governmental studies, is disturbing. Fund shareholders, who are in charge of making their own investment decisions, are ignorant of important characteristics of the funds in which they invest, inattentive to risks, and insensitive to fund fees. Palmiter ends with a "trillion-dollar question": whether the legal regime charged with protecting fund investors and ensuring the viability of our private retirement system is up to the task.

Lyman Johnson considers how best to protect investors in mutual funds. In his chapter, he examines the variety of approaches taken on investor protection since 1940 and argues that making efforts on many fronts is the best—and probably the only politically viable—regulatory strategy. Specifically, Johnson considers board-centered, investor-centered, SEC-centered, and market-centered solutions. Though he finds that all are flawed by themselves, and that each could be improved, the medley of their combined effect may be the best protection for investors.

Quinn Curtis looks specifically at the history and current state of mutual fund fee litigation under Section 36(b) of the Investment Company Act. He finds little evidence that lawsuits are effective in lowering the fees of funds managed by defendant advisers of sued targeted funds or that plaintiffs target particularly expensive mutual funds. In his chapter, Curtis attempts to situate new developments in fee litigation within the larger context of the Section 36 legislation. Many problems afflicting the operation of Section 36(b) are traceable, he argues, to the compromises, limitations, and ambiguities that resulted from the competing efforts of the SEC and the Investment Company Institute during the adoption of the 1970 amendments to the Company Act.

In the next chapter, Anita Krug contemplates possible ways to improve the governance of mutual funds, focusing specifically on a new model. In this new governance model, multiple funds in a common family are not managed by a single investment adviser but rather by numerous advisers, each managing one or a small number of funds within the organization. Krug contends that although the new model produces novel risks, there are reasons to believe that it is as least as effective as the traditional model, and may in fact be superior in some ways. Specifically, because the new model produces fewer sources of conflicts of interest than the traditional one, it may strengthen the board's ability to uphold its fiduciary duties to fund investors.

Finally, James Fanto focuses on the burgeoning field of regulatory compliance, as it relates to mutual funds. Specifically, he examines three major developments: (1) the continuing confusion over potential supervisory liability for compliance officers; (2) the increasing use of technology by these officers; and (3) the possible integration of the compliance function into risk management, rather than compliance remaining as a standalone control function. Fanto argues that, although these developments highlight the importance and achievements of compliance in the fund area, each in its own way discourages arguably the most valuable contribution of compliance officers, the provision of advice and counsel. He thus contends that, rather than passively watching and accepting these developments as they unfold, compliance officers and others with a stake in effective compliance should examine the developments critically to preserve the effectiveness of regulatory compliance.

In Part III, we turn our attention to less orthodox funds, such as money market funds, ETFs, and private funds. To begin, Jill Fisch considers money market funds and the shadow banking debate by tracing their evolution from their inception in the 1970s. Fisch focuses particularly on the events of September 2008, when the bankruptcy of Lehman Brothers caused the Reserve Primary Fund to "break the buck" and triggered investors' redemptions from money market funds. She explains the political interplay among government regulators regarding the need for reform and the ensuing regulations adopted by the SEC. Fisch closes by offering thoughtful observations about the likely structure of the money market fund industry in the future.

Eric Roiter conducts a comprehensive analysis of exchange-traded funds. Specifically, he explores the design of ETFs, traces their growth, and reviews their trading and investment strategies. He then considers the newest development in the world of ETFs, the advent of "actively managed" ETFs. Finally, Roiter considers ETFs more broadly, to determine whether they pose a risk to the financial system that warrants greater regulation by the SEC and the Federal Reserve Board.

William Birdthistle explores the possibility of a new public or eleemosynary infrastructure to support private investment in funds. Specifically, Birdthistle proposes and explores the concept of an investment fund provided to citizens as a service with zero investment advisory fees. The viability and advisability of free funds turn on three large questions: first, whether mutual funds with no fee are financially viable; second, whether they ought to exist; and third, who or what entities should serve as their sponsor. Birdthistle argues that free funds are theoretically plausible, inasmuch as funds with very low expense ratios could offset remaining net expenses with revenues from operations such as securities lending. In light of the central role of private investing today, he argues for experimentation with pilot fund, under the aegis of a nonprofit or governmental sponsor.

Finally in this section, Wulf Kaal considers the growth of the hedge fund industry and retail alternative funds. He finds there is an emerging confluence of the two, which will have implications in various areas of the financial industry.

Part IV focuses on the regulation of mutual funds in jurisdictions other than the United States. Dirk Zetzsche begins by providing a comprehensive analysis of pan-European investment law. By providing an overview of European Union sources of law and regulatory objectives, he offers a thorough introduction to a large and growing market that rivals the United States in global economic importance. Zetzsche explores the unique features of the two key pillars of European fund governance: UCITS (broadly corresponding to public funds like mutual funds in the United States) and Alternative Investment Funds (broadly corresponding to private US funds, such as hedge or private equity funds). Importantly, Zetzsche explains the European Passport, the license to engage in cross-border fund distribution and fund management in Europe, and the feature that first created the investment fund market in the European Union and European Economic Area. The type of passport for a collective investment scheme depends on whether the scheme meets the UCITS or AIF definition. Zetzsche also offers an analysis of the future trajectory of European investment fund law.

Blanaid Clarke and Mark White then consider governance aspects of mutual funds in Ireland, a disproportionately important international jurisdiction for wealth management. They examine the variety of attributes that make Ireland an attractive domicile for funds and asset managers, including the country's infrastructure, technology, and investment expertise, as well as its well-developed common law and legal system that provides parties with legal certainty. Ireland also offers a 12.5 percent corporate tax rate and no taxes on funds or investors. Clarke and White close by considering the possible effects of Brexit arising from the large financial market across the Irish Sea.

Iris H-Y Chiu provides another comprehensive country-specific analysis with her chapter on the regulation of collective retail investment funds in the United Kingdom. In discussing the market for such funds, Chiu argues that their regulatory framework has been shaped largely by European market integration and the need to brand pan-European collective investment products. She reflects on the need for a coherent regulatory framework for non-Undertakings for Collective Investment in Transferable Securities ("UCITS") and unconventional retail investment schemes, particularly in the wake of the great uncertainties unleashed by the United Kingdom's vote to leave the European Union.

In the final chapter, Pamela Hanrahan and Ian Ramsay look outside Europe to analyze the unique legal and regulatory framework for collective investments, including mutual funds, that Australia has developed over the past two decades. The Australian framework is built around a single "responsible entity" that combines the role of fund sponsor and adviser with that of the trustee. Hanrahan and Ramsay explain three key features of this system: the fiduciary duties imposed on the responsible entity and its officers; the limited role of an independent party to monitor or oversee the responsible entity's conduct of the fund; and the availability of investor "self help" mechanisms, including information rights, voting rights, enforcement rights, and exit rights.

We would like to thank all the authors for their fine contributions to this volume.

PART I

THE ROLE AND REGULATION OF INVESTMENT FUNDS

1. Why do investment funds have special securities regulation?

*John Morley**

America's securities laws are generic. We have only a single body of securities law for all types of companies. The two centerpieces of American securities regulation, the Securities Act of 1933 and the Securities Exchange Act of 1934, regulate almost every industry imaginable, from software making to clothing retail to food service, banking, coal mining, insurance, for-profit higher education, hotels, book publishing, art dealing, and real estate investing. American securities regulation contains multitudes.

Except, that is, for one very special industry: the investment company industry. Unlike all other companies, mutual funds, closed-end funds, hedge funds, and private equity funds have their own special securities regulatory regime in the form of the Investment Company Act of 1940. This act is administered by the Securities and Exchange Commission, the same agency that administers the other securities laws, but it imposes a different body of regulation in place of (and sometimes on top of) the generic securities regulation that applies to every other kind of company. No other large industry has a special securities regulatory scheme of this scope and magnitude.[1] The investment company industry is one of a kind.

But why? What exactly makes an investment company so different from every other kind of company that it alone deserves special securities regulation? Surprisingly, the answer has never been very clear and (in living memory, at least) even the question has never been directly posed.

This chapter tries to find an answer. My conclusion is that, whatever the historical rationales for investment company regulation, the most compelling rationale for investment company regulation today is an investment company's unique organizational structure. An investment fund almost always has a separate legal existence and a separate set of owners from the managers who control it. A fund investor thus relates to her managers in a radically different way from an investor in every other kind of company. Though this pattern of organization is often efficient in investment funds, it is

---

* I thank Matthew Chou, John Jo, and Alex Resar for research assistance and William Birdthistle for comments.

[1] To be sure, other industries are subject to distinctive regulation, and financial industries such as banking and insurance are subject to regulation of financial disclosures. But these industry-specific regulations are different from securities regulation. Industry-specific regulations are designed to protect customers or third parties rather than investors. And none of these industry-specific regulatory regimes supplants the regular securities regime. An insurance company, a travel agency, and a pet store chain each face different industry regulations but they nevertheless all make the same annual and quarterly disclosures to their investors under the Securities Exchange Act. Not so for a registered investment company, which has its own special disclosure regime under the ICA.

nevertheless often imperfect and it poses an array of serious problems that call out for regulation. The special job of the Investment Company Act is to provide that regulation.

Before we consider what makes a fund's organization so special, though, let us first turn to some other possible accounts of why an investment fund deserves special regulation. I will review several of these alternatives before arguing for the importance of organization.

1 SECURITIES OWNERSHIP

On first impression, the main thing that seems to make an investment company different is its tendency to *invest*. An investment company doesn't operate businesses; it invests in them. The trouble with this intuition, though, is that every company invests in something—whether land, factories, or brands. And so investing is not distinct to an investment fund. The next impulse is thus usually to take the intuition about investing and extend it a bit further to say that although an investment company may not be the only kind of business that invests, it is nevertheless the only kind of business that invests in a particular kind of asset, namely *securities*. On this telling, the thing that differentiates the Fidelity Magellan mutual fund from, say, Microsoft is that the Magellan fund invests in the securities of other companies, whereas Microsoft invests in branding and intellectual property.

This focus on securities gains support from no less an authority than the Investment Company Act of 1940 (the "ICA"), which is the special securities regulatory statute that supplants the regular securities regulatory regime for investment companies. The ICA regulates publicly registered mutual funds and closed-end funds as well as private investment vehicles, such as hedge funds and private equity funds.[2] Though the ICA uses the technical term "investment company," it regulates most of the vehicles that we commonly call "investment funds."

Section 3(a)(1) of the ICA is consistent with the securities-based definition of an investment company, because it tells us that an investment company is a business that "is ... engaged primarily ... in the business of investing ... in securities." Section 3(a)(2) alternatively gives a bright-line test that looks explicitly at securities ownership, saying that a company can also be an investment company if it "owns ... investment securities having a value exceeding 40 per centum of the value of such issuer's total assets." To simplify, a company is an investment company if its assets or intentions consist largely of investments in securities.

This focus on securities ownership seems to provide an answer to the question that began this chapter—why regulate investment companies differently—but the policy logic of this answer is dubious. Securities make sense as a focus of regulation only if there is something truly special about securities. There has to be some characteristic of securities, in other words, that is not also shared by other kinds of assets, such as food, machinery, or trademarks. What could that be?

---

[2] Of course, private vehicles can avoid complying with the ICA by virtue of their private status. Investment Company Act, Pub. L. No. 76-768, §§ 3(c)(1), (7), 54 Stat. 789 (1940) (codified as amended at 15 U.S.C. §§ 80a–1 to 80a–64 (2012)).

The answer is not clear, but one could imagine a few possibilities. One is that securities are highly liquid—they can be easily bought and sold. Another is that securities are hard to value. Yet another is that perhaps there is something unique about the way securities are owned and accounted for that poses special risks.

The trouble with each of these possible accounts of security specialness is that none of them is either unique or universal to securities. Many other kinds of assets exhibit these features, and many securities do not.

Consider liquidity. Liquidity is not unique to securities. Cash is even more liquid than securities, and many businesses hold vast amounts of cash. In 2016, Apple, the computer and smartphone maker, was sitting on some $230 billion in cash and cash equivalents, which exceeds the total assets of any mutual fund in America. See Tepper, "Apple's cash on hand decreased for the first time in nearly two years," *TechCrunch* (2016); "Performance for the 25 Largest Mutual Funds," *Lipper Performance Report* (2017). So should Apple be regulated as an investment company? Besides not being *unique* to securities, liquidity is also not *universal* to securities. Some of America's largest mutual funds invest primarily in corporate and government bonds, which can be very difficult to sell.

Difficulty in valuation is also neither unique nor universal to securities. It isn't unique to securities, because other assets are hard to value, too. An iron mine, for example, is as hard to value as almost any security. And difficulty in valuation isn't universal to securities, because securities are often quite easy to value. The stock of an iron mining company is paradoxically much easier to value than the iron mine itself, because the stock may be publicly quoted on a stock exchange every millisecond.[3] Difficulties in accounting are also neither unique nor universal to securities. Other assets also exist primarily in electronic ledgers—many businesses work on the electronic credit of their customers—and difficulties in accounting are so widespread that we already have an elaborate body of rules to address them: the Generally Accepted Accounting Principles, or GAAP.

Whatever special features we might imagine for securities thus appear on deeper reflection not to be so special after all. And even if these features were special, it is difficult to see why they would merit a full-blown special regulatory system. Even if securities did pose special problems, they would surely not be the only assets to do so. Every asset is at least a little bit special, but they do not all warrant their own separate securities regulations. Even if we accepted that a feature such as liquidity was unique to securities, for example, we could also imagine other features of seemingly similar importance that are unique to other kinds of assets. Copyright protections are uniquely important for book publishers, and spoilage is a special problem for meat processors. So do book publishers and meat producers deserve special securities regulation? Surely not. Every asset has its risks, and the risks of securities are not spectacularly special.

A further problem with basing investment company regulation on securities ownership is that even the bare fact of securities ownership is not unique or universal to investment companies. Securities ownership is not unique to investment companies,

---

[3] Of course, the valuation of the stock just raises the question of the valuation of the underlying asset. But at least for the kinds of ministerial purposes that concern regulation—accounting and disclosure—the valuation of a public company's stock is quite simple.

because many businesses invest in securities—often in huge amounts. In the early days of Microsoft, Bill Gates raised millions of dollars in cash to fund the company's research and development activities. It took a while before Gates could spend this hoard, so while he was waiting to use it on research, he invested it—where else?—in securities.[4] At the time that Microsoft made these investments, however, it had few other assets on its balance sheet besides these securities, since its business then consisted only of speculative interests in software that had no accounting value. There was thus a point early in Microsoft's history when a huge portion of its accounting value consisted of securities, making it indistinguishable from a closed-end bond fund. Microsoft nevertheless asked the SEC for a special exemption from the ICA and the SEC gave it, though the SEC was incapable of offering reasons other than Microsoft's own representations that it intended to run a business—which, of course, just begged the question about what it meant to run a business as distinct from an investment fund.

Further, not only are securities not unique to investment funds, but they are also not universal to investment funds. Consider the SPDR Gold Shares Exchange Traded Fund. The fund's marketing materials describe the fund as an "exchange-traded fund" and the fund is commonly ranked by the financial press as one of the largest ETFs in the world. See "SPDR Gold Shares," *State Street Global Advisors*, available at www.spdrgoldshares.com (accessed July 29, 2017); also see "Largest ETFs: Top 100 ETFs by Assets," *ETFdb.com* (accessed June 23, 2017); Murphy, "The 15 Most Important ETFs," *ETF.com* (2015). But the fund is not technically an "investment company" within the meaning of the ICA, because it does not invest in securities; it invests in physical bars of gold. And so even though almost everyone—including the fund's managers—considers Gold Shares a "fund," the ICA does not apply, and the fund is regulated only by the ordinary securities laws that apply to General Motors and Amazon.

Over the years, Congress and the SEC have sewn on various patches to smooth over the mismatch between the ICA's emphasis on securities ownership and our deeper intuitions about what makes a business an investment fund. In the late 1990s, for example, the SEC adopted a special rule exempting companies such as Microsoft from the Investment Company Act even if they also own large quantities of securities, so long as they spend large amounts of money on research and development.[5] And when Congress first passed the Investment Company Act in 1940, it added a special provision exempting businesses that invested in securities representing control stakes rather than minority stakes, so as to exclude industrial conglomerates like PepsiCo.[6]

These patches, however, are just that—patches. They are ad hoc bits of duct tape and superglue that no one can fully justify if we take seriously the notion that securities ownership is the measure of an investment fund. The exemption for Microsoft-style tech companies, for example, is plainly unprincipled, because it singles out only one

---

[4] See in the Matter of Microsoft Corporation c/o Martin E. Lybecker, Esquire Ropes & Gray, Release No. IC-16,467, 41 SEC Docket 472 (July 5, 1988) (order granting exemption); Microsoft Corp.; Application, Release No. IC-16,430, 41 SEC Docket 205 (June 10, 1988) (notice of application for order).
[5] 17 C.F.R. § 270.3a-8.
[6] Investment Company Act, Pub. L. No. 76-768, § 3(b).

kind of business—a research and development company—for special exemption from the ICA, even though many other kinds of businesses face the same problems. Movie studios, clothing companies, and sharing economy businesses would all like to raise cash and invest it in securities while they wait to spend it, but for some reason the SEC has given this privilege only to companies that invest in research and development. Why? No one can provide a principled answer.

A further problem is that a focus on securities ownership cannot explain why the Investment Company Act of 1940 does not apply to pension funds. Pension funds are pools of money that invest in securities for the purpose of paying out retirement benefits to the employees for whose benefit the money was originally contributed. Examples include the California Public Employees Retirement system pension fund and the large pension funds run by unions such as the Teamsters. If what we care about is securities ownership, then these pension funds should clearly be regulated by the same statute as mutual funds and other investment companies, since the assets of pension funds and many ICA registered mutual funds are essentially identical.

One might argue that pension funds should not be regulated by the ICA, because pension funds have their own distinct regulatory statute in the Employee Retirement Income Security Act (ERISA). But this just raises the question *why* pension funds have a different regulatory statute. The answer cannot have to do with securities investing, because although there are surely important differences between a pension fund and a mutual fund, securities investing is not one of them. The real difference between a pension fund and a mutual fund must be something other than securities ownership, which suggests that maybe securities ownership is not the real motivation for investment company regulation.

2 SMALL INVESTORS

Another theory of what makes an investment company special is the small size and limited sophistication of its investors. Some mutual fund investors are large, sophisticated institutions, but many others are small investors who lack professional expertise in investment. Mutual funds thus arguably need a special regulatory regime to ensure that shrewd investment managers do not take advantage of their small and unsophisticated clients.

This theory is consistent with some of the evidence about who owns mutual funds. Recent data show that mutual funds are popular in the portfolios of household savers. Small investors commonly invest in mutual funds through their 401(k) and other tax preferred retirement accounts. Small investors also commonly invest directly in mutual funds to meet non-retirement savings goals, such as home down payments and college tuition. Mutual funds have become so popular with small investors that they now account for almost a quarter of household financial assets and half of all retirement assets. See "2017 Investment Company Fact Book," *Investment Company Institute* (2017), pp. 11–12.

An emphasis on the importance of small investors is useful because it explains why the Investment Company Act differentiates between *public* and *private* funds. Sections 3(c)(1) and 3(c)(7) of the ICA provide that only funds that sell securities widely to the

14 *Research handbook on the regulation of mutual funds*

general public are subject to regulation under the Act. Funds that sell securities only to small numbers of wealthy individuals and institutions, such as private equity and hedge funds, are not required to comply with the ICA's many demands, even though they would otherwise fit the definition of an investment company.[7]

The problem with this focus on small investors as a justification for the special regulation of investment companies is that small investors are not unique to investment companies. Just like the ICA, the Securities Act of 1933 and the Securities Exchange Act of 1934 draw a line between public and private companies based on the number and size of their investors, and a company that chooses to comply with these laws can go public by accepting investment from anyone. A small investor with only $100 to spare can thus invest her money not just in the Vanguard 500 mutual fund, but also in General Electric and Microsoft. Small investors are thus a universal feature of all public companies.

One might reply that although small investors can buy stock in ordinary operating companies *in theory*, these investors *in fact* tend to invest disproportionately in investment companies. There is a great deal of truth to this claim, but it has a number of problems. One is that the facts that motivate it are of remarkably recent vintage. The mutual fund industry did not come close to its present popularity with small investors until the 1990s—a decade or two after the rise of 401(k) and IRA accounts transformed retirement saving, and more than 50 years after the ICA was passed.[8] And even now, many household investors still dabble in direct investing through brokerage accounts and similar devices. And so although it may be true that small investors invest primarily through investment companies nowadays, this was not the case for most of the history of investment company regulation and it is not universally the case even now.

3 COLLECTIVE BRANDING

Investment company regulation may be useful not just for protecting investors, but also for protecting the industry that markets to them. Like almost any regulation, the regulation of investment companies reflects the lobbying efforts of the industry it regulates. As I have argued elsewhere (Morley 2011), when the Investment Company Act was first passed in 1940, the investment company industry vigorously supported it. Congress voted to approve the act while the German army was blitzing across France, and the only way the industry could divert Congress' attention long enough to pass the act was by pleading with Congress to vote for it.

I have argued that the industry's motivation, at least in part, was to build what I have called a "collective brand": a single way of doing business that would come to define

---

[7] Similarly, some newer ICA administrative regulations, such as the ones applicable to money market funds, now differentiate between institutional and retail investors. See "SEC Adopts Money Market Fund Reform Rules: Rules Provide Structural and Operational Reform to Address Run Risks in Money Market Funds," *U.S. Securities and Exchange Commission* (2014).

[8] In 1980, only 5.7 percent of American households held shares in a mutual fund. In 1990, the number was 25.1 percent and in 2016 it was 54.9. See "2017 Investment Company Fact Book," *Investment Company Institute* (2017), p. 112 fig. 6.1.

the entire industry and give it a single image in the eyes of the investing public (Morley 2011). In seeking to build a collective brand, the investment company industry wanted to make sure that the public associated all investment companies with a single mode of operation, so that a small, unsophisticated investor would not be scared away from investing in an investment company by the risk that she might be confused into investing in something unusual. The largest players in the industry had a vision of what most small investors wanted, and although some investors might rationally have preferred something else, the largest players wished to ensure that the industry offered a single cohesive brand that catered to the majority of investors' preferences.

The clearest example of this branding impulse was borrowing. Although some investors might reasonably have preferred for their funds to borrow large amounts of money—this is now a core strategy of private equity and hedge funds—the investment company industry's largest players nevertheless lobbied for tight restrictions on borrowing in order to project an industry-wide image of caution and conservatism. The industry feared that if some investment companies borrowed too much, investors might come to associate borrowing with the entire industry and might avoid investing in the entire industry, for fear that they might not be able to sort the funds that borrowed from those that did not. The industry's goal was thus not simply to ensure the basic trustworthiness and honesty of a varied and diverse investment company industry, but to legislate a specific and contestable vision of what an investment company ought to be.

This industry politics-based explanation of ICA regulation goes further than the securities- and investor-based explanations in accounting for the existence of the ICA, but it still has limits. One is that it does not account for why the industry was able to form a sense of identity as a distinct industry. Saying that the "industry" wanted regulation presupposes that we know what the "industry" was. We can only believe that regulation served the purposes of a group of funds if we can identify the funds and their common purposes. But we still have not seen a clear concept of what could define a fund and what could unite the sponsors of different funds.

A further limitation of the industry politics account is that it is purely descriptive, rather than normative. It tells us how the ICA came into being, but not whether this was a good thing. It leaves open the question whether we, as rational policy designers today, should continue to want the entire industry to be forced into a single narrow vision of what an investment company should be.

And there are reasons to doubt the value of collective branding as a normative matter. The trouble is that the brand imposed by the ICA might be inconsistent with what many investors want. Even if most investors want a fund that complies with the ICA, some might want something else—especially now that the rise of 401(k) accounts has so dramatically expanded interest in mutual funds and changed the purposes for which people invest. Indeed, a desire to invest outside of the ICA is what has motivated the massive rise of ICA-exempt private equity and hedge funds. The ICA thus has the effect of making it impossible for many investors to get what they want—and may very well make them worse off as a result.

The normative desirability of collective branding thus rests on conjecture about how closely the desires of the investment company industry in 1940 conform to the desires of investors today. If the degree of conformity is high, the case for collective branding is strong. If the degree of conformity is low, the case is weak. Sadly, this empirical conjecture is extremely difficult to verify.

4 SYSTEMIC RISK

In trying to build a collective brand, the industry sought to benefit itself and its investors. But investment company regulation may also be justified by the benefits it offers to an entirely different set of people and institutions: the participants in the broader financial system. Like all large financial institutions, some of the biggest investment funds arguably pose risks to the financial system. Like the collapse of a large bank, the collapse of a large investment fund could, under the wrong conditions, send contagion spreading through the financial system, with consequences for a vast array of people who may never have interacted with the fund at all. Investment companies, in other words, may pose a problem of externalities.

Aspects of investment company regulation seem to have been designed to address this concern. The most relevant restrictions appear in Section 18 of the ICA, which limits how much an investment company can borrow.[9] Closed-end funds can issue only three classes of securities—preferred stock, bonds, and common stock—and only in fairly limited amounts. Open-end funds can issue only one class of security—common stock. Open-end funds can also borrow from banks, but the extent of the permissible borrowing is limited. The SEC has thickened these restrictions in recent years by trying to limit investment companies' investments in derivative securities that resemble borrowings and also by limiting open-end funds' investments in illiquid securities.[10]

Though the systemic risk-based justification for investment company regulation may seem at first to be compelling, its problems are myriad. The first and most obvious is that it does little to explain the great bulk of the ICA, which has nothing to do with borrowing, liquidity, or systemic risk. A concern for systemic risk offers no justification for limiting conflict of interest transactions or requiring disclosure of fees, for example. Systemic risk is, at most, a justification for Section 18 of the ICA and nothing more.

A further problem is that a concern for systemic risk is deeply at odds with the distinction in the ICA between public funds and private funds. As noted above, the ICA exempts so-called "private funds," which would otherwise qualify as investment companies, but do not have to comply with the ICA because they accept investments only from a small number of wealthy investors and institutions. The exemption for private funds relieves these funds from all of the requirements of the ICA, including the restrictions on borrowing. Thus, under the ICA, a private fund can borrow indiscriminately.

This free pass for private funds makes sense if the logic of the public/private distinction is to protect a fund's investors, since the original thinking behind the public/private distinction was that it was the investors in public funds who were most

---

[9] For a description of the rules, see Morley (2013).
[10] See Use of Derivatives by Registered Investment Companies and Business Development Companies, 80 FR 80883 (proposed Dec. 28, 2015) (to be codified at 17 C.F.R. §§ 270, 274); Investment Company Liquidity Risk Management Programs, 17 C.F.R. §§ 210, 270, 274 (2016).

vulnerable to exploitation. But if, as we have stipulated here, the concern is not about small investors but about the broader *financial system,* then the distinction no longer makes any sense. The number and sophistication of equity investors in a particular fund is irrelevant if our real concern is about the vast community of financial actors who may never have directly dealt with a fund at all. And a private fund poses just as much risk to the financial system as a private fund. A billion dollars of borrowed money poses more or less the same threat to the financial system whether it was borrowed by a private investment company or a public one. Systemic risk is often compared to environmental pollution in its tendency to damage third parties through externalities. And what we have in the ICA, essentially, is a system that says only rich people can dump toxins into rivers. If we were to take seriously the notion that systemic risk regulation is the rationale for regulating investment funds, therefore, we would have to apply the same regulations to hedge funds and private equity funds that we apply to mutual funds.[11]

A still further problem with systemic risk as a theory of investment company regulation is that, like the other concerns we have already addressed, systemic risk is not unique to investment companies. Though it would certainly be bad for the financial system if a large mutual fund were to go bankrupt, it would be bad for the financial system if *any* large company were to go bankrupt. When Enron collapsed in 2001, it sent shockwaves through the financial system, as did Chrysler when it filed for bankruptcy in 2009 and Puerto Rico when it began its slow motion implosion in 2015. So unless we can identify something truly distinctive about the capital structure of an investment company, the argument for regulating borrowing by a registered investment company boils down to nothing more than the argument for regulating borrowing by any large institution.

5 ORGANIZATIONAL STRUCTURE

A final possibility—and the one that seems most compelling—is that investment companies are distinct because of their organizational structure. Every type of investment company in the ICA orbit adopts a peculiar pattern of organization that I have elsewhere called the "separation of funds and managers" (Morley 2014). It is perhaps this pattern, more than anything else, that attracts the bulk of the ICA's concern.

An investment company is distinct because it separates its fund from its managers. It does so by establishing the fund and the managers as distinct legal entities with distinct groups of owners that are related to each other solely (or primarily) by contract. In the Fidelity asset management complex, for example, the manager is Fidelity itself. Fidelity is a corporation, owned privately by its founding family. Fidelity earns its money by charging management fees to hundreds of different funds, including mutual

---

[11] It is still uncertain how the new SIFI designations will affect private investment companies, but it remains clear that whatever restrictions emerge for hedge funds and private equity funds will likely be much less severe than the restrictions that the ICA imposes on registered investment companies.

funds, hedge funds, and private equity funds. Fidelity established each of these funds at various times, and each has its own distinct corporate existence and its own distinct group of owners, who were recruited by Fidelity's marketing efforts. Fidelity makes money by causing each fund early in its life—when it is wholly owned by Fidelity—to sign a contract with Fidelity under which Fidelity controls every aspect of the fund's operations. The fund has no ability to fire individual employees of a manager and (in a hedge fund or private equity fund) may not even have the ability to remove the management as a corporate entity. The net effect is that the funds each own their own investments, but have no employees or operational assets and no meaningful authority to manage their own affairs.

This pattern of organization is common to virtually everything we think of as part of the investment company regulatory system. Hedge funds, private equity funds, mutual funds, exchange-traded funds, and closed-end funds all adopt some variant of this pattern of organization.

Elsewhere, I have explained why this pattern is uniquely efficient in investment funds. See Morley (2014). The reasons are complicated, but they boil down to the way that this pattern limits a fund investor's involvement in the business of the management company and the management company's other funds. Because a fund investor does not own the management company, she cannot control the management company. And because a fund's assets do not belong to the same entity as a management company, the fund's investors do not face any risk of loss or gain from the management company's debts and cash flows. These limits on a fund investor's involvement in the management business tend to make sense because fund investors tend to have other rights that substitute for control over the management (such as the right to redeem), and also tend to have uniquely strong desires for precision in the tailoring of risk. The separation between funds and managers thus generally tends to be the most efficient pattern of organization available to most investment funds. See Morley (2014).

The separation of funds and managers nevertheless poses major challenges for regulators. Although this pattern tends to be the *most* efficient way to organize an investment fund, it is nevertheless not a *perfectly* efficient way to organize an investment fund. The value of separating a fund from its manager can vary from fund to fund and circumstance to circumstance. And although the separation of funds and managers may be the best available form of organization for many funds, it is not divinely ordained, and it can break down whenever the conditions that make it efficient fail to materialize. The main job of investment company regulation is thus to address the many risks that the separation of funds and managers inevitably poses and to single out for regulatory scrutiny the situations where these risks are most profound.

The risks are numerous. One is that a manager's many funds may come into conflict with one another. The legal separation between a fund and its manager permits the manager simultaneously to operate dozens or even hundreds of different funds at the same time, raising difficult questions about how the manager should allocate scarce resources among these different clients. When Fidelity comes across an opportunity to invest in a hot technology start-up, for example, Fidelity has to decide which of its hundreds of funds will get the opportunity. A related problem is the constant possibility that a manager may mix its clients' assets with its own. A fund manager is like a lawyer who might be tempted to dip into a trust account that actually belongs to a client. An even more serious problem is the risk that exit rights will break down. Because the separation of funds and managers cuts off a fund investor's right to control the management company, many investment funds compensate by offering their investors redemption rights, periodic liquidations, and other rights that permit them to remove their money from a manager's control. If an investor cannot control her manager, she can at least take away her money. But what happens if these exit rights cease to work? What if investors lack the sophistication or knowledge to redeem, or what if a manager suddenly decides to suspend the right of redemption? Or what if, like a closed-end fund, a fund offers no right to redeem or liquidate at all?

These and myriad other problems call out for regulation, and the job of the ICA is to provide it. The ICA has a provision to address each one of these and many other problems that arise from the separation between funds and their managers. Organizational structure thus offers a holistic explanation of what makes an investment company distinct and why the ICA might be necessary to regulate it.

An investment fund's peculiar pattern of organization does not just pose a particular kind of business risk—it sets up an altogether different way of relating to a company. This pattern of organization thus warrants a distinct body of securities regulation, because securities regulation is, after all, about governance. Securities law is fundamentally a way of regulating how shareholders relate to their companies. And so if shareholders relate to their companies in a radically unusual way, they may very well need a special form of securities regulation to protect them.

This focus on organization helps resolve a number of difficulties in how we understand the ICA. Among other things, a focus on organization explains why mutual funds are regulated differently from pension funds.[12] As we have seen, mutual funds and pension funds both tend to own large amounts of securities, and so if we focus only on securities ownership, a mutual fund and a pension fund look the same. But if we focus instead on organization, the difference becomes obvious, because pension funds do not have a separate corporate existence from their managers. Pension fund investors also lack the package of rights—such as redemption rights—that often makes the separation of funds and managers efficient in mutual funds and other vehicles regulated by the ICA. Pension funds have their own distinctive pattern of organization, which warrants its own distinctive regulatory statute.

The peculiar pattern of organization we find in investment companies is thus the central concern of investment company regulation. And many of the other possible accounts of fund regulation make more sense when we view them through the lens of organization. Consider, for example, the desire to protect small investors that we considered earlier. Small investors are a common focus of all securities statutes, but the Investment Company Act may be necessary to address a particular kind of problem faced by small investors. Unlike the other securities laws, for example, the ICA places numerous restrictions on conflicts of interest, requires advisory fees to be disclosed in a specified format, and restricts how much a manager of an open-end fund can limit redemptions. Obviously, these requirements exist to protect small investors, but their main effect is to protect small investors *from the peculiar risks of investment company*

---

[12] Pension funds are excluded from the ICA. Investment Company Act, Pub. L. No. 76-768, § 3(c)(11).

organization. The only reason a manager faces so many conflicts of interest, for example, is because the manager simultaneously works for so many different funds. And the only reason an advisory fee can be stated as a single number is because a fund does not directly cover the wide variety of operating expenses that would make it impossible to express expenses in a single number. Instead, a fund covers its expenses by paying a single fee to an external service provider. In other words, the ICA regulates the special set of risks to small investors that come from investing in such an unusually structured organization.

Stepping back, we can see that one way to understand the ICA is to say that it is not a form of securities regulation at all—it is actually a form of product or service regulation. This analogy makes sense mainly because of the importance of exit rights in investment funds. In many funds that adopt the separation of funds and managers, exit rights cause investors to look more like customers than regular equity holders. Recall that in order to compensate for the restrictions on control rights introduced by the separation of a fund from its manager, many investment funds give their investors strong exit rights, such as the power to withdraw their money by redeeming. And many funds also strongly restrict or even eliminate their investors' voting rights. As a result, an investor in an open-end mutual fund tends to relate to her fund in much the same way that a customer relates to an ordinary company selling products or services. In the same way that a customer of H&R Block, the consumer tax preparation service, can decide every year whether or not to hire the company again, so too can an investor in a mutual fund decide every day whether or not to leave her money with the fund and its management. And so in the same way that an H&R Block customer is protected by contract and regulation rather than by the right to elect the firm's directors, so too is a mutual fund investor protected mainly by contract, regulation, and fiduciary duty rather than by the right to vote for the directors of the fund's advisor.[13] The ease of exit enjoyed by customers has often been used in economic theory to define who counts as a customer (rather than an investor) and to explain why a customer receives different protections than an investor. See Hansmann (2000); Williamson (1983).

The product/service analogy is useful because it addresses the question that began this chapter, which is why investment companies deserve their own distinct body of regulation. If we view investment company regulation as a form of securities regulation, then carving out a special regime for investment companies looks quite unusual, since securities regulation is otherwise so monolithic. But if instead we view investment company regulation as a form of product or service regulation, then it seems quite ordinary, because unlike securities regulation, product and service regulation is highly variable. Though we have a single body of securities regulation for almost every kind of company, we have dozens—maybe hundreds—of different bodies of regulation for

---

[13] Mutual fund investors technically have a right to vote for directors in their own funds, but they do not have a right to vote for directors in their advisor. And even the right to vote for directors in their own funds is meaningless, because mutual fund investors never use it. Small investors do not vote, because they lack the sophistication; and large investors do not vote, because they lack the incentive. A large investor who becomes dissatisfied with a fund will almost always choose to redeem, rather than to vote. The net effect is that no director election has ever been contested by shareholders in the nearly 90-year history of the open-end mutual fund industry. See Morley & Curtis (2010).

products and services. Insurance companies, car makers, bakeries, cable TV providers, hospitals and computer manufacturers each have the same securities regulation but different product regulations. Product and service regulation is almost as varied as the industries it regulates.

6 CONCLUSION

When we ask why American law provides a distinct body of securities regulation for investment funds and not other businesses, the most obvious answers fail us. The tendency of investment funds to own securities, the small size of fund investors, the industry's need for collective branding, and the threat the industry poses to the financial system all prove inadequate to make sense of the special status of investment funds under American law. The most compelling answer thus turns out to be a surprising feature of investment funds that was only recently identified: their peculiar pattern of organization. An investment fund's tendency to maintain a distinct corporate existence and a distinct set of owners from its management radically transforms how investors relate to their managers and warrants a special body of regulation quite different from the rest of American securities law.

BIBLIOGRAPHY

"2017 Investment Company Fact Book," *Investment Company Institute* (2017).
Grow, Natalie R., The "Boston-Type Open-End Fund"—Development of a National Financial Institution: 1924–1940, Unpublished Ph.D. dissertation (Harvard University, 1977).
Hansmann, Henry, *The Ownership of Enterprise* (Belknap Press, Cambridge, MA, 2000).
"Largest ETFs: Top 100 ETFs by Assets," *ETFdb.com*.
Morley, John D., Collective Branding and the Origins of Investment Management Regulation: 1936–1942, *Virginia Law and Business Review* 6, 341–402 (2011).
Morley, John D., The Regulation of Mutual Fund Debt, *Yale Journal on Regulation* 30, 343–76 (2013).
Morley, John D., The Separation of Funds and Managers: A Theory of Investment Fund Structure and Regulation, *Yale Law Journal* 123, 1228–87 (2014).
Morley, John D. and Quinn Curtis, Taking Exit Rights Seriously: Why Governance and Fee Litigation Don't Work in Mutual Funds, *Yale Law Journal* 120, 84–142 (2010).
Murphy, Cinthia, "The 15 Most Important ETFs," *ETF.com* (Oct. 6, 2015).
"Performance for the 25 Largest Mutual Funds,", *Lipper Performance Report* (July 27, 2017).
"SEC Adopts Money Market Fund Reform Rules: Rules Provide Structural and Operational Reform to Address Run Risks in Money Market Funds," *U.S. Securities and Exchange Commission* (July 23, 2014).
"SPDR Gold Shares," *State Street Global Advisors*, available at www.spdrgoldshares.com.
Tepper, Fitz, "Apple's Cash on Hand Decreased for the First Time in Nearly Two Years," *TechCrunch* (July 26, 2016).
Williamson, Oliver E., *Markets and Hierarchies: Analysis and Antitrust Implications* (Free Press, New York, 1983).

2. The rise and fall of the mutual fund brand
Mercer Bullard[*]

Between 1980 and around 2000, the mutual fund was the most popular brand in the financial services marketplace. Ownership of mutual funds among households rose from 5.7 percent to 48.9 percent. Mutual funds represented 6.7 percent of household financial assets in 1999; by 2000 their share increased to 18.4 percent. Conventional wisdom might attribute the popularity of mutual funds to market forces, with regulatory reforms serving only to constrain the industry's growth. This chapter suggests the alternative explanation that regulatory innovation created the modern mutual fund and is substantially responsible for its popularity. The mutual fund brand could be considered a government brand, thereby turning on its head the cliché that regulation invariably interferes with market preferences.

Mutual funds are regulated under the Investment Company Act of 1940 (the "Act"), an extremely prescriptive statute under which mutual funds had achieved only limited market penetration up to 1980. However, the Act grants broad exemptive authority to the Commission, which it has exercised aggressively over the past 35 years. In fact, during that period the Commission has created a *bona fide* shadow Investment Company Act that materially alters virtually every major requirement under the Act (Bullard 2008). In some cases, SEC rules impose heightened requirements, but in most the Commission has substantially reduced or entirely eliminated requirements in fostering many variations on the statutory mutual fund, including money market funds, funds of funds, multiclass funds and, most recently, exchange-traded funds. This period of innovation coincides closely with the rise of the mutual fund brand, which this chapter contends may reflect a causal relationship.

However, growth in the mutual industry has stagnated since the turn of the century. This chapter suggests that this stagnation, like the industry's previous growth, may be attributable to government policy—a contemporaneous suspension of the SEC's program of aggressive regulatory innovation. Since 2000, SEC inaction in the face of threats to the mutual fund brand has, in some cases, damaged the value of the mutual fund brand. For example, the Commission should have anticipated and acted to preempt the mutual fund market timing scandal of 2003 and the run on money market funds in 2008, both of which tarnished the brand and resulted in a reduction in industry assets. Just as a proactive SEC in the past century accompanied robust growth in the mutual fund industry, an inactive SEC in this century has accompanied stagnation in the popularity of the mutual fund brand.

---

[*] The author thanks William Birdthistle and John Morley for their helpful comments, and Butler, Snow, O'Mara, Stevens, and Cannada for their research support.

1 INTRODUCTION

When one thinks of the iconic brands in America, names such as Apple, Coca-Cola and Starbucks may quickly come to mind. More mature respondents might name Pan Am, Woolworth's, RCA, and *Life* magazine—iconic brands whose claim to distinctive excellence has withered over time. If asked to name an iconic government or public brand, the question might at first cause hesitation. Brands are usually thought of as products of the private marketplace. But NASA, the Marines and the US Post Office exhibit the characteristics of an iconic brand. A financially attuned answer might include the government-operated Thrift Savings Plan, or TSP, which is the largest pension plan in the world.

Not many would answer "mutual fund," yet no government brand's demonstrated success in the free market has ever approached the success of the mutual fund, the most popular investment product the world has ever seen.[1] The regulatory construct that is the mutual fund dominates the most advanced financial market in the world. Stop any American on the street and ask for an investment recommendation, and one is likely to be advised to buy a mutual fund—not a particular *sponsor* of a mutual fund, but the thing that the public knows at some level as the most trusted set of operational rules through which a retail investor can access the capital markets.

1.1 The Mutual Fund as a Government Brand

The mutual fund is a government brand that has been created largely by government bureaucrats (Morley 2011; Bullard 2006). Prior to the Investment Company Act's ("the Act") becoming law in 1940, mutual funds had virtually no market presence; they remained a minor player on the financial landscape for 40 years. The modern mutual fund did not exist until around 1980, when SEC rulemaking created the foundation for it.[2]

The concept of a popular, government-created brand runs against the grain. In the United States, capital allocation and consumer purchases are generally left to laissez-faire forces, in keeping with the general view that respecting market preferences, rather than bureaucrats' judgments, will maximize net social welfare. The government's role in the economy typically focuses on the enforcement of various property rights and commercial antifraud rules, and on health, safety, and welfare regulation. Designing financial products falls far afield of these core governmental activities.

Mutual fund regulation represents an extraordinarily intrusive, prescriptive exception to prevailing free market policies. The Act does not simply prohibit leverage, but rather

---

[1] A mutual fund is, under the Investment Company Act, an open-end management investment company. 15 U.S. Code §§ 80a–4(3) & 5(a). An exchange-traded fund is a type of mutual fund. Closed-end funds and unit investment are also investment companies under the Act. 15 U.S. Code §§ 80a–4(2), 4(3) & 5(a).

[2] One significant pre-1980 reform was the adoption of the forward pricing rule in 1968, which required that mutual funds sell shares at the next computed per share net asset value. 17 C.F.R. § 270.22c-1.

sets a specific percentage limit on borrowing and establishes specific hedging requirements for activities that have the effect of creating leverage. The Act does not simply require that shares be redeemable, but rather dictates how quickly funds must execute a redemption request and with what type of proceeds the redemption may be honored. The Act does not simply prohibit multiple classes of shares, but prohibits precisely defined superior rights that include esoteric derivatives and other de facto leveraging arrangements. The Act (with other securities laws) does not simply prohibit excessive sales compensation; it sets, through administrative fiat, specific limits on various combinations of commissions and asset-based fees. The Act does not simply prohibit transactions with a fund sponsor's affiliates, but rather identifies numerous discrete transactions that are permitted under elaborate sets of conditions, and defines affiliates to include a range of relationships the mapping of which resembles the complexity of a large financial institution's corporate structure. Mutual fund regulation represents financial engineering nonpareil.

Corroborating conventional wisdom, the Act's exceptionally intrusive model did not result in Americans embracing the financial product that it created. That happened after the Commission began granting exemptions from many of the Act's prohibitions around 1980. These exemptions could simply represent agency capture, consistent with the generally conservative turn of the courts and Congress after the more liberal private claim creating in the 1960s and 1970s. But their impetus does not affect this chapter's thesis—that regulatory action can increase net social wealth based on market metrics such as industry growth.

There are compelling, well-worn market-based arguments for the government's assuming the role of financial architect. The mutual fund represents a field of securities regulation, one general justification for which is that mandatory rules can create efficiencies that would exist if markets were left alone. For example, price transparency enhances market efficiency, but free markets may not produce the optimal level of price transparency. Mandatory disclosure rules save investors the cost of gathering information that might not otherwise be collected because of the collective action problem.

Market failure can also occur when investors make bad decisions that decrease net social wealth. They may choose investments that are too risky or too expensive, or they may simply abjure choice altogether by making overly safe investments that inevitably lose purchasing power over time. They may choose illiquid investments because they underestimate the risk of life events that require immediate liquidity. They may underestimate or misunderstand the costs of conflicts of interest and the myriad forms these conflicts assume. These social costs may result not from the collective action problem, but from cognitive limits and biases that cause investors to fail to develop information or to act rationally when information is easily obtainable. Investors' innate behavioral tendencies may reduce net social wealth by rewarding inefficient pricing, risk management, and conflicts.

Mutual fund regulation mitigates this kind of market failure by establishing default rules that, in effect, make key decisions for investors where the risk of error may be greatest and most costly. For example, a mutual fund's authority to assume leverage is very limited. Mutual fund default rules also seek to prohibit the most costly conflicts of interest, such as by banning many types of affiliated transactions. Mutual fund default rules reduce search costs by standardizing investment performance reporting and fee disclosure, and mitigate the effects of bad judgment by requiring a minimum of portfolio diversification.

1.2 Popularity of the Mutual Fund Brand

Mutual fund default rules have become so widely accepted by the market that the term "mutual fund" has become as much a part of the American vernacular as the term "life insurance." Life insurance is usually more important to an individual's financial security than mutual funds, but the ownership of individual life insurance policies declined 15 percentage points leading up to 2010, while the household ownership of mutual funds skyrocketed from less than 5 percent in 1980 to more than 45 percent in 2010.[3] The mutual fund is arguably the most popular brand in the history of the financial services industry.

Yet the claim that the mutual fund brand reflects the revealed preferences of investors requires closer analysis. The concept of market approval assumes that investors are free to choose mutual funds over less or differently regulated alternatives. If mutual funds operated under a set of true or "default" rules, then investors would be free to opt out of many, if not all, of the rules. If consumers can only buy apples that are grown with pesticides and cannot buy apples that are not, then it is hard to evaluate consumers' true preference for apples grown with pesticide because they have no opportunity to purchase pesticide-free apples. Market approval for a set of default rules only reflects genuine consumer preferences when consumers are able to choose their own rules.

Corporate law operates in a kind of marketplace of default rules where the choice of jurisdiction implies, at least to some degree, a bona fide market preference (or to some, a race to the bottom). For example, Delaware law includes a default rule that shareholders shall not have preemptive rights. However, that policy is only what Richard Thaler and Cass Sunstein might call a "nudge" (Thaler and Sunstein 2009). Delaware law permits corporations to opt out of the default rule and grant preemptive rights. Delaware also imposes a number of mandatory rules, but even then a company can opt out by organizing in a different jurisdiction.

Others have argued that securities law should operate similarly by allowing companies to choose the securities rules under which they operate (for example, Romano 1998). But they generally do not test that argument by evaluating the extent to which there are, in fact, de facto securities law markets in which issuers and investors can opt out of many securities law requirements. Trillions of dollars are invested through securities offerings that are exempt, to varying degrees, from securities regulation. To understand whether securities regulation operates in a laissez-faire market, one must evaluate the actual preferences reflected by issuers and investors when they make choices in different offering and purchasing contexts.

Similarly, it may be possible to test issuers' and investors' real preference for mutual fund regulation by considering the existence and popularity of unregulated or differently regulated substitutes. If substitutes exist, the degree of their acceptance by issuers and investors should provide insight into whether investors' decisions to invest in

---

[3] THE LIFE INSURANCE COVERAGE GAP, THE PRUDENTIAL INSURANCE COMPANY (2011) (decline from 59 percent in 1960 to 44 percent in 2010); 2015 ICI Fact Book at 114.

mutual funds reflect genuine preferences. Indeed, all policy debates regarding securities regulation are implicitly framed by assumptions about the market for substitutes to the extent that efficiency justifications for securities regulation has any purchase. Understanding mutual fund regulation, as well as other areas of securities regulation, in terms of the validity of revealed preferences for a particular set of default rules could improve regulators' decisionmaking.

2 MUTUAL FUND SUBSTITUTES

2.1 What is a Mutual Fund Substitute?

Before considering substitutes for mutual funds, the thing for which a substitute is being sought must be defined. Exactly what would an unregulated alternative to a mutual fund be a substitute *for*? Rather than investing in a mutual fund, an investor could purchase hundreds or thousands of stocks and bonds and manage her account in the same way that a mutual fund would manage its portfolio. This relatively unregulated substitute for a mutual fund might be cost effective for extremely wealthy individuals, but it is an expensive option for retail investors. However, retail investors' preference for this impractical investment model says little about the true market appeal of the mutual fund because it lacks many key features of a mutual fund, such as professional management and comparatively frictionless transactions.

Alternatively, retail investors can directly purchase stocks and bonds in small, preselected portfolios that, while not precisely mirroring particular asset classes, are statistically designed to match the performance of an asset class. This approach avoids the impracticability of buying, selling, and holding thousands of securities while providing the benefits of diversification, optimal asset allocation, and enhanced tax efficiency. The earliest popular seller of such "mini-accounts," Foliofn, specifically advertised them as mutual fund substitutes (and the fund industry sued to stop them), but Foliofn's folios have not been widely embraced by the market.[4] Is that a positive reflection on the mutual fund brand? Or is a mini-account something entirely different? Have mini-accounts experienced limited market penetration because they lack market appeal or presence, or because they are subject to oppressive regulation?

2.2 Mini-Accounts

A mini-account could be viewed as an attempt to offer the benefits of a mutual fund while opting out of mutual fund regulation. One might evaluate this possibility by positing a set of hypothetical investor preferences and identifying how regulation affects investors' ability to obtain them. For example, imagine an investor who seeks to invest in a diversified, managed pool of securities in a particular asset class by:

---

[4] Folio*fn* Investments., Inc., is a wholly owned subsidiary of FOLIO*fn*, Inc., which was founded by former SEC Commission Steven M.H. Wallman.

(1) making an initial batch purchase of individual operating company securities based on a third-party model portfolio (a "folio"),
(2) as to which the investor only has the right to:
    (a) direct pro rata purchase and sales of the entire portfolio (not individual securities) and the reinvestment or distribution of interest and dividends,
(3) where the portfolio manager has the authority to buy and sell portfolio securities to:
    (a) match the performance of the asset class and
    (b) minimize each investor's taxes based on information that they provide to the manager.

Modern technology would allow for a cost-effective version of this fund, or alternatively an actively managed version where changes in the core holdings are subject to the fund manager's discretion.

The Commission permits the offering of such mini-accounts without complying with mutual fund regulation, but only if the firm offering the account allows investors to exercise some degree of discretionary control over holdings and transactions in the account and has regular contact with the investor. Regardless of whether the investor wants these rights, the mini-account sponsor must comply with the rights and must be able to show some evidence that investors actually exercise them in practice.[5]

Thus, investors cannot opt out of mutual fund regulation by investing through mini-accounts without paying a kind of penalty. The cost of operating a mini-account is necessarily increased by the SEC requirement that investors be afforded some degree of discretionary control and personal contact. Fundamental principles of economics tell us that raising the cost of a product (the mini-account) will reduce demand for the product and increase demand for substitutes (for example, mutual funds). Just as an increase in the price of mozzarella will move the demand curve for both pizza and hamburgers, taxing mini-accounts should move the demand curve for both mini-accounts and mutual funds, assuming that hamburgers and mutual funds are, in fact, correct substitutes in the relevant product market. To the extent that the mini-account penalty artificially increases demand for mutual funds, mutual funds' popularity may be attributable not to investors' market preferences, but to the visible hand of government regulation.

One could view the mini-account penalty as a kind of anticompetitive practice whereby the government gains an unfair market advantage by taxing competitors' offerings. The anticompetitive practices analogy might be a useful one in identifying market substitutes for mutual funds. In identifying the relevant market in which alleged anticompetitive effects should be evaluated under antitrust law, the Supreme Court has found that the "outer boundaries of a product market are determined by the reasonable

---

[5] Bloomberg, *Hype from a Financial Guru?* (May 9, 2004) (discussing lawsuit alleging that mini-accounts were not individualized).

interchangeability of use or the cross-elasticity of demand between the product itself and substitutes for it."[6]

Investors may view mini-accounts as interchangeable investment options and cross-elasticity between mutual funds and mini-accounts may exist. However, the small size of the mini-account market suggests that, even if the mini-account penalty artificially reduces the demand for mini-accounts and inflates the demand for mutual funds, the effect is not large enough to show that *overall* demand for mutual funds is artificial. That hypothesis would require substantially more evidence of artificial displacement of demand for mutual fund substitutes than is suggested by the artificial displacement of mini-accounts alone. Other potential mutual fund substitutes may provide such evidence.

2.3 Hedge Funds, Separate Accounts and Collective Investment Trusts

There are three categories of diversified pools of securities in which individuals invest substantial assets that could be viewed as mutual fund substitutes. Natural persons invest in private investment funds ("hedge funds"),[7] separate accounts, and collective investment trusts ("CITs"), each of which may be operated free of mutual fund regulation. However, none provides clear insight into how mutual funds fare against market substitutes. Hedge funds can be offered publicly to individuals, but purchasers must be accredited investors who have at least $1 million in investments or very high incomes (they represent, approximately, only 10 percent of US households). Individuals need not be accredited investors to invest in separate accounts or CITs, but neither of these products can be offered publicly. Retail investors own hedge funds, CITs and separate accounts in retirement plans,[8] but the exercise of free choice in this context is constrained by the intervening role of a plan fiduciary that may limit the number of investment options to only a handful. Plan fiduciaries may be weak proxies for genuine investor preferences.

Separate accounts and CITs may opt *out* of mutual fund regulation, but only by opting *into* an alternative regulatory structure. Separate accounts are subject to insurance regulation, and CITs to banking regulation. Inside retirement plans, hedge funds are subject to the Employee Retirement Income Security Act of 1974 ("ERISA")

---

[6] *Brown Shoe Co. v. U.S.*, 370 U.S. 294, 325 (1962); *United States v. E.I. du Pont de Nemours & Co.*, 351 U.S. 377, 395 (1956) (product market consists of "commodities reasonably interchangeable by consumers for the same purposes").

[7] The term "hedge funds" as used herein includes private equity funds and other privately offered investment vehicles that are investment companies under the Investment Company Act.

[8] The use of CITs in retirement plans has been growing. From 2009 to 2015, pension plan assets in CITs increased from $1.3 trillion (16 percent) to $2.4 trillion (12.7 percent) of total assets. Tergesen, *Some Funds in Your 401(k) Aren't Really Mutual Funds After All*, WALL. ST. J. (Sep. 28, 2015). The CIT industry claims that, from 2012 to 2014, the percentage of retirement plans offering CIT options increased from 48.3 to 60.0, while the percentage for mutual funds declined from 92.0 to 88.2, and the percentage of separate accounts increased from 42.5 to 42.7. COLLECTIVE INVESTMENT TRUSTS, COALITION OF COLLECTIVE INVESTMENT TRUSTS at 6 (2015). Some have suggested that liquidity requirements proposed by the Commission, if adopted, would cause some retirement plans to shift from mutual funds to separate accounts or CITs. Baert, *SEC Proposal Could Alter Use of Mutual Funds in DC Plans*, PENSIONS & INVESTMENTS (Feb. 8, 2016).

if plan assets comprise more than 25 percent of the fund's assets, whereas mutual funds are never subject to ERISA. It is difficult to evaluate the revealed preference for mutual funds when their competitors are weighed down by their own regulatory ankle weights.

Hedge funds may nonetheless provide a useful benchmark for investors' preference for mutual funds. Although they do not reflect the preferences of retail investors, they do reflect the preferences of accredited investors. Every accredited investor who chooses to invest in a hedge fund has chosen not to invest the same assets in mutual funds. Investment adviser regulation of hedge funds includes virtually none of the core requirements of the Act. Hedge funds therefore offer a mutual fund substitute where investors may pick and choose the mutual fund rules they prefer, as a kind of à la carte menu, as well as invest in portfolios that are not permitted for mutual funds.

Hedge funds therefore reflect accredited investors' revealed preferences for an investment pool that not only is free of mutual fund rules but also, importantly, incorporates few or none of those rules in practice. If accredited investors choose hedge funds that replicate few or none of the principal rules that apply to mutual funds, this revealed market preference raises the question of whether the trillions of dollars in mutual funds reflect the genuine preferences of retail investors.

However, there are a number of caveats to the hedge fund comparison. First, accredited investors are likely to have substantial assets in mutual funds as well as hedge funds. The hypothesis that mutual fund rules reflect market preferences would actually be supported if accredited investors' mutual fund assets exceeded their hedge fund investments. The amount and allocation of their mutual fund and hedge fund investments is not known, but one might crudely extrapolate from related data.

For example, only about 10 percent of accredited investors have made investments in private offerings generally, and hedge funds represent only part of that market, which means that an even smaller percentage of accredited investors has invested in hedge funds. In comparison with the near majority of US households that hold mutual funds, this rough approximation of hedge fund investments suggests that accredited investors overwhelmingly prefer mutual funds. But this claims too much, for investments in private offerings have been artificially suppressed by their being offered only privately. Mutual funds have had an enormous, unfair advantage as a result of hedge funds being prevented from making public offerings. In the JOBS Act of 2012, Congress required that the Commission permit the public offering of hedge funds, leading to the possibility of hedge funds gaining market share at the expense of mutual funds. But the JOBS Act's liberalizing of hedge fund regulation may have been neutralized by the Dodd–Frank Act of 2010's expansion of the SEC's authority to regulate hedge funds.

Even if the public marketing of hedge funds has increased their popularity, they still can only be sold to accredited investors, which limits the conclusions that can be drawn from growth in the market share of hedge funds. F. Scott Fitzgerald's observation that "the very rich ... are different from you and me" is certainly true of accredited investors' risk characteristics. For example, a substantial part of accredited investors' investment portfolios may be intended for future generations, which means that they can endure much longer periods of volatility than retirement investors, whose focus is generally their own lifetime.

These differences suggest two reasons that accredited investors would choose to opt out of mutual fund rules where retail investors would not. Mutual funds require daily liquidity, whereas hedge funds can set their own redemption terms. Hedge funds therefore can hold a less liquid portfolio (for example, nontraded debt and equity instruments held for years) and pay investors an ostensible illiquidity premium that mutual funds cannot offer. But opting out of the mutual fund liquidity rule necessarily holds much less appeal for retail investors because they have a greater need for liquidity. Similarly, retail investors are less able to benefit from the increased leverage that hedge funds may employ, and enjoy potentially higher returns that leveraging (and, arguably, nonfulcrum performance fees) may generate, because retail investors have less capacity than accredited investors to weather higher volatility.

In short, many retail investors would not benefit from some of the key features that hedge funds offer but mutual fund rules do not permit. They therefore might not opt out of these rules even if they had the option to do so. But that does not mean that retail investors would never make irrational choices in a laissez-faire market. Nor does this mean that retail investors would not opt for a class of hedge funds that were only mildly more illiquid and volatile than mutual funds. If hedge funds could be sold to retail investors, a market of low leverage, low volatility hedge funds might develop that would displace a substantial amount of mutual fund sales. In a large, public marketplace, hedge funds could be expected to develop rule-based brands of their own to compete with the mutual fund brand, although these rules would be contractual in nature, not regulatory.

Nor does the foregoing mean that retail investors could not rationally segment their asset allocation strategy to make room for a high leverage, high volatility hedge fund consistent with an investor's likely risk characteristics. In this respect, SEC rules permit an investor with $1 million in investments to invest and lose all of it in a single privately offered hedge fund, while an investor with only $999,999 in investments cannot allocate 5 percent of her portfolio to the same hedge fund. In other words, the Commission prohibits some investors from allocating a tiny percentage of their portfolios to hedge funds while permitting other, similarly situated investors to bet 100 percent of their assets on a single hedge fund. In light of modern portfolio theory, the SEC's disregard of the role of diversification is irrational, and it undoubtedly reduces hedge fund investments by properly diversified retail investors that pose minimal risk (Bullard 2013). Altering this rule to reflect a coherent theory of asset allocation would result in further displacement of mutual funds by hedge funds, although the incremental effect might be small.[9]

A full analysis of the degree to which mutual fund rules reflect investors' genuine revealed preferences is beyond the scope of this chapter, but such an analysis is needed. The law and economics literature has benefited regulatory analysis by questioning empirical assumptions regarding claimed efficiencies created by regulation. However, the same literature too often fails to test its own assumption that rules do not reflect market preferences. This assumption may be inaccurate, as illustrated in the following discussion of the ways in which the evolution of mutual fund regulation from 1980 to 2000 can be fairly characterized as a continuous, market-based attempt to maintain and strengthen the mutual fund brand as a diversified line of investment products.

---

[9] Congress adopted a diversification-based standard in the JOBS Act of 2012 for crowdfunding investors. 15 U.S.C. § 77d(a)(6).

3 THE SHADOW INVESTMENT COMPANY ACT: 1980–2000

This chapter has thus far framed the question of the legitimacy of mutual funds' market dominance in terms of the mutual fund as a single product *vis-à-vis* interchangeable substitutes in the financial services marketplace. In fact, the Commission has authorized many regulatory variations on the statutory mutual fund envisioned by Congress. As discussed above, variations on existing types of hedge funds, that is, alternative hedge fund brands, might develop if the Commission allowed them to be publicly offered to retail investors. One could argue that the Commission has done exactly that in the mutual fund context, that is, allowed the development of variations on the mutual fund brand, by accommodating investors' desire to opt out of certain mutual fund rules through a deliberate program of exemptive rules that mirror a strategy of market-based product differentiation. Money market funds, multiclass funds, funds of funds and target-date funds are examples of mutual fund products that have been created, in effect, by exemptive rulemaking.

The mutual fund statutory regime is designed to facilitate regulatory innovation. The most distinct characteristic of mutual fund regulation is that most of the substantive law that applies to mutual funds is based on a set of administrative exemptions. Over the past 35 years, the Commission has created a *bona fide* shadow Investment Company Act that materially alters virtually every major requirement under the Act (Bullard 2008). In some cases, SEC rules impose heightened requirements, but in most cases the Commission has substantially reduced or entirely eliminated requirements in fostering many variations on the statutory mutual fund.

The Act grants the Commission broad discretion to exempt mutual funds and their affiliates from its mandates.[10] Under this authority, the Commission has altered virtually every material requirement under the Act, with many exemptions reflecting a strong commitment to regulatory innovation in response to changing market demands. The Commission has repeatedly reinvented the statutory mutual fund by rolling out new products that have, in most cases, been met with resounding approval by issuers and investors. Some of these products are discussed below.

---

[10] Under Section 6(c), the Commission has broad authority to grant an exemption from the Act "if and to the extent that such exemption is necessary or appropriate in the public interest and consistent with the protection of investors and the purposes fairly intended by the policy and provisions of this subchapter." Section 3(b) authorizes the Commission to exempt an issuer from the Act upon a finding that the issuer is "primarily engaged in a business or businesses other than that of investing, reinvesting, owning, holding, or trading in securities." Section 12(d)(1)(J) authorizes exemptions from the Act's fund of funds restrictions "if and to the extent that such exemption is consistent with the public interest and the protection of investors." Section 17(b) authorizes the Commission to grant exemptions from Section 17(a)'s affiliated transaction prohibitions under the Act if the terms of the relevant transaction are "reasonable and fair," "consistent with the policy of each [fund] as recited in" its filings, and "consistent with the general purposes" of the Act.

3.1 Multiclass Funds and 12b-1 Fees

The multiclass mutual fund is a prominent example of regulatory innovation. Under the Act, today's "alphabet soup" of mutual funds' Class A, B, C, I, R1, R2, R3, and Z shares would not exist. The Act prohibits mutual funds from issuing senior securities, which generally include any class of shares with rights that are superior to any other class of shares. This prohibition was based on Congress's concern that among other things, complex capital structures facilitated wealth transfers from fund investors to insiders holding special classes of shares.

When the mutual fund industry complained that this restriction limited the flexibility of distribution arrangements, the Commission responded by granting hundreds of individual exemptions to permit the issuance of multiple classes of shares. These individual exemptions were codified in Rule 18f-3 in 1995. Multiclass funds initially enabled different combinations of front-end and contingent deferred commissions and asset-based sales charges. More recently, funds have introduced separate classes for investors who purchase shares through a financial adviser or retirement plan.

The incorporation of asset-based sales charges in mutual fund multiclass structures reflects a market innovation that has paralleled the development of multiclass funds. In the 1970s, the Commission took the position "that it is generally improper under the Investment Company Act of 1940 ('Act') for mutual funds to use their assets, directly or indirectly, to finance the distribution of their shares."[11] After a series of public hearings in which the fund industry complained that the SEC's position left funds unable to counter significant net redemptions of fund shares,[12] the Commission adopted Rule 12b-1, which permits funds to use fund assets to pay for distribution pursuant to a so-called 12b-1 plan.

Funds initially used 12b-1 fees for advertising and mailing fund prospectuses and literature to prospective investors (Goldberg and Bressler 1998). These activities have come to account for a tiny fraction of the use of 12b-1 fees, almost all of which are now paid to distributors as selling compensation.[13] More than two thirds of funds charge 12b-1 fees,[14] and funds collect more than $10 billion in 12b-1 fees annually.[15] Rule 12b-1 fees have become a central component of the brokers' compensation model.[16] The combination of SEC exemptions permitting multiclass shares and 12b-1 fees exemplify the SEC's history of regulatory innovation in the mutual fund marketplace.

---

[11] Bearing of Distribution Expenses by Mutual Funds, Rel. No. IC-9915 (Aug. 31, 1977).
[12] Advance Notice of Proposed Rulemaking, Rel. No. IC-10252 (May 23, 1978).
[13] *How Mutual Funds Use 12b-1 Fees*, 14 Investment Company Institute Fundamentals (Feb. 2005) (2 percent of 12b-1 fees used for promotion and advertising).
[14] INVESTMENT COMPANY INSTITUTE, REPORT OF THE GROUP ON RULE 12B-1 at 4 (May 2007) (as of 2006, more than 70 percent of funds charged 12b-1 fees).
[15] Steverman, *The Worst Deal in Mutual Funds Faces a Reckoning*, BloombergBusiness (Apr. 13, 2012) (investors paid $10.5 billion in 12b-1 fees in 2010).
[16] DIVISION OF INVESTMENT MANAGEMENT, U.S. SECURITIES AND EXCHANGE COMMISSION, REPORT ON MUTUAL FUND FEES AND EXPENSES, at text accompanying note 133 (Dec. 2000) ("Rule 12b-1 plans are integral to these arrangements—they are the means by which the brokers that sell fund shares under these arrangements are paid").

3.2 Money Market Funds

The Commission has also used its exemptive authority to create new products, of which the money market fund is the most prominent example. The Act requires that mutual funds value their portfolio securities at their fair market value, which the Commission interprets to prohibit funds from valuing debt securities at par. This prevented mutual funds from offering a cash-like product with a stable net asset value to compete with bank accounts. Such a fund would hold only very short-term debt securities, but even these money market instruments fluctuate in value enough to cause changes in a fund's per share value.

The potential benefits of offering a money market fund were heightened during the 1970s, when interest rates were very high and banks were prevented from sharing high rates with their customers because Regulation Q limited interest rates paid on deposits. Fund companies began offering money market funds that passed through high interest rates earned on the funds' investments to their shareholders, but their appeal was constrained because their value fluctuated while the value of bank accounts remained constant.

The fund industry lobbied the Commission to allow constant NAV funds that invest in money market instruments as a means of competing more effectively with banks. In 1983, the Commission responded with a rule permitting money market funds to value their portfolio securities at their amortized cost, and to round their per share NAVs to the nearest penny—that is, at $1.00 per share—provided that they met certain diversification, safety and maturity requirements.[17] Rule 2a-7 was a stunning success. While banks remained hamstrung by the lingering effect of Regulation Q's limits on interest paid on deposits,[18] Rule 2a-7 money market funds ("MMFs") took off, reaching $234 billion in assets by the end of 1983 and increasing every year until 2001.[19]

Money market funds represent one of the most significant developments in the financial markets in the past century. At the end of 2014, they held $3 trillion in assets,[20] including almost one quarter of nonfinancial businesses.[21] Money market funds hold more than one third of all open market commercial paper, 8 percent of municipal securities and loans, 5 percent of agency and GSE-backed securities, and 3 percent of US treasuries.[22] More personal assets were held in MMFs than checkable

---

[17] 17 C.F.R. 270.2a-7 (2015).

[18] Although Congress repealed limits on deposit interest rates in 1980, banks continued to be constrained by legacy, longer-term loans that paid interest rates that were too low to offer competitive interest rates on deposits. See Depository Institutions Deregulation and Monetary Control Act of 1980. Congress provided additional relief in the Garn–St. Germain Depository Institutions Act of 1982, which substantially liberalized the kinds of the loans that banks could offer and interest rates they could charge.

[19] ICI 2014 Fact Book at Table 35. Prior to the adoption of Rule 2a-7, MMFs held $3 billion in assets in 1976 and $80 billion in assets in 1980 (Markham 2002).

[20] U.S. Securities and Exchange Commission, Money Market Fund Statistics (July 29, 2015).

[21] 2015 ICI Fact Book at text accompanying figure 1.5.

[22] Historical Annuals, 2005–2014 Federal Reserve Board Flow of Funds at Tables L.208–211 (June 11, 2015).

bank deposits at the end of every year from 1998 to 2010.[23] Measured by their popularity with investors, MMFs have been a regulatory success story.[24]

3.3 Funds of Funds, Master-Feeder Funds and Multimanager Funds

With significant assistance from Congress, the Commission also created master-feeder funds and funds of funds. Funds of funds, as the term suggests, are a structure in which a fund invests its assets in underlying funds, each of which typically invests in a single asset class or subclass. A master-feeder fund reverses this structure; multiple funds invest in a single master fund to create a hub-and-spoke structure.[25] Originally, the Act generally restricted mutual funds' ability to invest in other funds.[26] Congress was concerned, among other things, about the top funds and underlying funds charging duplicative fees.[27]

In 1970, Congress amended the Act to permit funds to invest in other funds provided that they invested *all* of their assets in other funds.[28] The industry did not take advantage of this innovation until the first registration of a master fund in 1990. Master-feeder funds are now quite common. They allow for investors with different tax, regulatory, jurisdictional, marketing and other characteristics to invest in a single underlying portfolio, which avoids unnecessary duplication of portfolio management and administrative services. Master funds are not publicly offered, which means that their shares do not have to be registered under the Securities Act. They are not required to register under the Investment Company Act because they have a small number of shareholders and/or sell only to qualified purchasers.

With encouragement from the Commission, Congress amended the Act in 1996 to permit affiliated funds of funds, that is, funds of funds that invest only in underlying funds that are part of the same family of funds, and authorized the Commission to grant

---

[23] *Id.*; Historical Annuals, 1995–2004 Federal Reserve Board Flow of Funds at Table L.10 (June 11, 2015).

[24] Some would contend that the relative popularity of money market funds is due to the competitive advantage of not having to pay insurance premiums to the Federal Deposit Insurance Commission while offering an implied guarantee of principal similar to that offered by banks. This issue is beyond the scope of this analysis.

[25] U.S. SECURITIES AND EXCHANGE COMMISSION, "HUB-AND-SPOKE" FUNDS: A REPORT PREPARED BY THE DIVISION OF INVESTMENT MANAGEMENT (June 2, 1993).

[26] Section 12(d)(1)(A) of the Act generally prohibits funds from acquiring more than 3 percent of another fund's voting securities or investing more than 5 percent of its assets in a single fund or more than 10 percent of its assets in funds in the aggregate. Section 12(d)(1)(B) of the Act generally prohibits funds from selling securities if doing so would result in a single acquiring fund owning more than 3 percent of its voting securities or all acquiring funds in the aggregate owning more than 10 percent of its voting securities.

[27] Fund of Funds Investments, Rel. No. IC-26198, 68 F.R. at 58227 (Oct. 8, 2003) (fund of funds structures had been exploited by controlling persons who abused their positions, in some cases "when fund shareholders paid excessive charges due to duplicative fees at the acquiring and acquired fund levels") (citing INVESTMENT TRUSTS AND INVESTMENT COMPANIES, REPORT OF THE SECURITIES AND EXCHANGE COMMISSION, pt. 3, ch. 7, H.R. Doc. No. 136, 77th Cong., 1st Sess. at 2725–39, 2760 – 75 (1941)).

[28] ICA § 12(d)(1)(E); "HUB-AND-SPOKE" FUNDS, *supra*, at 4–5.

The rise and fall of the mutual fund brand 35

further funds of funds exemptions.[29] The Commission has since granted numerous individual exemptions and adopted rules that have expanded funds' options to adopt a fund of funds structure.[30] For example, Rule 12d1-2 allows intra-family funds of funds to invest in funds that are not in the same fund family.

Funds of funds have proliferated, most recently in the form of target-date funds, which typically invest in a mix of underlying funds that is intended to match the risk characteristics of an investor who expects to retire in the same year as the fund's target date. Since 2005, target-date fund assets have grown from less than $10 billion to more $600 billion (Yang and Lutton 2014).

In a vein similar to the fund of funds structure, the Commission has granted exemptions to permit funds to employ a manager or managers, or "multimanager." Under a multimanager structure, a fund's primary investment adviser oversees one or more subadvisers and hires and/or fires them based on their performance. Section 15(a) of the Act requires that investment advisers to mutual funds serve pursuant to a contract approved by the fund's shareholders, which necessitates a costly shareholders meeting and vote.[31] In addition, the Act requires that the contract precisely describe the compensation to be paid, which means that fees negotiated with subadvisers must be publicly disclosed.

The Commission has granted more than 200 individual exemptions to permit multimanager funds to hire subadvisers without shareholder approval and without disclosing the subadvisers' fees.[32] In 2003, multimanager fund assets exceeded $400 billion. The multimanager fund, like the MMF, fund of funds and master-feeder fund, represents yet another example of a positive market response to a successful regulatory innovation.

3.4 Exchange-Traded Funds

The SEC's latest creation—the exchange-traded fund ("ETF")—is perhaps its most successful as measured by market acceptance. One of the longstanding weaknesses of mutual funds has been the cost associated with offering redeemable securities. This requirement of the Act necessitates that funds hold a higher percentage of liquid assets than would otherwise be ideal in order to meet shareholder redemptions. When funds must sell portfolio securities to meet redemptions, they incur portfolio trading costs, and their shareholders incur passthrough tax liabilities as a result of the attendant capital gains inside the fund.

One potential solution to this problem is the closed-end fund, which has been permitted under the Act since its inception. Closed-end funds do not sell redeemable

---

[29] ICA § 12(d)(1)(G).
[30] Fund of Funds Investments, Rel. No. IC-27399 (June 20, 2006) (adopting Rules 12d1-1, 12d1-2, and 12d1-3).
[31] Exemption from Shareholder Approval for Certain Subadvisory Contracts, Rel. No. IC-26230 (Oct. 23, 2003).
[32] DIVISION OF INVESTMENT MANAGEMENT, U.S. SECURITIES AND EXCHANGE COMMISSION, MULTI-MANAGER FUNDS—AGGREGATE ADVISORY FEE RATE (Feb. 2014). In 2003, the Commission proposed to codify these exemptions, but that proposed rule has not been adopted. Exemption from Shareholder Approval for Certain Subadvisory Contracts, *supra*.

shares, which means that they do not incur the costs of meeting shareholder redemptions. However, a mutual fund's liquidity is an important feature for many investors, and closed-end funds therefore are poor mutual fund substitutes. Additionally, closed-end fund shares are traded in the secondary market, which means that fund share prices do not necessarily equal the pro rata value of the fund's net assets. This has been a persistent problem for closed-end funds, which often trade at large premiums and discounts to their NAV. As a result of these product flaws, closed-end funds do not hold a large amount of assets and their net new share issuances are approaching zero.[33]

The Commission has grappled with the mutual fund liquidity problem for years. For example, in 1990 the Commission granted an exemption to the SuperTrust for Capital Market Fund. The Fund was organized as a unit investment trust ("UIT") that invested in a single underlying mutual fund and issued shares that were redeemable only for orders of at least $5,000, which were called "SuperUnits."[34] SuperUnits traded on the American Stock Exchange; individual shares, called "SuperShares," were traded on the Chicago Board Options Exchange.[35] Although the SuperTrust can lay claim to having the first ETF shares on the market, there was nothing super about it. By late 1995, the SuperTrust had liquidated.[36] Its failure may have been related to its association with a trio of academics who were known as the "fathers of portfolio insurance," a disastrous financial experiment of the late 1980s for which many blamed the market crash of 1987.[37]

The Commission fared no better with its second effort. In 1993, the Commission adopted Rule 23c-3, which permitted closed-end funds to operate as so-called interval funds.[38] The rule was intended, like the exemptions granted later to allow ETFs, to mitigate that disruptive effect of ongoing redemptions. As is often the case with a new

---

[33] Since 2004, closed-end fund assets have increased from $253 billion to $289 billion and the number of funds has declined from 618 to 568. 2015 ICI Fact Book at figure 4.1. Net new share issuances have declined from $28 billion in 2007 to $5 billion in 2014. *Id.* at figure 4.3.

[34] SuperTrust Trust for Capital Market Fund, Inc., Rel. Nos. IC-17613 (Jul. 25, 1990) (notice) & IC-17809 (Oct. 19, 1990) (order).

[35] Petruno, *SEC Gives Tentative OK to New Market Hedge Securities*, L.A. TIMES at 4 (July 26, 1990). SuperShares were conceived by UC Berkeley professors as a form of portfolio insurance, not as alternative means of investing in mutual funds. Metz, *Investing in the S&P 500's Performance*, TULSA WORLD at G5 (Dec. 27, 1992); Pender, *UC Professor's SuperTrust an Investment Innovation*, SAN FRANCISCO CHRON. AT C1 (Mar. 3, 1989); *Leland O'Brien Offers Safe Opportunity in SuperShares*, AUSTRALIAN FIN. REV. at 42 (Dec. 2, 1988).

[36] SuperTrust Trust for Capital Market Fund, Inc., Rel. No. IC-21991 (May 29, 1996).

[37] Wilstein, *New Investment Fund Takes on Wall Street*, TULSA WORLD at G4 (Apr. 2, 1989); Frantz, *Leland O'Brien's Image Marred in "Meltdown" Pioneer Portfolio Insurers on the Defensive as Role in Market Skid Is Questioned*, L.A. TIMES at 1 (Nov. 2, 1987).

[38] Repurchases by Closed-End Management Investment Companies, Investment Company Act Rel. No. 19399 (Apr. 7, 1993) (adopting Rule 23c-3); Periodic Repurchases by Closed-End Management Investment Companies; Redemptions by Open-End Management Investment Companies and Registered Separate Accounts at Periodic Intervals or With Extended Payment, Investment Company Act Rel. Nos. 18869 (July 28, 1992) (proposing Rule 23c-3).

product rollout, the interval fund flopped. There are now almost no interval funds on the market.[39]

The SEC's third try was the charm. In 1992, it granted an exemption to State Street to offer shares in a UIT that were redeemable only in extremely large "creation units."[40] As a practical matter, only institutional investors had the capital necessary to redeem a creation unit, which meant that the fund did not have to deal with retail investor redemptions. The fund's shares traded in the secondary market, which provided liquidity to retail investors, and redemptions could be paid in kind, which meant that the fund need not sell portfolio securities.

The key feature that solved the closed-end fund premium/discount problem was the arbitrage created by the creation unit redemption right. When a premium or discount developed, arbitrageurs would, respectively, buy or redeem creation units to capture the difference between the trading price and the underlying value of the fund's NAV. The arbitrage was also facilitated by the constituents of the fund's index-based portfolio being publicly known.

Thus, the first successful ETF was launched: Standard & Poor's Depository Receipts, which are widely known by the moniker "SPDRs." State Street's Standard & Poor's 500 Index SPDR has since gathered more than $176 billion in assets, placing it among the five largest ETFs. However, no other State Street ETF places in the top 25. One reason for State Street's flagging success may be its use of the UIT structure, which must strictly replicate the index on which it is based. A UIT ETF does not reinvest dividends, engage in securities lending, employ derivatives, or use sampling to replicate its benchmark, which inevitably reduces its investment returns relative to a mutual fund ETF.[41] Since the 1990s, virtually all ETFs have therefore opted for the mutual fund structure (Yoder and Howell 2013).[42]

Exchange-traded funds had a slow start, gathering less than $34 billion in assets by the end of the 1990s.[43] However, ETF assets increased to $66 billion in 2000, and from 2003 to 2014 ETF assets grew more than 1,300 percent, from $151 billion to $2 trillion.[44] Net new issuance of ETF shares reached a record of $241 billion in 2014, compared with mutual funds' net new share issuance of $148 billion.[45]

---

[39] SharesPost 100 Fund: Frequently Asked Questions (2014): fund redeems up to 5 percent of shares each quarter). Recent reports suggest that intervals may yet find a niche in the investment company marketplace. Crowe, *The Rise of Interval Funds: Mutual Funds for Alternative Investing*, INVESTMENT NEWS (May 6, 2014).

[40] SPDR Trust, Rel. Nos. IC-18959 (Sept. 17, 1992) (notice) and IC-19055 (Oct. 26, 1992) (order).

[41] To illustrate, Barclay's iShares S&P 500 ETF, a mutual fund, has consistently outperformed SPDRs by far more than the 0.025 percent difference in fees between the two. Zhang, *Why Your Choice of S&P 500 ETF Matters*, MARKETWATCH (Mar. 19, 2013).

[42] The first ETFs operated as mutual (open-end) funds were the CountryBasket Index Funds. In the Matter of CountryBasket Index Funds, Inc., Investment Company Act Rel. Nos. 21736 (Feb. 6, 1996) (notice) and 21802 (Mar. 5, 1996) (order).

[43] Actively Managed Exchange Traded Funds, Rel. No. IC-25258 at text accompanying note 1 (Nov. 8, 2001).

[44] *Id.*; 2015 ICI Fact Book at figure 3.2.

[45] 2015 ICI Fact Book at figures 2.13 and 3.5.

Until 2008, the Commission granted exemptions only to index-based ETFs, out of concern that, among other things, the arbitrage mechanism would not work if the market did not know what was in the fund's portfolio.[46] That year, the Commission granted exemptions to permit actively managed ETFs on the condition that they publicly disclose their portfolios.[47] This fourth iteration of the ETF has not been popular with fund managers, who have expressed concern that publicly disclosing their portfolios will expose their funds to front running and reveal proprietary trading strategies.

In 2015, the Commission created yet another new product, the *nontransparent*, actively managed ETF, or "ETMF."[48] The ETMF trades on an exchange, but only at the fund's end of day NAV plus or minus the amount the broker agrees to be paid in connection with the transaction. It has yet to be determined whether the brokers and investors will embrace this novel pricing mechanism and trust the arbitrage mechanism in the absence of a fully transparent portfolio.[49] There is no denying, however, that the SEC's innovations are continuing apace. If ETMFs succeed, this latest iteration of the mutual fund brand may ultimately overtake the original.

3.5 Transactional Exemptions

Although they do not create new mutual fund brands, the SEC's roster of transactional exemptions are no less indicative of the agency's responsiveness to market preferences. The Act's affiliated transaction prohibitions prevent funds from engaging in a wide range of transactions, from principal trades between funds, to investments in IPOs in which an affiliate participates, to joint insurance policies covering fund directors and fund company executives. In each case, the Act assumes that the cost of potential self-dealing by fund affiliates exceeds the potential benefit of better trade execution, lower prices, and other efficiencies.

The Commission has adopted a wide range of exemptions that substantially mitigate potential losses resulting from the Act's ban on affiliated transactions. For example, Rule 17a-7 permits transactions between funds in the same fund complex. Rule 17a-9 permits a fund affiliate to purchase securities from a money market fund at the higher of its amortized cost of market value. Rule 10a-3 permits funds to purchase securities in an underwriting in which an affiliate participates. Rule 17d-1 permits funds, their

---

[46] Actively Managed Exchange Traded Funds, *supra*, at text accompanying note 33; Rule 6c-11 Proposal at note 20 (listing exemptive orders).

[47] *See* Actively Managed Exchange Traded Funds, *supra*, at 240.

[48] American Beacon NextShares Trust, et al., Rel. Nos. IC-31498 (Mar. 16, 2015) (notice) and IC-31542 (Apr. 1, 2015) (order). The Commission has denied applications for non-transparent, actively managed ETFs submitted by BlackRock Inc. and Precidian Investments. Hunnicutt, *SEC Denies Active ETF Proposal as NextShares Launches Salvo against Competitors*, INVESTMENT NEWS (July 27, 2015).

[49] *SEC Denies Active ETF Proposal*, *supra* (questioning brokers' acceptance of ETMF pricing mechanism). Envestnet was the first major broker-dealer to enlist to sell ETMFs. Hunnicut, *Nextshares Wins Its First Adviser Platform Partner with Envestnet*, INVESTMENT NEWS (Aug. 18, 2015).

directors, and fund company executives to obtain joint liability policies.[50] Rule 17e-1 permits affiliated brokers to receive commissions and other compensation without complying with Section 17(e)'s restrictions on such arrangements. Rule 17g-1 similarly permits funds and fund companies to obtain joint fidelity bonds.

The Commission has also adopted exemptions that simplify and reduce the cost of fund operations. For example, the Act requires the prior approval of a contract under which a firm acts as an investment adviser to a fund. Rule 15a-4 generally permits firms to act as an investment adviser to a fund on an interim basis following an assignment of the advisory contract. The Act generally prohibits the issuance of senior securities, which the Commission believes may occur if some but not all shareholders are granted the right to receive redemptions in kind. Rule 18f-1 permits such in-kind redemptions. The SEC's earliest exemptive order, published just 16 days after the attack on Pearl Harbor, permits a fund's independent public accountant to be approved by a majority of the board, rather than a majority of the fund's independent directors.[51]

These exemptions do not implicate as directly the question of whether investors have a de facto right to opt out of mutual fund rules. No investor ever sought out a fund that, for example, made it easier for the advisory contract or independent public accountant to be approved. Nonetheless, the exemptions reflect the kind of tinkering that product developers engage in to ensure that their products remain competitive in the marketplace.

4 MUTUAL FUND REGULATION AND GROWTH: 2000–2014

4.1 Stagnating Regulatory Innovation

The future of the mutual fund brand may depend on the SEC's maintaining its commitment to regulatory innovation, but there are signs that its commitment is flagging. The foregoing discussion of the Commission as entrepreneur generally applies only to developments from 1980 to 2000. During the past 15 years, both the SEC's commitment to the mutual fund brand and the fortunes of the mutual fund industry have been in decline.

In many cases, the SEC appears to have lacked the will to follow through on its own proposals. In 2003, the Commission proposed a rule that codified the terms of hundreds of multimanager exemptions, but no final action has been taken.[52] Nor has the Commission adopted proposed Rule 6c-11, which would codify ETF exemptions.[53]

---

[50] Rules promulgated under Section 17(d) technically are not exemptions from the Act. Section 17(d)'s prohibition against joint transactions involving funds and their affiliates is not self-executing, that is, the prohibition operates only to the extent that the Commission has prohibited joint transaction. Thus, these SEC exemptions are exemptions from the SEC's own prohibitions.

[51] Rule Conditionally Exempting One Class of Investment Companies from Certain Requirements of the Act Relating to the Selection of Independent Public Accountants, 6 F.R. 6631 (Dec. 23, 1941) (adopting Investment Company Act Rule 32a-1).

[52] *See* Rule 15a-5 Proposal, *supra*.

[53] *See* Exchange-Traded Funds, *supra*.

40 *Research handbook on the regulation of mutual funds*

Both multimanager fund and ETF sponsors therefore still must obtain individual exemptions. Giving new meaning to the word "temporary," the Commission adopted a "temporary" exemption from principal trading provision of the Advisers Act in 2007 with an expiration date of December 31, 2009,[54] which it extended in 2009, 2010, 2012, and 2014.[55] After issuing a concept release on actively managed ETFs in 2001,[56] the Commission took 13 years to grant an exemption to allow this structure, and even then to only one fund complex. Some of these initiatives have been supported by the industry and some have been opposed; all have been left unresolved.

The Commission has been passive in the face of newly permitted public advertising by hedge funds. The JOBS Act of 2012 required that the Commission allow public advertising of private offerings under Regulation D provided that the only purchasers were accredited investors (an innovation the Commission could have instituted). The Commission interpreted this provision to apply to hedge funds, but, in amending Regulation D as ordered by Congress, failed to resolve any of the issues regarding the effect of public advertising of hedge funds on the market for mutual fund substitutes. Instead, at the same time that the Commission allowed public advertising of hedge funds to proceed, it proposed a number of related reforms of hedge funds.[57] When the Commission issued the proposal, Chair Mary Jo White stated that she was "firmly committed to keeping consideration of this proposal on track so that the Commission is able to make an appropriate and timely regulatory response to the operation of the new rule permitting general solicitation."[58]

Nonetheless, more than three years later the proposal was still pending.

In important respects, since the turn of the millennium, the SEC's role in maintaining the mutual fund brand and promoting product innovation has weakened. As discussed further below, the SEC's lapsed commitment has been particularly prominent in the

---

[54] *See* Advisers Act Rule 206(3)-3T; Temporary Rule Regarding Principal Trades with Certain Advisory Clients, Rel. No. IA-2653 (Sep. 24, 2007). This rulemaking affects the ability of broker-dealers to operate wrap accounts and mini-accounts in competition with mutual funds and, therefore, investors' ability to opt out of mutual fund rules.

[55] Temporary Rule Regarding Principal Trades with Certain Advisory Clients, Rel. Nos. IA-3948 (Dec. 17, 2014) (Dec. 31, 2016 expiration date), IA-3522 (Dec. 20, 2012) (Dec. 31, 2014 expiration date), IA-3128 (Dec. 28, 2010) (Dec. 31, 2012 expiration date), and IA-2965 (Dec. 23, 2009) (Dec. 31, 2010 expiration date).

[56] Actively Managed Exchange Traded Funds, Rel. No. IC-25258 (Nov. 8, 2001). In 2008, the Commission proposed to codify the terms of ETF exemptions and to require daily portfolio disclosure for ETFs, but it has not taken final action on that proposal. Exchange-Traded Funds, Rel. No. IC-28193 (Mar. 11, 2008). In 2015, the Commission requested comment on ETFs and other exchange-traded products. Request for Comment on Exchange-Traded Products, Rel. No. 34-75165 (June 12, 2015).

[57] Amendments to Regulation D, Form D and Rule 156, Rel. No. 33-9416 (July 10, 2013). The Commission also stated that it would "monitor and study the development of private fund advertising and undertake a review to determine whether any further action is necessary." Eliminating the Prohibition Against General Solicitation and General Advertising in Rule 506 and Rule 144A Offerings, Rel. No. 33-9415 at 51–2 (July 10, 2013).

[58] Statement of Mary Jo White, Chair, U.S. Securities and Exchange Commission (July 10, 2013).

context of rules affecting mutual fund market timing, money market funds, and fund distribution arrangements.

4.1.1 Market timing

The earliest clear sign of the SEC's slipping commitment to the mutual fund brand was the market timing scandal in 2003. Mutual funds are required to price their shares based on their portfolio securities' current fair market value. In the late 1990s, some investors began noticing that funds were selling and redeeming shares based on stale values. For example, funds priced securities that traded in Asian markets based on closing prices at the close of trading on Asian exchanges at around 2:00 am EST. These prices were up to 14 hours old when funds used them to effect sales and redemptions in fund shares at 4:00 pm EST. When US markets rose after the close of Asian exchanges, investors bought fund shares on the assumption that the Asian securities had also increased in value. Funds therefore were, in effect, selling their shares at discount prices, thereby allowing them to obtain a relatively risk-free profit.

The Commission had been put on notice about this practice at least by October 1997, when a large bounce in the US markets left the shares of Asian funds substantially undervalued. Many investors exploited this opportunity and earned profits of up to 10 percent on a single day's investment. Investors in Fidelity funds were disappointed because Fidelity, unlike other funds, had corrected its funds' prices to reflect the change in market conditions, as required by the Act. These investors lost the 3 percent commission that they paid, and Fidelity was widely criticized for doing exactly what funds are required to do, which is to update stale prices in order to prevent dilution of shareholders' shares. The Commission conducted a study of the 1997 timing arbitrage event and found that timing arbitrage was widespread, but it did not require funds to stop using stale prices.

Not surprisingly, the pricing arbitrage problem grew, finally exploding in 2003. Over the years, some timing arbitrageurs arranged to buy fund shares *after* the shares had been priced. This practice violated the requirement that orders be executed at a fund's *next* computed price, but some funds agreed to permit late trading in return for investors agreeing to maintain a minimum balance in the fund sponsors' hedge funds. There is no evidence that the Commission was aware of late trading, as opposed to pricing arbitrage. A whistleblower informed New York Attorney General (NYAG) Eliot Spitzer about both practices, and he took immediate action. The NYAG, and eventually the Commission, brought dozens of enforcement actions against, and collected billions of dollars in penalties from, more than 20 different complexes. The NYAG also used the opportunity to negotiate a reduction in fund fees that he believed were excessive.

The market timing scandal was widely publicized and generally considered to be the biggest black mark on the mutual fund brand in history. Yet it reflected illegal conduct of which the Commission had been aware for years. This is understandable. A regulator is not responsible for maintaining the value of a particular brand; inaction on reports of timing arbitrage could be justified as a matter of prioritizing the allocation of SEC resources or in light of other regulatory considerations. The point here is that it reflected the abandonment of a role that the Commission had adopted successfully over the preceding two decades.

4.1.2 Money market funds

Although the effect of SEC inaction in the face of market timing is hard to measure, there is no doubt that the effect of its inaction regarding MMFs in 2007 and 2008 will have long-term repercussions. Net MMF inflows were negative $1.2 trillion from 2009 to 2011, a decline that is partly attributable to the SEC's failure to maintain and strengthen this mutual fund sub-brand.[59] Massive withdrawals of MMF assets began with the failure of the Reserve Primary Fund in September 2008. Previously, no retail MMF (and only one institutional MMF) had ever experienced a loss of principal. Although MMFs had seen their intraday NAVs drop below $1.00 on hundreds of occasions, they had a near perfect record primarily because their sponsors routinely obtained ad hoc, oral no-action relief from SEC staff to purchase bad debt from their MMFs in order to restore their $1.00 per share NAV. An exemptive process that relies on reaching key staff members on the phone is obviously fraught with risk and this became perilous as money markets experienced increasing stress in mid- to late 2007.[60]

At the same time, the Commission had no mechanism in place to evaluate the accuracy of prices at which MMFs valued their portfolios. Mutual funds have an incentive to inflate the value of their portfolios, which is heightened for MMFs because of the imperative to maintain a $1.00 per share NAV. The Commission also apparently had no systematic program of reviewing the MMFs that were most likely to be taking excess risk as reflected in their relative performance and attendant growth. Studies show that MMFs are essentially commodities, with virtually all variance in performance explainable by fees and risk, as opposed to management skill. The highest performing funds therefore are far more likely to fail, especially because they tend to attract hot money that is quick to redeem.[61] Finally, the Commission apparently had no systematic program of reviewing MMFs that were sponsored by firms that lacked the deep pockets that may be necessary to bail out their funds pursuant to the ad hoc no-action relief discussed above.

The threat to MMFs was widely known more than a year before the Reserve Primary Fund failed. Requests for no-action relief to bail out funds had reached an all-time high, with at least 44 fund companies buying securities from their MMFs' portfolios in late 2007.[62] A $5 billion cash fund operated by GE for its pension plans and was similar to an MMF failed in late 2007, ultimately paying investors 96 cents on the dollar.[63] A $27 billion state-run cash fund actually experienced a run in which $8 billion in assets were redeemed over a two-week period.[64] In January 2008, this

---

[59] There was preexisting market concern about money market funds, which had net negative inflows of $466 billion from 2002 to 2004. *See* 2015 ICI Fact Book at figure 2.3.

[60] Financial Crisis Inquiry Report, National Commission on the Causes of the Financial Economic Crisis in the United States at figure 13.1 (2011) (decline in outstanding asset-backed commercial paper from mid to later 2007 approximately equaled decline from 2008 to 2010).

[61] For example, in August 2007 the per share NAV of the top performing MMF during the preceding 12 months, which had goosed its performance by investing in structured finance products, declined below $1.00. Financial Crisis Inquiry Report at 254. The sponsor bought $5.7 billion of the $25 billion fund's assets. *Id.*

[62] *Id.* at 254–5.

[63] *Id.* at 255.

[64] *Id.*

author's advocacy group, along with other advocacy organizations, submitted a rulemaking petition to the Commission asking that it reconsider its ad hoc no-action process and requesting that MMFs be required to electronically file their portfolios with the Commission to enable the systematic review of MMF portfolio valuations.[65]

In light of these factors, the failure of the Reserve Primary Fund was quite predictable and preventable. The Fund's sponsor was not part of a large financial services firm and therefore less likely to be able to bail out its MMFs. The Fund reported the highest yield in the MMF industry in September 2008,[66] and was the "fastest-growing money market fund complex in the United States in 2006, 2007 and 2008—doubling in the first eight months of 2008 alone"[67]—as the fund company's owner prepped the firm for sale. The Fund therefore had an extremely high risk of breaking a dollar. The particular securities that caused this to happen were issued by Lehman Bros, one of the five largest investment banks and a close competitor of Bear Stearns, which the Fed had bailed out in March 2008.[68] If the Commission had implemented electronic pricing surveillance of MMFs, the valuation of Lehman-issued securities would have been red-flagged.

The SEC's most significant failure may have been its system of managing bailouts through ad hoc phone requests to SEC staff. Subsequent litigation revealed that the fund company's chairman and owner initially believed that the company could raise the cash necessary to bail out the fund and informed the Fund's board that he intended to seek the Commission's approval of a credit support agreement.[69] In contemporaneous, internal communications, the company's President had written that the fund company "intended to protect the NAV on the Primary Fund to whatever degree is required. We

---

[65] Letter from Fund Democracy, Consumer Federation of America, Consumer Action, AFL-CIO, Financial Planning Association, and National Association of Personal Financial Advisors to Nancy Morris, Secretary, U.S. Securities and Exchange Commission (Jan. 16, 2008).

[66] Stecklow and Gullapalli, *A Money-Fund Manager's Fateful Shift*, WALL ST. J. (Dec. 8, 2008). Proving the adage that pride goeth before a fall, Bent had frequently chastised other funds for investing in the same commercial paper that brought down his fund. *Id.* ("'Commercial paper is anathema to the concept of the money fund,' Mr. Bent told Reuters in 2001. 'People prostituted the concept by putting garbage in the funds and reaching for yield.' The following year, he told Investor's Business Daily that 'we don't drink, smoke or buy commercial paper.'").

[67] Financial Crisis Inquiry Report at 356.

[68] Federated Investors, one of the largest MMF managers, had dropped Bear Stearns from its list of approved counterparties for unsecured commercial paper in October 2007. Financial Crisis Inquiry Report at 283. Fidelity and State Street soon followed suit, around the same time that the Commission found that "no evidence of any deterioration in the firm's liquidity position." *Id.* at 284. On July 10, 2008, Federated announced that it would no longer pursue additional business with Lehman. *Id.* at 328. Fed Chairman Benjamin Bernanke has noted the connection between Lehman's distress the Reserve Fund's failure. *Id.* at 329. When it failed, the Reserve Fund held $785 million in Lehman commercial paper, equal to 1.2 percent of its assets. *Id.* at 356.

[69] *See In re Reserve Fund Sec. & Derivative Litig.*, 2013 WL 5432334At *3 (S.D.N.Y. 2013).

have spoken with the SEC and are waiting [for] their final approval which we expect to have in a few hours."[70]

Regardless of whether the Fund's sponsor could have raised sufficient assets to bail out the Fund, the dysfunctional nature of such a last-minute, phone-based no-action system is self-evident.

The Commission was not prepared to handle a true MMF liquidity crisis, notwithstanding the many signs that such a crisis was already underway. The Commission deserves significant credit for creating the MMF industry, but it also bears significant responsibility for the failure of the Reserve Primary Fund and MMF assets' shrinking by almost 25 percent since 2008.[71] The Commission has adopted MMF reforms, which are shrinking industry assets further, that were largely driven by the demands of the Treasury Department.[72] Just as the Commission left the handling of mutual fund market timing to the NYAG, it appears to have substantially deferred to banking regulators in reforming MMF rules.

4.1.3 12b-1 fees and revenue sharing

In two important respects, the Commission has not kept pace with developments in mutual fund distribution arrangements. First, the Commission has not addressed the disclosure of 12b-1 fees paid by investors, although it has conceded for more than 15 years that current disclosure requirements are inadequate. The mutual fund confirmation shows the amount of the commission charged, that is, the dollar amount subtracted from the investment before the fund shares are purchased, but it does not show the 12b-1 asset-based fees that investors pay on an ongoing basis. Nor does any other document show the amount deducted from shareholders' accounts to cover 12b-1 fees. This omission has been exacerbated by the broker-dealer industry's shift, over the past two decades, from commissions toward asset-based fees. Commissions on mutual funds have steadily declined, while 12b-1 fees have become the functional equivalent of a deferred or installment commission. In 2008, SEC Chairman Christopher Cox promised that "in coming days, you can look for the SEC to open up the hood of this old jalopy and start cleaning out the gunk. When the overhaul is done, I predict there won't be a 12b-1 in there anymore."[73] Seven years later, and five years after the

---

[70] *Id.* at *3. Notably, the Commission did not challenge the assertion that he had contacted the staff. Sponsors of other MMFs successfully bailed out their funds by buying their Lehman commercial paper (Fisch and Roiter 2012).

[71] Collins, Gallagher, Heinrichs, and Plantier, *Money Market Mutual Funds, Risk, and Financial Stability in the Wake of the 2010 Reforms*, 19 ICI Research Perspective (Jan 2013) (MMFs held almost $3 trillion in assets at their peak in 2008).

[72] As a technical matter, it is a committee of regulators, the Financial Stability Oversight Council ("FSOC"), that has ultimate authority to force the Commission to adopt rules relating to money market funds. However, in this author's view FSOC operates as a de facto extension of the Treasury Department. Additionally, the Treasury Department has been the most outspoken critic of SEC money market fund systemic risk regulation.

[73] Comments by Christopher Cox, Chairman, U.S. Securities and Exchange Commission, at the Investment Company Institute 4th Annual Mutual Fund Leadership Dinner, Washington, D.C. (Apr. 30, 2008).

Commission proposed reforms to the mutual fund confirmation, the SEC's "pending repeal or reform of rule 12b-1"[74] was still pending.[75]

Second, fund companies now routinely pay for fund distribution through revenue sharing arrangements. "Revenue sharing" refers to payments made by fund companies to broker-dealers for distribution services and for what are called "training and education" events for financial advisers. These payments generally comprise a percentage of the transaction amount and an ongoing percentage of fund assets held at the broker-dealer. Industry participants have been sued by private parties, state securities regulators, and the Commission itself regarding the disclosure of revenue sharing arrangements,[76] yet the Commission has not articulated standards for the disclosure of revenue sharing payments. The Commission proposed rules to address this issue in 2004 that would have mandated disclosure to investors at the time of the transaction ("point of sale").[77] More than a decade later, no final action has been taken on the SEC's point of sale proposal.

Again, the Commission left regulatory reform to another agency. In 2010, the Department of Labor put the Commission on notice with a proposed rulemaking to require, among other things, disclosure of revenue sharing arrangements.[78] Although the Department subsequently indicated its intention to withdraw the proposed rulemaking, it made it clear that a reproposal would be forthcoming. The Department proposed new rules in April 2015, which prompted belated calls from financial services for the Commission to take action.[79] The Commission did nothing, and the Department

---

[74] *Id.*

[75] Some Rule 12b-1 adjustments are simple and noncontroversial. For example, when it adopted the rule, the Commission imposed a de facto requirement that directors formally consider certain factors when evaluating a 12b-1 plan, including, for example, consideration of the "nature of the problems or circumstances which purportedly" necessitated the plan. Bearing of Distribution Expenses by Mutual Funds, Investment Company Act Release No. IC-11414 (Oct. 28, 1980). There is virtual unanimity that these factors reflect the original purpose of 12b-1 fees, which was to stem the tide of redemptions that occurred in the 1970s, and not their current purpose of paying for distribution. Yet the Commission has been unable to withdraw this requirement, and fund directors continue to paper their files with anachronistic findings. *See* Mutual Fund Distribution Fees; Confirmations, Rel. No. IC 29367 at 15 16 (July 21, 2010) ("12b-1 Fee Proposal").

[76] *Capital Research and Mgmt. Co. v. Brown*, 147 Cal.App.4th 58 (2007); *In the Matter of Focus Point Solutions, Inc.*, Admin. Proc. File No. 3-15011 (Sep. 6, 2012); Wiese, *Settlement Approved in A.G. Edwards Case*, MO. L. MEDIA (June 20, 2010) (describing settlement of private claims based on failure to disclose revenue sharing).

[77] Confirmation Requirements and Point of Sale Disclosure Requirements for Transactions in Certain Mutual Funds and Other Securities, and Other Confirmation Requirement Amendments, and Amendments to the Registration Form for Mutual Funds, Rel. No. IC-26341 (Jan. 29, 2004); Point of Sale Disclosure Requirements and Confirmation Requirements for Transactions in Mutual Funds, College Savings Plans, and Certain Other Securities, and Amendments to the Registration Form for Mutual Funds, Rel. No. IC-26778 (Feb. 28, 2005) (requesting additional comments).

[78] Definition of the Term "Fiduciary," 75 Fed. Reg. 65263 (Oct. 22, 2010).

[79] The rulemaking comprised a number of proposals, of which the expansion of the Department's definition of "fiduciary" is the most significant. Definition of the Term "Fiduciary," 80 Fed. Reg. 21928 (Apr. 20, 2015).

adopted final rules in April 2016.[80] The Commission ignored years of signs that undisclosed mutual fund fees needed to be addressed, thereby abdicating its regulatory role to another agency, just as it had left MMF reform to banking regulators and mutual fund market timing to the NYAG.

4.1.4 Conflicts of interest in broker-dealer compensation

The Commission has also failed to address the perception that broker-dealer compensation creates financial incentives for financial advisers to give investors bad advice. For example, broker-dealers compensation can vary greatly depending on the particular mutual fund that its financial advisers recommend to clients, which has fueled calls to impose a fiduciary duty on broker-dealers when providing retail investment advice.[81]

Congress, FINRA and the Department of Labor have taken action on this issue, but the Commission has seemed paralyzed by indecision. In 2010, the Dodd–Frank Act amended the Exchange Act to require the Commission to "examine and, where appropriate, promulgate rules prohibiting or restricting certain sales practices, conflicts of interest, and compensation schemes for brokers, dealers, and investment advisers."[82]

The Commission has taken no action under this provision. The Dodd–Frank Act required the Commission to issue a report on the difference in regulations between broker-dealers and investment advisers.[83] The completed study includes no discussion of compensation conflicts and offers no related recommendations.[84] The Dodd–Frank Act authorized the Commission to impose a fiduciary duty on broker-dealers that would have addressed such conflicts of interest.[85] SEC Chair Mary Jo White indicated that she supported a fiduciary rulemaking, but no other SEC action has been forthcoming.

---

[80] Definition of the Term "Fiduciary," 81 Fed. Reg. 20945 (Apr. 8, 2016).

[81] Ironically, the SEC's early response to conflicts in broker-dealer compensation structures was not to expand but to *eliminate* the fiduciary duty for many broker-dealers. The Commission currently takes the position that broker-dealers that charge an asset-based fee for investment advice are investment advisers under the Investment Advisers Act of 1940, which then subjects the broker-dealer to a fiduciary duty under the Act. However, in 1999 it proposed to exempt such broker-dealers from the Act as a means of encouraging less conflicted investment advice. Certain Broker-Dealers Deemed Not To Be Investment Advisers, Investment Advisers Act Rel. No. 1845 (Nov. 4, 1999). The Financial Planning Association challenged the SEC's authority to adopt what became known as the "Merrill Rule," and the U.S. Court of Appeals for the D.C. Circuit vacated the rule in 2005. *Financial Planning Assoc. v. SEC*, 482 F.3d 481 (2005). In yet another ironic twist, this precedent will likely be applied in upcoming challenges to the Department of Labor's rulemaking, which seeks to *expand* the number of broker-dealers that are subject to a fiduciary duty. Temple-West, *After Hearings, Labor Department on Track to Finish Fiduciary Rule by Year's End*, POLITICO PRO (Aug. 14, 2015) (reporting that Primerica had retained counsel to challenge the rulemaking).

[82] Dodd–Frank Act Section 913(g) (adding new subparagraph (l) to Exchange Act Section 15).

[83] *Id.* at Section 913(d).

[84] Study Regarding Obligations of Brokers, Dealers, and Investment Advisers, Exchange Act Release No. 34-62577 (July 27, 2010).

[85] Dodd–Frank Act Sections 913(g) (adding new subparagraph (k)(1) to Exchange Act Section 15) and 913(f) (authoring SEC rulemaking pursuant to findings of study mandated under Section 913(b)).

In 2014, FINRA strengthened its suitability standard to be more akin to a fiduciary standard and stated its view that broker-dealers must act in their customers' best interests (Bullard 2011). It has also implemented an inspection program targeted at ensuring that broker-dealers have adopted procedures that are designed to mitigate conflicts of interest. FINRA also proposed rules that would require more disclosure of revenue, but they have not been approved by the Commission. Nor has the Commission taken final action on its own 2004 proposal to improve revenue sharing disclosure at the time of the sale to the client, as noted above.

The SEC's inaction recently came to a head when the Department of Labor took matters into its own hands. As discussed above, in April 2016 the Department adopted rules that prohibit the payment of certain forms of financial adviser compensation. The rules create very different regulatory regimes for individual retirement accounts ("IRAs") and taxable accounts.[86] Faced with the unpleasant prospect of creating separate compliance systems for IRAs under DOL rules and taxable accounts under SEC rules, financial services firms are likely to subject all of their accounts to the higher DOL standard. The Commission is the primary regulator for mutual funds, but the Department now controls much of the mutual fund regulatory space.

4.1.5 Fixed pricing under Section 22(d)

As illustrated by the 12b-1 fee, multimanager, and point of sale proposals cited above, the Commission has continued to make attempts at innovation. A particularly promising example is its proposal to repeal, in effect, Section 22(d) of the Act. Section 22(d) requires funds to sell their shares at the price stated in the prospectus, which means that brokers cannot be paid different commissions on transactions in the same fund. As the Commission has noted, Section 22(d) "effectively prohibits competition in sales loads on mutual fund shares at the retail level"; such anticompetitive price fixing "would normally be a violation of the antitrust laws."[87] In 2010, the Commission proposed to allow funds to sell shares for which broker-dealers determined the commission. However, as has been the case with a number of promising SEC initiatives, the Commission has taken no final action on the proposal. Unlike the other unfinalized proposals discussed above, the effective repeal should have substantial industry support.

5 STAGNATING INDUSTRY GROWTH

With the exception of actively managed ETFs, since 2000 the Commission appears to have abdicated its role as keeper of the mutual fund flame. Perhaps the SEC's lapse reflects nothing more than the inevitable ups and downs of what still remains an iconic brand in the financial services industry. Or its inaction could reflect the nature of

---

[86] The rulemaking comprised a number of proposals of which the expansion of the Department's definition of "fiduciary" is the most significant. *See* Definition of the Term "Fiduciary," 75 Fed. Reg. 65263 (Oct. 22, 2010).

[87] 12b-1 Fee Proposal, *supra*, at 87 and n.266 (citing *U.S. v. National Ass'n of Sec. Dealers, Inc.*, 422 U.S. 694, 701 (1975)) (antitrust immunity is afforded to sales made pursuant to Section 22(d)).

needed reforms having transitioned from rules that the industry supported, from 1980 to 2000, to rules that the industry opposed, from 2000 to the present. Yet some of the latter reforms should (or likely would) have been supported by the industry; rulemaking that prevented the market timing scandal and/or the run on money market funds would unquestionably have benefited the industry. Rather than regulatory capture of the Commission by the industry, perhaps both were captured by a shared fear of upsetting the status quo, a theory that may explain many of the developments leading up to the financial crisis of 2008.

Periods of regulatory innovation and regulatory paralysis from 1980 to 2014 appear to have coincided with periods of industry growth and stagnation. The brand-enhancing reforms described above occurred during the 1980s and 1990s, a period of strong mutual fund growth. During the subsequent period in which the SEC's commitment to the mutual fund brand appears to have waned, mutual funds' growing popularity has slowed or come to a standstill. To illustrate, net inflows for mutual funds from 2002 to 2014 totaled $2 trillion, or an average of $157 billion annually.[88] Net inflows from 1990 to 2001 totaled $3.3 trillion, or an average of $272 billion annually.[89] Adjusting for inflation, the average net inflow in current dollars for each period was $181 billion and $406 billion, respectively.[90]

The weakening of net mutual fund inflows also coincides with stagnating market penetration. In 1990, mutual funds comprised 6.7 percent of household financial assets.[91] This share peaked at 18.4 percent in 2000, for an average annual increase of 1.06 percentage points. In 2014, mutual funds' share stood at only 20.9 percent,[92] for an average annual increase of 0.23 percentage points. In 1980, only 5.7 percent of households held mutual funds. Mutual funds' market penetration jumped to 27 percent by 1991 and to 48.9 percent by 2001 (Burnham, Bogdan, and Schrass 2013).[93] In contrast, from 2002 to 2013 household market penetration ranged from 43.7 to 47.1 percent. In 2014, the percent of households holding mutual funds fell to 43.3 percent, the lowest level since 1999.[94] Since 2001, mutual fund household market penetration has declined 5.6 percentage points, after increasing 21.9 percentage points during the preceding decade. Had the Commission taken steps to prevent the market timing scandal and/or run on money market funds, for example, it is very likely that the performance of the fund industry would have been substantially better during this period.

The declining market penetration of mutual funds has not been mitigated by expanding market penetration through ETFs. The data on ETFs held by households that

---

[88] 2015 ICI Fact Book at figure 2.3.
[89] 2003 ICI Fact Book at 108.
[90] These data are based on the Department of Labor's CPI Inflation Calculator at www.bls.gov/data/inflation_calculator.htm.
[91] 2015 ICI Fact Book at figure 1.3.
[92] *Id.* at figures 1.1 and 1.3.
[93] The actual amounts are somewhat higher, as pre-2000 excludes large categories of mutual fund assets. The data exclude mutual funds in retirement plans prior to 1994, in variable annuities prior to 1998, and in IRAs prior to 2000 (Burnham, Bogdan, and Schrass 2013). This has no effect, however, on the overall decline in household penetration after 2000.
[94] 2015 ICI Fact Book at figure 6.1.

do not hold mutual funds is limited, but that number appears to be very small. In 2013, ETFs were held by about 5.7 million households, but the vast majority of these households also held mutual funds.[95] When ETFs, UITs, and closed-end funds are included with mutual funds for 2013, household ownership rises to only 47.1 percent from the 46.3 percent of households holding mutual funds.[96] In other words, while the mutual fund brand is expanding through the sale of ETFs, these gains are largely cannibalizing the brand's overall market presence.

The fact that the declining value of the mutual fund brand since 2000 has been coextensive with SEC inaction on a range of brand-affecting issues is consistent with the view that SEC inaction has contributed to this decline. Admittedly, maintaining and strengthening a market brand is not a conventional regulatory responsibility, but neither is the Investment Company Act a conventional regulatory statute. As discussed above, the extraordinarily intrusive, prescriptive nature of the Act supports the view that Congress intended the Commission to extend the principles underlying the Act through ongoing exemptive rulemaking. The SEC actively embraced this role from 1980 to 2000, which coincides with the mutual fund brands' becoming the strongest brand in the financial services industry. The agency reverted to a narrower, more traditional role in the new millennium, which coincided with a period of stagnation for the mutual fund brand.

At the same time, other regulators have stepped into the SEC vacuum. The NYAG tackled market timing abuses, the Treasury Department has forced MMF reforms, and the Labor Department has overhauled the structure of distribution compensation for mutual funds. In each of these examples, both the mutual fund industry and the Commission have suffered reputational harm. In each case, the problems that led to other regulators' actions were longstanding and publicly known. The Commission could have taken proactive measures to address these situations, but it chose not to do so.

As of this writing, the SEC is extending its period of paralysis in the area of ETF regulation. The next potential game change is the actively managed ETF, which would be allowed to operate without disclosing its portfolio on an ongoing basis. Actively managed ETFs present an opportunity for the Commission to re-assert its role as keeper of the mutual fund brand by restructuring the mutual fund distribution model. This model was relatively unaffected by early ETFs because they were index funds, and brokers generally sell actively managed funds. Since 2008, the sale of actively managed ETFs with fully disclosed portfolios has been limited because most active managers believe that full portfolio disclosure would compromise their proprietary trading strategies and create front running risk.

In contrast, actively managed ETFs with undisclosed portfolios could transform the industry. These ETMFs would allow the same types of funds for which a small investor would pay a $1,000 commission to be purchased for a commission of less than $100. Marketing materials for the first ETMFs list their advantages over mutual funds, and the first item on that list is that there are "[n]o sales loads or distribution or services

---

[95] More than 80 percent of households that held ETFs or closed-end funds also held mutual funds. *See* Ownership of Mutual Funds, *supra*, at 3–4.
[96] *Id.* at 3.

fees."[97] The use of ETMFs would allow broker-dealers to sidestep the brunt of the DOL's fiduciary rulemaking. With the exception of Eaton Vance's NextShares, the Commission has repeatedly denied exemptive relief to permit other types of non-disclosing, actively managed ETFs. Eaton Vance claims intellectual property rights to certain aspects of its funds, which may inhibit growth that is based on the Eaton Vance model.

While the Commission seems uninterested in allowing the development of a market for actively managed ETFs, it is ignoring a vital threat to the integrity of the ETF pricing mechanism. The Commission has long misunderstood the critical importance of the degree and transparency of premiums and discounts in ETF prices. The Commission allowed ETFs to claim near perfect trading price and market value correlations until this author provided evidence to the contrary and forced Barclays, by requesting a hearing on its exemptive application, to agree to disclose premiums and discounts on its website. The Commission incorporated this disclosure condition into subsequent exemptive orders.

However, experience has demonstrated that the mandated disclosure of end of day premiums and discounts is inadequate to convey the large premiums and discounts at which the most liquid ETFs may trade. Rather than improving disclosure—or proposing operational reforms designed to mitigate deviant ETF trading prices—the Commission *eliminated* the requirement that ETFs disclose premiums and discounts. The Commission thereby aggravated a growing problem.

6 SEC ABANDONMENT OF THE MUTUAL FUND BRAND

As the foregoing discussion illustrates, the mutual fund brand comprises much more than a single set of default rules. Pursuant to the SEC's program of innovation through exemption, investors can opt out of many of the most restrictive mutual fund rules under the Act. They can mix and match distribution models, organizational structures, and liquidity and pricing options to create a broad matrix of options that, while not representing products created in an open market, reflect an array that has the characteristics of a market for regulation similar to that offered under state corporate law.

The SEC's role in creating this market looks very much like that of an entrepreneur adjusting product features in an attempt to maintain and strengthen a position of market dominance. The evolution of today's ETF began with consecutive flops, the SuperTrust and interval fund, followed by the successful release of the imperfect UIT model, SPDRs, and the ultimate delivery of today's ETF, a veritable mutual fund industry iPhone. Like many innovative businesses, the Commission tinkered with a new product until it found a regulatory mix that would appeal to investors. Two trillion dollars later, the success of ETFs represents only the most recent illustration of regulatory innovation through mutual fund exemptive rules.

---

[97] Introducing NextShares, www.nextshares.com (Aug. 23, 2015) ("Unlike most mutual fund share classes, NextShares don't charge sales loads or pay distribution and service (12b-1) fees. All investors have access to a single, low-cost share class").

The SEC's regulatory innovations have created an expansive internal market of products within the mutual fund space. Multiclass funds, funds of funds, multimanager funds, and ETFs offer ways for investors to opt out of mutual fund default rules yet stay within the mutual fund fold. SEC rulemaking could be viewed as creating multiple means by which investors can benefit from the inherent advantages of investing in investment pools run by professional managers. The same can be said for securities regulation generally, such as the set of offering rules under which issuers can raise capital and investors are permitted to invest in such issuers. While it is difficult to determine the extent to which investors' choices to invest in mutual fund substitutes reflect their revealed preferences for mutual fund rules, it is beyond cavil that regulatory innovation has created significant opt-out opportunities under the umbrella of the mutual fund brand.

Regulatory innovation and the vibrant market of mutual fund variants that it has created illustrate how regulation can effectively respond to market preferences. Popular critiques of federal securities regulation treat it as inconsistent with, if not antithetical to, laissez-faire market forces when in fact it comprises a richly diverse set of regulatory models that have accommodated a broad range of investor preferences. The primacy of the mutual fund brand in the marketplace of investment funds may be largely attributable to the SEC's historical role in maintaining and strengthening the mutual fund brand.

Among their many insightful comments on this chapter, William Birdthistle and John Morley have noted the rich vein of public choice issues that this chapter admittedly has left largely unplumbed. For example, a common explanation applied to agency action is regulatory capture, that is, the theory that agencies may be captive to the industries they regulate. The SEC's regulatory program over the past three decades may reflect nothing more than a policy of appeasement.

What prompts the SEC to act or refrain from acting is important, but this chapter is not so ambitious as to attempt to answer that question. This chapter's narrower purpose has been to provide a novel positive description of developments in mutual fund regulation and the mutual fund industry, and to suggest that these developments undermine, first, general skepticism regarding the capacity of regulation to reflect market preferences, and second, the more specific critique that securities regulation would necessarily be more efficient if structured as a regulatory marketplace similar to the market for state corporate law. The past three decades of mutual fund regulation challenge the popular mantra that regulating an activity will necessarily mean that there is less of it.

Although this chapter does not take any position as to *why* the Commission has adopted one policy or another, it would be helpful to know why the Commission does what it does. Legal analysis has practical utility to the extent that it sheds light on how and to what extent law furthers normative social goals. For example, a compelling normative case can be made that increasing mutual fund assets at the expense of mutual fund substitutes or other means of investing would generate net social benefits. Assuming such a normative goal, this chapter contends that the Commission will necessarily play a critical role in achieving it. Understanding what motivates the

Commission therefore would be helpful in creating the conditions under which it is most likely to enhance the mutual fund brand or take steps to protect the brand from harm.

Public choice theory, specifically agency capture, offers an appealing explanation for SEC action and inaction. Regulatory innovation prior to 2000 generally took the form of freeing funds and their affiliates from certain legal requirements. The reforms that this chapter contends the Commission should have undertaken after around 2000 generally would have entailed imposing new restrictions on the fund industry. One might contend that the industry would naturally support the former and oppose the latter, which would mean that the correlation described in this chapter between SEC action or inaction and industry growth or stagnation may have been nothing more than a coincidental byproduct of agency capture.

However, in some respects agency capture is a poor fit. Since 2000, the Commission has adopted a number of rules that the industry has opposed, which is inconsistent with the view that agency capture was pervasive. With respect to mutual funds, the industry opposed SEC rules requiring that mutual funds disclose how they vote proxies and disclose their portfolios more frequently, and that their boards be chaired by an independent director and at least two thirds composed of independent directors (the industry successfully challenged the latter two requirements in court). If the Commission were subject to agency capture, it is not clear why it would have chosen to adopt these rules while taking no action on problems that had far more profound implications for the fund industry and, in the case of MMFs, played a major role in the financial crisis of 2008. Conversely, agency capture does not explain why the Commission failed to take actions favored by the industry, such as finalizing its proposal to codify the terms of ETF exemptions. But agency capture need not be pervasive to be real; there may be certain types of regulatory initiatives that are more susceptible to its influence.

Agency capture may oversimplify rulemaking dynamics by implying the existence of common industry interests, when in fact industry interests conflict. For example, market timing arrangements benefited some fund complexes at the expense of their competitors. Fidelity endured a substantial amount of negative publicity for imposing internal rules that prevented market timing; it may well have been a vocal supporter of SEC action to bring other fund complexes into line. Many fund companies may have supported tightening pricing rules as a means of leveling the playing field. Similarly, the Reserve Primary Fund substantial asset gains prior to its collapse were obtained at the expenses of competitors that invested more conservatively. However, differing industry interests can be consistent with agency capture. The most intense industry lobbying generally comes from the industry groups with the most to lose, which would have been fund complexes that benefited from market timing and lax MMF regulation.

Agency capture must explain why some agencies are captured and others are not. As discussed above, the NYAG and Labor and Treasury Departments took action in areas where the Commission is the primary regulator. Why would the Commission have been captured but not the others? Agency capture may depend on intra-agency dynamics. The Office of the NYAG and the Labor and Treasury Departments are each run by a single individual, whereas the Commission makes decisions on rules as a committee and therefore may be more liable to agency capture. Congress's attempts to convert the very activist Consumer Financial Protection Bureau to a committee structure like that of the SEC may reflect the view that committees are structurally less effective.

Agency capture is not the only public choice theory of agency conduct that may help explain SEC policy. The SEC's inaction may reflect a public choice model in which bureaucrats seek to maximize their jurisdiction. However, SEC inaction opened the door for other government actors to regulate in areas where the Commission has primary responsibility. The Labor Department's fiduciary rulemaking may transform mutual fund distribution and IRA investing at the expense of SEC power. The same NYAG who took action against fund companies for permitting market timing also used his leverage in negotiating settlements of market timing charges to negotiate fee reductions, another area in which the Commission has historically abdicated responsibility (around the time of the market timing scandal, the NYAG also usurped the SEC's responsibility for analysts' conflicts). The run on MMFs opened the door for FSOC to intrude in MMF rulemaking. Yet SEC inaction could be viewed as a means of protecting its regulatory turf on the premise that regulatory activism may incite Congressional calls to reduce the SEC's budget. Like its committee structure, the SEC's dependence on Congressional appropriations—"budgetary capture"—may explain SEC inaction.

What motivates the Commission is particularly important in the mutual fund context. The extraordinarily prescriptive nature of investment company regulation, coupled with the SEC's expansive exemptive authority, ineluctably place the Commission in the position of a kind of mutual fund czar. This chapter suggests that the Commission should recognize and embrace its role, and that those who criticize virtually every form of regulation should recognize the potential for the SEC to increase net social wealth. These normative views are consistent with the theory of public choice that justifies the delegation of decisions to unelected independent agencies on the ground that they have the special expertise and reduced susceptibility to short-term political pressure to enable the degree of legal specificity required by certain subject matter (for example, Spence and Cross 2000). The SEC's rulemaking pattern in the past century arguably realized this vision of an effective administrative state; its failures in this century illustrate what happens when an agency abjures its inescapable role.

7 CONCLUSION

This chapter evaluates the efficiency of mutual fund regulation from a market perspective by considering whether investor preferences for potential market substitutes for mutual funds (e.g., hedge funds, separate accounts, CITs, mini-accounts) provide insights into whether mutual fund regulation is responsive to such preferences. Continuing on the theme of the regulatory market, this chapter also posits that SEC rulemaking played a major role in the creation and maintenance of the mutual fund brand from 1980 to around 2000, when mutual funds became the most popular investment vehicle in America. During the same period, the Commission adopted a number of exemptive rules permitting the creation and sale of money market funds, funds of funds, multimanager funds, and ETFs and authorizing arrangements such as 12b-1 fees. This chapter also suggests that the mutual fund's industry's relative stagnation since 2000 may reflect a contemporaneous stagnation in SEC rulemaking. The Commission was on notice of problems that led to both the market timing scandal of 2003 and the run on money market funds during the financial crisis of 2008, yet it took no steps to address these problems. In other respects, the Commission has let simmering regulatory problems fester, most recently leading to rulemaking by the Department of Labor that substantially supplants the Commission as the primary regulator of mutual funds and broker-dealers.

The Commission should consider reclaiming its role as regulatory entrepreneur in the mutual fund space. The pervasively prescriptive nature of the Investment Company Act did not and could not provide the conditions for mutual funds to become a leading financial product. The Act's grant of broad exemptive authority to the Commission allowed it to modify the Act to establish the mutual fund as the strongest, most popular brand in US financial services. Having assumed the de facto role of mutual fund czar, the Commission can only abdicate that role at the expense of the mutual fund brand, which will stagnate and ultimately whither in a vacuum of SEC paralysis. Some might argue that this would be a positive development, but the market for effective mutual fund substitutes is limited. There is a compelling case to be made that the dissipation of the mutual fund brand would have adverse effects on net social wealth and Americans' financial security.

BIBLIOGRAPHY

2003 Fact Book, Investment Company Institute.
2014 Fact Book, Investment Company Institute.
2015 Fact Book, Investment Company Institute.
Baert, Richard, *SEC Proposal Could Alter Use of Mutual Funds in DC Plans*, Pensions & Investments (Feb. 8, 2016).
Bullard, Mercer, *The Mutual Fund as a Firm: Frequent Trading, Fund Arbitrage and the SEC's Response to the Mutual Fund Scandal*, 42 Houston L. Rev. 1271 (2006).
Bullard, Mercer, *Regulating Hedge Fund Managers: The Investment Company Act as a Regulatory Screen*, 13 Stanford J. L. Bus. & Fin. 286 (2008).
Bullard, Mercer, *The Fiduciary Study: A Triumph of Substance over Form?* 30 B.U. Rev. Banking & Fin. L. 171 (2011).
Bullard, Mercer, *On Regulating Investors: The JOBS Act and the Accredited Investor Standard*, ssrn.com/abstract=2468031 (July 2013).
Burnham, Kimberly, Bogdan, Michael, and Schrass, Daniel, Ownership of Mutual Funds, Shareholder Sentiment, and Use of the Internet, 2013, 19 ICI Research Perspective (Oct. 2013).
Collective Investment Trusts, Coalition of Collective Investment Trusts (2015).
Collins, Sean, Gallagher, Emily, Heinrichs, Jane, and Plantier, Chris, *Money Market Mutual Funds, Risk, and Financial Stability in the Wake of the 2010 Reforms*, 19 ICI Research Perspective (Jan. 2013).
Comments by Christopher Cox, Chairman, U.S. Securities and Exchange Commission, at the Investment Company Institute 4th Annual Mutual Fund Leadership Dinner, Washington, D.C. (Apr. 30, 2008).
Crowe, Scott, The Rise of Interval Funds: Mutual Funds for Alternative Investing, Investment News (May 6, 2014).
Financial Crisis Inquiry Report, National Commission on the Causes of the Financial Economic Crisis in the United States (2011).
Fisch, Jill, and Roiter, Eric, *A Floating NAV for Money Market Funds: Fix or Fantasy?* U. Ill. L. Rev. 1003 (2012).
Frantz, Douglas, *Leland O'Brien's Image Marred in "Meltdown": Pioneer Portfolio Insurers on the Defensive as Role in Market Skid Is Questioned*, L.A. Times (Nov. 2, 1987).

Goldberg, Joel H., and Bressler, Gregory N., *Revisiting Rule 12b-1 Under the Investment Company Act*, 31 Rev. Sec. and Commodities Reg., 147 (1998).

Historical Annuals, 2005–2014 Federal Reserve Board Flow of Funds (June 11, 2015).

How Mutual Funds Use 12b-1 Fees, 14 Investment Company Institute Fundamentals (Feb. 2005).

Hunnicutt, Trevor, *SEC Denies Active ETF Proposal as NextShares Launches Salvo against Competitors*, Investment News (July 27, 2015).

Hunnicut, Trevor, *Nextshares Wins Its First Adviser Platform Partner with Envestnet* Investment News (Aug. 18, 2015).

Hype from a Financial Guru? Bloomberg (May 9, 2004).

Introducing NextShares, www.nextshares.com (Aug. 23, 2015).

Leland O'Brien Offers Safe Opportunity in SuperShares, Australian Fin. Rev. (Dec. 2, 1988).

Letter from Fund Democracy, Consumer Federation of America, Consumer Action, AFL-CIO, Financial Planning Association, and National Association of Personal Financial Advisors to Nancy Morris, Secretary, U.S. Securities and Exchange Commission (Jan. 16, 2008).

Markham, Jeremy W., 1 *A Financial History of the United States: From Christopher Columbus to the Robber Barons* (Routledge, 2002).

Metz, Robert, *Investing in the S&P 500's Performance*, Tulsa World (Dec. 27, 1992).

Morley, John, *Collective Branding and the Origins of Investment Management Regulation: 1936–1942*, Va. Law & Econ. Research Paper No. 2011-01 (March 3, 2011).

Pender, Kathleen, *UC Professor's SuperTrust an Investment Innovation*, San Francisco Chron. (Mar. 3, 1989).

Petruno, Tom, *SEC Gives Tentative OK to New Market Hedge Securities*, L.A. Times (July 26, 1990).

Report of the Working Group on Rule 12b-1, Investment Company Institute (May 2007).

Romano, Roberta, *Empowering Investors: A Market Approach to Securities Regulation*, 107 Yale L. J. 2359 (1998).

Spence, David B., and Cross, Frank, *A Public Choice Case for the Administrative State*, 89 Geo. L. J. 97 (2000).

Statement of Mary Jo White, Chair, U.S. Securities and Exchange Commission (July 10, 2013).

Stecklow, Steve and Gullapalli, Diya, *A Money-Fund Manager's Fateful Shift*, Wall St. J. (Dec. 8, 2008).

Steverman, Ben, *The Worst Deal in Mutual Funds Faces a Reckoning*, BloombergBusiness (Apr. 13, 2012).

Temple-West, Patrick, *After Hearings, Labor Department on Track to Finish Fiduciary Rule by Year's End*, Politico Pro (Aug. 14, 2015)

Tergesen, Anne, *Some Funds in Your 401(k) Aren't Really Mutual Funds After All*, Wall. St. J. (Sep. 28, 2015).

Thaler, Richard H., and Sunstein, Cass R., *Nudge* (Yale University Press, 2009).

The Life Insurance Coverage Gap, The Prudential Insurance Company (2011).

Wiese, Kelly, *Settlement Approved in A.G. Edwards Case*, Mo. L. Media (June 20, 2010).

Wilstein, Steve, *New Investment Fund Takes on Wall Street*, Tulsa World (Apr. 2, 1989).

Yang, Janet, and Lutton, Laura Pavlenko, *2014 Target-Date Series Research Paper*, Morningstar.

Yoder, John, and Howell, Bo, *Actively Managed ETFs: The Past, Present and Future*, 13 J. Bus. & Sec. L. 231 (2013).

Zhang, J.J., *Why Your Choice of S&P 500 ETF Matters*, MarketWatch (Mar. 19, 2013).

US Department of Labor

Definition of the Term "Fiduciary," 75 Fed. Reg. 65263 (Oct. 22, 2010).
Definition of the Term "Fiduciary," 81 Fed. Reg. 20945 (Apr. 8, 2016).

US Securities and Exchange Commission

Actively Managed Exchange Traded Funds, Rel. No. IC-25258 (Nov. 8, 2001).
Actively Managed Exchange Traded Funds, Rel. No. IC-25258 (Nov. 8, 2001).
Advance Notice of Proposed Rulemaking, Investment Company Act Rel. No. 10252 (May 23, 1978).
Amendments to Regulation D, Form D and Rule 156, Rel. No. 33-9416 (July 10, 2013).
American Beacon NextShares Trust, et al., Investment Company Act Rel. Nos. 31498 (Mar. 16, 2015) (notice) & IC-31542 (Apr. 1, 2015) (order).

56 *Research handbook on the regulation of mutual funds*

Bearing of Distribution Expenses by Mutual Funds, Investment Company Act Rel. No. 9915 (Aug. 31, 1977).

Bearing of Distribution Expenses by Mutual Funds, Investment Company Act Release No. IC-11414 (Oct. 28, 1980).

Confirmation Requirements and Point of Sale Disclosure Requirements for Transactions in Certain Mutual Funds and Other Securities, and Other Confirmation Requirement Amendments, and Amendments to the Registration Form for Mutual Funds, Investment Company Act Rel. No. 26341 (Jan. 29, 2004).

Eliminating the Prohibition Against General Solicitation and General Advertising in Rule 506 and Rule 144A Offerings, Rel. No. 33-9415 (July 10, 2013).

Exchange-Traded Funds, Investment Company Act Rel. No. 28193 (Mar. 11, 2008).

Exemption from Shareholder Approval for Certain Subadvisory Contracts, Investment Company Act Rel. No. 26230 (Oct. 23, 2003).

Fund of Funds Investments, Rel. No. IC-26198, 68 F.R. at 58227 (Oct. 8, 2003).

"Hub-and-Spoke" Funds: A report Prepared by the Division of Investment Management, U.S. Securities and Exchange Commission (June 2, 1993).

In the Matter of CountryBasket Index Funds, Inc., Investment Company Act Rel. Nos. 21736 (Feb. 6, 1996) (notice) & 21802 (Mar. 5, 1996) (order).

Money Market Fund Statistics, U.S. Securities and Exchange Commission (July 29, 2015).

Multi-Manager Funds—Aggregate Advisory Fee Rate, Division of Investment Management, U.S. Securities and Exchange Commission (Feb. 2014).

Mutual Fund Distribution Fees; Confirmations, Investment Company Act Rel. No. 29367 (July 21, 2010).

Periodic Repurchases by Closed–End Management Investment Companies; Redemptions by Open–End Management Investment Companies and Registered Separate Accounts at Periodic Intervals or With Extended Payment, Investment Company Act Rel. No. 18869 (July 28, 1992).

Point of Sale Disclosure Requirements and Confirmation Requirements for Transactions in Mutual Funds, College Savings Plans, and Certain Other Securities, and Amendments to the Registration Form for Mutual Funds, Investment Company Act Rel. No. 26778 (Feb. 28, 2005).

Report on Mutual Fund Fees and Expenses, Division of Investment Management, U.S. Securities and Exchange Commission (Dec. 2000).

Repurchases by Closed–End Management Investment Companies, Investment Company Act Rel. No. 19399 (Apr. 7, 1993).

Request for Comment on Exchange-Traded Products, Exchange Act Rel. No. 75165 (June 12, 2015).

Rule Conditionally Exempting One Class of Investment Companies from Certain Requirements of the Act Relating to the Selection of Independent Public Accountants, 6 F.R. 6631 (Dec. 23, 1941).

SPDR Trust, Investment Company Act Rel. Nos. 18959 (Sept. 17, 1992) (notice) and 19055 (Oct. 26, 1992) (order).

Study Regarding Obligations of Brokers, Dealers, and Investment Advisers, Exchange Act Release No. 34-62577 (July 27, 2010).

SuperTrust Trust for Capital Market Fund, Inc., Rel. Nos. IC-17613 (Jul. 25, 1990) (notice) & IC-17809 (Oct. 19, 1990) (order).

SuperTrust Trust for Capital Market Fund, Inc., Rel. No. IC-21991 (May 29, 1996).

Temporary Rule Regarding Principal Trades with Certain Advisory Clients, Rel. No. IA-2653 (Sep. 24, 2007).

Temporary Rule Regarding Principal Trades with Certain Advisory Clients, Rel. Nos. IA-3948 (Dec. 17, 2014), IA-3522 (Dec. 20, 2012), IA-3128 (Dec. 28, 2010) & IA-2965 (Dec. 23, 2009).

3. Fiduciary contours: perspectives on mutual funds and private funds
Deborah A. DeMott

1 INTRODUCTION

All fiduciaries owe obligations that include distinctive duties of loyalty, in addition to duties of care or performance. To say more requires knowing more about a particular fiduciary's circumstances; any further inquiry turns on the specific content of the fiduciary's duties and the consequences of breach.[1] Thus, the content of a fiduciary's duty necessarily underlies the legally significant determination of whether and when the fiduciary breached the duty.[2] The thesis of this chapter is that in the mutual fund context, the specifics of fiduciary duty reflect the distinctive qualities of this form of investment in securities, conventionally understood to involve an investment company that issues shares sold to public investors.[3] The specific contours that shape fiduciary duties reflect many factors, including the highly prescriptive regulatory structure of the Investment Company Act of 1940 ("ICA") that is distinctly applicable to mutual funds. To sharpen its depiction of the fiduciary distinctiveness of mutual funds, the chapter draws contrasts with two other avenues or vehicles for investment through which an investor delegates investment choice: (1) "private" funds, that is, vehicles for pooled investment that are not subject to the full regulatory regime applicable to mutual (or "public" funds); and (2) nonfund investment management relationships through which an investment adviser undertakes to manage an investor's individual securities account. In addition to their regulatory consequences,[4] management relationships geared to an individual account implicate the doctrines and concepts of common law agency. This chapter's overarching thesis is that assessment of the role and significance of fiduciary obligation as applied to investment funds, whether mutual funds or private funds, necessarily turns on their distinctive characteristics, including those prescribed by

---

[1] SEC v. Chenery Corp., 318 U.S. 80, 85–6 (1943) ("to say that a man is a fiduciary only begins analysis; it gives direction to further inquiry. To whom is he a fiduciary? What obligations does he owe as a fiduciary? In what respect has he failed to discharge those obligations? And what are the consequences of his deviation from duty?").

[2] Tibble v. Edison Int'l, 135 S. Ct. 1823, 1827 (2015) (whether beneficiaries of employee savings plan brought timely suit against plan fiduciaries under ERISA, 29 U.S.C. § 1113, requires consideration of "the nature of the fiduciary duty," which under trust law standards incorporated by ERISA included an ongoing duty to monitor plan investments and remove imprudent investments).

[3] The regulatory structure for mutual funds requires registration with the SEC, as discussed *infra* n. 11.

[4] Chief among them is whether the manager must register as an investment adviser under the Investment Advisers Act of 1940, discussed *infra* n. 14.

regulation. Moreover, these contrasts are timely. As I explain, the population of investment advisers now registered with the SEC includes many who advise at least one private fund. Newly available information about private funds' practices calls into question whether they are always consistent with fund managers' fiduciary duties to investors, as do data concerning practices of hedge fund managers during the financial crisis.

In this chapter I also articulate a more general perspective on mutual funds. The distinctively hybrid quality of investment that mutual fund vehicles enable can be viewed through three different lenses. First is an initial lens grounded in organizational or entity governance, stemming from the fact that mutual funds are generally organized in entity form.[5] A mutual fund's structure interposes the fund itself between investors and the fund's assets, liabilities, and managers. Prior scholarship examines governance features distinctive to entities, including boards of directors and voting rights conferred on fund investors, whether required by regulation or by contract, with some scholars investigating the function and efficacy of governance institutions in the mutual fund context. The second lens is grounded in the insight that shares in mutual funds are often characterized as products consisting of specified investment services that are packaged and sold by or on behalf of a fund to investors who may sell the shares, whether by exercising redemption rights against the fund itself or by selling into secondary markets for securities.[6] Understanding a mutual fund's investors as purchasers or consumers of a product carries implications for the duties owed by the fund's managers on an ongoing basis. It also highlights the importance of disclosure furnished when shares are purchased, as well as the robustness of investors' redemption rights. The third lens—even if relevant only by way of contrast—views the ongoing tripartite relationship between a mutual fund's manager, the fund's assets, and the fund's investors through the lens of common law agency. As the law defines agency relationships, the agent owes fiduciary duties to the principal throughout their relationship, and the principal has both an ongoing right of control over the agent and the power to terminate the relationship. Seen this way, investors are clients and thus principals of the actors who advise them or manage their financial assets, not (or not only) consumers of a product or service. In the same vein, one might think that physicians have patients, not (or not just) customers for medical services.[7] As agents, managers owe duties that are distinctively fiduciary and that apply on an ongoing basis. From this vantage point the

---

[5] The specific forms of organization include business corporations, common law trusts, and statutory business trusts, discussed *infra* nn. 25–6. As discussed *infra* n. 9, the operative definition for regulatory purposes is "investment company," which includes "an association" and "any organized group of persons whether incorporated or not." ICA § 2(a)(32); 15 U.S.C. § 80a-2(a)(32). If an investment adviser invests the assets held in individual client accounts in an identical fashion, the SEC may determine that an investment company exists. See In re Clarke Lanzen Inv. Firm, Rel. IC 21140, 1995 WL 374552 (1995), discussed in Roiter at 12 and n. 36.

[6] For the "product" characterization, see Morley at 1233; Roiter at 13. Mutual funds that issue redeemable shares are conventionally termed "open-end" funds, in contrast to "closed-end" funds. For further discussion, see *infra* n. 16.

[7] And one might think that the conduct of investment bankers who refer to their clients as "muppets" is more likely to fall short of meeting fiduciary (and other) standards. Zingales at 1348.

distinctiveness of the fiduciary issues associated with mutual funds is evident because what can seem relatively unproblematic from the perspective of entity governance or product sales may be troubling when viewed through an agency lens.

Let's begin by sketching the basic characteristics of mutual funds, private funds, and individual-account management relationships. Although this chapter in no way purports to exhaust the technical complexities, it notes salient aspects of applicable regulatory schemes for each investment vehicle or relationship, focusing on the Investment Advisers Act of 1940 ("Advisers Act") and the Investment Company Act of 1940 ("ICA").[8] Following these sketches, the chapter examines the contours of fiduciary duty applicable to each vehicle or relationship, whether stemming from regulation or generally applicable law, highlighting specific contrasts as between mutual funds and private funds. The next section identifies a few implications flowing from these contrasts, followed by a brief conclusion.

2 MUTUAL FUNDS, PRIVATE FUNDS, AND INDIVIDUALIZED INVESTMENT MANAGEMENT

2.1 Mutual Funds

Like much of the specialized terminology used in connection with asset management, "mutual fund" and "private fund" are widely used labels that -like the notoriously undefinable "hedge fund"—are not legal or regulatory terms of art. Mutual funds are generally understood to offer retail investors the opportunity to invest in pooled investment vehicles. The starting point for regulatory purposes is the ICA's opening definition of "investment company," which is an issuer of securities that "is or holds itself out as being engaged primarily ... in the business of investing, reinvesting, or trading in securities" or proposes to become such an issuer.[9] Alternatively, and often inadvertently, an issuer may become an investment company when 40 percent of the value of its total assets on an unconsolidated basis (but excluding government securities and cash items) consists of investment securities.[10] An investment company must register with the SEC unless the ICA excepts its type of company from registration, or the SEC exempts the particular company from registration.[11] Mutual funds are managed by "investment advisers," typically through a contract with the fund in which the adviser regularly furnishes advice concerning investing.[12] Managing an investment company generally requires that the investment adviser itself register with the SEC under the Advisers Act.[13] As discussed later, the Advisers Act itself defines "investment

---

[8] The chapter does not cover state-level regulation of investment advisers.
[9] ICA § 3(a)(1)(A); 15 U.S.C. § 80a-3(a)(1)(A).
[10] ICA § 3(a)(1)(c); 15 U.S.C. § 80a-3(a)(1)(c).
[11] ICA § 8(a).
[12] ICA § 2(a)(20).
[13] Advisers Act § 203(a); 15 U.S.C. § 80b-3(a). The Advisers Act contains several exemptions from its registration requirement, some of which are discussed infra nn. 40–1.

adviser" and may require registration by an investment manager that does not serve as an adviser to any mutual fund.[14]

The ICA classifies investment companies into two types depending on whether the securities issued are redeemable,[15] a typology that conforms to the generally used distinction between "open-end" and "closed-end" funds.[16] Investors in open-end mutual funds may sell their shares by exercising their rights of redemption; such shares, unlike those issued by closed-end mutual funds, are not listed for trading in secondary markets. Upon redemption, the shareholder in an open-end fund receives a cash payment equal to the shareholder's proportionate interest in the fund, commonly known as the "NAV," or net asset value. Additionally—but less frequently—an investment company may be organized as a unit investment trust ("UIT"), which before making a public offering of its shares assembles an investment portfolio and designates a date for its dissolution and liquidation.[17] Issues specific to UITs are outside the scope of this chapter, as are issues specific to exchange traded funds ("EFTs"): as open-end funds, EFTs are generally structured as index funds based on various equity- and industry-based indices. Although EFT shares trade on securities exchanges, they are also redeemable by the fund but only in large blocks, known as "creation units."[18]

Central to the definition and operation of a mutual fund is whether the fund makes a public offering of its shares. The ICA's broad definition of "investment company," quoted above, is inapplicable to any issuer with no more than one hundred beneficial owners of its long-term securities and "which is not making and does not presently propose to make a public offering of its shares."[19] To meet ongoing obligations to redeem outstanding shares, mutual funds ordinarily conduct continual public offerings of their shares to generate the cash requisite to satisfy redemption requests without

---

[14] Advisers Act § 202 (a)(11); 15 U.S.C. § 80b-2(11).

[15] ICA § 5(a) (defining "open-end company" as "a management company which is offering for sale or has outstanding any redeemable securities of which it is the issuer" and "closed-end company" as "any management company that is not an open-end company").

[16] Other types of investment vehicles may share functional characteristics with these basic forms. For example, publicly traded private equity firms have been characterized as "essentially closed-end funds" although private-equity funds are a categorical example of private funds. See Phalippou at 124. Indices based on these funds' listed securities were launched in the past decade. Id.

[17] ICA § 4(2); 15 U.S.C. § 80a-4(2).

[18] ETF redemptions occur through an in-kind tender of a basket of specified securities. If an ETF invests in assets other than securities, it is not an investment company under the ICA. On ETFs generally, see Kirsch ch. 35. One attraction of ETF shares is that the price at which an investor may sell is determined at the time of sale into the market, while the NAV at which mutual-fund shares are redeemed is determined at the end of the trading day. When securities markets rapidly decline—as on August 24, 2015—sell-side pressures may be so overwhelming that ETF prices decline substantially more than the prices of the securities the fund owns. For more on ETFs, see Birdthistle ch. 12; Roiter (this volume).

[19] ICA § 3 (c)(1); 15 U.S.C. § 80a-3(c)(1).

contracting in size.[20] Mutual funds honor redemption requests on a daily basis and the fund may impose a redemption fee.[21]

A significant element in the hybridity of mutual funds consists of governance characteristics that partially mimic those of a generic business corporation. However organized under state law, the operations of a mutual fund are, as is evident above, managed by the fund's investment adviser.[22] Indeed, investors may perceive the fund's association with a particular adviser as a "brand" on which the investor can rely, much more so than would be the case with either the composition or the functions of the fund's board of directors. This perception is consistent with the finding that, performance aside, mutual funds suffer declines in investment flows following merger or acquisition events that change their investment advisers.[23] Nonetheless, compliance with the ICA requires that the fund have a board of directors, composed of members no more than 60 percent of whom may be interested persons of the fund. The ICA's long definition of "interested person" encompasses (among others) any interested person of the fund's investment adviser or securities underwriter.[24] Although a mutual fund's directors do not manage the fund's investment portfolio, the ICA specifies functions to be performed by directors, including, most significantly, an annual review of the fund's contract with its investment adviser. If organized as corporations, mutual funds incorporate in Maryland.[25] Trust form funds mostly organize in Massachusetts as common law trusts or in Delaware as statutory business trusts.[26]

Again, regardless of chosen state law form, the federal ICA mandates that the fund have a board. As in generic corporations, fund shareholders have voting rights over the board's composition.[27] Additionally, the ICA requires that shareholders vote to approve

---

[20] Roiter at 12.
[21] The investor may also have paid an upfront "sales load" to the distributor of the fund's shares, or the investor may be charged a "back end" sales load at the point of redemption to be deducted from the proceeds.
[22] In contrast, in a generic corporation incorporated in Delaware, the corporation's "business and affairs" are by statute managed "by or under the direction of" the board of directors. Del. Code Ann., tit. 8, § 141 (a).
[23] Flows into mutual funds declined by 7 percent of fund assets during the year following an announced change in ownership of an investment adviser following a merger or acquisition event. See Kostovetsky. One might wonder how much this effect resembles ordinary business corporations that are closely identified with their CEOs, such that a change in CEO is a significant event. On Berkshire Hathaway Corp., an outlier on the spectrum of identification, see Lawrence A. Cunningham, *Berkshire's Blemishes. Lessons for Buffett's Successors, Peers, and Policy*, COLUM. BUS. L. REV. 1 (2016). More generally, scholars of CEO turnover find mixed results for stock prices. *See* Margarethe Wiersema, *Holes at the Top: Why CEO Firings Backfire*, HARV. BUS. REV. (Dec. 2002).
[24] ICA § 2(a)(19)(iii); 15 U.S.C. § 80a-2(a)(19)(iii).
[25] Maryland's general corporation statute accommodates continual issuances of shares and permits the insulation of funds within the same fund family from liabilities incurred by their fund siblings. Roiter at 62, citing Md. Code Ann., Corps and Assn's, § 2-208.1 and § 2-208.2.
[26] Roiter at 62–3.
[27] But in trust-form funds, shareholder voting rights are operative at the level of the trust, not the lower-level funds within the trust. Roiter at 58.

the fund's initial contract with its investment adviser, as well as subsequent modifications to the contract, and requires that the fund's registration statement and prospectus state all investment policies that can be changed only by shareholder vote.[28] Although prior scholarship suggests that shareholder voting for mutual fund directors lacks much functional significance,[29] ongoing litigation illustrates the potential peril to a fund's advisers and directors generated by unilateral deviations from fundamental investment objectives. In *Northstar Financial Advisors, Inc. v. Schwab Investments*, a class of mutual fund investors alleged that they were injured when the fund deviated from two fundamental investment objectives, which were to track a specific bond index and invest no more than 25 percent of the fund's assets in any one industry unless necessary to track the specific index.[30] The Ninth Circuit held that the investors stated claims against the fund for breach of contract, as well as against its adviser and directors, all of which claims were grounded in a "structural relationship" between the investors and the fund comparable to a provision in a corporation's charter. The deviations injured fund shareholders directly when actions were taken unilaterally that required shareholder approval.[31] And the defendants conceded at oral argument that the investors' allegations stated a claim for breach of fiduciary duty.[32]

More generally, *Northstar* is not entirely consistent with viewing mutual fund shares as products because it is difficult to visualize how a more typical product seller could effect postsale modifications in the product itself that would be comparable to unilaterally adopted alterations in investment policies. This weakens the plausibility of the product metaphor, unless one imagines a product that unilaterally morphs into something very different. More plausibly, *Northstar* is consistent with viewing a mutual fund as an instrumentality through which to effect an investment management relationship in which share ownership creates an agency relationship of sorts between fund investors and the fund's adviser. On this view, unilateral deviations from fundamental investment policies are comparable to actions for which an agent lacks authority. Lacking actual authority to bind the principal, the agent is subject to liability to the principal for injury stemming from third-party reliance on the agent's appearance of authority.[33] And, when the agent's unauthorized actions are self-interested, they are garden variety breaches of an agent's duty of loyalty to the principal.

2.2 Private Funds

In one sense, the ICA defines the universe of private funds as a negative space, one occupied by funds encompassed within the broad ICA definition of "investment company" but nonetheless excepted from the definition. This chapter focuses on private funds for which the rationale for exclusion from the ICA is that the funds "seem to be

---

[28] ICA § 80a-8(b).
[29] Morley at 1250.
[30] 779 F.3d 1036 (9th Cir. 2015).
[31] 779 F.3d at 1059. This reasoning overcomes the obstacle that the fund's shareholders themselves were not parties to the fund's contract with its adviser.
[32] 779 F.3d at 1056.
[33] Restatement (Third) of Agency § 8.09.

sufficiently controlled by their investors."[34] However, the history recounted in this chapter calls into question whether all such funds have in fact been "sufficiently controlled." Most prominently, private funds encompass hedge funds as well as private equity and venture capital funds. In general, hedge funds require a substantial initial investment, to be invested by the fund's manager in a portfolio of assets of a type as specified in the fund's prospectus or offering memorandum, which typically contemplates that the adviser will have substantial discretion in making investment decisions. To generate above-market returns, hedge fund managers may expose their investors to complex forms of risk, augmented in complexity from the investor's standpoint by the relatively nontransparent style of hedge fund investing.[35] Private equity funds differ in significant ways from venture capital funds. In investment strategy, venture capital funds invest in relatively new companies, while private equity funds, also known as buyout funds, focus on acquiring and holding controlling stakes in established companies. Both structures contemplate that the fund will liquidate after a stated period, typically after all the firms in the fund's portfolio have themselves enjoyed a liquidation event, such as through an IPO or a strategic acquisition.[36] Managers of private equity funds market themselves to two distinct constituencies: to prospective investors in the fund, but also to incumbent owners of companies into which the fund may invest. Private funds with advisers registered with the SEC as of September 2014 had around $7.4 trillion in regulatory assets under management ($5.4 trillion for advisers to hedge funds and $2 trillion for advisers to at least one private equity fund).[37] Although this number represented a fraction of overall assets under management ("AUM") in the United States (roughly $50 trillion),[38] the private fund segment of the asset management industry is significant in many ways, not least among which is its capacity for developing innovative and complex vehicles for investment, and, in some cases, generating systemic risk.[39]

Private funds rely on two ICA provisions that exclude certain issuers from the broad definition of "issuer": (1) an issuer that has no more than one hundred beneficial owners of its outstanding securities and that does not make or propose to make any public offering of its securities;[40] and (2) an issuer that does not make or propose to

---

[34] Frankel (2011) at 127. Other bases for exclusion are not recounted here.

[35] In addition to potential returns higher than those of mutual fund investing, hedge funds "also offer more complex risk exposures that vary according to style and market circumstances," including illiquidity and lack of transparency stemming from the proprietary nature of hedge fund trading strategies. Getmansky et al. at 484.

[36] Morley at 1235–6.

[37] Champ at 1. The term "regulatory assets" means that the adviser may have under management other assets that are outside the regulatory scheme. These are the latest full-year data available. As of third quarter 2015, the comparable statistic for hedge funds was around $6.2 billion. See Private Funds Statistics, available at www.sec.gov/divisions/investment/private-funds-statistics-2015-q3-accessible.pdf.

[38] In 2014, the global fund industry reportedly controlled $120 trillion in investor assets, with managers in the United States accounting for $50 trillion in AUM. Healy and Greer at 302.

[39] A memorable instance is the late 1990s collapse of Long Term Capital Portfolio, L.P., which prompted a recapitalization involving 16 financial institutions conducted under the supervision of the Federal Reserve Bank.

[40] ICA § 3(c)(1); 15 U.S.C. § 80a-3(c)(1).

make any public offering of its securities if all of its outstanding securities are owned by persons—of any number—who at the time of purchase were "qualified purchasers."[41] To be a qualified purchaser requires meeting statutorily prescribed financial tests; for example, a natural person is a qualified person if the individual owns no less than $5 million in investments.[42] Wealth, like income, is not a complete proxy for investment acumen, whether the focus is an individual or an entity or other institution.[43] Although wealth should enable an investor's access to expert advice and capacity to absorb financial losses, it does not necessarily ensure that the advice will be sound, that the investor will follow it, or that either the investor or the adviser will discern all that is material when an investment vehicle is opaque in material respects. But wealth is more readily measurable than are these propensities and probabilities. Moreover, some of the limitations inherent in quantitative definitions of investor sophistication in an opaque environment became evident recently in large public pension funds' acknowledgment of their failure to ask or disclose how much private equity funds kept in fees when reported investment returns seemed high enough to allay any curiosity or concerns about the toll imposed by fees.[44]

Although the ICA may itself exclude a private fund from its general registration requirement—and thus from the substantive constraints imposed by it that are discussed later in this chapter—it is a separate question whether the private fund's adviser must register with the SEC as an investment adviser. The Advisers Act long contained an exemption from registration known as the "private adviser exemption," available to advisers which had had fewer than fifteen clients over the preceding twelve months, did not advise a mutual fund (or other registered investment company), and did not hold out as an investment adviser to the public. Many advisers to hedge funds and private equity funds relied on this exemption, which permitted each fund to be treated as a single "client." Effective July 2011, the Dodd–Frank Act eliminated the exemption for advisers in the United States with $100 million or more assets under management. If an adviser advises *only* funds excluded from the ICA definition of investment company—that is, only private funds—the adviser is exempt from required registration under the Advisers Act so long as it has less than $150 million in assets under management.[45] To

---

[41] ICA § 3(c)(7); 15 U.S.C. § 80a-3(c)(7). The National Securities Markets Improvement Act of 1996 added this additional exclusion, which enabled a new type of private fund that may have an unlimited number of investors so long as each meets the "qualified purchaser" criterion. For the history, see Frankel (2011) at 146–51.

[42] ICA § 2(51)(A); 15 U.S.C. § 80a-2(51)(A).

[43] Whether the focus on wealth as a proxy for investor sophistication is entirely adequate when an investor is an institution that itself owes fiduciary duties to its own beneficiaries is beyond the scope of this chapter. For recent assessments of possible ways to specify investor sophistication, see Securities and Exchange Commission (2015) and United States Government Accountability Office (2013).

[44] Gretchen Morgenson, *Challenging Fees Tucked in Footnotes*, N.Y. TIMES, Oct. 18, 2015; Timothy W. Martin, *Pension Funds Tackle Fee Mystery*, WALL ST. J. (Nov. 23, 2015), at C1.

[45] Advisers Act § 203(m); 15 U.S.C. § 80b-3(m). Dodd–Frank created a narrowly defined exception (to the general registration requirement) for "foreign private advisers" who must satisfy several criteria geared to determine that they have no significant presence in the United States or significant following among US investors. See Advisers Act § 202 (a)(30)(defining 'foreign private adviser') and § 203 (a)(3)(registration requirement inapplicable to foreign

Fiduciary contours: perspectives on mutual funds and private funds 65

register, an adviser must complete and file a disclosure document—Form ADV—with the SEC, along with a brochure to be given to clients; the brochure requires narrative answers concerning specified items for disclosure.[46] Since 2011 the SEC has also required most registered advisers to file Form PF to report such matters as counterparty risk and leverage. Information reported on Form PF is not publicly available.[47]

A separate question is how a prospective investor in a private fund obtains sufficient information to choose among available private funds. For prospective investors in hedge funds, comparative information about hedge fund performance comes from a cottage industry of private data vendors.[48] Although the regulatory bar against general advertising by hedge funds that necessitated their services was lifted in 2013,[49] only with reluctance have hedge funds embraced the resultant opportunities for advertising.[50] Many (but not all) hedge funds self-report information about their returns to private vendors, who sell their data to potential investors.[51] Much research has identified the vulnerability of such self-reported return data to various biases, including an observed propensity for funds to commence reporting following a period of outperformance and to choose to "delist" from the database when the fund lacks capacity to absorb new investment or has suffered poor performance.[52] Additionally, standard commercial databases do not provide other information relevant to investors' choices, such as whether the fund's manager used its discretionary authority to restrict withdrawals from the fund,[53] as discussed below. For prospective investors in private equity funds, data on the performance of funds associated with a particular sponsor or investment adviser may prove elusive. Private equity sponsors prepare private placement memoranda in a process geared to attract new investors and exercise discretion about the information to be shared with prospective investors. Many private equity sponsors use private placement agents to market new funds.[54]

---

private advisers). For discussion, see Greene and Adams at 362–3. Nonetheless, for large advisers, the perception of adverse reputational consequences, combined with the less than onerous registration process, may not justify the expenditure of much energy to avoid registration.

[46] For more about Form ADV, see DeMott and Laby at 418–19.

[47] The SEC adopted Form PF jointly with the Commodities Futures Trading Commission. Although Form PF information is primarily intended to assist the Financial Stability Oversight Council in monitoring systematic risk, the SEC has also used the information in regulatory and examination programs and to facilitate its understanding of risks posed to investors. Champ at 2.

[48] Getmansky et al. at 491.

[49] Securities Act Rule 502(c).

[50] Section 201 of the 2012 JOBS Act directed the SEC to lift the general prohibition, which required it to revise Advisers Act Rule 506. Under revised Rule 506(c), a hedge fund may advertise so long as all investors are accredited, but it must verify their accreditation. Associated uncertainties make robust advertising unlikely. For a full account, see Kaal at 1173.

[51] Getmansky et al. at 491.

[52] Getmansky et al. at 492. Additionally, the fact that some data bases do not include funds that are "extinct" generates a survivorship bias because poorly performing funds choose to shut down and thus are no longer represented in the data. This affects the estimated mean and volatility of hedge-fund returns overall. Id. at 493.

[53] Aiken et al. at 200.

[54] On private placement agents, see Cain et al.

From 2011 to present, much changed for private fund advisers and their clients, triggered by the Dodd–Frank registration mandate and its aftermath.[55] The Advisers Act subjects registered advisers to constraints relevant to fiduciary duty issues, as I discuss below. Just as significantly, registration as an adviser exposes the registrant to the SEC's examination process.[56] In its initial round of examinations of newly registered fund advisers, the SEC identified numerous deficiencies in policies, procedures, and disclosure practices. For example, reportedly 40–60 percent of newly registered private equity advisers were deficient in some regard, most prominently in terms of insufficient disclosure of fees and allocation of fees and expenses as well as problematic conduct concerning portfolio companies.[57] As drafted, many limited partnership agreements created "an enormous grey area" that allowed advisers to "charge fees and pass along expenses that are not reasonably contemplated by investors."[58] In one egregious instance, the SEC alleged in an enforcement action that an adviser, without providing adequate disclosure to its investors, allocated to the funds it manages millions of dollars attributable to its own expenses, including its CEO's salary and bonus, as well as causing the funds to borrow money from the adviser at unfavorable rates in order to pay the adviser's expenses.[59] And by continuing to manage legacy funds, "zombie" advisers unable to raise additional funds may disserve investors' best interests in various ways and without proper disclosure.[60]

More generally, the initiation of the SEC examination process and subsequent enforcement proceedings elicited media engagement with issues that previously had been "relatively opaque," given the confidentiality of private equity documentation.[61] Less opacity led to new due diligence procedures for private equity investors, as well as changes in advisers' fee and allocation practices.[62] The SEC's scrutiny of the hedge fund industry was significantly shaped by its Aberrational Performance Inquiry designed first to identify funds that consistently outperformed standard market indices and then to focus more closely on those funds. The SEC's inquiry led to enforcement actions against fund managers who had overvalued their funds' returns.[63] For advisers to private funds now registered under the Advisers Act, additional regulatory scrutiny now figures largely in the environment, as do investors' reactions to revelations about problematic conduct.

---

[55] As the then director of the SEC's Division of Investment Management characterized matters in 2014, "[i]t is difficult to overstate how much the regulatory landscape for hedge fund managers has changed over the past four years." *See* Champ at 1. Much changed as well for managers of private equity funds. *See* Wyatt.
[56] These consequences are detailed in DeMott and Laby at 419–20.
[57] Rendón et al. at 1351.
[58] Bowden at 4.
[59] In re Clean Energy Capital LLC, SEC Rel. No. 3955, 2014 WL 7662742 (Oct. 17, 2014).
[60] Bowden at 4.
[61] Rendón *et al.* at 1352. In particular, the *Wall Street Journal* reported on the relationship between private equity firm Kohlberg Kravis Roberts & Co. and its related entity, Capstone, having obtained portions of a limited partnership agreement. The *WSJ* opined that KKR may have breached terms in the agreement by not sharing fees earned by Capstone. *See KKR Error Raises a Question: What Cash Should Go to Investors?* WALL ST. J. (May 21, 2014).
[62] *See* Wyatt at 4.
[63] Healy and Greer at 303.

Private funds are not subject to the mandatory governance structures that the ICA imposes on mutual funds. Hedge funds—many organized as limited partnerships or limited liability companies (LLCs)—generally do not have boards of directors.[64] However, the organizational structures for hedge funds may provide for committees chosen by investors with the assigned function of approving or disapproving transactions in which the adviser has a conflict, as explored in Section 3.3. Even when hedge funds do have boards of directors—typically because a fund is organized in the Cayman Islands, which requires a board—the functional substance of the board is open to question. Directors of Caymans-based hedge funds, at least as of 2012, often served on the boards of dozens of unrelated funds.[65] In contrast, the governance of private equity funds incorporates more investor input, but not control. Private equity funds—often structured as limited partnerships—often have investor-chosen advisory committees empowered to veto certain types of transactions, such as conflict transactions, and to trigger votes by investors on designated matters.[66]

Private funds do not confer redemption rights comparable to those of an open-end mutual fund.[67] Private equity funds, as noted above, liquidate periodically (typically every five or ten years) and are not structured to create interim redemption rights.[68] A limited partner in a private equity fund may always request an early withdrawal, but whether to grant the request is within the general partner's discretion.[69] Private equity structures, although seeming severe in this way, are nonetheless relatively straightforward. In contrast, redemption rights in hedge funds can share the same complexity associated with other aspects of hedge fund vehicles. For example, new investors in a fund are often subject to a one-year "lockup" period that prohibits any withdrawal of funds.[70] Any redemption requires advance notice, typically from 30 days up to as long

---

[64] Morley at 1243.

[65] Research made possible by hedge fund registrations under the Advisers Act revealed patterns of board staffing in the Caymans. Unlike directors of mutual funds who may serve on multiple funds with the same adviser within the same family of funds, many directors of Caymans-based funds each populated numerous boards of funds under unrelated management. Azan Ahmed, *In the Caymans, It's Simple to Fill a Hedge Fund Board*, N.Y. TIMES (July 1, 2012). Many directors also served their funds as lawyers or otherwise worked for the fund, distinct from board service. *Id.*

[66] Morley at 1255. The long lock-in period for investors' capital may explain why these rights are present.

[67] Although investors lack the ability to sell private-fund shares into secondary markets comparable to those for ETFs or closed-end mutual funds, a secondary market exists for interests in private equity funds. *See* William Alden, *A Boom in Private Equity's Secondary Market*, N.Y. TIMES (Feb. 18, 2015).

[68] Morley at 1254.

[69] When such requests are granted, other partners may object to the valuation that underlies the pro rata share of a hypothetical liquidation of the fund that the exiting limited partner receives. Typically, limited partners who wish to exit propose to transfer their interest to a new limited partner; the general partner is more likely to consent to a transfer than a withdrawal, and a transfer holds less potential stigma for the exiting limited partner contemplating whether it will be permitted to invest in other sponsors' funds in the future.

[70] Getmansky *et al.* at 489.

as a year and limited to quarterly or annual periods for redemption.[71] More significantly for the purposes of this chapter, hedge funds may incorporate mechanisms that confer discretion on fund managers to restrict redemptions, which if exercised can stymie an investor's desire to achieve liquidity. Most hedge fund agreements permit the manager to impose temporary "gates" on redemption during periods of high investor demand for exit by restricting how much an investor (or all investors) may redeem within a period of time.[72] Additionally, some hedge funds incorporate "side pockets" that enable the fund's manager to segregate relatively illiquid assets from the principal fund, to be distributed to investors as payments in kind, typically through the distribution of interests in a newly created special purpose vehicle.[73] Once placed in a side pocket, an asset may remain there for a long time, which can distort how investors understand the returns reported by the fund.[74]

A manager's discretionary power to restrict redemptions can create a conflict between investors' interests and those of the manager. Wishing to prolong the fund's life and protect its fees (and not just guard the fund's investors against fire sales of relatively illiquid assets), the manager may impose the gate and side-pocket assets to serve its own interests and sacrifice those of the fund's investors, who may strongly prefer the certainty of liquidity in times of market turmoil. Indeed, the SEC brought postcrisis enforcement proceedings against a hedge fund manager who side-pocketed assets for his own use.[75] More generally, the long duration and relative illiquidity of an investment in a hedge fund—or for that matter in any private fund—underscore the importance of disclosure at the point of sale, as well as subsequent compliance by fund managers with ongoing disclosure protocols governing matters such as valuation of fund assets.[76]

Nonetheless, looking forward, hedge fund investors who are surprised by how a manager has used its discretion may sanction funds in fund families that restricted withdrawals. Investors may decline altogether to invest, or invest only if the manager lowers its fees. Recent research confirms that investors, not having anticipated the widespread use of discretion to limit redemptions during the financial crisis, responded postcrisis in a manner that sanctioned funds within fund families that deployed discretionary restrictions on redemptions. Funds within families with tainted reputations experienced difficulties raising capital and were more likely to have cut their fees than funds in a control group that did not impose discretionary restrictions on redemptions.[77] Additionally, funds that imposed discretionary restrictions on redemption were no more likely to have sold illiquid assets than funds in a control group that

---

[71] *Id.*
[72] Aiken *et al.* at 198.
[73] *Id.* at 199.
[74] Additionally, the side pocket can enable a manager to insulate a difficult-to-value asset from a market in which it would perform poorly, later to triumph when the asset achieves superlative returns. See Aiken et al. at 199, discussing incident recounted by Michael Lewis in *The Big Short* 189–99 (2010).
[75] In re Lawrence Goldfarb, SEC News Digest 2011-85, 2011 WL 1662366 (May 3, 2011).
[76] John Cannon and Kathleen Marcus, *Disciplined Compliance with Investor Disclosures Protects Funds from SEC Enforcement*, 47 SEC. REG. & L. REP. 2361 (2015).
[77] Aiken *et al.* at 198.

did not impose such restrictions, which "casts doubt on the proposition that [such restrictions] served investor interests by preventing costly fire sales."[78] Thus, it is plausible that prospective investors would understand a fund family in which fund managers imposed discretionary restrictions on redemption as one in which the overall ethos may depart from loyalty to investors' interests, as made evident at the most acute point of conflict between the investors' interests and the manager's self-interest. Thus, just as private fund registration under the Advisers Act and its aftermath made less opaque the environment for private funds and their investors, how fund managers deployed their discretionary power to restrict withdrawals during the 2008 financial crisis revealed information relevant to managers' loyalties that proved to be salient to investors' decisions.

2.3 Individualized Investment Management

Investing in a fund managed by an investment adviser is, of course, not the sole route through which an investor may delegate investment decisions. An investor may establish an individual management account. Typically in the United States individual account management services are offered by "retail" firms that otherwise manage mutual funds and pension funds, but not by "institutional" asset management firms, which manage private funds.[79] For regulatory purposes, managers of individual accounts have long been defined as investment advisers and as such may be required to register with the SEC or a state securities authority.[80]

The key point for the purposes of this chapter is that an individual-account investment manager is a common law agent who is also subject to duties defined by the Advisers Act (or its state law counterpart), when applicable. As a common law agent, an investment manager owes fiduciary duties to its client. Moreover, as the principal in a relationship of common law agency, the client holds rights and powers that do not typify investors in funds as delineated above. It is constitutive of agency—integral to the definition—that the principal holds a power and right of interim control over the agent.[81] Even if the principal's exercise of control contravenes a contract with the agent, the principal retains a power of control albeit that its exercise constitutes a breach of contract.[82] Investing instead through a fund vehicle interposes the fund itself as the principal; a fund investor may have governance rights but those are different from a principal's more direct powers and rights of control. Additionally, as a principal in a relationship of agency with an investment manager, an individual-account investor has the power to terminate the relationship notwithstanding any agreement to the contrary.[83] To be sure, some individual-account advisers may impose termination fees

---

[78] Aiken *et al.* at 209.
[79] Healy and Greer at 303.
[80] For the details, see DeMott and Laby at 416–18.
[81] Restatement (Third) of Agency § 1.01 and cmt. f ("[a]n essential element of agency is the principal's right to control the agent's actions), quoted in Hollingsworth v. Perry, 133 S. Ct. 2652, 2666 (2013).
[82] *Id.* cmt. f.
[83] *Id.* § 3.10.

on clients but most do not, and a prospective management client presented with an agreement that charges for exit may decide to seek management services elsewhere.[84]

The vantage point of the principal–agency relationship created by individual-account management helps illuminate the distinctiveness of mutual funds. As just seen, investors in mutual funds, unlike principals, lack powers of interim control over the fund's managers. Indeed, interim control seems inimical to the advantages of investing through a pooled investment vehicle, especially when the vehicle serves a large number of investors. This feature of mutual fund investing is congenial to viewing shares in a mutual fund as products or as comparable in some respects to equity investment in a publicly held corporation, especially when the investor in question does not hold a controlling position. On the other hand, investors in open-end mutual funds have ongoing rights to exit from their relationship with the fund manager by redeeming their shares, subject to any applicable charges such as back-end sales loads.[85] The right to redeem thus functions as an equivalent to a client-principal's power to terminate the agency relationship with the manager of an individual account.[86]

These contrasts and similarities also serve to illuminate the distinctiveness of private funds. As detailed above, like investors in retail mutual funds, investors in private funds lack the powers and rights of direct control that are constitutive of a relationship of common law agency, as well as lacking the smidgens of mandatory governance rights held by investors in mutual funds. Investment in a private fund is also "stickier" than mutual fund investment because exit can be a long-term prospect. Additionally, for hedge fund investors, exit is both complex and subject to the vagaries of a fund manager's discretion to restrict redemptions. Developments in the private fund environment that followed Advisers Act registration for many fund managers imply that the relative opacity that previously characterized many private funds came with drawbacks, including obstacles to pricing the potential impact of managerial discretion, amplified by an opaque informational environment. And market developments for hedge funds illustrate that investors, having failed fully to anticipate how hedge fund managers might use their discretion in times of crisis, sanction funds in families associated with discretionary limits on redemptions.

---

[84] Jason Zweig, *Should You Have to Pay a Fee to Fire an Adviser?*, WALL ST. J. (July 26–27, 2014). The SEC has not addressed the question of termination fees by rule but in general is believed to disfavor termination fees that exceed a reasonable estimate of the costs of setting up and maintaining the client's account. If an adviser does not charge a termination fee, it's likely that the client may owe a portion of the annual account management fee for the pre-departure tenure of the client's funds with the manager.

[85] Roiter at 15–16. Professor Roiter notes that such charges appear not to impose "major obstacles" to redemption because "[w]hether overall market performance in a given year is strong or not, gross redemptions remain relatively close to gross new sales." *Id.* at 16–17. To be sure, redeeming early may trigger unpleasant tax consequences, and reinvesting in the context of a 401(k) plan confronts whatever limits on investment choice the plan imposes.

[86] Roiter at 14 ("Just as an investor can terminate the services of a personal investment manager, so, too, can a mutual fund investor terminate reliance on the fund's adviser by redeeming her shares").

3 CONTOURS OF FIDUCIARY DUTY

3.1 Fundamental Distinctions and Institutions

For mutual funds, as for private funds, the significance of fiduciary duties necessarily turns on many factors, including the structural and market characteristics sketched above, as well as regulatory prescriptions. This section begins with a few foundational distinctions and commonalities, followed by selected specifics. In general, a central objective of regulating asset managers (regardless of their categorization) is reducing agency costs.[87] Toward this end, regulation in the United States is structured around the segmentation of investors through qualifications that establish barriers to investor eligibility. However, as the history recounted above illustrates, even investors who, for regulatory purposes, are deemed sophisticated may be vulnerable to risks of self-interested managerial behavior. Informational vacuums aggravate these risks.

On questions specifically relevant to fiduciary duties, overall the Advisers Act is a principles-based regime: beyond specific restrictions and requirements imposed by the statute itself, much turns on the interpretation and application of general fiduciary principles.[88] The Supreme Court established the foundational significance of general fiduciary principles for investment advisers in *SEC v. Capital Gains Research Bureau*, holding that an adviser who published a subscription newsletter breached its fiduciary duty through a practice of "scalping" its clients.[89] The adviser recommended securities for purchase in anticipation of selling its own recently acquired holdings once the clients had acted on the recommendation and the market price rose. A majority of the Court agreed with the SEC that the scalping practice constituted a fraud or deceit on the adviser's clients that violated Advisers Act section 206 (1)–(2). Although the adviser may have given honest advice it believed sound, its fiduciary duty as an adviser required that it disclose to clients the material fact of the scalping strategy.[90]

A legacy of *Capital Gains* is the general recognition that an investment adviser's fiduciary position requires that the adviser avoid conflicts of interest or, at a minimum, disclose them to clients and obtain the client's informed consent, apart from specific requirements imposed by the Advisers Act itself, discussed below.[91] In contrast, although the ICA regime incorporates general fiduciary principles, it also prescribes much through substantive restrictions.[92] The differences between the two regimes—in overall orientations of managers subject to them as well as specifics—may tend to segment advisers, perhaps making it challenging for a private fund adviser to transition smoothly into the ICA environment with new registered funds.[93]

---

[87] DeMott at 424.
[88] For the "principles-based" characterization, see Champ at 3, 6.
[89] 375 U.S. 180 (1963).
[90] 375 U.S. at 197.
[91] DeMott and Laby at 422–3.
[92] Champ at 6.
[93] Champ at 6. Mr. Champ, then the Director of the SEC's Division of Investment Management, cautioned hedge fund advisers "to proceed carefully and thoughtfully before becoming advisers to registered funds," detailing major differences between the relevant regulatory regimes. *Id.* "Consider carefully your reasons for taking on a registered fund client,

Related to fiduciary duty issues but with a broader reach, the two regimes also differ in their frameworks for internal compliance. For example, it is mandatory for an ICA-registered fund that the fund's chief compliance officer (CCO) report directly to the fund's board, which has sole power to appoint and remove the CCO (but not the adviser).[94] A direct relationship with the fund's board can further the CCO's capacity to act independently by formally insulating the CCO from the adviser's senior management.[95] Internal compliance processes and personnel are highly significant to fiduciary duties when an actor is a complex organization. In part this is because official or formal enforcement of the law and regulation is necessarily subject to limits. As is well known, governmental institutions like the SEC with assigned enforcement functions are constrained by limited resources. Client-initiated enforcement is also subject to constraints; for example, there is no private right of action based on the antifraud provisions of the Advisers Act.[96] Additionally, in opaque environments, a client who may have a viable claim (such as a state law claim for breach of fiduciary obligation) may lack sufficient awareness of the adviser's practices to assert the claim. Finally, as I detail more fully below, the extent to which fiduciary duties may be modified or eliminated through investment management agreements or otherwise is a significant and overarching question.

3.2 Principal Transactions

Prohibitions on self-dealing are at the core of the fiduciary duty of loyalty. For example, it is well established that as a fiduciary "[a]n agent has a duty not to deal with the principal as or on behalf of an adverse party in a transaction connected with the agency relationship."[97] Consent given by the principal to a self-dealing transaction is

---

and the potential conflicts with your existing business ... Merely "tacking on" new [compliance] policies and procedures to the adviser's existing program, without considering the overall impact on the adviser's business model, may increase the risk of compliance weaknesses, deficiencies or violations." *Id.* at 6–7.

[94] The ICA compliance rule, Rule 38a-1, was adopted at the same time as Advisers Act Rule 206(4)-7. Rule 38a-1 requires that the fund's board approve the fund compliance program and those of its adviser and service providers. Under the rule, a fund must have its own chief compliance officer (CCO), whom only the board may appoint and remove. The CCO must report directly to the board. In contrast, Rule 206(4)-7 makes fewer specific demands. Rule 206(4)-7 requires the designation of a CCO, plus the adoption and implementation of policies and procedures reasonably designed to prevent violations of the Advisers Act by advisers and the persons they supervise. One basis for the difference is relatively greater heterogeneity among private fund advisers.

[95] On the other hand, a CCO's position is weakened when the CCO is an employee at will who may be fired by the adviser's CEO. *See* Sullivan v. Harnisch, 969 N.E.2d 758 (N.Y. 2012) (CCO fired by CEO after CCO alleged CEO's personal transactions constituted front running of clients' transactions; as employee at will under New York law, CCO had no tort claim for wrongful discharge in violation of public policy).

[96] Transamerica Mortg. Advisors, Inc. v. Lewis, 444 U.S. 11, 18–19 (1979) (limiting private suits to actions under Advisers Act section 215, which makes void contracts in contravention of Act and contracts performance of which would contravene Act).

[97] Restatement (Third) of Agency § 8.03.

ineffective unless the agent acts in good faith in obtaining the principal's consent and discloses all material facts to the principal, and the consent concerns either a specific act or transaction or transactions of a specified type that reasonably would be expected to occur within the agency relationship's ordinary course.[98] Against this common law backdrop, it is noteworthy that both the ICA and the Advisers Act—and despite the latter's "principles-based" style—deal explicitly with principal transactions, that is, transactions through which a fund's investment adviser, for its own account, buys securities from or sells securities to a fund.

Their divergent regulatory styles are manifest in the differences between the ICA and the Advisers Act. The ICA's stance on principal transactions, articulated in ICA section 17(a), is generally prohibitory.[99] Any such transactions with the adviser itself are prohibited, as are transactions with any affiliate of the adviser, any affiliate of the fund, and any affiliate of an affiliate of the fund. Additionally, under ICA section 17(d) and SEC Rule 17d-1, an adviser to a registered fund may not participate in any "joint enterprise or other joint arrangement or profit-sharing plan" in which the fund is a participant without first obtaining an exemptive order from the SEC. These broadly drawn prohibitions apply to advisers who manage funds registered under the ICA in addition to private funds.[100] The ICA's prohibitory treatment of principal transactions, unlike the common law of agency, does not contemplate consent to such transactions, even if effected through a vote by fund investors approving the transaction. Viewing a share in a mutual fund as akin to a product that an investor purchases, the ICA's prohibition on principal transactions resembles a form of product safety regulation effected by specifying acceptable (and unacceptable) characteristics in product design. But the product metaphor, as explained above, does not capture the hybrid complexity of mutual fund investment, which represents as well an ongoing relationship akin to common law agency that warrants the imposition of fiduciary norms.

In contrast, section 206(3) of the Advisers Act permits principal transactions when the client approves them in advance and in writing, having received disclosure of the proposed transaction and the capacity in which the adviser will act.[101] Advance consent can be difficult to obtain when markets are dynamic, with the consequence that many advisers refrain from principal transactions with their clients.[102] Some hedge fund advisers address the statutory requirement of consent through "conflict committees" charged with reviewing and determining whether to approve conflicted transactions on behalf of the fund. To be effective, it is important that the committee's members themselves not be conflicted. In *In re Paradigm Capital Management, Inc.*, the conflicts committee consisted of the adviser's CFO and CCO, and the adviser's CFO

---

[98] *Id.* § 8.06 (1).
[99] ICA § 17(a); 15 U.S.C. § 80a-17(a).
[100] The SEC has pursued enforcement actions against advisers who, without a prior exemptive order, caused hedge funds they managed to sell illiquid bonds to a registered fund to reduce the hedge funds' liquidity problems. *See* In re Ruffle, SEC Rel. No. IC-31066, 2014 WL 2447729 (June 2, 2014), discussed in Champ at 6.
[101] Advisers Act § 206(3); 15 U.S.C. § 80b-6(3). This provision is expressly inapplicable to transactions with a customer of a broker-dealer if the broker-dealer does not act as an investment adviser in connection with the transaction. *Id.*
[102] DeMott and Laby at 422.

served in the same role at an affiliated broker-dealer. The SEC found that this structure did not provide effective written consent, as section 206(3) requires, to transactions conducted by the adviser's owner on behalf of a hedge fund client through a broker-dealer also controlled by the adviser's owner.[103] *Paradigm* is better known for the SEC's subsequent award of $600,000 through its whistleblower reward program to the broker-dealer's head trader who reported the trading activity.[104]

3.3 Fees

Concerns focused on fees surround investment management relationships, whether regulated under the Advisers Act or the ICA, but differ in focus and specifics. Section 205 (a)(1) of the Advisers Act prohibits fee structures calculated "on the basis of a share of capital gains ... or capital appreciation" achieved for all or any portion of the client's funds. This prohibition expressly does not apply to contracts with registered investment companies or investments of assets in excess of $1 million when the contract incorporates a "fulcrum" fee, which both increases and decreases in amount over time as performance is measured against an appropriate index.[105] Otherwise, the regulatory strategy of the Advisers Act relies on an adviser's duty to make full and fair disclosure of fees to its clients. An adviser would breach its fiduciary duty by charging one client more than another for substantially the same service without disclosing the discrepancy.[106]

The ICA addresses mutual fund fees explicitly in section 36(b), which deems an investment adviser to have a fiduciary duty to fund investors "with respect to the receipt of compensation for services, or payments of a material nature," paid by the fund or its investors to the adviser or any affiliate. This duty situates a mutual fund's investment adviser in an agency relationship of sorts with the fund's investors. So situated, one might wonder how—consistent with well-established agency law doctrine—a mutual fund's adviser could justify taxing the fund itself, and thus its present investors, with the costs of distributing new shares.[107] After all, the fund's adviser, paid a management fee typically calculated as a percentage of the fund's assets, has an interest in enticing new investors to augment the fee.[108] The SEC resolved the obstacle posed by ICA section 12(b)—which prohibits a fund from paying for its own costs of distribution absent exemptive action by the SEC—in 1980 through Rule 12b-1, which lifts the statutory prohibition by permitting

---

[103] In re Paradigm Cap. Mgmt., Advisers Act Rel. No. 3657, 2014 WL 2700783 (June 16, 2014). In at least 83 principal transactions, the adviser's owner caused it to sell securities with unrealized losses from the hedge fund to the affiliated broker-dealer, with the objective of realizing losses to offset the fund's realized gains.
[104] The firm retaliated against its head trader after he reported problematic principal transactions to the SEC. The firm and its owner settled the SEC's anti-retaliation enforcement action for $2.2 million.
[105] Advisers Act § 205(b)(2). On fulcrum fees generally, see Bieber and Price.
[106] DeMott and Laby at 427.
[107] Frankel (2007) at 377–86.
[108] Roiter at 32.

fund directors wider latitude in allocating distribution costs.[109] The results were mixed: fund directors seemed willing to approve fee requests, regardless of circumstances.[110]

Private funds, in contrast, are not subject to the prohibition on performance-geared fees stated in Advisers Act section 205(a)(1).[111] Simplifying greatly, a commonly used structure for hedge funds consists of an annual management fee of 1–2 percent plus an annual performance fee calculated as 20–50 percent of net trading gains.[112] For private equity funds, an annual management fee of 1–2 percent of committed capital is typical,[113] plus an 80 percent–20 percent division of profits as between the fund's limited partner investors and the fund's general partner. As discussed above, postcrisis developments confound the precrisis view that these proportionate allocations and their amounts (along the lines of "two and twenty"), akin to facts of nature, were immutable. Additionally, by 2015, the sharp increase in institutional investing in hedge funds was pressuring traditional fee structures, led by investors with greater bargaining power.[114] Distinct from fees explicitly paid to an investment adviser, the adviser's fiduciary duty applies also to how it allocates expenses it incurs, for example as between the funds it manages and investors who coinvest with the fund. In June 2015, the SEC charged a prominent private equity firm, Kohlberg Kravis Roberts & Co., under Advisers Act section 206(2) alleging the misallocation of over $17 million in expenses attributable to buyout opportunities that failed. The firm had allocated all of these expenses to funds it managed but none to coinvestors with the funds, a cohort that included KKR's own executives.[115] The firm settled for $30 million, inclusive of a $10 million penalty, as widely noted in news media.[116]

---

[109] Roiter at 40.

[110] Roiter at 43. In the aggregate, Rule 12b-1 fees benefited advisers through growth in fund size, while benefits for fund shareholders did not follow through decreased expenditures via economies of scale or lower fund flow volatility. Lori Walsh, The Costs and Benefits to Fund Shareholders of 12b-1 Plans: An Examination of Fund Flow, Expenses and Returns (2004), *available at* www.sec.gov/rules/proposed/s70904/lwalsh042604.pdf.

[111] Advisers Act § 205 (a)(4) (prohibition on performance fees inapplicable to investment advisory contract with investment company excepted from ICA registration by ICA § 3(c)(7)).

[112] In this structure, the performance fee typically is subject to a "high water mark," which means that losses must be made up before the performance fee becomes applicable to gains. Some fund managers were known for especially high fees: SAC Capital charged a 3 percent management fee and a performance fee of up to 50 percent. Peter Lattman and Ben Protess, *$1.2 Billion Fine for Hedge Fund SAC Capital in Insider Case*, N.Y. TIMES (Nov. 4, 2013).

[113] The fund "calls" or requires the payment of committed capital only when it has identified investments to make.

[114] Kaal at 1168. In Professor Kaal's assessment, the 2/20 structure no longer typifies private funds.

[115] In re Kohlberg Kravis Roberts & Co., Rel. No. Ia-4131, June 29, 2015, 2015 WL 4123730.

[116] See e.g., Alexandra Stevenson, *KKR Settles Over "Broken Deal" Expenses*, N.Y. TIMES (June 29, 2015).

3.4 Exculpatory Provisions

A general question about duties is whether or to what extent parties may modify or eliminate duties that the law imposes, or mitigate the otherwise applicable consequences of breach of duty. Once again, the contrast between the ICA and the Advisors Act is informative. ICA section 17(i) explicitly prohibits the use in investment advisory agreements of provisions that protect a person against otherwise applicable liability "by reason of willful misfeasance, bad faith, or gross negligence, in the performance of his duties, or by reason of his reckless disregard of his duties" under the agreement.[117] An implication is that exculpatory provisions—in this context termed "hedge" clauses—may protect against liability for lesser breaches of duty, including ordinary negligence.

The principles-based Advisers Act does not explicitly address hedge clauses. In interpreting the Act's general prohibitions on fraud, the SEC long disapproved of hedge clauses in investment advisory contracts, reasoning that such clauses were likely to mislead investors into believing that they had waived all rights against the adviser. To be sure, early hedge clauses condemned by the SEC were problematic on many grounds, such as one stating that "'no liability is assumed'" by the adviser for the accuracy of information given to its clients.[118] More recently, the SEC's staff indicated that by using a hedge clause, an adviser does not necessarily violate the Adviser Act's antifraud provisions. The hedge clause in question, which came to the staff's attention during a routine examination, purported to exculpate the adviser from liability stemming from conduct that was not "grossly negligent, reckless, willfully improper, or illegal" and that did not constitute a material breach of the advisory contract or action beyond the scope of the adviser's authority.[119] Like provisions permitted by ICA section 17(i), this language would exculpate the adviser from liability stemming from ordinary negligence. The SEC's staff stated that although using the language would not constitute a per se violation of the Advisers Act, only by considering the full facts and circumstances, focused on the particulars of each client, could the adviser's proposed deployment of a hedge clause be assessed.

4 IMPLICATIONS

Four implications emerge from the material recounted in this chapter. First, the amount and quality of information available to investors matters. Just how, and how much, information can matter is evident in the postcrisis history of private funds. Second, it is an open question how long lessons learned from the crisis and its aftermath will be retained. Memories may endure longer, though, when they concern epoch-defining events, especially those that came as a negative surprise and that are shared by many who lived through the epoch. Tellingly, even general news media have not forgotten

---

[117] ICA § 17(i); 15 U.S.C. § 80a-17(i).
[118] DeMott and Laby at 449.
[119] Heitman Cap. Mgmt., 2007 WL 789073 (Feb. 12, 2007).

which hedge funds imposed discretionary restrictions on redemptions.[120] Third, much of the regulatory architecture applicable to investment funds turns on carefully segmenting investors into groups that can be readily typified. One might wonder whether, by segmenting investors, the regulatory architecture also segments advisers, who may find it challenging to transition from a principles-based regime to the prescriptive ICA regime. Fourth, scholars who focus on mutual funds place considerable weight on the power held by mutual fund investors to redeem their shares. This emphasis may suggest the vulnerability to critique of the discretionary power over redemption held by many hedge fund managers. To be sure, memories of crisis-era conduct may endure and continue to inform choices made by investors in private funds. Even granting that assumption, investors' choices are always made on the basis of information, and the private fund context can prove opaque.

5 CONCLUSION

In his presidential address, the incoming President of the American Finance Association, Professor Luigi Zingales, addressed a broad question that may not have been equally welcome to all in the audience: "Does Finance Benefit Society?" To be sure, Professor Zingales did not much engage with the asset management industry.[121] Tellingly, though, he emphasized the importance of scholarly identification of the "rent-seeking components of finance,"[122] the importance of acknowledging that poor general repute has a role in shaping regulation and governmental intervention,[123] and the widespread consequences that follow problematic conduct in the finance sector. This chapter does not question the proposition that investment funds, however structured, can be—and often are—widely beneficial. But the chapter does identify reasons to question whether, at any particular time, all is optimal.

BIBLIOGRAPHY

Aiken, Adam L., Clifford, Christopher P., and Ellis, Jesse A., Hedge Funds and Discretionary Liquidity Restrictions, 116 J. Fin. Econ. 197–218 (2015).
Bieber, Sander M. and Price, Lisa R., Fulcrum Fees: Registered Funds' Alternative Fee Structure, 21 Inv. Lawyer, no. 9 (Sept. 2014).
BIRDTHISTLE, WILLIAM A., EMPIRE OF THE FUND. THE WAY WE SAVE NOW (2016).

---

[120] For a recent example, see Rob Copeland, *Citadel's Ken Griffin Leaves 2008 Tumble Far Behind*, WALL ST. J. (Aug. 3, 2015) (characterizing funds' gating in 2008 as "still grating" to some observers). And Claren Road's more recent delay in paying out withdrawal requests, characterized as "unusual since the financial crisis ended," nonetheless "rankled some investors." Juliet Chung, *More Withdrawals for Carlyle Group's Claren Road*, WALL ST. J. (Dec. 22, 2015) at C4.
[121] He did point out that for business-school case studies critical of venture capital, "one has to read marketing cases, not finance ones." Zingales at 1359.
[122] Zingales at 1343.
[123] Zingales at 1328.

Bowden, Andrew J., Spreading Sunshine in Private Equity, May 6, 2014, available at www.sec.gov/news/speech/2014-spch05062014ab.html
Cain, Matthew D., McKeon, Stephen B., and Davidoff Solomon, Steven, Intermediation in Private Equity (May 2015), available at http://ssrn.com/abstract=2586273
Champ, Norm, Remarks to the Practicing Law Institute, Hedge Fund Management Seminar 2014, Sept. 11, 2014), *available at* www.sec.gov/News/Speech/Detail/Speech/1370542916156
DeMott, Deborah A., Regulatory Techniques and Liability Regimes for Asset Managers, 7 Cap. Mkts L. J. 423–31 (2012).
DeMott, Deborah A., and Laby, Arthur B., The United States of America, in LIABILITY OF ASSET MANAGERS 411–55 (Busch, D. & DeMott, D. eds 2012).
Frankel, Tamar, United States Mutual Fund Investors, Their Managers and Distributors, in CONFLICTS OF INTEREST (Thévenoz, Luc and Bahar, Rashid eds. 2007) 363–94.
Frankel, Tamar, Investment Management Regulation (4th ed. 2011).
Getmansky, Mila, Lee, Peter A., and Lo, Andrew W., Hedge Funds: A Dynamic Industry In Transition, 7 Ann. Rev. Fin. Econ. 483–577 (2015).
Greene, Nathan and Adams, John, US Regulation of Investment Advisers and Private Investment Funds—A Concise Overview, in RESEARCH HANDBOOK ON HEDGE FUNDS, PRIVATE EQUITY AND ALTERNATIVE INVESTMENTS (Athanassiou, Phoebus ed.) 355–78.
Healy, Robert and Greer, Amy, In the Crosshairs: The Asset Management Industry, 46 Sec. Reg. & L. Rep. 302–06 (2014).
Kaal, Wulf A., The Post Dodd–Frank Act Evolution of the Private Fund Industry: Comparative Evidence from 2012 and 2015, 71 Bus. Law. 1151–1206 (2016).
KIRSCH, CLIFFORD, MUTUAL FUNDS AND EXCHANGE TRADED FUNDS REGULATION (3rd ed. 2015).
Kostovetsky, Leonard, "Whom Do You Trust?" Investment-Advisor Relationships and Mutual Fund Flows, 29 Rev. Fin. Studies 898–936 (2016).
Morley, John, The Separation of Funds and Managers: A Theory of Investment Fund Structure and Regulation, 123 Yale L.J. 1228–87 (2014).
Phalippou, Ludovic, Private equity funds' performance, risk and selection, in RESEARCH HANDBOOK ON HEDGE FUNDS, PRIVATE EQUITY AND ALTERNATIVE INVESTMENTS (Athanassiou, Phoebus, ed. 2012) 113–37.
Rendón, Veronica E., Fleishhacker, Ellen Kaye, Lavin, Kevin J., Esser, Meredith B. and Kurzman, Jennifer S., Private Equity Management of Fees and Expenses: A Cautionary Tale, 46 Sec. Reg. & L. Rep. 1351–53 (2014).
Roiter, Eric D., Disentangling Mutual Fund Governance from Corporate Governance, 6 Harv. Bus. L. Rev. 2 1–82 (2015).
Securities and Exchange Commission, Staff Report on the Review of the Definition of "Accredited Investor," Dec. 18, 2015, *available at* www.sec.gov/corpfin/reportspubs/special-studies/review-definition-of-accredited-investor-12-18-2015.pdf
United States Government Accountability Office, Alternative Criteria for Qualifying As An Accredited Investor Should Be Considered, July 2013, *available at* www.gao.gov/assets/660/655963.pdf
Wyatt, Marc, Private Equity: A Look Back and a Glimpse Ahead, May 13, 2015, available at www.sec.gov/news/speech/private-equity-look-back-and-glimpse-ahead.html
Zingales, Luigi, Presidential Address: Does Finance Benefit Society, 70 J. Fin. 1327–63 (2015).

4. The fiduciary structure of investment management regulation

*Arthur B. Laby**

1 INTRODUCTION

The investment management industry is enormous, dynamic, and growing. As of mid-2018, investment managers registered with the US Securities and Exchange Commission ("SEC" or "Commission") numbered 12,659, with more than $72 trillion in assets under management. Another 17,635 investment advisers are registered with states. Still another 3,587 managers, although not registered, must file reports with the Commission.[1] As of the end of 2017, there were over 16,000 registered investment companies with assets exceeding $22 trillion.[2] The industry is developing new products, such as new forms of exchange-traded funds and alternative or "alt" funds, and it is increasingly using derivatives and other alternative strategies.

Regulatory developments in the fund industry garner significant attention from lawyers, academics, and others, but little attention is paid to the underlying structure of investment management regulation. What are regulators trying to achieve, and what are their primary concerns? This chapter addresses one aspect of these questions—the relationship between investment managers' fiduciary obligation and regulators' efforts to control the investment management industry through rules and enforcement actions that comprise much of investment management law.

An investment manager owes a fiduciary obligation to clients, including both institutional clients, such as mutual funds, and individual clients, such as retail investors. The fiduciary obligation includes duties of loyalty and care. A persistent question is what precisely is required by these duties. What does loyalty mean in the fiduciary context? How can one ensure loyalty to a principal? Similarly, under the duty of care, an investment manager might ask about the amount of diligence to be undertaken on a client's behalf with regard to management of client assets. How much time and effort must an investment manager expend to satisfy the duty of care? These questions have no clear answers. To reply that an investment manager must use reasonable efforts, or act as a reasonably prudent professional, hardly provides meaningful guidance.

---

* I am grateful to Barry Barbash, William Birdthistle, Jay Feinman, Robert Plaze, and Eric Roiter for comments.

[1] Proposed Commission Interpretation Regarding Standard of Conduct for Investment Advisers; Request for Comment on Enhancing Investment Adviser Regulation, 83 Fed. Reg. 21203, 21209 (May 9, 2018).

[2] *See* Investment Company Institute, 2018 Investment Company Fact Book, at 32, 52 (58th ed. 2018).

In this chapter, I shall argue that much of investment management law is a response by regulators to the uncertainties inherent in the fiduciary obligation. The claim is that regulators design investment management law to guide investment managers regarding the proscriptions imposed by the duty of loyalty and the diligence required by the duty of care. On one issue after another, regulators attempt to specify what precisely is required of investment managers in the context of exercising their fiduciary duty to clients.

Regulators specify the fiduciary duty through agency rulemaking, agency enforcement actions, and other formal and informal statements offered by agency officials. As to rulemaking, the Investment Advisers Act of 1940 authorizes the SEC to adopt rules to guard against fraud and the SEC has used this authority to prescribe detailed conduct for investment managers. In many cases, the SEC has outlined specific steps managers must take in carrying out their fiduciary responsibility. Absent these steps, the SEC will consider a manager to have breached its fiduciary duty and to have engaged in fraudulent conduct. Examples discussed below include requirements to disclose information, vote proxies for shares held by clients, and establish compliance policies and procedures. In each context, the SEC uses its rulemaking authority to outline specific steps managers must take to fulfill their fiduciary obligation.

The second way in which regulators address an investment manager's fiduciary duty is through agency enforcement actions. The Advisers Act is the primary federal statue regulating investment managers. Although there is only a limited private right of action under the Advisers Act,[3] the SEC and the Department of Justice ("DOJ") actively enforce the law.[4] Moreover, under the Advisers Act, mere negligent conduct is sufficient for fraud liability.[5] Thus, if the SEC deems an investment manager's conduct, or lack of conduct, to be inappropriate, the SEC can bring an enforcement action under the negligence provision of the Advisers Act's antifraud section.[6] With negligence as the standard, such cases often are not difficult to prove.

Moreover, the vast majority of SEC actions settle,[7] resulting in an SEC statement or order reviewing the misconduct and explaining that it is inconsistent with the Advisers Act. Such SEC statements, while not packing the same legal punch as litigated cases, are followed closely by members of the investment management bar, who counsel investment managers and funds on their behavior. Such statements are also followed by industry groups, which prepare best practices and other industry guidance drawn in large part from settled actions. The Commission, therefore, uses the potent weapon of an enforcement action to announce to the industry the level of conduct the SEC believes to be consistent with investment managers' fiduciary obligation.

---

[3] Transamerica Mortg. Advisors, Inc. (TAMA) v. Lewis, 444 U.S. 11, 24 (1979).

[4] *See* SEC, AGENCY FINANCIAL REPORT: FISCAL YEAR 2015 154–56.

[5] SEC v. Capital Gains Research Bur., Inc., 375 U.S. 180, 195 (1963) (quoting Investment Advisers Act § 206(2)).

[6] The SEC can enforce an investment adviser's fiduciary duty through Advisers Act section 206. Section 206(1) requires a showing of intent; section 206(2) requires a showing of negligence. SEC v. Steadman, 967 F.2d 636, 641–43 & n.5 (D.C. Cir. 1992).

[7] JAMES D. COX, ET AL., SECURITIES REGULATION: CASES AND MATERIALS 834 (2013) ("Most SEC enforcement proceedings (over 90 percent) are settled, not litigated").

Viewing investment management law as I propose in this chapter leads to important insights and challenges an alternative view of the fiduciary obligation. Some writers claim that detailed rules prescribing or proscribing conduct effectively displace fiduciary duties. According to this approach, regulators prepare conduct rules as an alternative to fiduciary duties.[8] Under this approach, once Congress or the SEC has spoken on a topic, there is no place for fiduciary duties, which serve to fill a gap in the *absence* of detailed rules. This chapter demonstrates that, far from being an alternative to the fiduciary obligation, investment management law serves to explicate what the fiduciary obligation entails. Such rules are not a substitute for the fiduciary duty; they help compose its essence.

This chapter proceeds as follows. Section 2 describes the fiduciary duties of loyalty and care. It explains how the duties differ, as well as the difficulties in specifying what they entail. Section 3 demonstrates that investment management law, both administrative rules and agency enforcement actions, explicates and instantiates what is required by the fiduciary duties of loyalty and care. Section 4 examines the alternative view that detailed rules displace fiduciary duties and explains why it is not compelling. Section 5 concludes.

2 THE FIDUCIARY DUTIES OF LOYALTY AND CARE

Although disagreement exists over the definition of a fiduciary relationship, for the purposes of this chapter a fiduciary duty generally arises when one person agrees to act on behalf of and for the benefit of another.[9] Investment managers typically owe a fiduciary duty to their clients. More than 50 years ago, the US Supreme Court, in *SEC v. Capital Gains Research Bureau, Inc.*, stated that investment managers must adhere to a strict fiduciary standard, including duties of utmost good faith and full and fair disclosure of material facts, and an obligation to use reasonable care to avoid misleading clients.[10]

---

[8] *See* Mercer Bullard, *The Fiduciary Study: A Triumph of Substance over Form?* 30 REV. OF BANKING & FIN. L. 171, 175 (2011). As discussed below, this is arguably the approach taken in the United Kingdom. *See infra* note 132 and accompanying text.

[9] *See* Arthur B. Laby, *The Fiduciary Obligation as the Adoption of Ends*, 56 BUFF. L. REV. 99, 129–37 (2008); Larry E. Ribstein, *Fiduciary Duty Contracts in Unincorporated Firms*, 54 WASH. & LEE L. REV. 537, 542 (1997). The definition of "fiduciary" and the determination of when fiduciary duties arise are controversial but that controversy need not detain us here because, as discussed below, investment managers are generally considered fiduciaries to their clients.

[10] *Capital Gains*, 375 U.S. at 194.

2.1 Duties of Loyalty and Care

2.1.1 Differentiating loyalty from care

The fiduciary obligation divides neatly into the duty of loyalty and the duty of care.[11] This division is based in part on the risks attendant to fiduciary relationships. The relationship exposes the principal to a risk of malfeasance, such as misappropriation, and to a risk of nonfeasance, such as neglect. The duty of loyalty addresses the risk of the first; the duty of care addresses the risk of the second.[12]

The duty of loyalty, therefore, is largely negative. It is a duty to prevent misconduct, refrain from self-interested behavior, and avoid conflicts of interest.[13] Under "Duty of Loyalty," the *Restatement (Second) of Trusts* states that a fiduciary must not profit at the beneficiary's expense and must not compete with the beneficiary without consent.[14] By contrast, the duty of care is largely positive. It is a duty to pursue the beneficiary's interests with diligence and skill, and it mandates good behavior.[15] The *Restatement (Third) of Agency* states that an agent has a duty of care, competence, and diligence normally exercised by agents in similar circumstances.[16] The *Restatement* explains that the duty of care expressed in section 8.08 is a duty to make reasonable efforts to achieve a result.[17] An investment adviser, for example, has a duty to clients to undertake a reasonable investigation before providing information to investors.[18]

The negative component of the duty of loyalty and the positive component of the duty of care form the keystone of the Prudent Investor Rule, which governs the investment of trust funds.[19] According to the *Restatement (Third) of Trusts*, the duty of loyalty in trust law prohibits the trustee from investing or managing trust assets in a way that will lead to a conflict of interest.[20] The duty of care requires the trustee to exercise reasonable effort and diligence in making and monitoring investments, paying attention to the trust's objectives.[21]

---

[11] Air Line Pilots Ass'n Int'l v. O'Neill, 499 U.S. 65, 75 (1991) (explaining that the fiduciary duty consists of a duty of care and a duty of loyalty).

[12] Robert Cooter and Bradley J. Freedman, *The Fiduciary Relationship: Its Economic Character and Legal Consequences*, 66 N.Y.U. L. REV. 1045, 1047 (1991).

[13] *See* Deborah A. DeMott, *Disloyal Agents*, 59 ALA. L. REV. 949, 952 (2007); D. Gordon Smith, *The Critical Resource Theory of Fiduciary Duty*, 55 VAND. L. REV. 1399, 1406–11 (2002); Julian Velasco, *A Defense of the Corporate Law Duty of Care*, 40 J. CORP. L. 647, 664 (2015).

[14] RESTATEMENT (SECOND) OF TRUSTS § 170 CMT. A (2012); *see* Arthur B. Laby, *Resolving Conflicts of Duty in Fiduciary Relationships*, 54 AM. U. L. REV. 75, 100–06 (2004).

[15] Velasco, *supra* note 13 at 664.

[16] RESTATEMENT (THIRD) OF AGENCY § 8.08 (2006).

[17] *Id.* at § 8.08 CMT. D.

[18] *See* SEC v. Blavin, 557 F. Supp. 1304, 1314 (E.D. Mich. 1983), *aff'd*, 760 F.2d 706 (6th Cir. 1985).

[19] *See* RESTATEMENT (THIRD) OF TRUSTS § 90 (2007).

[20] *See Id.* at § 90 CMT. C.

[21] *Id.* at CMT. D.

The Prudent Investor Rule can be traced to the 1830 case of *Harvard College v. Amory*.[22] The court in that case stated that trustees should "observe how men of prudence, discretion and intelligence manage their own affairs, not in regard to speculation, but in regard to the permanent disposition of their funds."[23] As should be apparent, neither the positive nor the negative formulation of the fiduciary duty, nor the Prudent Investor Rule, provides clear guidance for investment managers who seek to satisfy their fiduciary obligation.

2.1.2 The need to specify the duties of loyalty and care

The term "fiduciary duty" lacks clarity and its meaning often depends on context.[24] The 2009 edition of *Black's Law Dictionary* observes that "fiduciary" is a "vague term, and it has been pressed into service for a number of ends."[25] As the Supreme Court famously remarked in *SEC v. Chenery*, "to say that a man is a fiduciary only begins analysis; it gives direction to further inquiry."[26] This uncertainty holds true for both the duty of loyalty, which is primarily negative, and the duty of care, which is primarily positive. Each presents challenges in specifying the duties that an investment manager must perform in the asset management context.

2.1.2.1 The duty of loyalty The duty of loyalty is more precise than the duty of care in terms of what it demands of a fiduciary: Do not engage in theft, fraud, or self-dealing; avoid conflicts of interest, or if a conflict of interest cannot be avoided, it must be disclosed. Notwithstanding the precise nature of the obligation, enforcement of the duty of loyalty poses problems because of the subtle opportunities that arise for theft or self-dealing, and because conflicts of interest can affect a fiduciary's conduct in ways he or she might not fully understand. The US Supreme Court recognized this difficulty in *Capital Gains*, stating that the Advisers Act reflects a Congressional intent to eliminate or, at a minimum, to expose conflicts of interest that could lead an adviser "consciously or unconsciously" to provide conflicted advice.[27]

Subtle temptations to engage in deception offered in fiduciary relationships are well recognized. Courts respond by imposing prohibitions to ensure that an investment manager who is tempted by wrongdoing, or who might unconsciously step over the

---

[22] Harvard College v. Amory, 26 Mass. 446 (Mass. 1831); *See* RESTATEMENT (THIRD) OF TRUSTS, Prudent Investor Rule, General Note (describing origin of Prudent Investor Rule).

[23] *Harvard College*, 26 Mass. at 461.

[24] Wall Street and Fiduciary Duties: Can Jail Time Serve as an Adequate Deterrent for Willful Violations, Hearings Before the S. Subcomm. on Crime and Drugs, 111th Cong. 1 (2010) (statement of Larry E. Ribstein, Mildred Van Voorhis Jones Chair, University of Illinois College of Law) ("'Fiduciary duty' is one of the most amorphous concepts in the law"); Donald C. Langevoort, *Brokers as Fiduciaries*, 71 U. PITT. L. REV. 439, 456 (2010) ("[A]n open-ended broker fiduciary obligation is so loaded with unanswered questions that baseline predictability would come slowly, if at all").

[25] Fiduciary, BLACK'S LAW DICTIONARY 702 (9th ed. 2009) (quoting D.W.M. Waters, *The Constructive Trust: The Case for a New Approach in English Law* 4 (1964)); *see also* Velasco, *supra* note 13 at 664.

[26] SEC v. Chenery, 318 U.S. 80, 85–86 (1942).

[27] *Capital Gains*, 375 U.S. at 191–92.

line, is unable to do so. A persistent theme in fiduciary relationships is the high cost of detecting whether and when a fiduciary will engage in misappropriation.[28] In *U.S. v. Chenery*, the Supreme Court stated that corporate position and access to information present temptations to wrongdoing. The law can only address such temptations through prohibitions unconcerned with the fairness of a transaction.[29]

The concern over temptation is particularly severe when an investment manager has discretion over investment assets. When a manager has discretion, the manager has authority to make investment decisions on a client's behalf without notifying the client in advance.[30] John Langbein has explained that a trust relationship places trust beneficiaries at the mercy of the trustees' misconduct, such as misappropriation and mismanagement, and that trust law's central concern is to guard against such dangers.[31]

Langbein further explained that as trustees have gained additional discretionary authority over trust assets, fiduciary law has replaced old safeguards, such as limitations on investments and disempowering trustees from engaging in particular conduct. Discretion presents risk of harm as well as investment opportunity. The fiduciary duties of loyalty and care, according to Langbein, developed to replace former restrictions on trustees and serve to protect investors from abuse.[32] But this development leaves open the question of which conduct should be prohibited, or limited, by the fiduciary duty of loyalty. The legal list of acceptable investment assets, while providing clarity, is a historical artifact.[33] A general injunction to act in a client's best interest, however, is insufficient guidance to fulfilling one's duty of loyalty.

2.1.2.2 The duty of care The duty of care is different from the duty of loyalty and even more prone to uncertainty. The duty of care is generally positive; it focuses on process and the diligence a fiduciary must undertake.[34] Some situations require more process than others.[35] Under "Duties of Care, Competence, and Diligence," the *Restatement (Third) of Agency* explains that the duty of diligence is a duty to make "reasonable efforts" to achieve a result, as opposed to a duty to achieve the result regardless of the effort expended. As long as an agent makes "reasonable" efforts, the

---

[28] *See, e.g.*, Tamar Frankel, *Fiduciary Duties as Default Rules*, 74 OR. L. REV. 1209, 1217–18 (1995); Frank H. Easterbrook & Daniel R. Fischel, *Contract and Fiduciary Duty*, 36 J.L. AND ECON., 425, 427 (1993).

[29] *Chenery*, 318 U.S. at 92; *see also* Reading v. Regum, [1948] 2 All ER 27 (explaining that agent must disgorge his profits regardless of whether the principal has lost profit or suffered any other damage).

[30] Securities Exchange Act of 1934, § 3(a)(35), 15 U.S.C. § 78c(a)(35) (2012).

[31] John H. Langbein, *The Contractarian Basis of the Law of Trusts*, 105 YALE L.J. 625, 629 (1995).

[32] *Id.* at 642.

[33] HARVEY E. BINES & STEVE THEL, INVESTMENT MANAGEMENT LAW AND REGULATION 15 (2nd ed. 2004).

[34] *See* Velasco, *supra* note 13 at 664 (2015); Brehm v. Eisner, 746 A.2d 244, 264 (Del. 2000).

[35] Velasco, *supra* note 13 at 666.

agent will not be subject to liability even if the agent does not achieve the principal's desired objectives.[36]

The difficulty lies in specifying what is "reasonable." Corporate law cases recognize that a director's duty to be informed does not require the director to have detailed knowledge about all facets of the corporation's business.[37] In *Barnes v. Andrews*, Judge Learned Hand stated that a director's duty to pay attention to the corporation's affairs is "uncertain." He remarked that courts content themselves with vague statements. A director, for example, must give reasonable attention to the corporation's affairs.[38] Legal tests in a variety of contexts ask whether an individual is "fully informed" of all relevant facts.[39] A state of being "fully informed," however, is difficult to achieve. The complete truth on any topic is unknowable, or would take weeks or months of explanation.[40]

The uncertainty inherent in the fiduciary duty of care is one reason why the duty is seldom enforced. Although the duty of loyalty is often enforced aggressively, fewer cases allege breach of the duty of care.[41] In the corporate law context, the lack of duty of care cases might be due to the presence of the business judgment rule, which often protects directors from such claims.[42] The business judgment rule, however, is generally inapplicable outside of corporate law. Trust law, for example, lacks an analog to corporate law's business judgment rule.[43] And investment managers can be liable for breach of the duty of care in a variety of contexts.[44] But care cases are seldom brought, because of the difficulty in proving that what the manager *failed* to do was the cause of harm.

The investment manager's fiduciary duty, composed of the duties of loyalty and care, is imprecise. The fiduciary obligation alone does not provide an investment manager with certainty about what behavior is prohibited by loyalty or prescribed by due care.

---

[36] RESTATEMENT (THIRD) OF AGENCY § 8.08 CMT. D (2006).

[37] *See* In re Caremark Int'l, Inc., 698 A.2d 959, 972 (Del. Ch. 1996).

[38] Barnes v. Andrews, 298 F. 614, 615 (S.D.N.Y. 1924); *see also* BINES & THEL, *supra* note 33 at 24.

[39] U.S. v. O'Brien, 18 F. Supp. 3d 25, 32 (D. Mass. 2014) (judicial recusal standard); Campbell Harrison & Dagley L.L.P. v. Lisa Blue/Baron and Blue, 843 F. Supp. 2d 673, 688–89 (N.D. Tex. 2011) (client release in attorney-client relationship).

[40] SISSELA BOK, LYING: MORAL CHOICE IN PUBLIC AND PRIVATE LIFE 4 (1999); *see* Laby, *supra* note 14 at 114–16.

[41] *See* BINES & THEL, *supra* note 33 at 24; *see also* Christopher M. Bruner, *Is The Corporate Director's Duty of Care A "Fiduciary" Duty? Does it Matter?*, 48 WAKE FOREST L. REV. 1027, 1029 (2013).

[42] Velasco, *supra* note 13 at 649; *see* Bruner, *supra* note 41 at 1030.

[43] *See* Howard v. Shay, 100 F.3d 1484, 1489 (9th Cir. 1996) ("The business judgment rule is a creature of corporate, not trust, law"); *see also* Melanie Leslie, *Trusting Trustees: Fiduciary Duties and the Limits of Default Rules*, 94 GEO. L.J. 67, 96, 99 (2005) ("Courts adjudicating [trust law] cases alleging breach of the duty of care never developed a doctrine analogous to the business judgment rule").

[44] *See, e.g.*, SEC No-Action Letter, Institutional Shareholder Services, Inc., pub. avail., Sept. 15, 2004 (proxy voting context.).

A well-functioning regulatory scheme requires more clarity than a general directive to act in another's best interest.[45]

3 MAPPING INVESTMENT MANAGERS' FIDUCIARY OBLIGATION

Investment managers are fiduciaries, subject to the duties of loyalty and care discussed above. An investment manager's fiduciary obligation is embodied in Advisers Act section 206, the general antifraud provision of the Act. Unlike section 10(b) of the Securities Exchange Act of 1934, Advisers Act section 206 is considered more than an antifraud provision; it is viewed as establishing a fiduciary duty for advisers.[46] The fiduciary duty is imposed on investment managers because of the nature of the relationship between the manager and the client, including a fund client, and it is enforced through section 206 of the Advisers Act.[47]

Under the regulatory scheme outlined above, investment managers owe clients a fiduciary duty regardless of any SEC rule governing the investment management industry. Thus, in substantive areas, such as disclosure, proxy voting, and custody, managers would be required to exercise their fiduciary duty even if no relevant rule were adopted. By adopting rules and prosecuting enforcement actions, however, the SEC fills in the details of what is required by the fiduciary duties of loyalty and care, and brings uniformity to the industry.

As a result of the SEC's activity, investment managers know how to behave and clients know what to expect. Although a client might bargain for additional protections, administrative rules provide a fiduciary floor—rules that managers must follow. In other words, requirements that are set forth in applicable rules help to clarify a manager's fiduciary responsibilities, and failure to follow them often constitutes an independent breach of fiduciary duty.

3.1 Rules

Rules governing a profession or an industry are often detailed prescriptions or proscriptions, which put individuals on notice, ex ante, of what they can and cannot do. Rules are contrasted with standards, which also govern behavior, but which typically provide a general sense of what is required and leave discretion, ex post, for

---

[45] *Cf.* REINIER KRAAKMAN, ET AL., THE ANATOMY OF CORPORATE LAW 103 (2nd ed. 2009) (stating that "the injunction to boards to pursue their corporations' interests is less a species of equal sharing than, at best, a vague counsel of virtue, and, at worst, a smokescreen for board discretion").

[46] *See* Morris v. Wachovia Sec., Inc., 277 F. Supp. 2d 622, 644 (E.D. Va. 2003). For an historical discussion of how this view arose *see* Arthur B. Laby, SEC v. Capital Gains Research Bureau *and the Investment Advisers Act of 1940*, 91 B.U. L. REV. 1051 (2011).

[47] *See generally* Arleen W. Hughes, Exchange Act Release No. 4048 (Feb. 18, 1948), *aff'd sub. nom.* Hughes v. SEC, 174 F.2d 969 (D.C. Cir. 1949); *see also* Robert E. Plaze, Regulation of Investment Advisers by the U.S. Securities and Exchange Commission, June 2018, at 40, www.proskauer.com/professionals/robert-plaze.

adjudicators to determine whether a violation has occurred.[48] In some contexts, standards are preferable. Specific regulation might be harmful and render decision-making wooden and not necessarily in investors' best interests.[49] In those cases, standards are necessary to instruct a manager that he must act in the investor's best interest but provide the manager with the flexibility to exercise discretion as appropriate.[50]

Consider, for example, regulation of an investment manager's discretion regarding securities selection. It would be difficult to specify exactly what an investment manager must do before deciding whether to buy or sell one security or another. By contrast, there are many areas where regulators can and do require minimum conduct necessary to fulfill the fiduciary duties of loyalty and care. I shall provide three examples to illustrate how regulators prescribe what the fiduciary duty entails for investment managers: disclosure, proxy voting, and compliance programs.

3.1.1 Disclosure

An investment manager's duty to disclose can be viewed as arising under both the duty of loyalty and the duty of care, depending on the context.[51] When a manager discloses information to address a conflict of interest, the manager is disclosing information to refrain from fraudulent conduct.[52] As a result, one can view such disclosure as a means to satisfy the fiduciary duty of loyalty. Recall that the duty of loyalty is primarily negative—a duty to avoid self-dealing and conflicts of interest. Thus, to the extent that disclosure addresses a conflict, one can place the disclosure squarely under the duty of loyalty. By contrast, when a manager discloses information about the manager and its business, which allows a client to decide whether to select the manager, one can place the disclosure under the fiduciary duty of care.[53]

In either case, a difficult consideration for any investment manager is what types of facts must be disclosed and what level of detail is necessary. Provide too little information and an investor will have insufficient data to determine whether to engage a particular asset manager or consent to a conflict of interest. Provide too much and the

---

[48] See, e.g., Louis Kaplow, *Rules Versus Standards: An Economic Analysis*, 42 DUKE L.J. 557 (1992); KRAAKMAN, ET AL., *supra* note 45 at 39–40; see also Duncan Kennedy, *Form and Substance in Private Law Adjudication*, 89 HARV. L. REV. 1685 (1976). A large body of work, including the articles cited here, discusses rules versus standards. The issues are complex and assessing them in detail is not necessary for my analysis.

[49] *Cf.* Velasco, *supra* note 13 at 668.

[50] *Cf. id.*

[51] See, e.g., Bd. of Trs. of AFTRA Ret. Fund v. JPMorgan Chase Bank, N.A., 806 F. Supp. 2d 695 (S.D.N.Y. 2011) (duty of prudence and care); Metro Commun. Corp. BVI v. Advanced Mobilecomm Tech., Inc., 854 A.2d 121, 157 (Del.Ch. 2004) (a "duty of disclosure" is a component of the fiduciary duty of loyalty).

[52] See Plaze, *supra* note 47 at 41.

[53] I recognize that the line can blur. Disclosure about the manager's business, which also references a conflict, might move the disclosure back to the duty of loyalty.

investor will be buried under an avalanche of useless data, unable to separate the wheat from the chaff.[54]

In responding to the question of what information must be disclosed, one might point to the SEC's injunction to disclose all facts material to an engagement and avoid misleading clients.[55] The problem, of course, lies in the definition of "material." Materiality turns on whether there is a "substantial likelihood" that a reasonable client would consider the information important.[56] There are no clear rules regarding materiality; it is a "facts and circumstances" test.[57] The SEC has concluded that it is not appropriate to define materiality or provide a bright line test.[58]

In the absence of a definition of materiality, the SEC has adopted detailed rules describing the information an investment manager must disclose. The Commission has set forth these requirements in Part 2 of Form ADV, the general registration form for investment managers that register with the SEC. Part 2 of the form is the section designed for, and delivered to, clients.[59] Form ADV Part 2 includes detailed categories of information that must be disclosed, such as fees and compensation (Item 5), types of clients (Item 7), methods of analysis (Item 8), disciplinary information (Item 9), and brokerage practices (Item 12). The form elucidates additional information that must be disclosed within each category. Under disciplinary information, for example, the form sets forth in detail particular criminal actions, civil actions, administrative proceedings, and self-regulatory organization proceedings that the adviser must reveal (Item 9).

The SEC has clarified that an investment manager has a fiduciary obligation to disclose material information to clients, and that failure to make such disclosure can result in a violation of the Advisers Act.[60] Form ADV's detailed requirements specify the disclosure necessary for the investment manager to fulfill its fiduciary duty. According to the instructions prepared by the SEC, "much of the disclosure required in Part 2A addresses an adviser's conflicts of interest with its clients, and is disclosure that the adviser, as a fiduciary, must make to clients in some manner regardless of the form requirements."[61] Thus, disclosure required by Form ADV is meant to codify an adviser's fiduciary obligation, not displace it.

---

[54] TSC Indus., Inc. v. Northway, Inc., 426 U.S. 438, 448–49 (1976) (expressing the concern that "bury[ing] the shareholders in an avalanche of trivial information" is "a result that is hardly conducive to informed decisionmaking"); Susanna Kim Ripken, *The Dangers and Drawbacks of the Disclosure Antidote: Toward a More Substantive Approach to Securities Regulation*, 58 BAYLOR L. REV. 139, 160 (2006) (explaining that too much information can result in confusion, cognitive strain, and poor decision-making, and is worse than receiving too little information).

[55] See *Capital Gains*, 375 U.S. at 200; Arleen W. Hughes, Exchange Act Release No. 4048.

[56] *TSC Indus.*, 426 U.S. at 449; Sullivan v. Chase Inv. Serv. of Boston, Inc., 79 F.R.D. 246, 259 (N.D. Cal. 1978); *see also* Amendments to Form ADV, 75 Fed. Reg. 49234, 49237 n.35 (Aug. 12, 2010).

[57] *See, e.g.,* In re Moody's Corp. Sec. Litig., 274 F.R.D. 480, 489 (S.D.N.Y. 2011) ("materiality is not definitively established by an impact on price alone, rather it is an inquiry that looks at all the facts and circumstances of a particular case").

[58] *Id.*

[59] Part 1 of Form ADV, although publicly available, is designed to assist the SEC with the regulation of asset managers; it is not designed with client needs in mind.

[60] Amendments to Form ADV, 75 Fed Reg. at 49240 and n.89.

[61] *Id.* at 49236.

The fiduciary structure of investment management regulation 89

According to the SEC, an investment manager can use the disclosure statement required by Form ADV Part 2 to satisfy its fiduciary duty to disclose information to clients.[62] This stance regarding the relationship between investment manager's fiduciary duty and the SEC's disclosure rules is not new. When the SEC adopted a predecessor rule, Advisers Act Rule 206(4)-4, it stated that the rule was intended to "codify" an investment manager's fiduciary duty to disclose material facts to clients regarding financial and disciplinary information.[63]

Moreover, the SEC has explicitly instructed advisers that the detailed disclosures required by Form ADV Part 2 do not displace an ongoing fiduciary obligation. The instructions for completing Form ADV state as follows:

> Under federal and state law, you are a fiduciary and must make full disclosure to your clients of all material facts relating to the advisory relationship. As a fiduciary, you also must seek to avoid conflicts of interest with your clients, and, at a minimum, make full disclosure of all material conflicts of interest between you and your clients that could affect the advisory relationship. This obligation requires that you provide the client with sufficiently specific facts so that the client is able to understand the conflicts of interest you have and the business practices in which you engage, and can give informed consent to such conflicts or practices or reject them. To satisfy this obligation, you therefore may have to disclose to clients information not specifically required by Part 2 of Form ADV or in more detail than the brochure items might otherwise require.[64]

That the SEC's rules codify an investment manager's fiduciary duty is made plain by the SEC's attitude toward investment advisory relationships not covered by the disclosure rules. The Commission has clarified that investment managers owe a general duty to disclose financial and disciplinary information to clients, including clients to whom they are not required to deliver the specific information set forth in its rules. This clarification demonstrates that an investment manager's fiduciary duty is universal, that the duty includes a requirement to disclose financial and disciplinary information, and that the SEC, using its regulatory authority, has set forth what is entailed for an adviser to satisfy its fiduciary duty of disclosure.[65]

The SEC staff has made the same point in another disclosure context. Investment Advisers Act section 206(3) addresses an adviser's trading as a principal with advisory clients.[66] The provision prohibits an adviser from trading as a principal absent written disclosure and consent. Although the provision is quite specific, the staff has explained

---

[62] Id. at 49234–35.
[63] Financial and Disciplinary Information That Investment Advisers Must Disclose to Clients, Investment Advisers Act Release No. 1083 (Sept. 25, 1987), 52 Fed. Reg. 36915 (Oct. 2, 1987).
[64] Amendments to Form ADV, General Instructions for Part 2 of Form ADV, 75 Fed. Reg. 49234, Appendix C.
[65] See Amendments to Form ADV, 75 Fed. Reg. at 49245–46, n.191 ("[A]n adviser's fiduciary duty of full and fair disclosure, however, may require it to continue to disclose any material legal event or precarious financial condition promptly to all clients, even clients to whom it may not be required to deliver a brochure or amended brochure").
[66] Investment Advisers Act § 206(3), 15 U.S.C. § 80b-6(3) (2012).

90 Research handbook on the regulation of mutual funds

in a no-action letter that the statutory language is not a complete statement of an adviser's fiduciary duty in this context. According to the SEC staff:

> While section 206(3) of the Investment Advisers Act of 1940 ("Act") requires disclosure of such interest and the client's consent to enter into the transaction with knowledge of such interest, the adviser's fiduciary duties are not discharged merely by such disclosure and consent. The adviser must have a reasonable belief that the entry of the client into the transaction is in the client's interest.[67]

Thus, the disclosure required by section 206(3) does not satisfy the adviser's obligations with respect to the relevant principal transaction. The adviser must be mindful of its background fiduciary obligation, which continues to govern the purchase or sale.

Members of the investment management industry understand that the SEC rules are designed to implement the fiduciary obligation. Commenters on the SEC's proposed disclosure requirements argued that certain disclosure was already required by a manager's general fiduciary duty.[68] In responding to such comments, the SEC did not deny the premise that an investment manager's fiduciary obligation required general disclosure of the particular topic. (In this case the topic was additional compensation received by a manager provided by someone other than a client.) The SEC stated, however, that disclosure that might appear in response to one's general fiduciary obligation was insufficient. The SEC believed it was important for investment managers to make the particular detailed disclosure prescribed in its new rules.[69]

3.1.2 Proxy voting

Investment managers that exercise voting authority over client securities must vote in clients' best interest and not in the manager's interest. The SEC adopted a rule, Investment Advisers Act Rule 206(4)-6, which sets forth requirements for asset managers that have such voting authority. The premise underlying the rule is that investment managers are fiduciaries subject to the duties of loyalty and care. The securities laws, however, do not address how an asset manager should exercise its proxy voting authority for clients.[70] As a result, the SEC has stepped into the breach and clarified the conduct.

---

[67] Rocky Mountain Financial Planning, Inc., SEC No-Action Letter (Feb. 28, 1983), 1983 WL 31004 (Feb. 28, 1983).

[68] *See* Amendments to Form ADV, 75 Fed Reg. at 49250 & n.245; *see also* Letter from Justine Kirby, Legal and Compliance Division, Morgan Stanley & Co., Inc. to Nancy M. Morris, Secretary, Securities and Exchange Commission (May 16, 2008) ("To the extent that advisory representatives receive compensation or other economic benefits that may constitute a conflict of interest, these must be disclosed under the general law relating to fiduciary obligations"); Letter from David Riggs, Vice President and Associate General Counsel, Charles Schwab & Co., Inc. to Jonathan G. Katz, Secretary, Securities and Exchange Commission (June 13, 2000) ("objecting to requirement to deliver brochure 'stickers'" and stating that "adviser's fiduciary duty to fully disclose to its clients all material facts and the broad antifraud provisions of the Advisers Act and state securities laws currently require an adviser to timely disclose material changes to clients").

[69] *See* Amendments to Form ADV, 75 Fed Reg. at 49250.

[70] Proxy Voting by Investment Advisers, 68 Fed. Reg. 6585, 6586 (Feb. 7, 2003).

When adopting the proxy voting rule, the SEC began with the observation that an investment manager is a fiduciary and owes duties of loyalty and care with respect to all of its activities, including proxy voting.[71] Under the duty of loyalty, a manager must vote proxies consistent with a client's best interest and the manager cannot subrogate the client's interests to the manager's interests. Under the duty of care, the manager must monitor corporate events and vote.[72] The rule establishes a fiduciary floor for investment managers regarding proxy voting. The SEC made clear that nothing in the rule is intended to reduce or change the fiduciary responsibility of any investment manager, or person associated with an investment manager.[73]

Under the rule, an investment manager cannot exercise voting authority with respect to proxies unless it does the following: (1) adopt and implement written policies and procedures reasonably designed to ensure that the manager votes client securities in the clients' best interest, including procedures that address how the manager addresses conflicts of interest in the voting context; (2) disclose to clients how they can obtain information about the manager's proxy voting; and (3) disclose to clients the manager's proxy voting policies and how they can obtain a copy.[74] Thus, this rule, unlike others with more precise prescriptions or proscriptions, forces each investment manager that votes proxies to deliberate about how it can ensure that it will fulfill its duty of loyalty and vote proxies in the clients' best interest.

According to the rule, the procedures must include methods by which the manager addresses conflicts of interest between the manager and its clients in the voting context. Further, disclosing the manager's record of voting to clients will likely lead managers to pay greater attention to their fiduciary responsibilities. According to the SEC, fully informed clients will "serve as a check" on managers carrying out their obligations with respect to voting.[75] Moreover, in its adopting release, consistent with the fiduciary duty of care, the SEC clarified that once an investment manager has assumed the responsibility of voting proxies, it cannot refrain from doing so; it must actually vote.[76]

The premise of the rule is that investment managers, as part of their general fiduciary obligation, owe clients a duty to vote proxies in the clients' best interest and to provide them with information on how their proxies were voted. This obligation exists absent an SEC proxy voting rule.[77] As the SEC explained in its proposing release, many investment managers previously had adopted policies to ensure they voted proxies properly, avoided conflicts of interest, and otherwise fulfilled their fiduciary duties. Other managers did not take these steps. The SEC therefore proposed the proxy voting rules to ensure that all registered investment managers acted consistently with their fiduciary obligation.[78] A policy of disclosing conflicts of interest to clients and obtaining their consent to the conflict before voting fulfills the manager's fiduciary

---

[71] *Id.*
[72] *Id.*
[73] *Id.* at 6586 n.8.
[74] *See* 17 C.F.R. § 275.206(4)-6.
[75] Proxy Voting by Investment Advisers, 68 Fed. Reg. at 6589.
[76] *Id.* at 6588 n.23.
[77] *Id.* at 6586 and n.8.
[78] Proxy Voting by Investment Advisers, 67 Fed. Reg. 60841, 60847 (Sep. 26, 2002).

obligation under the Advisers Act.[79] This rule is meant not as a substitute for the fiduciary obligation, but rather to help ensure that investment managers carry out their fiduciary obligation.

In the proxy voting rule, the SEC attempted to codify what it believed was already the law under an investment manager's fiduciary obligation. In the proposing release, where the agency takes the time to explain the background and reasons behind a rule, the SEC stated that under the Advisers Act, an investment manager with a material conflict of interest must disclose the conflict to a client before voting proxies.[80] The SEC explained that preexisting law (the law before the proxy voting rule was adopted) entitled clients to the benefits of the fiduciary duties of loyalty and care in connection with proxy voting. It also entitled clients to information about how the manager voted the proxies—and some managers had previously adopted policies and procedures regarding proxy voting.[81]

The SEC, however, was concerned because some, but not all, managers had adopted policies and procedures to ensure that proxies were voted properly, that conflicts were avoided, and that managers' fiduciary duties were otherwise fulfilled. Of those managers with such policies and procedures, not all made them available to clients, and not all managers who voted disclosed their voting record to clients. The SEC explained that the importance of voting by investment managers and the potential conflicts in voting demonstrate a need for the SEC to address proxy voting in a rule.[82] Thus, a fiduciary duty governing proxy voting existed before the SEC adopted its proxy voting rule; the rule clarifies what the fiduciary obligation entails but nothing in the rule changes the overarching fiduciary obligation.

3.1.3 Compliance programs

The requirement for SEC-registered investment managers to adopt a compliance program is another example of where the Commission has defined what is required by the fiduciary obligation. Under the SEC's compliance rule adopted in 2003, registered investment managers and registered investment companies must adopt and implement written policies and procedures to prevent violation of the federal securities laws.[83] In addition, these entities must designate a chief compliance officer ("CCO") to administer the firm's compliance policies and procedures. The SEC explained that each investment manager should identify the risks presented by its respective firm and design policies and procedures to address those risks. To give additional guidance, the SEC wrote that a firm's procedures should address particular issues, if relevant, such as portfolio management processes, trading practices, valuation practices, safeguarding client assets, and business continuity.[84]

---

[79] Proxy Voting by Investment Advisers, 68 Fed. Reg. at 6587.
[80] Proxy Voting by Investment Advisers, 67 Fed. Reg. at 60842.
[81] *Id.* at 60847.
[82] *Id.* at 60842–43.
[83] *See* Compliance Programs of Investment Companies and Investment Advisers, 68 Fed. Reg. 74714 (Dec. 24, 2003).
[84] *Id.* at 74716.

The SEC adopted this rule in the wake of its discovery, alongside state regulators, of unlawful conduct such as inappropriate market timing, late trading, and misuse of material nonpublic information about fund portfolios.[85] The SEC began its analysis by explaining that, in some instances, investment managers' personnel have placed their personal interests ahead of their clients' interests. The SEC indicated that it would aggressively pursue any persons who violated the securities laws and breached their fiduciary obligations. The SEC also said it would take stock of its rules to determine what changes might be made to prevent misconduct.[86] Under the compliance rule, it is unlawful for a registered investment manager to provide investment advice unless it has adopted the policies and procedures referred to above.

This rule, although meant to sketch a manager's fiduciary obligation, is different in character from the disclosure and proxy voting rules discussed above. The compliance rule requires that investment managers actually consider their fiduciary obligations and formalize procedures to satisfy them.[87] The compliance rule for both managers and funds is meant as a prophylactic to help ensure no breach of fiduciary duty occurs.

Take the example of business continuity plans, which is one area where the SEC said it expected a firm to have policies and procedures. When preparing a business continuity plan, the SEC stated that an investment manager's fiduciary duty includes the duty to protect client assets from being put at risk as a result of the inability to provide services after a natural disaster or the loss of key personnel. Clients would be at risk if an adviser ceased operations.[88] As a result, an investment manager's fiduciary duty, even absent this rule, would, according to the Commission, require it to address business continuity. Thus, the requirement of policies and procedures in this context is nothing more than the SEC clarifying for managers what is already required by a preexisting fiduciary obligation.

The three rule areas discussed above—disclosure, proxy voting, and compliance policies and procedures—are examples demonstrating that the SEC is effectively clarifying what is required by an investment manager's fiduciary duty. In each of these areas, the fiduciary obligation places requirements on investment managers absent an SEC rule. The adoption of a rule does not remove the applicability of the fiduciary duty to act in a client's best interest in the context of the areas addressed by the rules.

3.2 Enforcement Cases

Regulators also elucidate investment managers' fiduciary obligation through enforcement actions. I shall focus exclusively on actions brought by the SEC, the primary regulator of the investment management industry, under the Investment Advisers Act of 1940, the primary federal law regulating investment managers. There is no private right of action under the Advisers Act's antifraud provision and therefore only the SEC (or the DOJ in criminal cases) can bring a fraud action under the Act.[89] If the SEC deems

---

[85] *Id.* at 74714.
[86] *Id.* at 74715.
[87] *Id.*
[88] *Id.* at 74716 n.22.
[89] *Transamerica Mortg. Advisors*, 444 U.S. at 24.

an investment manager's conduct to be a breach of fiduciary duty, the SEC and courts equate the breach of fiduciary duty with a violation of the antifraud provision of the Act.[90] Consequently, the SEC, through enforcement actions, guides the investment management industry on conduct necessary to fulfill one's fiduciary duty.

3.2.1 Litigated cases

The seminal SEC enforcement action against an investment adviser under the Advisers Act was the *Capital Gains Research Bureau* case mentioned above, which continues to be the leading case under the Advisers Act.[91] In that case, the Capital Gains firm, which published investment newsletters, engaged in a practice known as scalping. It purchased certain securities for the firm's own account and, at the same time, advised clients to buy those same securities. The firm, however, did not disclose its ownership of the securities to clients. After the price of the shares increased, the firm sold its shares at a profit.[92]

The SEC alleged that this conduct violated sections 206(1) and 206(2) of the Advisers Act. The US Supreme Court agreed. It reversed the court of appeals and held that the conduct operated as a fraud and deceit on clients or prospective clients.[93] The Court, quoting the venerable Louis Loss, stated that the Advisers Act reflected a congressional recognition "of the delicate fiduciary nature" of the investment management relationship and a congressional intent to address conflicts of interest.[94] A later Supreme Court case, *Santa Fe Industries v. Green*, relying on *Capital Gains*, stated that "Congress intended the Investment Advisers Act to establish federal fiduciary standards for investment advisers."[95] Although evidence of this congressional intent is scant,[96] subsequent courts and the SEC have embraced the language in *Santa Fe* and it is now often said that Congress created a federal fiduciary duty for investment managers.[97]

---

[90] Barry Barbash and Jai Massari have argued that, in the early 1990s, the SEC became more aggressive in bringing cases against investment advisers engaging in conduct that the SEC viewed as inconsistent with advisers' fiduciary duties. Barry P. Barbash & Jai Massari, *The Investment Advisers Act of 1940: Regulation by Accretion*, 39 RUTGERS L.J. 627, 634 (2008).

[91] *Capital Gains*, 375 U.S. 180; *see* Belmont v. MB Inv. Partners, Inc., 708 F.3d 470, 502–03 (3d Cir. 2013) ("Half a century later, courts still look primarily to Capital Gains Research for a description of an investment adviser's fiduciary duties.").

[92] *Capital Gains*, 375 U.S. at 181.

[93] *Id.*

[94] *Id.* at 191–92 (citing 2 LOUIS LOSS, SECURITIES REGULATION 1412 (2nd ed. 1961)).

[95] Santa Fe Industries v. Green, 430 U.S. 462, 471 n.11 (1977).

[96] *See* Laby, *supra* note 46. The lack of Congressional intent is unsurprising because, as the *Capital Gains* Court recognized, an adviser had a preexisting fiduciary duty to clients. *Capital Gains Research Bureau*, 180 U.S. at 191–92. There is little evidence that Congress intended the Advisers Act to "establish" federal fiduciary duties for advisers.

[97] *See* Financial Planning Ass'n v. SEC, 482 F.3d 481, 490 (D.C. Cir. 2007) ("The overall statutory scheme of the IAA addresses the problems identified to Congress ... by establishing a federal fiduciary standard to govern the conduct of investment advisers, broadly defined ..."); Political Contributions by Certain Investment Advisers, Advisers Act Release No. 3043, 75 Fed. Reg. 41,018, 41,022 (adopted July 10, 2010) (final rule) ("The Supreme Court has construed section 206 as establishing a Federal fiduciary standard governing the conduct of advisers.");

In subsequent decades, the SEC has examined investment managers' conduct and determined whether it violated fiduciary principles and, accordingly, the Advisers Act. The cases are too numerous to discuss here, but a good example is *Geman v. SEC*.[98] In that case, a registered investment adviser and broker-dealer, in need of additional income, changed its business model and began to execute customer trades as a principal as opposed to acting only as an agent. Over an 18-month period, the firm executed more than 8,000 trades as a principal, generating profits of more than $460,000.[99]

In *Geman*, customers consented to a modification of an agreement to allow the firm to trade as a principal. The firm's fatal flaw, however, was the failure to disclose its intent to profit from the principal transactions. The firm said merely that the change was due to new regulatory interpretations and improvements to its technological capabilities. The firm, however, adduced evidence of neither regulatory changes nor technological improvements.[100] The SEC staff alleged that the purported reasons for the change were not actually factors in the firm's decision to change its business model. Moreover, this conduct constituted a breach of the firm's fiduciary duty of full disclosure. The SEC agreed.[101]

Step back and examine the move that the SEC made in the *Geman* case. Recall that the firm disclosed it would be acting as a principal in certain customer trades. Geman emphasized this point in litigation.[102] The SEC, however, believed that the fiduciary obligation required more than disclosure of the firm's role as principal. The SEC argued that when a firm has a fiduciary relationship with a customer, it cannot execute trades as a principal absent full disclosure of the capacity in which it is trading, and full disclosure of additional information bears on the desirability of the transaction from the

---

F.X.C. Inv. Corp., SEC Release No. 218, 2002 WL 31741561 (Dec. 9, 2002) (ALJ decision) ("Section 206 establishes "federal fiduciary standards" to govern the conduct of investment advisers.").

[98] 334 F.3d 1183 (10th Cir. 2003); *see also* SEC v. Slocum, Gordon, & Co., 334 F. Supp. 2d 144 (D.R.I. 2004) (finding breach of fiduciary duty for failure to disclose comingling of firm and client assets); SEC v. Moran, 922 F. Supp. 867, 896–98 (S.D.N.Y. 1996) (holding that the defendants negligently put their interests ahead of clients' interests in breach of fiduciary duty); SEC v. Treadway, 430 F. Supp. 2d 293, 338-39 (S.D.N.Y. 2006) (market timing); Medcap Mgmt. & Research LLC, Investment Advisers Act Release No. 2802 (Oct. 16, 2008) ("portfolio pumping"); Strong Cap. Mgmt., Inc., Investment Advisers Act Release No. 2239 (May 20, 2004) (undisclosed short-term trading in portfolio managers' own managed funds); Hennessee Group LLC, Investment Advisers Act Release No. 2871 (Apr. 22, 2009) (failure to conduct due diligence evaluations); Scwendiman Partners, LLC, Investment Advisers Act Release No. 2043, WL 1484401 (2002) (taking advantage of investment opportunities); Barr Rosenberg, Investment Advisers Act Release No. 3285 (Sept. 22, 2011) (failure to disclose risk modeling error); Dawson-Samberg Cap. Mgmt., Inc., Investment Advisers Act Release No. 1889 (Aug. 3, 2000) (failure to disclose soft dollar or other brokerage practices).

[99] *Geman*, 334 F.3d at 1186–87. Trading as a principal presents a conflict of interest with clients because the firm, as principal, is conflicted between seeking the best terms for itself and at the same time acting in the best interest of its customer, with whom it is transacting.

[100] *Id.* at 1187.
[101] *Id.*
[102] *Id.* at 1189.

customer's perspective.[103] The appellate court agreed with the Commission, stating that the firm did not live up to its duties of disclosure "as a fiduciary."[104]

The SEC has a critical role to play in defining an investment manager's fiduciary obligation. The US Supreme Court, in *Herman & MacLean v. Huddleston*, explained that the antifraud provisions of the federal securities do not merely codify common law fraud.[105] As the Court stated, a primary purpose of the securities laws is to address deficiencies in the common law of fraud and establish higher standards of conduct in the securities industry.[106] Precisely what those higher standards should be is not answered in the statute. Thus, it is through agency rulemaking and enforcement cases, such as *Geman*, that the SEC can give precise guidance on the standards applicable to the investment management industry. Because the courts give the SEC deference to interpret the federal securities laws, the SEC's view of what is required by the fiduciary duty has broad and deep influence on investment management law.[107]

3.2.2 Settled actions

Although the matters discussed above were litigated cases, the vast majority of SEC actions settle.[108] Settled actions result in a Litigation Release for federal court matters and an administrative order for administrative proceedings. These materials review the relevant misconduct and explain why the Commission believes the misconduct is illegal. Settlements are closely watched by the investment management industry. They are also carefully analyzed by investment management lawyers, who advise clients on how to adjust their behavior so that it is permissible in the eyes of the Commission and its staff.

Among other reasons, the SEC uses settled enforcement actions as a means to explain to the industry the conduct that the Commission believes to be consistent with a manager's fiduciary obligation.[109] An example of the Commission using settlements to clarify conduct it believed to be a breach of a manager's fiduciary duty is a series of actions addressing market timing. Market timing is the frequent purchase and sale of mutual fund shares with the intent to profit from arbitrage between the net asset value of the fund and the value of the fund's underlying portfolio securities.[110] Market timing can harm fund shareholders (other than the market timer) by diluting the value of their

---

[103] *Id.*
[104] *Id.* at 1189–90.
[105] Herman & MacLean v. Huddleston, 459 U.S. 375, 388–89 (1983).
[106] *Id.*
[107] Chevron U.S.A., Inc. v. NRDC, 467 U.S. 837 (1984); *see also* Kornman v. SEC, 592 F.3d 173, 181 (D.C. Cir. 2010) ("The Commission's interpretation of its authorizing statutes is entitled to deference under the familiar two-pronged test set forth in *Chevron* …").
[108] COX, ET AL., *supra* note 7 at 834 ("Most SEC enforcement proceedings (over 90 percent) are settled, not litigated").
[109] Lori A. Richards, Director, Office of Compliance Inspections and Examinations, U.S. Sec. & Exch. Comm'n, Fiduciary duty: Return to First Principles, Remarks at Eighth Annual Investment Adviser Compliance Summit (Feb. 27, 2006), https://www.sec.gov/news/speech/spch022706lar.htm; Anne C. Flannery, *Time for Change: A Re-examination of the Settlement Policies of the Securities and Exchange Commission*, 51 WASH. & LEE L. REV. 1015 (1994).
[110] *See* THOMAS P. LEMKE, GERALD T. LINS, & THOMAS A. SMITH, III, REGULATION OF INVESTMENT COMPANIES § 9.02[2][a][5][A] (2015).

holdings, increasing transaction costs, disturbing the fund's management strategy, and forcing the fund to hold excess cash.[111]

Market timing is not necessarily illegal. Although the practice was often discouraged in fund prospectuses, by 2003 many fund managers did not stop market timing in their funds, and some fund managers may have encouraged it.[112] The opportunity to engage in market timing apparently was used by mutual fund managers to attract investment from certain hedge funds, thereby increasing the funds' assets under management and the managers' compensation.[113] In a surprise move in September 2003, New York Attorney General Eliot Spitzer announced a settlement for $40 million against a hedge fund called Canary Capital Partners, LLC for abusive practices in the trading of mutual funds, including market timing and late trading.[114]

The SEC then launched its own investigation of this conduct and brought and settled cases against numerous investment management firms for a breach of fiduciary duty and a violation of the Advisers Act's antifraud provision.[115] There were several ways in which mutual fund firms allowing market timing violated fiduciary principles. First, mutual funds which state that they prohibit or discourage market timing while privately encouraging or allowing it to occur are deceiving investors. In addition, market timing arrangements violated fiduciary principles to the extent that fund managers benefited from market timing at investors' expense.[116] Thus, these cases provide a clear example of the SEC using its prosecutorial authority to explain why market timing was a breach of fiduciary duty and a violation of the antifraud provisions.

A closer look at one of these cases illustrates the SEC's attempt to demonstrate a fiduciary breach. Take the 2005 settlement with Banc of America Capital Management,

---

[111] *Id.*

[112] Banc of America Capital Management, LLC, et al., Advisers Act Release No. 2355 (Feb. 9, 2005); Alliance Cap. Mgmt., L.P., Investment Advisers Act Release No. 2205 (Dec. 18, 2003); Pilgrim Baxter & Assoc., LTD., Investment Advisers Act Release No. 2251 (June 21, 2004); *see also* Massachusetts Fin. Servs. Co., Investment Advisers Act Release No. 2213 (Feb. 5, 2004); Banc One Inv. Advisors Corp., Investment Advisers Act Release No. 2254 (June 29, 2004).

[113] *See* Richard A. Booth, *Who Should Recover What for Late Trading and Market Timing?* 1 J. BUS. & TECH. L. 101, 109 (2006).

[114] New York Attorney General, Press Release, State Investigation Reveals Mutual Fund Fraud, Sept. 3, 2003, www.ag.ny.gov/press-release/state-investigation-reveals-mutual-fund-fraud.

[115] *See, e.g.*, Securities and Exchange Commission, Press Release, Strong Capital Management and Founder Richard Strong Agree to Pay $140 Million to Settle Fraud Charges Concerning Undisclosed Mutual Fund Trading, May 20, 2004, www.sec.gov/news/press/2004-69.htm; Securities and Exchange Commission, Press Release, SEC Brings Enforcement Action Against Banc of America Securities for Repeated Document Production Failures During a Pending Investigation, March 10, 2004, https://www.sec.gov/news/press/2004-29.htm; Securities and Exchange Commission, Press Release, Massachusetts Financial Services Co. Will Pay $225 Million and Make Significant Governance and Compliance Reforms to Settle SEC Fraud Charges Concerning Mutual Fund Market Timing, Feb. 5, 2004, www.sec.gov/news/press/2004-14.htm. For a discussion of the SEC's use of Advisers Act section 206 to prosecute market timing, *see* Barbash & Massari, *supra* note 90 at 645–49.

[116] *See* James J. Park, *The Competing Paradigms of Securities Regulation*, 57 DUKE L. J. 625, 661–62 (2007).

LLC ("BACAP").[117] BACAP was the investment manager for mutual funds in the Nations Funds investment company complex. BACAP allowed certain market timing clients to engage in short-term or excessive trading in the Nations Funds and did not disclose the arrangement to other investors. BACAP entered into arrangements with two entities, TransSierra Capital, LLC and Canary Capital Partners, LLC, and allowed them to engage in short-term trading in 13 funds in the Nations Funds complex. BACAP permitted this arrangement although it knew that the trading could be harmful to other Nations Funds' shareholders. The arrangements increased investment management fees earned by BACAP.[118]

In bringing its action, the SEC stated that market timing is not per se illegal.[119] BACAP, however, had a fiduciary duty to act in the best interest of Nations Funds and its shareholders. Tracking the language of *Capital Gains*, the SEC stated that BACAP had an affirmative obligation to Nations Funds' shareholders to act with utmost good faith and provide full and fair disclosure of all material facts. It had an affirmative obligation to act with reasonable care to avoid misleading prospective Nations Funds investors.[120] The SEC concluded that by placing its interest in enhancing fees above the interests of Nations Funds shareholders, and by failing to disclose the arrangements and the attendant conflicts of interest, BACAP breached its fiduciary duty to shareholders of the funds in which the trading occurred.[121]

That the SEC was concerned with BACAP's breach of fiduciary duty is clear from the undertakings required in the settlement. As part of the settlement, the Nations Funds mutual funds agreed to designate an independent compliance officer to assist the fund board of directors in monitoring BACAP's compliance with its fiduciary duties owed to fund shareholders. Furthermore, the compliance officer was required to report to the fund board of directors on any material breach of fiduciary duty of which the compliance officer became aware.[122] Although I have highlighted the matter against Banc of America, the SEC also brought similar claims of breach of fiduciary duty against other fund managers.[123]

In addition to SEC rules, the Commission has the ability, through enforcement actions, to communicate to the parties and to the investment management industry the scope of an investment manager's fiduciary obligation. As the law has developed, the SEC has been given the authority to enforce breaches of fiduciary duty under section 206 of the Advisers Act because a breach of fiduciary duty constitutes a violation of the Act. In addition, the SEC can bring section 206 cases alleging breach of fiduciary duty

---

[117] In re Banc of America Capital Management, LLC, et al., Advisers Act Release No. 2355 (Feb. 9, 2005). The case against BACAP was broader than described here. It included allegations against BACAP Distributors, distributor and fund administrator, and against BAS, a Bank of America subsidiary. Moreover, the action included allegations of late trading in addition to market timing.
[118] *Id.* at ¶1–2.
[119] *Id.* at ¶19.
[120] *Id.* at ¶5.
[121] *Id.* at ¶6.
[122] *Id.* at ¶134(h).
[123] *See supra* note 114; *see also* In re Columbia Mgt. Advisors, Inc. and Columbia Funds Distributor, Inc., Advisers Act Release No. 2351 (Feb. 9, 2005).

where the conduct was merely negligent and not intentional. Thus, by bringing breach of fiduciary duty cases under Advisers Act section 206, the SEC, since the *Capital Gains* case more than 50 years ago, has continued to explain, refine, and clarify the standard of conduct to which a fiduciary must adhere.

4 CODIFYING FIDUCIARY NORMS

The preceding section demonstrated that much of investment management regulation consists of detailed rules that implement and clarify the fiduciary duties of loyalty and care. When regulators adopt investment management rules, or prosecute enforcement actions, they are often explicating or clarifying the investment manager's fiduciary obligation in a particular context. They are not, as some argue, preparing conduct rules as an alternative to the fiduciary obligation. The overarching fiduciary duty does not vanish with the appearance of a detailed rule. In this section, I shall examine this opposing view—that specific conduct rules displace fiduciary standards—and explain why it is less compelling.

4.1 Conduct-Based Rules as an Alternative to the Fiduciary Obligation

Let us explore the opposing view that a conduct-based rule is an alternative to the fiduciary obligation as opposed to an embodiment of it. According to this view, the fiduciary duty is principles-based regulation that establishes standards—a series of requirements—developed through case law.[124] The fiduciary duty governs misconduct not addressed by rule and, therefore, addressed only by the common law.[125] Under this view, when regulators decide, by rule, that particular conduct is required or prohibited, the rule displaces fiduciary duties.[126] Regulating conduct by rule removes the conduct from the ambit of what the fiduciary obligation entails. Accordingly, as Professor Mercer Bullard writes, "the essence of the fiduciary duty is conduct that is not prohibited by rule."[127]

Additional evidence of this approach is found in the text of the federal securities laws. Advisers Act section 211(d) provides, "No provision of this title imposing any liability shall apply to any act done or omitted in good faith in conformity with any rule, regulation, or order of the Commission."[128] The Investment Company Act has a similar provision.[129] These provisions, however, do not appear to be invoked in federal securities law litigation. Moreover, the SEC staff has invoked them to state only that reliance on SEC orders or no-action letters will preclude an SEC action or private

---

[124] See Bullard, *supra* note 8 at 173–74.
[125] *Id.* at 174.
[126] See Bullard *supra* note 8; Velasco, *supra* note 13 at 667.
[127] Bullard, *supra* note 8 at 175.
[128] Investment Advisers Act § 211(d), 15 U.S.C. § 80b-11(d) (2012).
[129] Investment Company Act § 38(c), 15 U.S.C. § 80a-37 (2012).

action for acts taken in reliance on the order.[130] In other words, if a party applies for an exemption from the law, which is granted, the SEC will not subsequently take enforcement against the same party for conduct specifically exempted by the order. In addition, it is noteworthy that applicants seeking a legal exemption recognize their ongoing fiduciary obligations in the context of their business operations.[131]

This opposing view, where rules displace fiduciary standards, was looked upon favorably by courts in the United Kingdom as a possible approach. In the UK, compliance with particular trading rules might act as a safe harbor and satisfy applicable fiduciary duties. According to a UK Law Commission Consultation Paper, where a regulatory rule permits a lower level of disclosure than that required by fiduciary standards, a court might hold that an implied term of the relevant customer contract is that the customer is entitled only to the disclosure required by the rule.[132]

This same opposing view, whereby rules displace general standards, is followed in the United States in certain contexts, but not in the fiduciary duty one. Under the Truth in Lending Act ("TILA"), for example, disclosure requirements are quite detailed.[133] As long as the required TILA disclosures are made, I am unaware of any comprehensive principle stating that the creditor must disclose all material facts about its relationship with the customer. Customers are entitled only to the disclosures set forth in the applicable regulations; they cannot fall back on an all-embracing standard, such as a generalized duty of a bank to provide complete information or not to mislead. There is no reason, however, why the opposing view should always prevail. As we shall see, in many familiar instances, detailed rules do not displace generalized standards.

4.2 The Relationship between Conduct-Based Rules and Generalized Standards

Rules and standards touching the same subject can coexist. A detailed rule can prescribe or proscribe particular conduct, and a generalized standard can continue to exist in the background to address conduct not specifically addressed by rule. Take the familiar example of our traffic laws. A speed limit on a roadway is a rule that sets forth in advance the maximum speed allowed. The speed limit, however, does not displace applicable principles, such as the principle stating that no person shall drive at a speed greater than is prudent under current conditions and with regard to hazards that might

---

[130] See Elizabeth G. Osterman, Investment Company Registration and Compliance, ALI-ABA Course of Study, SP019 ALI-ABA 467 (July 16, 2008).

[131] See, e.g., Alex. Brown Cash Reserve Fund, Inc., et al., Application for an Order Granting Exemptions, Investment Company Act Release No. 14220 (Oct. 31, 1984); Shearson Lehman/Coast Savings Housing Partners, Limited, et al., Application for an Order for Exemption, Investment Company Act Release No. 14185 (Oct. 9, 1984); Wingate Housing Partners, Ltd. II and Continental Wingate Co., Inc., filing of Application for an Order Granting Exemption from all Provisions of the Act, Investment Company Act Release No. 13243 (May 13, 1983).

[132] The Law Comm'n, Fiduciary Duties and Regulatory Rules 44–45 (Law Com No. 236, Dec. 1995).

[133] See Content of Disclosures, 12 C.F.R. § 1026.18 (2016).

exist at the time.[134] The specific speed restriction does not displace the generalized standard of prudent behavior, and the standard can form the basis for liability even if the motorist drives under the posted limit.

The same relationship between rules and standards appears in the federal securities laws. The securities industry is governed by both rules aimed at specific misconduct and standards potentially applicable to a wide range of conduct.[135] Above, I discussed the relationship between an investment manager's particular disclosure obligations set forth in Form ADV and the ongoing fiduciary obligation to disclose information not necessarily covered by the Form.[136] The fiduciary obligation, however, is only one such generalized standard; another is the antifraud prohibition that exists in several of the securities acts.[137] In the Securities Exchange Act context, the US Supreme Court has explicitly described the antifraud provision as a "catchall."[138]

Other examples abound. A disclosure rule under the federal securities laws states that, in addition to information "expressly required" in a registration statement, the registration statement must include additional information necessary to make the required statements not misleading.[139] In other words, making the required disclosure is insufficient. As the SEC expressed in *In the Matter of Franchard Corporation*:

> The registration forms promulgated by us are guides intended to assist registrants in discharging their statutory duty of full disclosure. They are not and cannot possibly be exhaustive enumerations of each and every item material to investors in the particular circumstances relevant to a specific offering. The kaleidoscopic variety of economic life precludes any attempt at such an enumeration. The preparation of a registration statement is not satisfied, as registrant's position suggests, by a mechanical process of responding narrowly to the specific items of the applicable registration form.[140]

Similarly, in a broker-dealer antimanipulation rule, the SEC has stated that the scope of the broker-dealer antifraud provision will not be limited by specific definitions of the terms manipulative, deceptive, or fraudulent device or contrivance contained in other rules adopted under section 15(c).[141]

---

[134] *See, e.g.*, NY Vehicle and Traffic Law, Article 30, § 1180, http://ypdcrime.com/vt/article30.htm.

[135] Park, *supra* note 116 at 640.

[136] *Supra* note 64 and accompanying text.

[137] Securities Act § 17(a), 15 U.S.C. § 77q(a) (2012); Securities Exchange Act § 10(b), 15 U.S.C. § 78j(b) (2012); Investment Advisers Act § 206, 15 U.S.C. § 80b-6 (2012).

[138] Ernst & Ernst v. Hochfelder, 425 U.S. 185, 202–03 (1976) ("The section was described rightly as a 'catchall' clause to enable the Commission 'to deal with new manipulative (or cunning) devices'") (quoting Hearings on H.R. 7852 and H.R. 8720 before the House Committee on Interstate and Foreign Commerce, 73d Cong., 2d Sess., 115 (1934)).

[139] *See* Securities Act Rule 408(a), 17 C.F.R. § 230.408(a) (2016).

[140] In the Matter of Franchard Corp., 42 SEC 163 (1964); *see also* In re WorldCom, Inc. Sec. Litig., 346 F. Supp. 2d 628, 689 (S.D.N.Y. 2004) ("[N]on-disclosure of an underwriter or issuer's conflicts of interest can constitute material omissions, even where no regulation expressly compels the disclosure of such conflicts"); Brady v. UBS Fin. Serv., Inc., 2013 WL 1309250 (N.D. Okla., March 26, 2013) (ruling that defendants are not entitled to summary judgment on multiple omissions in a registration statement).

[141] *See* 17 C.F.R. § 240.15c1-2(c).

Regulators have prosecuted misconduct not prohibited by rule, but which violated generalized standards.[142] In the 1990s, the National Association of Securities Dealers (now the Financial Industry Regulatory Authority) addressed several sales practices, such as laddering and spinning, through detailed rules. A risk in adopting such rules is that they could be viewed as an exhaustive list of prohibited practices. These rules, however, were not prepared with this intent and the rules should not be viewed as safe harbors, displacing the general prohibition on deceptive practices. As Thomas Hazen has explained, such rules must be viewed as supplementing, not replacing, general principles and standards that apply to broker-dealers.[143]

Accounting rules addressing misconduct work this way too. Detailed accounting rules are set forth in Generally Accepted Accounting Principles ("GAAP"). Strict compliance with GAAP rules, however, will not preclude an enforcement action alleging violation of a standard, which states that the financial statements must fairly present the financial condition of the audited company.[144] In a Second Circuit decision in the accounting context, Judge Henry Friendly addressed the interaction between detailed rules and generalized standards. The defendants sought jury instructions providing that they could be guilty only if they willfully did not follow GAAP. The trial judge did not agree, stating that the "critical test" was whether the financial statements as a whole "fairly presented" the company's financial position. Proof of GAAP compliance was evidence of good faith, but not conclusive. The rules did not displace the standard, and the court of appeals agreed.[145]

Although I shall not present a comprehensive argument regarding why a detailed rule does not displace a general standard, one can easily see that rules can be underinclusive and a rule displacing a standard could lead to evasion. A standard, such as the fiduciary obligation, addresses situations where most people agree that conduct should be prohibited, but where the actor has tailored his or her conduct to avoid the application of a detailed rule.[146] In that case, while a rule may no longer be applicable because conduct falls outside it, the general principle will continue to apply and act as a prophylactic to inhibit the conduct before it causes injury.

4.3 The Case of *Meinhard v. Salmon*

In many cases where courts apply a fiduciary standard, the operative principle can be converted into a detailed rule. This conversion, however, does not eliminate the underlying fiduciary duty. An example is the well-worn case of *Meinhard v. Salmon*.[147] I reference this case because writers often refer to *Meinhard* to support their view of

---

[142] See Thomas Lee Hazen, *Are Existing Stockbroker Standards Sufficient? Principles, Rules, and Fiduciary Duties*, 2010 COLUM. BUS. L. REV. 710, 757 ("Even without explicit rules, severe sanctions may be imposed against brokerage firms that engage in … improper IPO practices").
[143] *Id.* at 758.
[144] U.S. v. Simon, 425 F.2d 796 (2d Cir. 1969).
[145] *Id.* at 805–06.
[146] See Joseph A. Franco, *Of Complicity and Compliance: A Rules-Based Anti-Complicity Strategy under Federal Securities Laws*, 14 U. PA. J. BUS. L. 1, 29 (2011).
[147] 164 N.E. 545 (N.Y. 1928).

The fiduciary structure of investment management regulation 103

the fiduciary relationship.[148] Professor Bullard maintains that Judge Cardozo's articulation of a "punctilio of honor" standard is a general principle that can be realized only through particular cases.[149] It is true that, where conduct is not addressed by a rule, determination of whether one has fulfilled her fiduciary duty takes place after the fact. The existence of a relevant rule, however, does not mean that the fiduciary standard cannot be applied to facts potentially covered by the rule.

Consider *Meinhard*. Once *Meinhard* and similar cases were decided, a principle of law developed providing that a coadventurer (or partner) cannot, absent disclosure, take advantage of a partnership opportunity during the partnership term. When a similar case appears, one could safely say, based on *Meinhard*, that a partner has a fiduciary duty, absent disclosure, not to take advantage of a partnership opportunity that arises during the partnership. Moreover, if this principle were codified in a partnership statute, the statutory obligation not to take advantage of one's partner would not displace the partners' fiduciary duty. Codification in that case would implement the fiduciary duty, not displace it; a codified standard and the fiduciary obligation would continue to live side by side.

Viewing SEC rules and enforcement cases as implementing an investment manager's fiduciary duty is consistent with the SEC's implementation of the Advisers Act, as discussed in Section 3 of this chapter. One might argue that the fiduciary obligation is not necessary to regulate conduct that otherwise violates the antifraud provision of the Advisers Act.[150] In a narrow sense, this is true. As Professor Bullard writes, "[t]he fiduciary duty is not needed to regulate misconduct that otherwise violates anti-fraud rules."[151] If conduct violates an SEC rule, there is no need for regulators to fall back on a general fiduciary obligation to demonstrate liability. The SEC can rely on the particular antifraud rule and ignore an adviser's supervening fiduciary obligation.

This enforcement result, however, does not defeat the claim that the rule instantiates the fiduciary duty. Fiduciary principles support the particular rule at hand and the rule can be viewed as an efficient mechanism for a regulator to enforce the fiduciary standard of conduct. Enforcement of a clear rule is easier and more efficient than repeatedly demonstrating that misconduct occurred and that the misconduct should be considered a breach of fiduciary duty. A rule promotes ease of enforcement; it does not eliminate the background fiduciary obligation.

Moreover, the fiduciary obligation plays an important role as the supporting structure for a statutory or rule-based claim. Recall that an investment manager's breach of fiduciary duty is tantamount to committing fraud under section 206 of the Advisers Act. Thus, in determining which antifraud rules to adopt, the SEC, as discussed in Section 2 of this chapter, determines which conduct constitutes a breach of fiduciary duty. In any

---

[148] Kristina A. Fausti, *A Fiduciary Duty for All?* 12 Duq. Bus. L.J. 183, 188 (2010); William Sanders, *Resolving the Conflict between Fiduciary Duties and Socially Responsible Investing*, 35 Pace L. Rev. 535, 548-50 (2014); Kenneth M. Rosen, *Financial Intermediaries as Principals and Agents*, 48 Wake Forest L. Rev. 625, 640–41 (2013); Jay Youngdahl, *The Time has Come for a Sustainable Theory of Fiduciary Duty in Investment*, 29 Hofstra Lab. & Emp. L.J. 115 (2011).
[149] Bullard, *supra* note 8 at 174.
[150] *See id.* at 175.
[151] *Id.*

given case, reference to the fiduciary duty might not be necessary to regulate misconduct otherwise addressed by an antifraud rule, once the rule is adopted. Regulators, however, must continually assess when some new form of misconduct results in a breach of fiduciary duty and constitutes a violation of the antifraud provision. Such misconduct might result in an enforcement case today, but the enforcement case might also be codified in a future rule prohibiting the misconduct. In many instances, the SEC will bring a number of enforcement actions in a given area and then codify those cases by adopting a rule.[152] The codification does not make the misconduct any less of a fiduciary breach.

4.4 The Challenge of *Press v. Quick & Reilly, Inc.*

To support the opposing approach, Professor Bullard references the Second Circuit case of *Press v. Quick & Reilly, Inc.*[153] An examination of the *Press* case, however, reveals that it is not applicable in the fiduciary duty context. In *Press*, broker-dealer customers complained that a broker placed their uninvested assets (such as cash resulting from a sale of securities) into poorly performing money market funds, which the broker-dealer selected because the funds and their advisers made payments to the broker.[154] The payments represent a classic potential conflict of interest: the defendants' decision as to where to invest the plaintiffs' assets might be influenced by payments the defendants received from the funds and their advisers. The specific allegation was that the defendants violated Exchange Act Rule 10b-5, a general antifraud rule, because the defendants failed to disclose payments they received from third parties. Such disclosures are arguably required by Exchange Act Rule 10b-10, a rule requiring delivery of a confirmation of each securities trade to a customer.[155]

The case might be relevant to the various approaches discussed in this chapter for the following reason: Although the defendants did not mention the conflict of interest in the context of their Rule 10b-10 disclosures, information about the payments was available to investors in the money market fund prospectuses and Statements of Additional Information.[156] The district court dismissed the Rule 10b-5 claim because the fund prospectuses and SAIs provided sufficient information to negate an inference of fraud.[157] The SEC submitted an amicus brief in the case stating that the defendants could, in fact, rely on statements in the fund prospectuses and SAIs to satisfy their

---

[152] See Financial and Disciplinary Information that Investment Advisers Must Disclose to Clients, Investment Advisers Act Release No. 1035 (Sept. 19, 1986) (explaining that disclosure rule codified investment managers' fiduciary obligation to disclose certain information to clients); Amendments to Regulation M: Anti-Manipulation Rules Concerning Securities Offerings, Securities Act Release 8511 (Dec. 9, 2004) (explaining that the proposed rule would prohibit by rule certain conduct previously addressed through enforcement actions).
[153] 218 F.3d 121 (2d Cir. 2000); see Bullard, supra note 8 at 181.
[154] *Press*, 218 F.3d at 123.
[155] *Id.* at 123–24.
[156] *Id.* at 124.
[157] *Id.* at 126.

obligations under Rule 10b-10.[158] The SEC did not separately opine on the existence of a Rule 10b-5 violation.[159]

The Second Circuit, per then Judge Sotomayor, disagreed that the defendants did not adequately disclose the conflict of interest under Rule 10b-10. The court looked to the SEC's interpretation stating that general disclosures in fund prospectuses and SAIs satisfied the defendants' duty under Rule 10b-10 to disclose third party payments.[160] Moreover, when analyzing the Rule 10b-5 claim, the court explained that the SEC has decided what disclosure is necessary to address a conflict of interest resulting from third party payments to broker-dealers. Therefore, the court stated that it would not undermine the SEC by requiring greater disclosure about the conflict in the Rule 10b-5 context.[161] The SEC's detailed disclosure rule, in other words, was the final word on the scope of disclosure required.

Professor Bullard suggests that *Press* demonstrates that the presence of a specific rule means no additional disclosure is required under a generalized standard.[162] The court, according to this view, looked at the SEC rule and determined that its requirements were a ceiling on what must be disclosed. Under this view, once the SEC adopts a specific rule, it displaces a set of generalized disclosure requirements called for under the general antifraud provision.

There is a crucial difference, however, between *Press* and the rules and enforcement cases discussed in Section 3 of this chapter. *Press* was not a case addressing what is required by a fiduciary. There is no reason to believe that the *Press* brokers were acting as fiduciaries. The general rule is that broker-dealers do not act in a fiduciary capacity with respect to their customers.[163] Moreover, when the SEC adopted Exchange Act Rule 10b-10, it did not state or even imply that the rule was intended to capture fiduciary obligations of broker-dealers.[164]

Thus, the result in *Press* in the Rule 10b-10 context is not relevant to the discussion in Section 3 of this chapter, where the SEC clarified that advisers subject to Advisers Act rules continue to owe a fiduciary obligation to clients. It is no surprise that, in the Rule 10b-10 context, a court would examine an SEC rule to understand what is required of market participants. In the *Press* context, there is no background fiduciary obligation. Perhaps *Press* supports the argument that the general antifraud standard of Exchange Act section 10 is limited in scope in the face of specific rules. *Press*, however, does not implicate the application of a fiduciary standard in the face of a specific rule.

---

[158] *Id.* at 127.
[159] *Id.* at 128.
[160] *Id.* at 129.
[161] *Id.* at 131.
[162] Bullard, *supra* note 8 at 101.
[163] *See* SEC. & EXCH. COMM'N STAFF, STUDY ON INVESTMENT ADVISERS AND BROKER-DEALERS AS REQUIRED BY SECTION 913 OF THE DODD-FRANK WALL STREET REFORM AND CONSUMER PROTECTION ACT 54 (2011).
[164] *See* Securities Confirmations, Securities Exchange Act Release No. 13508 (May 5, 1977), 42 Fed. Reg. 25318 (May 17, 1977).

5 CONCLUSION

The underlying structure of investment management regulation is in large part the implementation of an investment manager's fiduciary obligation—to explain and explicate what is required by the fiduciary duties of loyalty and care. The fiduciary obligation is not clear-cut; it is not easy to say precisely what conduct is prohibited by the fiduciary duty of loyalty nor what conduct is required by the fiduciary duty of care.

To say that an investment manager should act in a client's best interest, or should act prudently under the circumstances, provides little guidance to an investment manager, or her lawyer, trying to follow the law in good faith. Questions are legion: what rises to the level of a material conflict of interest? What level of disclosure is sufficient? How much diligence must be employed consistent with one's duty as an investment manager? These are questions investment managers and their lawyers face every day, and invoking a best interest standard provides little help.

Consequently, the SEC provides guidance on what the fiduciary obligation entails through a series of administrative rules and agency enforcement actions. When the agency adopts a rule, however, the investment manager's fiduciary duty does not vanish. At most, the fiduciary obligation recedes slightly into the background as the relevant rule becomes the SEC's weapon of choice to address misconduct covered by the rule.

There is an alternative view that an administrative rule displaces the fiduciary duty addressing similar conduct. In some cases, a detailed rule may constitute the entirety of the relevant law, including the substance of various duties imposed. In those cases, as long as one follows the rule, no liability ensues—there is no overarching standard to fall back on to ground liability. In the context of investment management regulation discussed in this chapter, the exclusivity of specific rules is insufficient for regulation. A fiduciary duty is painted with broad strokes on a larger canvas, which is then dotted with detailed rules. The fiduciary obligation does not disappear in the presence of a detailed rule. Rather, rules coexist with the fiduciary obligation, which can continue to serve as the basis for liability.

BIBLIOGRAPHY

Air Line Pilots Association International v. O'Neill, 1991, 499 U.S. 65, 75.
Alex Brown Cash Reserve Fund, Inc., et al., 1984, Application for an Order Granting Exemptions, Investment Company Act Release No. 14220 (Oct. 31).
Barbash, Barry P. & Jai Massari, The Investment Advisers Act of 1940: Regulation by Accretion, *Rutgers Law Journal* 39 (2008).
Barnes v. Andrews, 1924, 298 F. 614, 615 (S.D.N.Y.).
Belmont v. MB Inv. Partners, Inc., 2013, 708 F.3d 470, 502-03 (3d Cir.).
Bines, Harvey E. & Steve Thel, Investment Management Law and Regulation (2nd ed., 2004).
Black's Law Dictionary, Fiduciary 702 (9th ed., 2009).
Board of Governors of the Federal Reserve System, 2016, Content of Disclosures, 12 C.F.R. § 1026.18.
Board of Trustees of the Aftra Retirement Fund v. JPMorgan Chase Bank, N.A., 2011, 806 F. Supp. 2d 695 (S.D.N.Y.).
Bok, Sissela, Lying: Moral Choice in Public and Private Life (1999).
Booth, Richard A., 2006, Who Should Recover What for Late Trading and Market Timing? *Journal of Business and Technology Law* 1.

Brady v. UBS Financial Services, Inc., 2013, 2013 WL 1309250 (N.D. Okla., March 26).
Brehm v. Eisner, 2000, 746 A.2d 244, 264 (Del.).
Brunner, Christopher M., 2013, Is The Corporate Director's Duty of Care A "Fiduciary" Duty? Does it Matter? *Wake Forest Law Review* 48, 1027, 1029, 1030.
Bullard, Mercer, 2011, The Fiduciary Study: A Triumph of Substance over Form? *Review of Banking & Financial Law* 30.
Campbell Harrison & Dagley L.L.P. v. Lisa Blue/Baron and Blue, 2011, 843 F. Supp. 2d 673, 688–89 (N.D. Tex.).
Chevron U.S.A., Inc. v. NRDC, 1984, 467 U.S. 837.
Cooter, Robert & Bradley J. Freedman, 1991, The Fiduciary Relationship: Its Economic Character and Legal Consequences, *New York University Law Review* 66.
Cox, James D. et al., 2013, Securities Regulation: Cases and Materials.
DeMott, Deborah A., 2007, Disloyal Agents, *Alabama Law Review* 59.
Easterbrook, Frank H. & Daniel R. Fischel, 1993, Contract and Fiduciary Duty, *Journal of Law and Economics* 36.
Ernst & Ernst v. Hochfelder, 1976, 425 U.S. 185, 202–03.
Fausti, Kristina A., 2010, A Fiduciary Duty for All? *Duquesne Business Law Journal*, 12, 183, 188.
Financial Planning Association v. SEC, 2007, 482 F.3d 481, 490 (D.C. Cir.).
Flannery, Anne C., 1994, Time for Change: A Re-Examination of the Settlement Policies of the Securities and Exchange Commission, *Washington & Lee Law Review* 51.
Franco, Joseph A., 2011, Of Complicity and Compliance: A Rules-Based Anti-Complicity Strategy under Federal Securities Laws, *University of Pennsylvania Journal of Business Law* 14, 1, 29.
Frankel, Tamar, 1995, Fiduciary Duties as Default Rules, *Oregon Law Review* 74.
Geman v. SEC, 2003, 334 F.3d 1183, 1186–87, 1189, 1190 (10th Cir.).
Harvard College v. Amory, 1831, 26 Mass. 446 (Mass.).
Hazen, Thomas Lee, 2010, Are Existing Stockbroker Standards Sufficient? Principles, Rules, and Fiduciary Duties, *Columbia Business Law Review* 710.
Herman & MacLean v. Huddleston, 1983, 459 U.S. 375, 388–89.
Howard v. Shay, 1996, 100 F.3d 1484, 1489 (9th Cir.).
In re Caremark International, Inc., 1996, 698 A.2d 959, 972 (Del. Ch.).
In re Moody's Corp. Sec. Litig., 2011, 274 F.R.D. 480, 489 (S.D.N.Y.).
In re WorldCom, Inc. Securities Litigation, 2004, 346 F. Supp. 2d 628, 689 (S.D.N.Y.).
In the Matter of Franchard Corp., 1964, 42 SEC 163.
Investment Advisers Act of 1940, 2012, § 206, 211(d), 15 U.S.C. § 80b-6, 80b-11(d).
Investment Company Act of 1940, 2012, § 38(c), 15 U.S.C. § 80a-37.
Investment Company Institute, 2018, Investment Company Fact Book, 32, 52 (58th ed.).
Kaplow, Louis, 1992, Rules Versus Standards: An Economic Analysis, *Duke Law Journal* 42.
Kennedy, Duncan, 1976, Form and Substance in Private Law Adjudication, *Harvard Law Review* 89.
Kirby, Justin, 2008, Letter to Nancy M. Morris, Secretary, Securities and Exchange Commission (May 16).
Kornman v. SEC, 2010, 592 F.3d 173, 181.
Kraakman, Reinier, et al., 2009, The Anatomy of Corporate Law.
Laby, Arthur B., 2004, Resolving Conflicts of Duty in Fiduciary Relationships, *American University Law Review* 54.
Laby, Arthur B., 2008, The Fiduciary Obligation as the Adoption of Ends, *Buffalo Law Review* 56.
Laby, Arthur B., 2011, *SEC v. Capital Gains Research Bureau* and the Investment Advisers Act of 1940, *Boston University Law Review* 91, 1051.
Langbein, John H., 1995, The Contractarian Basis of the Law of Trusts, *Yale Law Journal* 105.
Langevoort, Donald C., 2010, Brokers as Fiduciaries, *University of Pittsburgh Law Review* 71.
Lemke, Thomas P., Gerald T. Lins, & Thomas A. Smith, III, 2015, Regulation of Investment Companies § 9.02[2][a][5][a].
Leslie, Melanie, 2005, Trusting Trustees: Fiduciary Duties and the Limits of Default Rules, *Georgetown Law Journal* 94.
Meinhard v. Salmon, 1928, 164 N.E. 545.
Metro Communication Corp. BVI v. Advanced Mobilecomm Tech., Inc., 2004 854 A.2d 121, 157 (Del. Ch.).
Morris v. Wachovia Sec., Inc., 2003, 277 F. Supp. 2d 622, 644 (E.D. Va.).
New York Attorney General, 2003, Press Release, State Investigation Reveals Mutual Fund Fraud, Sept. 3.
New York State, 2016, NY Vehicle and Traffic Law, Article 30, § 1180.

Osterman, Elizabeth G., 2008, Investment Company Registration and Compliance, ALI-ABA Course of Study, SP019 ALI-ABA 467 (July 16).
Park, James J., 2007, The Competing Paradigms of Securities Regulation, *Duke Law Journal* 57.
Plaze, Robert E., 2018, Regulation of Investment Advisers by the U.S. Securities and Exchange Commission.
Press v. Quick & Reilly, Inc., 2000, 218 F.3d 121, 123–24, 126–29, 131 (2d Cir.).
Reading v. Regum, 1948, 2 All ER 27.
Restatement (Third) of Agency, 2006, § 8.08.
Restatement (Second) of Trusts, 2012, § 170 cmt. a.
Restatement (Third) of Trusts, 2007, § 90, Prudent Investor Rule, General Note.
Ribstein, Larry E., 1997, Fiduciary Duty Contracts in Unincorporated Firms, *Washington & Lee Law Review* 54.
Ribstein, Larry E., 2010, Wall Street and Fiduciary Duties: Can Jail Time Serve as an Adequate Deterrent for Willful Violations, Hearings Before the Senate Subcommittee on Crime and Drugs, 111th Cong. 1.
Richards, Lori A., 2006, Fiduciary Duty: Return to First Principles, Remarks at Eighth Annual Investment Adviser Compliance Summit (Feb. 27).
Riggs, David, 2000, Letter to Jonathan G. Katz, Secretary, Securities and Exchange Commission (June 13).
Ripken, Susanna Kim, 2006, The Dangers and Drawbacks of the Disclosure Antidote: Toward a More Substantive Approach to Securities Regulation, *Baylor Law Review* 58.
Rosen, Kenneth M., 2013, Financial Intermediaries as Principals and Agents, *Wake Forest Law Review* 48, 625, 640–41.
Sanders, William, 2014, Resolving the Conflict Between Fiduciary Duties and Socially Responsible Investing, *Pace Law Review* 35.
Santa Fe Industries v. Green, 1977, 430 U.S. 462, 471 n.11.
SEC v. Blavin, 1983, 557 F. Supp. 1304, 1314 (E.D. Mich.).
SEC v. Capital Gains Research Bur., Inc., 1963, 375 U.S. 180, 181, 191–92, 194, 195, 200.
SEC v. Chenery, 1942, 318 U.S. 80, 85–86, 92.
SEC v. Moran, 1996, 922 F. Supp. 867, 896–98 (S.D.N.Y.).
SEC v. Slocum, Gordon, & Co., 2004, 334 F. Supp. 2d 144 (D.R.I.).
SEC v. Steadman, 1992, 967 F.2d 636, 641–43 & n.5 (D.C. Cir.).
SEC v. Treadway, 2006, 430 F. Supp. 2d 293, 338–39 (S.D.N.Y.).
Securities Act of 1933, 2012, § 17(a), 15 U.S.C. § 77q(a).
Securities Exchange Act of 1934, 2012, §§ 3(a)(35), 10(b) 15 U.S.C. § 78c(a)(35), 78j(b).
Shearson Lehman/Coast Savings Housing Partners, Limited, et al., 1984, Application for an Order for Exemption, Investment Company Act Release No. 14185 (Oct. 9).
Smith, D. Gordon, 2002, The Critical Resource Theory of Fiduciary Duty, *Vanderbilt Law Review* 55.
Sullivan v. Chase Inv. Serv. of Boston, Inc., 1978, 79 F.R.D. 246, 259 (N.D. Cal.).
The Law Commission, 1995, Fiduciary Duties and Regulatory Rules 44–45 (Law Com No. 236).
Transamerica Mortgage Advisors, Inc. (TAMA) v. Lewis, 1979, 444 U.S. 11, 24.
TSC Industries, Inc. v. Northway, Inc., 1976, 426 U.S. 438, 448-49.
U.S. v. O'Brien, 2014, 18 F. Supp. 3d 25, 32 (D. Mass.).
U.S. v. Simon, 1969, 425 F.2d 796, 805-06 (2d Cir.).
U.S. Securities and Exchange Commission, 1948, Arleen W. Hughes, Exchange Act Release No. 4048, (Feb. 18), aff'd sub. nom. Hughes v. SEC, 1949, 174 F.2d 969 (D.C. Cir.).
U.S. Securities and Exchange Commission, 1977, Securities Confirmations, Securities Exchange Act Release No. 13508, 42 Fed. Reg. 25318 (May 17).
U.S. Securities and Exchange Commission, 1983, No-Action Letter, Rocky Mountain Financial Planning, Inc. (Feb. 28).
U.S. Securities and Exchange Commission, 1986, Financial and Disciplinary Information That Investment Advisers Must Disclose to Clients, Investment Advisers Act Release No. 1035, 51 Fed. Reg. 34229 (Sept. 26).
U.S. Securities and Exchange Commission, 2000, Dawson-Samberg Cap. Mgmt., Inc., Investment Advisers Act Release No. 1889 (Aug. 3).
U.S. Securities and Exchange Commission, 2002, Scwendiman Partners, LLC, Investment Advisers Act Release No. 2043, 2002 WL 1484401 (July 11).
U.S. Securities and Exchange Commission, 2002, Proxy Voting by Investment Advisers, 67 Fed. Reg. 60841, 60842–43, 60847 (Sep. 26).

U.S. Securities and Exchange Commission, 2002, F.X.C. Inv. Corp., SEC Release No. 218, 2002 WL 31741561 (Dec. 9).

U.S. Securities and Exchange Commission, 2003, Proxy Voting by Investment Advisers, 68 Fed. Reg. 6585, 6586, 6588 n.23, 6589 (Feb. 7).

U.S. Securities and Exchange Commission, 2003, Alliance Capital Management, L.P., Investment Advisers Act Release No. 2205 (Dec. 18).

U.S. Securities and Exchange Commission, 2003, Compliance Programs of Investment Companies and Investment Advisers, 68 Fed. Reg. 74714, 74715, 74716 (Dec. 24).

U.S. Securities and Exchange Commission, 2004, Press Release, Massachusetts Financial Services Co. Will Pay $225 Million and Make Significant Governance and Compliance Reforms to Settle SEC Fraud Charges Concerning Mutual Fund Market Timing, Feb. 5.

U.S. Securities and Exchange Commission, 2004, Massachusetts Financial Services, Co., Investment Advisers Act Release No. 2213 (Feb. 5).

U.S. Securities and Exchange Commission, 2004, Press Release, SEC Brings Enforcement Action Against Banc of America Securities for Repeated Document Production Failures During a Pending Investigation, March 10.

U.S. Securities and Exchange Commission, 2004, Strong Cap. Mgmt., Inc., Investment Advisers Act Release No. 2239 (May 20).

U.S. Securities and Exchange Commission, 2004, Press Release, Strong Capital Management and Founder Richard Strong Agree to Pay $140 Million to Settle Fraud Charges Concerning Undisclosed Mutual Fund Trading, May 20.

U.S. Securities and Exchange Commission, 2004, Pilgrim Baxter & Associates, LTD., Investment Advisers Act Release No. 2251 (June 21).

U.S. Securities and Exchange Commission, 2004, Banc One Investment Advisors Corp., Investment Advisers Act Release No. 2254 (June 29).

U.S. Securities and Exchange Commission, 2004, No-Action Letter, Institutional Shareholder Services (Sept. 15).

U.S. Securities and Exchange Commission, 2004, Amendments to Regulation M: Anti-Manipulation Rules Concerning Securities Offerings, Securities Act Release 8511 (Dec. 9).

U.S. Securities and Exchange Commission, 2005, Banc of America Capital Management, LLC, et al., Advisers Act Release No. 2355 (Feb. 9).

U.S. Securities and Exchange Commission, 2005, In re Columbia Mgt. Advisors, Inc. and Columbia Funds Distributor, Inc., Advisers Act Release No. 2351 (Feb. 9).

U.S. Securities and Exchange Commission, 2008, Medcap Mgmt. & Research LLC, Investment Advisers Act Release No. 2802 (Oct. 16).

U.S. Securities and Exchange Commission, 2009, Hennessee Group LLC, Investment Advisers Act Release No. 2871 (Apr. 22).

U.S. Securities and Exchange Commission, 2010, Political Contributions By Certain Investment Advisers, Advisers Act Release No. 3043, 75 Fed. Reg. 41,018, 41,022 (July 14).

U.S. Securities and Exchange Commission, 2010, Amendments to Form ADV, 75 Fed. Reg. 49234–35, 49236, 49237 n.35, 49240, 49245–46, n. 191, 49250, n. 245, Appendix C (Aug. 12).

U.S. Securities and Exchange Commission, 2011, Study on Investment Advisers and Broker-Dealers as Required by Section 913 of the Dodd-Frank Wall Street Reform and Consumer Protection Act 54.

U.S. Securities and Exchange Commission, 2011, Barr Rosenberg, Investment Advisers Act Release No. 3285 (Sept. 22).

U.S. Securities and Exchange Commission, 2015, Agency Financial Report, 154–56.

U.S. Securities and Exchange Commission, 2016, Investment Advisers Act Rule 206(4)-6, 17 C.F.R. § 275.206(4)-6.

U.S. Securities and Exchange Commission, 2016, Securities Exchange Act Rule 15c1-2c, 17 C.F.R. § 240.15c1-2(c).

U.S. Securities and Exchange Commission, 2016, Securities Act Rule 408(a), 17 C.F.R. § 230.408(a).

U.S. Securities and Exchange Commission, 2018, Proposed Commission Interpretation Regarding Standard of Conduct for Investment Advisers; Request for Comment on Enhancing Investment Adviser Regulation, 83 Fed. Reg. 21203, 21209 (May 9).

Velasco, Julian, 2015, A Defense of the Corporate Law Duty of Care, *Journal of Corporate Law* 40.

Wingate Housing Partners, Ltd. II and Continental Wingate Co., Inc., 1983, Filing of Application for an Order Granting Exemption from all Provisions of the Act, Investment Company Act Release No. 13243 (May 13).

Youngdahl, Jay, 2011, The Time has Come for a Sustainable Theory of Fiduciary Duty in Investment, *Hofstra Labor & Employment Law Journal* 29.

PART II

IDENTITY AND BEHAVIOR OF MUTUAL FUND INVESTORS

5. Who are mutual fund investors?
Alan Palmiter

This chapter offers an overview of the mutual fund market and the investors who inhabit it. The purpose is to provide a framework for understanding the regulatory protections for mutual fund investors, including the fiduciary duties of fund directors, professional advisers, and fund management companies.

On the supply side, mutual funds hold $16 trillion in financial assets and have become the largest component of our private retirement system. On the demand side, mutual fund ownership has become widespread, with 90 million fund-owning households composed mostly of middle-class, educated, and older investors.

The portrait of mutual fund investors that has been painted by a large and consistent body of academic and government studies over the past few decades is disturbing. Fund investors, who have been largely tasked with making investment decisions about the funds in which they invest, are mostly ignorant of the fund characteristics, inattentive to risks (and opportunities) of different asset classes, and often insensitive to fund fees. Instead, fund investors tend to chase past returns and attempt to time the market. As a result, the average returns for fund investors (both in stock and bond funds) have significantly trailed benchmark market returns—in some studies by several percentage points. Over time, these "lost" returns wreak devastation on the portfolios of fund investors.

The role of financial intermediaries in the mutual fund market has also been disconcerting. Often, financial advisers give fund investors conflicting advice, leading them to choose high cost, underperforming funds on which the advisers garner commissions. Although some employers are shifting employees to low cost, risk-appropriate balanced funds, many 401(k) plans remain less than optimal. Moreover, fund companies tout higher cost actively managed funds, despite growing evidence that most, if not all, fund managers are unable to beat the market.

Meanwhile, the fund industry continues to portray fund investors as well informed and well advised, exerting pressure on fund companies to provide an optimal mix of cost and performance. The SEC, despite studies to the contrary, has assumed that, with appropriate disclosure, fund investors are capable of fending for themselves.

Yet there are reasons for hope. Recently, many fund investors have moved to lower cost index funds—reflecting both a new sensitivity to the importance of low costs and the empty promise of active fund management. Target date funds have also established a beachhead in the 401(k) market. The recent clarion calls of the financial press reinforce these trends, as a growing drumbeat of stories emphasizes the importance of fund fees, the counterproductivity of trying to beat the market, the emptiness of chasing past fund performance, and the foolishness of trying to time the market.

1 MUTUAL FUND MARKET

A mutual fund pools multiple investors' money into a single investment portfolio created and managed by a fund management company. Investors who purchase shares in the fund are entitled to the proportionate return from the assets held by the fund. (The focus here is on open-ended mutual funds, which allow investors to buy and redeem directly from the fund; funds that investors trade on the market, such as closed-end funds and exchange-traded funds, are generally not part of tax-preferred retirement plans, and are not covered here.)

1.1 Mutual Fund Categories

As of June 2016, US mutual funds held $15.9 trillion in assets, representing about one fourth of the total value of the US equity and bond markets (ICI, Trends, 2016). Investors have a great number of mutual funds to choose from—8,115 as of June 2016 (ICI, Trends, 2016). Broadly speaking, there are two types of mutual funds: longer-term (stock and bond) funds and shorter-term money market funds. Stock (or equity) funds account for more than half (52 percent) of total mutual fund assets (ICI, Fact Book, 2016), with most focused on US equities (41 percent) but a significant portion focused on non-US equities (15 percent). Then come bond funds (22 percent) and money market funds (16 percent), with the remaining categorized as hybrid funds (8 percent) (ICI, Fact Book, 2016).

1.2 Fundholding Households

Ownership of mutual funds is widespread, although household ownership of mutual funds has remained relatively steady since 2000 (ICI, Fact Book, 2016). Of the 124.6 million households in the United States, about 53.6 million (or 43 percent) own mutual funds—far more than hold individual stocks and bonds (ICI, Fact Book, 2016). The percentage of households holding mutual funds has reduced in relatively recent years, however, having peaked in 2013 at 46.3 percent (ICI, Fact Book, 2016).

Reflecting the importance of mutual funds to US savings and retirement funding, most households that hold mutual funds have moderate income and wealth. The median household income of mutual fund investors is $87,000, with most fund-owning households (55 percent) having incomes below $100,000 and many (20 percent) having incomes below $50,000 (ICI, Fact Book, 2016).

The median fund-owning household has total financial assets (excluding its home) of $200,000, with approximately $120,000 held in mutual funds. Mutual funds are many households' primary form of financial investment. The majority (67 percent) of fund-owning households hold over half of their total financial assets invested in mutual funds (ICI, Fact Book, 2016).

Fund investors tend to come from more stable, slightly older, better educated households. According to an ICI survey of 6,000 fund investors, nearly three fourths (71 percent) live in married or two-partner households (ICI, Profile of Mutual Fund Shareholders, 2016). Fund ownership is concentrated among older households, with about 42 percent of fund-owning households headed by someone over 55, and only

5 percent headed by someone younger than 35. Finally, fund investors tend to be better educated than the general US population, with 78 percent of fund-owning households headed by a person with some college or more (ICI, Profile of Mutual Fund Shareholders, 2016).

1.3 Importance of Mutual Funds to Retirement Savings

Mutual fund ownership has become widespread largely because mutual funds have become a primary way that Americans save for retirement. This rise in fund ownership has corresponded to the switch among employers, over the past 40 years, from providing traditional, defined benefit (DB) pension plans to providing defined contribution (DC) retirement plans, such as 401(k) plans. Typically, mutual funds are among the investment options available to the employees in a defined contribution plan (ICI, Retirement Market, 2015).

Nearly all fund investors (91 percent) cite retirement as their primary reason for investing in mutual funds, with emergency funds (50 percent), current income (30 percent), and education (24 percent) less important (ICI, Profile of Mutual Fund Shareholders, 2016). Reflecting this, most mutual fund assets (53 percent) are held in tax-deferred retirement accounts, such as DC plans and Individual Retirement Accounts (IRAs).

As of March 2016, US retirement assets totaled $24.1 trillion, constituting 34 percent of all household financial assets. In the past 35 years, the proportion of retirement assets held in DC plans and IRAs has grown from 20 percent to nearly 60 percent, while the proportion held in DB plans (traditional pensions) has shrunk from nearly 70 percent of retirement assets to only 35 percent today (ICI, Retirement Market, 2016).

Importantly, mutual funds constitute a significant and growing proportion of US retirement assets. As of 2015, about $6.8 trillion (28.2 percent) of retirement assets were in defined contribution plans, and more than half of the assets (54 percent) in these plans ($3.7 trillion) were invested in mutual funds—up from 34 percent and $263 billion in 1995. The story is similar for IRAs. As of 2015, IRAs constituted an estimated $7.4 trillion (30.5 percent) of all retirement assets, with $3.5 trillion (47 percent) of IRA assets invested in mutual funds—up from $498 billion (34 percent) in 1995 (ICI, Retirement Market, 2016; ICI, Annual Report, 1997).

Defined contribution plans and IRAs are intricately linked, as most of the money flowing into IRAs comes from rollovers from employer-based retirement plans, not direct IRA contributions (White House, 2015). For example, IRA rollovers were $300 billion in 2012, compared to direct IRA contributions of $30 billion in that year. As employees move from job to job, the way in which IRA rollovers are made and then managed is of continuing and growing importance.

In summary, our nation relies on mutual funds. Ownership of mutual funds has become widespread, with about half of US households owning mutual funds. These funds constitute a significant and increasing portion of our savings and are a particularly important component of our private retirement system.

2 "IRRATIONAL" FUND INVESTORS

Given the importance of mutual funds in our national savings and retirement systems, it is important to consider the "efficiency" of the demand side of the mutual fund market. Toward this end, a rich financial literature over the past two decades has looked at how fund investors make decisions concerning their mutual fund investments.

The evidence shows that mutual fund investors are generally unable to perform the disciplining role that one would expect in an "efficient" market. Whether investing on their own (mostly with the help of financial professionals) or through employer-provided retirement plans, fund investors choose the funds in which they invest—and they often choose poorly. Based on consistent findings of academic studies over the past two decades, reinforced in government reports, fund investors need much more help than they currently receive.

The studies reveal that fund investors are generally ignorant of the attributes, risks, and expenses of the funds in which they invest. Fund investors chase past performance, a weak (if not downright misleading) signal of future fund performance. Although fund investors have become somewhat attentive to frontend sales loads, they remain mostly oblivious to continuing 12b-1 marketing fees. Fund investors chase the past performance of funds, despite overwhelming evidence that there is no performance persistence among any mutual funds. Fund investors, like other investors, also engage in futile market timing. The overall result is that fund investors are often in the wrong fund for them, generally paying excessive costs, and too often buying high and selling low.

In the meantime, the fund industry has staked the position that fund investors behave rationally and exert pressure on fund companies to lower fees and offer investor-friendly products. And the SEC has assumed that fund investors can protect themselves with proper information.

2.1 Ignorance of Fund Characteristics

A 200-page study prepared by the SEC (as mandated by the Dodd–Frank Act of 2010) concluded that "American investors lack basic financial literacy." According to the study, investors (including fund investors) do not understand basic concepts such as diversification, investment costs, inflation, and compound interest (SEC Study, 2012).

This also appears to be true of mutual fund investors. According to the consistent findings of studies over the past two decades, most fund investors do not know the basic characteristics of the mutual funds they own. For example, a random telephone survey, conducted in the 1990s, of almost 3,400 households that invest in mutual funds found that 72 percent of the surveyed investors did not know if their primary fund invested in domestic or international securities, and 75 percent did not know whether the fund invested in equity or fixed income securities (Capon et al., 1996).

A 2005 study on investor reaction to fund name changes—which often accompany a shift in the investment objectives of a fund—also reflected this general ignorance among fund investors. Looking at investors' reactions to 332 style-name changes in equity mutual funds, the study found that funds that changed their names to reflect a more popular investment style experienced a large increase in net fund flows. The study found flow increased even when the fund changed only its name, without actually changing its investment style—further evidence that fund investors are unaware of the holdings of their mutual funds (Cooper et al., 2005).

2.2 Inattention to Risk (and Asset Diversification)

Fund investors, according to academic studies, generally are also unaware of fund risks and do not take them seriously. For example, in an experimental study of how investors choose stock mutual funds, the fund's beta (price variability) was the least important characteristic in their choice (Wilcox, 2003).

Although investors personally do not focus on a fund's risk, many investors say that they use published fund ratings or rankings—such as those from Morningstar—that often incorporate some measure of risk. An ICI survey, for example, found that 35 percent of investors review a fund's rating from a mutual fund rating service before purchasing the fund, and 19 percent call it "very important" to their final decision to invest (ICI, Investor Preferences, 2006). But reliance on third-party advice does not appear to markedly increase investors' sensitivity to fund risk. Although there is a positive relationship between flow and funds' risk-adjusted returns, studies show it is not as strong as the positive relationship between flow and nonadjusted returns. That is, fund investors pay much more attention to fund performance than to fund risk (Del Guercio and Reuter, 2014).

2.3 Inattention to Fund Expenses

Fund investors generally pay little attention to fund fees and expenses, particularly the regular costs that funds incur, such as management fees and trading costs. Even though fund expenses have dramatic effects on investor returns over time, the evidence suggests that most investors ignore or misunderstand the impact of fund fees.

For example, an investor who invests $5,000 per year from age 25 to age 65 could expect a quite comfortable nest egg of $2.3 million (assuming average annual returns of 9.8 percent, the historic return for the S&P 500), while that same investor bearing expenses of 2.5 percent (an average for actively managed equity funds) would have only half an egg: $1.15 million (Bogle, 2008).

Surveys over the past couple of decades show that fund investors give little weight to fund fees and expenses. For example, in a 1998 survey sponsored by the SEC and the Office of the Comptroller of the Currency of 2,000 randomly selected mutual fund investors, only 19 percent of those surveyed could give even an estimate of the expenses of their largest mutual fund holding. In addition, only 43 percent claimed to have known the fund's expenses at the time they first purchased the fund (Alexander et al., 1998).

A 2003 study asking fund investors to choose among hypothetical stock mutual funds based on six characteristics found that investors identified the fund's management fee as only the fourth most important factor, ahead only of the fund's load and its beta (price volatility) (Wilcox, 2003).

Confirming the findings of academic surveys of fund investors, other academic studies looking at actual investor behavior find that fund investors generally have not considered fund fees and expenses to be important. In fact, studies of how investors actually behave—rather than surveys relying on self-reported behavior—have painted a portrait of fund investors who pay little attention to ongoing fund fees and expenses.

Studies of actual investor behavior in the 1990s and before generally found that higher expense ratios did not reduce fund flows—that is, fund investors did not differentiate low cost and high cost funds. For example, a study looking at investments in diversified US equity mutual funds from 1970 to 1999 found "at best, no relation between operating expenses and flows and, at worse, a perverse positive relation between expenses and flows for large funds" (Barber et al., 2005). In addition, the study looked at instances when customers of a large discount broker had sold one fund and then purchased another fund within a three-week period, finding that operating expenses of the purchased funds were generally higher than those of the sold funds, indicating that investors do not switch funds to reduce the expenses they are paying.

A recent study comparing retail and institutional investors in mutual funds finds that institutional fund investors are more sensitive to high fees and poor risk-adjusted performance than retail fund investors, who tend to respond to (counterproductive) signals such as past performance. Looking at "twin funds" (funds with the same manager and similar portfolios, but sold separately to institutional and retail investors), the study found that retail funds with an institutional twin outperformed similar retail funds without an institutional twin by 1.5 percent on risk-adjusted basis. The study's authors suggest that institutional investors provide an important disciplining effect on fund managers that is lacking in retail markets (Evans and Fahlenbrach, 2012).

While the recent growth of low cost index funds suggests that many retail fund investors are becoming more aware of the importance of fund expenses, the continuing success of high cost index funds provides continuing evidence that investors still underweight expenses. Although it is understandable that investors might buy high expense, actively managed funds in the hope that the fund manager's stockpicking skills will more than compensate for the higher expenses, a high expense index fund makes little sense. Index funds do not attempt to pick high performing securities, but rather just hold the securities in a specific market index. A rational fund investor should buy the index fund that has the lowest expense ratio.

Strangely, however, this is not how many investors choose among index mutual funds. In a study of flows into different S&P 500 index funds from 1996 to 2001, investors did not move from high expense to low expense index funds. Instead, a large amount of new cash flow went to the poorest performing funds—that is, the index funds with the highest fees. Fund companies may play to the assumption among fund investors that "paying more buys you more." During the period of the study, new index funds that entered the market had higher expense ratios (0.77 percent, with a maximum of 2 percent) compared to the average index fund (0.44 percent) (Capon et al., 1996).

Although the industry has argued that different service levels explain the move to high cost index funds, an experimental study involving Wharton MBA and Harvard College students casts doubt on the conclusion. The study found that even these presumably savvy investors chose high cost index funds, even when the services offered by all index funds were identical. In the experiment, the students were presented with the prospectuses of four S&P 500 index funds with different expense ratios, and were asked to allocate an investment among these funds. Participants were told they would maximize their compensation for participating in the experiment if they picked the fund with the highest future return, which for index funds is the fund with the lowest expense ratio. All that mattered were returns (and thus expenses) (Choi et al., 2006).

Nevertheless, more than 95 percent of the participants failed to pick the fund that minimized expenses. Instead, they gravitated to funds based on stated past performance—which varied depending on the fund's starting date. The experiment suggests that fund investors do not choose high cost index funds because of additional services, but because of perceptions of past performance (Choi et al., 2006).

To add to the burden borne by fund investors who choose an actively managed fund, such funds often significantly understate their "true" management fee—that is, the amount charged for the fund's stockpicking services. The reason: many actively managed funds are actually "closet indexers." For example, Fidelity's Contrafund® so closely tracked a Large Growth Index that the 0.64 percent that fund investors were paying in management fees was mostly to ensure the fund tracked its index, not beat it.

Given that many actively managed funds seek mainly to imitate the market, one study sought to "unbundle" the stockpicking of actively managed funds and to identify how much is simply tracking a market benchmark and how much trying to beat the benchmark (Miller, 2007). On the assumption that the "passive expense ratio" for the tracking portion of the fund should be that of a low cost index fund, the fund's "active expense ratio" is actually much larger than the fund's overall expense ratio. For example, the study estimates that Fidelity Magellan's expense ratio of 0.70 percent is better understood as an amalgam of a 5.87 percent "active ratio" for the small actively managed portion of the fund and a 0.20 percent "passive ratio" for the indexed portion. According to the study, the average "active expense ratio" of actively managed funds, rather than the stated 1.15 percent, is closer to 6.99 percent.

2.4 Inattention to Loads (Including 12b-1 Fees)

Fund investors, although generally insensitive to fund expenses, increasingly pay attention to fund loads, which were once prevalent in the fund industry, but are now the exception (Palmiter and Taha, 2008).

Fund investors may be more sensitive to loads than to other expense charges. Loads are more salient than ongoing operating fees, which are often masked by the volatility of equity returns. When an investor buys a fund with a frontend load, the investor feels the effect of the load immediately and vividly. The investor's initial account statement will show less money than the investor sent to the fund company. On the other hand, the investor never directly sees the effect of fund operating expenses, the effect only perceptible as reduced returns over time. As a result, investors tend to underestimate the effect of operating expenses compared to loads.

This explanation also finds support in fund investors' lower aversion to 12b-1 fees than to loads (permitted since 1980, 12b-1 fees are marketing fees capped by SEC rule at 1.0 percent per year that cover both fund marketing expenses and commissions paid to financial advisers for steering clients to the fund). Like operating expenses, 12b-1 fees are smaller, ongoing charges deducted from fund assets rather than directly from investors' accounts. In short, fund investors seem to notice when struck by a club, but not when slowly bled to death.

2.5 Chasing Past Performance

Although mutual fund investors pay little attention to a fund's risk and operating expenses, they pay great attention to a fund's historical returns. Surveys of fund investors and studies of their actual behavior find that this may be the most prominent component of their investing profile.

Studies gauging investor views uniformly identify the importance of a fund's past returns. For example, a 2003 experiment asking investors to choose between hypothetical mutual funds found that a fund's returns over the past ten years and over the past year are the two most important factors for investors (Wilcox, 2003). Also, a survey of fundholding households found that a fund's "investment performance track record" is the most important factor in investors' choice of funds (Capon et al., 1996). In addition, the ICI survey of fund investors found that 69 percent of respondents stated they reviewed a fund's "historical performance" before investing in a fund (ICI, Investor Preferences, 2006).

Similarly, numerous studies of actual investor behavior have found that investors chase past fund performance. For example, a fund's past return has a strong positive effect on flow into the fund (Del Guercio and Tkac, 2002). And this positive relationship was strongest for funds with the highest returns, indicating that investors especially chase returns. Similarly, other studies find that equity funds with higher returns garner more flow, particularly the highest performing quintile of funds.

The tendency of investors to chase returns manifests itself not only in buying specific high performing funds, but also extends to buying the types of funds that have recently performed well. For example, a 2005 study found that funds changing their name to reflect a hotter investment style receive a dramatic increase in flow. This increase in flow occurs even if the fund doesn't actually change to the investment style suggested by the name change (Cooper et al., 2005).

Although investors flock to funds that have produced the highest returns, there is little reason for them to do so. Numerous (including recent) studies in the finance literature testing the relationship between past performance and future fund returns uniformly conclude that past performance lacks "predictive ability for future returns." In other words, there is little evidence of returns persistence; top performing funds generally do not continue to outperform other funds (Wilcox, 2003).

Instead, studies find that investment expenses almost completely explain persistence in equity fund returns. Funds with lower expenses have better returns than funds with higher expenses. Despite claims that some fund managers have "hot hands" that produce high performance, their high performing funds rarely continue to be high performing. As one study concluded, "The results do not support the existence of skilled or informed mutual fund portfolio managers" (Carhart, 1997, 57).

2.6 There Is No *Alpha*

Among financial economists there is a clear consensus: actively managed funds on average generate negative after-fee, risk-adjusted returns (Gruber, 1996; Carhart, 1997; French, 2008; Fama and French, 2010). In study after study, financial economists find there is no "*alpha*." That is, there are no funds (or fund managers) that can regularly beat the market, and the outliers achieve their market beating returns by chance. In fact, the studies find that the typical actively managed US equity fund earns a negative after-fee *alpha*—that is, once fees are included, fund investors can expect performance of their actively managed funds to be below market (Berk and van Binsbergen, 2012).

The most extensive of these studies, by Nobel laureate Eugene Fama and Kenneth French, finds that although the *aggregate portfolios* in US equity funds tend to perform close to the overall market, the actual fund returns are below market because of the high costs of active management (Fama and French, 2010). Running multiple simulations to identify funds that beat the market (a positive *alpha*), the study finds that few actively managed funds produce returns sufficient to cover their costs. But these market beating funds are few and nearly impossible to identify. As the authors conclude, "For fund investors the simulation results are disheartening ... true *alpha* in net returns to investors is negative for most if not all investors" (Fama and French, 2010, 1916). That is, there may be no actively managed funds (at least, that can be identified) that provide investors market beating returns after costs.

Studies on return persistence—that is, the ability of market beating funds to continue to beat the market—come to the same conclusion. It is impossible to identify actively managed funds that will perform better than a low cost index fund. For example, a recent study shows that among actively managed funds that had been in the top quintile at the end of 2007, only a tiny portion of these funds (12 percent) were still in the top quintile in 2013, and most (28 percent) had fallen to the bottom quintile at the end of 2013—or, perhaps out of shame, had ceased to exist (14 percent) (Buttonwood Column, 2014). That is, not only is there a reversion to mean among high-flying funds, there is actually a tendency for them to burn and crash!

Another study looking at return persistence found that successful performance in the first five years of a fund manager's career is not predictive of success in the following five years (Porter and Trifts, 2014). Nonetheless, early success in a fund manager's career leads to greater career longevity—that is, the fund industry eats its own (bad) cooking. According to the study, fund managers who outperform their peers (measured on a style adjusted basis) keep their jobs, while underperforming managers lose their jobs. But the surviving managers of any tenure—even those who manage their funds for ten or more years—generally do not outperform the market or their style benchmarks, and do not display consistently superior performance. The study concluded, "even long-term managers show no ability to beat the market on a risk-adjusted basis. The key to a long career in the mutual-fund industry seems to be related more to avoiding underperformance than to achieving superior performance" (Porter and Trifts, 2014, 70).

In summary, from all evidence (at least in the past 20 years), no actively managed funds can be identified that consistently beat the market, particularly after costs. Actively managed funds have been selling a magic elixir—and one that has yet to work.

2.7 Investors Continue to Chase Past Returns

Studies also show a tendency (if not a characteristic) of investors to overemphasize a fund's past returns (Palmiter and Taha, 2008). Fund investors who chase past returns—a cognitive bias manifested in the *representativeness heuristic*—try to predict whether a fund will perform well in the future by giving great weight to how it has performed in the past. They assume, as is true in so many other aspects of life, that "past is prologue."

Interestingly, many mutual fund investors say they recognize that past performance is not predictive of future performance. In a 2000 survey by the SEC and the Office of the Comptroller of the Currency, 71 percent of fund investors surveyed expected that a fund with "good performance" in the previous year would have only "about average" performance the next year. Yet, fund investors continue to be mesmerized by past returns.

An experiment from 2006 demonstrated the extent to which investors will irrationally chase high returns. In the experiment, which asked Wharton MBA and Harvard undergraduate students to choose among S&P 500 index funds with different expense ratios and different inception dates, participants were mesmerized by past returns. Although higher expense funds (in the experiment) had higher past annualized returns—but only because they had different inception dates—participants nonetheless chose the high return index funds, even though these higher expense funds would (by definition) be outperformed in the future by the lower expense funds (Choi et al., 2006).

The representativeness heuristic also may help explain fund investors' choice of asset classes. Investors tend to be optimistic about future stock prices during bull markets and pessimistic about them during bear markets. Thus, it is unsurprising that aggregate fund flows into equity mutual funds increase following stock market increases. But future returns do not tend to be higher following market rises than market declines. Exuberant behavior, though irrational for fund investing, is human.

2.8 Buy High and Sell Low (Market Timing)

Related to the phenomenon of fund investors chasing past performance is the tendency of fund investors to attempt to "time the market." Despite overwhelming evidence that all investors – whether professionals or not—are unable to predict market movements, fund investors regularly enter funds when markets rise and exit funds when they fall. The result is that fund investors tend to "buy high and sell low."

An example illustrates. Suppose a fund has a price of $20 at the beginning of the year, and a fund investor buys 50 shares for $1,000. When in midyear the price rises to $30, the excited investor buys another 50 shares for $1,500. But the fund falls and ends the year at $22—a 10 percent return for the fund. The investor, now disappointed, sells. For the investor her return is not plus 10 percent, but instead negative: she bought her 100 shares for $2,500 and sold for $2,200—a minus 12 percent return. The reason: misguided market timing!

The gap between *actual returns* for fund investors and *stated* fund returns provides marketwide evidence of failed market timing by fund investors. In a 2014 study, Morningstar found a uniformly negative gap between actual investor returns and average fund returns for the ten-year period from 2004 to 2013 for different fund categories—strong evidence of endemic, misguided market timing by fund investors. The study looked at monthly fund flows and calculated the dollar weighted returns for investors, compared to the stated returns for the funds (Strauts, 2014). The gap varied from minus 3.14 percent for sector equity funds (such as health, technology, energy) to minus 1.66 percent for US equity funds. For all funds, Morningstar identified a gap of minus 2.49 percent.

Other studies comparing actual investor returns and stated fund returns confirm the Morningstar results: the gap is negative and in some studies surprisingly large. For example, a study by John Bogle compared asset-weighted returns and stated returns at the 200 equity funds with the largest cash inflows from 1996 to 2005 (Bogle, 2008). While concluding that fund investors "usually chase good performance, and then abandon ship after bad performance" (p.96), the actual returns for these fund investors trailed the returns reported by the funds by an "astonishing" 6.4 percentage points. While the studied funds reported overall returns of 133 percent (8.8 percent per year) for the ten-year period, investors in these funds actually saw overall returns of only 27 percent (2.4 percent per year).

Although more recent studies suggest the gap may be shrinking, studies continue to find that actual returns for fund investors remain lower than state fund returns. A study from 2007 found the gap between actual investor returns and stated fund returns to be between 100 and 200 basis points (Friesen and Sapp, 2007). And the gap appears to be larger for load funds that make conflicted payments, a result confirmed by recent studies finding that conflicted advisers often do not discourage excessive trading by their clients (Hackethal, 2012b).

Not surprisingly, a gap between actual and stated returns (evidence of failed attempts to time or beat the market) exists not for just fund investors, but for *all* investors and in nearly *all* stock markets. According to a landmark 2007 study comparing actual returns and stated returns for stock investors—that is, all stock investors (retail and institutional), in all international markets—dollar weighted returns are systematically lower than "buy and hold" returns in equity markets in the United States and around the world (Dichev, 2007). The gap varied depending on the time period and market, but was uniformly negative (except for Canada). For example, the study found a return differential (using monthly data) of 5.3 percent for NASDAQ stocks from 1973 to 2002, though of only 1.3 percent for NYSE/AMEX stocks from 1926 to 2002. That is to say: the false belief that one can beat the market is a phenomenon that reaches beyond US mutual funds!

In summary, fund investors seem generally to "buy high and sell low." Thus, in addition to suffering all of the other drags on mutual fund performance—expense ratios, trading costs related to portfolio turnover, marketing costs (such as 12b-1 fees), performance chasing by fund investors, and underperformance of actively managed funds—fund investors bear the burden of their own misguided attempts to time the market.

2.9 Actual Investor Returns vs Market Performance

Ultimately, the question is how the combination of the many drags on returns for fund investors affects their overall returns, compared to market benchmarks. Although studies vary in quantifying the gap between actual investor returns and benchmark market returns, they uniformly identify a significant gap. That is, inattentive, performance chasing, market timing fund investors earn less (and apparently much less) than if they had adopted a simple "buy and hold" for a diversified mix of low cost index funds.

Studies comparing actual returns for fund investors (that is, dollar weighted returns of mutual funds) and market performance arrive at jawdropping conclusions. According to the widely cited Qualitative Analysis of Investor Behavior (QAIB) study, actual returns for mutual fund investors over the past 30 years have trailed market benchmarks by significant margins.

For example, the QAIB study for 2014 finds that actual *equity fund* returns for the 20-year period from 1995 to 2014 have been 5.19 percent per year, compared to average annual returns in the S&P 500 (a broad measure of US equity market performance) of 9.85 percent per year—a 4.66 percent gap. And the gap has been increasing. Although dropping to an "admirable" 2.41 percent during the ten-year period from 2005 to 2014, the gap increased to 5.26 percent in the five-year period from 2009 to 2014, then to 5.59 percent in the three-year period from 2011 to 2014, and then climbed to a staggering 8.19 percent in 2014! That is, rather than becoming more "efficient," the market in equity mutual funds seems to be moving toward less efficiency.

The gap between actual and stated returns in *bond mutual funds* identified by the Dalbar study of the same year is even more dramatic, with actual returns for bond fund investors trailing a widely recognized market benchmark by 5.40 percent over 20 years—and also trailing inflation by 1.48 percent. That is, bond fund investors would have done better to have spent their money rather than to have invested it in mutual funds! Although the gap for bond funds has narrowed recently—falling to 4.02 percent over ten years, 3.34 percent over five years, and 1.94 percent over three years—returns to investors in bond funds have continued to trail inflation. Only in 2014 did investors in bond mutual funds have returns (1.16 percent) that exceeded inflation (0.75 percent), but the gap between these returns and the bond market benchmark was still a stunning 4.81 percent.

Although the QAIB study has been criticized—among other things, for looking at purchases and redemptions on an *annualized* basis rather than at more reliable monthly or even daily data—its findings are consistent with the few other studies comparing actual fund investor returns and market benchmark returns.

In summary, comparisons of actual returns for fund investors and market returns tell a disconcerting story of investor "irrationality." Various longitudinal studies come to the consistent conclusion that actual returns for fund investors significantly lag behind benchmark indices. That is, burdened by fund expenses and a longing to "beat the market," fund investors are doomed to trail the market by a wide margin.

3 ROLE OF FINANCIAL INTERMEDIARIES

Given the "only human" nature of fund investors, the question arises whether financial intermediaries can ameliorate investors' irrational tendencies. Perhaps financial advisers (stock brokers and investment advisers), companies offering 401(k) retirement plans, and even fund companies themselves help temper the seeming indifference of fund investors to high costs and hidden marketing fees, their insensitivity to risk and misallocation among asset classes, and their chasing of past performance and misguided market timing.

The evidence here is mixed. While financial advisers seem to help fund investors overcome some of their cognitive biases and may help improve saving habits, these advisers are often conflicted and exhibit their own biases. Stock brokers and commission-paid investment advisers ("conflicted advisers," as they are called) tend to steer fund investors to the funds that pay advisers commissions, leading them to minimize to their clients the importance of fund expenses and instead to focus on past fund performance. The results are predictable: clients of conflicted advisers end up in higher cost funds that are often wrong for them and generally with (much) weaker performance (White House, 2015).

In addition, although companies have begun to offer their employees 401(k) plans that include low cost, life cycle funds, the plans continue to hide unnecessary fees and have not discouraged investors from performance chasing and market timing.

Finally, fund companies continue to advertise in ways that encourage performance chasing and investment in actively managed funds, despite the now consistent finding from a still growing body of studies that there is *no* performance persistence among mutual funds and that *no* fund manager is able to beat the market. While fund disclosures and advertising include the statement that "past performance does not guarantee future results," the warning is not strong enough (Mercer, 2010, 456). And the warning does not capture the reality that strong past performance for actively managed funds is simply a matter of luck.

3.1 Financial Advisers

Many fund investors (outside of employer retirement plans) use financial advisers. According to one survey, roughly half of traditional IRA-owning households have a retirement strategy created with the help of a professional financial adviser (Holden and Schrass, 2015). A 2006 ICI survey found that the most common source of information consulted by a mutual fund investor is a professional financial adviser (though no distinction was made between commission based and fee based), with 73 percent of those surveyed responding that they consulted a professional financial adviser before buying a fund (ICI, Investor Preferences, 2006). Other researchers have made similar findings (Capon et al., 1996).

Financial advisers are compensated for their services either by receiving payments that depend on actions taken by their client ("conflicted payments") or by charging an hourly rate or a fee based on percentage of assets ("nonconflicted payments"). Some advisers received compensation in both ways. Conflicted advisers—both stock brokers (who execute client trades) and investment advisers (who do not execute trades)—represent about one fourth of the mutual fund market.

Conflicted payments may be invisible to clients, given that advisers are often paid by financial companies for directing their clients to their products. In surveys, most households state their satisfaction with their advisers, though they also express confusion about the fees they are charged and make mistakes regarding the different titles, legal obligations, and consumer protections that exist in the advice industry (White House, 2015).

3.1.1 Conflicted advice

A survey of 530 professional financial advisers asked them to rank the importance of 14 fund characteristics played in their mutual fund recommendations to clients (Jones, 2005). First, the good news. Financial advisers ranked the fund's objective as the second most important factor in their recommendations and the fund's risk as the third most important factor. (By comparison, as we have seen, fund investors generally pay little attention to a fund's asset mix and risks.)

But other results of the survey of financial advisers are less encouraging. Financial advisers admit to emphasizing a fund's cost less to their clients, ranking fund expenses (excluding commissions) as only the eighth most important factor and the fund's load and 12b-1 fees as the least important factor. This last finding, though not surprising, is disturbing. Taken at their word, financial advisers are less sensitive to expenses, loads, and fees than fund investors themselves.

In addition, financial advisers (like investors) place great emphasis on the fund's past performance. In surveys, advisers rank a fund's past returns compared to similar funds as the most important factor. Thus, following the advice of their financial advisers, fund investors are doomed to chase performance—a losing proposition. Studies uniformly find that fund investors relying on financial advisers are as likely to chase past performance as investors who buy funds through direct channels (Bergstresser, 2009; Chalmers and Reuter, 2015).

An extensive study comparing returns from 1996 to 2004 for investors who bought through commission-paid brokers and those who bought funds through direct channels found that broker directed investors paid higher marketing fees, had higher expense ratios, and ended up in lower performing funds (Bergstresser, 2009). Even without taking account of marketing fees, the study found that broker-sold domestic equity funds underperformed comparable direct-sold funds by 77 basis points, and bond funds by 90 basis points. All told, for the period of the study, fund investors who relied on brokers averaged returns in their equity funds of 8.3 percent, compared to returns of 10.5 percent for investors who invested on their own—a gap of 220 basis points.

Similarly, a 2012 study found not only that investment advisers directed more of their clients' money to funds that shared upfront marketing fees with the advisers, but also that the returns of these funds were poor compared with alternatives (Christoffersen, 2012). Another 2014 study found the same relationship, with higher payments to advisers leading to higher inflows to funds, but with net returns to fund investors falling by 50 basis points for every 100 basis points shared with advisers. The study further found that intermediary-sold funds underperformed direct-sold funds between 1993 and 2009 by 115 basis points per year (Del Guercio and Reuter, 2014). And comparing actively managed and passively managed funds sold through intermediaries, the study found that the actively managed funds (which pay higher commissions) underperformed the lower cost, passively managed funds by 112 to 132 basis points per year. That is, conflicted advisers just cannot help but point clients toward higher cost, underperforming funds—if they're paid commissions to do so.

The White House's Council of Economic Advisers, focusing on professional advice that fund investors receive about their IRA investments, quantified the cost of "conflicted advice"—that is, advice to IRA investors from advisers who receive payments from the funds they recommend. According to the Council, such "conflicted advice" caused returns for IRA investors to fall by 1.0 percent (White House, 2015). Estimating that $1.7 trillion of IRA assets are invested in funds that generate conflicted advice payments, the report concluded that conflicted advice costs IRA investors at least $17 billion per year. To put this in more meaningful terms, retirees receiving conflicted advice when rolling a 401(k) balance into an IRA would suffer portfolio losses that would result in their running out of savings five years earlier than similar IRA investors who had not received conflicted advice.

Conflicted advice not only puts clients in underperforming funds, it also encourages clients to engage in performance chasing and market timing—and, thus, excessive trading and underperformance. Not only do conflicted advisers sometimes benefit directly by having clients move from one fund to another, but they also create the impression they are actively serving the client's interests by recommending counter-productive investment strategies. Studies indicate that conflicted advisers tend to steer clients toward excessive trading (Hackethal, 2012b). As a result, the gap between actual investor returns and fund returns (evidence of misguided market timing) is larger among load funds (Friesen and Sapp, 2007).

In a mystery shopper study, researchers sent hypothetical investors to conflicted advice financial advisers (Mullainathan et al., 2012). The shoppers presented four portfolios to the advisers: a return chasing portfolio, an employer stock portfolio, a diversified low fee portfolio, and a cash portfolio. The study found that advisers generally recommended a change to actively managed funds, even when the investor's current investment strategy had been a diversified low fee portfolio. The study concluded that advisers "seem to support strategies that result in more transactions and higher management fees" (Mullainathan et al., 2012, 12) even when clients appear to hold the optimal portfolio.

But perhaps fund investors who rely on intermediaries get something. On the assumption that savers who seek out advisers distrust their own investing skills, a recent "controlled" study of similar savers looked at whether or not receiving investment advice was helpful. The study compared the outcomes for two groups of participants in a university-sponsored retirement plan, one group who received conflicted advice and another group who (after a change in the plan) directed their own plan investments (Chalmers and Reuter, 2015). The returns of the two groups were compared to the returns of a hypothetical low cost, target date fund. Advised participants had returns 298 basis points below the hypothetical fund, while the returns for self-directed participants were 125 basis points below. In short, the participants who received conflicted advice had returns of about 1.7 percent below those of self-directed participants, who nonetheless would have been better off if they had chosen a low cost, target date fund. According to the study, "brokers significantly increased annual fees, significantly decreased annual after-fee returns, and slightly increased risk-taking relative to the [default] portfolio."

In summary, many investors follow the advice of financial advisers when picking a mutual fund. There is little evidence that financial advisers provide tangible benefits to fund investors. In fact, the evidence is quite the opposite: financial advisers direct their clients to high cost, low performing funds.

3.1.2 Fee-based advisers

Besides giving questionable advice, financial advisers also overcharge for their advice. Most advisory fee arrangements (79 percent) are based on assets under management, rather than the advice given. In effect, asset based fees—which typically run at between 1 and 2 percent of assets under management—are a "tax on wealth" (Zweig, 2015b). For example, technology is now available (and is offered by some fund groups) for people to form their own fund portfolios, complete with online help and an online manager, for an annual fee of less than 0.1 percent.

While investment advisers cover the basics, many investors need more extensive advice for complicated investments involving such matters as minimizing income and estate taxes and financing requirements. However, the financial advisers do not charge extra for these services. An automatic 1 percent is often taken out of investors' financial assets regardless of what services the financial adviser is providing. Even more worrisome is that many investors may not be fully aware of how much they are being charged. For example, when a client with a $5 million investment portfolio was told that his current adviser charged him 1.5 percent, the client assumed he was paying "$7,000 or $8,000 per year," when the adviser was actually collecting $75,000 (Zweig, 2015b).

3.2 Company 401(k) Plans

Company 401(k) plans often match a certain percentage of what employees invest into their company 401(k). This gives investors the opportunity to increase their investment in such plans, sometimes by as much as 150 percent.

3.2.1 Rollovers

When an employee retires or leaves the company, rolling the 401(k) plan into an IRA can have important investment and tax implications. The options are typically to leave their savings in the current plan, roll them over into a new employer's plan, or roll them over into an IRA. Often advisers recommend inappropriate rollovers to plan participants to collect fees for managing the assets. A recent government report found that advisers can earn $6,000 to $9,000 with an IRA rollover, but only $50 to $100 if the same participant invested within the employer plan (GAO 2011). Advisers frequently encourage clients to roll over funds to an IRA with minimal knowledge of the client's financial situation, without acknowledging other options, and without discussing fees (GAO 2013).

3.3 Mutual Fund Advertising

In addition to financial advisers, investors pay attention to mutual fund advertisements. Unfortunately, studies have shown that these advertisements do not help investors make better fund choices, but instead tend to exploit investors' tendency to chase past returns.

According to a survey of fund investors, fund advertising was identified as the second most important source of information (Capon et al., 1996). Advertising's importance to investors is suggested by studies that conclude that mutual fund advertising works. For example, a 2000 study examined fund flows into 294 equity mutual funds that advertised in *Barron's* or *Money* magazines. The study found that these advertised funds experienced approximately 20 percent greater flow than did similar funds that did not advertise in the publications (Jain and Wu, 2000).

There is little evidence that advertising is correlated with benefits to investors. One study found, not surprisingly, that advertised funds tend to be those that have significantly outperformed their relevant benchmarks in the year prior to the advertisement (Jain and Wu, 2000). However, after being advertised, the funds—predictably—tended to underperform the benchmarks. Fund advertising may also have a disturbing side effect. There is evidence suggesting that financial publications in which fund families place their ads exhibit a bias in their fund recommendations. In particular, one study found that a fund's family's advertising expenditures increased the probability of the family's funds being recommended in each of three popular personal finance magazines: *Money*, *Kiplinger's Personal Finance*, and *SmartMoney* (Reuter and Zitzewitz, 2006).

An experimental study on how potential investors perceive the warning required by the SEC in fund advertising—namely, that "past performance is not a guarantee of future results"—found it actually leads investors to focus even more on past performance in selecting a fund, compared with advertising without the warning (Mercer, 2010). The study found that investors do heed a warning that past performance is most likely a matter of luck and unlikely to persist, but the SEC has shown little interest in requiring "truth in advertising."

In summary, advertising works—investors buy funds that are advertised, and they especially buy heavily advertised funds. But advertising doesn't provide investors useful information, as fund advertising often exploits investors' proclivity for performance chasing and advertised funds tend to underperform unadvertised funds going forward. Advertising, even with the warnings required by the SEC, encourages investors' pursuit of past returns. No doubt because of this tendency, mutual fund families advertise funds that have performed well in the past.

4 CONTRASTING PORTRAITS OF FUND INVESTORS

The portrait of fund investors painted by the financial literature stands in stark contrast to the rosy views adopted by the mutual fund industry and largely accepted by the SEC. While the fund industry portrays fund investors (with the help of investment professionals) as capable of making informed decisions about mutual funds, and the SEC portrays fund investors as needing to only be reminded to pay appropriate attention to important fund characteristics, the academic literature portrays many, if not most, fund investors as ill equipped to make mutual fund investment decisions.

4.1 The Industry's Portrait of Fund Investors

The fund industry's portrait of the typical mutual fund investor is painted mostly by the industry's trade association, the Investment Company Institute (ICI). Established in 1940, the ICI touts its members (mostly fund companies) as serving 90.4 million individual investors (ICI, Annual Report, 2015).

The ICI has consistently maintained that the mutual fund industry is highly competitive, with fund choices, services, and fees determined by a robust market of sophisticated and informed mutual fund investors (Palmiter and Taha, 2008). For example, relying on the results of a 2006 survey conducted by the ICI of investors who had purchased mutual funds outside of retirement plans, the ICI has asserted that fund investors seek out and examine important fund information before investing, including the fund's investment objectives, fees and expenses, historical performance, and risk. The ICI survey concluded that investors obtain information about mutual funds from a variety of sources, and most receive guidance from professional financial advisers.

In other settings, the ICI has presented a slightly more cautious portrait of mutual fund investors. In its publications, speeches by its officials, and comments it has made to the SEC, the ICI has regularly supported simplifying and standardizing required disclosure by mutual funds. Implicit in this has been a recognition of the limitations and lack of sophistication of many mutual fund investors.

The portrait of mutual fund investors offered by the ICI, it is worth noting, relies almost exclusively on the ICI's own studies, without reference to academic studies of fund investor knowledge and behavior. For example, the ICI has never responded to studies identifying the lack of performance persistence of actively managed funds or the "gap" between actual returns for fund investors and benchmark market performance.

The ICI regularly claims that cost-sensitive investors impose a strong market discipline on mutual funds (ICI, Competition, 2008). Thus, the "[i]ncreased investor demand for low-cost funds accounted for more than half of the decline in the asset-weighted average expense ratio [in 2005]" (ICI, Fees and Expenses, 2006).

Interestingly, while pointing to the scope of information available to fund investors, the ICI has also asserted that most investors may be receiving too much information about funds. Thus, the ICI has supported steps taken by the SEC to reduce, simplify, summarize, and standardize the information in the fund disclosure documents. In addition, the ICI has sometimes opposed disclosure reforms on the grounds that investors can obtain the information from other sources. For example, while supporting an NASD (now FINRA) requirement that annual expense ratios be disclosed in performance advertisements, the ICI argued again the disclosure of the actual dollar amount of expenses that would be incurred by a hypothetical fund investor. The ICI argued that "fund advertisements are not intended to be the exclusive source for investors of information about the fund."

In summary, although sometimes inconsistent, the ICI's profile of fund investors should be comforting to regulators. Whether on their own or with the assistance of financial advisers, fund investors are said to be well informed and to impose market discipline on the mutual fund industry. At the same time, however, the ICI warns that investors generally will only read and understand disclosure that is concise and clear, and the ICI does not view loads, expenses, and fees to be relevant to investor education.

4.2 SEC Portrait of Fund Investors

The SEC, although less sanguine than the industry, also has painted a portrait of fund investors that implies a well-functioning mutual fund market. The SEC shares the industry view that fund investors consider a variety of important information before investing. The SEC also agrees that fund investors can become confused while navigating the sea of information about mutual funds and thus can benefit from fund information presented in a concise, readable, and standardized form. Unlike the industry, however, the SEC has specific concerns about investor sophistication, worrying that fund investors pay insufficient attention to fund fees and expenses, and too much attention to past returns. The agency's solution is generally more and better disclosure.

Capturing the SEC's view, then SEC Chairman Arthur Levitt testified before Congress in 1998: "The Commission should not be the arbiter of the appropriate level of fund fees. Whether fund fees are too high or too low is a question that we believe must be answered by competition in the marketplace, not by government intervention." That is, despite the underlying premise of the Investment Company Act of 1940 that fund investors cannot fend for themselves, the agency has assumed that demand side market forces (properly informed) are sufficient to discipline any supply side excesses.

The SEC's portrait of "rational" fund investors can be distilled from a number of sources, especially the disclosure the SEC requires in fund prospectuses, profiles, and advertising. Nonetheless, the ongoing attempts by the SEC to educate fund investors also reveal an awareness of investors' limitations. That said, the SEC—as shown in its releases accompanying its mutual fund rulemakings over the past 20 years—has been influenced significantly by industry comments and studies, and is close to oblivious to the findings of the academic literature on fund investor behavior, which it rarely cites.

Mandated by the Dodd–Frank Act, the SEC staff in 2012 conducted a study of financial literacy among retail investors, especially fund investors, with the goal of improving investor disclosures. In particular, the study looked at how well investors understood fund expenses and conflicted advice from financial advisers.

The SEC staff study, based on a review of other studies and a commissioned investor survey, confirmed the results of the past two decades' financial literature. First, retail investors lack basic financial literacy, have only a weak grasp of elementary financial concepts (such as compound interest and inflation, diversification, and the difference between stocks and bonds), and lack critical knowledge of ways to avoid investment fraud. Second, retail investors do not understand fee disclosures. Although many surveyed investors claimed to understand them, most lacked the comprehension to compute actual dollar charges on the value of their assets under management or the commissions paid to their investment adviser. Third, retail investors are often unaware that their financial advisers have conflicts of interest. About half of the survey respondents who were presented with transaction confirmations and account statements failed to understand the existence, nature, and extent of their investment advisers' conflicts of interest.

Rather than call on the Commission to undertake a fundamental review of its regulation of the fund industry, to begin enforcement proceedings against misleading advice by financial advisers, or to compel actively managed funds to disclose that their results are a matter of luck, the SEC staff's report concluded in the same way as so many other SEC initiatives: with additional recommendations for more and better disclosure. Among the recommendations for fund investors, the staff report repeated much of what is already happening—namely that investors receive disclosures before investing about fees, investment strategies, and conflicts of interest in summary documents written with bullets, tables, and graphs, and in plain English. And to educate fund investors, the report recommended "Promoting Investor.gov as the primary federal government resource for investing information" (p.vii).

The SEC staff report thus continued the close to neurotic (doing the same thing, expecting different results) approach that the agency has pursued for the past two decades: more and simplified point-of-sale disclosure, along with investor education. The effort, largely a regulatory flop, is illustrated by the "summary prospectus," a simplified disclosure document that the SEC permitted for funds to satisfy their prospectus delivery obligations. According to the SEC staff report, most survey respondents admitted they did not read either the statutory or the summary prospectus (too long, complicated, or boring), and about one third said instead they relied on their broker or financial adviser.

In the end, the SEC has not wanted to discombobulate the mutual fund market. Although fund investors turn to financial advisers and financial publications for comparative information—after all, there are more mutual funds than there are publicly traded corporations—the SEC requires virtually no comparisons. Except for data on an "appropriate" market index, the fund prospectus (and summary prospectus) need not provide any comparative information on performance, loads, fees, expenses, or portfolio turnover. That is, fund investors must search elsewhere for how a particular fund compares to others. Instead, the SEC assumes fund investors, left to their own devices, can determine how a fund's performance and costs compare to those of other funds.

In summary, like the ICI, the SEC believes that a variety of information is important to most mutual fund investors. Also like the ICI, the SEC believes that not only the substance of this information, but also its format, is important to investors. The SEC believes fund investors are more likely to understand clear, concise, and standardized disclosure of information in plain English or in graphical or tabular form. But in terms of getting important information to investors—and undertaking a real education campaign through the regulation of what investors must see before they invest, what they see when they receive account statements, and what fund companies can say when they advertise—the SEC has not shown itself to be serious about fund disclosure and investor education.

5 REASONS FOR HOPE: RECENT SHIFTS IN THE RETAIL FUND MARKET

So fund investors, to whom the investment of their own retirement savings has been entrusted, are mostly on their own. They must deal with their own financial illiteracy, and their tendencies to disregard fund costs, to chase past performance, and to seek to time the market.

There are glimmers of hope. Low cost index funds are growing in popularity, while dollar weighted fund fees are falling. Employers are increasingly offering target date funds that generally keep costs down, provide age-appropriate asset balancing (and rebalancing). And the financial press is becoming more strident in its admonition to fund investors to keep an eye on fees, not to chase "hot funds," and to be wary of "buying high and selling low."

5.1 Decline of High Cost, Actively Managed Funds

Fund investors, at least many of them, have been doing their homework and have begun to move out of high cost, actively managed funds to lower cost funds—increasingly, passively managed (index) funds. Jack Bogle (2014) has predicted this trend will strengthen.

5.1.1 Lower fee ratios

Average expenses paid by mutual fund investors have fallen over the past decade. According to Morningstar, the average mutual fund investor (on a dollar weighted basis) paid in fund expenses fell from 0.95 percent in 2000 to 0.71 percent in 2013—a 25 percent decline. Interestingly, the average fund's expense ratio fell from 1.41 percent in 2000 to 1.25 percent in 2013—a decline of only 11 percent (Morningstar, 2014). Clearly, fund investors are moving their money to low cost funds, even as most funds continue to charge high fees.

The ICI has identified similar (and even greater) declines in average expense ratios, with average expense ratios for equity funds on a dollar weighted basis falling from 99 basis points in 2000 to 68 basis points in 2015—a 31 percent decline. (ICI, Fact Book, 2016). The decline in fees charged by index equity funds has been particularly impressive, falling from 27 basis points in 2000 to 11 basis points in 2015—a 59 percent decline!

Both Morningstar and the ICI have explained declining expense ratios in terms of a combination of greater economies of scale and competition. As fund assets have risen, expense ratios have fallen, given that many fund costs are fixed, such as transfer agency fees, accounting and audit fees, and directors' fees. And as fund investors have shifted toward low cost funds, some funds have lowered fees to meet the demand. For example, although the expense ratio in 2015 for the *average* equity fund was 1.31 percent, the asset-weighted average (that is, looking at where fund investors actually put their money) was 0.68 percent (ICI Fact Book, 2016).

But the real story may be that investors (not the funds themselves) are embracing lower cost funds. For 2015, the ICI identified that 74 percent of all equity fund assets are held in funds whose expense ratios are in the lowest quartile (ICI, Fact Book, 2016). It would seem that investors have found the low cost funds, not the other way around. A recent study of how investors choose among funds confirms this greater sensitivity to fees. Using a simulated investment game asking participants to allocate a hypothetical retirement account among ten mutual funds, participants recognized that higher fees affect performance. And when instructed about fees and offered a simplified fee disclosure, subjects allocated more money on average to higher value funds—that is, low fee funds offering the same asset mix (Fisch and Wilkinson-Ryan, 2014).

Complete victory, however, is still elusive. For example, 15 percent of assets in index equity funds are still held in funds whose fees are in the highest three quartiles—why an investor would hold a high cost S&P 500 index fund remains baffling.

5.1.2 Growth of low cost index funds

A major reason for the decline in expense ratios has been the increasing popularity of index funds, which attempt to match rather than beat the returns of a particular index, such as the S&P 500. Not only are management fees for index funds lower, because their managers need not seek to identify and research particular stocks that they believe will perform well, but index funds generally have less portfolio turnover, resulting in lower transaction costs.

According to the ICI, index funds now account for 22 percent of US equity mutual fund assets (ICI, Fact Book, 2016). Since 2007, investors have added $1.2 trillion to passively managed equity index funds, while withdrawing $835 billion from actively managed equity funds—a swing of nearly $365 billion in investor preferences.

Others have noted the trend, with a study of net flows in 2014 finding that index based funds accounted for 68 percent of mutual fund flows (Rekenthaler, 2014). Looking at this data, a US News story summarized what is happening: "investors concluded the cost of active management was so high, and the potential for incremental returns so low, that it was not a game worth playing" (Solin, 2014).

5.2 Growth of Target Date/Lifecycle Funds

Another development has been the emergence in the retirement savings market of target date funds, also known as lifecycle funds, which delegate asset allocation decisions to the fund manager. These target date funds blend particular asset types (such as stocks and bonds) to match investors' risk tolerance and investment horizon, rebalancing the portfolio with market swings and shifting the asset mix over time in light of the investor's retirement target date. As the target date approaches and then passes, the fund portfolios become less focused on growth and more focused on income.

Target date funds have grown dramatically in the past few years—from $160 billion in 2008 to $763 billion in 2015 (after taking a 12.5 percent loss between 2007 and 2008). And over the past ten years, target date funds have had net inflows of $433 billion.

Target date funds have become widely available in 401(k) plans, with the proportion of 401(k) plans offering such funds growing from 57 percent to 72 percent in the past eight years, and the proportion of 401(k) participants holding such funds growing from 19 percent to 48 percent in the same period. At yearend 2014, target date funds accounted for 18 percent of 401(k) assets, up from 5 percent at yearend 2006 (ICI, Fact Book, 2016).

Target date funds have been particularly popular with younger retirement savers. The proportion of recently hired 401(k) participants who chose target date funds increased from 28.3 percent in 2006 to 47.6 percent in 2010 (Employee Benefit Research Institute, 2011).

The main impetus for the growth in target date funds was the adoption of the Pension Protection Act of 2006, which directed the Department of Labor to define qualified default investments for employer-provided defined contribution plans. Target date funds, along with balanced accounts and managed accounts, were among the three default options chosen by the Labor Department—and as of 2015 nearly three quarters of employer defined contribution plans make target date funds the default option for newly enrolled employees, offering on average nine target funds to choose from (ICI, Fact Book, 2016).

Despite their growth, as of 2015 target date funds still constituted less than 3 percent of retirement assets (ICI, Retirement Market, 2015). And the offerings vary widely from fund family to fund family, with the different target date funds creating significantly different allocations (and investment records). For example, the ICI compared the "glide paths" of two representative target date funds, finding that one anticipated a 50 percent allocation to equity at retirement that declined to 20 percent, while another fixed the equity allocation at 32 percent for the entire retirement period, with no allocation to short-term money market investments.

In addition, besides wide differences in allocations and glide patterns, target date funds (which tend to be funds of funds that combine other funds offered by a fund family) have wide differences in their fee structures and allocation to different types of equity (US and international), bond (government, corporate, international), and actively managed and passively managed funds.

5.3 Investor Education: Financial Press

In the last several years, the financial press has increased its reporting on the caustic effect of high mutual fund fees, especially on a retirement portfolio, as well as the pitfalls of chasing past performance and the questionable promise of active fund management. The stories regularly cite to the "latest study" on the effect of fees, the pitfalls of performance chasing, and the problems of market timing.

One missing (and telling) element of the stories has been the absence of both the SEC and the fund industry. For whatever reason, the financial press does not include commentary from SEC sources, such as speeches by commissioners or interviews with staff about the foibles of fund investors, perhaps reflecting the agency's continuing obliviousness about how broken its disclosure model is. And, despite the often withering criticism in the stories of the fund industry—for continuing to tout past performance and to sell high cost, active fund management—industry sources are rarely mentioned. At most, the ICI is cited as a source for fund industry statistics.

5.3.1 Focus on fees

The popular media has also been giving greater attention to the benefits of index funds, which, the financial press is slowly recognizing, generally outperform actively managed funds as a group. Popular publications such as *Money* magazine and the "Getting Going" and "The Intelligent Investor" columns in *The Wall Street Journal* have frequently touted the wisdom of buying index funds.

For example, the *New York Times* ran an op-ed piece in March 2015 (for a time the most emailed story among the newspapers' subscribers) that described in graphic terms the effect of fees on mutual fund returns. The piece began with the caution that "odds are you will run out of money in retirement," in large part because "Wall Street is bleeding savers dry." The piece then pointed to a Federal Reserve study that found a typical working household headed by somebody 55–64 years old has only $104,000 in retirement savings, not enough (according to Boston College's Center for Retirement Research) for most US households to maintain the living standards to which they were accustomed before retirement.

The *New York Times* piece described the importance of fees for retirement savings, stating that although the "standard prescription is that Americans should put more money aside in investments, this recommendation glosses over a critical driver of unpreparedness"—namely, high fund fees. The piece pointed to a study by Jack Bogle, published in the *Financial Analysts Journal*, which found that costs to investors in actively managed equity funds (expense ratio, transaction costs, and distribution costs) add up to 2.27 percent per year. The story illustrated the significance of these costs: a typical 30-year-old worker making $30,000 a year and saving 10 percent per year would have $561,000 at age 70 by investing in an actively managed fund, while that same worker would have $927,000 (65 percent more) by investing in a low cost passive index fund. (This assumed, perhaps optimistically, that the portfolio of the actively managed fund before expenses would match the market.)

Over the past several years, as investors have begun to pay more attention to fees, the fund industry has responded by not only lowering fees generally, but in some instances slashing fees below 10 basis points ($10 per $10,000 invested). According to a Morningstar survey, more than 100 mutual funds and ETFs in 2015 cost less than 10 basis points, up from 40 in 2010—all of this to attract "cost-obsessed" investors (Zweig, 2016).

5.3.2 Futility of chasing past performance

Another *New York Times* story reported on the futility of fund investors focusing on past returns. The story pointed to "updated findings" that no active fund managers have managed to beat their market benchmarks (Sommer, 2015). A senior director of global research and design at S&P was quoted as saying that past performance numbers give no indication of future fund performance or evidence as to whether there is skill involved in managing a successful fund. Even if the fund manager is skilled—which he believed some of them to be—what the managers do and how the funds perform is really just luck. The story concluded that the 2,862 actively managed funds investing in S&P stocks would likely have produced better results if they had been managed by flipping a coin.

5.3.3 Emptiness of active management

In a similar vein, other stories have looked at whether active management is a viable investment choice. A recent *Wall Street Journal* story, profiling the debate on active versus passive fund management, concluded that the evidence is overwhelming: active management simply is not worth it (WSJ, 2015). Another story by US News came to the same conclusion: the debate over active versus passive money management is now over (Solin, 2014): "According to S&P Dow Jones Indices data for the end of 2013, the majority of active managers across all domestic equity categories did not provide investors with returns higher than their benchmarks over three or five-year investment horizons. There is also no reliable way to identify funds likely to repeat stellar past performance." Another *New York Times* story described a Morningstar study that found that funds that had performed well in the past discontinued that performance (Sommer, 2014). Still another *New York Times* story, this one in 2016, reported on a study finding that the average actively managed fund in each of 29 asset categories (from stocks to fixed income instruments) underperformed its benchmark over the previous decade. The story drummed home the point: low cost index funds outperform the average actively managed fund in all categories (Sommer, 2016).

Lately, investors seem to be paying attention. In 2015, the movement toward passively managed funds picked up, with investors pulling about $200 billion from actively managed stock and bond funds and moving $400 billion to passively managed funds—a remarkable $600 billion swing against active management. Perhaps most remarkable was that the swing toward lower cost, passively managed funds happened in a year when actively managed funds (for the first time since 2012) outperformed their market cloning competitors (Zweig and Krouse, 2016).

5.3.4 Market timing

The financial press has also begun to highlight the foolishness of market timing. Some stories have described the "gap" between actual returns for fund investors and available market returns. For example, a *Wall Street Journal* story in 2014 summarized the annual Dalbar Qualitative Analysis of Investor Behavior that identified a 4.2 percent gap between actual returns for equity fund returns and benchmark market returns (Zweig, 2014). The story used a dramatic chart showing that while the S&P 500 had produced annualized returns of 9.22 percent over a 20-year period, the average equity mutual fund investor realized annualized returns of only 5.02 percent. And the average fixed income mutual fund investor realized annualized returns of a meager 0.71 percent—well below the Barclay's aggregate bond index for the same period of 5.74 percent, and also below inflation of 2.37 percent. The clear message of the story was that the "gap" between actual returns and available market returns should be reason for real concern. Other stories summarized Morningstar's 2014 finding of a 2.49 percent gap between average returns for investors in equity funds and stated fund returns (Waggoner, 2014).

6 CONCLUSION

In summary, our private retirement system has come to depend on mutual funds, with the choice of funds in 401(k) plans and IRAs left largely to individual investors. From the evidence, mutual fund investors tend to engage in a variety of counterproductive investment strategies: choosing higher cost, actively managed funds, while chasing past performance and timing the market.

Financial intermediaries, rather than tempering these tendencies, have often aggravated them—at least before the recent introduction of new fiduciary standards applicable to those who advise on 401(k) plans and IRAs. The fund industry and the SEC, despite evidence of the foibles of fund investors, have been largely oblivious. Meanwhile, though, the financial press has begun to report in more strident terms on the caustic effect of fund expenses, the empty promise that actively managed funds can beat the market, and the disastrous effects for investors who chase performance and attempt to time the market.

The trillion dollar questions that arise from gap between the returns that fund investors have actually earned—particularly in their retirement accounts—and what was available to them in low cost, risk-appropriate balanced index funds are: Has the legal regime charged with protecting fund investors and ensuring the viability of our private retirement system been up to the task? Can it be?

BIBLIOGRAPHY

Alexander, Gordon, Jonathan D. Jones, and Peter Nigro, 1998. Mutual Fund Shareholders: Characteristics Investor Knowledge, and Sources of Information, *Financial Services Review* 7, 301–9.

Barber, Brad, Terrence Odean, and Lu Zheng, 2005. Out of Sight, Out of Mind: The Effects of Expenses on Mutual Fund Flows, *Journal of Business* 78, 2095–2107.

Bergstresser, Daniel, John Chalmers, and Peter Tufano, 2009. Assessing the Costs and Benefits of Brokers in the Mutual Fund Industry, *Review of Financial Studies* 22, 4129–56.

Benartzi, Shlomo, and Richard H. Thaler, 2001. Naive Diversification Strategies in Defined Contribution Saving Plans, *American Economic Review* 91, 79–98.

Berk, Jonathan, and Jules van Binsbergen, 2012. Measuring Economic Rents in the Mutual Fund Industry, *NBER Working Paper 18184*, Stanford University.

Bogle, John, 2008. A Question So Important That It Should Be Hard to Think About Anything Else, *The Journal of Portfolio Management*, 95–102. Available at: http://johncbogle.com/wordpress/wp content/uploads/2010/04/JPM-Question-so-Important.pdf.

Bogle, John, 2014. Future of Investing: Rise of the Shareholders, *Wall Street Journal*, July 7, 2014.

Bollen, Nicolas, and Jeffrey A. Busse, 2004. Short-Term Persistence in Mutual Fund Performance, *Review of Financial Studies* 18, 594–5.

Buttonwood Column, Practice Makes Imperfect: Even Experienced Fund Managers Don't Beat the Market, *The Economist*, August 8, 2014.

Capon, Noel, Gavan J. Fitzsimmons, and Russ Alan Prince, 1996. An Individual Level Analysis of the Mutual Fund Investment Decisions, *Journal of Financial Services Research* 59, 59–77.

Carhart, Mark M., 1997. On Persistence in Mutual Fund Performance, *Journal of Finance* 52, 57–82.

Chalmers, John, and Jonathan Reuter, 2015. Is Conflicted Investment Advice Better than No Advice? *University of Oregon and Boston College Working Paper*. Available at: www2.bc.edu/~reuterj/research/ORP_201503.pdf.

Choi, James, David Laibson, and Brigitte C. Madrian, 2006. Why Does the Law of One Price Fail? An Experiment on Index Mutual Funds. Available at: www.som.yale.edu/faculty/jjc83/fees.pdf.

Consumer Financial Protection Bureau (CFPB). 2013. Senior Designations for Financial Advisers: Reducing Consumer Confusion and Risks. Available at: http://files.consumerfinance.gov/f/201304_CFPB_OlderAmericans_Report.pdf.
Cooper, Michael, Huseyin Gulen, and P. Raghavendra Rau, 2005. Changing Names with Style: Mutual Fund Name Changes and Their Effects on Fund Flows, *Journal of Finances* 60, 2825–6.
Christoffersen, Susan, Richard Evans, and David K. Musto, 2012. What Do Consumers' Fund Flows Maximize? Evidence from Their Brokers' Incentives, *Journal of Finance* 68(1), 201–35. Available at: SSRN: http://papers.ssrn.com/sol3/papers.cfm?abstract_id=1393289.
de Souza, Andre, and Anthony W. Lynch, 2012. Does Mutual Fund Performance Vary over the Business Cycle? *NBER Working Paper* 18137. Available at: www.nber.org/papers/w18137.
Del Guercio, Diane, and Paula A. Tkac, 2002. The Determinants of the Flow of Funds of Managed Portfolios: Mutual Funds v. Pension Funds, *Journal of Finance* 37, 523–38.
Del Guercio, Diane, and Jonathan Reuter, 2014. Mutual Fund Performance and the Incentive to Generate Alpha, *Journal of Finance* 69(4), 1673–1704.
Dichev, Ilia, 2007. What Are Stock Investors' Actual Historical Returns? Evidence from Dollar-Weighted Returns, *American Economic Review* 97, 386–40.
Evans, Richard and Rudiger Fahlenbrach, 2012. Institutional Investors and Mutual Fund Governance: Evidence From Retail-Institutional Twin Funds, *Review of Financial Studies* 25, 12. Available at: www.istfin.eco.usi.ch/index/fahlenbrach-186797.pdf.
Fama, Eugene F., and Kenneth R. French, 2010. Luck versus Skill in the Cross-Section of Mutual Fund Returns, *Journal of Finance* 65, 1915–47.
Fisch, Jill E. and Tess Wilkinson-Ryan, 2014. Why Do Retail Investors Make Costly Mistakes? An Experiment on Mutual Fund Choice, *University of Pennsylvania Law School* 162, 605–47. Available at: http://papers.ssrn.com/sol3/papers.cfm?abstract_id=2086766.
Foerster, Stephen, Juhani T. Linnainmaa, Brian T. Melzer, and Alessandro Previtero, 2014. Retail Financial Advice: Does One Size Fit All? *National Bureau of Economic Research Working Paper 20712*. Available at: www.nber.org/papers/w20712.
Frazzini, Andrea, and Owen A. Lamont, 2008. Dumb Money: Mutual Fund Flow and the Cross-Section of Stock Returns, *Journal of Finance* 88, 299–319.
French, Kenneth R., 2008. The Cost of Active Investing, *Journal of Finance* 63, 1537–73.
Friesen, Geoffrey C., and Travis R.A. Sapp. 2007. Mutual Fund Flows and Investor Returns: An Empirical Examination of Fund Investor Timing Ability, *Journal of Banking and Finance* 31(9), 2796–2816.
Gallaher, Steve, Ron Kaniel, and Laura T. Starks, 2006. Madison Avenue Meets Wall Street: Mutual Fund Families, Competition and Advertising. Available at: http://ssrn.com/abstract=879775
Glode, Vincent, 2011. Why Mutual Funds "Underperform," *Journal of Financial Economics* 99, 546–59.
Government Accountability Office (GAO). 2009. "Conflicts of Interest Can Affect Defined Benefit and Defined Contribution Plans." GAO-09-503T. Available at: www.gao.gov/assets/130/122042.pdf
Government Accountability Office (GAO). 2011. 401(K) Plans: Improved Regulation Could Better Protect Participants from Conflicts of Interest." *GAO-11-119*. Available at: www.gao.gov/assets/320/315369.html
Government Accountability Office (GAO). 2013. "401(K) Plans: Labor and IRS Could Improve the Rollover Process for Participants." *GAO-13-30*. Available at: www.gao.gov/assets/660/652881.pdf
Gruber, Martin J., 1996. Another Puzzle: The Growth in Actively-Managed Mutual Funds, *Journal of Finance* 51, 783–810.
Hackethal, Andreas, Michael Haliassos, and Tullio Jappelli. 2012a. Financial Advisers: A Case of Babysitters? *Journal of Banking and Finance* 36(2), 509–24.
Hackethal, Andreas, Roman Inderst, and Steffen Meyer. 2012b. Trading on Advice. University of Frankfurt. Available at: http://papers.ssrn.com/sol3/papers.cfm?abstract_id=1701777.
Holden, Sarah, and Daniel Schrass, 2015. The Role of IRAs in U.S. Households' Saving for Retirement, 2014. *ICI Research Perspective* 21(1). Available at: www.ici.org/pdf/per21-01.pdf.
Hung, Angela A., Noreen Clancy, Jeff Dominitz, Eric Talley, Claude Berrebi, and Farrukh Suvankulov, 2008. Investor and Industry Perspectives on Investment Advisers and Broker-Dealers, *RAND Corporation*. Available at: www.rand.org/pubs/technical_reports/TR556.html.
Investment Company Institute, 2005. Fees and Expenses of Mutual Funds. Available at: www.ici.org/pdf/fm-v15n4.pdf.
Investment Company Institute, 2006. Research Commentary: Competition in the Mutual Fund Business. Available at: www.ici.org/stats/res/rc_competition.pdf.
Investment Company Institute, 2007, Annual Report. Available at: www.ici.org/pdf/07_ici_annual.pdf.

Investment Company Institute, 2014, Investment Company Fact Book. Available at: www.ici.org/pdf/2014_factbook.pdf.
Investment Company Institute, 2014, Ownership of Mutual Funds, Shareholder Sentiment and Use of the Internet, *ICI Research* 20(8), 1–44. Available at: www.ici.org/pdf/per20-08.pdf.
Investment Company Institute, 2015, Investment Company Fact Book. Available at: http://www.icifactbook.org/.
Investment Company Institute, 2015, Profile of Mutual Fund Shareholders, 2014 (March 2015). Available at: www.ici.org/pdf/rpt_15_profiles.pdf.
Investment Company Institute, 2015, Statistics and Research, Trends in Mutual Fund Investing. Available at: www.ici.org/research/stats/trends/trends_05_15.
Investment Company Institute, 2015, The U.S. Retirement Market. Available at: www.ici.org/research/stats/retirement/ret_15_q1.
Investment Company Institute, 2016, About ICI. Available at: www.ici.org/about_ici.
Investment Company Institute, 2016, Investment Company Fact Book. Available at: https://www.ici.org/pdf/2016_factbook.pdf.
Investment Company Institute, 2016, Profile of Mutual Fund Shareholders, 2015 (March 2016). Available at: www.ici.org/pdf/rpt_16_profiles.pdf.
Investment Company Institute, 2016, Trends. Available at: www.ici.org/research/stats/trends/trends_06_16.
Jain, Prem and Joanna Shuang Wu, 2000. Truth in Mutual Fund Advertising: Evidence on Future Performance and Fund Flows, *Journal of Finance* 55, 937–57.
Jones, Michael A., Vance P. Lesseig, and Thomas Smythe, 2005. Financial Advisors and Mutual Fund Selection, *Journal of Financial Planning* 18(3), 64–70.
Kinnel, Russel, 2014, Mutual Fund Expense Ratio Trends June 2014. *Morningstar*, 1–18. Available at: http://corporate.morningstar.com/US/documents/researchpapers/Fee_Trend.pdf
Mercer, Molly, Alan R. Palmiter, and Ahmed E. Taha, 2010. Worthless Warnings? Testing the Effectiveness of Disclaimers in Mutual Fund Advertisements. *Journal of Empirical Legal Studies*, 7, 429–59. Available at https://mycourses.aalto.fi/pluginfile.php/112996/mod_resource/content/1/Mercer%20%20Palmiter%20%20Taha.pdf
Miller, Ross M., 2007. Measuring the True Cost of Active Management by Mutual Funds, *Journal of Investment Management*, 5, 29–49. Available at SSRN: https://ssrn.com/abstract=972173
Mullainathan, Sendhil, Markus Noeth, and Antoinette Schoar, 2012. The Market for Financial Advice: An Audit Study, *National Bureau of Economic Research Working Paper 17929*.
Palmiter, Alan R. and Taha, Ahmed E., 2008. Mutual Fund Investors: Divergent Profiles, *Columbia Business Law Review* 3, 934–1020. Available at http://dx.doi.org/10.2139/ssrn.1098991
Porter, Gary and Jack W. Trifts, 2014. The Career Paths of Mutual Fund Managers: The Role of Merit, *Financial Analysts Journal* 70(4), 55–71.
Porto, Eduardo, Americans Aren't Saving Enough for Retirement, But One Change Could Help, *New York Times, Economic Scene*, March 3, 2015, 1.
Rekenthaler, John. Do Active Funds Have a Future? *Morningstar*, August 6, 2014. Available at: www.morningstar.com/advisor/t/95469765/do-active-funds-have-a-future.htm.
Reuter, Jonathan and Eric Zitzewitz, 2006. Do Ads Influence Editors? Advertising and Bias in the Financial Media, *Quarterly Journal of Economics* 121, 197–98.
Savov, A., 2014. The Price of Skill: Performance Evaluation by Households, *Journal of Financial Economics* 112(2), 213–31
SEC staff, 2012. Study Regarding Financial Literacy among Investors. Available at: www.sec.gov/news/studies/2012/917-financial-literacy-study-part1.pdf.
Solin, Daniel, 2014. The Active or Passive Fund Debate is Over, *U.S. News and World Report, Money*, December 11, 2014. Available at: http://money.usnews.com/money/blogs/the-smarter-mutual-fund-investor/2014/12/11/the-active-or-passive-fund-debate-is-over.
Sommer, Jeff, 2014. Rules of the Fund Road: Watch the Fees, and Don't Look Back, *New York Times*, May 31, 2014. Available at www.nytimes.com/2014/06/01/your-money/rules-of-the-fund-road-watch-the-fees-and-dont-look-back.html.
Sommer, Jeff, 2015. How Many Mutual Funds Routinely Rout the Market? Zero. *New York Times*, March 14, 2015. Available at: www.nytimes.com/2015/03/15/your-money/how-many-mutual-funds-routinely-rout-the-market-zero.html.
Sommer, Jeff, 2016. The High Fees You Don't See Can Hurt You, *New York Times*, Apr. 23, 2016.
Strauts, Timothy, 2014. Bad Timing Costs Investors 2.5% a Year, *Morningstar*, June 11, 2014.

Swedroe, Larry, Kevin Grogan, and Tiya Lim, 2010. *The Only Guide You'll Ever Need for the Right Financial Plan: Managing Your Wealth, Risk, and Investments*, Bloomberg Press/John Wiley & Sons, Inc.

Waggoner, John, 2014. Investors' Miscues Sap Returns—again, USA TODAY (Feb. 27, 2014). Available at https://www.usatoday.com/story/money/markets/2014/02/27/investor-miscues-sap-returns/5860713/

West, Sandra, and Victoria Leonard-Chambers, 2006. Understanding Investor Preferences for Mutual Fund Information. *Investment Company Institute*, 1–47. Available at: http://ici.org/pdf/rpt_06_inv_prefs_full.pdf

White House, Council of Economic Advisers, 2015. The Effects of Conflicted Advice on Retirement Savings. Available at: www.whitehouse.gov/sites/default/files/docs/cea_coi_report_final.pdf

Wilcox, Ronald, 2003. Bargain Hunting or Star Gazing? Investors' Preferences for Stock Mutual Funds, *Journal of Business* 76, 645.

Wilkinson-Ryan, Tess and Jill E. Fisch, 2014. Why Do Retail Investors Make Costly Mistakes? An Experiment on Mutual Fund Choice, *University of Pennsylvania Faculty Scholarship Paper 415*.

Zweig, Jason, 2005. What a Fund Is Really Worth to You, *Money Magazine*, Oct. 12, 2005.

Zweig, Jason, 2014. The Intelligent Investor: Just How Dumb Are Investors? *Wall Street Journal*, May 9, 2014.

Zweig, Jason, 2015a. Bogle vs. Grant in the Great Fund Debate, *The Wall Street Journal*, May 3, 2015. Available at: www.wsj.com/articles/bogle-vs-grant-in-the-great-fund-debate-1430709409.

Zweig, Jason, 2015b. Connect, Why You're Paying Too Much in Fees, *Wall Street Journal*, June 20, 2015. Available at: http://blogs.wsj.com/moneybeat/2015/06/19/why-youre-paying-too-much-in-fees/.

Zweig, Jason and Sarah Krouse, 2016. Fees on Mutual Funds and ETFs Tumble toward Zero, *Wall Street Journal*, Jan. 26, 2016. Available at: www.wsj.com/articles/fees-on-mutual-funds-and-etfs-tumble-toward-zero-1453858966.

6. Protecting mutual fund investors: an inevitable eclecticism
*Lyman P.Q. Johnson**

1 INTRODUCTION

After 75 years of experience with the Investment Company Act,[1] improving investor protection remains an ongoing, multifaceted, and frustratingly elusive endeavor. Certain regulatory approaches have been emphasized to a greater or lesser degree over the years, but today we still lack an agreed-upon singular "silver bullet" for assuring investor protection and must, of necessity, pursue an ever evolving, eclectic approach to that central policy goal. Our understanding of open-end investment companies (mutual funds) has been greatly enriched in recent years by theoretical and empirical scholarship, but how best to achieve protection of investors remains pragmatically highly contentious, and no more tractable.

This chapter describes the various approaches taken to investor protection since 1940 and argues that moving on many, admittedly imperfect, fronts is the best regulatory strategy today, and probably the only politically viable one in any event. Board-centered, investor-centered, SEC-centered, and market-centered solutions are all flawed standalone responses, and each of the four can be incrementally improved, but unless broad consensus forms around emphasizing only one or two approaches, investors are best protected through a medley of efforts. Given the dynamics of today's mutual fund industry, regulatory stances must be adaptive and diverse, with each of the four approaches working in tandem with, not in opposition to, the others.

Section 2 of the chapter identifies the industry abuses that animated enactment of the federal Investment Company Act of 1940 (the "Company Act" or the "Act"). Although the historical particulars of those investor vulnerabilities have changed, the essential plight of the modern investor in a mutual fund remains the same, given the inherent organizational structure of investment companies. Mutual funds are organized under state law—typically that of Maryland corporate law or Massachusetts or Delaware trust law—and thus are subject to state law as well as federal regulation. But state statutes are notoriously lax and do not provide meaningful investor protection.[2] State common

---

* The author thanks Stacy Louizos for excellent guidance on technical issues, Arthur Laby for help on a historical point, and Andrew Christensen for research assistance. The Frances Lewis Law Center at Washington and Lee University provided financial support.

[1] Investment Company Act of 1940, Pub. L. No. 76-768, 54 Stat. 789 (1940) (codified as amended at 15 U.S.C. §§ 80a-1 to 80a-64 (2012)).

[2] In 1996, the National Securities Market Improvements Act significantly preempted state regulation of mutual fund operations and substantive disclosures. States may still require notice filings and payment of certain fees, and they may bring actions relating to fraudulent activity.

141

law fiduciary duties also govern mutual fund boards of directors, as they do directors of regular corporations and other business entities, but these too have generally proven to be of little remedial significance.[3] It is federal law—the Act—that remains the regulatory heart of the investor protection objective.

Section 3 of the chapter canvases the four key approaches to investor protection, all of which are both understandable and faulty. A board-oriented approach should be retained, but with a reconceived vision of the mutual fund board as the investors' representative, pure and simple, not truly a "company" governance body. This is because, unlike the traditional business corporation, mutual funds are not operating companies but are collective action mechanisms, and mutual fund governance is not "boardcentric" but "advisorcentric." The organizational structure of a fund, in which fund assets and management assets are housed in separate vehicles, when coupled with ease of investor exit, undoubtedly makes the mutual fund board far less effective than analogies to corporate governance suggest, as Professor Morley has insightfully observed.[4] Nonetheless, the board's enhanced, if narrowed, effectiveness remains important for several reasons, including the need to take seriously the conflicted advisor's fiduciary duties, particularly in shaping salutary ex ante norms in fund–advisor dealings.

As to investor-oriented approaches, the redemption right will always be the most robust investor protection mechanism, but it tends to be a backward-looking ex post solution, and many investors demonstrably stay in high-fee funds, notwithstanding cheaper options offering equivalent returns. Investor-oriented options can be incrementally improved, however, with the key policy issue being whether § 36(b) should be substantially bolstered or remain only of ex ante force, with a candid acknowledgment that it currently affords scant hope for meaningful ex post remedial relief. SEC-centered regulation can substantively curb new abuses and offer both guidance to and investigations of directors and advisors, and provide agency enforcement on behalf of investors that goes well beyond § 36(b). And although market forces are constrained in some ways, to be sure, industry competition is not insignificant, and recent investor migration toward passive low fee funds somewhat mitigates the concern over fund expenses—a central concern in the quest for investor protection.

---

[3] Lyman Johnson, *A Fresh Look at Director "Independence": Mutual Fund Fee Litigation and Gartenberg at 25*, 61 VAND. L. REV. 497 (2008). A recent Ninth Circuit decision, however, held, somewhat unusually for mutual funds, that a fund's investors could bring a breach of fiduciary duty action against a fund's trustees and investor advisor as a direct rather than derivative action with respect to a mutual fund organized as a Massachusetts business trust. *Northstar Financial Advisors Inc. v. Schwab Investments*, 779 F.3d 1036 (9th Cir. 2015).

[4] John Morley, *The Separation of Funds and Managers: A Theory of Investment Fund Structure and Regulation*, 30 YALE L.J. 1228 (2014).

2 THE INVESTMENT COMPANY ACT AT 75 AND THE CHALLENGE OF INVESTOR PROTECTION TODAY

The Act was adopted in the wake of the SEC's 1938 and 1939 Reports on Investment Trusts and Investment Companies.[5] Those Reports noted the dependence of the shell-like mutual funds on their third party investment advisors and also chronicled a litany of investment fund abuses that harmed investors. These included rampant self-dealing practices, lax custody of securities, inadequate investor information, lack of effective shareholder control over investment objectives or strategies, excessive leverage and inadequate capital, and others.[6] To combat these, the stated purpose of the original Act was "to mitigate and, so far as is feasible, to eliminate the conditions … which adversely affect the national public interest and the interest of investors."[7] Of course, abusive practices have not been altogether eliminated, as the late trading and market timing scandals of the past decade attest.[8] Troubling as various investor-harming practices are, however, they do not cost investors nearly as much as substantial, ongoing management fees[9]—a persistent and perplexing policy concern.

Regulatory efforts, of course, are always a step (or more) behind fast moving market actors, but the decades-long conundrum of protecting mutual fund investors stems from an unusual, core feature of fund organizational structure—a feature identified long ago by the SEC,[10] noted by the Supreme Court,[11] and recently theorized as central to understanding funds and their regulation by Professor John Morley.[12] The investment company exists as a separate corporation or trust formed under state law, it obtains funds from investors (and issues securities in return), and it has a board of directors (or trustees), much like other companies. Management of investment company assets, however, is not undertaken internally, but instead is provided by an external investment advisor pursuant to an advisory contract negotiated and approved by the fund's board of directors.[13] Typically, moreover, it is the advisor itself that establishes and sponsors

---

[5] H.R. Doc. No. 75-707 (1938) (Part I); H.R. Doc. No. 76-70 (1939) (Part II); H.R. Doc. No. 76-279 (1939) (Part III).

[6] *Id. See generally* Eric D. Roiter, *Disentangling Mutual Fund Governance from Corporate Governance*, 6 HARV. BUS. L. REV. 1, 5 (2015).

[7] Investment Company Act, § 1(a)(b). The Act today requires that SEC rulemaking action, besides protecting investors, should consider the promotion of efficiency, competition, and capital formation. Investment Company Act, § 2(c).

[8] For a description of these practices, see William A. Birdthistle, *Compensating Power: An Analysis of Rents and Rewards in the Mutual Fund Industry*, 80 TUL. L. REV. 1401, 1453–56, 1458–60 (2006).

[9] *See* Johnson, *supra* note 3 at 503, n. 28 (collecting authorities).

[10] See collected federal documents, *supra* note 5.

[11] *Burks v. Lasker*, 441 U.S. 471, 480 (1979) (recognizing the potential for abuse inherent in the structure of investment companies).

[12] *See* Morley, *supra* note 4; *see also* John Morley & Quinn Curtis, *Taking Exit Rights Seriously: Why Governance and Fee Litigation Don't Work in Mutual Funds*, 120 YALE L.J. 84 (2010).

[13] Section 15(c) of the Act requires that the advisory contract be approved annually by a majority of the directors on the fund's board and by a majority of the "non-interested" directors. Act, § 15(c) (2014).

the investment company and then contracts with it to provide all necessary personnel, facilities, and expertise, and make all investment decisions. The company itself, albeit possessing a distinct legal identity, essentially is merely a pool of portfolio securities, options, futures, loans, cash, or cash equivalents.[14] Thus, investor funds are combined via the mutual fund company and portfolio securities are housed in the mutual fund structure, but all management-related assets are located in the separately organized investment advisor, thereby achieving a sharp partitioning of essential assets, quite unlike most other business corporations. The advisor manages its own and the company's assets, and quite clearly stands in a dominant and controlling position with respect to the fund and its investors.[15]

From an organizational structure standpoint, this institutional reality has led some to describe mutual funds as "products," not traditional companies or securities,[16] with an urging that regulatory policy reflect that difference. From a governance standpoint, mutual funds are neither boardcentric nor shareholdercentric, but instead are advisor-centric. The central organizational and regulatory concern is that the all powerful advisor will act to promote its own interests by extracting excessive fees from fund assets, rather than faithfully serving the interests of investors, leading the Supreme Court to note both "the potential for abuse inherent in the structure of investment companies"[17] and the Act's efforts to address the obvious advisor conflicts.[18]

The advisory contract typically charges a fee based on a percentage of assets managed and not on fund performance. Investors benefit from a lower percentage while the advisor obviously prefers a higher percentage. Moreover, advisors have an incentive to maximize assets under management because that alone raises the aggregate fee even when the performance of the fund falters. Investors, on the other hand, gain only by enhanced fund performance—that is, higher investment returns—and lower expenses, or both.

---

[14] See Birdthistle, *supra* note 8 (2006) at 1409–10.

[15] The SEC has expressed its continuing concern that "many boards continue to be dominated by their management companies." Investment Company Governance, Investment Company Act Rel. No. 26, 520, 69 Fed. Reg. 46,378, 46,381 (Aug. 2, 2004).

[16] See Morley and Curtis, *supra* note 12, at 103; *see also* Jill E. Fisch, *Rethinking the Regulation of Securities Intermediaries*, 158 U. PA. L. REV. 1961, 2027–35 (2010). Professor Anita Krug somewhat relatedly advocates a financial services model of regulation because she sees mutual fund investors more as customers than shareholders of a firm. *See* Anita Krug, *Investment Company as Instrument: The Limitations of the Corporate Governance Regulatory Paradigm*, 86 S. CALIFORNIA L. REV. 263 (2013). For an acknowledgement of that characterization but also a criticism of it from a regulatory perspective, see Donald C. Langevoort, *Private Litigation to Enforce Fiduciary Duties in Mutual Funds: Derivative Suits, Disinterested Directors, and the Ideology of Investor Sovereignty*, 83 WASH. U. L. Q. 1017, 1037 (2005) ("Once the mutual fund is viewed as a product to be marketed ... then any notion that the producer is a 'fiduciary' is awkward and disorienting."). This issue will be returned to in section 3.

[17] *Burks*, 441 U.S. at 480.

[18] *Daily Income Fund, Inc. v. Fox*, 464 U.S. 523, 536-41 (1984). See also, *Jones v. Harris Assoc., L. P.*, 559 U.S. 333, 338 (2010).

Academic literature has identified several conflicts between mutual fund investors and advisors as a result of fund structure.[19] These include differences in financial incentives, differences in investor and advisor risk tolerances, and cross-subsidization of funds within a fund complex.[20] A simple illustration of the first, drawn from an SEC study, highlights the problem:

> New mutual fund investments are highly sensitive to published reports of annual performance. Because greater performance implies greater net fund inflows and greater net inflows imply greater management fees, managers may alter the risk of the fund to indirectly maximize their won compensation. If a fund is ahead of expectations halfway into the reporting period, managers may "pull back" from the strategy preferred by investors and reduce the risk of the portfolio in order to lock-in the present level of returns, attract more assets and maximize fees from investors. Conversely, if the fund is underperforming during the year, managers may be tempted to "gamble" and increase the risk of the portfolio to try and catch up to the market so they can minimize the impact on fees.[21]

The extent to which the inherent structure of the fund–advisor relationship generates investor-harming conduct, in light of such mitigating factors as easy investor exit and some degree of competition in the mutual fund market, has been widely and inconclusively debated.[22] The innate conflict between advisors and investors is hard to deny, however, and is compounded by another common feature of investment companies: officers and employees of the investment advisor frequently serve on the investment company's board of directors. As members of the investment company board, they owe a duty of loyalty to fund investors.[23] As decisionmakers for the advisor, however, they both personally benefit from and are in a position to take actions that are good for the advisor but adverse to the interests of investors. The significance of this structural conflict of interest is significantly exacerbated by investor inability to directly observe or communicate with and influence the advisor, thus dampening investor self-help.

In addition to structural concerns, there are a limited number of investment advisors, notwithstanding that there are thousands of mutual funds. For example, in 2013, the vast majority of the 7,707 US mutual funds, having 23,353 different series, were managed and advised by the top 300 investment advisors.[24] Thus, investor movement away from a particular fund is not necessarily movement away from an advisor. And individual directors frequently serve on more than one company board within a mutual

---

[19] Memorandum from Chester Spratt, Chief Economist, Office of Economic Analysis, SEC, to Inv. Co. File S7-03-04, at 10 (Dec. 29, 2006) [hereinafter OEA Study] (reviewing literature), *available at* www.sec.gov/rules/proposed/s70304/oeamemo122906-litreview.pdf.

[20] *Id.* at 5–7 (describing conflicts and academic literature).

[21] *Id.* at 5 (citing literature); *see also* Jeff D. Opdyke, *Mutual Funds Avoid Risk to Lift Ratings*, WALL ST. J., Feb. 28, 2007, at D2 (describing a Goldman Sachs study indicating that large-company equity mutual funds sidestep risk to reduce price volatility and gain higher Morningstar ratings so as to attract and retain assets under management).

[22] *See* Morley & Curtis, *supra* note 12, at 92, n. 11 (citing literature). *See infra* section 3.4.

[23] *See* Johnson, *supra* note 3 at 507.

[24] FT Special Report: Top 300 Investment Advisers (June 26, 2014), *available at* http://ft-static.com/content/images/6c30552e-fb45-11e3-8959-00144feab7de.pdf.

fund complex managed by the same advisor. A 2014 survey, for example, revealed that 86 percent of fund families under the same advisor had "unitary boards," where the same individuals served on the board of every fund in the family.[25] Thus, problems with conflicts between one company and its advisor likely plague all funds in the same family.

In sum, the two warring constants since 1940 have been the centrality of investor protection as a policy goal and the conflict-prone, advisor-controlled organizational structure of mutual funds.[26] The various regulatory initiatives historically aimed at augmenting investor welfare in light of this institutional reality are traced below.

3 VARIED, CONCURRENT APPROACHES TO INVESTOR PROTECTION

Today, protection of mutual fund investors is sought through various approaches. These approaches have evolved over 75 years and include board-centered efforts, investor-focused efforts, direct SEC regulation, and reliance on the workings of competitive markets. All of these initiatives have clear shortcomings upon which commentators have eagerly pounced, and, to different degrees, most are changing on an ongoing basis, with investor-oriented efforts being the most stagnant in recent decades. Given the inherent structural conflict at the heart of mutual fund organization, the current multifront regulatory stance is, Sisyphus-like, inevitably fated to be inadequate, while also being overall a pragmatic strategy likely to endure unless consensus for a fresh approach forms among various powerful constituencies associated with the industry.

3.1 Board-Centered Efforts

3.1.1 The overloaded, conflicted but unavoidable mutual fund board

A mutual fund board plays an important but far more limited governance role than does a typical corporate board. This stems from the fact that, as noted in Section 2 of this chapter, the fund's assets are entirely managed by the investment advisor. In fact, the advisor organizes the fund and, owning the initial securities of the fund, appoints directors and approves the advisory contract between the fund and itself. Only then, with the chief governance mechanism already in place, does the fund sell securities to

---

[25] INVESTMENT COMPANY INSTITUTE AND INDEPENDENT DIRECTORS COUNCIL, OVERVIEW OF FUND GOVERNANCE PRACTICES: 1994–2014, 5 (2015) https://www.idc.org/pdf/pub_15_fund_governance.pdf. This is up from 81 percent in 2007. INVESTMENT COMPANY INSTITUTE AND INDEPENDENT DIRECTORS COUNCIL, OVERVIEW OF FUND GOVERNANCE PRACTICES, 1994–2006 (2007), *available at* www.ici.org/pdf/rpt_07_fund_gov_practices.pdf. *See generally* Sophie Xiaofei Kong and Dragon Yongjun Tang, *Unitary Boards and Mutual Fund Governance*, 31 J. FIN. RES. 193 (2008).

[26] Professor Morley argues that the organizational structure of mutual funds—what he calls the "separation of funds and managers"—benefits fund investors and is a central and long-standing feature of fund structure for that reason. *See* Morley, *supra* note 4 (2014) at 1232, 1279. At the same time, the structure presents a pointed clash of interests, with the relevant issue being whether one or more regulatory approaches best addresses that clash.

outside investors. In short, the advisor, not outside investors or an independent fund board, is the moving party with respect to hiring fund management.

The chief responsibilities of the board under the Act are to annually evaluate and approve the advisory agreement, with a majority of independent directors so voting;[27] annually approve distribution arrangements, including Rule 12b-1 plans permitting the use of fund assets to pay distribution expenses;[28] value securities for which market quotations are not readily available;[29] approve of an auditor;[30] make arrangements for third party custody of securities;[31] and monitor affiliated transactions.[32] Boards also must oversee risk management and monitor fund compliance programs—recently bolstered by SEC rules requiring funds and advisors to have Chief Compliance Officers[33]—and they must adopt proxy voting guidelines. Boards, however, do not chart the investment strategy of the fund or actually manage fund assets, both of which are done by the advisor. Boards have the right to terminate an advisor, but apparently never do. Changing advisors requires a shareholder vote—deeply problematic, as Professor Morley notes[34]—and industry norms make it essentially taboo. After all, investors choose funds because of their advisors, not because of their directors.[35] Mutual fund governance, in short, is decidedly "advisorcentric," not "boardcentric," in thrust.

Acknowledging the reality of the advisor-primacy nature of fund governance,[36] and preserving broad advisor control over fund management, the Act permits up to 60 percent of board positions to comprise directors affiliated with the investment advisor.[37] In other words, only 40 percent of the fund directors must not be "interested persons." Moreover, the concept of "interestedness" under the Act is far narrower than the concept of "independence" under Delaware corporate law,[38] and certain types of directors who lack independence under the latter would be considered independent under the Act.[39] Thus, not only does the Act require fewer directors, numerically, to be independent, the Act has a more generous definition of independence than does Delaware corporate law in key conflict contexts, such as self-dealing transactions, dealing with derivative litigation, and addressing mergers and sales. Whatever one

---

[27] Investment Company Act, § 15(a), (c).
[28] 17 C.F.R. § 270.12b-1 (2012).
[29] Investment Company Act, § 2(a) (41).
[30] *Id.*, § 32.
[31] *Id.*, § 17(f).
[32] *Id.*, §§ 10(f), 17 (a), (d), (e).
[33] 17 C.F.R. § 270.38a-1.
[34] See generally Morley, *supra* note 4.
[35] Investors in most business corporations likely base their investment decisions on who the company's managers are, not who the directors are. Given the boardcentric nature of corporate governance, coupled with more engaged investor voting and activism in that milieu, disenchantment with managers frequently leads to management departure, whereas with advisorcentric mutual funds and easy investor exit, such disenchantment is more likely to lead to investor departure.
[36] Roiter, *supra* note 6 at 20–3.
[37] Investment Company Act, § 10(a).
[38] *Id.* at § 2(a)(19); *see generally* Johnson, *supra* note 3.
[39] *Id.* (Investment Company Act).

thinks of the tendency to draw from corporate governance analogies,[40] for a body of federal law that exists to address an inherent conflict, the chief governance body for monitoring that conflict is not very strictly configured. Moreover, mutual fund directors, realistically, cannot truly *function* independently in the Delaware sense of retaining the power to say "no" to the investment advisor or its contract,[41] because the advisor is indispensable to the fund and investors purchase the fund because of its advisor, not because of its directors.

Notwithstanding the Act itself, citing parallel developments in corporate governance generally,[42] in 2001 the SEC conditioned reliance on certain exemptive rules on a mutual fund board having a majority of independent directors.[43] Besides requiring a majority of independent directors in order to rely on those exemptive rules, the independent directors must select and nominate other independent directors, counsel for the independent directors must be independent, boards must conduct annual self-assessments, and independent directors must meet in executive session at least quarterly.

Due to various onerous substantive restrictions in the Act that require express SEC waiver, the ability to broadly rely on a host of exemptive rules is very significant to funds and their advisors. This agency action on the independent director front, however, followed rather than caused the industry's own movement toward boards with a majority of independent directors, likely the result of evolved corporate norms generally. This eventual industry trend toward greater independence was given strong judicial endorsement in 1979 when the Supreme Court characterized independent directors as the "cornerstone" of efforts to address fund conflicts.[44]

This policy initiative by the SEC reflected an effort to shift more of the burden of oversight of funds and their advisors to independent directors and away from the agency—a reversal of earlier agency skepticism about the efficacy of boards.[45] This may have stemmed from a sincere, if altered, belief that boards with a majority of independent directors were truly up to this monitoring task, but it no doubt was the product of necessity as well, because the SEC simply could not continue direct

---

[40] *See, e.g.*, Krug, *supra* note 16; Birdthistle, *supra* note 8; Langevoort, *supra* note 16; Alan Palmiter, *The Mutual Fund Board: A Failed Experiment in Regulatory Outsourcing*, 1 BROOK. J. CORP., FIN., & COM. L. 165 (2006a); Jerry W. Markham, *Mutual Fund Scandals—A Comparative Analysis of the Role of Corporate Governance in the Regulation of Collective Investments*, 3 HASTINGS BUS. L. J. 67 (2006).

[41] *See Kahn v. Tremont*, 644 A.2d 422 (Del. 1997); *In re First Boston S'holders Litig.*, 1990 WL 78836 (Del. Ch.) (describing "the power to say no").

[42] *See* Roiter, *supra* note 6 at note 172.

[43] Role of Independent Directors of Investment Companies, Investment Company Act Rel. No. IC-24816, 66 Fed. Reg. 3734 (Jan. 16, 2001).

[44] *Burks*, 441 U.S. at 482. *See also*, Mercer Bullard, Regulating Hedge Fund Managers: The Investment Company Act as a Regulatory Screen, 13 STANFORD J. LAW, BUSINESS & FINANCE 286 and 309 (2008).

[45] *See generally* Roiter, *supra* note 6.

oversight of the rapidly growing mutual fund industry.[46] A 2004 effort by the SEC to require that 75 percent of a fund's board members be independent and that the board have an independent chair was twice struck down on procedural grounds.[47]

In sum, today mutual fund boards have a growing number of responsibilities as the SEC looks to independent directors to play a larger role in protecting investors. For example, new regulation of money market funds—to be phased in beginning in July 2015—will require the board to decide whether and when to impose liquidity fees and redemption gates.[48] And the SEC recently brought actions against independent fund trustees for failure to satisfy their § 15(c) requirements in approving the advisory contract,[49] an obvious strong signal to fund boards generally to take seriously that baseline responsibility. Compliance and risk management also now loom large as key responsibilities of fund directors. But boards, as always, still lack real power over the fund's investment strategy, assets, and management because those are controlled by the advisor. Thus, more and more is expected of a body that does not grow in core strength. Perhaps the board, as proposed by Professors Morley and Curtis and Professor Krug, should be eliminated.[50] Or perhaps, like the mutual fund itself, the mutual fund board is misconceived.

3.2 Reconceiving the Misconceived Board

3.2.1 Mutual funds as collective action mechanisms

Although almost all mutual funds are organized as corporations or trusts, with each considered a "company" under the Act, any organized group of unincorporated persons also can be a "company."[51] As companies, mutual funds have distinctive legal personhood, and corporate personality necessarily entails important rights, as seen in the corporate context in the Supreme Court's 2014 *Hobby Lobby* decision.[52] In 2011 the Supreme Court took corporate personality quite seriously in the mutual fund context by holding that the board, not the advisor, had "ultimate authority" over a fund, and thus the advisor was not liable for "making" a statement for Rule 10b-5 purposes.[53]

---

[46] In 1990 there were 2,395 mutual funds but at the end of 2000 there were 6,876. Rob Silverblatt, *Are There Too Many Mutual Funds?*, U.S. NEWS & WORLD REPORT (June 10, 2013).

[47] Johnson (2008) at 498, nn. 3–5 (describing the litigation). Nonetheless, as of 2014, 83 percent of all fund complexes reported that 75 percent or more of their directors were independent. Overview of Fund Governance Practices, 1994–2014, Investment Company Institute and Independent Directors Council 1, 6 (2015).

[48] *See* Sean Graber and John J. O'Brien, *A Director's Guide to Understanding Liquidity Fee and Redemption Gate Responsibilities*, THE INVESTMENT LAWYER 1, 5 (2015).

[49] Commonwealth Capital Management, Investment Company Act Release No. 31678 (June 17, 2015). The SEC stated that "As the first line of defense in protecting mutual fund shareholders, board members must be vigilant": *Id.*

[50] *See* Morley and Curtis, *supra* note 12; Krug, *supra* note 16.

[51] Investment Company Act, § 2(a)(8).

[52] *Burwell v. Hobby Lobby Stores, Inc.*, 134 S.Ct. 2751 (2014).

[53] *Janus Capital Group, Inc. v. First Derivative Traders*, 131 S.Ct. 2296 (2011). The SEC has sought to limit the *Janus* holding in enforcement actions by interpreting it as applying only to claims under Rule 10b-5(b), and not to claims under Rule 10b-5(a) or (c). In re John P. Flannery & James D. Hopkins, Investment Company Act Release No. 31374, 2014 WL 7145625

As a matter of state law and the Act's definition, that ruling made sense; as a matter of organizational structure and market reality, it was absurd.[54] But in fact, the entire edifice of federal mutual fund policy is built on this same faulty predicate of misemphasizing the significance of the state law organizational form.

For a mutual fund, to be organized as a trust or corporation under state law is to be whole and sufficient as a legal entity. To be a functioning mutual fund, however, while legal existence is a necessary component, it is not sufficient without also engaging an investment advisor. Federal mutual fund policy, however, can take seriously the separate legal personality of state-created corporate/trust entities without also taking seriously their company governance regime, given that critical advisory services are external and not internal to the company. A mutual fund thus is a legally distinct entity, but as such it is best understood as an organizational mechanism for pooling investor assets and efficiently coordinating collective action by investors, who are the sole constituency. Such a fund is "mutual" in that it is the investors alone who stand in a common relationship to one another via the "fund" vehicle.[55] The fund, moreover, has no purpose other than to act in the investors' interest. Thus, there is no "corporate" business purpose separate and distinct from advancing investor interests; nor, therefore, is there any business necessity for "locking in" investor capital, which explains the easy redemption right and ability to withdraw fund assets at will. And the mutual fund also has no other noninvestor stakeholders, such as employees, consumers, and so on.

This characterization of mutual funds, while distinguishing them from corporations generally, does not however mean that investments in such funds are better understood as products, as some commentators contend.[56] Purchasing a security in a fund is the pathway to procuring a financial good, to be sure, but the security carries other attributes as well. Importantly, it includes the right, along with other investors, to have their dispersed, collective interests represented by a body (the board) owing fiduciary duties to them. This is not the case with purchasers of products. The security also carries a standing redemption right entitling the holder to exchange the security for cash from the fund, thereby withdrawing assets from the fund provider—also a feature unlike those of a typical consumer product. And even though the board does not govern in the same way as a traditional board that oversees a discrete enterprise requiring locked-in assets, the board nonetheless is the representative of investors in their dealings with the advisor, somewhat akin to a corporate board negotiating a sale with a third party tender offeror on behalf of investors. The mutual fund vehicle thus efficiently organizes and facilitates investor pooling of funds to a scalable investment level, and the retention of a board to act for investors in dealing with the advisor places in a small decision-making body a focused responsibility for those aspects of investor welfare not advanced by investor exit, thus reducing collective action and free-riding issues.

(Dec. 15, 2014), *vacated* 810 F.3d 1 (1st Cir. 2015); *accord* SEC v. Strebinger, 2015 WL 4307398 (N.D. Ga.).

[54] *See* Morley, *supra* note 4 at 1287, n. 145 (citing scholarly consensus).

[55] The term "mutual fund" is the customary marketplace term. The legal term is "open-end company." Investment Company Act, § 5(a)(1).

[56] *See generally* Morley, *supra* note 4; Fisch, *supra* note 16.

3.2.2 The mutual fund board as investor governance representative, not company directors

Correctly understanding a mutual fund as a distinct legal person defined under the Act as a "company," but one with a special, limited purpose of pooling investor assets and advancing investor interests, thus alters how we see the board of directors. The board does not advance some larger "corporate" purpose, as do regular business companies such as Apple or Ford or countless others, but that does not mean the board serves no purpose, as some contend,[57] only that its function differs from that of a typical corporate board. The board is the investors' representative, pure and simple.[58] Of course, the board's primary responsibility is the annual negotiation of the advisory contract. The widely dispersed investors cannot all interact with the advisor, just as bondholders cannot engage efficiently with an institutional borrower but must instead act through a trustee under a trust indenture. Negotiating the advisory contract is an especially central and financially important function given that the advisor itself stands in a fiduciary relationship to the investors with respect to its fees.[59] Courts always have strictly scrutinized self-dealing by fiduciaries and one meliorating consideration in the judicial review of such interactions is the interjection of an independent investor representative to bargain with the conflicted fiduciary.[60] Bargaining in the mutual fund setting may be constrained, but without a board the conflicted advisor would simply set its own fees.

Boards of regular business corporations could manage their companies if they chose to,[61] but in public companies they internally delegate that function to skilled officers, who are employees of the company itself. Boards of mutual fund companies, by way of contrast, cannot manage the fund internally; they hire no employees, but instead contract with the advisor for all operational aspects. Moreover, the Act substantially limits the board's role in setting investment strategy;[62] both structurally and operationally, the advisor controls strategy. Thus, mutual fund boards, as shareholder representatives only—not company directors—make no "business" decisions, and applying the business judgment rule to them makes no conceptual or policy sense. Courts therefore should not invoke that ill-suited doctrine in the mutual fund context.

Boards of mutual fund companies, in relation to investors, more closely reflect what Michael Jensen and William Meckling, in their seminal 1976 work,[63] term a "principal–agent" relationship. Jensen and Meckling, both nonlawyers, articulated an organizational theory to explain, generally, the relationship of shareholders to directors in a business firm. In using the simplifying terminology of principal–agent, they failed to capture legal reality, because corporate directors of operating companies are not

---

[57] *See generally* Morley, *supra* note 4; Fisch, *supra* note 16.
[58] *See generally* Roiter, *supra* 6.
[59] Investment Company Act, § 36(b).
[60] *See, e.g.,* Kahn v. M&F Worldwide Corp, 88 A.3d 635 (Del. 2014). Of course, in § 36(b) litigation such judicial scrutiny has been distressingly absent. *See also* Johnson, *supra* note 3.
[61] In many nonpublic companies there is considerable overlap of directors and managers.
[62] *See* Roiter, *supra* note 6 at 19–23.
[63] Michael C. Jensen & William H. Meckling, *Theory of the Firm: Managerial Behavior, Agency Costs and Ownership Structure*, 3 J. FIN. ECON. 305, 309 (1976).

agents of shareholders or of the companies they direct.[64] But in the mutual fund organizational structure, even though directors are not subject to direct control by shareholders, they have no purpose other than to advance investor interests and are much closer to Jensen and Meckling's conception of an "agent" for their "principal" (investors) than is a corporate board.

The board, functionally, mediates between the investors qua investors and the advisor. It represents the collective interests of the investors, and is to act on their behalf and solely in their best interest. It should be the consummate investor advocate, and, exercising broad discretionary power over the investors' nonexit relationship to the advisor via the advisory contract, the board stands in a fiduciary relationship and owes fiduciary duties.[65] Conceiving of boards in this way gives far sharper focus to their role—and the challenges they face—than does the faulty notion that they somehow govern a "company."

Conceiving of the mutual fund board as a representative (or agent) of investors via the vehicle of the fund itself accomplishes several purposes. First, it more realistically describes the narrowed function of the board than does the faulty business corporation director analogy. Second, it accounts for the persistent institutional and marketplace reality that mutual fund boards exist, however roundly criticized and constrained they may be. Third, of necessity, given an enduring fund structure employing external advisors, someone must, on behalf of investors, negotiate the advisory contract, lest the conflicted advisor simply set its own fee; that someone is the board. Fourth, and relatedly, as a fiduciary the advisor is better able to sustain a fee against investor attack if it bargained over that fee with an independent representative who itself is a fiduciary.[66] Fifth, although § 36(b) has proven to be a very anemic ex post remedial provision, likely the customary negotiating ritual between boards and advisors has generated industry norms and a culture that overall are better for investors than would be the case with unilateral advisor fee setting. And these norms can, in theory, constrain advisors and bolster board bargaining power ex ante. Finally, however easy fund-to-fund fee comparison is for most reasonably savvy investors, it appears that many mutual fund investors do not shop for low fee providers because high-fee funds continue to exist and continue to hold substantial assets,[67] notwithstanding recent inroads by passive low fee funds.[68] Thus, competition alone appears not to uniformly drive down fees. Therefore, the board, within acknowledged constraints, may be able to exert pressure to constrain or reduce fees in higher fee funds in a way market forces alone do not. A board-centered approach, however, whatever the arguments for

---

[64] *See* David Millon, *Radical Shareholder Primacy*, 10 U. St. Thomas L. J. 1013, 1022–23 (2014).

[65] *See* Ernest J. Weinrib, *The Fiduciary Obligation*, 25 U. Toronto L. J. 1 (1975) (explaining the rationale for a relationship being fiduciary in nature); but *see* Investment Company Act, § 36(a) (SEC may bring action only where breach of fiduciary duty involved personal misconduct).

[66] This is not to say that courts have done a good job on this point in the § 36(b) fee litigation context, because they have not, as discussed in section 2 of this chapter.

[67] *See* Morley and Curtis, *supra* note 12 at 109.

[68] This is described in section 4 of this chapter.

preserving efforts on this front, is inadequate by itself for assuring investor protection, and is only one component of a multifaceted strategy aimed at that goal.

3.3 Investor-Focused Efforts

Notwithstanding the SEC's modern return to focusing on boards as a pivotal means for enhancing investor protection, both the SEC and the Act itself have also emphasized investor-focused efforts. Although investors have long had certain voting rights and, since 1970, a potential claim against the advisor for excessive fees, these are of little governance or disciplinary significance. Other corporate accountability forces, such as a market for corporate control, activist institutional investors, and performance-based management compensation, are also largely absent from the mutual fund industry. Today, the investor redemption right is of paramount importance, and other investor-focused efforts have stagnated and need bolstering.

3.3.1 Voting and exit

Although the Act requires an investor vote on the advisory contract, this measure for protecting investors is sidestepped at the fund's formation by the advisor voting, as the initial investor, to approve the contract. Advisory contracts can be extended without an investor vote if independent directors annually vote to approve the agreement. Incumbent directors also may fill board vacancies as long as, thereafter, at least two-thirds of fund directors are elected by investors.[69] Any change in advisor, fees, or investment policies, however, would require a vote of existing investors.[70] This itself likely constrains a board's willingness to terminate, or threaten to terminate, an advisor in negotiations. The Act does not require annual shareholder meetings, and investor voting initiatives and director election contests are virtually unknown.[71] In short, investor suffrage plays a limited role in protecting mutual fund investors.

Mutual fund investors, unlike shareholders in regular business corporations, can withdraw cash from the fund by exchanging their securities. This redemption right is, in practice,[72] available on a daily basis and, in essence, means investors have a standing "put" option to liquidate their position. Professor Morley has argued at length that this exit right is the "dominant" investor strategy; that it almost completely eliminates investor incentives to use board representation, voting, and fee litigation; and that, therefore, those approaches are of limited value.[73] Assessing, on a cost/benefit basis, a disgruntled investor's choices among exit, activism, or doing nothing, Morley concludes that exit and doing nothing are more likely than an activist voting strategy.[74]

---

[69] Investment Company Act, § 16(a).
[70] Id., §§ 13(a)(3), 15(a).
[71] See Morley, *supra* note 4 at 57.
[72] As Professor Morley notes, the Act mandates only that investors be permitted to withdraw funds within seven days of demand: Investment Company Act, § 22(e); but, in practice, almost all funds permit daily redemption. Morley (2014) at 1247, n. 42.
[73] See Morley & Curtis, *supra* note 12, at 102–19; *and* Morley, *supra* note 4, at 10.
[74] See Morley, *supra* note 4, at 1251. Mutual funds themselves, however, are increasingly joining activists in seeking change at U.S. companies. David Benoit and Kirsten Grind, Activists' Secret Ally: Big Mutual Funds, WALL ST. J., Aug. 10, 2015, at A1.

Morley's analysis illuminates why activism is not an attractive option for investors, but it does not explain why some dissatisfied investors do nothing while others exit. These are starkly different responses and open the door to the need for other approaches to investor protection, given this phenomenon. As Morley acknowledges,[75] and an SEC study has confirmed, evidence establishes that some investors neglect their investments, with such inaction resulting in "sticky" fund assets, or they choose funds for the wrong reasons. This seems to be a significant behavioral hurdle to exclusive reliance on exit as a protective mechanism.

Moreover, even less supine mutual fund investors may not be as vigilant or adept as easy exit implies. Investors may exit for the wrong reasons, just as they may stay invested in pricey or underperforming funds for too long. And investors who exit cannot prevent already incurred high fees, wrongdoing, or poor performance, nor can they easily detect the latter two elements on an ongoing basis. Their exit option largely, at least from a dissatisfaction standpoint, is past-looking; it treats a problem but does not necessarily prevent it. And determining where to put funds, once withdrawn, requires time, effort, and study of the manifold possible investment options—itself daunting for many, and likely one factor leading to inertia for many investors. Exit is powerful and attractive, but it is not a panacea.

3.4 § 36(b) Litigation

3.4.1 Unlikely ex post remedies; ex ante norm shaping

After decades of a board-centered approach to investor protection, as supplemented by investor exit and voting rights, in 1970 Congress sought to bolster the investor-oriented approach.[76] Congress added § 36(b), which creates a cause of action against the investment advisor for excessive fees. This followed a 1966 study by the SEC that concluded it was "unrealistic" to believe independent directors could protect investors in their fee negotiations with the advisor,[77] for the simple reason that directors cannot realistically threaten to terminate the advisor, thus weakening their bargaining position.[78]

Section 36(b) specifies that an investment advisor of a registered investment company "shall be deemed to have a fiduciary duty with respect to the receipt of compensation for services."[79] The section provides that the SEC or a security holder of the company, but not the company itself, may bring an action on behalf of the company against the advisor or any affiliated person "for breach of fiduciary duty in respect of such compensation or payments paid by such registered investment company or by the security holders thereof to such adviser or person."[80] Strictly speaking, the action is not

---

[75] See Morley and Curtis, *supra* note 12 at 114.
[76] Investment Company Act of 1970 § 36, 15 U.S.C. § 80a-35(b).
[77] H.R. Rep. No. 89-2337, at 148 (1966).
[78] *Id.* at 131. Of course, in the early 2000s, the SEC once again argued that independent directors were important to investor protection. See *supra* notes 39–43 and accompanying text.
[79] Investment Company Amendments Act of 1970 § 36(b), 15 U.S.C. § 80a-35(b) (2000).
[80] *Id.*

a "derivative" action because the company itself cannot initiate a lawsuit.[81] This frees an investor from any need to make a demand on the board of directors before beginning the suit.[82] Section 36(b)(1) mandates that the plaintiff "shall have the burden of proving a breach of fiduciary duty."[83] Personal misconduct, however, is not an element of the claim.[84] No action may be brought against a person who is not the recipient of compensation, and any award of damages against such recipient is limited to actual damages resulting from the breach of fiduciary duty; punitive damages may not be recovered.[85] Damages cannot be recovered for any period prior to one year before the action is commenced.[86] Federal courts have exclusive jurisdiction,[87] and there is no right to a jury trial.[88]

In sum, as noted by the Supreme Court:[89] in 1970 Congress adopted a twofold regulatory approach to advisor conflicts. This strategy relied in part on "the structural requirement" of disinterested director negotiation with the investment advisor under § 15, and in part on meaningful private fiduciary duty litigation initiated by investors under § 36(b).[90] The court described this as a "policy choice" to provide "independent checks on excessive fees."[91]

Section 36(b) has been a remedial failure. No investor ever has obtained a verdict, and the SEC apparently has brought only two cases under that section, the latest in 1980.[92] The Second Circuit laid out a six-factor test to guide statutory analysis in the seminal case of *Gartenberg v. Merrill Lynch Asset Management*,[93] a test somewhat modified by the Supreme Court in 2010 in *Jones v. Harris Associates L.P.*[94] But in the several years since *Jones*,[95] no investor has yet obtained a verdict under § 36(b), and, although some cases settle, most end through defendants' motions to dismiss or motions for summary judgment.[96]

---

[81] *Id.*; *Daily Income Fund, Inc. v. Fox*, 464 U.S. 523 (1984).
[82] *Fox*, 464 U.S. at 527–28.
[83] 15 U.S.C. § 80a-35(b)(1).
[84] *Id.*
[85] *Id.* § 80a-35(b)(3).
[86] *Id.*
[87] *Id.* § 80a-35(b)(5).
[88] *Krinsk v. Fund Asset Management, Inc.*, 875 F.2d 404 (2d Cir. 1989).
[89] *Fox*, 464 U.S. at 538–41.
[90] *Id.*
[91] *Id.* at 541.
[92] James G. Cavoli, et al., *The SEC's Mutual Fund Fee Initiative: What to Expect*, 16 SEC. LITIG. & REG., Issue 14, at p. 2, nn. 8–9 (2010).
[93] Gartenberg v. Merrill Lynch Asset Mgmt., Inc., 694 F.2d 923 (2nd Cir. 1982).
[94] *Jones v. Harris Associates L. P.*, 559 U.S. 333 (2010). The Court indicated that courts may compare an advisor's fees charged to retail investors with the advisor's fees to institutional clients. 559 U.S. at 349.
[95] On remand from the Supreme Court in *Jones*, the Seventh Circuit again entered summary judgment for the defendants. 611 Fed. App'x. 359 (7th Cir. 2015).
[96] In an August 2015 decision, one federal district court did deny defendants' motion for summary judgment in the first "manager of managers" case to reach that stage where plaintiff challenged fees charged by an advisor that delegated substantial duties to subadvisors. *Sivolella v. AXA Equitable Insurance Co.* No. 3:11-CV-04194 (D. N. J. 2015).

156 *Research handbook on the regulation of mutual funds*

The threat of § 36(b) litigation may have a salutary ex ante constraining effect on advisory fees, but behavioral deterrence of excessive fees would be far stronger with at least an occasional outright investor victory. A liability section that never leads to verdicts should be reassessed, either to be scrapped as a failure or to be bolstered. Several changes are in order.

3.4.2 Reform

First, the SEC should initiate § 36(b) claims or suggest the section's repeal. Its failure to pursue claims indicates either a lack of belief in the section or a misguided belief that private litigation is sufficient. The agency should address this supposedly core feature of regulatory strategy, and it can do so without heeding faulty assertions that its actions would comprise rate regulation of advisory fees.[97] Second, as this author has argued (Johnson 2008), courts using the *Gartenberg* factors should be far more demanding as to what constitutes an "independent" director, and place the burden of production of evidence (not the ultimate burden of proof) on the advisor with respect to this factor under § 36(b)(2).[98] Doing so will help judicial review of mutual fund litigation catch up with corporate governance norms that have outstripped lagging mutual fund practices. The Supreme Court in *Jones* noted that a measure of deference to the mutual fund board was appropriate only depending on circumstances; a nonindependent board should receive little or no judicial deference. Third, the current remedy under § 36(b), being restitutionary in nature, simply requires restoration of ill-gotten gains and does not sufficiently compensate investors or deter advisors. The sanction should be stiffened.[99] Fourth, the investment advisor can readily be characterized as an agent of the mutual fund, thereby owing the array of duties, including loyalty, automatically owed by an agent to its principal.[100] This affords additional remedies and applies to subadvisors and portfolio managers as well; as subagents, they too owe an ultimate duty of loyalty to fund investors.[101] Fifth, arbitration of § 36(b) claims is worth a try, either on a voluntary or pilot program basis. Perhaps investors will fare no better but they will likely fare no worse. Of course, neither advisors nor plaintiffs' lawyers may be keen on this change if it is perceived as adverse to their interests. Finally, recovery under § 36(b) should go to the affected investors, not to the fund itself, as the damage incurred and recovery obtained are mismatched when the fund recovers. After all, the important exit right is an individual investor right and excessive fees directly damage investors who may have exited the fund, as well as those who stayed in, while they are a windfall to later investors. Therefore, an action to

---

[97] The SEC, but not private investors, may also bring an aiding and abetting action against those who substantially assist another in violating § 36(b) or other provisions of the Company Act. Dodd–Frank Wall Street Reform and Consumer Protection Act, 55. Pub. L. No. 111-203, § 929M (2010).
[98] *See* Johnson, *supra* note 3, at 527.
[99] For a description of various remedies available upon a breach of fiduciary duties, *see* Deborah A. DeMott, *Disloyal Agents*, 58 ALA. L. REV. 1049, 1056–61 (2007).
[100] RESTATEMENT (THIRD) OF AGENCY § 8.01–§ 8.13 (2006) (describing agent's duties).
[101] *Id.* at § 3.15(i) & cmt. d (defining subagent and its duty of loyalty).

recover damages should be direct in nature and the verdict/settlement should be paid to affected investors to align the damage and remedy.[102]

Overall, § 36(b) has not lived up to its promise.

3.5 Ongoing Regulation by the SEC

The regulatory philosophy of the Company Act differs markedly from that of state corporate law and that of other federal securities laws, such as the Securities Act of 1933 and the Securities Exchange Act of 1934. State corporate law leaves most important decisions in the hands of boards of directors, with very little substantive regulation or constraint. The Securities Act and the Exchange Act likewise impose few substantive constraints, largely relying instead on a policy approach of full disclosure.

In sharp contrast, the Act contains extensive regulatory mandates from which only the SEC, not the mutual fund board, may grant exemptive relief. For example, most fund transactions with advisors are prohibited, capital structures are restricted (as by forbidding preferred stock and limiting leverage),[103] and the pricing and process of distributing securities are regulated. The SEC alone may provide waivers and exemptions.[104] This reflects the dominance of the advisor-primacy model of governance over the board-primacy one, as further augmented by requiring direct governmental approval, rather than board consent or investor approval. Too, it credits easy entrance and exit by investors as conveying some level of satisfaction with or relief from fund activities, but at the same time it reflects deep suspicion of board judgments on key issues even as boards are entrusted with the most critical issue of all—the advisor contract.

The severity of this regulatory approach has been used by the SEC as a lever to advance its reform agenda. Thus, in order to obtain exemptions from ten rules[105]—including that for Rule 12b-1 fees—mutual funds must comply with the SEC's "suggested" governance standards, including a board with a majority of independent directors, independent counsel for those directors, mandatory quarterly executive sessions, and so on.

Government regulation of mutual funds is inescapably extensive and ongoing, rather than episodic, both because of board weakness due to inherent dependence on the advisor and rational investor apathy toward governance efforts due to easy exit. For the SEC, the key policy question is where, in a dynamic and complex industry, the agency can most effectively focus its efforts at any particular time, in light of investment trends (such as, for example, the emergence of alternative mutual funds following hedge fund-like strategies) and shifting market conditions. This requires, first of all, gathering "market intelligence," not just systemically but with specific respect to large numbers

---

[102] Northstar Financial Advisors Inc. v. Schwab Investments, 779 F.3d 1036 (9th Cir. 2015) (describing recent Ninth Circuit case ruling that investors may bring a direct action in a non-§ 36(b) context).

[103] Professor Morley has argued in favor of permitting debt/leverage by funds. *See generally* John Morley, *The Regulation of Mutual Fund Debt*, 30 YALE J. REG. 343 (2013).

[104] Investment Company Act, § 6(c). *See also* Act, §§ 17(a), (b).

[105] For a list of these rules, *see* Roiter, *supra* note 6 at n. 175.

of individual providers. Much focus here, rightly, should be on rules directed at, and frequent investigations of, the advisor itself, under the Investment Advisor Act,[106] both because of advisor importance and because the most significant advisors are far fewer in number than mutual funds themselves. But companies themselves, according to SEC Chair Mary Jo White,[107] must provide the agency and investors with more data on fund investment in derivatives, liquidity, securities lending practices, and valuation of their holdings. Toward this end, in May 2015 the SEC proposed new rules requiring monthly reporting by mutual funds on their use of derivatives contracts, to aid investors in identifying fund-specific risk and the SEC in monitoring industrywide risk.[108] In addition, the proposed rules require greater disclosure with respect to fund securities lending practices, liquidity and valuation of portfolio holdings, and certain basic risk metrics relating to fund exposure to changes in asset prices.[109] The SEC also proposed liquidity risk management rules in September 2015. Among other requirements, a new proposed Rule 22e-4 would require funds to establish a liquidity risk management program and determine a minimum percentage of assets that must be converted to cash within three days.[110] A Department of Labor Rule imposing a uniform fiduciary duty standard on investment advisors and broker-dealers serving retirement accounts was also adopted, but was struck down in federal court.[111] And of course, new money market rules were adopted in July 2014 and phased in starting in July 2015.[112] They require certain institutional funds to price and transact at a "floating" net asset value (NAV), charge liquidity fees, and impose redemption gates temporarily limiting withdrawals during periods of market stress.

The SEC's role in mutual fund regulation goes beyond formal rulemaking. The agency also provides extensive ex ante guidance, both informally and through no-action letters and regular Investment Management Guidance Updates. The latter provide clarification and advice, offer staff summaries, occasionally carry stern admonitions, and frequently address significant matters such as the unbundling of proxy proposals and the nature and presentation of prospectus disclosures, along with the usual run of agency reminders.

Finally, ex post enforcement of the Act and agency rules by the SEC through its Asset Management Unit is essential. Private investor litigation, as noted, is largely ineffective from a remedial standpoint. The SEC is more nimble, has greater resources

---

[106] The Investment Advisers Act of 1940, codified at 15 U.S.C. § 80b-1 through 80b-21.

[107] Mary Jo White, Chair, Enhancing Risk Monitoring and Regulatory Safeguards for the Asset Management Industry, Address at the *New York Times* Dealbook Opportunities for Tomorrow Conference (Dec. 11, 2014), *available at* www.sec.gov/News/Speech/Detail/Speech/1370543677722.

[108] Investment Company Reporting Modernization, Investment Company Act Release No. 31,610, 80 Fed. Reg. 33,589 (May 20, 2015).

[109] *Id.*

[110] SEC, Open-End Liquidity Risk Management Programs, Investment Company Act Release No. 31835 (September 22, 2015).

[111] Chamber of Commerce v. U.S. Department of Labor, 885 F.3d 360 (5th Cir. 2018).

[112] *Money Market Fund Reform: Amendments to Form PF*, Investment Company Act Release No. 31166 (July 23, 2014). *See* Michael Caccase, et al., *SEC Adopts Final Rules Governing the Structure and Operation of Money Market Funds*, 21 INV. LAW. 1, 4–16 (2014).

and regulatory leverage to pursue sanctions for wrongdoing, and can engage in informal "rulemaking through enforcement." That sustained agency initiatives in fund enforcement activities are needed can be seen in the ongoing, egregious nature of many practices in this industry. For example, early in 2015 three advisors were sanctioned for falsely reporting a basic metric, "assets under management."[113] And in April 2015 BlackRock agreed to be censured and pay a penalty under the Act because one of its top portfolio managers formed a joint venture with a public company held in his managed funds, a remarkable fact not disclosed to the fund's board of directors or its clients.[114] Investors, of course—and likely boards themselves—simply are unable to detect this kind of intra-advisor wrongdoing.

As with all government enforcement, the recurrent issue is selecting priorities. Advisor conflicts of interest are, as recently described by the cochief of the Asset Management Unit, an "overarching, perennial priority."[115] Again, this simply acknowledges the reality of board failure and investor ineptitude in policing this basic problem. A steady flow of fund wrongdoings such as deviating from investment guidelines, pursuing undisclosed investment strategies, overstating performance of and assets under management, and finding creative ways to use fund assets to pay intermediaries outside of a fund's Rule 12b-1 plan, as seen in the SEC's 2015 Distribution-in-Guise Initiative,[116] to cite a few, all ensure that direct government oversight of mutual fund activity in the name of investor protection will not disappear soon.

3.6 The Competition Debate: Constraints; Passive Low Fee Funds

The debate about the degree to which competitive forces in the mutual fund industry serve to protect investors is longstanding and ongoing. Certain factors, as a theoretical matter, might serve to align investor and advisor interests without regulatory (or at least without additional regulatory) intervention. For example, the mutual fund industry is said to be competitive, with more than 7,700 funds in existence at the end of 2013. Advisors seeking to enhance their reputations in order to attract greater fund inflows and facilitate their own advancement in the advisor labor market have an incentive to perform well on behalf of investors. The ability of investors to redeem mutual fund shares at net asset value also may impose discipline on fund managers because investors can exit the fund without dampening the price of fund shares. These factors lead some, such as Professor Paul Mahoney and Professors John Coates and Glenn

---

[113] Peter D. Fetzer, *Recent SEC Enforcement Actions Target False Reporting by Investment Advisers regarding Assets under Management*, LEXOLOGY (April 30, 2015), www.lexology.com/library/detail.aspx?g=57a60dc7-ee31-4250-92d2-34b0965371d3.

[114] Philip Shecter, *Investment Adviser Conflicts of Interest—Blackrock Censured; Compliance Officer Personally Liable*, LEXOLOGY (April 21, 2015).

[115] Julie M. Riewe, Speech, *Conflicts, Conflicts Everywhere*, Feb. 26, 2015, available at www.sec.gov/news/speech/conflicts-everywhere-full-360-view.html#.VRsP7phO4-A.

[116] In September 2015, the SEC charged First Eagle Investment with improperly using fund assets to pay distribution expenses, outside the company's board-adopted 12b-1 plan. First Eagle settled for about $40 million. SEC Press Release 2015-198, SEC Charges Investment Adviser With Improperly Using Mutual Fund Assets to Pay Distribution Expenses, www.sec.gov/news/pressrelease/2015-198.html.

Hubbard,[117] to argue that fund markets are "consistent with competition,"[118] and thus to favor reliance on competition as a means for reducing the adverse effects of investor–advisor conflicts.

The competitive goal for fund providers is to maximize the assets under management, because advisory fees are set as a percentage of that number. High performance and/or low expense ratios may be a means to that end—though they are not necessarily so—but the goal itself is substantial assets under management. From the investor's perspective, the goal is net gain, which is simply investment returns minus expenses. Theoretically then, the competition argument goes, investor assets should flow to those funds that offer the best gains, via a combination of investment performance and/or low expenses. Those funds, then having more assets under management, will in turn necessarily generate higher fees for their advisors.

As noted in an important SEC study, however, several constraints may inhibit the effectiveness of competitive forces in mitigating conflicts between investors and advisors.[119] These include lack of investor knowledge about management and how to assess managerial skill; high search and switching costs in fund selection; tax considerations on selling shares; and excessive reliance on reputation, trends, and recommendations. To many, these constraints demonstrate substantial shortcomings in a strategy relying only on market forces to align investor and advisor interests.[120] For example, one study found that Morningstar rankings are inaccurate predictors of future fund performance,[121] yet investors may still chase performance. Moreover, Professor Langevoort has identified several other ways in which market forces, possibly at work to some degree in corporate law, are lacking in the mutual fund industry.[122] Salient differences include the lack of stock or stock option grants to align investor and management interests, the absence of active institutional investors advocating governance reforms, the absence (at least in mutual funds, though not in closed-end funds) of a market for corporate control (that is, no hostile takeovers), and manager compensation based on the value of assets (that is, size, not performance). Overall, these features may lead to mutual fund assets being "sticky" rather than mobile, as market

---

[117] Paul Mahoney, *Manager-Investor Conflicts in Mutual Funds*, 18 J. ECON. PERSP. 161 (2004); John C. Coates IV & R. Glenn Hubbard, *Competition in the Mutual Fund Industry: Evidence and Implications for Policy*, 33 J. CORP. L. 151 (2007).
[118] Coates & Hubbard, *supra* note 117 at 151, 163.
[119] OEA Study, *supra* note 19 at 8–10.
[120] *Id. See* John P. Freeman & Stewart L. Brown, *Mutual Fund Advisory Fees: The Cost of Conflicts of Interest*, 26 J. CORP. L. 609, 651 (2001).
[121] Christopher R. Blake & Matthew R. Morey, *Morningstar Ratings and Mutual Fund Performance*, 35 J. FIN. & QUANTITATIVE ANALYSIS 451 (2000) (noting exceptions for low-rated funds); *see* Alan Palmiter, *The $7 Trillion Question: Mutual Funds & Investor Welfare*, 1 J. BUS. & TECH. L. 23, 26 (2006b) http://digitalcommons.law.umaryland.edu/cgi/viewcontent.cgi?article=1008&context=jbtl ("[T]he [Morningstar] rating is a very powerful predictor of future performance—but negatively!").
[122] *See generally* Langevoort, *supra* note 16.

theory posits.[123] Congress recognized as much in 1970: "But in the mutual fund industry ... these marketplace forces are not likely to operate as effectively."[124]

The regulatory debate invariably centers on whether advisor fees are somehow "excessive" in light of essentially fixed costs, or are simply the natural outgrowth of offering investments that, in aggregate, many investors find attractive. Given capital mobility, coupled with the demise of about 7 percent of funds every year even as new funds emerge,[125] fund managers contend that they face heady competition to hold assets. This dynamic, at least recently, seems to have been at work to some extent. A 2015 Morningstar study reveals that retail investors have gravitated toward lower cost funds such as index funds.[126] In fact, 95 of the 100 lowest cost funds in 2014 were index funds.[127] Vanguard Group, the largest provider of index-tracking funds, gained $216 billion of the $244 billion moved into passively managed funds in 2014.[128] Recently, moreover, passively managed, low fee funds have generally outperformed actively managed, higher fee funds.[129] Whether investors will continue to adhere to a low fee fund strategy if tempted by higher returns from high-fee funds remains unknown. In spite of improved investor understanding that, unlike the children of Lake Wobegon, by definition not all investors can achieve above average returns, many individuals—perhaps a dwindling but still significant number—likely will try.

As noted, moreover, advisors benefit from the higher fee revenue generated simply by the influx of investor assets. Yet, given economies of scale, if costs trail the heightened revenue, overall net fee income increases nonetheless. Thus, for example, overall fee revenue rose 75 percent over the decade prior to 2014, but the asset-weighted expense ratio declined only 27 percent, spurring net income.[130]

Professor Stewart Brown seized on advisor profit margins and other financial measures to support a position he has long advocated: that the mutual fund advisory industry is extraordinarily profitable and such evidence is consistent with a lack of price competition in the industry.[131] Brown sets out specifically to refute the claim of

---

[123] OEA Study, *supra* note 19 at 9. Professor Sendhil Mullainathan observes that "investors often choose what to do with their money once, and leave it there for a long time." *Investing in the Dark*, N.Y. TIMES, July 12, 2015, BU 11.

[124] S. REP. NO. 91-184, 5 (1970), as reprinted in 1970 U.S.C.C.A.N. 4897, 4901.

[125] Silverblatt, *supra* note 46 (citing numbers provided by John Bogle).

[126] Jeff Sommer, *Fees on Mutual Funds Fall. Thank Yourself*, N.Y. TIMES, May 10, 2015 at B3 (describing the Morningstar report, "2015 Fee Study: Investors Are Driving Expense Ratios Down").

[127] *Id.* Professor Mullainathan notes, however, that index funds can have as much variability in fees as actively managed funds. Mullainathan, *supra* note 123.

[128] Kirsten Grind, *Vanguard Sets Record Funds Inflow*, WALL ST. J., Jan. 4, 2015. Through October 2015, Vanguard had taken in an additional $196 billion of investor cash and was on pace to exceed its record-breaking 2014 performance. Sarah Krouse, Vanguard Group Took in $196 billion of Investor Cash through October, WALL ST. J., Nov. 15, 2015, www.wsj.com/articles/vanguard-group-took-in-196-billion-of-investor-cash-through-october-1447440046.

[129] Grind, *Id.*

[130] Sommer, *supra* note 126.

[131] Stewart L. Brown, *Gartenberg: Some Empirical Clarity* 17 (2015) *retrieved from* http://ssrn.com/abstract=2616347.

Coates and Hubbard that mutual fund markets are "consistent with" competition.[132] Citing industrywide data on operating profit margins, along with other profitability and return on equity metrics for a subset of publicly traded firms providing advisory services, Brown concludes that the growth in assets under management, without corresponding fee reductions, is not "consistent with" price competition.[133]

He argues too that a significant percentage of mutual fund investors are not knowledgeable about fund fees and that we do not know what percentage of total fund assets are fee sensitive. Although Morley and Curtis argue that what matters most is that at least some funds are competitive,[134] from a regulatory standpoint that still leaves many investors consistently paying high fees, and there remains the persistent policy challenge of what, if anything, to do about that fact. Brown's study, and expected forthcoming industry counterarguments, will keep the competition debate alive and unresolved for at least the near future, if not long beyond.

4 CONCLUSION

The unsettled competition debate, along with dynamic industry flux, occurs quite apart from the intrepid activities of investment company boards and the SEC. Both bodies are equipped to curb certain advisor abuses and they can help shape more salutary institutional norms and practices, but they cannot finetune fees or change investor behavior. And § 36(b) litigation as it stands today may shape industry norms ex ante, but it is of little remedial significance to fees and capital flows, leaving exit as the key investor-oriented protection. Still, however flawed, the Act's eclectic approach to protecting mutual fund investors seems likely to endure both on pragmatic grounds and for lack of a demonstrably better approach.

BIBLIOGRAPHY

Barnett, Larry D. (2006), "When Is a Mutual Fund Director Independent? The Unexplored Role of Professional Relationships under Section 2(a)(19) of the Investment Company Act," *DePaul Business & Commercial Law Journal*, 4, 155–88.
Birdthistle, William A. (2006), "Compensating Power: An Analysis of Rents and Rewards in the Mutual Fund Industry," *Tulane Law Review*, 80, 1401–65.
Birdthistle, William A. (2010), "Investment Indiscipline: A Behavioral Approach to Mutual Fund Jurisprudence," *University of Illinois Law Review*, 2010, 61–108.
Blake, Christopher R. & Matthew R. Morey (2000), "Morningstar Ratings and Mutual Fund Performance," *Journal of Financial and Quantitative Analysis*, 35, 451–83.
Brown, Stewart L. (2015), "Gartenberg: Some Empirical Clarity," retrieved from http://ssrn.com/abstract=2616347.
Bullard, Mercer (2006), "The Mutual Fund as a Firm: Frequent Trading, Fund Arbitrage and the SEC's Response to the Mutual Fund Scandal," *Houston Law Review*, 41, 1271–1331.
Bullard, Mercer (2008), "Regulating Hedge Fund Managers: The Investment Company Act as a Regulatory Screen," *Stanford Journal of Law, Business & Finance*, 13, 286–333.

---

[132] *Id.*; *see also* Coates & Hubbard, *supra* note 117.
[133] Brown, *supra* note 131, at 39.
[134] *See* Morley & Curtis, *supra* note 12.

Coates, John C. IV & R. Glenn Hubbard (2007), "Competition in the Mutual Fund Industry: Evidence and Implications for Policy," *Journal of Corporation Law*, 33, 151–222.

Cox, James D. & John W. Payne (2005), "Mutual Fund Expense Disclosures: A Behavioral Perspective," *Washington University Law Quarterly*, 83, 907–38.

DeMott, Deborah A. (2007), "Disloyal Agents," *Alabama Law Review*, 58, 1049–68.

Fisch, Jill E. (2010), "Rethinking the Regulation of Securities Intermediaries," *University of Pennsylvania Law Review*, 158, 1961–2041.

Frankel, Tamar & Ann Taylor Schwing (2004), *The Regulation of Money Managers: Mutual Funds and Advisers* (2nd ed.), Gaithersburg, MD: Wolters Kluwer Law & Business.

Freeman, John P. & Stewart L. Brown (2001), "Mutual Fund Advisory Fees: The Cost of Conflicts of Interest," *Journal of Corporation Law*, 26, 609–73.

Freeman, John P., Stewart L. Brown, & Steve Pomerantz (2008), "Mutual Fund Advisory Fees: New Evidence and a Fair Fiduciary Duty Test," *Oklahoma Law Review*, 61, 83–153.

Graber, Sean & John J. O'Brien (2015), "A Director's Guide to Understanding Liquidity Fee and Redemption Gate Responsibilities," *The Investment Lawyer*, May 2015, 1–11.

Hubbard, R. Glenn, Michael F. Koehn, Stanley I. Ornstein, Marc Van Audenrode, & Jimmy Royer (2010), *The Mutual Fund Industry: Competition and Investor Welfare*, New York: Columbia Business School Publishing.

Hurst, Thomas R. (2005), "The Unfinished Business of Mutual Fund Reform," *Pace Law Review*, 26, 133–54.

Jensen, Michael C. & William H. Meckling (1976), "Theory of the Firm: Managerial Behavior, Agency Costs and Ownership Structure," *Journal of Financial Economics*, 3, 305–60.

Johnson, Lyman (2008), "A Fresh Look at Director 'Independence': Mutual Fund Fee Litigation and Gartenberg at Twenty-Five," *Vanderbilt Law Review*, 61, 497–542.

Kong, Sophie Xiaofei & Dragon Yongjun Tang (2008), "Unitary Boards and Mutual Fund Governance," *Journal of Financial Research*, 31, 193–224.

Krug, Anita (2013), "Investment Company as Instrument: The Limitations of the Corporate Governance Regulatory Paradigm," *Southern California Law Review*, 86, 263–319.

Langevoort, Donald C. (2005), "Private Litigation to Enforce Fiduciary Duties in Mutual Funds: Derivative Suits, Disinterested Directors and the Ideology of Investor Sovereignty," *Washington University Law Quarterly*, 83, 1017–44.

Lybecker, Martin E. (2005), "Enhanced Corporate Governance for Mutual Funds: A Flawed Concept that Deserves Serious Reconsideration," *Washington University Law Quarterly*, 83, 1045–93.

Mahoney, Paul (2004), "Manager–Investor Conflicts in Mutual Funds," *Journal of Economic Perspectives*, 18, 161–82.

Markham, Jerry W. (2006), "Mutual Fund Scandals—A Comparative Analysis of the Role of Corporate Governance in the Regulation of Collective Investments," *Hastings Business Law Journal*, 3, 67–155.

Millon, David (2014), "Radical Shareholder Primacy," *University of St. Thomas Law Review*, 10, 1013–44.

Morley, John (2013), "The Regulation of Mutual Fund Debt," *Yale Journal on Regulation*, 30, 343–76.

Morley, John (2014), "The Separation of Funds and Managers: A Theory of Investment Fund Structure and Regulation," *Yale Law Journal*, 123, 1228–87.

Morley, John & Quinn Curtis (2010), "Taking Exit Rights Seriously: Why Governance and Fee Litigation Don't Work in Mutual Funds," *Yale Law Journal*, 120, 84–142.

Nagy, Donna M. (2006), "Regulating the Mutual Fund Industry," *Brooklyn Journal of Corporate, Financial & Commercial Law*, 1, 11–44.

Palmiter, Alan (2006a), "Conference, The $7 Trillion Question: Mutual Funds & Investor Welfare," *Journal of Business & Technology Law*, 1, 23–43.

Palmiter, Alan (2006b), "The Mutual Fund Board: A Failed Experiment in Regulatory Outsourcing," *Brooklyn Journal of Corporate, Financial & Commercial Law*, 1, 165–208.

Ribstein, Larry (2010), "Federal Misgovernance of Mutual Funds," *Cato Supreme Court Review*, 2010, 301–32.

Roiter, Eric D. (2015), "Disentangling Mutual Fund Governance from Corporate Governance," *Harvard Business Law Review*, 5, retrieved from http://ssrn.com/abstract=2568392.

Warburton, A. Joseph (2008), "Should Mutual Funds Be Corporations? A Legal & Econometric Analysis," *Journal of Corporation Law*, 33, 745–76.

Weinrib, Ernest J. (1975), "The Fiduciary Obligation," *University of Toronto Law Journal*, 25, 1–22.

Yeung, Amy Y. & Kristen J. Freeman (2010), "Gartenberg, Jones, and the Meaning of Fiduciary: A Legislative Investigation of Section 36(b)," *Delaware Journal of Corporate Law*, 35, 483–513.

7. The past and present of mutual fund fee litigation under section 36(b)
Quinn Curtis

Section 36(b) of the Investment Company Act permits mutual fund investors to sue funds for charging excessive asset management fees. This liability for excessive fees has proven to be one of the more problematic areas of mutual fund regulation.[1] Fund complexes view the suits largely as unpredictable nuisances unrelated to fee levels, while for those concerned about mutual fund fees, section 36(b) has never resulted in a verdict for plaintiffs. The extremely factbound nature of the excessive fee standard as articulated in the seminal *Gartenberg* and *Jones* cases makes obtaining early dismissal of suits difficult and litigation lengthy and expensive.[2] Settlements are common. There is little evidence that suits are effective in bringing fees down in sued funds or that such suits target particularly expensive funds.[3]

The goal of this chapter is to situate new developments in mutual fund fee litigation in the larger context of the history and development of section 36(b). Many of the problems that have plagued the operation of 36(b) are traceable to the compromises, limitations, and ambiguities that resulted from the competing efforts of the SEC and Investment Company Institute (ICI) during the adoption of the 1970 amendments. I argue that the *Gartenberg* standard, as essentially approved in *Jones*, reflects the type of liability that the SEC hoped to create when it encouraged Congress to enact 36(b) as part of the 1970 amendments. In particular, it was clearly the intention of the SEC to put most of the fund industry in play for potential fee suits and to give little weight to the fees of comparable funds or the approval of fees by boards. But the absence of clear guidance for courts evaluating fees, combined with the stringent standard for finding funds actually liable, has led to a "worst of all worlds" arrangement in which strike suits are hard to dismiss, but meritorious suits are almost impossible to win. The result has been a litigation environment dominated for much of the section's history by less than credible claims.

Attention to 36(b) is timely because the industry is in the midst of a new wave of mutual fund fee suits characterized by novel theories of liability based on subadvisory agreements.[4] These new suits take up *Jones*'s implicit invitation for plaintiffs to rely on comparisons between mutual fund fees and other types of money management, but they raise a number of potential concerns.

---

[1] For criticism of Section 36(b) see Curtis and Morley (2015); Coates (2010); Henderson (2010); Johnsen (2010); and Ribstein (2010).
[2] Gartenberg v. Merrill Lynch Asset Mgmt., Inc., 694 F.2d 923, 928 (2d Cir. 1982); Jones v. Harris Assocs. L.P., 559 U.S. 335 (2010).
[3] Curtis and Morley (2014).
[4] ICI Mutual (2016). These cases are discussed in more detail in section 4.

The chapter proceeds by reviewing the history of the adoption of 36(b) in section 1 and the major developments in its judicial interpretation, in section 2. Section 3 outlines how 36(b) has tended to function in practice and section 4 discusses recent developments since the *Jones* case. Section 5 concludes.

1 THE ORIGINS OF 36(b)

The shortcomings of contemporary 36(b) litigation are rooted in issues that arose as the section was being drafted and have never been truly resolved. It is therefore helpful to begin with the origins of the section.[5] Section 36(b) provides for a unique form of securities liability. Unlike most claims in securities law, liability under 36(b) arises not from inaccurate or incomplete disclosure, but from a determination that a mutual fund's expenses, though fully disclosed, were unjustifiably high. The threshold for liability is not expressed as a cap, or even in terms of reasonableness, but instead takes the form of a fiduciary duty flowing from the mutual fund adviser, the recipient of the management fee, to the mutual fund itself. Thus a mutual fund adviser is placed in the position of owing a fiduciary duty to its counterparty in setting its own compensation. It is perhaps not surprising that such a standard for liability arose out of a legislative compromise.

1.1 Growing Concerns about Fund Fees

Section 36(b) has its roots in the explosive growth of the mutual fund industry in the 1950s and early 1960s.[6] The eventual adoption of 36(b) can be traced to the confluence of two factors. First, state law mechanisms that might have provided an outlet for fund investors to challenge fees as excessive were judicially limited in ways that made them, in the view of industry critics, an ineffective check on fund costs. Second, as more and more money flowed into the relatively small number of open-ended funds available at the time, concern grew that portfolio managers were receiving ever growing compensation for performing portfolio management duties whose costs did not scale with assets under management in a linear way. Both of these developments are detailed below.

Investors in the pre-36(b) era turned to state corporate law as a weapon against allegedly excessive fees.[7] The claims in these suits were similar to many modern 36(b) suits and amounted to allegations that funds were agreeing to pay fees that resulted in excessive profits to fund advisers. Since these suits were brought by fund shareholders and argued that fund board members had breached a duty to the fund by agreeing to pay excessive compensation to the fund adviser, they were derivative in nature. While only a handful of state law claims for excessive fees were fully litigated, it was apparent that courts were reluctant to inquire deeply into the quality of asset management services, arguing that what investors were purchasing was not a fixed

---

[5] The brief historical overview provided here draws on Yeung and Freeman (2010); Fink (2008); and Rogers and Benedict (1982).
[6] Fink (2008), p. 66.
[7] Yeung and Freeman (2010).

effort on the part of the adviser, but the adviser's financial expertise and wise management.[8]

Conceivably, a number of corporate law standards could apply to such lawsuits. If the adviser of the fund was treated as a separate, unrelated provider of management services to the fund, then the deal struck with the adviser might simply be a matter of business judgment, with the fund board receiving the deference of the business judgment rule. Alternatively, given the close relationship between the fund board and the adviser, the advisory contract might be considered a conflict transaction, with the burden on the fund board to establish that the terms are fair to the fund investors.[9]

Ultimately, mutual fund fee derivative suits ran up against a fundamental problem of state corporate law in *Saxe v Brady*.[10] Since the initial mutual fund fee agreement must be approved by the shareholders,[11] standard corporate law doctrine holds that the fee payments are not subject to review for fairness or even to business judgment review. Instead, because the shareholders had ratified the fees, the *Saxe* court argued that such agreements could be struck down only if they amounted to a waste of corporate assets. The standard would be, as the *Saxe* court put it, "whether what the corporation has received is so inadequate in value that no person of ordinary, sound business judgment would deem it worth what the corporation has paid."[12] Since the application of the waste standard followed from the shareholder ratification of the advisory contract, and shareholder approval of the advisory contract is mandatory under section 15(a) of the ICA, the *Saxe* decision and its ilk established a nearly insurmountable burden for mutual fund investors challenging funds' fees using shareholder derivative suits: fees could only be challenged if they amounted to waste of a fund's assets.

While state law avenues to challenge fees were closing down, concern over the size of the fund industry was beginning to mount. The growth of the mutual fund industry initially raised regulatory concerns about financial stability.[13] The SEC commissioned the famous Wharton study of the mutual fund industry in 1958, and the study eventually expanded to encompass questions about whether investors were well served by the close relationship between funds and advisers.[14] The report, which was delivered in 1962, was critical of the fee structure of the industry, finding that most mutual funds were charged a 0.5 percent flat fee (ironically, low by modern standards) while other money management clients paid less.[15] The Wharton report placed the blame for this fee differential on the conflicting interests of mutual fund boards in negotiating fees. Since mutual funds are created by their advisers, and the initial boards are chosen by these advisers, mutual funds have a close relationship with their advisers that is difficult to square with conventional notions of arm's length bargaining. The notion that a mutual fund board's "choice" to do business with the adviser that created it deserves the same deference as the decision of an ordinary corporation to purchase services in an

---

[8] Id.
[9] Id.
[10] Saxe v. Brady, 40 Del. Ch. 474 (1962).
[11] 15 U.S.C. § 80a-15(a) (1964).
[12] Saxe v. Brady, 40 Del. Ch. 474 at 486.
[13] Fink (2008), p. 66.
[14] Yeung and Freeman (2010), p. 494.
[15] Id.

impersonal market is indeed difficult to defend, even if other competitive forces may obviate the need for such competition.

The SEC followed the Wharton study with a study of its own that was also critical of the fund industry and was clearly aimed at driving a reform agenda.[16] The issue of fees had received significant attention after the release of the Wharton report, and this attention led to some changes in the industry, including the adoption of size-contingent sliding scale rate structures. Nevertheless, the SEC found that "[t]he 0.50 percent annual advisory fee rate was still prevalent in the mutual fund industry during 1965," even though, by mid-1966, mutual fund assets had tripled from the time the Wharton School began its study.[17] Thus, in the view of the SEC, fund fees remained a problem.

Two aspects of the SEC report are notable, insofar as they motivated particular aspects of the legislative reforms the SEC would seek. First, the SEC, like the Wharton report, highlighted the comparative fees charged to other purchasers of asset management services, finding that advisers charged their mutual fund clients substantially higher fees than their private, non-fund clients for comparable asset levels.[18] According to the SEC report, in 1965 mutual fund expenses were almost double those of internally managed investment companies of comparable size. It argued that "the higher management expenses ... cannot be attributed solely to cost factors," noting that "advisors' profit margins [were] higher on their mutual fund accounts than on non-fund accounts."[19] Second, the SEC also took to task, albeit indirectly, the *Saxe* decision and the resulting limitations on state law intervention, noting "[t]he shareholder protections created by the Act have been construed under [s]tate law as precluding judicial inquiry into the reasonableness of advisory fees."[20]

Finally, in what would be a recurring theme of concerns about fund fees, the SEC argued that mutual fund advisers do not face real competition for management services from other fund advisers because "mutual funds are formed by, and generally remain under, the effective control of their advisers."[21] Of course, and as has been argued elsewhere,[22] investors can generally leave an open-ended mutual fund if they are dissatisfied with its costs. As such, market competition can be a powerful check on the power of fund advisers to extract excessive fees, at least for a substantial portion of the fund market. But competitive dynamics in the mid-1960s fund market were different than for modern funds: Options were fewer and transaction costs, load fees in particular, were higher in this era of the mutual fund business. The SEC noted the potential of high load fees to create a lock-in problem for investors: "the prospect of paying another sales load and possibly a capital gains tax is likely to deter [a shareholder] from switching to another fund with a lower advisory fee."[23] With loads both common and ranging up to 8 percent, this was not an idle concern. Thus, the

---

[16] SEC, PUBLIC POLICY IMPLICATIONS OF INVESTMENT COMPANY GROWTH (1966).
[17] SEC (1966), p. 11.
[18] Id.
[19] Id.
[20] Id.
[21] Id.
[22] Morley and Curtis (2010).
[23] Rogers and Benedict (1982), p. 1079 (quoting the SEC Report at 126).

competition for investor dollars that might provide some protection was subject to considerable friction.

1.2 The Adoption of 36(b)

The SEC's report made it clear that the SEC found the regulatory scheme around fees deficient and state law remedies inadequate. Proposals for legislative reform soon followed. The legislative debates pitted the SEC against the ICI, the most prominent mutual fund trade group. The three-year struggle would end with the adoption of the Investment Company Amendments Act of 1970 (ICAA of 1970), which included the compromise language of section 36(b).

The SEC's opening volley was based on a reasonableness standard with respect to investment company fees, with the plaintiff bearing the burden of proving the fees unreasonable.[24] The SEC regarded this standard as a compromise between the waste standard, which offered essentially no hope of plaintiff success, and the view that mutual fund fee-setting was a conflict transaction subject to review for entire fairness with the burden placed on the defendant directors.[25] The SEC apparently felt that requiring the plaintiff to show fund fees were unreasonable to be sufficient protection against vexatious litigation.

The ICI objected to the reasonableness standard, worrying that it was ambiguous and therefore would result in costly litigation.[26] A reasonableness standard would also give little deference to the judgment of mutual fund boards, and "the courts might feel called upon to substitute their business judgment for that of the directors of the fund" and "determine *de novo* on a case-by-case basis whether [an adviser fee] was in any particular case, in fact, 'reasonable.'"[27] The ICI did not want courts to become free-ranging fee regulators. In place of the reasonableness proposal, the ICI suggested increasing the independence of mutual fund boards as a way to protect investors against excessive fees.[28]

The result of the back and forth between the ICI and the SEC was a compromise bill, which included the language that is now 36(b). Several aspects of the final language of 36(b) are notable, and it is worth setting out the statutory language at some length:

> **(b)** For the purposes of this subsection, the investment adviser of a registered investment company shall be deemed to have a fiduciary duty with respect to the receipt of compensation for services ... An action may be brought under this subsection by the Commission, or by a security holder of such registered investment company ... for breach of fiduciary duty in

---

[24] Yeung and Freeman (2010), p. 500.
[25] "Whenever the fairness of a transaction involving a conflict of interest is challenged, the burden is usually placed upon those who seek to uphold the transaction." Schiffman (1979), p. 185).
[26] *Id.*
[27] Dec. 17, 1969 Letter from Robert L. Augenblick, President and General Counsel of the Investment Company Institute, to the Hon. John E. Moss, Chairman of the Subcommittee on Commerce and Finance of the Interstate and Foreign Commerce Committee [hereinafter Augenblick Letter].
[28] Yeung and Freeman (2010), p. 503.

respect of such compensation or payments ... With respect to any such action the following provisions shall apply:

> **(1)** It shall not be necessary to allege or prove that any defendant engaged in personal misconduct, and the plaintiff shall have the burden of proving a breach of fiduciary duty.
>
> **(2)** In any such action approval by the board of directors of such investment company of such compensation or payments, or of contracts or other arrangements providing for such compensation or payments, and ratification or approval of such compensation or payments, or of contracts or other arrangements providing for such compensation or payments, by the shareholders of such investment company, shall be given such consideration by the court as is deemed appropriate under all the circumstances.
>
> **(3)** No such action shall be brought or maintained against any person other than the recipient of such compensation or payments, and no damages or other relief shall be granted against any person other than the recipient of such compensation or payments. No award of damages shall be recoverable for any period prior to one year before the action was instituted. Any award of damages against such recipient shall be limited to the actual damages resulting from the breach of fiduciary duty and shall in no event exceed the amount of compensation or payment received from such investment company, or the security holders thereof, by such recipient.

Section 36(b) creates a right of action for shareholders in the fund, as well as the SEC, to bring suits alleging excessive fees. Section 36(b)(1) establishes that the burden of proof to establish a breach will be on the plaintiff, rejecting the notion that the defendants would need to establish fairness as in a conflict transaction, while also making explicit that the fiduciary breach need not amount to fraud or other misconduct.

While the SEC was deeply skeptical about the decisions of fund boards, which it viewed as captive, being given deference, the ICI hoped that board approval would be accorded some weight by the courts. These competing goals resulted in the language of section 36(b)(2) that the approval of the advisory contract "shall be given such consideration by the court as is deemed appropriate under all the circumstances."[29] This section leaves to the courts the debate over the importance of fee approval by the board, essentially punting on this critical issue and converting what might have been a matter of law into a factual matter for courts to determine on a case by case basis. Section 36(b)(2) also overturns *Saxe*'s waste-type standard, saying that shareholder ratification will not automatically insulate advisory contracts from challenge, while again calling upon the courts to give shareholder ratification whatever weight they see fit. While this section may have been seen as a compromise relative to what the SEC sought, it vastly expanded the factual issues to be litigated in 36(b) claims and, as a result, the cost and length of litigation.

Since a fiduciary duty is typically regarded as especially stringent, it is perhaps surprising that the ICI apparently preferred a fiduciary standard over a reasonableness standard, but the ICI felt that the fiduciary language connoted that the "adviser is running a business which is a commercial enterprise, albeit subject to high standards of conduct."[30] The ICI believed that the language would cause courts to "look to the general law of fiduciary relationships which involve the negotiating of fees by a

---

[29] *Id.* at § 80a-36(b)(2).
[30] Augenblick Letter, *supra* note 27.

fiduciary with the other party to the particular transaction. In such situations it would appear that there is no question that a fiduciary can negotiate for his fee."[31] The ICI felt the language would focus the courts on the adviser's conduct, instead of the fee itself, causing them "to try the adviser, not the fee, and find out qualitatively whether people in the negotiation behaved unreasonably."[32] Moreover, the ICI anticipated that courts would be more reluctant to find a fiduciary breach than to declare a fee unreasonable, because of the implication of wrongful behavior in the event of a fiduciary breach.[33]

While the ICI hoped to avoid free-ranging judicial oversight of fees and reduce litigation through the compromise wording of 36(b), the SEC felt that the fiduciary language sacrificed little relative to a reasonableness standard. The SEC argued that "the effect of the shift in language from 'reasonableness' to 'breach of fiduciary duty' is primarily procedural and not substantive. It was designed to assure reasonable fees just as the original language of S. 34 was meant to do."[34] The SEC felt that the new standard was "a significant and meaningful improvement over the existing law and at least as helpful as the reasonableness standard of S.34."[35]

The language also limits recovery of fees to a scant one year prior to the bringing of the suit, sharply limiting the fees that could be put at issue in an individual 36(b) suit. While this statute of limitations has received relatively little attention, it greatly reduces recoveries, and therefore the incentive to bring suits. It is this stringent limit on recoveries, more than perhaps any other aspect of the law, that has shaped the actual practice and impact of 36(b) litigation. Lowering the stakes of an individual suit—alongside the compromise language of 36(b)(2), which greatly increased the expense of litigation—made frequent settlements all but inevitable.

All told, 36(b) reflects less a legislative compromise between competing agendas, more an abdication of policymaking from Congress to the courts. The fiduciary standard is not a true compromise *standard* in the sense of adopting an intermediate threshold of liability between two extremes, but rather compromise *language*, sufficiently ambiguous that the SEC and ICI hung vastly different interpretive hopes on it. Working out that interpretation was left to the courts. Section 36(b) left the significance of board approval of fees in determining liability entirely undefined, leaving courts to decide, on a case by case basis, what board approval should mean for the satisfaction of the 36(b) fiduciary duty. The largely dysfunctional operation of 36(b) throughout its existence can be traced to this original failure. Without clear guidance, courts were left to interpret and implement this new form of liability on their own. The result has been a legal framework that is satisfactory to no one.

---

[31] Id.
[32] Rogers and Benedict (1982), p. 1085 (quoting ICI general counsel David Silver).
[33] Id.
[34] Note, Private Rights (1971).
[35] H.R. Rep. No. 91-1382, 91st Cong. 2d Sess. 8 (1969).

2 THE JUDICIAL APPROACH TO 36(b)

2.1 The *Gartenberg* Decision

Whatever the hopes of the SEC, the ICI, and Congress with respect to fund fees in adopting the 1970 act, the functioning of 36(b) was largely left to the courts, and the pivotal moment in the interpretation of 36(b)'s fiduciary language was the *Gartenberg* decision in 1982. *Gartenberg* involved a fee challenge against a Fidelity money market fund. The *Gartenberg* court referred to the statutory history as "tortuous,"[36] and clearly struggled to give meaning to the fiduciary terminology. The *Gartenberg* court essentially sided with the SEC's view of the 36(b) holding that "the substitution of the term 'fiduciary duty' for 'reasonable,' while possibly intended to modify the standard somewhat, was a more semantical than substantive compromise, shifting the focus slightly from the fund directors to the conduct of the investment adviser-manager."[37] In the case's most oft-cited passage the court framed the reasonableness standard thus:

> [T]he test is essentially whether the fee schedule represents a charge within the range of what would have been negotiated at arm's-length in the light of all of the surrounding circumstances
>
> ...
>
> To be guilty of a violation of § 36(b), therefore, the adviser-manager must charge a fee that is so disproportionately large that it bears no reasonable relationship to the services rendered and could not have been the product of arm's-length bargaining.[38]

While the *Gartenberg* court did not make much of the distinction between 36(b)'s fiduciary standard and a reasonableness standard, this language requires plaintiffs to satisfy the considerable burden of establishing not just that fees could have been lower but that they "could not have been the product of arms'-length bargaining," and makes reference to a "range of what would have been negotiated." It could be fairly read as a more stringent "reasonableness-plus" test for liability.

While this reading of the fiduciary duty can be seen as defendant-friendly, the court proceeded to reject market-based comparisons as a basis for defense in a move that would permanently alter the character of 36(b) litigation. It is worth considering the passage in its entirety:

> We disagree with the district court's suggestions that the principal factor to be considered in evaluating a fee's fairness is the price charged by other similar advisers to funds managed by them ... Competition between money market funds for shareholder business does not support an inference that competition must therefore also exist between adviser-managers for fund business. The former may be vigorous even though the latter is virtually non-existent. Each is governed by different forces. Reliance on prevailing industry advisory fees will not satisfy § 36(b).[39]

---

[36] Gartenberg v. Merrill Lynch Asset Mgmt., Inc., 694 F.2d 923, 928 (2d Cir. 1982).
[37] *Id.* at 928.
[38] *Id.*
[39] *Id.* at 929.

The lower court had explicitly drawn on market comparison to similar funds to establish the reasonableness of the fund's fees.[40] Such comparisons may seem perfectly natural in the context of the modern mutual fund market, but the 1970 amendments were explicitly motivated by the general perception that mutual fund prices were subject to an industry-wide conflict of interest due to the close relationship of advisers and boards, and so no prices could be used as a market benchmark. Indeed, the stubborn staying power of the largely standardized 0.5 percent fee structure despite the growth of the industry meant that market comparables at the time of the Wharton and SEC fee studies would have largely been useless. If the *Gartenberg* court's concern was the intention of the adopters of 36(b), it is almost certainly true that rejecting the fees of comparable funds as a basis for avoiding liability was a correct reading of their intention.

But the court's *reasoning* for this rejection was and remains problematic. The lack of competition among advisers for funds to advise is irrelevant if the market is sufficiently competitive that investors can easily move between funds. This was less relevant at the time that 36(b) was adopted because, as noted above, load fees were high enough that they may have been an obstacle to competition for investor dollars. But the money market fund in *Gartenberg* carried no sales loads and investors could easily shift assets out of the fund.[41] Nevertheless, the court seemed to view competition for investors as an imperfect substitute for competition for asset management services by the funds themselves. Vigorous competition among advisers for the business of funds has never been a feature of the mutual fund market. The result of the *Gartenberg* decision's treatment of competition was to put, essentially, the entire mutual fund market into play for 36(b) complaints. Since charging a market-average fee was not a defense against a finding that the fee was unreasonable, even a fund with modest fees was not safe from potential challenge.

The final significant contribution of *Gartenberg* was the identification of several factors that are relevant to the determination of liability. The so-called *Gartenberg* factors have taken on a life of their own as the key touchstones for mutual fund fee evaluation. One recapitulation of them is found in *Krinsk v. Fund Asset Mgmt*:

> (1) the nature and quality of services provided; (2) the profitability of the fund to the adviser-manager; (3) fall-out benefits; (4) economies of scale; (5) comparative fee structures; and (6) the independence and conscientiousness of the trustees.[42]

Thus, the excessiveness of fees turns on a number of considerations regarding the fund itself, the fund complex, and the behavior of the fund board in approving the specific advisory agreement.

Stepping back, *Gartenberg* created a standard that functions as follows: To establish excessiveness, a plaintiff must show that the fee levels of the fund are outside the realm of what might have been produced in some counterfactual negotiation. Indeed, the

---

[40] Gartenberg v. Merrill Lynch Asset Mgmt., Inc., 528 F. Supp. 1038, 1048 (S.D.N.Y. 1981), aff'd, 694 F.2d 923 (2d Cir. 1982).
[41] The *Gartenberg* court expressly rejected the notion that no load funds should be subject to a more generous standard for fee liability, a possibility floated by the district court. *Id.* at 930.
[42] Krinsk v. Fund Asset Mgmt., Inc., 875 F.2d 404, 409 (2d Cir. 1989).

standard seems to envision a range of potential negotiated outcomes, with the plaintiff bearing the burden of establishing that fees are outside of such a range. The actual arm's length bargaining between fund boards and advisers that this standard asks courts to use as a benchmark is not an observed feature of the mutual fund market. The notion of arm's length fees is therefore a wholly judicial construction. In lieu of an actual arm's length benchmark, the reasonableness of fees will rely on the consideration of a number of factors related to operational details of the mutual fund, including factors such as "fall out benefits" or the profitability of the individual fund to the adviser, which might not even be part of the adviser's internal financial calculations.

The extremely factbound nature of the *Gartenberg* factors interacts with notice pleading to create a litigation framework that is satisfying to neither side. Section 36(b) cases are almost trivially easy to bring, with a credible threat of surviving the motion to dismiss because the factors required to be considered are difficult to ascertain without discovery. And since—consistent with the Wharton study's view that the market may be broadly overpriced—having market-average fees does not ensure that a claim will fail, such suits can be brought against a huge swath of the mutual fund industry. But—because the *Gartenberg* factors are also difficult to evaluate even *with* the benefit of discovery, and the reasonableness standard is, in practice, fairly stringent—36(b) suits have never ended in a trial victory for plaintiffs. *Gartenberg* produces, then, a substantial amount of costly litigation, but no real deterrence.

2.2 The *Jones* case

Despite its flaws, the *Gartenberg* opinion provided the unchallenged guiding principles for fund fee litigation for decades,[43] until Judge Easterbrook in the Seventh Circuit created a striking circuit split in a decision that aimed to greatly curtail the *Gartenberg* standard and move sharply in the direction of the pre-1970 amendments *Saxe* ruling. Easterbrook based his rejection of *Gartenberg* on a narrower reading of the word "fiduciary":

> A fiduciary must make full disclosure and play no tricks but is not subject to a cap on compensation. The trustees (and in the end investors, who vote with their feet and dollars), rather than a judge or jury, determine how much advisory services are worth.
>
> Section 36(b) does not say that fees must be "reasonable" in relation to a judicially created standard. It says instead that the adviser has a fiduciary duty. That is a familiar word; to use it is to summon up the law of trusts. And the rule in trust law is straightforward: A trustee owes an obligation of candor in negotiation, and honesty in performance, but may negotiate in his own interest and accept what the settlor or governance institution agrees to pay.[44]

Easterbrook's reading would certainly have narrowed 36(b) and may have read 36(b) out of existence as an independent basis for liability. After all, if fraud or deceit were alleged, there would be a basis recovery in other areas of securities law.

---

[43] See Jones v. Harris Associates L.P., 537 F.3d 728, 729 (7th Cir. 2008) ("*Jones* is the only appellate opinion noted in Westlaw as disagreeing with *Gartenberg*").

[44] Jones v. Harris Associates L.P., 527 F.3d 627, 632 (7th Cir. 2008) (internal citations omitted).

This reading of 36(b) is obviously at odds with the SEC's view, contemporaneous with the 1970 amendments, that the "fiduciary" language was insubstantially different from a reasonableness standard. Moreover, it is difficult to square the notion that the obligation of a fiduciary is only "to make full disclosure" and "play no tricks" with a statutory framework that creates other liability for disclosure deficiencies and expressly states, in 36(b)(1), that there is no need for plaintiffs to "prove that any defendant engaged in personal misconduct."

On the other hand, Easterbrook's narrow view of 36(b)'s "fiduciary" language is arguably consistent with the ICI's hopes at the time of the passage of the 1970 amendments that courts would "look to the general law of fiduciary relationships which involve the negotiating of fees by a fiduciary with the other party to the particular transaction. In such situations it would appear that there is no question that a fiduciary can negotiate for his fee."[45] The *Jones* circuit split can therefore be read as reflecting, decades later, the original disagreement between the SEC and ICI over the appropriate standard for review of mutual fund fees. The fiduciary language was deliberately ambiguous, and the *Jones* and *Gartenberg* split merely highlights this ambiguity.

Easterbrook discussed at length the significant changes in the mutual funds since the 1970 amendments and the increasingly competitive nature of the marketplace:

> Statements made during the debates between 1968 and 1970 rest on beliefs about the structure of the mutual-fund market at the time ... Today thousands of mutual funds compete ... New entry is common, and funds can attract money only by offering a combination of service and management that investors value, at a price they are willing to pay.[46]

In so arguing, Easterbrook recognized, correctly, that competition between funds for investor dollars could provide market discipline even if funds never changed advisers.[47] Given these changes, the *Gartenberg* and SEC concerns about board independence are significantly less worrisome.[48] This is not to say that there is no lingering worry that some funds charge supracompetitive fees, but as an argument that market-average fees ought to receive considerable weight in evaluating whether a fund is overcharging, Easterbrook's argument is sensible as a matter of policy.

Nevertheless, Easterbrook's view would not long influence the interpretation of 36(b). In light of the stark circuit split, the case was taken up by the Supreme Court.

---

[45] Dec. 17, 1969 Letter from Robert L. Augenblick, President and General Counsel of the Investment Company Institute, to the Hon. John E. Moss, Chairman of the Subcommittee on Commerce and Finance of the Interstate and Foreign Commerce Committee.

[46] 527 F.3d 633–4.

[47] The argument that the modern mutual fund market is broadly competitive has been advanced by Coates and Hubbard (2007) and Hubbard *et al.* (2010). Fisch (p.1989, 2010) notes, though, that the considerable dispersion of mutual fund fees is inconsistent with a fully competitive market.

[48] Easterbrook also rejected the notion that the presence of unsophisticated investors ought to undermine competition, but in doing so relied on work in bargaining theory that is not a direct analog of mutual fund markets. Since complexes can offer similar mutual funds at different price points, it is not inevitable that a fund complex will respond to price pressure by lowering the price of an existing fund (thereby benefiting price-insensitive investors) when it has the option of creating a new, low-cost fund to capture price-sensitive investors.

Interestingly, both parties before the Court, as well as the ICI in an amicus brief, argued for keeping the *Gartenberg* standard intact. It is hardly surprising, then, that the Supreme Court's *Jones* decision was largely an endorsement of *Gartenberg*, with a few inflections that have led to important subsequent developments in fee litigation. The *Jones* decision entrenched *Gartenberg*'s skepticism regarding intra-fund fee comparison, stating that "courts should not rely too heavily on comparisons with fees charged to mutual funds by other advisers. These comparisons are problematic because these fees, like those challenged, may not be the product of negotiations conducted at arm's length."[49] In so stating the court effectively endorsed the SECs skepticism of four decades earlier, when the fund market was orders of magnitude smaller.

More importantly, the *Jones* case went beyond *Gartenberg* in explicitly paving the way for courts to compare fees with respect to different types of money management. The parties disagreed over the admissibility of "comparisons between the fees that an adviser charges a captive mutual fund and the fees that it charges its independent clients."[50] The *Gartenberg* court had rejected a comparison between the fees that the adviser charged a money market fund and the fees that it charged a pension fund. The *Jones* court said, echoing 36(b)'s treatment of the role of boards, that courts should treat such comparisons on a case by case basis:

> We do not think that there can be any categorical rule regarding the comparisons of the fees charged different types of clients. Instead, courts may give such comparisons the weight that they merit in light of the similarities and differences between the services that the clients in question require, but courts must be wary of inapt comparison.[51]

Thus, the court further expanded the already broad factual considerations that could enter into 36(b) claims to include not just the costs of other types of money management services, but also the "similarities and differences" between those types of services.

But *Jones* was not, by any means, a straightforward expansion of 36(b) liability. In language that seems designed to focus courts on the role of the board, Alito's opinion emphasized that a robust, well-informed fee approval process ought to be given some weight by courts within the statutory framework. While it seems unlikely that courts could afford mutual fund boards full business judgment deference with respect to the fee approval process and still fulfill the spirit of 36(b), one commentator has referred to the *Jones* standard as "business judgment lite."[52]

This raises the question, post-*Jones*, of how far removed the standard for establishing fee liability is from the *Saxe* case. *Saxe*, after all, set the adoption of 36(b) in motion—and if *Jones* indeed signals a move toward increased deference to fund boards' decision to approve advisory contracts, and the *Gartenberg* standard has already proved all but impossible for plaintiffs to satisfy, then has fee litigation approached the status quo ante regarding 36(b)? Time will tell, but, as detailed below,

---

[49] Jones v. Harris Associates L.P., 559 U.S. 335, 350–1 (2010).
[50] Id.
[51] Id.
[52] Knickle (2011), p. 307.

176 *Research handbook on the regulation of mutual funds*

36(b) litigation post-*Jones* has not withered away. Quite the contrary, there has been a significant new wave of complaints.

The *Jones* opinion can be seen as continuing the tradition, dating back to the adoption of 36(b), of holding competing goals in tension, and perhaps in conflict. While 36(b) failed to settle the debate between the ICI and the SEC over what exactly ought to give rise to liability, and the *Gartenberg* court crafted a standard nearly impossible to satisfy and made it almost trivially easy to state a claim, *Jones* both expanded the permissible theories of liability and emphasized the defensive value of board approval. It seems unlikely that *Jones* did much to alter the fundamental dynamic of 36(b) litigation, except to further expand the factual inquiries with which courts and litigants must grapple.

3 THE REAL-WORLD OPERATION OF 36(b)

Both anecdotal and empirical evidence suggest that the operation of 36(b) has been problematic, regardless of one's opinion on the question of fees. It is clear that cases are easy to bring, almost impossible to win, and frequently settle for undisclosed sums that are likely consistent with strike value. Suits frequently target low and moderately priced funds, and are clearly driven by plaintiffs' attorneys rather than investor concerns. The current state of section 36(b) litigation is, in short, a disappointment to everyone. For defenders of the fund industry, suits are a random nuisance; for those concerned about costs, suits have been an ineffective tool.

3.1 Section 36(b) Litigation

Gartenberg is widely thought to have erected an insurmountable barrier to plaintiff success in 36(b) cases. According to one practitioner, over 40 years, only seven cases, out of about one hundred filed, went to trial, and all of these were decided in favor of defendants.[53] On the other hand, many 36(b) cases have survived the motion to dismiss: a fact not surprising in light of the factbound *Gartenberg* standard. With many suits moving to discovery, and only a handful being taken to trial or decided at the summary judgment phase, it is clear that many 36(b) cases settle.

The details of 36(b) settlements are not public, nor must they be approved as fair and reasonable by a court. Settlement is an attractive option for 36(b) cases because the short statute of limitations keeps potential recoveries low, but litigation can be lengthy and expensive. Many 36(b) cases drag on for years with substantial discovery involved, with many recent cases taking more than five years to litigate and *Jones* itself taking more than ten years. Moreover, litigation is painful for the adviser and directors. While independent fund directors are not defendants in 36(b) cases, their testimony is the key factor in evaluating the deference owed to the board's decision to approve the

---

[53] ICI Mutual (2014).

management contract, and so they are often extensively deposed and their decision-making process is subject to intense scrutiny.[54] Even if the outcome at trial is likely to result in a verdict for defendants, the impulse to settle is understandable.

The empirical evidence squares with practitioners' impressions. A study of 91 36(b) claims filed between 2000 and 2009, comprising all cases brought during the period, confirms practitioners' impression of mutual fund fee litigation as described above.[55] Lawsuits tended to target large fund families, with nearly half of cases targeting an entire fund family rather than specific funds. As a result of this broad targeting strategy, nearly a quarter of funds in the industry were targeted at least once during the period. The fees of the targeted funds, if compared based on simple means, were not substantially higher than the universe of mutual funds, but sued funds were larger and came from larger families than unsued funds. Only when fund fees were adjusted for fund size was any difference in fees between sued and unsued funds observable.

Consistent with plaintiffs' attorney-driven litigation, cases tended to proceed in waves based on different theories of liability. A total of 25 cases, nearly all of which were brought by Milberg LLP, alleged that funds impermissible paid kickbacks to brokers; a handful of cases alleged that funds failed to participate in class action settlements; and a third group of claims focused on 12b-1 fees in funds closed to new investors. Excluded from the sample was a set of cases related to the market timing scandal, which seemed to have no apparent connection to fee excessiveness.

A wave of 12 cases beginning in 2004 made more direct excessive fee allegations. All of these cases were brought by two law firms, and this wave of litigation included the *Jones* case which would, years later, come to the Supreme Court. While these cases alleged that fees were excessive, the basis for the allegation was not always clear from the complaint. Moreover, these complaints never specified which share classes were alleged to have excessive fees, even though different share classes have different fees. On the whole, the excessive fee allegations amounted to cursory statements that the fees were excessive, with little theory or analysis, or even an idea of what the baseline might be.

Notably missing from the 36(b) landscape are suits against very expensive funds that could conceivably meet the *Gartenberg* standard. While bringing suit against the costliest funds may seem like an attractive strategy, most very expensive funds are small and are from small families, and therefore collect less in asset management fees than larger funds in absolute terms. This effect, combined with the one-year limit on fees at issue and the potentially protracted nature of 36(b) litigation, means that even a very expensive small fund may be a less attractive target than a large fund with average fees.

This focus on size rather than fees creates substantial incentive problems for fund families. In the Curtis and Morley study previously cited, the likelihood of being sued was not very sensitive to the fees charged. Indeed, a fund would have to drop from the top decile to well below the median before any statistically significant reduction in the likelihood of being sued could be obtained. As such, lowering fees is not a viable strategy for lowering the likelihood of suit. While small funds were likely to escape

---

[54] ICI Mutual (2014).
[55] Curtis and Morley (2014).

the notice of plaintiffs' attorneys, no fund—as one practitioner noted—is going to shed assets to reduce the likelihood of a 36(b) suit, nor would any public policy be served by inducing them to do so.[56]

This shotgun approach to pleading might have some benefit to investors if it produced lower fees at least in the funds that were sued, but the study found no evidence of such a trend. Despite the relatively high rate of settlement, there was no downward trend in fund expenses in the three years after funds were sued. It is therefore not clear, then, that 36(b) cases produced even specific deterrence with respect to funds whose fees were alleged to be excessive.

Section 36(b) cases in the study proved hard to resolve. Of the 78 cases in the study that had been resolved as of 2010, 28 had been dismissed, and another three cases were adjudicated on summary judgment. The remaining 47 had likely settled.[57] A substantial number of the settled claims had been pending for more than three years.

While the *Gartenberg* standard created stringent requirement for establishing fund liability, the empirical evidence suggests that this standard has not led to a world in which cases are brought only against extremely high-fee funds against which that burden has a chance of being carried. Nor has the "could not have been the product of arm's-length bargaining" language insulated moderately priced funds from the risk of costly settlements. The essentially random distribution of suits means that funds can do little to reduce the risk of being targeted, even if they were willing to accept lower management fees. Thus, *Gartenberg* seems to have resulted in a "worst of all worlds" middle ground wherein the motion to dismiss mechanism is ineffective at screening out low-merit suits, but even high-merit suits will ultimately fail. In such a world, the incentive of plaintiffs is to bring suits that have high settlement value.

3.2 Section 36(b) and Fund Boards

The results described above highlight the difficulty in bringing successful 36(b) claims, but the lack of plaintiff success does not mean that 36(b) has had no effect on how funds operate. Ironically, 36(b), which creates a fiduciary duty for fund *advisers*, seems to have had the most significant impact on the operation of fund *boards*. This is because the *Gartenberg* factors have been incorporated in the 15(c) process whereby directors approve fund advisory agreements. Fund boards spend considerable effort in ensuring that they document and consider the *Gartenberg* factors when negotiating fees.

Section 15(c) was added to the ICA as part of the 1970 amendments' focus on fund costs. The section states, in part, "It shall be the duty of the directors of a registered investment company to request and evaluate, and the duty of an investment adviser to such company to furnish, such information as may reasonably be necessary to evaluate the terms of any contract whereby a person undertakes regularly to serve or act as investment adviser of such company." The goal was to provide a robust role for fund boards in monitoring adviser compensation and to ensure that advisers provided boards

---

[56] ICI Mutual (2014).
[57] Since settlements in 36(b) suits are not publicly disclosed public information, it is difficult to conclusively determine that a case was settled.

the necessary information to evaluate advisory agreements.[58] While 15(c) does not contain a private cause of action, the SEC has brought cases alleging dysfunction in the 15(c) process.[59]

Since 15(c) makes explicit the duty of fund directors to evaluate advisory contracts, and *Gartenberg* outlines the factors that are legally relevant in making that evaluation, there is a close connection between 36(b) and 15(c), and mutual fund directors tend to focus in carrying out the 15(c) process on the *Gartenberg* factors as outlined above.[60] Moreover, the 36(b) language, stressed in *Jones*, that courts should give "whatever weight appropriate" to the board's decision to approve the fee agreement means that fund boards have incentives to take the *Gartenberg* factors seriously when approving adviser agreements, and typically do so.

It may be that the most important legacy of 36(b) is not the fiduciary duty it creates for advisers but the role it has played in focusing the attention of mutual fund directors on issue of fund costs, and also the *Gartenberg* factors, particularly in overseeing advisory agreements. Whatever the structural flaws of 36(b), it can at least be said to have focused the minds of mutual fund directors on costs when the advisory contract is approved. The 15(c) process is taken quite seriously by directors, by all accounts, and the information gathered by directors with respect to the *Gartenberg* factors may play a role in surfacing administrative problems.

4 THE CURRENT STATE OF FUND FEE LITIGATION

Post-*Jones*, we are now in the midst of a new wave of 36(b) cases. The cases brought as part of this new wave of claims look different than those seen in the pre-*Jones* era, and it is fair to say that the theories of liability underlying these claims reflect a better-developed notion of fee excessiveness than did most pre-*Jones* suits. Between 2013 and 2015, 13 new suits were brought, nine of which focused on the disparity between fees paid to advisers for fund management and fees paid to subadvisers of funds.[61] This new wave of post-*Jones* cases takes up the *Jones* opinion's explicit invitation to compare the cost of different types of money management in order to support a claim of overcharging by focusing on the use of subadvisers to manage fund portfolios.

4.1 Subadvisory Suits

Mutual fund complexes frequently offer mutual funds with portfolios that are managed by third parties, or subadvisers. These third parties, often other mutual fund companies, enable a complex to expand its menu of fund styles even if the complex does not possess the inhouse management expertise to offer the particular fund. The subadviser will be charged with day to day management of the fund portfolio, while the

---

[58] Knickle (2011), p. 271.
[59] *Id.* at 286–96.
[60] *Id.*
[61] ICI Mutual (2015).

investment adviser will remain responsible for the administration of the fund and monitoring the performance of the subadviser. In some cases, the portfolio management provided by the subadviser will be identical or substantially identical to the portfolio of another fund offered by the subadviser complex. Such arrangements provide benefits to both the adviser and the subadviser, as the adviser is able to expand its menu, while the subadviser is able to expand the assets under management by managing the subadvised assets alongside an inhouse fund.

A complex that both provides subadvisory services and offers to the general public a fund with a similar or the same portfolio is offering asset management services as a subadviser to third parties and as an adviser to its own fund. Subadvisory fees tend to be lower than fees charged to the public, sometimes substantially so. This is to be expected because the inhouse fund requires additional administrative support (though the amount and cost of such services is a matter of dispute) and marketing, while these services for a subadvised fund are provided by the primary adviser.[62] But the attraction of these cases for plaintiffs seems clear: The *Jones* opinion explicitly approved the consideration of comparisons between different asset management services, at least on a case by case basis, and subadvising presents a comparative context in which two different prices are charged for delivering the same or similar portfolio. The question becomes whether the administrative overhead justifies the difference between the inhouse fee and subadvisory fee. Plaintiffs are, naturally, skeptical that the administrative costs of the inhouse fund justify the price differential between the inhouse fund and the subadvised pool. As one fund critic put it, "If a management fee is higher than the subadvisory fee and the sub-advisers are doing all of the work, you really have to ask yourself what the management company is doing for its fee."[63] The question for litigation, of course, is whether the subadviser is really "doing all the work."

An example will be helpful. The BlackRock Global Allocation Fund is one of the funds that is the basis of a 36(b) lawsuit filed against BlackRock Investment Management (BRIM).[64] Per the complaint, BlackRock Global Allocation pays fees to BRIM of 0.66 percent of assets, which is the expense investors in the fund would bear. BRIM also provides subadvisory services to a number of other "global allocation funds" that offer substantially similar portfolios. For example, the Transamerica Global Allocation Fund contracts BRIM for portfolio services and pays fees between 0.44 percent and 0.32 percent depending on the size of the subadvised portfolio. The crux of the lawsuit, which has survived the motion to dismiss, is that the difference between the 0.66 percent charged to the BlackRock Global Allocation Fund and the lesser fee charged by BRIM to the Transamerica Fund cannot be justified as a reasonable expense. The complaint goes on to allege that many of the necessary administrative services are provided by BRIM, along with portfolio management.

---

[62] It bears noting that the subadvised fund will be offered to the public at a cost higher than the subadvisory fee, since the administrative overhead must be recouped with respect to that fund as well.

[63] Braham, *Lawsuit Shines a Harsh Light on Subadvisory Fund Fees*, BLOOMBERG BUSINESS (2013).

[64] In re Blackrock Mut. Funds Advisory Fee Litig., No. CIV.A. 14-1165 FLW, 2015 WL 1418848 (D.N.J. Mar. 27, 2015).

While many 36(b) claims in the pre-*Jones* era were sloppily drafted and imprecise, these new suits focus on specific, facially plausible measures of what it might mean for a fund to overcharge. These subadvisory cases are unique among 36(b) cases in that the subadvisory agreement represents a contract for management services that is negotiated between two fund complexes, and therefore can be understood as an arm's-length bargain for at least a portion of the services involved in running a mutual fund. Since the days of the Wharton study, the absence of arm's-length bargaining has plagued attempts to characterize excessive fees, but subadvisory agreements put an arm's-length price on a major component of fund management.

This is not to say that subadvisory cases involve clear examples of overcharging. There is more to running a mutual fund, after all, than simply managing the portfolio. Payments in and out of the fund must be processed, there are administrative costs at the fund level, and there are overheads associated with operating a mutual fund complex.[65] The subadvisory agreement captures only part of these costs, and so it is an incomplete picture of the funds' expenses. Judiciously choosing and overseeing a subadviser can also be understood as part of the hard-to-price services provided by the parent fund. In comparing the subadvisory fees to the fees paid by mutual fund investors, plaintiffs are inviting courts to weight an incomplete expense against the full cost of running the fund, a comparison that BlackRock's attorneys argued was "apples and oranges."[66] Indeed, it is notable that the Transamerica Global Allocation Fund currently charges fees to its public investors of between 0.77 percent and 1.02 percent, both higher than the 0.66 percent that BlackRock's Global Allocation Fund investors pay. The BlackRock fund is actually cheaper for investors all in, but it is the target of the excessive fee suit.

One might wonder whether a 36(b) suit might be brought against the fund family purchasing the subadvisory services. After all, in the example above, the argument is that BlackRock is providing essentially all of the necessary services to the Transamerica Global Allocation Fund, while charging investors in its inhouse fund more. Taking these allegations at face value, how would a subadvised fund justify charging a premium over the subadvisory fee? Such arguments have been the basis of a number of claims.[67] In these cases, the difference between the advisory fee and the

---

[65] Among the responsibilities typically retained by the fund contracting for subadvisory services are: "(i) supervising the general management and setting the overall investment strategies of the fund; (ii) evaluating, selecting, and recommending sub-advisers to manage all or a part of the fund's assets; (iii) allocating and reallocating the fund's assets among multiple sub-advisers; (iv) monitoring and evaluating the portfolio management services provided by each sub-adviser, and the investment performance of the fund, or portion thereof managed by the sub-adviser; (v) advising and consulting with the board of directors of the fund with respect to matters relating to the investment operations of the fund, including matters relating to the selection, evaluation, retention, and possible termination of each sub-adviser; (vi) implementing procedures reasonably designed to ensure that the sub-advisers comply with the fund's investment objectives, policies, and restrictions; and (vii) regularly reporting to the board of directors of the fund with respect to the foregoing matters." Davis *et al.* (2013), pp. 42-3–42-4.

[66] In re Blackrock Mut. Funds Advisory Fee Litig., 2015 WL 1418848, at 5 (D.N.J. Mar. 27, 2015).

[67] ICI Mutual (2016) provides a list of suits that target subadvised funds.

subadvisory fee of a subadvised fund is argued to be excessive in light of the amount of delegation to the subadviser. As with claims brought against the *providers* of subadvisory services, these claims against the *purchasers* of subadvisory services turn on the details of the services provided by the parent fund and the subadviser, and, as a result, such cases raise factual issues that are difficult to resolve on the pleadings.

4.2 Potential Problems with Subadvisory Suits

It is a simple fact of the mutual fund market that advisory fees will be higher than subadvisory fees. They cannot—obviously—be lower, or the adviser would lose money. And if the fees were the same there would be little point in maintaining the fund. Regardless of the degree to which services are contracted out, ultimate legal responsibility for operating the fund, which includes identifying a suitable subadviser, rests with the parent fund. It is hard to put a price on bearing that sort of liability. While it may be that the differential charged by fund complexes for advisory fees as compared with subadvisory fees reflects rent seeking, making this determination entails costly litigation to, essentially, evaluate the profitability of a business against an extremely vague set of factors.

A concerning issue with subadvisory cases is that they create legal risk for fund complexes that either offer or purchase subadvisory services. A truly high cost fund with no subadvisory agreements with outside complexes may present a more difficult target than a moderately priced fund with a low cost subadvisory agreement. If complexes deal with the issue of subadvisory suits by cutting back on subadvising, this would be detrimental to mutual fund investors in two ways. First, there would be a direct effect in terms of reduced choice, as it would be harder for complexes to offer funds based on subadvisory agreements to the extent that such agreements create legal risk. Second, and more subtly, subadvisory agreements create economies of scale for fund complexes that offer them, effectively increasing assets under management. Complexes that lose subadvisory revenues may make up those losses through increased fees. Finally, the legal risk of a lawsuit could induce a complex to manage a fund in house that could be more efficiently (and cheaply) managed through a subadvisory agreement, leaving both the complex and investors worse off.

At a more general level, these lawsuits reflect the confused incentives created by section 36(b) and the problems rooted in its legislative history. Because 36(b) calls on courts to consider a broad range of factual issues, but provides no clear guidance on the meaning of excessive fees, litigants focus on targets that solve the evidentiary problems posed by the *Gartenberg* and *Jones* standards rather than on the most egregiously priced funds. The "apples and oranges" comparison of advisory and subadvisory fees gets traction, while the more fundamental comparison of what investors in similar funds actually pay does not.

The BlackRock and Transamerica global allocation funds provide a particularly stark example. Both funds provide substantially the same portfolio, and the Transamerica fund is more costly to investors. An investor worried about fees who was seeking a fund that provides the exposure of the Global Allocation portfolio would naturally gravitate to the BlackRock fund and avoid the Transamerica option. But the BlackRock fund is the target of a 36(b) suit because BlackRock offers subadvisory services to

Transamerica, and can thus be called upon to justify the price differential of its (lower cost) retail fund. A more rational regime might call upon the Transamerica Global Allocation Fund to explain why its consumer investors pay more than BlackRock's investors for the same market exposure, but *Jones* discounts the apples to apples comparison of two retail funds while opening the door to the apples to oranges comparison of a retail fund with a subadvisory contract.

The post-*Jones* fee litigation landscape is still developing, and the contours of 36(b) in the aftermath of *Jones* are, at this point, still unclear. While subadvisory suits reflect a new, more sophisticated theory of liability under 36(b) than was seen in most pre-*Jones* cases, the ultimate success of these suits remains highly uncertain.

5 CONCLUSIONS

Legislative compromises resulting in vague legal standards are hardly rare, and such compromises need not lead to broken regulatory schemes. The problem with 36(b) is not that it was the product of compromise, but that the compromise was to treat areas of conflict as factual issues for courts to weigh on a case by case basis. The clash between the ICI and SEC was "resolved" by throwing the matter to the courts to sort out, with fiduciary language clearly admitting both the SEC's and ICI's hoped-for interpretations and the issue of board approval to be settled by discovery in every suit brought to bar. The result of this legislative abdication was a standard wherein strike suits are easy to bring and settle and meritorious suits are impossible to win. *Jones* has continued the ambiguity by essentially reinforcing the *Gartenberg* factors, while further increasing the factual issues to be determined through ever more complex litigation.

Section 36(b) would function better if we could move beyond the concerns that dominated at the time of its adoption. While the SEC strongly felt that the entire fund industry could be overpriced, Easterbrook's arguments about subsequent changes in the fund industry and the importance of market competition are well taken, at least with respect to average fund fees. More to the point, it is inconceivable that 36(b), at least as it has been constructed in the decades since its adoption, could function as a tool to bring down fees across the industry; it is, at best, capable of targeting the worst offenders. We would do better to simply acknowledge this reality, and admit evidence of comparative fees both for the purposes of creating and defending against liability. Such a shift would focus 36(b) litigation on funds that are actually very expensive. While this would to some degree eschew the historical concerns that motivated fee liability, it would almost certainly produce a better functioning framework for litigation.

REFERENCES

Coates IV, John C., 2010, The Downside of Judicial Restraint: The (Non-)Effect of Jones v. Harris, *Duke Journal of Constitutional Law & Public Policy* 6, 58–64.

Coates IV, John C., and Hubbard, R. Glenn, 2007, Competition in the Mutual Fund Industry: Evidence and Implications for Policy, *Journal of Corporation Law* 33, 151–222.

Curtis, Quinn, and Morley, John, 2014, An Empirical Study of Mutual Fund Excessive Fee Litigation: Do the Merits Matter? *Journal of Law, Economics, and Organization* 30, 275–305.

Curtis, Quinn and Morley, John, 2015, The Flawed Mechanics of Mutual Fund Fee Litigation, *Yale Journal on Regulation* 32, 1–44.

Davis, Gregory C., Chanda, Rahib, and Laws, Renee E, Mutual Fund Use of Sub-Advisers, in *Mutual Funds and Exchange Traded Funds Regulation*, vol. 2 (Clifford E. Kirsch ed., 3d ed. 2013) (Practicing Law Institute, New York), § 42.

Fink, Matthew P., 2008, *The Rise of Mutual Funds: An Insider's View* (Oxford University Press, New York).

Fisch, Jill E., 2010, Rethinking the Regulation of Securities Intermediaries, *University of Pennsylvania Law Review* 158, 1961–2041.

Henderson, Todd M., 2010, Justifying "Jones," *The University of Chicago Law Review* 77, 1027–53.

Hubbard, R. Glenn, Koehn, Michael F., Ornstein, Stanley I., Van Audenrode, Marc, and Royer, Jimmy, 2010, *The Mutual Fund Industry: Competition and Investor Welfare* (Columbia University Press, New York).

ICI Mutual, 2014, Trends in Fee Litigation: Actions Brought under Section 36(b) and ERISA.

ICI Mutual, 2016, Section 36(b) Litigation since *Jones v. Harris*: An Overview for Investment Advisers and Fund Independent Directors.

Johnsen, Bruce D., 2010, Myths about Mutual Fund Fees: Economic Insights on Jones v. Harris, *Journal of Corporation Law* 35, 561–614.

Knickle, H. Norman, 2011, The Mutual Fund's Section 15(C) Process: Jones v. Harris, the SEC and Fiduciary Duties of Directors, *Review of Banking and Financial Law* 31, 265–340.

Morley, John, and Curtis, Quinn, 2010, Taking Exit Rights Seriously: Why Governance and Fee Litigation Don't Work in Mutual Funds, *The Yale Law Journal* 120, 84–142.

Note, 1971, Private Rights of Action Against Mutual Fund Investment Advisers: Amended Section 36 of the 1940 Act, *University of Pennsylvania Law Review* 120, 143–64.

Ribstein, Larry, 2010 Federal Misgovernance of Mutual Funds, *Cato Supreme Court Review*, 301–32.

Rogers, William P., and Benedict, James N.,1982, Money Market Fund Management Fees: How Much Is Too Much? *New York University Law Review* 57, 1059–1125.

Schiffman, Howard, 1979, The Relationship between the Investment Advisor and the Mutual Fund: Too Close for Comfort, *Fordham Law Review* 45, 183–201.

SEC, Public Policy Implications of Investment Company Growth, House Report Number 89-2337 (1966).

Yeung, Amy Y., and Freeman, Kristen J., 2010, Gartenberg, Jones, and the Meaning of Fiduciary: A Legislative Investigation of Section 36(B), *Delaware Journal of Corporate Law* 35, 483–514.

8. Toward better mutual fund governance
*Anita K. Krug**

1 INTRODUCTION

Governance of mutual funds is structured not unlike governance of most public companies and many private ones, in that it is board-centered.[1] That is perhaps not surprising, given that most mutual funds are organized as corporations or statutory trusts,[2] formed under state laws that contemplate a board of directors or trustees (collectively, "directors") to oversee and control all aspects of the entity's operations.[3] Nonetheless, in the mutual fund context board-centered governance was not inevitable because, in that context, most aspects of board oversight—most board obligations, that is—do not arise from state law, which for the most part is merely enabling and, indeed, contains few true "obligations."[4]

Rather, these board obligations arise from federal securities laws and rules,[5] and, consistent with the securities laws as a whole, exist to protect investors and promote market integrity.[6] And securities law, unlike state corporate and trust law, does not

---

* The author notes, in the interest of complete disclosure, that she is on the boards of trustees of various mutual fund groups, variously structured using both the "traditional model" and the "new model."

[1] Alan R. Palmiter, *The Mutual Fund Board: A Failed Experiment in Regulatory Outsourcing*, 1 BROOK. J. CORP. FIN. & COM. L. 165, 168–69 (2006) (observing that a mutual fund must have "a board of directors (or its equivalent) to oversee" the fund's operations).

[2] *See id.* at 167–68 (noting that U.S. mutual fund regulation "assumes that mutual funds will be organized as (or along the lines of) a corporation" but that it does not mandate that mutual funds be formally organized as corporations).

[3] *See id.* at 167 ("The board of directors is a defining feature of the corporate structure that was adopted by the U.S. mutual fund industry at its inception").

[4] *See* Frank H. Easterbrook & Daniel R. Fischel, *The Corporate Contract*, 89 COLUM. L. REV. 1416, 1417 (1988) ("The corporate code in almost every state is an 'enabling' statute ... [that] allows managers and investors to write their own tickets, to establish systems of governance without substantive scrutiny from a regulator and without effective restraint on the permissible methods of corporate governance").

[5] *See* David E. Riggs, Robert C. Rosselot, & Melanie Mayo West, *Securities Regulation of Mutual Funds: A Banker's Primer*, 113 BANKING L.J. 864, 865 (1996) ("To protect investors in mutual funds, the federal securities laws impose several layers of regulation in the form of disclosure requirements, statutory restrictions on activities, and the oversight of a fund's Board of Directors").

[6] *See* Edith Hollan Jones, Comment, *An Interest Analysis Approach to Extraterritorial Application of Rule 10b-5*, 52 TEX. L. REV. 983, 993 (1975) ("The broad goal of United States securities laws is the promotion of securities markets whose integrity and reliability will protect investors and warrant their confidence"); INV. CO. INST., UNDERSTANDING THE ROLE OF MUTUAL FUND DIRECTORS 3 (1999), www.ici.org/pdf/bro_mf_directors.pdf [hereinafter ICI, ROLE OF

depend for its force or effect on the fact that mutual funds typically take the form of corporations or trusts. Indeed, it does not even depend on the fact that mutual funds are entities. There is no particular reason why securities law—the Investment Company Act of 1940 (the "Investment Company Act"), in particular[7]—could not have designated another person or body as primarily responsible for ensuring that a mutual fund operates in a way that satisfies the Investment Company Act's mandates. There is, in other words, no necessity to the corporate governance mode of mutual fund regulation.

Focusing on that observation, a prominent argument in recent scholarship on mutual fund regulation has been that the prevailing model of regulation is inadequate. Among the ailments that scholars have observed are that mutual fund boards cannot adequately fulfill their obligations—or, at least, cannot fulfill them to the same the extent as boards of public companies that pursue noninvestment-related business activities, such as manufacturing widgets or developing new technologies.[8] Some scholars have contended that, in light of this circumstance, regulation should be less (or differently) board-centered, even if a role for the board remains.[9] Other scholars, going further, have contended that mutual funds are sufficiently different from other public companies that it makes little sense to speak of governance at all and that regulation, to be effective, must take a wholly different form.[10]

The critiques begin from differing perspectives and end with differing visions of what reform should look like, but many of them share a common assumption—namely, that mutual fund boards are beholden to a "sponsoring" investment advisory firm that is

---

DIRECTORS] ("Unlike the directors of other corporations, mutual fund directors are responsible for protecting consumers, in this case, the fund's investors").

[7] 15 U.S.C. §§ 80a-1 to 80a-64 (2012).

[8] *See, e.g.*, Lyman Johnson, *A Fresh Look at Director "Independence": Mutual Fund Fee Litigation and Gartenberg at Twenty-Five*, 61 VAND. L. REV. 497, 505–06 (2008) (arguing that an inadequate conception of director independence has served to weaken mutual fund boards' role as fiduciaries to shareholders); Donald C. Langevoort, *Private Litigation to Enforce Fiduciary Duties in Mutual Funds: Derivative Suits, Disinterested Directors and the Ideology of Investor Sovereignty*, 83 WASH. U. L.Q. 1017, 1031 (2005) ("Mutual funds are not enough like business corporations for there to be any more than a facile analogy"); John C. Bogle, *Re-Mutualizing the Mutual Fund Industry—The Alpha and the Omega*, 45 B.C. L. REV. 391, 418–19 (2004) (arguing that the external management structure of most mutual fund complexes benefits managers to the detriment of shareholders and that mutual funds should instead be mutualized, with a fund's "shareholders and their directors … in working control" of the fund) (internal quotation omitted).

[9] *See* Eric D. Roiter, *Disentangling Mutual Fund Governance from Corporate Governance*, 6 HARV. BUS. L. REV. 1, 4 (2016) ("[T]he primary role of fund directors is not to exercise an all-encompassing business judgment over a fund's operations, but instead to monitor the fund adviser for compliance with legal and fiduciary duties"); Anita K. Krug, *Investment Company as Instrument: The Limitations of the Corporate Governance Regulatory Paradigm*, 86 S. CAL. L. REV. 263, 308–09 (2013) (arguing that the regulatory focus in the mutual fund context should be primarily on investment advisers, rather than on boards).

[10] *See* John Morley & Quinn Curtis, *Taking Exit Rights Seriously: Why Governance and Fee Litigation Don't Work in Mutual Funds*, 120 YALE L.J. 84, 131 (2010) (arguing that mutual funds should be regulated as products, rather than as investments); Jill E. Fisch, *Rethinking the Regulation of Securities Intermediaries*, 158 U. PA. L. REV. 1961, 2028 (2010) ("Mutual funds and comparable alternatives should be regulated as products, not investments").

responsible not only for creating the funds that a board oversees but also for the directors' appointments to their positions.[11] In this model of fund governance (the "traditional model," for purposes of this chapter), moreover, a single group of directors typically serves as the board of multiple discrete funds managed by that investment adviser.[12]

However, although the traditional model remains the dominant one, it has been losing ground to a second governance model, one that is centered not on the investment adviser but instead on a third party that is typically unaffiliated with the adviser. This third party is usually—but not always—an administration firm that assumes the role of the funds' administrator after the funds begin operating. Like the traditional model, this alternative model similarly contemplates the creation of multiple funds—that is, a fund group. However, in contrast to the traditional model, it eschews a single investment adviser charged with managing each fund's assets. Rather, the model is defined by the involvement of numerous advisers, each managing one or a small number of funds within the group.[13]

The emergence and growth of this second model—the "new model," for purposes of this chapter—makes sense when one considers the dramatic increase in investment advisers over the past two decades.[14] That development, in turn, is attributable to, and arguably is also responsible for, the increasing popularity of hedge funds and investors' use of financial intermediaries to pursue their activities in the financial markets.[15] Many of these advisers, who are smaller (in terms of assets under management) than advisers who sponsor traditional model funds, are looking to expand their investment approaches into the retail investor market. The new model allows them to do that because it enables them to avoid some of the costs they otherwise would bear if they were to sponsor an entire fund group.

This chapter evaluates the implications of the new model for effective mutual fund governance and regulation. Although the new model portends an improvement over the

---

[11] See Laura Lin, *The Effectiveness of Outside Directors as a Corporate Governance Mechanism: Theories and Evidence*, 90 Nw. U. L. REV. 898, 910 (1996) ("[A mutual] fund's investment advisers usually form, sell, and manage the fund and appoint the fund's initial board of directors").

[12] See Business Roundtable v. S.E.C., 647 F.3d 1144, 1154 (D.C. Cir. 2011) (observing that "[t]he boards of the funds in a [mutual fund] complex" are typically organized as either "a 'unitary board,' comprising one group of directors who sit as the board of every fund in the complex," or as "'cluster boards,' comprising two or more groups of directors, with each group overseeing a different set of funds within the complex").

[13] See Press Release, U.S. Sec. & Exch. Comm'n, *SEC Charges Gatekeepers of Two Mutual Fund Trusts for Inaccurate Disclosures about Decisions on Behalf of Shareholders* (May 2, 2013), www.sec.gov/News/PressRelease/Detail/PressRelease/1365171514096 ("Some trusts are created as turnkey mutual fund operations that launch numerous funds to be managed by different unaffiliated advisers").

[14] See Christopher Condon, *The Rise of the Registered Investment Adviser*, BLOOMBERG (Mar. 3, 2011), www.bloomberg.com/news/articles/2011-03-03/the-rise-of-the-registered-investment-adviser (discussing the significant growth in the number of registered investment advisers from 1999 to 2009).

[15] See id. (observing that investment advisers "emerged to challenge stockbrokers in the 1990s when individuals with growing portfolios sought out affordable and reliable guidance").

traditional model in many respects, questions arise as to whether it introduces concerns of its own and whether those concerns are more or less manageable than those to which the traditional model gives rise. The chapter contends that, although the new model produces risks not associated with the traditional model, there are reasons to believe that, as a governance structure, it is at least as effective as the traditional model and may be superior in some respects. Specifically, because the new model produces fewer sources of conflicts of interest as compared with the traditional model, it may strengthen the board's ability to uphold its fiduciary responsibilities to shareholders.

2 BOARD GOVERNANCE

A mutual fund's board of directors is responsible for governing the fund and its operations, consistent with age-old corporate law principles.[16] Beyond that, however, the Investment Company Act provides that the board is primarily responsible for the fund's compliance with its regulatory obligations under the securities laws.[17] Those latter requirements, unlike the former, have nothing to do with the internal constitution of the fund ("control's" relationship to "ownership," in the classic formulation) and instead exist for the same reason as the securities laws generally—to promote the integrity of the securities markets and to protect investors.[18]

Accordingly, not only are fund boards tasked with such things as reviewing and approving all agreements to which a fund is a party (or delegating those functions) and appointing and removing the fund's officers, all of which are traditional board responsibilities under corporate law principles.[19] They also are obligated to ensure that the funds they govern, as public companies,[20] comply with the same disclosure and reporting requirements as those to which public companies that pursue (noninvestment-related) business objectives must adhere. In particular, as required by the Securities Act

---

[16] *See* Wallace Wen Yeu Wang, *Corporate Versus Contractual Mutual Funds: An Evaluation of Structure and Governance*, 69 WASH. L. REV. 927, 948 (1994) (observing that the U.S. mutual fund regulatory regime "impose(s) requirements that assume the standard structure of corporate democracy: a board of directors, whose function is to oversee the operations of the mutual fund and police conflicts of interest").

[17] *See* DIV. OF INV. MGMT., U.S. SEC. AND EXCH. COMM'N, PROTECTING INVESTORS: A HALF CENTURY OF INVESTMENT COMPANY REGULATION 255–56 (1992), www.sec.gov/divisions/investment/guidance/icreg50-92.pdf (describing the authority of boards of directors under the Investment Company Act); Riggs, Rosselot, & West, *supra* note 5, at 873 ("The [Investment Company] Act imposes a significant burden upon the Board of Directors of a mutual fund to act as the watchdogs for the fund's shareholders and to oversee the compliance of each of the managers of the fund ... with the requirements of the [Investment Company] Act").

[18] *See supra* notes 5–6 and accompanying text (describing the goals of securities regulation).

[19] These obligations are simply a product of the fact that, under the default rules of state corporate law, the board has management authority over the corporation: *see supra* notes 1–4 and accompanying text (noting that mutual funds are managed by boards of directors).

[20] *See* Stacey P. Slaughter, *Advising Clients in a Changing Securities Law Environment*, in NEW DEVELOPMENTS IN SECURITIES LITIGATION, 2014 WL 1245075 (noting that mutual funds are public companies and therefore were subject to aspects of the securities laws even before the enactment of the Investment Company Act).

of 1933 (the "Securities Act"),[21] a mutual fund (acting through its board) must prepare a registration statement, which the SEC must approve before the fund can commence its offering;[22] file annual reports with the SEC regarding, among other things, the fund and its activities, as well as its investment adviser and other service providers; and periodically disclose relevant information about the fund to shareholders.[23] Moreover, in order to obtain a vote of shareholders, the fund must comply with the proxy rules of Section 14 of the Securities Exchange Act of 1934 (the "Exchange Act")[24] and the SEC's proxy rules under the Exchange Act.[25]

Beyond complying with requirements imposed by the Securities Act and the Exchange Act, a mutual fund board must also contend with strictures contained in the statute that is the primary source of mutual fund regulation—namely, the Investment Company Act—and the associated SEC rules.[26] To name just a few: The board must ensure that the fund complies with portfolio concentration limitations, including the requirements that the fund not invest more than 5 percent of its assets in any other mutual fund or other registered investment company or own more than 10 percent of that other fund or company;[27] maintain policies and procedures that address risks arising from all aspects of the fund's activities;[28] adhere to limitations on the fund's use of leverage;[29] maintain certain types of books and records for minimum periods of time as specified by the SEC;[30] and determine the fair market values of any illiquid ("Level 3") securities or other instruments in the fund's portfolio.[31]

As the discussion above suggests, the board is responsible for all activities in which the fund might engage, be they regulatory compliance-related or not.[32] And permeating all that a board does as it relates to the fund is the corporate law principle that boards are fiduciaries to the fund and its shareholders and, as such, may not act in a manner

---

[21] 15 U.S.C. §§ 77a-77aa (2012).

[22] *See Investment Company Registration and Regulation Package*, U.S. SEC. & EXCHANGE COMMISSION, www.sec.gov/divisions/investment/invcoreg121504.htm (last modified Feb. 19, 2013) (noting that a mutual fund "must register its public offerings under the Securities Act" and describing the registration process).

[23] For example, under section 29 of the Investment Company Act, 15 U.S.C. § 80a-29(a) (2012), and SEC rule 30b2-1 thereunder, 17 C.F.R. § 270.30b2-1 (2016), on an annual basis a mutual fund board must, on behalf of the fund, file a comprehensive disclosure document (Form N-CSR) with the SEC. *See* 15 U.S.C. § 80a-29(c) (2012) (requiring that mutual funds deliver semi-annual reports to shareholders).

[24] *See* 15 U.S.C. § 78n (2012).

[25] *See* 17 C.F.R. §§ 240.41a-1 to 14a21 (2016).

[26] 17 C.F.R. §§ 270.0-1 to 270.60a-1 (2016).

[27] *See* 15 U.S.C. § 80a-12(d) (2012).

[28] *See* 17 C.F.R. § 270.38a-1 (2016).

[29] *See* 15 U.S.C. § 80a-18(f)(1) (2012).

[30] *See* 15 U.S.C. § 80a-30 (2012); 17 C.F.R. § 270.31a-1 (2016).

[31] *See* 17 C.F.R. § 270.2a-1 (2016).

[32] The Investment Company Act speaks in terms of what a mutual fund must, may, and may not do, and therefore obligates the board, as the governing body for regulatory purposes, to comply with the Act's requirements. It thereby leaves only a subsidiary role for others involved with the fund, such as the adviser, the administrator, and the distributor.

that serves their or others' interests to the detriment of those constituencies.[33] Importantly, then, transactions involving conflicts of interest—such as engaging a director's own employer to provide audit services to the fund[34] or allowing the fund to buy securities from another fund managed by the same investment adviser[35]—are either prohibited or subject to rigid constraints.

Of course, conflicted transactions similarly implicate directors' judgment and compliance with their fiduciary duties in the general corporate context. As an example, if the board of Acme Inc. causes the firm to enter into a contract with Widget Corp., of which one of the Acme directors is CEO, there arises the concern that the Acme board entered into the transaction not because doing so was in the Acme shareholders' best interests but because of the relevant director's relationship with Widget. These concerns often can be overcome, however, if the board follows certain procedures and the terms of the contract are fair to the firm.[36] In the mutual fund context, by contrast, most conflicted transactions are off limits, regardless of what procedures the board might follow or what consents it might procure. The requirements are prophylactic, which reflects that mutual funds are subject to a regulating statute (the Investment Company Act), not just an enabling one (the relevant state corporate code).[37]

3 THE TRADITIONAL MODEL

A mutual fund has only one purpose: to invest its capital according to a particular investment program, as directed by its investment adviser. Because of this, the adviser arguably has more to gain from being involved with the fund, in terms of revenue, name recognition, and prospects for business expansion, as compared with the fund's administrator, auditor, custodian, and other service providers.[38] This circumstance— mutual funds' close association with the advisers that manage them—has traditionally

---

[33] *See* Sam Mamudi, *The Unseen Figures of Your Funds*, WALL ST. J. (May 3, 2010), www.wsj.com/articles/SB10001424052748704100604575146040314631942 (discussing mutual fund boards' fiduciary obligations).

[34] *See* 17 C.F.R. § 210.2-01(c)(3) (2016) (Exchange Act Regulation S-X) (requiring that auditors of public companies meet strict independence requirements).

[35] *See* 17 C.F.R. § 270.17a-7 (2016) (setting forth procedures that a mutual fund must follow in order to enter into such so-called "cross transactions").

[36] *See* Claire Hill & Brett McDonnell, *Executive Compensation and the Optimal Penumbra of Delaware Corporation Law*, 4 VA. L. & BUS. REV. 333, 339 (2009) ("Corporate boards faced with a conflicted transaction are well advised to closely follow the prescribed procedures in the case law for achieving valid board or shareholder approval, because if they do not, they face a serious chance that their directors will be held liable in court").

[37] *See* ICI, ROLE OF DIRECTORS, *supra* note 6, at 17 ("The prohibitions placed on transactions with affiliates represent one very important way the Investment Company Act serves to protect investors").

[38] To be sure, other service providers may also benefit considerably from their relationships with a particular mutual fund.

supported an organizational structure in which the adviser sponsors the funds that it manages and effectively dominates their operations.[39]

In this model (the traditional model), therefore, the adviser sets the wheels in motion, engaging counsel on a proposed fund's behalf and arranging for the involvement of other service providers, including, importantly, the distributor and other firms and personnel that will market the fund to prospective shareholders.[40] In addition, the adviser's employees effectively serve as the fund's personnel—in most cases, the fund has none of its own—and, in that capacity, carry out most of the fund's activities.[41] Indeed, the adviser's role is so important that the fund not only would not have come into being without the adviser; it also would likely cease to exist in the event the adviser's relationship with it were ever terminated.

As part of its control over the fund's organization and launch, the investment adviser also seeks out candidates to serve on the fund's board.[42] Those candidates may be longtime friends of the adviser's principals or may be introduced to the adviser by others involved with the fund's organization. Moreover, before the fund has begun issuing shares to the public, the adviser, in its capacity as the fund's initial shareholder, also typically completes the formal act of electing those candidates as directors. Accordingly, it is no exaggeration to say that a mutual fund director in the traditional model may often, if not usually, credit its status as such to the adviser.

In part as a result of that circumstance, despite the vigilance that mutual fund regulation imposes on mutual fund boards—and the conscientiousness and seriousness with which most traditional-model boards carry out their responsibilities—the traditional model embodies conditions for incentivizing the board to weaken its fiduciary vigilance. As discussed below, those conditions, and the incentives to which they may give rise, form the core of the problems with the traditional model: Given how directors are typically appointed, a board may have incentives to inappropriately accede to the investment adviser's wishes. Similarly, if an adviser affiliate is a board member, the board may be unduly influenced by the views of that member because of his or her relationship to the adviser. Finally, if, as is usually the case, the board is a "unitary" board that oversees multiple funds managed by the adviser, the board may be

---

[39] See Johnson, *supra* note 8, at 503 (observing that a mutual fund's investment adviser "frequently … establishes and 'sponsors' the investment company and provides all necessary personnel, facilities, and expertise").

[40] See *id.* However, the fund's board, once it has been appointed, must ultimately approve any such arrangements, in its role as the fund's governing body. See *supra* notes 16–37 (discussing the role of mutual fund boards and a board's obligation to oversee all of the fund's activities).

[41] Although a board may appoint officers for a fund—and, under SEC rules, must appoint a chief compliance officer, 17 C.F.R. § 270.38a-1(a)(4) (2012)—in most cases those officers are employees of the adviser. See INDEP. DIRS. COUNCIL, FUNDAMENTALS FOR NEWER DIRECTORS 4 (2014), www.idc.org/pdf/idc_14_fundamentals.pdf.

[42] See Jones v. Harris Assocs., L.P., 559 U.S. 335, 338 (2010) (noting in its description of "mutual funds" that "[t]he adviser selects the fund's directors") (citations omitted); John C. Coates IV & R. Glenn Hubbard, *Competition in the Mutual Fund Industry: Evidence and Implications for Policy*, 33 J. CORP. L. 151, 158 (2007) ("[T]he fund's investment adviser … appoints the fund's initial board of directors").

influenced to focus on the fund group as a whole, at the expense of particular funds within the group.[43]

3.1 Adviser Influence

Perhaps the most problematic source of adverse incentives in the traditional model is the adviser's selection and appointment of the members of the boards that oversee the funds that the adviser manages. To the extent that directors wish to retain their positions indefinitely—a viable prospect given the associated compensation—or are simply grateful for having been appointed in the first place, the board could be in some sense beholden to the adviser. This does not mean that the board will do whatever the adviser wishes come what may, but it might mean that the board will too readily accede to those wishes, without sufficient critical analysis or questioning. Furthermore, this risk could be exacerbated by the fact that, unlike other types of public companies, mutual funds do not—indeed, cannot[44]—grant stock options to directors to better align their interests with those of shareholders,[45] and, in contrast to the shareholders of other public companies, mutual fund shareholders typically do not engage in activist activities that might help ensure board discipline.[46]

If a board were to base its actions on these incentives, moreover, the effects could be severe. For example, the board might agree to the adviser's proposed fee increase when it would not otherwise do so if its members were truly independent of the adviser's influence.[47] Or, the board might acquiesce to the adviser's proposal to permit a large shareholder to redeem shares more frequently than would otherwise be possible under the fund's governing documents.[48] Or, the board might too quickly defend an adviser whom shareholders have sued, construing relevant facts in a manner more favorable to

---

[43] It is worth emphasizing that most mutual fund boards carry out their obligations responsibly and in the furtherance of shareholders' best interests. Accordingly, the incentives that this chapter discusses are merely potential incentives—that is, incentives that the traditional model could facilitate and, in any event, does nothing to forestall.

[44] Section 22(g) of the Investment Company Act prohibits a fund from issuing shares as compensation for services or for any other noncash consideration. However, many fund groups encourage or require directors to buy shares of one or more funds.

[45] *See* Langevoort, *supra* note 8, at 1031–32 (noting that mutual fund directors "are typically paid all or mostly in cash" and that the use of stock options to align the board's interests with those of shareholders does not "operate[] with any power in the world of mutual funds").

[46] *See* Morley & Curtis, *supra* note 10, at 115–19 (observing that mutual fund shareholders "do not meaningfully elect or lobby boards of directors," tend not to vote—particularly not in director elections or matters involving fees or performance—and do not engage in litigation challenging advisory fees and prefer instead simply to redeem their shares).

[47] *See* Coates & Hubbard, *supra* note 42, at 158 (noting that a mutual fund board must approve the fees that the adviser charges the fund). Despite the common supposition that there is little competitive discipline governing the fee-setting process—*see id.*—John Coates and Glenn Hubbard have argued, based on their empirical study, that market forces do in fact limit advisory fees because "investors in mutual funds have contractual rights giving them the ability to 'fire' advisers on their own by redeeming their shares." *Id.* at 159.

[48] *See* William A. Birdthistle, *Investment Indiscipline: A Behavioral Approach to Mutual Fund Jurisprudence*, 2010 U. ILL. L. REV. 61, 65 (discussing how, during the years of the

the adviser than would otherwise be warranted. Finally, and perhaps most important, the board might not contemplate terminating the adviser, even if circumstances support its doing so.[49] After all, without the adviser, there likely also would be no fund or fund group or, therefore, board positions. Whatever the particular influence-induced decision or omission might be, the shareholders—those whom the board has a duty to protect—likely would not benefit from it.

3.2 Affiliated Directors

An investment adviser's overwhelming dominance of the fund group that it manages could produce a second type of adverse incentives, stemming from the fact that the adviser is typically the party that carries out each fund's day to day operations. Among other things, it executes trades on the fund's behalf; selects brokers and other intermediaries; addresses questions from marketers, auditors, and other service providers; and compiles performance reports and financial data in the first instance.[50] This role means, as noted above, that the adviser's personnel are effectively the fund's employees—a necessary circumstance, given that the fund has no employees of its own.

Consistent with the adviser's extensive role, the adviser usually desires representation on the fund's board and, accordingly, appoints one or more of its employees or other affiliates as directors.[51] In the traditional model, then, although a majority of directors are formally independent of the adviser, as generally must be the case under the Investment Company Act,[52] a minority of directors will often not be. Although the effect of this circumstance is unclear, it may produce a still stronger connection between the board and the adviser—a connection that could influence the independent directors in making decisions, even those in which the affiliated directors do not take part.[53] Of course, the presence of affiliated directors does not mean that the associated

---

mutual-fund market timing "scandal," various investment advisers "countenanced" institutional shareholders' market-timing transactions).

[49] See Jones, 559 U.S. at 338 ("Because of the relationship between a mutual fund and its investment adviser, the fund often cannot, as a practical matter[,] sever its relationship with the adviser").

[50] See Tannenbaum v. Zeller, 552 F.2d 402, 405 (2d Cir. 1977) (noting that "[t]he management of [a mutual fund] is largely in the hands of an investment adviser, an independent entity which generally organizes the fund and provides it with investment advice, management services, and office space and staff" and that "[t]he adviser either selects or recommends the fund's investments and rate of portfolio turnover, and operates or supervises most of the other phases of the fund's business").

[51] See Victoria E. Schonfeld & Thomas M.J. Kerwin, *Organization of a Mutual Fund*, 49 BUS. LAW. 107, 107–08 (1993) ("[A mutual fund's] sponsor also typically provides personnel to manage and operate the fund, including officers and affiliated directors"); Emily D. Johnson, Note *The Fiduciary Duty in Mutual Fund Excessive Fee Cases: Ripe for Reexamination*, 59 DUKE L.J. 145, 152 (2009) ("[A mutual fund's] sponsor, ... typically the investment advisor, appoints officers and affiliated directors to serve on the board").

[52] See 17 C.F.R. 270.0-1(a)(7)(i) (2016).

[53] See Johnson, *supra* note 8, at 505 (observing that affiliated directors, "[a]s decisionmakers for the adviser ... both personally benefit from and are in a position to influence a contract

potential incentives would necessarily guide the board's actions or, even if they did, that shareholders would be harmed as a result. However, if that presence—and the potential for conflicts that it creates—produces appreciable risks, then logically shareholders would be better off with an entirely independent board.

3.3 Unitary Board

A defining feature of the traditional model is that an investment adviser that starts one mutual fund usually will start several more.[54] Its doing so is simply a matter of efficiency, in that launching and managing a mutual fund are costly activities.[55] Expenses arise from the practical necessity that the adviser pay for some, perhaps many, of the fund's considerable expenses,[56] particularly in the startup phase, lest the fledgling fund be burdened with them at the same time that it is seeking to gather assets and produce strong performance.[57] A substantial portion of the startup costs consists of the fees charged by legal counsel for tasks such as drafting fund documents, forming the fund entity, completing regulatory filings, and responding to comments from SEC staff. Additional considerable expenditures are required on an ongoing basis to compensate service providers, as well as the adviser's employees, and to comply with the fund's and the adviser's respective regulatory obligations. Managing more funds (and, therefore, more assets) means that, if all goes well, the adviser will receive more advisory fees, while expenses should at some point diminish on a relative basis, as economies of scale emerge.[58] This is a viable prospect because each new fund typically

---

[between the fund and the adviser] that is good for the adviser but adverse to the interests of investors"). Shareholders suing boards and investment advisers based on excessive-fee allegations have made claims to this effect. *See* Meyer Eisenberg & Richard M. Phillips, *Mutual Fund Litigation—New Frontiers for the Investment Company Act*, 62 COLUM. L. REV. 73, 79 (1962) (discussing early excessive fee litigation and noting that some of the complaints "charge[d] that the affiliated directors dominate[d] or 'guide[d]' the unaffiliated directors of the board, thus assuring annual renewal of the advisory and underwriting contracts with firms in which the affiliated directors ha[d] an interest and thereby precluding any legitimate review or evaluation of the performance of the adviser").

[54] *See* Brown v. Calamos, 664 F.3d 123, 130 (7th Cir. 2011) (noting that "most advisors ... run[] multiple funds").

[55] *See* Tracey Longo, *Starting Your Own Mutual Fund*, FIN. ADVISOR (May 1, 2006), www.fa-mag.com/news/article-1393.html (describing the high costs associated with starting a mutual fund).

[56] *See* John Waggoner, *What Impels Someone to Start a Stock Mutual Fund Today?* USA TODAY MONEY (Feb. 8, 2012), http://usatoday30.usatoday.com/money/perfi/funds/story/2012-02-08/new-stock-mutal-funds-managers/53014508/1 (noting that "[s]tarting a fund can be complex and expensive" and listing some of the costs associated with a mutual fund's organization and ongoing operations).

[57] *Cf. Treatment of Organization and Offering Costs For New Open-End Funds*, BBD (Apr. 15, 2014), www.bbdcpa.com/investment-company-notebook/treatment-of-organization-and-offering-costs-for-new-open-end-funds/ ("In the process of establishing a new [mutual fund] ... organization costs will be borne so that the entity is legally able to operate.").

[58] *See* Michael Maiello, *Mutual Funds: Economics of Scale*, FORBES (Feb. 6, 2009), www.forbes.com/2009/02/05/mutual-fund-startup-intelligent-investing_0206_mutual_fund.html

engages the initial fund's counsel and other service providers, thereby allowing the service providers to view each new fund as but a new verse of the same song.[59]

Economies of scale not only counsel in favor of using the same service providers for each fund in the group, however; they also counsel in favor of having the same directors serve as such for each fund. Accordingly, another defining feature of the traditional model is that the board is not just the board of any given mutual fund; it is also the board of the entire group (or particular subgroups) of funds that the adviser manages.[60] Indeed, this approach is all but inevitable given that, as a formal matter, the fund group often comprises not numerous discrete funds but, instead, several smaller aggregations of funds. Each such aggregation takes the form of a legal entity (often a so-called series trust) that "houses" a number of the funds, each of which is a separate "series" of the entity.[61] Although, as a formal matter, the board is the board only of each of these more encompassing entities, or of particular encompassing entities, by virtue of that role it is also effectively the board of each fund within them.

Such a board is known as a "unitary board"[62] and is the third source of adverse incentives that could soften a board's fiduciary vigilance. These incentives stem from the basic principle that boards owe fiduciary duties to *each fund* they oversee—a principle that, alternatively stated, means that boards must act in the best interest of each such fund and its shareholders. A unitary board, however, is effectively also the board of the fund group as a whole and can, if it chooses, make decisions for the funds collectively.[63] To be sure, such decisions could potentially be in the best interest of every fund in the group. However, because different funds have different amounts of assets, different investment strategies, and possibly different types of shareholders, a board decision could both disproportionately advantage some funds while disproportionately disadvantaging others. Although one prominent jurist has expressly condoned this result,[64] suggesting that the board owes its obligations not to individual funds but

---

("In theory, it doesn't cost much more to manage $500 million than $50 million, so the greater the assets, the greater the profits to fund companies").

[59] See *Overview of Mutual Fund Governance*, INDEP. DIRECTORS COUNCIL, www.idc.org/idc/issues/governance/composition/faqs/overview_fund_gov_idc (last visited July 4, 2015) [hereinafter IDC, *Mutual Fund Governance*] (noting that "all of the funds within a fund complex usually receive necessary services from the same entities, are served by common personnel, and are organized around common operating features").

[60] See Brown, 664 F.3d at 130 ("Most mutual fund complexes have unitary boards"); IDC, *Mutual Fund Governance*, supra note 59 ("[F]und boards employ a 'unitary' board model (a single board overseeing all funds in the complex)").

[61] See *Organizing a Mutual Fund*, K&L GATES 4 (2013) www.klgates.com/files/Upload/DC_IM_03-Organizing_Mutual_Fund.pdf ("[A mutual fund] sponsor may use a single legal entity to offer multiple portfolios or 'series' of shares, each having different investment objectives, policies, and potential investors, *i.e.*, a 'series fund'").

[62] See id.

[63] Cf. *Brown*, 664 F.3d at 130 (observing that a unitary board is "responsible to the entire family of funds").

[64] According to Judge Posner: "A unitary board [is] responsible to the entire family of funds, including future funds because the present value of an enterprise is the discounted value of its future earnings. This responsibility may require the board to make tradeoffs to the disadvantage of investors in one of the funds for the sake of the welfare of the family a whole." *Id.*

to the fund group, such an approach arguably does not comport with either the Investment Company Act or the board's fiduciary obligations.[65]

4 THE NEW MODEL

Despite the fact that the traditional model has dominated the mutual fund industry virtually since its inception, over the past decade a second model has emerged and gained ground.[66] This alternative model, like the traditional model, centers on a corporate governance mode of regulation—indeed, given the content of the Investment Company Act, it cannot do otherwise.[67] However, the new model differs in several significant ways from the traditional model. Because of those differences, it also gives rise to the question of whether it might create fewer adverse incentives and be more effective in furthering corporate governance and securities regulatory objectives.

In the new model, although the concept of a fund group—and a single unifying sponsor—remains, the investment adviser is not the pivot around which the enterprise rotates. Rather, the group, which typically takes the form of a series trust or other "umbrella" entity, is tied together by a service provider, typically a mutual fund administration firm.[68] As the sponsor, the administrator is responsible for organizing each member fund. In addition—and not surprisingly—if the sponsor is the administrator, that firm performs administrative services for each of the funds, including reconciling the funds' securities trades, assisting with regulatory filings, calculating and paying service provider fees and other fund expenses, preparing each fund's financial statements, and preliminarily valuing the funds' portfolio holdings.[69] It also plays the

---

[65] Indeed, the notion that appointing the same board for each fund within a fund group produces cost efficiencies stands squarely in tension with the principle that a board should devote the same amount of time and attention to each fund that it oversees.

[66] The president of one firm that sponsors new-model fund groups estimates that the structures had attracted at least $150 billion as of mid-2016. This estimate is likely too low, however, given a report stating that, by mid-2013, assets in the series trusts sponsored by only five of the sponsoring administrators had exceeded $137 billion. See INFOVEST21, SPECIAL RESEARCH REPORT: SELECTING A SERIES TRUST 16 (Aug. 2012), http://library.constantcontact.com/download/get/file/1102801309343-498/Special+Research+Report+Selecting+a+Series+Trust.pdf [hereinafter SELECTING A SERIES TRUST].

[67] See supra notes 16–37 and accompanying text (describing the role of boards in the mutual fund regulatory structure).

[68] See U.S. BANCORP FUND SERVICES LLC, MSTs EXPERIENCE RECORD GROWTH 2 (2013), www.usbfs.com/usbfs/documents/2013/white-papers/USBFS_MST_whitepaper.pdf [hereinafter U.S. BANCORP, GROWTH OF MSTs] ("The [new-model fund] structure is typically sponsored by a service provider"). As of mid-2016, approximately eight administrators sponsored series trusts, with Gemini Fund Services, SEI Investment Manager Services, UMB Fund Services, and U.S. Bancorp Fund Services being among the more dominant firms in the sponsorship arena. Other administrators that act as series trusts sponsors are ALPS, Atlantic Fund Services, BNY Mellon, and Ultimus Fund Solutions.

[69] See id. at 3 (noting that new model funds within the same trust structure usually share the same service providers).

dominant role in marketing the structure to investment advisers that may be interested in launching one or more funds within it.

Accordingly, in the new model, there are multiple advisers—perhaps a dozen or more—managing assets within each umbrella entity,[70] with each adviser managing one or, eventually, a small handful of funds. The new model has blossomed in recent years in lockstep with the growth of the investment advisory industry, itself a product of strong financial markets and investors with sufficient capital to seek professional guidance with their investments. In what is now a competitive market for advisory services, many advisers, including many newer ones who were perhaps at first focused on managing hedge funds or separate accounts for sophisticated investors, have sought to make their investment strategies available to the much broader (and potentially lucrative) retail investor market.[71] Managing a mutual fund is one, if not the only, way to do that.[72]

Arguably the most formidable challenge facing these investment advisers—particularly the newer advisers, which are often smaller than more established ones—is a resources challenge. As noted in section 3, the mutual fund business is a cost-intensive one, particularly at the outset.[73] For a smaller adviser, therefore, the costs associated with starting such a business by launching its own traditional-model fund group will often be prohibitive.[74] By offering a cost-effective mutual fund structure, the new model provides a way for such an adviser to achieve its goal of managing retail investors' assets.[75] This solution not only works for the adviser, who, by not acting as

---

[70] *See id.* at 2 ("The [new-model] structure is … utilized by multiple, unrelated investment management firms to house their mutual fund products").

[71] *See* Corrie Driebusch, *Mutual Funds that Hire Hedge-Fund Managers*, WALL ST. J. (Dec. 4, 2013), www.wsj.com/articles/SB10001424052702304448204579183970188148750 ("[H]edge-fund managers are increasingly seeing the opportunity in the small-investor and defined-contribution spaces") (internal citation omitted).

[72] Christine Williamson, *Hedge Funds Zoom in on Mutual Funds*, PENSIONS & INV., Apr. 29, 2013, at 1, 1 www.pionline.com/article/20130429/PRINT/304299975/hedge-funds-zoom-in-on-mutual-funds ("Hedge fund managers are looking to the mutual fund industry for their next source of growth").

[73] *See supra* notes 55–59 (describing the costs associated with starting a mutual fund).

[74] *See Can Anyone Create a Mutual Fund?*, MOTLEY FOOL, www.fool.com/knowledge-center/can-anyone-create-a-mutual-fund.aspx (reciting some of the complexities of starting a mutual fund and noting that the associated costs can be prohibitive for many prospective sponsors).

[75] The new model may be confused with a common permutation of the traditional model, in which the sponsoring investment adviser does not directly manage the portfolios of the funds comprising the group but rather engages a number of other investment advisers—appropriately called subadvisers—to perform that role. In this structure, each subadviser manages a single fund or, as is often the case, part of the assets of one or more funds in the group. Although such a structure involves numerous advisers (the subadvisers), it differs from new model fund groups in that the subadvisers do not have "ownership" of the funds—or portions thereof—that they manage. Among other things, a subadviser typically does not have exclusive authority to determine the investment strategies that it will use to manage the allocated assets but, instead, must make those decisions in consultation with the sponsoring adviser. In addition, the subadviser is entitled to only a portion—usually less than 50 percent—of the management fee paid by the funds that it manages, rather than the full fee, as is the case for advisers managing

the sponsor of the entire enterprise, does not bear the brunt of overhead and startup costs;[76] it also serves the needs of retail investors, who increasingly seek access to "alternative" (hedge fund-like) investment strategies that previously were available only to sophisticated investors.[77]

Apart from the cost efficiencies that it permits, the new model allows an adviser to begin operating "its" funds in substantially less time than what would be required to build a fund group from the ground up. After all, the adviser is not responsible for organizing the umbrella entity and launching its operations—tasks that the sponsor will already have completed. In addition, in most cases, the adviser need not select an administrator, counsel, distributor, transfer agent, or auditor because the sponsor will already have done that. Nor does the adviser need to spend time negotiating the terms of any necessary agreement between its fund and any given service provider because such agreements are typically based on the agreements completed between the service providers and other funds that are already part of the group. Finally, the adviser need not spend time overseeing each service provider as it performs its responsibilities, at least to the extent that those responsibilities pertain to the umbrella entity or to other funds in the group.[78] As an SEI brochure notes, the new-model structure "potentially offers ... operational efficiencies through a leveraged platform, access to trust-level selling agreements, and a much shorter time to market."[79]

---

a new model fund. Further, the subadvisory relationship creates little branding or marketing benefit for the subadviser because the funds that it manages are squarely under the sponsoring adviser's aegis. Finally, from a more functional perspective, there is a limit to the number of subadvisers that may be involved with any particular traditional-model fund group and to the types of strategies those subadvisers may use—limits that the sponsoring adviser determines, based on the relevant funds' investment programs. By contrast, the number and types of advisers that may participate in a new model fund group are determined only by investor demand and the quality of services provided by the advisers, as indicated by their performance managing other accounts.

[76] See U.S. BANCORP, GROWTH OF MSTS, *supra* note 68, at 3 (listing as one of the advantages of the new model the fact that a new-model fund "provides economies of scale for certain fund startup and annual operating costs," in part because "certain annual operating expenses for a [new-model] fund ... are reduced due to the allocation of certain costs across all funds within the Trust").

[77] *Cf.* Williamson, *supra* note 72 ("The [Investment Company Act] has real, tangible benefits for retail investors, and you will see some world-class hedge funds entering the liquid alternatives space") (quoting Neil Siegel of Neuberger Berman Group LLC).

[78] The respective obligations of the adviser and the sponsor are typically set forth in an agreement that the parties sign at the outset of the relationship and therefore may differ in various respects from the general description here. Under that agreement, moreover, the adviser is usually obligated to pay the sponsor an upfront fee and to bear certain costs, such as the fees that fund counsel charges for registering the offering(s) that the adviser's fund(s) will conduct. In addition, the adviser typically agrees to indemnify the sponsor for any losses the sponsor may suffer as a result of its activities under the agreement, other than those arising from its own negligence or misconduct.

[79] THE RETAIL ALTERNATIVES PHENOMENON: WHAT ENTERPRISING PRIVATE FUND MANAGERS NEED TO KNOW 21 (2013), www.seic.com/IMS/SEI-IMS-RetailAlternatives-US-2013.pdf.

Like the traditional model, the new model relies on boards of directors for meeting securities regulatory requirements.[80] However, a new-model board differs in an important way from traditional-model boards, a product of the fact that each adviser participating in a new-model fund group is but one small component of the group: Each director is typically independent of all of the advisers within the fund group,[81] meaning that none of them is an employee or other affiliate of any adviser. Moreover, the procedures through which advisers typically are selected to join the group reinforce this independence. In particular, although the board must evaluate and approve each new adviser,[82] the board usually has no involvement in the administrator's efforts to recruit new advisers to the group—and, therefore, typically does not have a say in determining what advisers will come before it for consideration. Accordingly, in at least two respects, the new model promises to serve the interests of effective regulation and sound corporate governance better than the traditional model does.

Because of these differences between the new model and the traditional model, the board in the former should have no incentives to comply with any adviser's wishes, at least not without analysis and discussion consistent with its fiduciary obligations. Nor should it be prone to avoid terminating a fund's advisory contract with an adviser (thereby terminating the adviser's involvement with the fund group) when doing so would be in shareholders' best interests. Rather, the board is able to uphold its fiduciary duties in its decisions pertaining to advisers without any possible concern that it will jeopardize its status by doing so.

5 NEW MODEL ANALYSIS

The new model is, perhaps, an improvement over the traditional model in several important respects, but is it ideal? Perhaps not. For purposes of assessing which model is the better one, in terms of promoting corporate governance and regulatory objectives, the inevitable question is whether the new model harbors its own structural risks. If it does, the further question is whether those risks are more or less substantial than risks associated with the traditional model—and, if so, whether there is a better approach.

A few structural risks—once again, in the realm of conflicts of interest—are apparent. As an initial matter, because, in the new model, the role of the administrator-as-sponsor has supplanted the all important role of the investment adviser-as-sponsor, the new-model board may be afflicted with incentives similar in kind to those plaguing the traditional model. After all, just as an adviser in the traditional model is, in its capacity as sponsor, often responsible for appointing directors, so it is in the new

---

[80] *See* U.S. BANCORP, GROWTH OF MSTS, *supra* note 68, at 4 (observing that "[t]he responsibilities of [new-model] Board members are identical to those of a proprietary fund trustee" and listing some of the responsibilities of new-model boards).

[81] *See id.* ("[New-model] Trustees are entirely independent of the advisers within the Trust, creating a true 'arm's length' arrangement between the fund and the adviser").

[82] *See* 15 U.S.C. § 80a-15(c) (2012) (requiring board approval of an investment adviser's contract with a mutual fund); ICI, ROLE OF DIRECTORS, *supra* note 6, at 15 ("A majority of the independent directors must vote in person at a specially designated meeting to approve the advisory contract and its renewal every year").

model: The administrator, as the sponsor, generally has appointment discretion, at least as to the initial directors (although, in setting the slate of candidates it may rely on recommendations from the initial adviser, fund counsel, or other director candidates).[83] Yet if the directors' status as such is primarily attributable to the administrator, then might the board be somewhat more inclined than it otherwise would be to accede to the administrator's wishes? Furthermore, for the same reason, might the board be somewhat more hesitant than it otherwise would be to terminate the administrator's status as administrator in favor of a competing administration firm? Finally, to the extent that the funds' distributor or other service providers are affiliates of the administrator, might the board be more willing than it otherwise would be to retain them as service providers as well?

This author is inclined to answer "no" to those questions. This is not because the administrator's role in the new model is not equivalent to the adviser's role in the traditional model or because adverse consequences from a new-model board's defying the administrator's wishes could not be severe. It is, and, at least in theory, they could be. Rather, the reason that adverse incentives are muted in the new model is that the advisers are where the money is. Without the firms that manage the assets, there is no enterprise.[84] If an adviser is successful, its performance record attracts additional investors and additional capital from existing investors, and everyone (hopefully) benefits, from the service providers who receive higher fees from servicing larger, more complex funds to the board, whose compensation may also increase commensurately for largely the same reasons.[85]

---

[83] The appointment process is similar to that used for a traditional-model fund group, in that the initial shareholder appoints the initial directors. *See supra* note 42 and accompanying text. Although the sponsoring administrator could serve as the initial shareholder, the initial investment adviser in the group often fills that role. In most cases, however, it is merely a formal role, in that the adviser simply elects the candidates that the administrator has chosen, based on its own preferences and possibly also recommendations from other involved parties. Telephone interview with Thomas Westle, Partner, Blank Rome LLP (July 25, 2016).

[84] Of course, this might be said of other types of service providers to mutual funds. In that regard, the firms that market a mutual fund, in particular, come to mind. After all, the distribution mechanisms these firms provide are responsible for bringing investors (and their all-critical capital) to the fund. However, even marketers are not as important as the fund's adviser, evidenced by the fact that not all funds rely on them; rather, some funds obtain capital from other sources, such as investors who were already clients of the adviser before the funds began operating. Indeed, in those circumstances the adviser may have established the fund to provide a particular type of product to its existing clients.

[85] The importance of the investment adviser is evident in the emphasis that investors place on them in selecting the funds in which they will invest. *See* William J. Nutt, *A Study of Mutual Fund Independent Directors*, 120 U. PA. L. REV. 179, 223 (1971) (discussing the importance to mutual fund shareholders of the investment adviser's reputation and experience); Richard M. Phillips, *Mutual Fund Independent Directors: A Model for Corporate America?* INV. COMPANY INST. PERSP. 5–6 (Aug. 2003), www.ici.org/pdf/per09-04.pdf ("Since there usually are many funds with comparable investment objectives and investment strategies, [investors] choose the particular fund which, in their individual judgment, has the best possible manager to implement their chosen investment strategy and shareholder services suitable to their needs at an acceptable cost").

To be sure, advisers do not always perform well, and, therefore, the funds they manage are not always profitable—and, indeed, may be unprofitable for years on end. As discussed in section 3, in the traditional model, the board will likely hesitate to terminate even those advisers, given the incentives at play.[86] In the new model, however, there is little reason for the board to march in line with the administrator to the extent that profitability, efficiency, or other interests could be furthered by its refusing to do so. That is, in such cases, furthering shareholders' interests furthers everyone's interests, which is how the norms of corporate governance ideally should function.

Beyond the notion that conflicts could arise from the administrator's role in selecting directors is the possibility that, because the new model typically is characterized by a unitary board,[87] there could arise the same concerns as those to which a unitary board gives rise in the traditional fund structure. That is, just as a unitary board in the traditional model could—even if unwittingly—allocate costs or otherwise make decisions that disadvantage one fund and advantage another, so could a unitary board in the new model act so as to privilege some funds over others.[88]

However, on this question, too, there is reason to think that the structural risks presented by a new-model unitary board are not as great as those associated with a unitary board in the traditional model. This suggestion stems from the greater diversity of new-model funds within any given fund group as compared with traditional-model funds within a particular fund group. The latter are, as noted, managed by a single adviser and, because of that, in many cases have investment strategies that are very similar to the strategies of other funds within the group. The strategies might be aptly regarded as variations on a theme, with that theme being, for example, investing in ETFs, other mutual funds, US securities, international securities, or something else.

By contrast, because the new model is characterized by multiple advisers, each with its own investment strategy or set of strategies, one adviser's investment strategy will differ, perhaps significantly so, from the strategies of any other adviser participating in the fund group. This heterogeneity among funds and managers in new-model fund groups means that fewer board decisions (whether pertaining to cost allocations or other matters) apply to all funds within the group, and more decisions are relevant only for funds managed by a single adviser or group of advisers. For example, a new-model fund group is arguably more likely than a traditional-model fund group to have multiple auditors or custodians, depending on the needs of any particular fund and the preferences of any particular adviser. Accordingly, the board's allocation of fees charged by a custodian should involve only the funds to which the custodian provides services, thereby eliminating the risk that any other funds may be adversely affected by the allocation.

---

[86] *See supra* note 49 and accompanying text (describing boards' disincentives to terminate an adviser in the traditional model).

[87] *See* U.S. BANCORP, GROWTH OF MSTS, *supra* note 68, at 2–3 (noting that a board in a new model fund group serves as the board for all of the funds in the group).

[88] *See id.* at 3 (observing that certain costs in a new model fund group are typically allocated "across all funds within the [group]," including, among other things, "[t]rustee expenses, [t]rust level legal counsel costs … [and] [c]ertain state Blue Sky permit costs").

Nevertheless, although the new model may present fewer risks to shareholders in each of the areas elaborated in section 3, it may pose unique risks that are not present, or not present to the same extent, in the traditional model. For one thing, the prevalence of smaller advisory firms in new-model structures could create at least some risks, in the sense that smaller advisers have not been tested by time, at least not to the same extent as their better-established counterparts. Many of the advisers are not, in other words, "known quantities," in the way that Janus, Fidelity, or BlackRock are.[89] As a result, both their abilities and their business ethics present less certainty as compared with the established advisers' abilities and ethics.[90]

That concern is augmented, moreover, by the fact that smaller advisers almost universally have less well developed compliance infrastructures, as compared with larger advisers. After all, whereas advisers that manage mutual funds must be registered with the SEC as investment advisers, many advisers involved with new-model structures are sufficiently small that, prior to that involvement, they were not so registered.[91] This means, among other things, that these advisers likely did not have either a chief compliance officer or policies and procedures addressing risks arising from their businesses, both of which are required for SEC-registered advisers.[92] In short, they may not have cultivated the "culture of compliance" that regulators emphasize as critical among financial firm personnel, or at least not one as robust as what might be discernible in more established advisory firms.[93]

In the end, however, it is difficult to know whether these presumed differences between traditional model advisers and new model advisers present true risks to new-model shareholders or whether instead they are nothing more than differences, which for any new-model adviser will subside over time as the adviser becomes more

---

[89] *See* U.S. BANCORP, GROWTH OF MSTS, *supra* note 68, at 2 ("Historically, [new model fund structures] were utilized by advisers with limited assets under management as an inexpensive means of offering a mutual fund family with small assets").

[90] *See* Luke T. Cadigan, *The SEC's Aggressive New Approach to Exams and Investigations of Investment Advisers and Investment Companies*, THE INVESTMENT LAWYER, May 2012, at 5 (suggesting that the SEC has greater than average regulatory interest in "smaller advisers").

[91] Under the Investment Advisers Act of 1940 (the "Advisers Act"), a "small" adviser (based on assets under management) is not required—indeed, is not permitted—to register with the SEC as an investment adviser, *see* 15 U.S.C. § 80b-3a(a)(1)(A), except that an adviser, regardless of its size, must become registered if it manages a mutual fund or other fund registered under the Investment Company Act, *see* 15 U.S.C. § 80b-3a(a)(1)(B) (2012).

[92] That is, pursuant to the SEC's rules under the Advisers Act, an SEC-registered investment adviser must appoint a chief compliance officer to administer the firm's policies and procedures. *See* 17 C.F.R. § 275.206(4)-7 (2016); *Information for Newly-Registered Investment Advisers*, U.S. SEC. & EXCHANGE COMMISSION, www.sec.gov/divisions/investment/advoverview.htm (last modified Nov. 23, 2010).

[93] *See* Luis A. Aguilar, Comm'r, U.S. Sec. & Exch. Comm'n, Doing the Right Thing: Compliance that Works for Investors, Remarks at the Regulatory Compliance Association, Regulation, Operations & Compliance (ROC) 2013 Conference (Apr. 18, 2013), www.sec.gov/News/Speech/Detail/Speech/1365171515784 (noting that "[t]he SEC has long focused on requiring a strong compliance culture at investment advisory firms" and defining such a culture as "an environment where everyone understands that the firm values honesty, integrity, and takes compliance issues seriously").

experienced in the world of publicly offered funds. In any event, new-model fund groups, like their traditional counterparts, have their own strong regulatory compliance infrastructures, in the form of dedicated chief compliance officers and tailored policies and procedures designed to address fund-specific risks.[94] In addition, because a group's compliance risks are derivative of those of the investment advisers within the group, one of the responsibilities of the group's chief compliance officer is to monitor each adviser to ensure that it continues to comply with regulatory requirements. That strong compliance overlay may help shore up whatever compliance difficulties a particular adviser may experience.

6 CONCLUSION

The discussion in this chapter suggests that there are both advantages and disadvantages associated with each model of mutual fund governance and that the new model holds its own in comparison to the traditional one and may be better in certain respects and worse in others. As noted, of course, the new model also has the general policy advantage that it opens up a vastly larger world of investing to retail investors. Yet the discussion also indicates that neither model is ideal, thanks largely to the prospect of conflicts of interest and the incentives that those conflicts could produce—incentives that could adversely affect shareholders.

These observations may provide a reason to look for a better model of mutual fund regulation, one not centered on a board of directors and the associated corporate governance approach to regulatory oversight. To be sure, this suggestion is far from new. The varied critiques of board governance of mutual funds have focused on different factors and called for different solutions, but, by identifying problems arising from the board's formal responsibilities or the way it functions in practice, each has in some way taken to task the corporate governance basis of mutual fund regulation.[95]

Nevertheless, the circumstances out of which the new model emerged may justify that model's existence, at least to the same extent as any justification for the traditional model. This suggestion is a product of the criticism that a board-centered regulatory approach is insufficient because boards cannot have adequate oversight over the all-critical advisers. In the traditional model, after all, advisers are—or, more accurately, *the adviser* is—the epicenter of the fund group's activities, and the adviser's employees, by carrying out many of the funds' day to day activities, also effectively act as the *funds*' employees.[96] This structure is troublesome because one of the signal activities of a board, whether it be a mutual fund board or the board of another type of public

---

[94] See 17 C.F.R. § 270.38a-1(a) (2016) (requiring that mutual funds (and other funds registered under the Investment Company Act) appoint a chief compliance officer); U.S. BANCORP, GROWTH OF MSTS, *supra* note 68, at 4 (observing that new-model funds "provide an experienced Chief Compliance Officer for all funds within the Trust").

[95] See *supra* notes 8–10 and accompanying text (describing and listing previous scholarly work that evaluates the mutual fund regulatory structure).

[96] See *supra* note 41 and accompanying text (describing the extensive role of the investment adviser and its employees in carrying out the mutual fund's operations and activities).

company, is to oversee the entity's activities and the persons carrying them out.[97] However, in the mutual fund context, the board may be powerless to do that, given that it has no formal relationship or affiliation with the adviser.[98]

This structural challenge, which precludes traditional-model boards from fully and completely performing their oversight obligations, is arguably part and parcel of the structure-based incentives that characterize board governance in the traditional model.[99] That is, the possible effect of the board's inability to oversee the adviser's activities or to help set the adviser's business objectives is that the board will comply with whatever wishes or demands the adviser may have. The further possible effect is that it will fail to fully uphold shareholders' best interests.

Of course, as in the traditional model, each new-model adviser has substantial control over the particular fund or funds it manages, and its personnel are primarily responsible for those funds' day to day operations. Yet the new-model board can potentially be more effective by virtue of the muted power that any particular adviser wields. Moreover, if there were no unifying regulatory body in the new model—a body such as the board—it is difficult to envision how a fund group would be able to function efficiently, if at all. In other words, although new-model board governance is not perfect, for reasons articulated above, the board's regulatory role in the new context may present one of the strongest arguments for the board's continuing dominating role in the mutual fund regulatory regime.

---

[97] *See Frequently Asked Questions About Mutual Fund Directors*, INV. COMPANY INST., www.ici.org/pubs/faqs/ci.faq_fund_gov_idc.idc (last visited Aug. 12, 2016) ("Like the directors of a corporate board, mutual fund directors oversee the management and operations of a company (the fund) and have a fiduciary duty to represent the interests of shareholders").

[98] Or, more accurately, as mutual funds are usually structured today, the board has third party status vis-à-vis the adviser. As John Bogle has argued, however, that need not be the case and, indeed, has not always been the case. In the alternative structure that Bogle describes, managers are internal to the fund and operate not in their own interests but, rather, in the interests of shareholders. *See* Bogle, *supra* note 8, at 391 (observing that the first mutual fund, the Massachusetts Investors Trust, was a true "mutual" fund in the sense that it was "managed by its own trustees, who held the power ... to invest its assets" and who were compensated by the "current Boston rate for trustees") (internal quotation omitted).

[99] *See supra* section 2 (describing the adverse incentives that may be associated with board governance in the traditional model).

9. Mutual fund compliance: key developments and their implications

James Fanto

1 INTRODUCTION

The year 2003 saw the ten-year anniversary of the compliance rules for the Investment Advisers Act of 1940 and the Investment Company Act.[1] The period since the promulgation of the rules reflects significant progress for the compliance function in funds and for the compliance officers who staff it. The compliance officer now has an important control role in financial firms in general, and in investment advisers and companies in particular.[2] Compliance officers have moved from the back offices to occupy a more visible position in firms. In fact, the chief compliance officer ("CCO") is a significant executive and, as a result, has a seat at the management conference table.[3] Therefore, a look back over the situation of adviser and fund compliance in the ten or so years since the implementation of the compliance program rules compels the conclusion that the success of the compliance officer in the adviser and fund worlds mirrors the general rise in importance of compliance professionals more broadly in other firms and industries.[4]

However, even though their position in advisers and funds, as well as in other firms in the financial industry, is well established, compliance officers face several developments that may influence the direction of compliance practice. These are: (1) continuing confusion over potential supervisory liability for compliance officers; (2) the increasing use of technology by these officers; and (3) the possible integration of the compliance function into risk management, rather than compliance remaining as a standalone control function or within the legal department. As will be discussed in more detail later in the chapter, the developments are not new and to a certain extent reflect the enhanced position of compliance. Supervisory liability is an issue precisely because compliance officers have assumed more responsibilities in financial firms where they have been delegated managerial tasks. In addition, the developments are interrelated. For example, because technology enables compliance officers to become involved with a greater amount of firm matters, the following questions are raised: What exact role do the officers have with respect to a given transaction or decision? Are they in the supervisory chain? Moreover, as compliance officers become involved with more firm matters (again partly as a result of technology), the question naturally

---

[1] For the compliance rules, *see* Compliance Programs of Investment Companies and Investment Advisers (2003). Investment Advisers Act of 1940 hereafter Advisers Act.
[2] *See* SIFMA (2013) 1–2.
[3] *See* SIFMA (2013) 6–8.
[4] *See* Walsh (2015) 773–95 (discussing the growth of compliance as a profession).

arises as to where they fit into the increasingly dominant paradigm of financial firm management and regulation, or risk management.[5]

Although the developments will not likely undermine the success and achievements of the compliance function in advisers and funds, they are mutually reinforcing and thus powerful. The contention in this chapter is that they may be encouraging compliance officers to focus on a few of their tasks, chiefly monitoring or surveillance, while downplaying their equally important advisory and counseling responsibilities. While this distinction will be discussed more below, compliance exists to tell employees how to do their jobs in accordance with law, regulation, professional standards, and ethics, and then to ensure that they follow this direction. But its mission is also to enable compliance officers to offer counsel and advise employees when the application of legal and other standards is less than clear or is aspirational (for example, "put the customer's interests first"). These developments risk sacrificing certain benefits of this advisory function of a compliance program because they could push compliance officers to operate at a distance from business employees and to focus on their monitoring. Not only will some misconduct escape this remote surveillance, but in addition firm employees will lose the benefit of having a compliance officer who is "walking the halls" and can thus advise and counsel them as to the compliance implications of particular decisions, products, and strategies, and who, through this advice and counsel, can act as a model of compliant conduct and decisionmaking for these employees. The chapter thus argues that, rather than watching developments unfold, compliance officers and others interested in effective compliance, such as regulators, should make sure that they do not result in reduced effectiveness of compliance.

The chapter proceeds as follows. Section 1 reviews the origins of the compliance program rules in advisers and funds. It then discusses the requirements of the regulations and highlights the growth in the importance, and the establishment, of compliance in the adviser and fund sectors. Section 2 examines the statutory basis for a duty of supervision and thus of supervisory liability, and explains how jurisprudence of the Securities and Exchange Commission (SEC) broadened the definition of a supervisor so that it could be read to reach compliance officers performing established compliance tasks. The section argues that continuing uncertainty over the application of this liability to compliance officers could make them wary of engaging in advisory and counseling activities and lead them to focus on compliance work less likely to lead them to incur this liability. This is despite well-publicized efforts by the SEC and the Financial Industry Regulatory Authority (FINRA)[6] to assure compliance officers that they are not enforcement targets for supervisory liability.

Section 3 looks at the related development of the expanded use of technology by compliance officers, particularly in helping them to more efficiently perform their

---

[5] See SIFMA (2013) 8 (discussing compliance's relationship with other control functions).
[6] FINRA is the union of the former self-regulatory arms of the National Association of Securities Dealers (NASD), FINRA's actual predecessor, and the New York Stock Exchange (NYSE). This union occurred when the Nasdaq and NYSE stock markets became private companies, rather than member organizations. FINRA, like the NASD before it, is a registered securities association. Exchange Act 15A, 15 U.S.C. § 78o-3.

surveillance responsibilities. The section discusses how this use both increases their productivity in monitoring and distances them from business personnel by allowing them to remotely survey firm activities. It suggests that the use of technology reinforces the same trend as the uncertainty over supervisory liability: the distancing of compliance officers from business staff. Section 4 considers the effect of the increasingly significant risk management paradigm on the compliance function and speculates that, if compliance becomes a spoke in the risk management wheel, compliance officers will emphasize monitoring and controlling compliance "risks." As in the case of supervisory liability and the use of technology, compliance's adoption of this approach could undermine its advisory role, which may figure less prominently in the risk management paradigm. Section 5 concludes with suggestions as to how compliance officers, regulators, and others interested in maintaining an effective compliance function can respond to these developments.

2. THE COMPLIANCE PROGRAM RULES

While compliance became a legal requirement for investment funds and advisers only in 2004, it was not new to financial intermediaries in the securities markets. It was present in the broker-dealer industry from at least the 1970s.[7] The spur for the growth of compliance in broker-dealers was the establishment of a statutory supervisory liability for firms and for their supervisors as a result of the 1964 amendments to the federal securities laws.[8] Congress imposed the liability due to concern that the SEC did not have sufficient discretionary power over broker-dealers if a securities violation occurred in a firm—being able only to rescind their registration—and little power over firms' associated persons in relation to such violations.[9] Moreover, the imposition of supervisory liability was seen as a way to compel firms to use their managerial and organizational capabilities to ensure that their brokers were complying with the federal securities laws.[10] Under the applicable provision, if a broker committed a federal securities law violation, the SEC could charge the broker-dealer and the broker's supervisor for having "failed reasonably to supervise" the broker in question.[11] There were, however, important statutory defenses to supervisory liability. In particular, a broker-dealer could avoid liability by implementing reasonable supervisory procedures

---

[7] See *Guide to Broker-Dealer Compliance* (1974) 6–7 (early industry report on compliance commissioned by the SEC).

[8] See Securities Act Amendments of 1964 (1964) 565, 571–72 (for the predecessor provisions to those discussed below).

[9] "Associated person" would include supervisors, brokers, and others working at a broker-dealer who engage in its business. See Exchange Act § 3(a)(18), 15 U.S.C. § 78c(a)(18).

[10] I discuss this background elsewhere. See Fanto (2015) 134–44.

[11] See Exchange Act § 15(b)(4)(E), 15 U.S.C. § 78o(b)(4)(E). The provision imposes direct liability upon a broker-dealer for its failure to supervise its own brokers and other affiliated persons, and vicarious liability upon it for failure to supervise by its associated persons. The liability of supervisors arises under Exchange Act § 15(b)(6)(A)(i), 15 U.S.C. § 78o(b)(6)(A)(i), which cross-references Section 15(b)(4)(E). As is clear from the language, the statutory standard of conduct is reasonableness.

and a system for applying them "which would reasonably be expected to prevent and detect, insofar as practicable," the violations.[12] And the broker-dealer had to put the procedures and system "reasonably" into effect.[13]

Compliance became the specialized firm control function that drafted the supervisory policies and procedures; that told supervisors how to manage their business in accordance with law, regulations, and compliance policies and procedures; and that instructed brokers and other staff as to how to do their work in a legally compliant way. Compliance officers distributed, and trained supervisors and brokers in, these policies and procedures, and regularly provided information on, monitored compliance with, and investigated any potential violations of them.[14] The self-regulatory organizations (SROs),[15] chiefly what was then the NASD and the NYSE, imposed their own detailed requirements that broker-dealers have supervisory systems, which added to the growth of compliance in the brokerage industry.[16]

Compliance in investment advisers and funds came later, perhaps because there was (and still is) no SRO for advisers that would have promulgated detailed supervisory rules for them. Liability for a failure to supervise was imposed upon advisers and their associated persons only a few years after it had been placed on broker-dealers, by the Investment Company Amendments of 1970.[17] Indeed, the statutory language and the defenses were identical to those applicable to broker-dealers, and the legislative history indicates that Congress was conforming the Advisers Act to the Exchange Act on this and related issues.[18] The same regulatory goal of empowering the SEC with regard to advisers explained the conforming amendments.[19] As in the case of broker-dealers,

---

[12] See Exchange Act § 15(b)(4)(E)(i), 15 U.S.C. § 78o(b)(4)(E)(i).

[13] See Exchange Act § 15(b)(4)(E)(ii), 15 U.S.C. § 78o(b)(4)(E)(ii). The actual language was that "such person has reasonably discharged the duties and obligations incumbent upon him by reason of such procedures and system without reasonable cause to believe that such procedures and system were not being complied with."

[14] For a discussion of the role of compliance in broker-dealers, see Fanto (2014).

[15] Self-regulatory organizations are essentially markets or groups of financial professionals authorized under federal securities laws to regulate their own participants, which are generally broker-dealers operating in these markets, with this self-regulation subject to SEC oversight. See Exchange Act § 3(a)(26), 15 U.S.C. § 78c(a)(26) (definition of a self-regulatory organization).

[16] The main supervisory rules for FINRA are now in FINRA Rules 3110, 3120, and 3130. These rules have extensive requirements for supervisory and compliance systems in a broker-dealer.

[17] See (1970) 1431 (adding sections (e)(5) and (f) to Section 203 of the Advisers Act) (currently 15 U.S.C. §§ 80b-3(e)(6) and (f)).

[18] See Report of the House Committee on Interstate and Foreign Commerce, Investment Company Amendments of 1970 (1970) 40. The supervisory liability provision (as well as related others) was designed to give the SEC more disciplinary power over advisers and their associated persons, comparable to what the SEC had received for broker-dealers in 1964.

[19] There was a similar amendment with respect to investment companies. It made little sense to impose supervisory liability upon them, since they were set up and operated by investment advisers. Rather, the provision comparable to the imposition of supervisory liability upon an adviser was an amendment to Section 9 of the Investment Company Act, which, among other things, gave the SEC the power to bar a party from being associated with registered investment company if such person had willfully violated, or induced the violation of, the federal securities laws. See Investment Company Amendments of 1970 (1970) 1415–16.

compliance developed in advisers as a control function that would help the firm and supervisors satisfy their duty of supervision and avoid supervisory liability, even if investment advisers did not have the added requirement of having to comply with an SRO's supervisory rules.

Scandals in mutual funds in the early part of this century triggered the imposition of compliance program rules on advisers and funds that were comparable to SRO supervisory rules for broker-dealers. In these scandals, investment advisers, other mutual fund personnel, and service providers allowed favored clients to take advantage of fund shareholders generally through, among others, "market" timing of their orders, late trading, and use of insider information about funds.[20] In reaction to the scandals, the SEC required each fund and adviser to have a compliance program designed to prevent violations of the law and a CCO to administer the program. Indeed, at the same time that the SEC was promulgating the compliance program rules, it was approving SROs' efforts to enhance compliance programs in broker-dealers by, among other things, requiring a broker-dealer to do an annual assessment or audit of its supervisory system and to have a CCO in charge of the compliance program, which officer reported to a broker-dealer's senior executives and its board.[21]

The compliance program rules were Rule 206(4)-7 under the Advisers Act,[22] and Rule 38a-1 under the Investment Company Act.[23] They required each registered adviser and each fund to adopt and implement a compliance program with specified features, which in substance followed the broker-dealer model under SRO rules. An adviser was to have "written policies and procedures reasonably designed to prevent" violations of the Advisers Act and its rules by the adviser or by anybody under its supervision.[24] The policies and procedures also had to enable the adviser to detect violations that had occurred and to correct them promptly.[25] The SEC set out the kinds of compliance risks or issues that, in the SEC's view, an adviser typically had to address in the policies and procedures and that had in fact appeared in the scandals. These included portfolio management processes (for example, allocation of investment opportunities among clients), trading practices (for example, satisfying best execution responsibility), proprietary trading and personal trading of supervised persons, accuracy of disclosure

---

[20] The SEC discussed these scandals as background to the rules. *See* Compliance Programs of Investment Companies and Investment Advisers (2003) 74, 714–15. For example, a favored client might be allowed to profit from late-breaking favorable news concerning the securities in a fund's portfolio by purchasing fund shares after hours at a price not reflective of this positive news. And the scandals clearly shaped the specifics of the rules, as will be highlighted further below. For a discussion of the background to the compliance program rules, see Nagy (2006) 17–18.

[21] *See* Walsh (2008) 389–99 (discussing the reforms to the then NASD rules that imposed a CCO requirement on broker-dealers, together with an annual meeting between the CCO and the firm's chief executive (NASD Rule 3013), and an obligation to do an annual self-assessment of the supervisory system (NASD Rule 3012)).

[22] 17 C.F.R. § 275.206(4)-7 (2018).

[23] 17 C.F.R. § 270.38a-1 (2018).

[24] 17 C.F.R. § 275.206(4)-7(a) (2018).

[25] *See* Compliance Programs of Investment Companies and Investment Advisers (2003) 74, 716.

to clients and others, protection of client assets, recordkeeping, marketing, valuation, privacy, and business continuity.[26]

Rule 38a-1 essentially required investment fund boards to adopt and implement "written policies and procedures reasonably designed to prevent" violations of the federal securities laws by their funds.[27] In addition, these policies and procedures had to provide for the oversight of compliance on the part of service providers to funds, that is, advisers, underwriters, administrators, and transfer agents.[28] As the SEC explained, a fund had flexibility in satisfying this requirement. A fund's policies and procedures could cover itself and all its service providers; they could provide for the fund's approval of the policies and procedures of each service provider; or there could be a mix of the two (for example, they could provide for compliance of some service providers and oversight of compliance of others).[29] In addition, under this rule a fund's board (including a majority of its independent directors) had to approve the policies and procedures of the fund and of each of its service providers on the basis of a finding that they satisfied the foregoing "reasonably designed" criterion.[30] To do this appropriately, the board could consult with the fund's CCO, legal counsel, or compliance experts, or rely upon a third party report about the service provider's compliance program.[31] A fund's policies and procedures had also to address the same risks as those of advisers, as well as additional ones, many of which had appeared in the mutual fund scandals, such as pricing of portfolio securities and fund shares, processing of fund orders, identification of affiliated persons, prevention of insider trading, compliance with fund governance in board constitution, and market timing.[32]

As previously noted, the compliance program rules imposed an annual review and assessment requirement similar to the one that the SROs were placing upon broker-dealers at the same time.[33] Rule 206(4)-7 requires an adviser "no less frequently than annually" (and preferably on an interim basis as well) to review its policies and procedures for their adequacy and the effectiveness of their implementation.[34] This annual review requires an adviser to consider changes to the policies and procedures as a result of compliance events that had occurred, business developments, and/or new legal obligations imposed upon it.[35] Under Rule 38a-1, a fund should similarly conduct an annual review, which would include a review of the effectiveness of compliance programs in its service providers,[36] although the SEC suggested that the fund board

---

[26] See id. 74,716.
[27] 17 C.F.R. § 270.38a-1(a)(1) (2018).
[28] Id.
[29] See Compliance Programs of Investment Companies and Investment Advisers (2003) 74,717.
[30] 17 C.F.R. § 270.38a-1(a)(2) (2018).
[31] See Compliance Programs of Investment Companies and Investment Advisers (2003) 74,717.
[32] See id. 74,718–20.
[33] See Walsh (2008) 395–98.
[34] 17 C.F.R. § 275.206(4)-7(b) (2018).
[35] See Compliance Programs of Investment Companies and Investment Advisers (2003) 74,720.
[36] 17 C.F.R. § 270.38a-1(a)(3) (2018).

could rely upon a report on that subject by the CCO.[37] Again, any serious compliance breakdown, any significant new business activities, or a new law or regulation should trigger an interim review.[38]

The highlight of the compliance program rules—at least for the purposes of this chapter—was the requirement that a CCO be designated to administer the compliance program,[39] a requirement that mirrored the imposition of the same upon broker-dealers, albeit through an SRO rule.[40] The rules as to the CCO were slightly different in advisers and funds to reflect the reality of each. In an adviser, the CCO had to be a "supervised person" who should be "competent and knowledgeable" about the law and have the requisite authority to develop the policies and procedures and to compel others to follow them.[41] The CCO did not have to be just a compliance officer, but could have business responsibilities.[42] The fund rule imposed more requirements as to a fund's CCO in order to make that person independent from the management of the fund, that is, from the fund adviser.[43] Thus, the fund board (including a majority of the independent directors) had to approve the hiring and dismissal of the CCO and the CCO's compensation (and changes thereto).[44] Moreover, the CCO was required to meet with the board and to present an annual written report to it about the operation of the compliance policies and procedures during the year (and those of service providers), material changes to them, any recommendations for material changes made as a result of the annual assessment, and any "Material Compliance Matter" since the date of the last report.[45] The CCO had also to meet in executive session with the independent directors of the fund at least once a year, without the presence of anyone else, such as the adviser.[46] The Rule also tried to protect the fund CCO from undue influence by any of the fund directors, employees, or service providers.[47] Nevertheless, as was the case of a CCO for an investment adviser, the occupant of a fund CCO position could have

---

[37] See Compliance Programs of Investment Companies and Investment Advisers (2003) 74,720.
[38] See id.
[39] 17 C.F.R. § 275.206(4)-7(c) (2016); 17 C.F.R. § 270.38a-1(a)(4) (2018).
[40] See Walsh (2008) 390-91 (discussing the requirement among advisers, broker-dealers, and funds).
[41] See Compliance Programs of Investment Companies and Investment Advisers (2003) 74,720.
[42] See id. 74,720 n. 74.
[43] See id. 74,721.
[44] 17 C.F.R. § 270.38a-1(a)(4)(i) and (ii) (2018).
[45] 17 C.F.R. § 270.38a-1(a)(4)(iii) (2018). "Material Compliance Matter" is defined to refer to a matter that the board would reasonably need to know about with respect to its oversight of compliance and that involves a violation of the federal securities laws or the compliance policies and procedures by the fund or by a service provider, or a weakness in the design or implementation of the policies or procedures, or those of a service provider. 17 C.F.R. § 270.38a-1(e)(2) (2018).
[46] 17 C.F.R. § 270.38a-1(a)(4)(iv) (2018).
[47] 17 C.F.R. § 270.38a-1(c) (2018).

another position with a service provider; indeed, a fund CCO was assumed by the SEC to be an employee of the adviser or another service provider (and even the CCO of them).[48]

Certainly, the compliance program rules for advisers and funds and the comparable SRO rules for broker-dealers did much to establish and to enhance the position of compliance officers, particularly CCOs, in these firms. As is particularly evident in the fund context, but was also true for broker-dealers,[49] the CCO had by rule access to the highest legal authority of the firm, which made the CCO an important executive. This importance was reinforced by the authority given to CCOs to compel employees to follow the compliance policies and procedures and by the annual assessment, which brought the CCO and other senior executives together to discuss the adequacy and effectiveness of existing supervisory and compliance policies and procedures and the necessity for new ones as a result of business developments. In sum, the CCO had to have a seat at the CEO's executive table. Moreover, that the CCO needed to be knowledgeable and competent about compliance, not only to create and to administer the policies and procedures but also to adjust them to changing circumstances, meant that this position demanded an increasingly specialized expertise in compliance and could not be easily filled by a nonspecialist.[50]

If we fast forward to ten or so years after the promulgation of the compliance program rules, we see that, at least in broker-dealers, investment advisers, and investment funds, CCO is a well-established, and even well-compensated,[51] position.[52] There are now defined career paths and educational training and certification possibilities for compliance professionals.[53] Compliance officers have their own "professional"

---

[48] See Compliance Programs of Investment Companies and Investment Advisers (2003) 74,722 and n.88.

[49] See FINRA Rule 3130 (requiring a broker-dealer CEO to certify that compliance policies and procedures are in place to prevent violations of the federal securities laws; the CEO makes this certification after meeting with and receiving a report from the CCO, which report also goes to the firm's board).

[50] There also existed a longstanding rule that a fund have a code of ethics. See Prevention of Certain Unlawful Activities with Respect to Registered Investment Companies (1980) (promulgating Rule 17j-1). Among other things, this rule imposed a code of ethics requirement on an investment adviser to a fund. The code of ethics rule for an investment adviser as such came later, following the imposition of the compliance rule. See Investment Adviser Codes of Ethics (2004) (promulgating Rule 204A-1).

[51] See, e.g., Society of Corporate Compliance and Ethics (2012) 19 (indicating average compensation for CCOs in financial services to be approximately $165,000).

[52] Congress now follows this CCO model in other financial firms. For example, new section 15F(k) of the Exchange Act, enacted by Dodd-Frank, regulation mandates that a security-based swap dealer have a CCO to implement compliance. See 15 U.S.C. § 78o-10(k).

[53] One example in the broker-dealer/investment adviser world is the annual FINRA Institute at Georgetown, which trains and certifies compliance professionals in the Certified Regulatory and Compliance Professional ("CRCP") Program. See Certified Regulatory and Compliance Professional Program, www.finra.org/Industry/Education/UniversityPrograms/FINRAInstitute.

organizations with their own specialized conferences and journals.[54] Regulators such as the SEC and SROs such as FINRA pay regular attention, and devote considerable resources, to compliance professionals, enlisting them in their oversight of firms.[55] The story of compliance since the promulgation of the compliance program rules has thus really been one of the steadily growing importance of compliance officers, even if they were unable to prevent many of the scandals in broker-dealers and investment advisers that occurred since that time and if their overall effectiveness in preventing securities law violations has not been established. Yet there are developments in compliance that pose challenges to its position, and it is to these that the chapter now turns.

3 SUPERVISORY LIABILITY

The first compliance development to be discussed is the status of a compliance officer as a supervisor in an investment adviser or investment fund. More specifically, the question is whether, and when, supervisory liability can be imposed upon a compliance officer as a result of the performance of compliance tasks. As discussed previously in the chapter, supervisors in a broker-dealer or investment adviser are liable if they failed reasonably to supervise any person under their supervision who commits a securities law violation. And as was also examined previously, supervisory liability was originally imposed upon firm supervisors to encourage the "middle managers" in broker-dealer and investment adviser firms to police their employees' conduct. Compliance officers assist the firm and its supervisors by establishing and operating the supervisory and compliance systems that provide a defense to this liability. Supervisors need the assistance of compliance officers in order to satisfy their duty of supervision, and supervisors make disciplinary and other personnel decisions often based upon findings of compliance officers. Yet, in general, compliance officers are outside the supervisory chain of command.

Sometimes the line between the supervisor and the compliance officer gets blurred, or the positions overlap. In smaller adviser firms that do not have a compliance infrastructure, an employee with business responsibilities may well assume the CCO role. This overlap is permissible. In these cases, a CCO could incur supervisory liability based upon what the CCO did while wearing the supervisor's hat.[56] Even in larger firms, a compliance officer may be given a particular task that is clearly supervisory, such as approving personal trades by adviser personnel. If the officer negligently performs this task, he or she may incur supervisory liability. In addition, compliance tasks may have supervisory implications. A compliance officer may be assigned the responsibility for drafting policies and procedures to ensure that the law is complied with in a given area and then fail reasonably to do this job, which results in federal

---

[54] One example for compliance officers in broker-dealers and investment advisers is the National Association of Compliance Professionals, www.nscp.org, which sponsors conferences and publishes a regular journal.

[55] The SEC holds regular "compliance outreach" programs for broker-dealer and investment adviser compliance professionals. *See* www.sec.gov/info/complianceoutreach.htm.

[56] *See* Rubin & Firippis (2015) 741–42 (listing such cases).

securities law violations within the firm. For example, a compliance officer might be mandated to draft and implement insider trading policies and procedures for the firm, but may fail to do so or may do a substandard job, after which insider trading by firm employees occurs. In this case, the compliance officer would be liable as a supervisor for the violations.[57]

While supervisory liability for a compliance officer could be seen as just an issue that arises whenever *any* employee, including the officer, has managerial or operational authority in a firm, it raises a problem that goes to the heart of that compliance position. As discussed previously, compliance officers draft and help to implement compliance and supervisory policies and procedures, educate employees about them, monitor compliance with them, and, when necessary, investigate violations of them. The officers also spend a considerable amount of their time advising supervisors and other business employees about the application to specific factual situations of laws, regulations, professional standards, and even ethics.[58] For example, they provide advice on the compliance implications of a new product or business strategy, or make a recommendation as to the legal and regulatory factors arising from a particular business decision. In exercising this advisory function, compliance officers are providing business employees with a model of compliant thinking and conduct.[59] This is why it is important that compliance officers have a seat at the business table (and the CCO at the executive table), so that they can offer their advice on almost every major firm decision or project, and that they "walk the halls" in a firm.[60]

The problem with supervisory liability for compliance officers arises from the fact that in its administrative decisions over the years, the SEC gradually broadened the definition of a supervisor so that it could conceivably include someone like a compliance officer who is providing advice. Originally, a supervisor was considered to be a person in the firm who could hire, dismiss, and control the actions of the supervised person, that is, someone with clear managerial authority.[61] Then the SEC adopted a more flexible, indeed vaguer, standard that made a supervisor a person who could "affect the conduct" of the supervised person.[62] Certainly, the SEC's intent here was understandable: not to allow those in the managerial chain of command of a broker-dealer or investment adviser, such as a chief executive officer or another senior executive, to escape supervisory liability by claiming that they did not have immediate authority over the violator. However, the "affecting conduct" language is broad enough to pull within the supervisor definition all those involved in a supervisory or disciplinary matter, including those who, like a legal officer or a compliance officer, might provide advice about a recommended course of action that executives should take with respect to a particular violation or problem. In fact, there have been a few

---

[57] For a settlement involving a chief compliance officer's failure to put into place procedures dealing with employees' outside activities and the conflicts arising under them, see *In re* BlackRock Advisors, LLC & Bartholomew A. Battista (2015).

[58] See SIFMA (2013) 3.

[59] See Fanto (2014) 1164 (discussing the "internal" compliance approach).

[60] See Donohue (2016) (recommending that, as one of the ways to get comfortable with a firm, a compliance officer should "[w]alk the floor").

[61] See Arthur James Huff (1991) *9.

[62] *In re* John H. Gutfreund, et al. (1992) *15.

Mutual fund compliance: key developments and their implications 215

notorious cases (including the one announcing this "affecting conduct" standard) in which the SEC's enforcement division brought a "failure to supervise" charge against these kinds of officers.[63] Although these cases have been few, they suggest that the SEC accepts a broad definition of supervisor, which creates potential supervisory liability for compliance officers (as well as for others not in the business line) that would be at the discretion of enforcement officials.[64] Compliance officers and their advisers thus worry about whether the provision of advice by a compliance officer, even outside the context of counseling on a specific disciplinary matter, could be the basis for a charge of failure to supervise.

The SEC Commission and staff have tried to defuse this worry among compliance officers. They publicly assert that regulators have no intention of broadly imposing supervisory liability upon compliance officers.[65] They explain—correctly—that most enforcement actions against compliance officers deal with "bad" officers who are either themselves involved in a particular securities law violation or who condone it.[66] They point out how involving a compliance officer in an enforcement action requires a high-level SEC decision because of the concern that it could have adverse consequences on compliance officers.[67] They also regularly tell compliance officers that regulators are appreciative of their efforts and that they support compliance officers in

---

[63] The *Gutfreund* case involved the liability of the broker-dealer's general counsel, who was involved in discussions concerning the appropriate discipline for a banker who had engaged in securities law violations. The more recent notorious case involved Theodore Urban. In that case, Urban, who was a former member of the SEC's staff and the chief legal and compliance officer of a broker-dealer, participated in the firm's efforts to discipline a "rogue" broker, but his advice was overruled by business executives. For the administrative law judge's initial decision finding that Urban was a supervisor, but not liable, see *In re* Urban (2010a). The SEC declined summarily to affirm the judge's decision, *In re* Urban (2010b), but eventually let it stand because three Commissioners recused themselves and the other two were evenly divided, *In re* Urban (2012). For Urban's take on his own case and the issue of supervisory liability of compliance officers, see Urban (2015).

[64] An SEC enforcement action alone, regardless of its merits, might well be a "death sentence" for a compliance officer's career in the area. For an expression of this concern and overall defensive measures for compliance officers, see Jackson (2015).

[65] See, e.g., White (2015) ("To be clear, it is not our intention to use our enforcement program to target compliance professionals. We have tremendous respect for the work that you do. You have a tough job in a complex industry where the stakes are extremely high. That being said, we must, of course, take enforcement action against compliance professionals if we see significant misconduct or failures by them. Being a CCO obviously does not provide immunity from liability, but neither should our enforcement actions be seen by conscientious and diligent compliance professionals as a threat. We do not bring cases based on second guessing compliance officers' good faith judgments, but rather when their actions or inactions cross a clear line that deserve sanction.").

[66] See, e.g., Aguilar (2015a) (providing statistics on number of cases against CCOs of investment advisers and investment companies and explaining that they generally involved "dual-hatted" CCOs (i.e., those doing both business and compliance work) and CCOs directly engaged in misconduct).

[67] See id. (pointing out that the Commission decides to move against a CCO only after considerable deliberation). Commissioner Aguilar, calling for more clarity in SEC enforcement orders, used CCO cases as examples. See Aguilar (2015b).

the firms by, for example, disciplining business persons who fail to pay attention to, or who obstruct, compliance officers.[68] The SEC even appeared to walk back from its most expansive position on supervisory liability by encouraging compliance officers to do their advisory work without worrying about being deemed to be supervisors.[69]

Perhaps the threat of supervisory liability for compliance officers has diminished, at least for now. But enforcement priorities change, and it will only take an enforcement action or two against a compliance officer acting in his or her advisory role to cause compliance officers renewed anxiety. This is why some have called for a definitive resolution of the uncertainty over the supervisor status of compliance officers when the latter provide advice to business-line personnel, even on a disciplinary matter.[70] The resolution could be achieved by an official pronouncement, interpretation, or rulemaking, which would disavow the previously used expansive language in enforcement decisions and explicitly exempt compliance officers from the definition of supervisor when they are providing compliance advice and recommendations.

This resolution is important for the future position and stature of compliance officers in the financial industry, in general, and in investment advisers and funds, in particular. Compliance is at a crossroads. First, it could proceed down a technical or technological path. Technical here means tasks such as the drafting of policies and procedures, together with monitoring compliance with them, recordkeeping, reporting, inspecting, and investigating, all of which are designed to ensure that business personnel are compliant with the federal securities laws and regulations, as well as other relevant obligations. Although compliance officers need knowledge, skill, and experience to accomplish these tasks, increasingly some or parts of them can be automated and assisted by technology, as will be discussed in the following section.

One path for compliance officers would be for them to develop their technological role and skills and downplay their advice and counseling role. The continuing regulatory uncertainty about supervisory liability of compliance officers supports this path. The compliance officer, as a kind of back-office technocrat, would have less chance of being considered a supervisor. They would simply gather information from their surveillance and then pass it along to executives and other supervisors for the latter's own decisionmaking. Although compliance officers may be required to step away from their seat at the management table, or move from their place on the floor, if they proceed down this technological path, they may find this a small price to pay for the freedom from supervisory liability.

---

[68] See Aguilar (2015b) (citing *In re* Pekin Singer Strauss Asset Management Inc., Ronald L. Strauss, William A. Pekin, and Joshua D. Strauss, Advisers Act Rels. No. 4126 (June 23, 2015), and *In re* Carl D. Johns, Advisers Act Rels. No. 3655 (Aug. 27, 2013)).

[69] The SEC suggested that being a supervisor involves the power to hire, fire, and punish; to reassign; to affect very strongly the working conditions of an individual. See SEC Division of Market Regulation (2013). It also noted here that the *Urban* decision by the administrative law judge was of no precedential value.

[70] For example, former SEC Commissioner Daniel M. Gallagher called for an amendment or other official guidance to Rule 206(4)-7 to clarify that compliance officers should not be held responsible for violations occurring within their firms. See Gallagher (2015). Commissioner Aguilar's statement (2015a) cited above was issued partly in response to this statement by Commissioner Gallagher.

Mutual fund compliance: key developments and their implications 217

The second path would be to try to maintain the advisory and counseling role of compliance officers. Under this role, as explained previously, compliance officers help ensure that advisers, funds, and their associated persons conduct their business in accordance with law, regulation, and ethics, not just through monitoring, but through their advice and example-setting. Monitoring and inspection are essential as a check on bad actors and as a form of boundary setting for proper conduct for all business personnel. However, the effectiveness of compliance is enhanced when employees internalize the proper norms of conduct.[71] Compliance officers promote this internalization through their regular advice and counseling on business decisions, new products and strategies, where they provide examples of compliant thinking and conduct. This path also furthers the professional project of compliance officers, who wish to be recognized as independent professionals who provide compliance advice within firms.[72]

The SEC's lack of clarity about the application of supervisory liability to compliance officers arguably runs counter to effective compliance. Certainly, compliance officers should be liable as supervisors when they are engaged in actual supervision; when they fail to do a specific compliance task, such as preparing adequate policies and procedures; and even when they negligently provide incorrect advice. The liability here gives them an added incentive to do their job correctly and professionally. However, applying supervisory liability to compliance officers who provide proper advice to the business decision-makers, who are the true supervisors, detracts from compliance's mission, effectiveness, and professionalism. It is unclear whether the SEC will take the necessary action to clarify the nonsupervisory role of compliance officers. Not only does it have numerous regulatory matters on its plate,[73] but it is likely reluctant to relinquish any of its enforcement power over compliance officers, if only in order to retain the flexibility to address future situations involving them. As noted above, this legal state of affairs may push compliance officers down a technological path, but this leads to a discussion of a related development that is affecting compliance and that should be separately addressed.

4 COMPLIANCE AND TECHNOLOGY

Technology has always been synonymous with financial services in the United States and, not surprisingly, has also been used by compliance officers in this domain. Communications technology allowed securities markets and transactions to become national in scope by enabling investors to participate in deals and to trade in these markets even if they lived far away from financial centers.[74] Early data processing gave broker-dealers tools to rationalize order processing and to centralize information about clients and their portfolios, which facilitated the surveillance of orders and customer

---

[71] *See* Fanto (2014) 1163–64 (discussing the significance of this approach).
[72] On this professional mission of compliance officers, see Walsh (2015).
[73] *See* SEC (2016) 4–7 (discussing numerous regulatory issues and tasks for the SEC to complete).
[74] *See* SEC (1963) 294–95 (discussing use of technology by national broker-dealers).

assets. Compliance officers in broker-dealers used this technology for their monitoring and other oversight tasks.[75]

The compliance program rules assumed that technology would be an important aspect of adviser and fund compliance. As discussed previously, the rules release instructed firms systematically to identify and assess the compliance risks in their business so that they can design appropriate compliance policies and procedures to address them. Data management aided this gathering and evaluation of risks. Moreover, the SEC also directed funds and advisers to have their compliance programs deal with issues that were intertwined with technology, such as determining the appropriate value of assets held and traded in various markets, keeping watch over the activities of service providers, monitoring proprietary trading and trading by associated persons to prevent insider trading, keeping accurate records, safeguarding client records and information, and ensuring business continuity.[76] In addition, in the annual assessment or audit of the compliance policies and procedures for adequacy and effectiveness,[77] compliance officers had to collect data and run tests on it for this purpose. The SEC assumed that, in all but the smallest adviser, compliance testing required technological assistance.

Compliance today is characterized by its expanding use of technology. Compliance officers use technology particularly in their monitoring of transactions and employees to keep up with technological advances in the business.[78] Third-party vendors market all kinds of software and hardware that that can be used "out of the box" or adapted to the needs of a particular firm.[79] This is a fortunate development for compliance officers, who could not efficiently perform many of their surveillance or other tasks without the aid of technology. To take a few examples, it would be difficult for a compliance officer in any investment adviser to monitor personal trading by associated persons without technological aids to track and, where necessary, to block these trades.[80] Similarly, technology aids compliance officers when they check on an adviser's use of broker-dealers and market venues for trade execution.[81]

---

[75] *See Guide to Broker-Dealer Compliance* (1974) 267–72 (describing the uses of electronic data processing for tasks by the "Compliance Official").

[76] *See* Compliance Programs of Investment Companies and Investment Advisers (2003) 74,716, 74,718–20.

[77] *See id.* 74,720.

[78] *See* Kraskin & Spillane (2014) 12 (discussing, in the investment adviser context, the demands that the compliance department have technological capacities equal in sophistication to those used in the business and partner with its technology department). Elsewhere I have called this phenomenon "dashboard compliance." *See* Fanto (2016a, b).

[79] *See, e.g.,* Bloomberg Communications Compliance (providing real time review of electronic communications). *See also* Layette, et al. (2014) 19 (discussing how to select this software).

[80] An Adviser Act rule requires an adviser to monitor the personal trading of its supervised persons to prevent securities law violations and conflicts with clients. *See* 17 C.F.R. § 275.204A-1(a)(3) (2018).

[81] This is designed to satisfy the adviser's "best execution" obligation under 15 U.S.C. § 80b-6(2). *See, e.g., In re* Goelzer Investment Management, Inc. & Gregory W. Goelzer (2013) (among other things, faulting chief executive officer, who was also the CCO, for failing to adopt and implement policies and procedures for best execution of client trades).

The SEC encourages this use of technology by compliance officers because it is expanding its own technological capabilities for the surveillance of regulated firms, and it would prefer that they have technological systems that can supply data to the SEC's own surveillance systems. The SEC is championing the use of "big data" in its oversight of investment advisers and investment funds, as well as other market participants. Technological systems that are compatible with, and that feed into, the SEC's surveillance would enable the SEC ideally to keep an eye on market developments in the adviser and fund space or customer abuses and to identify problem firms.[82] As an additional justification for its access to firm data, the SEC explains that this data enables it better to tailor its inquiries and examinations of firms, making them more efficient.[83] Whatever the reasons for the SEC's enhanced data gathering, this trend puts additional pressure on compliance officers—who are often a firm's "point person" in dealing with the SEC—to expand their own use of technology.

But technology could end up being a double-edged sword for compliance officers. It certainly allows for more efficient surveillance and, as a result, more productive use of firm compliance resources. In the bottom-line world of finance, firms value the enhancement of compliance officers' productivity that comes with their use of technology.[84] Rather than just easing the burden on these officers, however, technology could expand their monitoring work, because they would have to spend more time reviewing the data feeds from various surveillance systems. More significantly, technology may encourage advisory firms to streamline their compliance functions in order to take advantage of the efficiencies gained from compliance technology and eliminate compliance staff who might formerly have collected the data and done other compliance tasks.[85]

This development may also distance the remaining compliance officers from day to day interactions with the business staff as they spend time evaluating "feeds" from their "dashboards."[86] They would deal with business personnel remotely and interact with them primarily electronically. Even advice giving could end up being automated, with compliance-related answers to transaction or other business questions being provided online, which is a form of "robo compliance."[87] Compliance officers would deliver the

---

[82] One example is its 2016 annual examination priorities release, where the SEC's Office of Compliance Inspections and Examinations observed that its use of data analytics enabled it to identify problematic firms. See SEC OCIE (2016) 4

[83] See SEC (2016) 5–6 (discussing this and other purposes for its enhanced use of technology and data gathering).

[84] See PWC (2015) 5 (explaining that firms in this industry have increased their budgets for compliance technology).

[85] See McKinsey (2015) 18, 20–21 (explaining that cost pressures are forcing firms to automate compliance, among other control functions). See also Engler (2016) (referring to industry sources who discuss this trade-off between automation and the number of compliance officers).

[86] I develop these arguments in more detail in Fanto (2016a, b).

[87] I owe this observation to Steven Lofchie, a partner at Cadwalader, Wickersham & Taft. Compliance education and advising could be automated, just as investment advice is. See Malito (2015) (discussing the growth of "robo" investment platforms).

education and training in compliance procedures that is the basis for advice and counseling electronically, for example through podcasts or other computer-based means.[88]

The efficiencies and enhanced productivity that technology offers compliance officers could well be liberating for them, just as the use of earlier forms of technology has been. It could well free them to do the higher value, satisfying work of looking into potential compliance problems and offering advice on business plans, rather than the tedious work of collecting and evaluating the data. Yet it may make sense to keep an eye on how technology is transforming compliance in order to make sure that the valuable contributions of the current compliance approach are maintained. For example, to avoid living in a world where every physical act or utterance is recorded, some employees escape technologically based surveillance and people find ways to game it.[89] Moreover, the exclusive use of compliance dashboards may lead compliance officers to become complacent about them, making them vulnerable to gaps, limits, and blind spots in that technology.[90] There may thus be a value to having compliance officers "onsite" because they can provide advice, counseling, and examples *and* do the kind of monitoring of the day-to-day activities of the firm that is not possible from a remote location.[91]

This caution about the use of technology by compliance officers returns us to the SEC, which has a role in this development in compliance just as it does with respect to the supervisory liability of compliance officers. The SEC's enthusiasm for technology is understandable, especially as its budget is limited while its regulatory tasks have increased as a result of Dodd–Frank,[92] and as, understandably, it does not want to appear unable to match the financial firms that it regulates in terms of its technological resources and sophistication. However, the SEC should at least balance its encouragement of the use of technology by compliance officers with a recognition that it may push them down a path that could have adverse effects on compliance.

---

[88] My conversations with compliance officers confirm that this is already a widespread practice.

[89] Other activities, securities-based or nonsecurities-based, by associated persons come to mind. A firm should know about them and might have to supervise some of them, but associated persons may fail to report these activities to their firms. Failure to supervise outside business activities was one of the issues in the *BlackRock* case (2015).

[90] It is common today to have enforcement actions that have, as their basis, an improper oversight of an automated system, which proves to be defective. *See, e.g., In re* Western Asset Management Company (2014) (security's designation is changed, which makes the automated system allow the security to be placed into ERISA accounts, even though it was non-ERISA eligible).

[91] *See* Donohue (2016). A good example of remote compliance having a negative effect is *In re* Citigroup Global Markets, Inc. (2015). There Citigroup proprietary trading desks got into trouble for, among other things, trading with the firm's advisory clients. This occurred when compliance for these desks was moved to a remote location (Buffalo, New York) to save on costs.

[92] The obligations have grown as a result of Dodd–Frank (2010).

5 COMPLIANCE AND RISK MANAGEMENT

Another development that may affect the future of compliance is the place of this control function in a firm. More specifically, the question is whether compliance will continue to be an important standalone control function or whether it will be subsumed within another such function in advisers and funds. In the early days (and still in some firms today), compliance officers reported to the legal department, and only in recent years has compliance operated as an independent control function.[93] Another control function, risk management, is now gaining importance in firms. Common in commercial banks, risk management initially focused on the credit risks of borrowers and then extended its coverage to market risks because banks held debt securities on their balance sheets.[94] Risk management officers determine and evaluate the risks associated with a bank's major activities (that is, lending and eventually securities investing and trading), propose to executives and the board a risk management statement or plan for the amount of risk that the firm will bear in these activities, and then implement a risk management framework so that the firm's operations stay within the risk parameters of the statement.[95] They also help determine the bank's amount of equity capital, which is proportional to the amount of risk reflected on, and even off, its balance sheet.[96]

The risk management approach has become a model for how every organization should govern itself. Today, firms are expected to use enterprise risk management, which means managing the risks in all of their operations.[97] In addition, the risks covered go beyond credit and market risk to include operational, legal, and compliance risks. The financial crisis led both financial institutions and their regulators to focus more on risk management.[98] Dodd–Frank explicitly mandates that bank regulators enhance risk management in large financial holding companies and nonbank systemically important institutions.[99] Regulators, such as the Board of Governors of the Federal Reserve System and the Office of the Comptroller of the Currency, have responded to this statutory mandate by, among other things, requiring financial holding companies and large banks to adopt risk appetite statements, risk management frameworks, and a governance structure to put the statements and frameworks into

---

[93] *See generally* SIA (2005) 1 (discussing the initial structure of compliance); SIFMA (2013) 17–18 (discussing the various compliance structures used). *See also* NYSE Governance Services (2014) 11–13 (presenting the survey results of the reporting line of the person responsible for a compliance program, where reporting to general counsel is less than 20 percent).

[94] *See generally* Basel Committee on Banking Supervision (2000) 1.

[95] *See generally* Basel Committee on Banking Supervision (2014) 22–27 (discussing risk management processes in the firm).

[96] This is the risk-based capital model that is now a part of banking regulation. *See generally* Broome & Markham (2011) 545–62.

[97] *See generally* Committee of Sponsoring Organizations of the Treadway Commission (2009) (discussing an "ERM" approach).

[98] The regulation of investment advisers and investment funds is not the same as banking regulation, a point that can be sensitive in the fund world. Yet banking regulation often points to issues that the regulation of other financial firms will eventually have to address.

[99] *See* Section 165(h), 124 Stat. 1429 (codified at 12 U.S.C. § 5365); Section 618(d), 124 Stat. 1619–20 (codified at 12 U.S.C. § 1850a).

action, as well as to monitor and control their implementation.[100] Compliance is seen to be a part of risk management because it "manages" the risk of legal and ethical noncompliance.[101]

The risk management approach to compliance has been part of investment adviser and investment fund compliance since the promulgation of the compliance program rules. To draft adequate policies and procedures, a CCO of an adviser or fund is required first to assess the compliance risks of the business.[102] Indeed, in the compliance program rules release, the SEC listed the kinds of compliance risks that the policies and procedures of an adviser or fund should address.[103] Compliance officers now embrace the risk management approach to the point that it has become common for many of them to think about their position in terms of managing compliance "risks."[104] As with the use of technology, the SEC is pushing this approach by its own actions. The SEC staff increasingly takes a risk-based approach in its oversight and examination of advisers and other regulated firms, and it encourages compliance officers to do the same when they are monitoring their own firms.[105]

It may well be that having compliance officers adopt a risk management approach will have little effect upon their performance or their position in advisers or funds. Compliance officers could work within the adviser's or the fund's enterprise risk management framework and still retain their functional independence. Alternatively, the compliance function could be completely subsumed into risk management, as a kind of spoke in the enterprise risk management wheel. This in fact already occurs in certain large financial institutions, where the reporting line of compliance can run to the firm's risk management function.[106] In either case, compliance officers would identify legal, regulatory, and ethical risks; manage them through the compliance policies and procedures; and contribute their efforts to the adviser's or fund's risk management. In theory, there should be no problem with the organizational location of compliance in the firm so long as the CCO has a seat at an important enough table to raise the compliance risk issues on particular transactions and operations. Indeed, in the

---

[100] See OCC Guidelines (2014) (setting forth the standards for risk governance for certain large national banks, codified at Appendix D, 12 C.F.R. pt. 30 (2018)); Federal Reserve System (2014) (standards include risk management guidelines; promulgating Regulation YY, 12 C.F.R. §§ 252.1 et al. (2018).

[101] See Federal Reserve System (2008) (supervisory letter on guidance on managing compliance risks).

[102] See Compliance Programs of Investment Companies and Investment Advisers (2003) 74,716 ("Each adviser, in designing its policies and procedures, should first identify conflicts and other compliance factors creating risk exposure for the firm and its clients in light of the firm's particular operations, and then design policies and procedures that address those risks").

[103] See id.

[104] See, e.g., Stork (2015) (discussing how to conduct a risk assessment of the compliance risks facing an adviser).

[105] See, e.g., SEC OCIE (2015) 1–3 (mentioning the risk-based approach of its examinations and observing that, by sharing its own risk-based areas of focus, it will encourage firms to look at their own policies and procedures in these areas).

[106] The approach of bank regulators arguably encourages this approach. For example, the Federal Reserve discusses compliance entirely as a function of the firm's risk management oversight, while recognizing its particular contributions. See Federal Reserve System (2008) 1–2.

investment adviser and fund worlds, compliance risks will always be significant (and thus the CCO important) because law and regulation inform most technical issues, such as pricing, valuation, and trading practices. Moreover, the compliance program rules ensure that the CCO has direct access to the adviser's CEO or the fund board, as the case may be, to discuss the compliance program and to raise particular compliance risk issues and problems, which guarantees that the CCO will not be buried in a risk management hierarchy.

The problem here, if problem it is, arises from the same issue that has been previously raised with respect to the other two developments affecting compliance, which is the downplaying of the importance of the advisory and counseling side of compliance. Risk management has a quantitative finance side, where its goal is to set finance-based parameters for business activities and to monitor that they are not exceeded, or to require that an explicit decision be taken when a transaction incurring risk beyond accepted parameters is allowed. To take an example from credit risk management, credit limits are established for a counterparty or client of a financial institution, with special approval needed to exceed them.[107] Aligning compliance with risk management may push the orientation of compliance officers toward a kind of quantitative-based risk monitoring. Indeed, the software-based monitoring systems for firm and employee transactions and communications are "risk based" (that is, they identify communications or transactions on the basis of specified risk factors).[108] Certainly, risk managers provide advice on risk management statements and frameworks and on risks arising from individual strategies and transactions, and they do nonquantitative scenario analysis to identify the outcomes of potential bad events.[109] However, given that supervisory liability and the use of technology may lead compliance officers to downplay their advisory and counseling role, it is important to be careful that the movement to subsume compliance within risk management does not do the same.

6 CONCLUSION

The chapter examined three developments that could affect the future of the compliance function in investment advisers and investment funds: (1) continued uncertainty over whether compliance officers might be liable for a failure to supervise when they provide advice; (2) consequences of the use of technology by compliance officers; and (3) situating the compliance function within a firm's overall risk management. There is a common theme that arises from this examination: that each of the developments may be encouraging compliance officers to focus more on their monitoring tasks and to downplay their advisory and counseling activities. The reluctance of the SEC officially to exempt compliance officers from supervisory liability when it provides advice could make compliance officers more wary about this activity and lead them to engage more in their monitoring activities, where there is less risk of this kind of liability.

---

[107] See Basel Committee on Banking Supervision (2000) 3–4.
[108] See Layette (2014).
[109] See OCC Guidelines (2014) 54,534 (discussing scenario analysis in risk management).

Compliance officers would review firm activities for compliance with supervisory and compliance policies and procedures and then notify supervisors of any issues or problems, in this way being careful to stay out of the supervisory chain of command. The use of technology reinforces this removal of compliance officers from the floor, for it enhances their surveillance powers and effectiveness, but increases their monitoring tasks as compliance dashboards feed more data to them. This could leave them less time for advice and counseling, although the possibility exists that the technology may liberate them from many time-consuming data gathering tasks. The SEC has also contributed to this development, because it encourages the use of technology by compliance officers whose monitoring results can be linked to the SEC's own oversight of advisers and funds. Finally, while adviser and fund compliance have used a risk management approach from the promulgation of the compliance program rules, this approach may also distance compliance officers from regular interaction with firm employees, the natural setting for advice and counseling, as they focus on establishing, and then monitoring compliance with, compliance risk metrics.

In encouraging compliance officers to use a technologically based, occasionally remote approach to their job, these developments could lead compliance officers to neglect one of the main functions of compliance: the provision of advice and counseling on legal, professional, and ethical issues. Not only does this advice giving and counseling define the compliance officer as a specialist and even a professional, who applies a body of knowledge to diverse factual scenarios presented by firm personnel, but these activities are also important for effective compliance. In doing them, compliance officers are guiding employees in compliant conduct and serving as models for the kind of thinking and conduct that the employees need to adopt. When they are close to business personnel, compliance officers are also able to identify problems or issues related to the firm or employees, which may be difficult for dashboard surveillance to detect. It is ironic that, just as compliance officers have attained a recognized status in investment advisers and funds, the developments discussed in this chapter may lead them to downplay the advisory and counseling tasks whose achievement contributed to their importance in their firms.

REFERENCES

Advisers Act, 15 U.S.C. §§ 80b-1, et seq.
Advisers Act Rules, 17 C.F.R. §§ 0-2, et seq.
Aguilar, Luis A., June 29, 2015a, The Role of Chief Compliance Officers Must Be Supported.
Aguilar, Luis A., Aug. 10, 2015b, Statement of the Importance of Clarity in Commission Orders.
Arthur James Huff, Mar. 28, 1991, Exchange Act Release No. 29,017, 1991 WL 296561.
Basel Committee on Banking Supervision, 2000, *Principles for the Management of Credit Risk*.
Basel Committee on Banking Supervision, Oct. 2014, *Corporate Governance Principles for Banks*.
Board of Governors of the Federal Reserve System, Oct. 16, 2008, Compliance Risk Management Programs and Oversight at Large Banking Organizations with Complex Compliance Profiles, SR 08-8.
Board of Governors of the Federal Reserve System, Mar. 27, 2014, Enhanced Prudential Standards for Bank Holding Companies and Foreign Banking Organizations, 79 Fed. Reg. 17,240-338.
Broome, Lissa L. & Jerry W. Markham, 2011, *Regulation of Bank Financial Service Activities: Cases and Materials* (4th ed.).
Committee of Sponsoring Organizations of the Treadway Commission, 2009, *Effective Enterprise Risk Oversight: The Role of the Board of Directors*.

Compliance Programs of Investment Companies and Investment Advisers (Dec. 24, 2003), Advisers Act Release No. 2204, 68 Fed. Reg. 74,714-30.

Dodd–Frank Wall Street Reform and Consumer Protection Act of 2010, July 21, 2010, Pub. L. No. 111-203, 124 Stat. 1376.

Donohue, Andrew J., SEC Chief of Staff, May 20, 2016, "New Directions in Corporate Compliance: Keynote Luncheon Speech," Rutgers Law School Center for Corporate Law and Governance, Camden, New Jersey.

Engler, Henry, July 13, 2016, "'Dashboard Compliance': Automation Push May Carry Unforeseen Risks," *Thomson Reuters Accelus* (online).

Exchange Act, 15 U.S.C. §§ 78a, et seq.

Fanto, James A., 2014, Surveillant and Counselor: A Reorientation in Compliance for Broker-Dealers, *B.Y.U. L. Rev.*, 1121–84.

Fanto, James A., 2015, The Vanishing Supervisor, 41 *J. Corp. L.* 41, 117–65.

Fanto, James A., 2016a, "Dashboard Compliance: Benefit, Threat or Both?" *Brooklyn J. Corp. & Comm. L.* 11, https://brooklynworks.brooklaw.edu/bjcfcl/vol11/iss1/1/.

Fanto, James A., 2016b, "Dashboard Compliance: What Will Be Its Consequences?" Compliance & Enforcement blog, NYU Program on Corporate Compliance and Enforcement, http://wp.nyu.edu/compliance_enforcement/.

FINRA, Certified Regulatory and Compliance Professional Program, www.finra.org/Industry/Education/UniversityPrograms/FINRAInstitute.

FINRA Rules 3110, 3120, and 3130, 2016.

Gallagher, Daniel M., June 18, 2015, Statement on Recent SEC Settlements Charging Chief Compliance Officers With Violations of Investment Advisers Act Rule 206(4)-7.

Guide to Broker-Dealer Compliance, Report of the Broker-Dealer Model Compliance Program Advisory Committee to the Securities and Exchange Commission, Nov. 13, 1974.

In re BlackRock Advisors, LLC & Bartholomew A. Battista, Apr. 20, 2015, Advisers Act Release No. 4065.

In re Citigroup Global Markets, Inc., Aug. 19, 2015, Exchange Act Release No. 75,729.

In re Goelzer Investment Management, Inc. & Gregory W. Goelzer, July 31, 2013, Exchange Act Release No. 70083.

In re John H. Gutfreund, et al., Dec. 3, 1992, Exchange Act Release No. 31,554, 52 S.E.C. Docket 2849, 1992 WL 362753.

In re Theodore Urban, Sept. 8, 2010a, SEC Initial Decision Release No. 402; Dec. 7, 2010b, SEC Admin. Proc. File No. 3-13655; Jan. 26, 2012, SEC Admin. Proc. File No. 3-13655.

In re Western Asset Management Company, Jan. 27, 2014, Advisers Act Release No. 3763.

Investment Adviser Codes of Ethics, July 9, 2004, Investment Advisers Act Release No. 2256, 69 Fed. Reg. 41,696-709.

Investment Company Act, 15 U.S.C. §§ 80a-1, et seq.

Investment Company Act Rules, 2016, 17 C.F.R. §§ 270.0-1, et seq.

Investment Company Amendments of 1970, 1970, Pub. L. 91-547, 84 Stat. 1413.

Jackson, J. Christopher, 2015, Seeking to Avoid Chief Compliance Officer Liability, *Modern Compliance: Best Practices for Securities & Finance* (David H. Lui & John H. Walsh, eds), 679–702.

Kraskin, Mitchel & Todd Spillane, Sept. 2014, Technology, Compliance and the Future of Fund Governance, *Institutional Investor: Fund Directions*, 23, 12–14.

Layette, Shannan, et al., July–Aug. 2014, Best Practices for Selecting Governance Risk and Compliance Software, *Practical Compliance & Risk Mgt for the Securities Industry*, 7, No. 4, 19.

McKinsey, Oct. 2015, *Two Routes to Digital Success in Capital Markets* (W.P. No. 10 on Corporate & Investment Banking).

Malito, Alessandra, Oct. 2, 2015, Indie B-Ds Late to the Robo Game, *Investment News* (online).

Nagy, Donna M., Regulating the Mutual Fund Industry, 2006, *Brook. J. Corp. Fin. & Com. L.* 1, 11–44.

National Association of Compliance Professionals, www.nscp.org

NYSE Governance Services, 2014, *Compliance and Ethics Program Environment Report*.

OCC Guidelines Establishing Heightened Standards for Certain Large Insured National Banks, Insured Federal Savings Associations, and Insured Federal Branches, Integration of Regulations, Sept. 11, 2014, 79 Fed. Reg. 54,518-549.

Prevention of Certain Unlawful Activities with Respect to Registered Investment Companies, Oct. 31, 1980, Investment Company Act Release No. 11,421, 45 Fed. Reg. 73,915.

PWC, 2015, *State of Compliance Survey 2015: Moving beyond the Baseline Asset Management Industry Brief*.

Report of the House Committee on Interstate and Foreign Commerce, Investment Company Amendments Act of 1970, 1970, H. Rep. No. 91-1382, 91st Cong., 2d Sess. 40.

Rubin, Brian L. & Irene A. Firippis, 2015, Enforcement Actions Against Chief Compliance Officers, *Modern Compliance: Best Practices for Securities & Finance* (David H. Lui & John H. Walsh, eds) 733–51.

SEC Division of Market Regulation, Sept. 30, 2013, "Frequently Asked Questions on Legal and Compliance Officers," www.sec.gov/divisions/marketreg/faq-cco-supervision-093013.htm.

SEC Office of Compliance Inspections and Examinations (OCIE), April 20, 2015, Never-Before-Examined Registered Investment Company Initiative, *National Exam Priority Risk Alert*, IV, Issue 5, 1–3.

SEC Office of Compliance Inspections and Examinations (OCIE), 2016, National Exam Program: Examination Priorities for 2016.

Securities Act Amendments of 1964, 1964, Pub. L. 88-467, 78 Stat. 565.

Securities and Exchange Commission (SEC), Compliance outreach, www.sec.gov/info/complianceoutreach.htm.

Securities and Exchange Commission, 1963, *Report of Special Study of Securities Markets of the Securities and Exchange Commission*, 88th Congress, Ist Session—House Document No. 95, Pt. 1.

Securities and Exchange Commission, 2016, *FY 2017 Congressional Budget Justification*.

Securities Industry and Financial Markets Association (SIFMA), 2013, *The Evolving Role of Compliance*.

Securities Industry Association (SIA), Compliance & Legal Division, Oct. 2005, *White Paper on the Role of Compliance*.

Society of Corporate Compliance and Ethics, 2012, *2012 Cross Industry Chief Compliance Officers Salary Survey*.

Stork, Veronica T., Sept.–Oct. 2015, Conducting a Functional Risk Assessment for Investment Advisers, *Practical Compliance & Risk Management for the Securities Industry*, 8, No. 5, 19–25.

Urban, Ted, 2015, Avoiding Supervisory Liability, *Modern Compliance: Best Practices for Securities & Finance* (David H. Lui & John H. Walsh, eds), 703–32.

Walsh, John H., 2008, Institution-Based Financial Regulation: A Third Paradigm, *Harv. Int'l L.J.* 49, 383–412.

Walsh, John H. 2015, Compliance as a Profession, *Modern Compliance: Best Practices for Securities & Finance* (David H. Lui & John H. Walsh, eds) 773–95.

White, Mary Jo, July 15, 2015, Opening Remarks at the Compliance Outreach Program for Broker-Dealers, Washington, D.C.

PART III

THE BROADER RANGE OF INVESTMENT FUNDS

10. Tales from the dark side: money market funds and the shadow banking debate*
Jill E. Fisch

1 INTRODUCTION

Since the financial crisis of 2008, the regulation of money market mutual funds (MMFs) has generated substantial controversy. MMFs were developed by the mutual fund industry in the 1970s as an alternative to bank accounts that allowed investors to enjoy larger returns. Over the next 40 years, MMFs grew to become a three trillion dollar business.[1] Both retail and institutional investors use MMFs to manage their short-term cash balances.[2] When the Reserve Primary Fund announced, on September 16, 2008, that it was breaking the buck after Lehman Brothers filed for bankruptcy, however, investors redeemed substantial amounts of money from MMFs, and policymakers responded with novel mechanisms designed to support MMFs and prevent further withdrawals (Fisch 2015).

These events led policymakers to view MMFs as a source of financial instability. Many critics termed MMFs an instrument of the nefarious shadow banking industry and targeted them for regulatory reform. The SEC's adoption of new rules on July 23, 2014 implementing dramatic changes with respect to most categories of MMFs only went into effect in October 2016.[3] As a result, it is difficult to anticipate their full impact and to predict the size and shape of the MMF industry in the future. The story of MMFs and the reform effort raise important issues, however, about the process of financial regulation in the United States.

This chapter will trace the evolution of MMFs from their inception in the 1970s. It will describe the events of September 2008, when the bankruptcy filing of Lehman Brothers caused the Reserve Primary Fund to "break the buck," and the ensuing redemptions by investors from MMFs. It will explain the political interplay among government regulators about the need for regulatory reform and describe the reforms adopted by the SEC. Finally, although the impact of recent reform efforts has not been fully realized, the chapter will conclude with a few observations about the likely structure of the MMF industry in the future.

---

* This chapter draws heavily from Fisch & Roiter (2012) and Fisch (2015).
[1] See Stevens (2012) (reporting that "Assets of money market funds achieved an all-time high of almost $3.9 trillion by February 2009.").
[2] See Investment Company Fact Book (2015) at 13 ("in 2008, U.S. nonfinancial businesses held 37 percent of their cash balances in money market funds"); Investment Company Institute (2013) (reporting that almost 35.5 million US households own MMFs).
[3] SEC (2014).

2 THE EVOLUTION OF MMFs

Henry Brown and Bruce Bent invented the first MMF in 1971 (Markham 2002). The concept was a response to existing regulatory restrictions. Businesses at that time were not allowed to have bank savings accounts, and banks were not allowed to pay interest on checking accounts (Fisch & Roiter 2012). In addition, Regulation Q capped the interest rates available on bank savings accounts,[4] and bank interest rates were substantially lower than the return that was available on short-term debt instruments such as Treasury bills (Stecklow & Gullapalli 2008). Brown and Bent realized that, by pooling assets, a mutual fund could be used to provide a convenient investment option for business cash balances and to enable small investors, who could not afford the minimum investment for a Treasury bill, to access those higher yields (Fisch & Roiter 2012).

Although Brown and Bent started their operations on a shoestring (Stecklow & Gullapalli 2008), the MMF idea took off rapidly. Brown and Bent's first fund, the Reserve Fund,[5] soon accumulated assets of more than $100 million (Markham 2002). Other mutual fund sponsors, including Fidelity, Dreyfus, and Merrill Lynch, launched their own MMFs. By March 1975, 36 sponsors had started MMFs,[6] and as of June 1976, the industry held $3 billion in assets (Markham 2002). Congress eliminated most interest rate controls on bank deposits in the early 1980s but, by that point, the MMF industry had been born.[7]

As of July 19, 2018, MMFs had more than $2.85 trillion in assets under management (Investment Company Institute 2018). Bank affiliates sponsor about half of MMFs; the remainder are sponsored by asset management firms (McCabe 2010). Fund sponsors can earn substantial fees from the management of their MMFs.[8] In addition, MMFs are an important tool enabling fund sponsors to retain customer assets. As one commentator explains, MMFs work "like glue ... keeping that cash within the [family]" (Rowland 2014).

MMFs are a type of mutual fund and, as such, are subject to the general regulatory requirements of the Investment Company Act.[9] The development of MMFs initially raised significant questions about the application of standard mutual fund rules to issues such as valuation of fund assets and the calculation of the fund's net asset value (NAV) (Fisch & Roiter 2012). Fund sponsors sought to use amortized cost accounting and penny rounding—tools that enabled MMF shares to be priced at a stable $1 share price (SEC 1982). The $1 NAV greatly enhanced the MMF's marketability as an alternative to a bank deposit account because it allowed investors to use MMFs as they

---

[4] See Wilmarth (2002) (describing interest rate regulation imposed by Regulation Q and resulting shift of assets to MMFs).
[5] It is perhaps ironic that the Reserve Fund was both the first MMF and the one that collapsed in 2008. See infra (discussing the events that caused the fund to break the buck).
[6] SEC (1975) n. 1.
[7] See Wilmarth (2002) at 240 ("Congress phased out all interest rate controls on bank deposits (except for demand checking accounts) between 1980 and 1986").
[8] See, e.g., Rowland (2014) (explaining that Fidelity earns about $650 million in annual revenue generated by its MMFs).
[9] Investment Company Act, 15 U.S.C. §§ 80a-1 to -64.

did bank accounts, with cash management features such as ATM withdrawals and check-writing. The SEC initially reacted negatively to this valuation approach and issued a release stating that funds should instead mark the value of their securities to market (SEC 1977). Numerous funds, however, petitioned the SEC for exemptive relief to permit the use of amortized cost accounting.[10] In 1983, the SEC bowed to these requests and adopted a special rule for the regulation of MMFs—Rule 2a-7 (SEC 1983).

Rule 2a-7 allowed MMFs to trade at a stable $1 share price by authorizing the use of amortized cost accounting rather than market price to value the securities in the MMF's portfolio. Use of amortized cost accounting was based on the fact that MMFs generally held high quality short-term debt securities and retained those securities until maturity. In order to ensure that amortized cost accounting was appropriate, Rule 2a-7 restricted MMFs by "limiting permissible portfolio investments of such funds to 'high quality' instruments which present minimal credit risks."[11] Fund boards were also authorized to use penny rounding—meaning that they could round the fund's NAV to $1 so long as the actual NAV was at least 99.5 cents and less than $1.05. This authorization was contingent on the board taking reasonable steps to assure that the fund's share price remained stabilized at $1.

Rule 2a-7 provided that the right to redeem at a stable $1 share price was conditional. If the board of directors determined that $1 did not fairly reflect the market-based net asset value of the MMF's portfolio, it was required to adjust the NAV and to purchase and redeem shares at the MMF's fair price.[12] This adjustment is called "breaking the buck" and, as the colloquial name suggests, is considered ominous for the health of the fund.

MMF sponsors have been successful in maintaining the stability of the $1 share price. In the 37 years from 1971 to 2008, only one MMF was required to deviate from the $1 share price due to a decline in the value of its portfolio (Fisch & Roiter 2012). The fund, the Community Bankers US Government Fund, was a small institutional MMF. It broke the buck in 1994 after investing a high percentage of its portfolio in derivatives (Phelps, et al., 2004). The fund was forced to liquidate, eventually paying its investors 96 cents per share.

MMF sponsors manage their portfolios to maintain a stable share price in several ways. First, they concentrate their portfolios in high quality, low risk assets, as Rule 2a-7 demands. Second, they seek to maintain sufficient liquidity to meet the redemption demands of their customers. Third, when circumstances have made it necessary, MMF sponsors provided support to their funds.[13] Sponsor support has taken various forms, including the purchase of assets by a sponsor to increase the MMF's liquidity,

---

[10] See SEC (1982) (describing requests for exemptive relief by more than 90 funds).
[11] SEC (1983).
[12] Id. at 32556.
[13] See Shilling (2010) (describing forms of sponsor support and reporting that at least 145 MMFs received sponsor support prior to 2007). See also Phelps et al. (2004) (observing that the sponsor of the Community Bankers Fund did not have the resources to support its fund but that other sponsors that employed similar investment strategies provided support and prevented their MMFs from breaking the buck).

Money market funds and the shadow banking debate 231

the guarantee of fund assets, the voluntary waiver of advisory fees, or the injection of capital.[14]

The success of MMFs is largely due to their ability to offer investors a stable $1 share price and higher interest rates than are available from banks.[15] MMFs provide a number of additional features, however. They typically offer investors cash management services such as check-writing, ATM access, and bill pay, often at a lower cost than would be available through a bank (Markham 2002). Brokerage firms and money market sponsors use MMFs as an investment option for excess customer funds through a sweep feature.[16] Businesses use MMFs to manage their short-term assets.[17]

MMFs also serve as important suppliers of short-term debt financing. MMFs are a "crucial source of short-term wholesale dollar funding used by large global financial firms."[18] Prior to the financial crisis, MMFs were the primary buyers of short-term commercial paper and, although these purchases have decreased, MMFs continue to be major holders of commercial paper.[19] Additionally, MMFs are a source of state and local financing through their purchases of municipal securities (Larrabee 2012).

3 THE FINANCIAL CRISIS AND MONEY MARKET FUNDS

On September 15, 2008, Lehman Brothers filed for bankruptcy. The bankruptcy filing came after an 11th-hour effort by regulators to engineer an acquisition or other form of rescue.[20] On the date that Lehman filed, the Reserve Primary Fund (the RPF) was holding 1.2 percent of its portfolio in short-term Lehman debt that carried Moody's highest short-term debt rating (Fisch 2015). When Moody's downgraded the debt in response to the bankruptcy filing, the RPF received redemption requests of $25 billion, an amount that constituted 40 percent of the fund's assets under management. The next day, the RPF broke the buck. The fund subsequently suspended redemptions and adopted a plan of liquidation. RPF investors eventually received approximately 99 cents on the dollar, but the liquidation process took 16 months (Fisch & Roiter 2012). The

---

[14] See Fisch (2015) at 980 (describing the frequency with which sponsors have provided support and defending such support as a mechanism for increasing MMF stability).

[15] A stable $1 share price means that each purchase and redemption occurs at the same price, which simplifies the tax and accounting of transactions and enables investors to use an MMF for cash management. See *id.* at 966 (noting that "most institutional investors [are] unwilling or unable to use a floating NAV product").

[16] See, e.g., Cash Sweep From Wells Fargo Advisors, www.wellsfargo.com/investing/cash-sweep/. See also Gibson (2012) (explaining that large financial institutions typically offer MMFs as a convenience for their customers).

[17] In 2014, MMFs managed 23 percent of U.S. businesses' short-term assets (Investment Company Institute 2015).

[18] See Hanson et al. (2015) at 4 (estimating that MMFs provide 35 percent of such funding).

[19] See Bush (2016) (describing size of the U.S. commercial paper market and changes in that market after 2007).

[20] See Baxter (2010) (describing the events that occurred over the Lehman weekend).

liquidation process involved shareholder litigation as well as SEC enforcement actions against the RPF's principals.[21]

With the Lehman bankruptcy, the RPF's announcement, and the credit markets freezing up, other MMF investors also sought to redeem their shares.[22] During the month after the Lehman bankruptcy, termed "Crisis Month" by the SEC staff, institutional investors withdrew $498 billion from prime MMFs (SEC 2012). Most of this money was redirected into government MMFs.[23] Fund sponsors attempted to reassure their investors, but even funds that had not invested in Lehman debt felt redemption pressure.[24] The redemption requests led MMF sponsors to shift to more liquid assets, which in turn reduced the availability of short-term credit for businesses.

Concerned about the "run" on MMFs and the broader effects on the economy, government policymakers intervened. The Treasury Department established the Temporary Guarantee Program for Money Market Funds—a $50 billion guarantee program that provided temporary government insurance for money invested in MMFs (U.S. Dept. of Treasury 2008).[25] The Federal Reserve Board created the Asset-Backed Commercial Paper Money Market Mutual Fund Liquidity Facility to provide liquidity in the short-term credit market by facilitating bank purchases of commercial paper. Both programs were widely viewed as successful. The pace of MMF redemptions slowed, no other MMF broke the buck, and the government did not have to pay out any funds under the guarantee program. In addition, the support of the Liquidity Facility stabilized the market for asset-backed commercial paper (Fisch 2015).

Commentators have since debated the reasons for the failure of the RPF. According to some critics, the fund's failure reflected a moral hazard problem leading to excessive risk-taking.[26] As one Treasury Department official observed, "in retrospect it seems reckless for a money market fund that portrayed itself as safe to have taken on the risk of a sizable exposure to Lehman securities" (Swagel 2013). It is true that, in the years leading up to 2008, the MMF industry became increasingly competitive and funds competed, especially for institutional investors, based on yields. As with most investments, of course, higher yields are correlated with increased risk.

Moreover, the RPF made a deliberate decision to adopt a riskier trading strategy in order to increase yields and attract additional assets.[27] In September 2006, having historically lagged behind its competitors due to a longstanding conservative approach, the RPF reversed its investment strategy and began investing in commercial paper

---

[21] The shareholder litigation was settled, and a jury found for the defendants on most of the SEC's securities fraud charges (Raymond 2013).

[22] Various factors likely contributed to the high volume of redemption requests. See SEC (2012) at 7–10 (discussing various factors that may have contributed to the redemption volume).

[23] See SEC (2012) at 7 (reporting that government fund assets increased by $409 billion).

[24] See Mamudi (2008) (reporting statements by sponsors such as Schwab that their funds did not hold any Lehman debt).

[25] Participating MMFs paid a total of $1.2 billion for this insurance.

[26] Notably, it was arguably excessive risk-taking, in the form of derivatives investments in an effort to boost yields during a period of low interest rates, that led to the failure of the Community Bankers Fund in 1994.

[27] See Hanson et al. (2015) (reporting that institutional investors reward MMFs for greater risk-taking with inflows of assets).

(Stecklow & Gullapalli 2008). Within a few months, the fund's holdings of commercial paper increased substantially and, by September 2008, the fund's average trailing 12-month yield was the highest among 2,100 money market funds tracked by Morningstar, and a full point above the average MFF yield (Dolan 2008). The strategy paid off in attracting investors. In two years, from September 2006 to September 2008, the size of the RPF had tripled (Stecklow & Gullapalli 2008).

It is unclear whether the RPF's investment in Lehman debt was inappropriately risky at the time it was made. The Lehman debt instruments that triggered the RPF's failure were rated prime-1, Moody's highest credit rating, up until the date that Lehman filed for bankruptcy.[28] Notably, too, Lehman was the only financial institution that the government failed to bail out. In light of the government's prior bailout of Bear Stearns, it may have been reasonable to expect that Lehman too would be rescued.[29]

4 POLITICAL RESPONSE TO THE RESERVE FUND

In 2010, the SEC responded to the financial crisis and the events at the RPF by amending Rule 2a-7 (SEC 2010). The 2010 amendments included a number of provisions designed to increase MMF stability. The rule required MMFs to invest in higher quality securities with shorter maturities and to meet new daily and weekly liquidity requirements. The SEC also mandated periodic stress testing of MMF portfolios and enhanced disclosure.

These rule changes were relatively modest in scope.[30] Many critics argued that the fragility of MMFs was a major factor contributing to the financial crisis and that a substantial reshaping of the MMF industry was required. The core of most reform proposals was either to eliminate the fixed NAV that allowed MMFs to serve as an alternative to bank accounts or to ensure that MMFs were regulated more like banks with some combination of reserves or capital buffers, a backup liquidity facility, and government insurance similar to the FDIC insurance applicable to bank accounts (PWGFM 2010). The requirement for MMFs to shift from a fixed to a floating NAV, in which the fund's shares would fluctuate on a daily basis to reflect changes in the value of the fund's portfolio holdings, was the dominant reform proposal (Fisch & Roiter 2012).

Banking regulators, in particular, urged the SEC to adopt additional reforms. Treasury Secretary Tim Geithner charged the President's Working Group on Financial Markets (PWGFM) with evaluating "whether more fundamental changes are necessary to further reduce the MMF industry's susceptibility to runs" (Geithner 2012). The PWGFM subsequently released a report finding that MMFs remained vulnerable to runs despite the SEC's 2010 reforms (PWGFM 2010). Federal Reserve Chair Ben

---

[28] On the issue of whether financial institution commercial paper such as the Lehman debt should have been viewed by MMFs as risky see Kacperczyk & Schnabl (2010).

[29] See Michel (2013) ("The Bear Stearns bailout set the expectation that Lehman would also be bailed out, setting up investors and creditors for a fall").

[30] Indeed, the mutual fund industry worked in conjunction with the SEC to draft the 2010 reforms. See Rowland (2014).

Bernanke stressed the continued vulnerability of MMFs and called for additional measures such as a floating NAV or required capital buffers (Bernanke 2012). Former FDIC Chair Sheila Bair testified before Congress that a floating NAV was "required" to address MMF's "structural weakness" (Bair 2013).

At the time that the SEC adopted the 2010 reforms, SEC Chair Mary Schapiro acknowledged that they might be insufficient, and she noted that the SEC was considering additional regulatory alternatives, including a requirement that MMFs utilize a floating NAV (Schapiro 2010). In 2012, the SEC developed an additional rulemaking proposal.[31] Several SEC commissioners questioned the need for additional regulation, however, as well as the utility of the measures then under consideration (Gallagher & Paredes 2012). Faced with the inability to obtain support for her proposal, in August 2012 Schapiro announced that the SEC would not adopt additional rules at that time (Schapiro 2012).

When the SEC failed to take further action, banking regulators turned to the Financial Stability Oversight Council (the FSOC), which Geithner chaired. On September 27, 2012, Geithner wrote a letter urging the FSOC "to use its authority … to recommend that the SEC proceed with MMF reform" (Geithner 2012). The authority to which Geithner referred was the FSOC's newly granted authority, under section 120 of Dodd–Frank,[32] to "provide for more stringent regulation of such financial activity or practice by issuing recommendations to a primary financial regulatory agency to apply new or heightened standards or safeguards."[33] At Geithner's prompting, the FSOC took the unprecedented step of releasing for public comment its own MMF reform recommendations.[34] Significantly, this was the first time that the FSOC used its authority under Dodd–Frank to issue recommendations to another regulatory agency.[35] The FSOC proposals, which it recommended that the SEC adopt individually or in combination, consisted of a floating NAV or a capital buffer combined with a required minimum balance at risk.[36]

The FSOC's proposals were more than mere recommendations; they were coupled with an implicit threat (Keen 2012). Geithner's letter urged the FSOC to step in and take over the regulation of MMFs "in the event the SEC is unwilling to act in a timely and effective manner" (Geithner 2012). The FSOC's most viable mechanism for doing so would have been to designate MMFs as systemically important financial institutions

---

[31] The SEC staff report concluded that, although the reforms had made MMFs "more resilient," they would not have been sufficient to prevent the Reserve Fund from breaking the buck in 2008.

[32] Dodd–Frank Wall Street Reform and Consumer Protection Act § 120(c)(2), 124 Stat. at 1409 (2010).

[33] *Id.* at 5.

[34] Financial Stability Oversight Council, Proposed Recommendations Regarding Money Market Mutual Fund Reform, Financial Stability Oversight Council, 77 Fed. Reg. 69455 (Nov. 19, 2012).

[35] See Keen (2012) (explaining that this was the first time that FSOC was being asked to use its power under Section 120).

[36] A required minimum balance at risk is the equivalent of holding back a percentage of an investor's account so that it is only available for redemption on a delayed basis.

(SIFIs) under the Dodd–Frank Act.[37] SIFI designation would subject MMFs to supervision by the Federal Reserve, as well as prudential regulation.[38] The Federal Reserve subsequently released a report floating the possibility of a SIFI designation for large asset managers (Financial Stability Board 2015).[39]

One important component of the FSOC effort was the role of the banking industry and bank regulators. As noted earlier in this chapter, MMFs emerged from a failure of the banking industry to meet investor needs. Since that time, banks and banking regulators have regarded the MMF industry as unfair competition due to its ability to offer a banking substitute without bank-like regulation or insurance premiums. This perception is what has led to the characterization of MMFs as a form of shadow banking. As former Federal Reserve Chair Paul Volcker testified: "I happened to be there at the birth of money market funds. It was pure regulatory arbitrage … It is a shadow bank. And do we need shadow banks, or are we making real banks?" (Volcker 2011).

The irony of the bank regulators' efforts is that bank prudential regulation has had only limited effectiveness in providing financial stability.[40] Long before the financial crisis, banks began to fail in increasing numbers.[41] In contrast to the single failure of the RPF in connection with the 2008 financial crisis, there has been an "explosion of bank failures starting in 2008."[42] Similarly, perceptions of instability have led to frequent "runs," despite extensive safety and soundness regulation, including reserve requirements and government insurance (Fisch 2015). Mutual fund regulation offers an alternative approach, and there is reason to believe that this approach has proven superior.

The FSOC proposal drew criticism. SEC Commissioner Gallagher noted the irony of bank regulators, who had "performed so poorly" during the financial crisis, seeking to impose bank-like regulation on the capital markets.[43] Perhaps more problematically, Commissioner Gallagher pointed out that FSOC's involvement in the regulation of MMFs was in tension with the political independence of the SEC (Gallagher 2013). The tension existed on two levels. First, the FSOC was dominated by banking regulators rather than securities or capital markets regulators. Second, the FSOC consists of political appointees who are members of the president's political party. In contrast, the SEC is an independent bipartisan agency—a structure that provides greater

---

[37] Dodd–Frank Act § 113.
[38] See Keen (2012) (describing this alternative and identifying but rejecting alternative approach of designation as systemically important financial market utilities).
[39] See Kupiec (2013) (criticizing the FSOC approach).
[40] See Garten (1989) (recounting history of bank regulation and explaining that it was more about ensuring bank profitability than risk reduction).
[41] See Miller (1992) at 743–44 ("Approximately 200 commercial banks per year have failed since 1987").
[42] See Nickel (2013) (citing FDIC statistics reporting 465 bank failures between 2008 and 2012).
[43] Gallagher (2015) (describing bank regulators as creating a "false narrative of the financial crisis" as a "ploy to wrest control of a hugely important sector of the capital markets from the SEC").

insulation from political influence. Commentators questioned the propriety of the FSOC, a "non-expert body," attempting to exercise control over a specialized capital markets regulator (Foley, 2012–13). The mutual fund industry also criticized the FSOC proposal and mounted substantial political opposition (Rowland 2014).

Despite the criticism, the FSOC proposal had the desired effect of pressuring the SEC to take further action.[44] The FSOC also applied pressure to the large mutual fund sponsors in an effort to deflect industry opposition to further regulatory reform. In September 2013, the Office of Financial Research of the US Treasury Department released a report to the FSOC warning that, because some activities engaged by asset managers were similar to those of banks, they might face regulation as SIFIs.[45] Subsequently, the FSOC announced that it was considering whether BlackRock and Fidelity—two of the largest mutual fund sponsors, and two highly vocal opponents to MMF reform—should be designated as SIFIs (Katz & Hamilton 2013).

Faced with the possibility that the FSOC would use the supposed instability of sponsors' MMFs as a justification for classifying them as SIFIs (Rowland 2013),[46] several large mutual funds shifted their position from total opposition to support of a compromise measure. The compromise measure included additional regulatory reforms but, critically, only imposed the most stringent reform, a floating NAV, on institutional MMFs. (Michaels 2013). Retail funds would face less substantial regulatory changes, the most significant of which was the authority to impose liquidity gates and fees. The compromise thus enabled the big mutual sponsors, such as Fidelity, Vanguard, and Charles Schwab—which focus on serving retail investors—to preserve a fixed NAV option for their customers.

On July 23, 2014, the SEC yielded to the FSOC pressure and adopted a new MMF rule by a divided 3–2 vote (SEC 2014). Chair Mary Jo White stated explained that "this strong reform package will make our financial system more resilient and enhance the transparency and fairness of these products for America's investors" (White 2014). Importantly, the new rule was an explicit compromise and, as such, a victory for the mutual fund industry, in that the most dramatic reform, a floating NAV, would be applied only to institutional prime MMFs and not to the rest of the market.

5 THE 2014 SEC RULES

The SEC's new MMF rules created two new categories of MMF—retail and institutional. The rules prohibit institutional MMFs from using a stable NAV. Instead, institutional MMFs are required to purchase and redeem shares at a floating NAV calculated to four decimal places (SEC 2014).

---

[44] Lynch (2013) (quoting former SEC Chairman Mary Schapiro as stating that "I don't think there is any doubt that, but for FSOC stepping in, this issue would have never continued to [be] part of the public debate and discussion").

[45] Office of Financial Research of the US Treasury Department (2013).

[46] Page one of the report expressly warned that "asset managers may create funds that can be close substitutes for the money-like liabilities created by banks." Office of Financial Research of the U.S. Treasury Department (2013).

Retail funds—which may only accept investments from natural persons—are exempt from the floating NAV requirement but instead are required to adopt redemption fees and liquidity gates. Redemption fees allow a fund, if it suffers a decrease in liquidity, to impose a fee of up to two percent on investors seeking to redeem their shares. A liquidity gate allows a fund to suspend redemptions for up to ten business days. Importantly, although the rules dictate the circumstances under which fees and gates can be used by specifying liquidity triggers,[47] the imposition of these restrictions is within a fund board's discretion (Fisch 2015). Additionally, retail funds are required to disclose a market-based shadow NAV, calculated to four decimal places, on a daily basis (SEC 2014).

Both institutional and retail funds are subject to enhanced stress testing requirements (Berkowitz 2015). Under the new rules, MMFs must test their ability to maintain weekly liquidity under adverse market conditions, conditions that include an increase in interest rates, a downgrade or default in portfolio securities, a widening of spreads, or an increase in shareholder redemptions from the fund (Bender 2015).

The SEC exempted government MMFs from both the floating NAV and the fees and gates requirement.[48] The new rules, however, adopted a new and more restrictive definition of a government MMF. To meet the definition, government MMFs must invest at least 99.5 percent of their assets in cash or US government securities (SEC 2014).

Finally, the SEC adopted extensive new disclosure requirements (Fisch 2015). MMFs are required to disclose their current and historical market-based NAV calculated on a daily basis and rounded to four decimal points, any past use of fees and gates, and historical sponsor support. Funds must disclose current and historical information about the percentage of daily and weekly liquid assets in their portfolios as well as current and historical information about net shareholder inflows and outflows.

The new rules have the potential to affect the viability and structure of MMFs as well as the short-term credit markets. Indeed, the SEC acknowledged that the rule changes could themselves trigger a run on MMFs (SEC 2014). As a result, the SEC provided a two-year implementation period. The new rules did not go into full effect until October 14, 2016.

The new rules raise a number of potential concerns in that they both reduce the value and increase the costs of investing in MMFs (Fisch 2015). As institutional investors consistently indicated during the rulemaking process, a floating NAV product is unsuitable for many of the businesses that have used MMFs for cash management because the variations in price create tax and accounting complexity (Investment Company Institute 2012).[49] As a result, institutional investments in prime MMFs have been substantially reduced. This, in turn, may affect the availability of short-term credit for business.

---

[47] The board's power to impose fees, gates, or both is triggered if a fund's weekly liquidity falls below 30 percent.

[48] The exemption did not extend to municipal MMFs (McDonald 2013).

[49] The SEC indicated its expectation, in its rulemaking release, that the IRS would modify its rules to simplify the compliance issues associated with a floating NAV. SEC (2014), at 47,781–82.

Although they have received less attention, fees and gates are equally problematic for retail investors in that they threaten the liquidity that is the key rationale for investing in an MMF. It is unclear whether retail investors will truly understand the structure of fees and gates and the circumstances under which they might be used, but any fund's implementation of such a redemption restriction is likely to trigger investor panic and generate a contagion effect (Stein 2014). Even absent a contagion effect, a sponsor that imposes a fee or gate is likely to suffer irreparable reputational harm from doing so.[50] Because of the likely adverse business consequences of imposing these restrictions, there are serious questions about whether fund boards will ever use fees and gates, limiting their utility in improving financial stability.

The anticipated benefits of the SEC's regulatory reforms are even less compelling. The most significant of the reforms was the imposition of floating NAV, but it is unclear that a floating NAV will increase MMF stability. The SEC was presented with a fair amount of evidence suggesting that a floating NAV was unlikely to reduce the risk of large redemptions from MMFs during times of economic stress. Indeed, prior experience with floating rate funds and short-term bond funds suggests that a floating NAV may, if anything, exacerbate redemption pressure (Fisch 2015; Johnson 2015). Similarly, although fees and gates may limit redemptions, if not redemption pressure, once imposed, the possibility that a fund will impose a fee or gate heightens redemption pressure in anticipation of its use. This instability is increased by potential investor uncertainty about the likelihood that a fund board will impose the fee or gate.

The new disclosure requirements also raise a host of issues (Fisch 2015). Requiring MMFs to calculate their NAV to four decimal places, for example, conveys both a synthetic volatility in what has historically been a highly stable investment product and a false sense of precision with respect to the fair value of the MMF's holdings. As one commentator warned the SEC, attempts to determine the fair value of MMF assets on a daily basis are, at best, "noisy guesstimates of true value" (Angel 2013, 4).

Perhaps most problematic was the SEC's treatment of sponsor support. Although sponsor support historically played a valuable role in enhancing MMF stability, the regulatory reforms view sponsor support with suspicion and the new disclosures seem intended to discourage sponsor willingness to provide such support (Fisch 2015). As a result, the extent to which sponsors will adhere to their prior practice of voluntarily supporting the $1 NAV through mechanisms such as fee waivers, guarantees, and the purchase of distressed assets remains unclear.

In sum, it is not clear that the SEC's 2014 reforms were necessary but, in any event, they were poorly designed for enhancing MMF stability. As such, they appear to reflect a greater concern about responding to the demands of bank regulators and the political environment than about protecting investors.

---

[50] See BlackRock (2014) at 6 (describing "the implementation of fees and gates as an event from which a sponsor's reputation will not easily recover").

6 THE FUTURE OF MMFs

MMFs and their sponsors have modified their operations to comply with regulatory reform.[51] In anticipation of the October 14, 2016 effective date, many funds began to implement changes, and those changes continue. From these changes, it is clear that the MMF industry will undergo significant evolution. The long-term effect of the reforms, however, may not fully be understood until a future financial crisis.

In the short run, mutual fund sponsors have focused on consolidation. Most sponsors have reduced the number of MMF options they offer and converted many of their existing funds to the most lightly regulated category: government MMFs.[52] Consolidation is a consequence of the new restrictions that make fewer fund offerings viable (Team 2015). For example, the restrictive definition of government MMFs means that there will be little if any market for MMFs that consist primarily of government securities but do not meet the requirement of 99.5 percent—such funds will be unlikely to be able to offer sufficiently higher yields to justify investor exposure to a floating NAV or fees and gates.

Institutional investors appear to be concentrating their money, at present, in government MMFs—the primary mechanism for avoiding a floating NAV as well as fees and gates.[53] This behavior is consistent with the prior survey data suggesting that most institutional investors are unwilling to invest in a floating NAV product.[54] The migration of MMF assets to government MMFs raises several concerns. Although US government securities have traditionally been very safe, an increased concentration of assets in government MMFs is potentially destabilizing in the event of an economic shock to that sector. Notably, the industry faced these concerns in 2013, when government borrowing approached the debt ceiling and created the risk that the government might default on its debt (Reid 2013).

The potential for government MMFs to satisfy the short-term cash management needs of investors in the long run also remains uncertain. One important consideration is that government MMFs typically offer investors a lower yield than other investment options (Flynn 2015). In the current low interest rate environment, investors do not pay a substantial penalty for choosing a government MMF. It is fair to conclude, however, that the current era of ultralow interest rates is an artificial environment that is unlikely to persist (Pozen 2010). Government MMFs will become less attractive if interest rates

---

[51] US regulatory reforms have sparked similar reform initiatives in Europe. See Hennebert et al. (2017).
[52] See, e.g., Fidelity Investments (2015a) (announcing conversion of three prime MMFs to government MMFs); Maxey (2015) (reporting product modifications by Federated and BlackRock). Fund sponsors have also taken the necessary steps to ensure that their fund documents comply with the new and more restrictive definition of government fund.
[53] The limitations on fixed NAV MMFs creates a business opportunity for banks to capture some of that excess cash. See Hooker (2015) (explaining that, if institutions have fewer cash management options, some of the money that has historically been invested in MMFs may move into banks).
[54] See Association for Finance Professionals (2014) (reporting that 50 percent of respondents would move some or all of their money out of floating rate MMFs).

increase and the spread between a government fund and other alternatives becomes economically meaningful. At the same time, if government yields remain low, it may become economically unattractive for sponsors to continue to subsidize their MMFs with fee waivers (Williams et al. 2015).[55]

Further, it is unclear that the supply of government securities is sufficient to meet the demands of a substantial migration of assets into government MMFs. The media has reported that increased demand has reduced the yield on government debt to zero or less (Burne 2015). Future interest rate increases and other economic developments could limit new issuances of short-term government debt, exacerbating the shortage (Flynn 2015).

If yields on government MMFs remain low when overall interest rates rise, how will institutional investors respond?[56] It is unclear whether and to what extent institutional demand for prime MMFs will exist—Fidelity posted results of a survey indicating that 60 percent of its institutional clients were "unsure" if they would continue to use prime MMFs when those MMFs moved to a floating NAV (Cranedata 2015). Investor demand for a floating NAV MMF may depend, in part, on the workability of tax and accounting accommodations that were announced as part of the new MMF rules but that have not yet been finalized (SEC 2014). Some fund sponsors have introduced new products designed to take advantage of exemptions in the regulatory requirements. These include sixty-day prime funds, which are not required to use a floating NAV, and seven-day prime funds, which do not have to impose fees and gates (Williams et al. 2015). These products are likely to increase in attractiveness as interest rates rise.

There is some debate about the extent to which institutions will embrace floating NAV products such as ultrashort bond funds, which offer investors higher yield but at an increased risk (Hunnicutt 2015). The problem, of course, with these alternatives is that, in many cases, they have the potential to cost investors a substantial loss in principal, which can be highly destabilizing and unsuitable for many types of institutions.[57] Additionally, substantial inflow into fixed income funds may increase systemic instability. In December 2015, the Third Avenue Focused Credit Fund experienced a wave of losses and redemption requests, leading the fund to announce that it would halt redemptions and liquidate its assets (Ackerman 2015). The actions bore an uncanny resemblance to the Reserve Primary Fund crisis. The broader impact of the Third Avenue fund closure is unclear, but commentators have expressed concern about the potential contagion effect in the corporate bond market (Wigglesworth 2015).

Alternatively, institutional investors may turn to unregistered investment options (McNamara & Fishman 2014). Several large fund sponsors are reportedly considering offering their institutional clients private funds that retain the characteristics of prime MMFs but are not subject to MMF regulation (Wilmer 2015). A move of substantial

---

[55] Continued low interest rates also create pressure for excessive risk-taking (Masson 2013).
[56] See Maxey (2015) (noting that investor willingness to shift from prime to government MMFs may change when interest rates rise).
[57] See Hunnicutt (2015) (reporting that the average ultra-short bond fund lost 7.89 percent of its value in 2008).

institutional money into private funds would limit the effectiveness of the regulatory changes while substantially reducing economic transparency (Fayvilevich 2015).

The implications for retail investors are less clear. The regulatory reforms preserve retail investor access to fixed NAV MMFs, ensuring that investors will not be faced with complex tax and accounting issues or concerns over the loss of principal. A greater concern for retail investors is the potential loss in liquidity created by the fees and gates provision. Consistent with the prediction in this chapter that the use of fees and gates is unlikely because of investor concern, sponsors appear to be taking steps to reassure investors that they will have unimpeded access to their money. Vanguard, for example, has advised its investors that "We expect to be able to manage our funds without fees and gates" (Vanguard 2014, 3). Similarly, Fidelity has approved statements in its MMF prospectus disclosure advising investors that it does not intend to use fees and gates for its government MMFs.[58]

Although the perception that MMFs represented unfair competition for deposits was a likely contributor to the banks' push for regulatory reform, the extent to which the regulation will cause retail investors to shift their money from MMFs to banks remains unclear (Hooker 2015). As noted previously, bank deposits have traditionally offered institutional investors limited safety due to the limits in deposit insurance, and new bank regulations have reduced the availability of accounts for institutional investors (Fayvilevich 2015). New banking regulations create additional incentives for banks to turn away deposits and impose higher fees (Capital Advisors Group 2015; Carney & Reilly 2015). Higher bank fees are likely to continue to make MMFs an attractive alternative for retail investors.[59] As a result, banks may benefit less than they anticipated from the results of the battle to regulate MMFs.

An additional question is the extent to which the SEC will focus its enforcement efforts on MMFs in order to identify broad-based compliance problems or excessive risk-taking. Low interest rates will continue to create powerful financial incentives for risk-taking. The Commission's administrative proceeding against Ambassador Capital Management in 2013 signaled the possibility that, going forward, MMFs will have to face greater enforcement attention as well as regulatory attention (Ambassador Capital Management 2013). The SEC initiated an action based on ACM's "deceiving the trustees of a money market fund and failing to comply with rules that limit risk in a money market fund's portfolio." As the evidence presented by the Commission indicated, ACM's activities raised concerns both because of the high risk reflected in the Ambassador Money Market Fund portfolio and in the fund's characteristics that made it particularly vulnerable in light of that risk.

Overall, the MMF industry will survive, but it is likely to look somewhat different. MMF sponsors are likely to find an accommodation for institutional money but that money may be segregated from retail money, and the risks associated with that

---

[58] Fidelity Investments, (2015b), at 1–2 ("the Board of Trustees for the funds has approved prospectus disclosure to notify investors of its intention not to impose fees or gates on Fidelity government and U.S. Treasury money market mutual funds").

[59] Indeed, fund sponsors have recently been able to raise MMF fees slightly (McLaughlin 2015).

investment may be less transparent to regulators and the public.[60] Retail investors are likely to be in the same position but perhaps less protected by sponsor support in the event of financial distress, and less able to evaluate the potential risks of their investment. Moreover, the possibility that sponsors will use fees and gates may heighten investor panic and accelerate redemptions in the event of a future crisis.

Significant changes in the size and composition of the MMF industry are also likely to have a substantial effect on the short-term credit markets. In particular, prime MMFs have traditionally been major purchasers of commercial paper (Carney 2015). A reduction in the demand for commercial paper will require many businesses to find alternative sources of short-term financing, and those alternatives may be more expensive. One issuer observed that its costs of borrowing would be as much as 500 percent higher in the event that the new rules eliminated its access to the commercial paper market (Natarajan & Janofsky 2014). Similarly, prior to the reforms, MMFs were the single largest purchase of municipal securities, holding 72 percent of the market in 2013 (McDonald 2013). The SEC's failure to exempt municipal MMFs from the floating NAV and fees and gates requirements may significantly reduce investor demand for municipal MMFs and increase funding costs for state and local governments.

7 CONCLUSION

The debate over MMF regulation produced little information on the stability of MMFs during times of financial distress or on the role of a fixed NAV or redemption restrictions on enhancing MMF stability. The fight between banking and capital markets regulators over the need for and the scope of regulatory reform offered little insight into the contributions of MMFs, if any, to the financial crisis, nor did it explore the critical role of MMFs in the short-term credit markets or the likely impact of reform on those markets. Instead, MMF reform was a turf war between bank regulators and the SEC over protecting their constituencies. In the end, neither side was entirely successful—the MMF industry survived, but will face the burden of new restrictions and an uncertain market response to those restrictions.

Framing MMFs as shadow banks mischaracterizes a critical structural difference between MMFs and banks, and overlooks the fact that MMF sponsors can and do provide financial support to stabilize their MMFs in a way that banks cannot (Fisch 2015). A more plausible motivation for imposing greater regulatory burdens on MMFs is to reduce their ability to compete effectively with banks for deposits. To the extent that banking interest groups pursued MMF regulation with the goal of gaining a competitive advantage, their efforts may be misguided if the regulation reduces the availability of short-term credit upon which banks have become highly dependent. Ironically, however, if the new MMF rules cause financial institutions to increase the term of their borrowing, they may ultimately enhance financial stability.

---

[60] Retail investors may be disserved by increased market segmentation as retail-only funds are likely to be less competitive and costlier. See Fisch (2015).

BIBLIOGRAPHY

Ackerman, Andrew, 2015, SEC Reviewing Third Avenue's Move to Bar Redemptions From Fund, Wall St. J., https://www.wsj.com/articles/sec-reviewing-third-avenues-move-to-bar-redemptions-from-fund-1450129681.
Ambassador Capital Management LLC., 2014, Admin. Proc. File No. 3-15625.
Angel, James, 2013, Letter to Sec. & Exch. Comm'n, www.sec.gov/comments/s7-03-13/s70313-228.pdf.
Association for Finance Professionals, 2014, 2014 AFP Liquidity Survey.
Bair, Sheila C., 2011, Securities & Exchange Commission, Unofficial Transcript: Roundtable on Money Market Funds and Systemic Risk.
Bair, Sheila C., 2013, Examining the SEC's Money Market Fund Rule Proposal, Testimony before the House Committee on Financial Services Capital Markets & Government Sponsored Enterprises Subcommittee.
Baxter, Jr., Thomas C., 2010, Too Big to Fail: Expectations and Impact of Extraordinary Government Intervention and the Role of Systemic Risk in the Financial Crisis, Testimony before the Financial Crisis Inquiry Commission, Washington, D.C.
Bender, Daniel, 2015, Money Market Funds, Ernst & Young, www.ey.com/Publication/vwLUAssets/EY-money-market-funds/$FILE/EY-money-market-funds.pdf.
Berkowitz, Jeremy, 2015, Money Market Mutual Funds: Stress Testing & New Regulatory Requirements, https://corpgov.law.harvard.edu/2015/07/14/money-market-mutual-funds-stress-testing-new-regulatory-requirements/.
Bernanke, Ben S., 2012, Fostering Financial Stability, www.federalreserve.gov/newsevents/speech/bernanke20120409a.htm.
BlackRock, 2014, Understanding Liquidity Fees and Redemption Gates, www.blackrock.com/cash/literature/whitepaper/understanding-liquditiy-fees-redemption-gates.pdf.
Burne, Katy, 2015, Money Funds Clamor for Short-Term Treasurys, Wall St. J., www.wsj.com/articles/money-funds-clamor-for-short-term-treasurys-1445300813.
Bush, Eric, 2016, The Structural Shift in the US Commercial Paper Market, https://www.advisorperspectives.com/commentaries/2016/04/25/the-structural-shift-in-the-us-commercial-paper-market.
Capital Advisors Group, 2015, The Transformation of Corporate Deposits in a New Regulatory Environment, https://capitaladvisors.com/wp-content/uploads/2016/12/The-Transformation-of-Corporate-Deposits-in-a-New-Regulatory-Environment.pdf.
Carney, John, 2015, Money Markets May Keep the Squeeze on Banks, Wall St. J., www.wsj.com/articles/money-markets-may-keep-the-squeeze-on-banks-heard-on-the-street-1423167586.
Carney, John & Reilly, David, 2015, J.P. Morgan Shows Why It Pays to Turn Money Away, Wall St. J., www.wsj.com/articles/j-p-morgan-shows-why-it-pays-to-turn-money-away-heard-on-the-street-1424813559.
Cash Sweep from Wells Fargo Advisors, www.wellsfargo.com/investing/cash-sweep/.
Cranedata, 2015, Fidelity Announces Major Changes to MMFs; Staying Stable, Going Govt, https://cranedata.com/archives/all-articles/5428/.
Dodd–Frank Wall Street Reform and Consumer Protection Act § 120(c)(2), 124 Stat. at 1409 (2010).
Dolan, Karen, 2018, A Large Money Market Fund Breaks the Buck, Morningstar, http://www.morningstar.com/articles/253485/a-large-money-market-fund-breaks-the-buck.html
Fayyilevich, Greg, 2015, Revisit Your Corporate Investment Policy, Treasury & Risk, www.treasuryandrisk.com/2015/07/30/revisit-your-corporate-investment-policy/?slreturn=20180430143011.
Fidelity Investments, 2015a, Fidelity Money Market Mutual Fund Changes.
Fidelity Investments, 2015b, Update Fidelity Money Market Mutual Fund Changes.
Financial Stability Board, 2015, Assessment Methodologies for Identifying Non-Bank Non-Insurer Global Systemically Important Financial Institutions (NBNI G-SIFIs).
Financial Stability Oversight Council, 2012, Proposed Recommendations Regarding Money Market Mutual Fund Reform, 77 Fed. Reg. 69455.
Fisch, Jill, 2015, The Broken Buck Stops Here: Embracing Sponsor Support in Money Market Fund Reform, North Carolina Law Review: 93: 935–992.
Fisch, Jill & Eric Roiter, 2012, A Floating NAV for Money Market Funds: Fix or Fantasy? University of Illinois Law Review 2012: 1003–1050.
Flynn, Alice, 2015, Challenges Facing Government Money Market Funds, Columbia Threadneedle.
Foley, Sean, 2012–13, Money Market Fund Reform & The Financial Stability Oversight Council, Rev. Banking & Fin. L. 32: 308–320.

Gallagher, Daniel M., 2013, Remarks at "The SEC Speaks in 2013", https://www.sec.gov/news/speech/2013-spch022213dmghtm.

Gallagher, Daniel M., 2015, Bank Regulators at the Gates: The Misguided Quest for Prudential Regulation of Asset Managers: Remarks at the 2015 Virginia Law and Business Review Symposium, https://www.sec.gov/news/speech/041015-spch-cdmg.html.

Gallagher Daniel M. & Troy A. Paredes, 2012, Statement on the Regulation of Money Market Funds, https://www.sec.gov/news/public-statement/2012-spch082812dmgtaphtm.

Garten, Helen A., 1989, Regulatory Growing Pains: A Perspective on Bank Regulation in a Deregulatory Age, Fordham L. Rev. 57: 501–577.

Geithner, Timothy F., 2012, Letter to Members, Fin. Stability Oversight Council, https://www.treasury.gov/connect/blog/Documents/Sec.Geithner.Letter.To.FSOC.pdf.

Gibson, Warren C., 2012, Money Market Funds: Success Must Not Go Unpunished, The Freeman, https://fee.org/articles/money-market-funds-success-must-not-go-unpunished/.

Hanson, Samuel G., David S. Scharfstein, & Adi Sunderam. 2015, An Evaluation of Money Market Fund Reform Proposals, IMF Economic Review, 63: 984–1023.

Hennebert, Nicolas et al, 2017, Deloitte, European Council Approved the New Rules on Money Market Funds, https://www2.deloitte.com/content/dam/Deloitte/lu/Documents/financial-services/IM/lu-rna-european-council-approved-new-rules-money-market-funds-31052017.pdf.

Hooker, Joe, 2015, Why Money Market Fund Reform Helps Banks, Banking Exchange, www.bankingexchange.com/news-feed/item/5203-why-money-market-fund-reform-helps-banks?Itemid=101.

Hunnicutt, Trevor, Money Market Reforms Force Advisers to Rethink Risk, *InvestmentNews* Feb. 19, 2015, http://www.investmentnews.com/article/20150219/FREE/150219912/money-market-reforms-force-advisers-to-rethink-risk.

Investment Company Act, 15 U.S.C. §§ 80a-1 to -64.

Investment Company Institute, 2012, U.S. Treasurers Will Leave Money Market Funds Should the SEC Change Regulation, According to Treasury Strategies Study, www.ici.org/policy/current_issues/12_news_tsi_study.

Investment Company Institute, 2015, Investment Company Fact Book, https://www.ici.org/pdf/2015_factbook.pdf.

Investment Company Institute, 2018, Money Market Fund Assets, https://www.ici.org/research/stats/mmf/mm_07_19_18.

Johnson, Steve, 2015, All Money Market Funds Are Created Equal, Says Moody's, Regulation & Governance, FT.com, www.ft.com/content/1557434c-de03-11e4-8d14-00144feab7de.

Kacperczyk, Marcin & Philipp Schnabl, 2010, When Safe Proved Risky: Commercial Paper during the Financial Crisis of 2001–2009, J. Econ. Persp. 24: 29–50.

Katz, Ian & Jesse Hamilton, 2013, BlackRock, Fidelity Face Initial Risk Study by Regulators, Bloomberg, www.bloomberg.com/news/articles/2013-11-05/blackrock-fidelity-face-initial-risk-study-by-u-s-regulators.

Keen, Steven A., 2012, FSOC and Money Market Fund Reform: A Path to Nowhere, www.reedsmith.com/en/perspectives/2012/10/fsoc-and-money-market-fund-reform-a-path-to-nowher.

Kupiec, Paul, 2013, Our Worst Fears about Dodd–Frank's FSOC Are Being Confirmed, Forbes, www.forbes.com/sites/realspin/2013/11/26/our-worst-fears-about-dodd-franks-fsoc-are-being-confirmed/.

Larrabee, David, 2012, Is a Floating NAV the Fix Money Market Funds Need? Enterprising Investor, https://blogs.cfainstitute.org/investor/2012/03/14/is-a-floating-nav-the-fix-money-market-funds-need/.

Lynch, Sarah N., Schapiro, 2013, U.S. Risk Council Gave Life to Money Fund Reforms, Reuters, www.reuters.com/article/us-sec-moneyfunds-schapiro-idUSBRE9530PY20130604.

Mamudi, Sam, 2008, Money Market Breaks the Buck, Freezes Redemptions, Marketwatch, www.marketwatch.com/story/money-market-fund-breaks-the-buck-freezes-redemptions.

Markham, Jerry W., 2002, *A Financial History of the United States*, Vol. III.

Masson, Paul, 2013, The Dangers of an Extended Period of Low Interest Rates: Why the Bank of Canada Should Start Raising Them Now, C.D. Howe Inst., Commentary No. 381.

Maxey, Daisy, 2015, Advisers Prepare for Changes to Money-Market Funds, Wall St. J., www.wsj.com/articles/advisers-prepare-for-changes-to-money-market-funds-1424267558.

McCabe, Patrick E., 2010, The Cross Section of Money Market Fund Risks and Financial Crises, Finance and Economics Discussion Series, Divisions of Research & Statistics and Monetary Affairs Federal Reserve Board, Washington, D.C.

McDonald, Dustin, 2013, Government Finance Officers, Association, Letter to SEC.

McLaughlin, Tim, 2015, U.S. Money-Market Funds Raise Fees after Years of Cutting Them, Reuters, www.reuters.com/article/funds-moneymarket-investors-idUSL1N11029O20150825.

McNamara, James A. & David Fishman, 2014, Letter to Kevin O'Neill, Deputy Sec'y, Sec. & Exch. Comm'n., https://www.sec.gov/comments/s7-03-13/s70313-383.pdf.

Michaels, David, 2013, SEC Money Fund Rule Changing $1 Share Faces Less Opposition, Bloomberg Business, https://onwallstreet.financial-planning.com/news/sec-money-fund-rule-faces-less-opposition-as-1-shares-debated.

Michel, Norbert J., 2013, Lehman Brothers Bankruptcy and the Financial Crisis: Lessons Learned, The Heritage Found. Issue Brief.

Miller, Geoffrey P., 1992, Book Review: Anatomy of a Disaster: Why Bank Regulation Failed, Northwestern Univ. L. Rev. 86: 742–752.

Natarajan, Sridhar & Adam Janofsky, 2014, Money Fund Rules Seen Triggering Commercial Paper Jam, Bloomberg Business, www.bloomberg.com/news/articles/2014-07-31/money-fund-rules-seen-triggering-commercial-paper-jam.

Nickel, 2013, Looking Back At Bank Failure Rates, Forbes, https://www.forbes.com/sites/moneybuilder/2013/03/25/looking-back-at-bank-failure-rates/#337c8afc581b.

Office of Financial Research of the US Treasury Department, 2013, Asset Management and Financial Stability.

Phelps, Jack M., et al., 2004, Effects of Interest Rates on Money Market Mutual Funds, FDIC White Paper.

Pozen, Richard, 2010, *Too Big to Save: How to Fix the U.S. Financial System*, https://www.amazon.com/Too-Save-U-S-Financial-System/dp/0470499052#reader_0470499052.

President's Working Group on Financial Markets (PWGFM), 2010, Money Market Fund Reform Options.

Raymond, Nate, 2013, Settlement reached in Reserve Primary Fund lawsuit, Reuters, Sept. 6, 2013, https://www.reuters.com/article/us-reserveprimary-lawsuit/settlement-reached-in-reserve-primary-fund-lawsuit-idUSBRE98604Q20130907.

Reid, Brian, 2013, Money Market Funds and the Debt Ceiling: What Do We Know?, ICI Viewpoints.

Rowland, Christopher, 2013, Fidelity Fought Washington over Money Market Funds—and Won, Boston Globe, www.bostonglobe.com/news/politics/2014/10/18/with-aggressive-strategy-fidelity-fought-washington-over-money-market-funds-and-won/3ZbsOGsb9rfMuPpx2wx58H/story.html.

Rowland, Gregory, 2013, Designation of Asset Managers and Funds as Systemically Important Non-Bank Financial Institutions: Process and Industry Implications: Part 1 of 2, Inv. Lawyer, www.davispolk.com/files/files/Publication/cc040be7-3426-4e3c-a555-0ef1fd595b25/Preview/PublicationAttachment/a52b978d-dd91-4238-8f85-1032ecf3c697/IL_March_2013_Rowland_article.pdf.

Schapiro, Mary, 2010, Statement on Money Market Funds Before the Open Commission Meeting, Securities & Exchange Commission.

SEC, 1975, Investment Company Act Release No. 8757.

SEC, 1977, Valuation of Debt Instruments by Money Market Funds and Certain Other Open-End Investment Companies, Investment Company Act Release No. 9786.

SEC, 1982, Investment Company Act Rel. No. 12206, 47 Fed. Reg. 5428.

SEC, 1983, Valuation of Debt Instruments and Computation of Current Price Per Share by Certain Open-End Investment Companies (Money Market Funds), Investment Company Act Release No. 13380.

SEC, 2010, Money Market Fund Reform, Investment Company Act Rel. No. 29132, 75 Fed. Reg. 10060.

SEC, 2012, Div. of Risk, Strategy, & Fin. Innovation, 2012, Response to Questions Posed by Commissioners Aguilar, Paredes, and Gallagher.

SEC, 2013, Press Release, SEC Announces Fraud Charges against Detroit Based Money Market Fund Manager.

SEC, 2014, Money Market Fund Reform; Amendments to Form PF, 79 Fed. Reg. 47,736.

Shilling, Henry, 2010, Sponsor Support Key to Money Market Funds, Moody's Investors Service, https://files.alston.com/files/docs/Moody%27s_report.pdf.

Stecklow, Steve & Diya Gullapalli, 2008, A Money-Fund Manager's Fateful Shift, Wall St. Journal, www.wsj.com/articles/SB122869788400386907.

Stein, Kara M., 2014, Statement of Commissioner Kara M. Stein, Securities & Exchange Commission, http://www.sec.gov/News/Speech/Detail/Speech/1370542347012.

Stevens, Paul Schott, 2012, Testimony before the U.S. Senate Comm. On Banking, and Urban Affairs, www.ici.org/pdf/12_senate_pss_mmf_written.pdf.

Swagel, Phillip, 2013, Why Lehman Wasn't Rescued, N.Y. Times, https://economix.blogs.nytimes.com/2013/09/13/why-lehman-wasnt-rescued/.

Team, Trefis, 2015, BlackRock Shakes Up Money Market Offerings Ahead Of Impending Regulatory Changes, Forbes, www.forbes.com/sites/greatspeculations/2015/04/07/blackrock-shakes-up-money-market-offerings-ahead-of-impending-regulatory-changes/#5f1879564ea8.

U.S. Dept. of Treasury, 2008, Press Release, Treasury Announces Temporary Guarantee Program for Money Market Funds, Sept. 29, 2008, https://www.treasury.gov/press-center/press-releases/Pages/hp1161.aspx.

Vanguard, 2014, Money Market Reform: What You Need to Know, Oct. 2014, https://personal.vanguard.com/pdf/VGMMR.pdf.

Volcker, Paul, 2011, Securities & Exchange Commission, Unofficial Transcript: Roundtable on Money Market Funds and Systemic Risk.

White, Mary Jo, 2014, Statement at SEC Open Meeting on Money Market Fund Reform, Securities & Exchange Commission.

Wigglesworth, Robin, 2015, Third Avenue Fund Closure Sends Shivers through Credit Markets, FT.com, https://www.ft.com/content/9fda3c7e-a01b-11e5-8613-08e211ea5317.

Williams, Alex, Mikaylee O'Connor, & John Roche, 2015, Impact of Money Market Regulatory Reform, RVK Investment Perspectives.

Wilmarth, J., Arthur E., 2002, The Transformation of the U.S. Financial Services Industry, 1975–2000: Competition, Consolidation, and Increased Risks, University of Illinois Law Review 2002: 215–476.

Wilmer, Sabrina, 2015, Federated, BlackRock Mull Private Money Funds amid Rules, BloombergBusiness, March 15, 2015, www.bloomberg.com/news/articles/2015-03-16/federated-blackrock-mull-private-money-funds-amid-rules.

11. Exchange-traded funds: neither fish nor fowl
Eric D. Roiter

1 INTRODUCTION

Since exchange-traded funds (ETFs) first appeared on the scene in the early 1990s, their growth has been impressive. By 2015, there were nearly 1600 ETFs, with total assets of more than $2.1 trillion.[1] For US stocks, the Standard & Poor's 500 index has long been the most closely followed index, and thus it is not surprising that the first ETF, launched in 1992 by State Street Global Advisers, tracks that index. Over the years, ETFs have proliferated to the point that virtually every recognizable stock and bond index in the US and abroad is tracked by at least one. The types of securities in which ETFs invest are as varied as the capital markets themselves.[2] Stock ETFs range across the various categories of market capitalization (large, medium, or small cap), different industries, and various geographic regions. A similar proliferation has unfolded with bond ETFs. As the strategy of passive investing has gained more adherents, and as conventional index mutual funds have themselves gained market share at the expense of actively managed funds, ETFs have grown as well. Indeed, much of the case made for ETFs is not unique but rather turns on the benefits—especially low fees, low portfolio turnover, and tax efficiency—inherent in passive investing.

ETFs, however, pose a fundamental policy question for the SEC. Unlike mutual funds and closed-end funds, ETFs are nowhere authorized in the governing federal statute, the Investment Company Act of 1940 (ICA). ETFs exist only because the SEC in its discretion has granted exemptions from core statutory provisions governing fund structure, pricing and operations. In so doing, the SEC has sought to reconcile investor protection and financial innovation, two goals that are not always complementary.

---

[1] Investment Company Institute, 2016 Investment Company Fact Book, at 60 (2016) ("ICI 2016 Fact Book"), www.ici.org/pdf/2016_factbook.pdf.

[2] It is beyond the scope of this chapter to address other types of exchange-traded products that do not convey ownership interests in securities pools. Chief among these are exchange-traded commodities funds and exchange-traded notes. The former, subject to the jurisdiction of the Commodities Futures Trading Commission, are pools investing in commodities (such as gold or oil), currencies, and commodity futures. In 2015, exchange-traded commodity funds held aggregate net assets of approximately $48 billion (compared to securities-based ETFs with net assets of $2.1 trillion). See ICI 2016 Fact Book, at 61, figure 3.2. Exchange-traded notes hold no investment pools of any sort. Rather, they are debt instruments whose variable interest rates are tied to the performance of a designated benchmark such as the S&P 500 index or a commodities index. See SEC, Request for Comment on Exchange-Traded Products, Rel. No. 34-75165 (June 12, 2015), 80 Fed. Reg. 34729 (June 17, 2015).

In this chapter, we will see how the SEC's efforts to balance investor protection and financial innovation have played out thus far. We consider the design of ETFs, trace their growth, and review trading and investment strategies. We then turn to the regulatory framework within which ETFs must be made to fit, the record of exemptive relief granted by the SEC, and the agency's inconclusive efforts to adopt rules for ETFs. We next take up issues posed by "actively managed" ETFs. While they now comprise a relatively small niche in the ETF universe, if ETFs are to offer a broad alternative to conventional mutual funds, actively managed ETFs must find a place. Finally, we consider ETFs from a wider perspective—whether they pose "systemic risk" to the financial markets, which could give rise to additional regulation, not only by the SEC, but by the Federal Reserve Board as well.

2 THE EVOLUTION OF ETFs

2.1 Precursors to ETFs: The Brief Life of Index Participations

In 1989, a commodities law case provided, inadvertently, an impetus to the development and growth of ETFs.[3] Three securities exchanges—the Philadelphia Stock Exchange, the American Stock Exchange, and the Chicago Board Options Exchange—had each obtained approval from the SEC to list for trading derivative instruments whose value would be based upon a designated stock index. In the version developed by the Philadelphia Stock Exchange, these instruments were called "index participations" (or "IPs"). The concept was to allow buyers and sellers to trade IPs as proxies for stocks making up a particular stock index, and for the buyer or the seller to profit from the upward or downward movement in the value of the index. The IPs did not represent ownership interests in securities pools and, indeed, the IPs themselves owned no underlying securities. But because IPs derived their price from the value of a given securities index, the market value of an IP would vary from day to day, and within a trading day, as the value of the index itself varied. IPs could thus serve as a hedge for investors holding underlying stocks or as a vehicle for speculation by traders who did not. The underlying stocks were not traded between the parties; when closing out a long position (as a buyer) or short position (as a seller), a party would pay or receive cash depending upon the movement of the IP's trading price over the holding period.

The Chicago Mercantile Exchange, a commodities exchange regulated not by the SEC but by a sister federal regulatory agency (the Commodity Futures Trading Commission or "CFTC"), brought suit against the SEC for approving the trading of these instruments on the three securities exchanges. The suit brought to the fore the

---

[3] Chicago Mercantile Exchange v. Securities and Exchange Commission, 883 F. 2d 537 (7th Cir. 1989). The first ETF approved by the SEC was the SPDR Trust, Series 1, known popularly as the SPDR S&P 500 ETF, an ETF designed to track the performance of the Standard & Poor's 500 Composite Stock Price Index. In its application for an exemption, State Street Bank and Trust Company explained that "SPDRs were developed in response to the suspension of trading in 'index participations' ('IPs')." Exemption Application of SPDR Trust, Series 1, Rel. No. IC-18959 (Sept. 17, 1992), 57 Fed. Reg. 43996 (Sept. 23, 1992).

competing mandates of the SEC (with jurisdiction over securities and options on securities) and the CFTC (with jurisdiction over futures and options on futures). At first glance, it would seem a bright jurisdictional line. But what about futures on securities (for example, US Treasury bonds) or on bundles of securities (for example, the S&P 500 Index)?

In earlier litigation, courts had upheld the CFTC's statutory grant of exclusive jurisdiction over all futures trading, even futures on securities or securities indexes. A dispositive issue in the *Chicago Mercantile* case, therefore, was whether IPs were futures contracts, on one hand, or stand-alone securities or options on securities, on the other. The instruments did not fit neatly in either category. As the court noted, "We must decide whether tetrahedrons belong in square or round holes." The court ultimately concluded, however, that IPs were in fact futures contracts (even if also securities), and therefore that the SEC had impermissibly encroached upon the CFTC's exclusive jurisdiction by approving the trading of IPs and similar instruments on the stock exchanges. In the wake of the adverse decision in the *Chicago Mercantile* case, the challenge for the securities industry thus became how to design a product that would fit properly within the SEC's jurisdictional purview. ETFs would meet these design requirements.

2.2 ETF Structure

ETFs are investment companies that, like conventional mutual funds (and unlike IPs), are pools of securities, investing in stocks or bonds or both, under the management of a professional investment adviser. ETF investors, like mutual fund investors, share in the investment gains and losses of their funds proportionate to their share ownership. ETFs and mutual funds, however, differ in one fundamental attribute: how their shares are traded. Mutual fund investors, when buying or selling shares, trade directly with their mutual fund, not with each other. ETF investors, on the other hand, generally trade with one another on a securities exchange or other trading venue.

Pricing differences follow. Mutual fund investors do not negotiate price but rather buy and sell at a single "forward" price reflecting the net asset value of the fund determined at the end of the trading day. ETF investors, in contrast, buy and sell at negotiated prices that typically fluctuate during a trading day in response to market forces, much like individual stocks. This defining feature of ETFs—negotiated trading at fluctuating prices in a secondary market—gives rise both to their appeal and their regulatory challenge.

In addition to liquidity and intraday trading, advocates for ETFs proffer other advantages. The preponderance of ETFs are passively managed to track the performance of a particular stock or bond index. Investment managers of ETFs (actually, their computers) perform this task at relatively low cost, and this leads to low fees for investors. ETFs provide exposure to some securities, such as foreign stocks, that most investors would find difficult to acquire directly. Portfolios of ETFs typically have low turnover because the trading of their shares in the secondary market obviates the need for ETFs to sell holdings to pay for share redemptions. Low turnover, in turn, can lead not only to greater investment efficiency but also to greater tax efficiency by limiting the realization of capital gains. By tracking specified indexes, ETFs can serve as efficient hedging vehicles and accommodate other types of trading strategies, fostering over the longer term capital formation, allocation of investment assets, and price discovery.

While most ETF investors do not buy shares from nor sell them back to the fund, it is critical to the structure of ETFs that some do. These are broker-dealers or large financial institutions who enter into contractual arrangements with an ETF and agree to act as "Authorized Participants" or "APs." In this capacity, they carry out the essential function of distributing ETF shares to investors in the secondary market. In basic economic terms, APs are wholesalers, purchasing in bulk from the producer, the ETF, and distributing to investors in the retail market.

The process of distribution begins with the purchase by an AP of a so-called "creation unit" of an ETF's shares, a block ranging in size from 25,000 to 250,000 shares, with a typical creation unit consisting of 50,000. The AP purchases "in kind" from the ETF, that is, the purchase price consists entirely or almost entirely of securities rather than cash. At the beginning of each trading day, an ETF specifies the securities that must be included in each creation unit basket for that day. For index-tracking ETFs, the creation basket mirrors the securities which make up the index in identity and weighting. In the case of a very broad index consisting of thousands of securities, the ETF manager may specify a creation basket consisting of a subset of securities replicating the investment performance of the index as a whole. It is not uncommon at the end of a trading day for the market value of securities in a creation basket to vary somewhat from the ETF's net asset value. In this event, the broker-dealer will pay to (or receive from) the ETF a comparatively small amount of cash to bring the purchase price precisely into alignment with the ETF's day-ending net asset value. The second step in the distribution process is the AP's resale of ETF shares from its inventory to investors in the secondary market. This is done over one or more days at market prices.

The process works in reverse as well. APs have a right of redemption, by which they can sell back to ETFs (and ETFs have an obligation to repurchase) ETF shares in one or more creation unit blocks. The redemption, too, is paid "in kind," with the ETF delivering a redemption basket of securities matching some or all of the ETF's portfolio, as specified by the ETF earlier on the trading day. The value of the securities (again often adjusted by a small cash payment to or from the AP) will match the ETF's net asset value at the end of the trading day. The in-kind purchases and in-kind redemptions of ETF shares through primary market (that is, direct) trades between ETFs and APs allow under ordinary conditions for expansion or contraction of an ETF's investment portfolio without forcing an ETF manager's hand in the timing of securities trades in the secondary market to invest or raise large amounts of cash.

The existence of both a primary market and a secondary market, however, inevitably creates deviation between an ETF's net asset value and fluctuating market prices for the ETF's shares. Here is where APs play a second important role—as arbitrageurs. For efficient arbitrage to take place, the market must have basic information about an ETF beyond its designated index or portfolio composition. For all ETFs, the exchange on which their shares trade must regularly (typically, every 15 seconds), throughout the trading day, update an ETF's net asset value per share (its "indicative intraday value" or "IIV"), reflecting the market value of the ETF's portfolio securities. Further, many APs operate their own proprietary pricing models to track changes in the value of an ETF's portfolio securities (and hence the ETF's net asset value) during the trading day, on what is close to a real-time basis.

An example illustrates how arbitrage can bring the net asset value and market price of an ETF's shares into close alignment. Take, for example, a situation where an ETF tracking the S&P 500 index has an IIV of $10 per share but on the exchange its shares are trading at $9.90, representing a discount from NAV of 1 percent. A broker-dealer can realize an arbitrage profit by purchasing ETF shares at prices lower than $10 per share and contemporaneously selling short the stocks in the S&P 500 index. The broker-dealer's purchases (together with that of others engaged in arbitrage) will tend to drive up the market price of the ETF's shares (by increasing demand and reducing supply), bringing the price closer to the ETF's NAV. At the end of the trading day, for example, the ETF's shares closing price might be $9.99, representing a NAV discount of only 0.1 percent.

As the foregoing example suggests, the AP earns an arbitrage profit by redeeming ETF shares in creation units and receiving an in-kind redemption basket comprising the stocks making up the S&P 500 index or a subset thereof (together with any cash adjustment) equal to the ETF's net asset value per share. Upon receiving the portfolio securities, the broker-dealer then delivers them to close out its short positions. The broker-dealer's arbitrage profits derive from the difference between the prices the broker-dealer paid to acquire ETF shares and the higher prices at which it sold the constituent stocks in the S&P 500 index.

The same arbitrage principles are at work when ETF shares trade at a premium to an ETF's NAV. APs purchase the individual securities in an ETF's portfolio (or a representative subset thereof) and contemporaneously sell short the higher priced ETF shares. The firm's short-selling of ETF shares will tend to drive down their market price, bringing it in closer alignment with the ETF's NAV per share price. At the end of the day, the broker-dealer will purchase from the ETF one or more creation units of ETF shares by delivering creation baskets of portfolio securities. It will use the ETF shares so acquired to close out its short positions.[4]

Over extended periods, arbitrage has kept the market price of the preponderance of ETFs in close proximity to their NAV price, especially for those with domestic securities portfolios. The SEC has found that for the latter half of 2014, the disparity between market price and NAV for domestic stock index-based ETFs was only 0.21 percent, and that for actively managed domestic stock ETFs only 0.38 percent. For

---

[4] The foregoing describes classical, riskless arbitrage. Firms engaged in ETF arbitrage often employ other techniques, using swaps or other derivatives. *See, e.g.*, Letter from Barbara Novick, Vice Chairman & Ira Shapiro, Managing Director, BlackRock to Brent J. Fields, Secretary, SEC (Aug. 11, 2015) ("[I]n BlackRock's experience, professional trading firms ... hedge their trading exposure to ETF shares by taking offsetting, correlated positions in derivative instruments, which are often considerably easier to trade quickly than the ETF In Kind Basket. Many market participants treat ETF trading positions as part of a global trading book, and offset long or short trading exposures to ETFs against aggregated exposures to correlated futures, swaps, structured notes or securities incurred through other parts of their trading business.").

that same period, the disparity for domestic bond index-based ETFs was 0.26 percent and for actively managed domestic bond ETFs only 0.19 percent.[5]

3 THE RISE AND GROWTH OF ETFs

However measured, the growth of ETFs over the past two decades has been remarkable. In 2015 alone, ETFs took in approximately $229 billion in net sales of shares, and assets under management in ETFs accounted for 12 percent of assets held in all investment companies, including conventional mutual funds.[6] From a standing start in 1993, ETFs grew to 80 funds with collective assets of $65.5 billion by 2000, to 869 funds and $891 billion by 2010, and to 1521 funds and $2.1 trillion by 2015.[7] By contrast, closed-end funds in 2015 held assets of $260 billion.[8] Indeed, ETFs are fast approaching the level of assets held in all money market funds.[9]

Types of ETF vary widely. By the end of 2015, among stock ETFs, there were 360 funds with broad-based, domestic stock portfolios, 266 ETFs with more narrowly focused sector or industry portfolios, and 592 investing in stocks on a global or international basis. There were also 274 bond ETFs and 21 hybrid ETFs, investing in both stocks and bonds.[10] While the great preponderance of ETFs track an index, tracking strategies themselves have taken different directions. Rather than tracking an index proportionally, more recent types of index ETFs use leverage to track an index exponentially, multiplying the index's gains or losses.[11] Other index ETFs, through short sales and derivatives trading, are designed to track inversely (proportionally or exponentially) the performance of a given index.[12] Further, many ETFs, rather than tracking a recognized, preexisting index, instead track a customized one created specifically to serve as the investment template for an index-tracking ETF. For example, whereas the S&P 500 index (and many others) is a "market cap" weighted index (increasing a stock's weighting in proportion to a company's market capitalization), ETFs have emerged to track indexes where equal weight is given to constituent stocks.

---

[5] SEC, Request for Comment on Exchange-Traded Products, Rel. No. 34-75165 (June 12, 2015), www.sec.gov/rules/other/2015/34-75165.pdf.
[6] ICI 2016 Fact Book, at p. 69, figure 3.7.
[7] Id. at 182–83, tables 11 & 12. These figures exclude ETFs not regulated under the Investment Company Act of 1940, which invest primarily in commodities, currencies and futures. In 2010 and 2015, there were 54 and 73 such ETFs, respectively. Id.
[8] Id. at 180, table 9.
[9] At the close of 2015, money market funds (both institutional and retail) collectively held $2.75 trillion in assets. Id. at p. 175, table 4.
[10] Id. at 183, table 12.
[11] For a discussion of the proliferation of index-tracking ETFs, see generally SEC, Request for Comment on Exchange-Traded Products, Rel. No. 34-75165 (June 12, 2015), 80 Fed. Reg. 34729 (June 17, 2015).
[12] See SEC, Leveraged and Inverse ETFs: Specialized Products with Extra Risks for Buy-and-Hold Investors, www.sec.gov/investor/pubs/leveragedetfs-alert.htm.

Perhaps the most dramatic development has been the growth of "smart beta" ETFs, which track a customized rather than an established index. A customized index selects for inclusion and assigns weights to stocks based on one or more factors. Some indexes might accord weight to stocks of companies identified as falling into the value rather than the growth category. Other indexes might give weight to stocks based, for example, upon a company's cash flow, sales, earnings, book value, or dividends, or a stock's low volatility or trading momentum. Among many examples of a smart beta ETF is the WisdomTree Total Dividend Fund, tracking a customized index of dividend-paying US companies. The index was designed by WisdomTree in 2006 specifically to serve as the benchmark index for its Total Dividend Fund ETF and its other smart beta dividend ETFs.

One reason for the appeal of smart beta ETFs is that they afford investors different avenues for diversification beyond that offered by capitalization-weighted index-tracking ETFs. Another reason advanced by proponents of smart beta is that markets not only are inefficient, but are systematically so. Smart beta ETFs, they say, take advantages of opportunities for above-market returns based on investment strategies that exploit pricing inefficiencies. Smart beta is thus a hybrid of passive and active management. It is passive in the sense that a smart beta ETF's portfolio manager is not making individualized investment decisions, but it is active in that the creation of the customized index itself—selecting some stocks and rejecting others—is an exercise of investment decision-making, setting the rules which then dictate how the ETF's investments are made.

A smart beta ETF's index is the product of backtesting, an effort to find how certain factors could (with the benefit of hindsight) have achieved investment results exceeding a capitalization-weighted index like the S&P 500. A smart beta index, once constructed, is not immutable. It can be revised based upon additional backtesting taking into account updated security trading prices. These changes then lead to rebalancing of a smart beta ETF's portfolio to conform it to the newly revised index. Whether smart beta strategies will prove successful over the longer term remains open to question.[13]

Rounding out the array of ETFs are those that are actively managed in the traditional sense where a portfolio manager makes individualized investing decisions to outperform a recognized benchmark index. In numbers and assets, actively managed ETFs have seen limited, yet gradual, growth. They were first permitted by the SEC in 2008, and there were 13 "conventional" actively managed ETFs in that year, 25 in 2010, and 134 in 2015.[14] By the end of 2015, actively managed ETFs held assets of over

---

[13] See, e.g., Denys Glushkov, How Smart Are Smart Beta ETFs? Analysis of Relative Performance and Factor Exposure (Sept. 22, 2015), http://papers.ssrn.com/sol3/papers.cfm?abstract_id=2594941 (finding that over the period from May 2003 to December 2014, "there is lack of empirical support for the hypothesis that [smart beta] ETFs outperform their risk-adjusted [passive cap-weighted] benchmarks"); Rob Arnott, Noah Beck, Vitali Kalesnik, and John West, How Can "Smart Beta" Go Horribly Wrong? (Feb. 2016), www.researchaffiliates.com/Production%20content%20library/How%20Can%20Smart%20Beta%20Go%20Horribly%20Wrong_pdf.pdf ("[M]any of these alpha claims are based on 10- to 15-year back-tests that won't cover more than a couple of market cycles").

[14] ICI 2016 Fact Book, at 183, table 12.

$27 billion.[15] Thus far, most of the successful (in terms of attracting assets) actively managed ETFs invest in bonds, rather than stocks.

4 TRADING AND INVESTMENT STRATEGIES FOR ETFs

Like conventional index mutual funds, index-based ETFs serve as a ready vehicle for investors, both retail and professional, to diversify across asset classes (for example, growth stocks, value stocks, investment grade bonds and high-yield bonds) and across different geographic regions. Investors can also buy shares in ETFs to gain exposure to narrower, discrete groups of securities, for example, stocks of a single industry or country.[16]

Index-tracking ETFs have emerged as widely used vehicles for investors to hedge other investments in their investment portfolios. ETFs are generally superior to conventional index mutual funds in this regard because investors can lock in an intraday trading price for their ETF positions to match against contemporaneous changes in other portfolio holdings. The ability to hedge all or part of an actively managed portfolio is, of course, crucial for professional asset managers (including mutual fund advisers) in a number of contexts, including where there is a need to "equitize" cash that has just come into the portfolio (for example, through net purchases of shares in a mutual fund). For example, a mutual fund near the end of a trading day might find itself with an impending net inflow of cash that might account for 1 percent of its total portfolio. The fund manager can ill afford to let that cash sit idle for one or more trading days, as she chooses which stocks to add to the portfolio. It is commonplace for the fund manager therefore to use the cash to purchase an index-based ETF whose designated index is the same (or substantially similar to) the benchmark index of the fund. This hedge allows the fund manager time to sift through and pick individual stocks for the fund's portfolio, while simultaneously reducing the size of the fund's ETF hedge.

ETFs, of course, can serve the very different investment strategy of market timing and gaining alpha. ETFs, in contrast to at least some of their portfolio securities, can offer more liquidity, can trade during US trading hours, and thus can afford investors the ability to trade in and out of positions within short time periods. In this regard, ETFs, like individual stocks, can be traded on margin, can be sold short, and can be the subject of puts, calls, and other derivatives trading—all features not afforded by conventional mutual funds, and all important to the active professional trading firm.

---

[15] *Id.* at 182, table 11.
[16] For extensive discussion of uses and trading strategies for ETFs, *see* Gary L. Gastineau, THE EXCHANGE-TRADED FUNDS MANUAL (John Wiley & Sons, Inc. 2d ed., 2010); David J. Abner, VISUAL GUIDE TO ETFs (Bloomberg Press, 2013). *See also* Josh Cherry, THE LIMITS OF ARBITRAGE: EVIDENCE FROM EXCHANGE TRADED FUNDS (2004), http://papers.ssrn.com/sol3/Papers.cfm?abstract_id=628061.

5 THE REGULATORY FRAMEWORK AND EXEMPTIVE RELIEF FOR ETFs

Because ETFs invest primarily in securities, they are subject to regulation as investment companies under the ICA, but they do not fit within the statutory mold of either of the two most important—a closed-end fund or a mutual fund. ETFs cannot qualify as closed-end funds because some investors—namely, APs—have a daily right of redemption.[17] On the other hand, without exemptive relief from the SEC, ETFs cannot qualify as mutual funds because redemption rights are not given to all fund investors.[18] The ICA, moreover, requires equal treatment of all mutual fund investors by prohibiting issuance of more than one class of common stock.[19] ETFs, however, depend for their existence upon the disparate treatment of investors. Nonetheless, the great preponderance of ETFs have been formed as mutual funds, with important exemptions granted by the SEC.

First, exemptive relief has been needed to allow ETFs to deny the right of redemption to most investors. Second, for secondary market trading to take place at negotiated prices, an exemption is needed from ICA Section 22(d) and Rule 22c-1, which require that both purchases and redemptions of shares be tied to a fund's net asset value per share calculated at a forward price at the end of the trading day.[20] Third,

---

[17] Sponsors, it appears, have never sought to organize ETFs as closed-end funds and seek exemptive relief to allow for redemptions by large holders. It is not altogether clear, however, why this approach has never been tried. The SEC has in fact shown flexibility with regard to closed-end funds, adopting in 1993 its so-called "Interval Fund" rule, Rule 23c-3, 17 C.F.R. § 270.23c-3. That rule permits closed-end funds to redeem at their NAV price a specified percentage of outstanding shares (at least 5 percent and not more than 25 percent), not on a daily basis, but at periodic intervals of 3, 6, or 12 months. The right to participate in these periodic redemptions must be extended to all shareholders, and a closed-end fund choosing to rely on the rule must adhere to its redemption policy unless holders of a majority of shares votes to terminate the policy. *See* Repurchase Offers by Closed-End Management Investment Companies, Rel. IC-19399 (April 7, 1993). As discussed *infra*, some ETFs have, with exemptive relief, been formed as unit investment trusts.

[18] The ICA requires that every fund share convey to its holder a redemption right, an option entitling the holder to put the share back to the fund and receive in return a payment that represents "approximately his proportionate share of [the fund's] current net assets, or the cash equivalent." ICA, § 2(a)(32). The ICA has other provisions governing mutual funds that reinforce the redemption right and provide other related protections to investors. Section 22(e) generally prohibits a fund from suspending the right of redemption or deferring the payment of redemption proceeds for longer than seven days. The SEC can grant temporary exceptions to these requirements if emergency conditions impair the fair valuation of a fund's assets or impede the liquidation of a fund's portfolio securities, but grants of exceptions have been exceedingly rare.

[19] ICA § 18(i), 15 U.S.C. § 80a-18(i).

[20] Rule 22c-1 requires "forward pricing" of mutual fund shares for both purchases and redemptions. At least once each trading day, a mutual fund must calculate its NAV, valuing all of its assets and liabilities, and assigning current market values to all securities in its investment portfolio if quotations are readily available. If a security lacks a current market value, the fund must assign a "fair value." Typically, mutual funds compute their NAVs once per day as of 4 p.m. (Eastern Time), when trading in stocks generally ends. An investor wishing to purchase or redeem mutual fund shares during any trading day must submit the order prior to the time as to

exemptive relief is needed to allow in-kind purchases and redemptions by APs, where payment consists of a basket of securities paid to or withdrawn from the ETF's portfolio rather than cash. In-kind transactions between ETFs and their APs are essential to arbitrage, but conflict with the ICA if the AP is an "affiliated person" of the ETF by virtue of owning 5 percent or more of the ETF's outstanding shares at the time of a trade. Absent an exemption, the ICA flatly prohibits an affiliated purchaser from selling securities to or purchasing securities from a fund.[21]

In addition to these three key aspects of exemptive relief, the SEC has granted ancillary relief from other regulatory requirements. Over the years, a fairly predictable path for obtaining favorable action has emerged, prompting the SEC to propose an exemptive rule to spare ETF sponsors the need to apply for exemptions on a case by case basis.

The SEC has prescribed two basic conditions for every ETF. One is that an ETF's portfolio be transparent to market participants on a daily basis. For ETFs tracking a well-known stock or bond index, this is readily achieved simply by identifying the index, such as the S&P 500 or the Russell 2000 index. Other ETF index funds have customized indexes which add or drop securities based upon preset rules that incorporate issuer-specific factors such as low volatility or dividend growth. For these ETFs, the SEC requires disclosure and explanation of these rules-based factors. What about ETFs that do not track an index, that is, actively managed funds? Thus far, the SEC has deemed investor protection to require daily disclosure of the actual holdings of the ETF's investment portfolio, an inhibiting factor for active managers.

The SEC's second condition for investor protection is effective arbitrage trading, ensuring that ETF shares trading in the secondary market do so at prices that closely approximate the ETF's net asset value. This, too, has been reasonably well achieved by ETFs tracking broad-based indexes whose constituent securities themselves trade in a liquid market. But newer generations of ETFs have emerged tracking narrow indexes comprising securities that, at least at times, have little liquidity, thereby hampering efficient arbitrage.

5.1 Index-Tracking ETFs

The first wave of ETFs granted exemptive relief, starting with the SPDR S&P 500 ETF, involved those that fully replicate their index, holding all of the index's securities. Because this obviates investment discretion, the SPDR S&P 500 ETF, as with other early ETFs, had no need for, and thus did not have, any investment adviser. Rather, the ETF's sponsor, acting as trustee, carried out the mechanistic role of constructing the ETF to match the index, adjusting the portfolio over time as stocks were added or dropped from the index or their weightings were adjusted.

The absence of an investment adviser has meant that the SPDR S&P 500 ETF, and other first generation ETFs, could take the form of a specialized type of investment

---

which NAV is calculated. If an order is received by a fund after that time, the investor's order (unless cancelled) is carried over to the next day and receives that next day's closing NAV price.
    [21] ICA, § 17(a)(1), (2). In this context, "securities" are those of third party issuers, not the fund itself.

company allowed under the ICA: a "unit investment trust" ("UIT"). A UIT, like a mutual fund, issues redeemable securities, but the ICA provides that those securities (unlike mutual fund shares) must represent undivided interests in "a unit of specified securities," thereby precluding exercise of investment authority or changes to the UIT's investment portfolio following launch.[22] The SEC's exemptive relief has required ETFs to disclose to the market, on a daily basis, the basket of securities (and their respective weightings) that an AP is required to deliver to acquire an ETF's creation unit of shares. Following the SEC's approval of the SPDR S&P 500 Index in October 1992, a wave of other "full replication" ETFs soon followed, gaining substantially similar exemptive relief from the SEC.

It was inevitable that index ETFs would migrate from UIT form and toward mutual fund form. First, any index ETF managed in order to achieve full replication suffers a disadvantage. An index represents only notional value. No account is taken of the various expenses—brokerage commissions, trustees' fees, SEC filings, and the like—of investing in securities. This means that full replication will invariably lead to tracking error, and that error will be under- rather than overperformance of the index.

Further, many securities indexes do not lend themselves to full replication. Well before ETFs emerged, conventional index mutual funds developed strategies to track an index without owning all constituent securities. It was natural therefore for a second generation of index ETFs to follow this same approach, purchasing a subgroup of securities in an index and sometimes even securities outside an index. One can rightly say that this is a form of "active" management because investment discretion is exercised even though the objective is to match rather than outperform an index's performance. Investment discretion, however, is antithetical to the UIT form of investment company, and this led ETF sponsors to switch to the mutual fund form. This brings three advantages. An index-tracking ETF organized as a mutual fund can vary the time when it purchases or sells portfolio securities, rather than simply matching the time when securities are added, dropped, or rebalanced in the index itself. This simple strategy can add an increment of gain to an ETF's portfolio, partially offsetting tracking error. Second, an ETF organized as a mutual fund can use derivatives—options, futures, and swaps—to add economic leverage, increasing the potential for gain but also loss. Finally, the mutual fund form allows an ETF to lend portfolio securities to others (typically short-sellers), and to reap interest on these loans. All of these strategies can increase an ETF's return and thus help narrow its index-tracking error.

One of the first exemptions for a second generation index ETF was granted to First Trust ETF in 2005.[23] The application sought approval for an unspecified number of different stock index ETFs. The first would be the First Trust Dow Jones Select Microcap Index ETF. The application stated that a representative sampling investment strategy might be used when a particular security in a given index is illiquid or when there might be practical difficulties or substantial costs in acquiring it. This would typically be a greater possibility with foreign securities. The exemptive application acknowledged that a sampling strategy would likely be less successful than full

---

[22] ICA § 4(2), 15 U.S.C. § 80a-4(2).
[23] First Trust ETF, Rel. No IC-27051, 70 Fed. Reg. 52450 (Sept. 2, 2005).

258 *Research handbook on the regulation of mutual funds*

replication in achieving close tracking of a designated index. Indeed, the application stated that tracking error in some cases might approach 5 percent.

Putting investment discretion aside, the First Trust ETF looked much like a first generation index ETF. APs would enter into in-kind purchases and redemptions of creation units with the ETF; daily disclosure would be made to the markets as to the composition and weightings of the securities of a portfolio deposit; and shares of the First Trust ETF would trade on a secondary market, namely Nasdaq, at negotiated prices. To guard against investor confusion, the First Trust ETF undertook not to represent or advertise itself as a mutual fund—even though, with the benefit of certain exemptions as explained, it is. This has long since become standard protocol for ETFs.

For the hundreds of smart beta and other ETFs that have customized indexes which add or drop securities based upon preset rules that incorporate issuer-specific factors such as sales or book value or market factors such as volatility or momentum, the SEC requires disclosure and explanation of these rules-based factors.[24] The SEC has also imposed conditions to require confidentiality surrounding the revisions to a customized index, including the rebalancing of weights given to constituent securities.

5.2 Actively Managed ETFs

An investor in a conventional mutual fund has the benefit of only limited transparency regarding fund holdings and net asset value. A mutual fund investor does not know the current holdings of the fund at the time of her purchase or redemption. SEC rules require that funds disclose their full portfolio holdings only on a quarterly basis; they allow a 60-day lag period for this disclosure. Many funds voluntarily make more frequent disclosures—typically monthly—but these are often limited to a fund's top ten holdings or allocations across industries, and have a lag time of ten days or so. Further, because of the SEC's forward pricing rule, a mutual fund investor does not know the net asset value price which she will pay or receive at the time of her trade and can learn that price only after the end of the trading day.[25] This is a remarkable departure from the normal workings of free and open markets, where agreement on price between transacting parties is key, if not essential.

The reasons for limited portfolio disclosure are well known. Fund investors may well wish to know what securities their fund is holding at any moment so that they can better allocate their own assets across a number of funds and accounts. Further, disclosure of a fund's current holdings (or increasing the frequency and reducing the delay of disclosure) helps a fund's investors evaluate how well the portfolio manager is adhering to the fund's investment policies. But while a fund's investors may want to know about current portfolio holdings, they do not want others to know. Opportunistic

---

[24] See, e.g., PowerShares Exchange-Traded Fund Trust, Release No. IC-25961 (March. 4, 2003); WisdomTree Investments, Release No. IC-27324 (May 18, 2006), 71 Fed. Reg. 29995 (May 24, 2006).

[25] See William A. Birdthistle, *The Fortunes and Foibles of Exchange-Traded Funds: A Positive Market Response to the Problems of Mutual Funds*, 33 DEL. J. CORP. L. 69, 78 (2008) ("[I]f, shortly after the opening bell, a remarkable piece of bad news sends the market into a precipitous fall throughout the entire business day, a mutual fund investor can do no more than place a sell order and ride the price of the fund all the way down until the closing bell").

short-term traders will "front run" a fund when they know, or even suspect, that the fund has embarked on a program to acquire or reduce a sizable position in a particular stock.[26] By buying up the stock earlier, these traders raise the price at which they can sell to the fund. "Free riders" also pose concerns. These are investors, unwilling to bear the expense of buying shares and being a shareholder in a mutual fund, who take advantage of the disclosure of a successful actively managed fund's holdings by mimicking the fund's investment decisions in their personal accounts.[27] Even with delayed disclosures by mutual funds, free riding occurs, but it is safe to assume that the practice would become greatly more pronounced and more prejudicial to mutual fund investors if daily full disclosure were mandated for mutual funds.

The exemptive relief granted by the SEC, however, has placed emphasis on the need for full disclosure to the markets of an actively managed ETF's current portfolio so that effective arbitrage trading can occur.[28] Among the first exemptions granted by the SEC in 2008 was that to PowerShares Capital Management,[29] which gained approval for a number of ETFs that would employ a quantitative investment management model, aimed at achieving long-term capital appreciation. Three proposed ETFs would invest in stocks and one in bonds.[30] Among the conditions accepted by PowerShares was that each ETF, prior to the start of each day's trading, would make full public disclosure on its website of all securities in its investment portfolio, including the weightings of each securities holding. Also, on a per share basis, each ETF would daily disclose (1) the prior day's NAV and bid/ask price in the secondary market and the discount (or premium) in relation to the prior day's NAV, and (2) a chart depicting the spread between NAV and bid/ask prices over the preceding four quarters.

To supplement this data, PowerShares represented that during the course of every trading day, the stock exchange where the ETF's shares would be traded would disseminate the NAV per share of the fund every 15 seconds, reflecting intraday

---

[26] *See, e.g.*, Markus K. Brunnermeier and Lasse Heje Pedersen, *Predatory Trading*, 60(4) J. FINANCE, 1825–1863 (2005).

[27] *See, e.g.*, Mary Margaret Frank, James M. Poterba, Douglas A. Shackelford, and John B. Shoven, *Copycat Funds: Information Disclosure Regulation and the Returns to Active Management in the Mutual Fund Industry*, 47(2) J. LAW AND ECONOMICS, 515–41 (2004).

[28] *See, e.g.*, Letter from James A. Brigagliano, Division of Trading and Markets, SEC, to Stuart M. Strauss, Clifford Chance, Class Relief for Exchange-Traded Index Funds (Oct. 24, 2006) (explaining that exemptive relief for equity index-based ETFs is appropriate only when secondary market prices of an ETF's shares do not deviate substantially from the ETF's NAV), www.sec.gov/divisions/marketreg/mr-noaction/etifclassrelief102406-msr.pdf. The SEC has explained that its concerns over misalignment of secondary market prices and ETFs extend not only to end-of-day prices but to intraday trading as well. SEC, Request for Comment on Exchange-Traded Products, Rel. No. 34-75165 (June 12, 2015), 80 Fed. Reg. 34729 (June 17, 2015).

[29] Notice of Exemption Application of PowerShares Capital Management LLC, Rel. No. IC-28140, 73 Fed. Reg. 7328 (Feb. 7, 2008).

[30] The three initial stock ETFs were PowerShares Active AlphaQ Portfolio, PowerShares Active Alpha Multi-Cap Portfolio, and PowerShares Mega-Cap Portfolio; the bond ETF was PowerShares Active Low Duration Portfolio (investing in US government and corporate bonds).

260 *Research handbook on the regulation of mutual funds*

changes in the market prices of the securities held in the ETF's portfolio.[31] With such near real-time transparency around each ETF's portfolio, the SEC was satisfied that conditions would likely be sufficient to support efficient arbitrage, thereby keeping negotiated prices in close alignment with each ETF's net asset value.[32]

5.3 SEC Rulemaking

After more than two decades of ETF trading, the SEC has yet to adopt a rule on ETFs.[33] The SEC has taken two halting steps forward over the last 15 years. The first was issuance of a "concept release" in 2001, where the SEC raised questions focusing on actively managed ETFs.[34] A central question raised by the SEC was whether efficient arbitrage could occur without full daily disclosure of the identity and weightings of every holding in an ETF's portfolio. Further, the SEC voiced concerns about *intraday* changes to the ETF's portfolio, noting that such changes would likely be more frequent and less foreseeable compared to an index-tracking ETF. The SEC, however, recognized that transparent portfolios would likely lead to front-running and free-riding abuses.

In short, the SEC wrestled with a dilemma: Should the agency accept lack of portfolio transparency to further the competing goal of greater investment performance by actively managed ETFs? For its part, the fund industry's trade group, the Investment Company Institute, in its comment letter to the SEC strenuously opposed, on grounds of fairness, selective disclosure of portfolio information solely to large firms who would be purchasing and redeeming creation units in the course of arbitrage trading.[35] An American Bar Association committee suggested a compromise, however: shield

---

[31] The SEC has approved the applications of three exchanges—NYSE Arca, the American Stock Exchange, and Nasdaq—to list and trade shares of actively managed ETFs on the condition (among others) that the intraday value of such ETFs' shares be disseminated at least every 15 seconds. See SEC Rel. Nos. 34-57619 (Apr. 4. 2008). 73 Fed. Reg. 19544 (Apr. 10, 2008); 34-57514 (Mar. 17, 2008), 73 Fed. Reg. 15230 (Mar. 21, 2008), and 34- 57800 (May 8, 2008). 73 Fed. Reg. 27874 (May 14, 2008).

[32] The SEC granted similar exemptive relief in early 2008 to a number of other ETF sponsors. See WisdomTree Trust, et al., Rel. Nos. IC-28147 (Feb. 6, 2008), 73 Fed. Reg. 7776 (Feb. 11, 2008)] (notice) ("WisdomTree Actively Managed ETF Notice") and IC-28174 (Feb. 27, 2008) (order) ("WisdomTree Actively Managed ETF"); Barclays Global Fund Advisors, et al., Rel. Nos. IC-28146 (Feb. 6, 2008), 73 FR 7771 (Feb. 11, 2008) (notice) and IC-28173 (Feb. 27, 2008) (order) ("Barclays Actively Managed ETF"); Bear Sterns Asset Management, Inc., et al., Release Nos. IC-28143 (Feb. 5, 2008), 73 FR 7768 (Feb. 11, 2008)] (notice) and IC-28172 (Feb. 27, 2008) (order) ("Bear Sterns Actively Managed ETF").

[33] In contrast, the SEC has adopted specific rules to govern the structure and operation of two other variants of investment company not explicitly recognized under the ICA—money market funds and interval funds.

[34] SEC Concept Release, Actively Managed Exchange-Traded Funds, Rel. No. IC-25258 (Nov. 8, 2001), 66 Fed. Reg. 57614 (Nov. 15, 2001) ("2001 Concept Release").

[35] Letter from Amy Lancelotta, Senior Counsel, ICI to Jonathan G. Katz, Secretary, SEC (Jan. 14, 2002), www.sec.gov/rules/concept/s72001/s72001-6.pdf. The ICI asserted that "[s]electively disclosing information to one group of investors—while keeping other investors in the dark would be fundamentally at odds with the core principles of the federal securities laws."

actively managed ETFs from disclosing their portfolio holdings but require them to disclose an ETF's net asset value throughout the trading day, thereby reflecting fluctuations in the aggregate trading prices of those holdings.[36]

The SEC took its second, inconclusive step toward rulemaking in 2008, shortly after approving exemptive applications for PowerShares and several other ETFs to be actively managed based on quantitative, computer-based investment models rather than fundamental investment strategies. The SEC proposed a new rule, Rule 6c-11, which would have imposed a number of conditions for exemptive relief, codifying in large part the conditions included in individual exemptive orders. Chief among these was a transparency condition. An ETF must disclose, prior to the start of trading each day, the identity and weightings of every security and other assets in its investment portfolio. An index-tracking ETF, however, could instead simply designate the index and disclose the identities and weightings of the securities and other assets in the index. The SEC pointed out that the exchange on which ETF shares would trade must undertake to disclose, at frequent intervals during the trading day (for example, every 15 seconds), the intraday net asset value of an ETF's shares, reflecting the intraday fluctuations of the securities and other assets in the ETF's portfolio.

In the SEC's view, full portfolio disclosure coupled with frequent intraday reporting of an ETF's NAV is essential for efficient arbitrage. Though any ETF not meeting these transparency conditions could not qualify for exemptive relief under proposed Rule 6c-11, the SEC explained that the ETF sponsor could separately apply for exemptive relief. In the seven years that have followed, the SEC has not acted upon Rule 6c-11, and it has not granted exemptive relief to any actively managed ETF that has not undertaken to provide full portfolio transparency.

5.4 SEC's Recent Denials of Exemptive Relief for Nontransparent, Actively Managed ETFs

In responding to exemption applications from Precidian ETFs Trust and Spruce ETF Trust in 2014,[37] the SEC signaled its unwillingness to allow the market to test the viability of actively managed ETFs not meeting the dual transparency requirements of daily portfolio disclosure and intraday reporting of the market value of their investment portfolios. Both applicants urged the SEC to require only the latter, asserting that broker-dealers, even in the absence of daily portfolio transparency, could infer enough information over a relatively short period of time to support efficient arbitrage trading, taking into account quarterly portfolio holdings disclosure. To avoid selective disclosure of portfolio holdings, the applicants proposed to place in-kind redemption

---

[36] Letter from Stanley Keller, Chair, Com. on Federal Regulation of Securities; Diane E. Ambler, Chair, and Jay G. Baris, Vice-Chair, Subcom. on Investment Companies and Investment Advisers, Section of Business Law of the American Bar Association to Jonathan G. Katz, Secretary, SEC (Feb. 1, 2002), www.sec.gov/rules/concept/s72001/keller1.htm.

[37] Exemption Application of Precidian ETFs Trust, Rel. No. IC-31300 (Oct. 21, 2014), 79 Fed. Reg. 63971 (Oct. 27, 2014); Exemption Application of Spruce ETF Trust, Rel. No. IC-31301 (Oct. 21, 2014), 79 Fed. Reg. 63964 (Oct. 27, 2014).

payments in blind trusts, whose third party trustees would then sell the deposited securities over time and remit the cash proceeds to the redeeming broker-dealer firms.

The question remained, however, whether arbitrage under these conditions would work well enough to narrow disparities between market and NAV prices for an ETF's shares. The SEC was not persuaded, pointing out that the ETF's portfolio value which would be reported intraday on a per share basis would only be, at best, an approximation of the ETF's net asset value per share and, even if reported every 15 seconds, would be stale in light of intraday portfolio turnover.[38] The SEC expressed doubt that broker-dealers could infer sufficient information to enable them to engage in the hedging activities in underlying securities necessary to engage in efficient arbitrage.

As a backstop, if price disparities were to become too wide, Precidian and Spruce undertook to extend redemption rights to retail investors. In particular, if an ETF's shares were to trade at a discount of 5 percent or more for ten consecutive days, Spruce ETF Trust proposed to allow retail investors the ability to redeem their shares at net asset value over the next 15 trading days. These redemptions, however, would come at a cost to the investor: a 2 percent redemption fee. The SEC took the view that this redemption fee would effectively preclude investors from exercising their redemption rights. The SEC pointed out that the average bid/ask spread for ETFs with domestic stock portfolios, for example, is only .04 percent. Accordingly, in many if not most instances, the SEC concluded that selling ETF shares in the secondary market would be far preferable to redeeming them subject to a 2 percent redemption fee.

The SEC's unwillingness to grant exemptive relief suggests concerns that go beyond whether efficient arbitrage can take place. The SEC stated that Section 22(d) of the ICA, and its forward pricing rule, Rule 22c-1, rest on a "foundational principle" that "shareholders be treated equitably."[39] Large investors—with their in-kind purchases and redemptions—would have been able to trade at an NAV price but retail investors would not have been able to trade at secondary market prices sufficiently close to NAV. For the SEC, this disparity means inequitable treatment.

The SEC's insistence on full transparency for actively managed ETFs stands in contrast to how closed-end funds operate. Closed-end funds offer neither NAV pricing nor current portfolio holdings transparency—and their shares often trade at not insubstantial discounts.[40] The SEC's position on actively managed ETFs dismisses (or

---

[38] Among other things, the portfolio value (called an "Indicative Intraday Value"), according to the SEC, would not include extraordinary expenses or liabilities booked during the trading day. Further, the SEC noted that some of the securities in an ETF's portfolio would lack a liquid secondary market and hence would need to be given a "fair value." Under ordinary circumstances, the making of fair value determinations is an exercise that cannot be readily performed until the close of a trading day.

[39] Spruce Trust ETF Application, *supra*, note 37.

[40] It is common for closed-end funds to trade at a persistent discount to their NAV, typically at prices 5 percent to 10 percent lower than NAV. The range of NAV discount can vary depending upon the securities in which a closed-end fund invests. At year end 2014, shares of closed-end funds investing primarily in taxable bonds traded at an average discount of 7.2 percent, those in U.S. stocks at 7 percent, and those in international stocks at 8.5 percent. Investment Company Institute, Research Perspectives, The Closed-End Fund Market 2014 at 3, www.ici.org/pdf/per21-02.pdf.

at least subordinates) the interests of investors who would place higher importance on warding off predatory front-running and free riding than on current portfolio transparency. Consistent with goals of "fairness," a strong case can be made that the SEC should allow investors to act on their own preferences, choosing not only among conventional mutual funds, closed-end funds, and ETFs, but among different types of ETFs as well. This would have the additional advantage of allowing the market to test the efficacy of arbitrage for actively managed ETFs shielding their current holdings and would allow for experimentation with various techniques to promote arbitrage, perhaps by making holding disclosures on a weekly rather than daily basis or by disclosing an ETF's portfolio characteristics (such as its beta) along with NAV updates every 15 seconds or fewer during the trading day. For any actively managed ETF, if deviation between market price and NAV were to become too wide, it could be expected that the ETF would fail to attract or retain assets and the market itself would thus self-correct.

5.5 ETFs and Systemic Risk

In response to the financial crisis of 2008, in 2010 Congress enacted legislation, the Dodd–Frank Act,[41] creating a vast array of new regulatory powers for the federal banking agencies and the SEC. A new, interagency federal body—the Financial Stability Oversight Council, chaired by the Secretary of Treasury—was created and assigned the responsibility of identifying large nonbank financial firms deemed to pose a systemic risk to the U.S. financial system. Upon designation by the FSOC as a "systemically important financial institution" (SIFI), such a firm is subjected to regulation by the Federal Reserve Board, which can impose capital requirements, liquidity levels, limits on leverage, short-term funding and concentration standards, and other prudential rules otherwise reserved for commercial banks and their parents.

Gazing across the capital markets in 2013, the FSOC's research staff issued a white paper examining whether mutual funds pose systemic risk.[42] The concern was that widespread redemptions in the largest mutual funds could trigger sudden and massive liquidations of portfolio holdings that would produce dramatic drops in the market values of many publicly traded securities. This could, in turn, lead to a downward spiral of follow-on fund redemptions driving down the securities markets even further. The response from the mutual fund industry was immediate and adamant, and the FSOC soon retreated from this foray. Turning from mutual funds to particular activities, the FSOC's next step was to solicit public comment about asset management products and services in an effort to determine whether any particular facet of asset management, notably redemption rights, poses systemic risk.[43]

---

[41] Dodd–Frank Wall Street Reform and Consumer Protection Act, Pub. L. 111-203, 124 Stat. 1376 (2010).

[42] U.S. Dept. of Treasury, Office of Financial Research, Asset Management and Financial Stability (Sept. 2013), http://financialresearch.gov/reports/files/ofr_asset_management_and_financial_stability.pdf.

[43] Financial Stability Oversight Council, Notice Seeking Comment on Asset Management Products and Activities (Dec. 24, 2014), www.treasury.gov/initiatives/fsoc/rulemaking/Documents/Notice%20Seeking%20Comment%20on%20Asset%20Management%20Products%20and%20Activities.pdf.

The comments submitted to the FSOC pointed out, among other things, the stark differences between the rights of redemption held by mutual fund shareholders and the withdrawal rights of bank depositors. The paradigmatic systemic risk, of course, is a "run on the bank," where depositors—that is, claimants with fixed debt obligations—call their debt. If too many depositors call their debt at the same time, a bank falls victim to the asset/liability maturity mismatch which is inherent in fractional banking, wherein banks carry relatively illiquid long-term loans and other assets while financed by short-term or callable debt. Mutual funds, however, have a distinctly different capital structure, wholly inapposite to the fractional banking model. Fund shareholders are equity claimants, not debt claimants. Upon purchasing shares in a mutual fund, they gain no right to a return of the amount of their investment. Their right of redemption conveys only a right to receive the value of the pro rata interest in a fund's NAV that their mutual fund shares represent. In short, mutual funds are designed for self-liquidation if many shareholders decide to redeem at once.[44] Whether fund shareholders upon redeeming get more or less than their original capital contribution is entirely dependent on the net asset value of the fund's investment portfolio upon the date that a redemption right is exercised.

If mutual funds, as a general proposition, pose little systemic risk (because they do not face a "run on the bank" risk), where does this leave ETFs, which limit redemption rights to a select group of investors, their APs? One of the key attributes of ETFs is the insulation of their portfolios from the trading activities of shareholders in the secondary markets, so it would appear to follow that if it is unlikely that conventional mutual funds would pose significant systemic risk to the nation's financial system, ETFs would be even less likely to do so. One concern, however, is that ETFs, whose shares are liquid, increasingly are investing in securities that have little liquidity. It is true that ETFs, to meet redemptions of their APs, pay in kind rather than in cash—this in many cases may simply transfer, rather than eliminate, a type of systemic risk. The redeeming AP might itself have to sell the securities received in its redemption of ETF shares, and may have to sell at fire sale prices if the securities have little liquidity.

Further, while arbitrage ordinarily leads to quite narrow deviations between an ETF share's NAV and its market price, ETFs are susceptible to market volatility that can give rise to sharp disparity between NAV and market price. A notable example of pricing dislocation occurred on August 24, 2015, when market volatility led to trading pauses on US exchanges for some individual stocks and ETFs, resulting in steep discounts from net asset value for certain ETFs, including the SPDR S&P 500 ETF. In a follow-up study, the SEC staff found that within 15 minutes of the stock market's opening at 9:30 am on August 24, stocks of more than 20 percent of companies in the S&P 500 index, and of 40 percent of those in the NASDAQ-100 index, reached daily lows more than 10 percent below their previous day's closing price. As for the SPDR

---

[44] For an extensive discussion of the orderly process entailed in the liquidation of a mutual fund, *see* Letter from Paul Schott Stevens, President & CEO, ICI to Patrick Pinschmidt, Deputy Assistant Secretary for the Financial Stability Oversight Council (March 25, 2015, www.regulations.gov/#!documentDetail;D=FSOC-2014-0001-0056.

S&P 500 ETF, at 9:30 its shares opened 5.2 percent below their previous day's close and by 9:35 had further declined to a daily low of 7.8 percent.[45]

The FSOC and SEC have yet to resolve issues over potential systemic risk posed by mutual funds and ETFs. The FSOC has suggested that in lieu of its designation of funds or ETFs as SIFIs, the SEC could adopt rules to address particular concerns relating to liquidity, redemptions, and leverage.[46] The SEC, taking its cue, has issued proposed rules on these very areas.[47] While new rules might well have salutary effects, we would do well to recognize the distinction between systemic risk and other issues relating to mutual funds and ETFs, particularly those holding stocks. As the bursting of the internet bubble at the turn of the twenty-first century illustrated, drastic drops in stocks' market values do not themselves forebode market failure or risk to the financial system. To the extent that there are concerns over ETFs investing in stocks, however liquid or illiquid those holdings might be, it is important to bear in mind that they hold equity rather than debt. Investors in these underlying securities have only a residual claim on earnings to the extent that there are any, and no fixed claims for payment of principal or interest. This stands in stark contrast to the debt claims that triggered the systemic crisis of 2008.

6 CONCLUSION

The emergence of ETFs as a new form of securities pool was certainly not anticipated when the Investment Company Act was enacted over 75 years ago. In many respects, ETFs are comparable to conventional mutual funds in offering to public investors collective investment management and a range of investment approaches, notably passive management. What sets ETFs apart is their trading on exchanges and other market venues, thereby allowing for negotiated pricing and intraday liquidity—features that have gained wide acceptance. However, ETFs pose unique regulatory challenges because they depend upon different treatment for two types of investors, with ETFS entering into direct sales and redemptions at net asset value prices with a small number of institutions (the APs), while leaving retail investors to trade only in the secondary markets. The SEC's efforts to balance policy goals of fairness to investors and capital markets innovation has, to date, been largely successful. Challenges remain, however,

---

[45] *See* SEC, Office of Analytics and Research, Research Note on Equity Market Volatility on August 24, 2015, www.sec.gov/marketstructure/research/equity_market_volatility.pdf ("OAR Research Note"). The staff noted that data suggests that the first 15 minutes of trading after a market's opening "typically are the least liquid portion of the trading day, with wider spreads, less quoted depth, and higher volatility. These patterns were observed on August 24, but with much larger trading volume than normal."

[46] FSOC, Update on Review of Asset Management Products and Activities (April 18, 2016), www.treasury.gov/initiatives/fsoc/news/Documents/FSOC%20Update%20on%20Review%20of%20Asset%20Management%20Products%20and%20Activities.pdf.

[47] SEC, Open-End Fund Liquidity Risk Management Programs and Swing Pricing, Rel. No IC-31835 (Sept. 22, 2015), www.sec.gov/rules/proposed/2015/33-9922.pdf; SEC, Use of Derivatives by Registered Investment Companies and Business Development Companies, Rel. No. IC-31933 (Dec. 11, 2015), www.sec.gov/rules/proposed/2015/ic-31933.pdf.

in two particular areas—establishing broadly applicable ground rules for actively managed ETFs and addressing the potential for systemic risk or market dislocations posed by ETFs.

BIBLIOGRAPHY

David J. Abner, VISUAL GUIDE TO ETFS (Bloomberg Press, 2013).
Rochelle Antoniewicz & Jane Heinrichs, Understanding Exchange-Traded Funds: How ETFs Work (Sept. 2014), http://papers.ssrn.com/sol3/Papers.cfm?abstract_id=2523540
Josh Cherry, The Limits of Arbitrage: Evidence from Exchange Traded Funds (2004), http://papers.ssrn.com/sol3/Papers.cfm?abstract_id=628061
Elroy Dimson & Carolina Minio-Kozerski, Closed-End Funds: A Survey (Sept. 1998), http://papers.ssrn.com/sol3/papers.cfm?abstract_id=135688 [surveying literature on NAV discounts].
Robert Engle & Debojyoti Sarkar, Pricing Exchange Traded Funds (May 2002), NYU Working Paper No. S-DRP-02-11, http://papers.ssrn.com/sol3/papers.cfm?abstract_id=1296379
Exemption Application of Precidian ETFs Trust, Rel. No. IC-31300 (Oct. 21, 2014), 79 Red. Reg. 63971 (Oct. 27, 2014).
Exemption Application of SPDR Trust, Series 1, Rel. No. IC-18959 (Sept. 17, 1992), 57 Fed. Reg. 43996 (Sept. 23, 1992).
Exemption Application of Spruce ETF Trust, Rel. No. IC-31301 (Oct. 21, 2014), 79 Fed. Reg. 63964 (Oct. 27, 2014).
Financial Stability Oversight Council, Notice Seeking Comment on Asset Management Products and Activities (Dec. 24, 2014), www.treasury.gov/initiatives/fsoc/rulemaking/Documents/Notice%20Seeking%20Comment%20on%20Asset%20Management%20Products%20and%20Activities.pdf
First Trust Exchange-Traded Fund, Notice of Application, Rel. IC-27051, 70 Fed. Reg. 52450 (Sept. 2, 2005).
Gary L. Gastineau, THE EXCHANGE-TRADED FUNDS MANUAL (John Wiley & Sons, Inc. 2d ed., 2010).
Investment Company Institute, Letter to Secretariat of the Financial Stability Board (May 16, 2011), www.ici.org/pdf/25189.pdf
Investment Company Institute, Understanding How Exchange-Traded Funds Work (Sept. 2014), www.ici.org/pdf/per20-05.pdf
Investment Company Institute, Exchange-Traded Funds Data (May, 2015), www.ici.org/research/stats/etf/ci.etfs_05_15.print
Investment Company Institute, The Role and Activities of Exchange-Traded Funds (March 2015), www.ici.org/pdf/ppr_15_aps_etfs.pdf
Doron Israeli, Charles M.C. Lee, & Suhas A. Sridharan, Is There a Dark Side to Exchange Traded Funds? An Information Perspective (July 26, 2015) http://papers.ssrn.com/sol3/papers.cfm?abstract_id=2625975
Letter from Gary L. Gastineau, Managing Director, Nuveen Investments to Jonathan G. Katz, Secretary, SEC (Jan. 14, 2002), www.sec.gov/rules/concept/s72001/gastineau1.htm
Letter from Stanley Keller, Chair, Com. on Federal Regulation of Securities; Diane E. Ambler, Chair, and Jay G. Baris, Vice-Chair, Subcom. on Investment Companies and Investment Advisers, Section of Business Law of the American Bar Association to Jonathan G. Katz, Secretary, SEC (Feb. 1, 2002), www.sec.gov/rules/concept/s72001/keller1.htm
Notice of Exemption Application of PowerShares Capital Management LLC, Rel. No. IC-28140, 73 Fed. Reg. 7328 (Feb. 7, 2008).
Office of Financial Research, Asset Management and Financial Stability (Sept. 2013), http://financialresearch.gov/reports/files/ofr_asset_management_and_financial_stability.pdf
Gary E. Porter, Rodney L. Roenfeldt, and Neil Sicherman, The Value of Open Market Repurchases of Closed-End Fund Shares, 72 J. of Business 257 (1999).
SEC, Concept Release, Actively Managed Exchange-Traded Funds, Rel. No. IC-25258 Nov. 8, 2001), 66 Fed. Reg. 57614 (Nov. 15, 2001).
SEC, Proposed Rule, Exchange-Trade Funds, Rel. No. IC-28193 (March 11, 2008), 73 Fed. Reg. 14618 (March 18, 2008).
SEC, Request for Comments on Exchange-Traded Products, Rel. No. 34-75165 (June 12, 2015), 80 Fed. Reg. 34729 (June 17, 2015).

12. Free funds: retirement savings as public infrastructure
William A. Birdthistle*

1 INTRODUCTION

The central component of retirement planning in the United States is personal saving. Pensions and social security do still exist, of course, though in something of an atrophied or stagnant state.[1] Each year, ever more trillions of dollars flow into individual retirement accounts (IRAs), 401(k) plans, and similar private investment vehicles.[2] In this chapter, I explore the extent to which governmental or nonprofit entities can and should assist with the project of personal saving by providing a public or open infrastructure for private investment. In particular, I propose the creation of free funds—that is, mutual funds that charge shareholders no fees.[3]

The viability and advisability of free funds turn on three large questions: first, whether mutual funds with no fee are financially viable; second, whether they ought to exist; third, who or what entities should serve as their sponsor.

To the first question, we already have something of an answer. Yes, a fund with an expense ratio of nil can exist—Fidelity recently began offering a suite of 13 "Flex Funds," which boast expense ratios of zero.[4] These "no-fee" funds are not truly free, however, as they are available only to investors in fee-based accounts with the firm's

---

* Professor of Law, Chicago-Kent College of Law. For their helpful questions and comments, I thank the participants of the Public Law & Legal Theory Workshop at the University of Chicago Law School, the 2017 Law and Entrepreneurship Association Retreat at Berkeley Law School, and the 9th Annual Berle Symposium: Investor Time Horizons at Georgia State University College of Law.

[1] *See, e.g.*, THE 2018 ANNUAL REPORT OF THE TRUSTEES OF THE FEDERAL OLD-AGE AND SURVIVORS INSURANCE AND FEDERAL DISABILITY INSURANCE TRUST FUNDS, June 5, 2018, at 2 (reporting that "Social Security's total cost is projected to exceed its total income in 2018 for the first time since 1982"); PENSION BENEFIT GUARANTY CORPORATION, 2017 ANNUAL PERFORMANCE REPORT, at 27 (reporting a combined deficit of almost $80 billion for the Pension Benefit Guaranty Corporation).

[2] *See* INVESTMENT COMPANY INSTITUTE, 2018 INVESTMENT COMPANY FACT BOOK (hereinafter "ICI FACT BOOK") at p. 85, figure 8.17 (reporting that IRA assets now surpass $9 trillion, up from $2.6 trillion in 2000); *see ibid* at p. 175, figure 8.10 (reporting growth in defined contribution plan assets, including 401(k) plans expanding from $1.7 trillion in 2000 to $5.3 trillion in 2017).

[3] With a coauthor, I explored the idea of a free fund in a recent op-ed. *See* William A. Birdthistle & Daniel J. Hemel, *Next Stop for Mutual-Fund Fees: Zero*, WALL STREET JOURNAL, June 10, 2018.

[4] Vicky Ge Huang, *Fidelity Unveils 13 No-Fee Funds, But There's a Catch*, CITYWIRE, April 12, 2018 (noting that Fidelity Go clients "will pay an annual advisory fee of 0.35%").

roboadviser, Fidelity Go. So although the fund itself may not charge a fee, Fidelity is collecting remuneration somewhere along the chain of managing their investors' assets. The greater challenge would be offering a fund that charges no fee to investors anywhere in that chain. I begin by exploring the logistical and financial challenges of offering such a fund. In particular, I consider the potential sources of revenue—such as from securities lending—available to large pools of investment that can offset their costs of operation.

The second question—whether free funds ought to exist—turns on the significance of mutual fund fees to America's investing public. That significance is high, if indeed not preeminent. Although some investors may care about performance or even a few of the more arcane fund factors discussed at great length in obligatory disclosure documents, no attribute of a mutual fund is more economically salient than its fee. The issue of fees is particularly critical today, as we witness the convergence of two relatively new phenomena in the world of individual investing: first, the consensus of scholarship demonstrating that none but the smallest minority of managers can consistently outperform the market;[5] second, our current tectonic shift into passively managed funds, which suggests that many investors are at last growing content to settle for the performance of a market index.[6] In this world of increased indexing, which eliminates active investment decisions by portfolio managers, the key remaining variable is the fee. A fund offering the reliable performance of an index, with none of the cost, would clearly be a boon to many millions of US investors. Americans pay approximately $100 billion per year in fees to the investment advisory industry to manage assets held in mutual funds, and any reduction in those fees would redound to the benefit of investors, both immediately and via future compounded returns.[7]

If we assume that such a reduction would be in the public interest, though not necessarily the investment industry's, we must then ask the third question: who should attempt to provide such an investment option? The investment industry already offers many indexed mutual funds and exchange-traded funds that charge fees of merely single-digit basis points. And, as the Fidelity example suggests, the industry is alive to at least the appearance of a no-fee fund. But a for-profit enterprise choosing to eliminate fees—and the substantial streams of revenue that come with them—seems both unlikely and worthy of suspicion. Accordingly, here I explore the possibility of a governmental or eleemosynary entity serving as the sponsor of such a fund. I conclude that such a project is far more practicable than it may first appear, and indeed strongly

---

[5] *See, e.g.*, Eugene F. Fama & Kenneth R. French, *Luck Versus Skill in the Cross Section of Mutual Fund Returns*, 65 J. FIN. 1915–47 (2010).

[6] *See, e.g.*, Dorothy Shapiro Lund, *The Case Against Passive Shareholder Voting*, J. CORP. L. (forthcoming 2018) ("American investors have begun to embrace the reality that academics have been championing for decades—that a broad-based, passive indexing strategy is superior to picking individual stocks or investing in actively managed funds.").

[7] *See* Landon Thomas Jr., *Why Are Mutual Fund Fees So High? This Billionaire Knows*, N.Y. TIMES, Dec. 30, 2017 ("While more than $1 trillion has left higher-fee funds in favor of passive competitors, that still leaves some $10 trillion. That generates about $100 billion in fees for fund companies").

advisable in our current system of saving, which delegates so much responsibility to America's population of investing amateurs untrained in the dangers of navigating fund fees.

2 CONSTRUCTING A FREE FUND

The project of creating a free fund comprises two closely related but distinct steps: step one, construct a very inexpensive fund; step two, find ways to eliminate any remaining net costs to operating such a fund. The first step is well trodden in today's investing environment; the second has never been done before. Fortunately, several key tools for reducing a fund's net operating expenses do already exist and could be put to work by a willing sponsor. The most significant challenge of offering a truly free fund has more to do with a sponsor's willingness to forego revenue than with any technical impediment.

2.1 Begin with Very Inexpensive Funds

Constructing a very inexpensive investment fund is not difficult. In just the United States alone, many such funds already exist and thrive. Approximately 450 of the nearly 8,000 mutual funds registered in the United States are index funds,[8] and they hold roughly $3.5 trillion in assets under management.[9] Another 1,832 funds—holding a further $3.4 trillion in AUM—are exchange-traded funds ("ETFs").[10] Like their actively managed alternatives, both index mutual funds and ETFs offer investors a professionally managed, diverse, and easily redeemable investment option. Today, the expense ratios of all mutual funds are at historical lows. Since the year 2000, the weighted average expense ratio for equity mutual funds has fallen from 0.99 percent (or 99 basis points) to 0.59 percent. In that same window, the cost of bond funds has fallen from 0.76 percent to 0.48 percent.[11]

Still, for index funds, the average costs are much lower. Since the turn of the millennium, the cost of index equity mutual funds has fallen from 0.27 percent to 0.09 percent. Index bond funds have dropped from 0.21 percent to 0.07 percent.[12] These average fees may be distorted somewhat by the recent success of a few extremely low cost funds offered by advisers such as Vanguard and Fidelity, which

---

[8] See ICI FACT BOOK at 251, table 44 (reporting a total of 453 index funds and 7,121 actively managed funds in 2017).
[9] See ibid at 42, figure 2.7 (reporting that index mutual funds held 18 percent of the total market of $19.2 trillion in fund assets in 2017).
[10] See ibid at 86 (noting that the US ETF market "account[s] for 72 percent of the $4.7 trillion in ETF total net assets worldwide").
[11] See ibid at 119, figure 6.1, "Expense Ratios Incurred by Mutual Fund Investors Have Declined Substantially since 2000."
[12] See ibid at 126, figure 6.7, "Expense Ratios of Actively Managed and Index Mutual Funds Have Fallen."

have enjoyed a massive inflow of investment in recent years.[13] Nevertheless, these fees do illustrate the key concept: the subset of indexed investment funds can and do charge considerably less than the average mutual fund, particularly actively managed alternatives. A closer look at one such fund helps to explain why.

Let us focus upon a prominent and extremely cheap fund currently offered in the United States: the Vanguard S&P 500 index fund. This fund charges just 4 basis points for investors in its Admiral class of shares, a price that Vanguard boasts "is 96% lower than the average expense ratio of funds with similar holdings."[14] By exploring the elements that makes this fund so inexpensive, we can try to establish the key elements that could be useful for creating a free fund. In this fund—and as is true of many Vanguard funds—two factors stand out immediately: first, the fund is a passive, index fund; second, it is massive.

By simply tracking an index rather than attempting to outperform the market, a passive fund can eliminate much of the cost associated with managing a mutual fund. Actively managed funds typically aspire to outperform the market. To do so, they typically hire human beings—portfolio managers—whose analytical judgment and labor are considered valuable and whose contribution must therefore be remunerated. Index funds, by contrast and as their name suggests, aspire only to replicate the performance of an index. To do so, an index fund needs only employ the services of a relatively simple computer algorithm to help keep the fund's holdings in line with whichever index the fund tracks.

With the Vanguard S&P 500 index fund, one can observe the relatively inexpensive operating costs by consulting the fund's financial statements in its publicly filed disclosure documents. The first interesting figure, reported in the fund's Statement of Additional Information, sets forth what the fund pays in brokerage commissions. Just like human investors, whenever a mutual fund buys or sells securities for its portfolio, it does so by employing the services of a financial broker. And just as individuals do, the fund must pay brokers a fee for their efforts in acquiring or liquidating investments. The typical actively managed fund trades relatively frequently in an effort to time developments in the investment markets: to buy low and to sell high. Index funds, by contrast, simply aim to maintain a portfolio identical to the composition of the index and therefore need not trade frequently. Most indices do not change their composition often and, when they do, change only a small number of their individual components. Much of the trading executed by index funds relates to rebalancing the fund to keep the relative weight of its components in line with the index. The financial records of the Vanguard S&P index fund reflect this phenomenon, reporting that in 2017, the fund paid the remarkably low figure of $1,812,000 in brokerage commissions.[15]

---

[13] *See, e.g.*, Karen Wallace, *The Top 25 Funds Investors Bought in 2017*, MORNINGSTAR, January 30, 2018 ("Six out of 10 funds with the highest estimated net inflows were index funds, and all six of them were Vanguard funds").

[14] Product Summary, Vanguard 500 Index Fund Admiral Shares, available at https://investor.vanguard.com/mutual-funds/profile/VFIAX.

[15] *See* Statement of Additional Information, Vanguard 500 Index Fund, April 25, 2018, at p. B-48, available at https://personal.vanguard.com/pub/Pdf/sai040.pdf?2210142850.

Free funds: retirement savings as public infrastructure 271

That number brings us to the second notable characteristic of the Vanguard fund: its size. As of December 31, 2017, the fund held total net assets of almost $400 billion, with more than $235 billion of those assets contributed by owners of the fund's so-called Admiral share class.[16] Size is not a useful attribute in its own right but is more helpful as an instrument for creating economies of scale. So when one revisits the aforementioned brokerage commissions and considers them as a percentage of the overall fund, the cost of buying and selling components of the fund's portfolio in 2017 was the infinitesimal amount of approximately 0.0008 percent.

What other expenses does a fund such as this incur? Certain administrative costs inhere in the operation of any fund but, again, their relative impact can be reduced to small percentages through economies of scale. So this Vanguard fund paid the following amounts in 2016, all of which were very small percentages of the hundreds of billions of dollars of AUM: $1.7 million in fees paid to the fund's custodian; $43,000 in auditing fees; and $582,000 for shareholders' reports.[17]

Eliminating these fees is practically impossible given the unshakable obligation of legal compliance, of course, but their overall impact is usually small in an index fund and, with massive scale, can be rendered negligible. Thus, incurring minimal operating expenses and spreading them across a massive asset base are two key components that allow Vanguard to offer this fund for as few as four basis points.

2.2 Making Inexpensive Funds Even Cheaper

Our project is not to create just another cheap fund, but to follow the asymptote all the way down to zero, or as close thereto as possible. So although we might begin by emulating Vanguard's structure, we must do something more to accomplish that goal. At least two key levers are available for reducing the net cost of running a fund. If used in combination, they might permit the creation of an entirely free fund.

2.2.1 Lowering expenses

First, the index tracked by an index fund does not have to be a well-known brand. A fund does not have to track the Standard & Poor's 500 index, for instance, in order to expose its investors to a prudently diverse array of notable US equity issuers. Indeed, much of the variability of an S&P 500 index comes from the market movement of a minority of its components. At times, as much as a third of the index's total return has been generated by the movement of just five of those 500 companies: Apple, Amazon, Facebook, Microsoft, and Google's parent, Alphabet. By adding just ten more stocks, one could replicate the returns of almost 50 percent of the overall index.[18] Accordingly, any competent investment adviser could select a custom basket of several dozen stocks that would come close to replicating far more well-known indices.

---

[16] *See* Annual Report, Vanguard 500 Index Fund, December 31, 2017, at pp. 19–20, available at www.vanguard.com/funds/reports/q400.pdf.
[17] *See ibid.*
[18] *See* Victor Reklaitis, *This Top-Heavy Rally Is Built on Just 5 Big Tech Stocks*, MarketWatch, May 26, 2017.

A generic index would lower fund expenses in two ways. The first is by reducing brokerage commissions. A fund with fewer components in its portfolio need not buy or sell as many different stocks to track its stated index. Second, a fund unconnected to a brand name index would eliminate its licensing fees. Consider one large ETF as an example. The SPDR S&P 500 ETF is the largest fund in the world that tracks the S&P 500 index. For the right to incorporate the S&P 500 name in its own name, the ETF pays Standard & Poor's more than $69 million on net assets of $249 billion—or 2.8 basis points—annually.[19] Those licensing expenses could be eliminated entirely by creating and following a bespoke index instead.

Second, the first truly free fund may also be able to capitalize substantially on free publicity. Even the aforementioned Fidelity funds, which are not actually free, enjoyed widespread coverage in a number of news articles discussing their attributes. That sort of attention can be a valuable benefit in a market with almost 8,000 competitors. The less a fund pays for advertising, the less shareholders in the fund need pay to invest. Consider, for example, that marketing added almost an entire basis point to the SPDR S&P 500 fund's expense ratio in 2017. The fund paid $18.4 million, again on net assets of $249 billion, which equaled 0.7 of a basis point.[20] Smaller funds generally expend an even greater share of their revenues on advertising. The first genuinely free fund should be able to surf a wave of media coverage in lieu of paying for marketing.

Finally, the largest expense in the financial statements for almost every investment fund is the management fee paid to its investment adviser. Certainly that is true with our Vanguard fund, in which $47 million went to Vanguard in connection with the Admiral class of shares, an expense that dwarfed the fund's combined outlay of $1.8 million in brokerage commissions, $1.7 million in fees to the custodian, $582,000 for shareholder reports, and $43,000 in auditing fees.[21] I discuss the nature of possible fund sponsors below, but one can immediately note how massive the impact upon price could be should a fund's adviser be willing to manage the fund for a far lower—or perhaps even no—management fee.

2.2.2 Generating revenue

Lowering expenses is, of course, only one side of the financial ledger. Let us also consider what might be the single most important accounting variable in our quest for a free fund: a source of income (other than via investment returns, which of course cannot be guaranteed). Contrary to what some investors might assume, operating a mutual fund does not consist solely in paying expenses; by managing a mountain of money, one can also generate money. To reduce *net* operating costs, a fund should explore these possible sources of revenue.

Mutual funds have already discovered ways to generate income from sources other than fees paid by investors. In 2017, for instance, the Vanguard Total International Stock Index Fund earned more than 63 percent of its expenses by lending securities in its portfolios to other market participants. The usual source of demand for these loans

---

[19] See SPDR S&P 500 ETF, Annual Report at pp. 9–10, September 30, 2017.
[20] See ibid.
[21] See Annual Report, Vanguard 500 Index Fund, December 31, 2017, at pp. 19–20, available at www.vanguard.com/funds/reports/q400.pdf.

Free funds: retirement savings as public infrastructure 273

is short sellers, who execute their bets against a stock by first borrowing shares, then selling them, with the hope that any subsequent decline in the stock's performance will allow them to buy shares at a lower price in future. They can return those more cheaply acquired shares to their original securities lender; in this case, a mutual fund. The annual report of this Vanguard fund lists revenues of $202.5 million from securities lending, compared to total expenses of $320 million—that is, revenues from securities lending alone offset more than 63 percent of the fund's total costs.[22]

Our financial sector does not, of course, enjoy an infinite demand for short selling and securities lending, so one should not overinflate the depth of this source of revenue. At some point, demand will be entirely satisfied, and no more revenue would be available to offset funds' operating expenses, so these limitations also limit the scalability of a free fund. Still, this source of income certainly exists today, and can be used to offset some or all fund operating expenses right now.

Investment advisers can also explore other sources of revenue that attend the management of massive amounts of money. Soft dollars, for instance, are the mutual fund equivalent of frequent flier miles or credit card points: in exchange for directing portfolio transactions to particular brokers, those brokers will reward the adviser with "soft dollars," which can be redeemed for products and services that also reduce the fund's operating expenses.[23] Offering a free mutual fund might also attract customers to whom financial institutions could cross-sell other products, such as annuities and life insurance.

Note that the Vanguard fund's more than $200 million of income easily dwarfed the combination of all expenses (other than advisory and management fees), which aggregated only to about $6 million. To be sure, these net savings were easily overtopped by more than $235 million in advisory fees.[24] But it need not necessarily be so. Here again we return to the nature of our adviser. With the right adviser, one willing to accept lower or no fees, we see that we could in fact operate a fund just like the Vanguard Total Stock Market Index Fund at zero net cost to the investors.

3 WHY CREATE A FREE FUND?

Having explored theoretical ways to create a free fund, the next question is why try so hard to reach zero. Certainly very inexpensive investment options already exist, as we have seen, so why push so hard to get to a free fund? Because zero is different.

---

[22] *See* Annual Report, Vanguard Total International Stock Index Fund, pp. 20–22, available at https://personal.vanguard.com/funds/reports/q1130.pdf?2210139988.

[23] *See, e.g.*, WILLIAM A. BIRDTHISTLE, EMPIRE OF THE FUND: THE WAY WE SAVE NOW at 89–98 (2016).

[24] *See* Annual Report, Vanguard Total International Stock Index Fund, pp. 20–22, available at https://personal.vanguard.com/funds/reports/q1130.pdf?2210139988.

3.1 Why Try?

Though the average fee of an equity fund is currently 59 basis points,[25] we have already seen that in certain sectors of the industry, fees compete at a far lower level. Vanguard, for instance, offers its S&P 500 index fund for just 14 basis points (or even just 4 basis points via its Admiral Shares),[26] while Fidelity does the same for 9 basis points (or 3.5 basis points via its Premium Class).[27] The existence of such low fees prompts one to wonder what additional benefit—beyond the marginal mathematical difference—might be obtained from lowering the fee all the way to zero.

The answer is difficult to know with certainty, as no such investing option is available to provide data, but two possible answers seem likeliest: not much or lots. Not much might happen if the investing public treats a reduction from 3 or 4 basis points to zero in the same way as they treat other fee variations of that magnitude. For instance, a reduction from 76 to 72 basis points or from 48 to 44 basis points is unlikely to move a large number of fund investors. A small number of price-sensitive and mobile investors might change their investments, but the overall migration is not likely to be particularly notable.

Or, by contrast, lots might happen if investors treat crossing from a very low fee to a completely absent fee as the crossing of an important psychological barrier, an event horizon. Zero is an absolute, a total void, and thus is a categorically different number from all others. As such, a zero fee might generate very different behavior in investors, even if those responses are irrational. Perhaps the fact that investors need not worry whatsoever about a fee, however large or small or however compounded over time, might encourage many new investors to come forward more freely with their savings. The cognitive load of considering investment costs—whether the performance is worth the price, whether the adviser is taking some sort of advantage of investors, whether a cheaper or better alternative might exist elsewhere—drops off a cliff when the fee falls to nothing.

Consider again the public benefits that might attend the press coverage and public interest in such a fund, which could significantly raise its profile and the entire concept of investing for nothing. To the extent that not enough Americans are contributing to their future savings, then a free fund that triggers a wave of new investment would be an important benefit to the health of our system of savings. The US reliance upon defined contribution plans suffers from many flaws, but perhaps the largest is that so many millions of Americans have no access to 401(k) plans or similar accounts.

Of course, a third, darker possibility also exists. On occasion, when people pay nothing for a service, they do not value the service. Some investors might similarly consider a free fund to be a worthless fund, and thus one to be shunned rather than embraced. The reputation of the fund manager, once again, could be an important factor in countering such conceptions and helping the success of such a fund. Nevertheless, the possibility of such perverse or unintended reactions to a free fund

---

[25] *See* ICI FACT BOOK at 117.
[26] *See, e.g.,* https://personal.vanguard.com/us/FundsSnapshot?FundId=0040&FundIntExt=INT&ps_disable_redirect=true.
[27] *See, e.g.,* https://fundresearch.fidelity.com/mutual-funds/summary/315911206.

counsel in favor of caution. A limited launch of the idea, with perhaps one or two funds from different types of sponsors, might be most prudent.

3.2 Low Fees Are Increasingly Popular

Another reason to offer such a fund is to capitalize on the increasing popularity of passive management. After many decades of exhortations to stop paying high fees to chase market-beating performance—an almost entirely futile project—index investing has finally gained wide popularity with retirement savers and retail investors. In 2000, index funds held 7.5 percent of assets in equity mutual funds. By 2017, they had grown to hold more than 21 percent, almost a threefold increase.[28] The remarkable growth of index investing suggests that Americans have come to appreciate the salience of paying low fees to portfolio managers, who have historically failed to beat the market.

3.3 So Are Free Services

There may be no such thing as a free lunch, but there are many services that are both excellent and without financial cost to their users. Anyone who ever experienced early search engines knows that Google search is a vast improvement, and perhaps the best internet search tool available—and it costs nothing to use. A free mutual fund would join Google and a quickly growing array of costless financial services already available to users.

More than 100 million Americans are already eligible to use free tax preparation software provided by the Free File Alliance, a consortium of companies that includes Intuit and H&R Block. The fact that only three million taxpayers actually take advantage of that service may provide a warning for free mutual funds: perhaps publicity of a free service is less potent than one might imagine, or biases against "free lunches" are more potent. Note, however, that Mint.com provides free bill payment services to more than ten million users, and Credit Karma furnishes complementary credit scores. Finally, the online financial broker Robin Hood provides free daytime trade execution to its more than four million users.[29]

4 WHO SHOULD OFFER A FREE FUND?

What sort of institution might be willing to operate a mutual fund for low or no advisory fees? Most evidently, one willing to subordinate its immediate desire for profit. That does not necessarily mean only an eleemosynary institution, as a for-profit enterprise might consider a free fund a loss leader useful for attracting assets to its broader fund complex. Eventually, however, a for-profit firm will be tempted to impose

---

[28] See ICI Fact Book at p. 249, table 42 (reporting 2017 totals of $3.3 trillion in index funds versus $12.5 trillion in actively managed funds; and 2000 totals of $0.384 trillion in index versus $4.74 trillion in actively managed funds).

[29] See *supra* note 3, Birdthistle & Hemel.

or raise fees on any such fund. The more likely candidate for a permanently free fund would be a charitable foundation, a university, or a government entity.

The reason for doing so might be either selfish or altruistic. A selfish institution—perhaps a university looking to entice the most talented academics to its faculty—might offer a free fund as an additional perquisite of employment. An altruistic institution might do so as a public service. The free fund would obviously save its own shareholders money while simultaneously placing market pressure on other funds. In addition, it could attract broader attention to the need for cheaper investment alternatives in a retirement system premised so intensely on the need for individuals to save their own money—and to pay for those savings.

A governmental entity might also consider serving as the sponsor. States such as California and Oregon have already begun to offer state defined contribution plans as a way to provide retirement planning options to employees without access to 401(k) plans.[30] A state legislature might reasonably conclude that a free investment fund is a logical extension of those services.

Indeed, perhaps one way to think of these mutual funds is not as free funds but as public infrastructure. Governments already provide the public with "free" roads, schools, lighting, and policing—of course, none of those items is free, each is provided for the good of the public and financed by taxes. In the project to help the American public save for its own retirement, the investment vector—such as a mutual fund—might simply be another component of the *civitas* provided via taxes for the commonwealth. The state provides the fund; investors provide the savings and keep the returns. As we have already seen, however, in this case the public good might pay for itself.

5 CONCLUSION

The mutual fund industry, like many others before it, is a particularly attractive target for disruptive change. Free funds would not, by themselves, solve America's retirement crisis, but they could be a critical tool in our national investing toolbox. Americans typically pay tens of thousands of dollars in mutual fund fees over their lifetime. Every dollar not paid in those fees would remain with investors, and grow through compounding, to help ensure more secure financial futures for more investors.

Lest we think that the idea of a free financial instrument such as a mutual fund seems preposterous, let us reflect on the history of banks, which for hundreds of years paid investors to manage their money. Though I do not suggest that mutual funds should pay investors to hold our savings, the goal of eliminating fees is both conceivable and commendable.

---

[30] *See* Ann Carns, *For Workers Without Retirement Savings, State-Run IRAs Can Pay Off*, N.Y. TIMES, April 20, 2018.

SELECT BIBLIOGRAPHY

2018 ANNUAL REPORT OF THE TRUSTEES OF THE FEDERAL OLD-AGE AND SURVIVORS INSURANCE AND FEDERAL DISABILITY INSURANCE TRUST FUNDS, June 5, 2018.

WILLIAM A. BIRDTHISTLE, EMPIRE OF THE FUND: THE WAY WE SAVE NOW at 89–98 (2016).

William A. Birdthistle & Daniel J. Hemel, *Next Stop for Mutual-Fund Fees: Zero*, WALL STREET JOURNAL, June 10, 2018.

Ann Carns, *For Workers Without Retirement Savings, State-Run IRAs Can Pay Off*, N.Y. TIMES, April 20, 2018.

Eugene F. Fama & Kenneth R. French, *Luck Versus Skill in the Cross Section of Mutual Fund Returns*, 65 J. FIN. 1915–47 (2010), available at https://fundresearch.fidelity.com/mutual-funds/summary/315911206.

Vicky Ge Huang, *Fidelity Unveils 13 No-Fee Funds, But There's a Catch*, CITYWIRE, April 12, 2018.

INVESTMENT COMPANY INSTITUTE, 2018 INVESTMENT COMPANY FACT BOOK.

Dorothy Shapiro Lund, *The Case Against Passive Shareholder Voting*, J. CORP. L.

PENSION BENEFIT GUARANTY CORPORATION, 2017 ANNUAL PERFORMANCE REPORT.

Victor Reklaitis, *This Top-Heavy Rally Is Built on Just 5 Big Tech Stocks*, MarketWatch, May 26, 2017.

SPDR S&P 500 ETF, Annual Report at pp. 9–10, September 30, 2017.

Statement of Additional Information, Vanguard 500 Index Fund, April 25, 2018, at p. B-48, available at https://personal.vanguard.com/pub/Pdf/sai040.pdf?2210142850.

Landon Thomas Jr., *Why Are Mutual Fund Fees So High? This Billionaire Knows*, N.Y. TIMES, Dec. 30, 2017.

Annual Report, Vanguard 500 Index Fund, December 31, 2017, at pp. 19-20, available at www.vanguard.com/funds/reports/q400.pdf.

Annual Report, Vanguard Total International Stock Index Fund, pp. 20-22, available at https://personal.vanguard.com/funds/reports/q1130.pdf?2210139988.

Karen Wallace, *The Top 25 Funds Investors Bought in 2017*, MORNINGSTAR, January 30, 2018.

13. Confluence of mutual and hedge funds
*Wulf A. Kaal**

1 INTRODUCTION

A combination of market forces and regulatory reform is calling into question the traditional distinctions between mutual and hedge funds (Citi Fund Services 2010; Papagiannis 2013). Mutual funds and hedge funds occupy distinct segments of the investment market, employ different investment strategies, and serve largely different classes of investors.[1] They are subject to different legal rules. However, several combinations of factors suggest that the traditional distinction between mutual and hedge funds may be eroding, resulting in a confluence of mutual and hedge funds. Market-driven factors contributing to this confluence include the emergence and proliferation of so-called retail alternative or hybrid funds, such as synthetic hedge funds and unconstrained mutual funds (Kaal & Anderson 2016). Other important confluence factors include the increasing side by side management of mutual funds and hedge funds, and public offerings of alternative asset managers, among others, in combination with the fundamental reshaping of the regulatory landscape for the hedge fund industry through the Dodd–Frank Act,[2] as well as the Jumpstart Our Business Startups Act ("JOBS Act").[3]

---

* The author would like to thank the editors, John Morley and William Birdthistle, as well as Quinn Curtis, Bentley Anderson, and the participants at the 8th Annual Investment Fund Roundtable at Boston University School of Law. The author is grateful for outstanding assistance provided by research librarians Nick Farris and Ann Bateson.

[1] The terms "private fund" and "mutual fund," as used throughout this article, are used as follows: a private fund is a fund with an (active) trading strategy run by human portfolio management staff (that is, investment recommendations are not based on an algorithm), and in most such private funds (unlike mutual funds) there is no substantive limitation on, for example, (1) the types of securities which the fund may trade, (2) the location of the markets where those securities may be traded, or (3) the degree of concentrated ownership of a security (or securities), or the degree of exposure to an industry or market that the fund may take on. By contrast, mutual funds can be (1) standard registered open-end investment management companies, (2) closed-end funds, (3) ETFs, and/or (4) UITs. The author recognizes that while the fund industry itself may use all of these offering types as synonyms, each in fact has substantively different legal and regulatory characteristics.

[2] Dodd–Frank Wall Street Reform and Consumer Protection (Dodd–Frank Act), Pub. L. No. 111-203, §§ 401-416, 124 Stat. 1376, 1571 (2010).

[3] Jumpstart Our Business Startups Act, Pub. L. No. 112-106, § 201(a)(1), 126 Stat. 306, 313–14 (2012).

The term "confluence," as used in this chapter in the context of mutual and hedge funds,[4] connotes a process associated with two separate yet connected phenomena with related consequences. Mutual funds are becoming more like hedge funds as a matter of investment strategy, while hedge funds are becoming more like mutual funds as a matter of the regulatory framework. This chapter conceptualizes confluence as a process and identifies a trend in which alternative mutual funds and other products that are fundamentally mutual funds are increasingly becoming more like hedge funds. It also shows that changes in the regulatory framework post-Dodd–Frank pertaining to hedge funds tend to render hedge funds and hedge fund-like vehicles more like mutual funds. This is not just a result of more stringent regulations enacted via the Dodd–Frank Act in the aftermath of the financial crisis; the liberalization of the advertising restrictions post-Dodd–Frank Act also makes hedge funds more like mutual funds.

Market forces are a significant factor in the emerging confluence of mutual and hedge funds (Mutual Fund Directors Forum 2014; McKinsey & Company 2014; Warren 2012). Changes to the capital markets precipitated by the financial crisis of 2007–8 and a very low interest rate environment, in combination with the enormous growth of hedge funds, created, and over time increased, the demand for retail alternatives (SEI 2013).[5] The net assets of mutual funds employing alternative strategies increased almost 200 percent from 2009 to 2014.[6] Evidence of a growing number of side by side management structures, in which an investment adviser manages both mutual funds and hedge funds (Nohel et al. 2010), further suggests that investment advisers are adjusting their operations to satisfy retail investor demand for alternative investments.[7]

The fundamental reshaping of the regulatory landscape for the hedge fund industry removed many of the legal differences separating the two industries. The Dodd–Frank Act and JOBS Act streamlined core legal requirements for the hedge fund industry, aligning them more closely with those applicable to the mutual fund industry and helping the hedge fund industry transition from secretive to less so, supported by a more widely recognized and influential group of investment managers (White 2013). The registration and increased disclosure requirements for certain hedge fund advisers under the Dodd–Frank Act subjects hedge fund investment advisers to similar registration and reporting obligations as mutual fund advisers. The registration requirement

---

[4] The term "private fund," as used in this article, is an umbrella term for any unregistered investment vehicle, including, among others, hedge funds, private equity funds, venture capital funds, liquidity funds, real estate funds.

[5] Retail alternatives are investment vehicles that offer the attractive features of mutual funds, such as significant diversification, relative stability, and transparency, with the more aggressive strategies—and the corresponding prospect of absolute returns—of private funds.

[6] Calculation (Rate of Growth) using the Investment Company Institute data in table 42 ("Alternative Strategies Mutual Funds: Total Net Assets, Net New Cash Flow, Number of Funds, and Number of Share Classes"). Final calculation was 192 percent growth in net assets between 2009 and 2014. Investment Company Institute 2015.

[7] For the year 2012: 53 percent of investors would consider using alternative investments; 74 percent of advisers now use alternative strategies; 75 percent of advisers in the past year have increased their allocation to alternative assets. SEI 2013.

under the Dodd–Frank Act, in combination with the removal of advertising restrictions for hedge fund advisers under the JOBS Act and the equal treatment of mutual and hedge funds for FSOC's systemically important financial institution (SIFI) designation, in effect assimilated legal requirements applicable to mutual and hedge funds.

The confluence factors identified in this chapter have implications for both the private and mutual fund industries (Kaal & Anderson 2016). The confluence of mutual and hedge funds affects the evolution of the hedge fund industry, rendering it a more widely recognized industry that is part of the finance mainstream. Confluence factors also make governance alternatives and possible governance improvements available for the mutual fund industry. Other implications include a positive effect on the growth of the retail alternative fund market and possible support for the proposition that the public/private distinction in federal securities regulation may be dissipating.

Section 2 of this chapter provides a short discussion of data on the growth of the hedge fund industry and, more specifically, the growth of so-called retail alternative funds. Section 3 evaluates historical differences between private and mutual funds and forms of nominal confluence. Section 4 examines market-driven factors of confluence and regulatory confluence of mutual and hedge funds, including the Dodd–Frank Act and the JOBS Act. Section 5 shows the impact of mutual and hedge fund confluence on the evolution of the hedge fund industry, the governance of the mutual fund industry, the growth of the retail alternative fund market, and the structure of federal securities regulation. Section 6 concludes.

2 PROLIFERATION OF PRIVATE AND RETAIL ALTERNATIVE FUNDS

The hedge fund industry has been growing consistently since the early 2000s (Stulz 2007). Although by comparison to the overall asset management industry, hedge funds still represent a small portion of business (Investment Company Institute 2015; BarclayHedge 2015), changing demands by institutional investors have had an astounding impact on alternative investments, precipitating growth reaching $2 trillion in assets under management (AUM) by the end of 2013 (Deutsche Bank 2014). Between 2013 and 2015, the private fund industry grew by 26 percent, increasing from just over 2 trillion dollars AUM in 2013 to 2.7 trillion dollars AUM through 2015 (BarclayHedge 2015). According to Hedge Fund Research/Preqin/McKinsey analysis, alternative investments, such as hedge funds and private equity, have grown twice as fast as traditional investments, such as mutual funds and closed-end funds, since 2005 (Baghai et al. 2015).

Retail alternative funds (retail alternatives) are a rapidly emerging sector in the asset management industry. For purposes of this chapter, retail alternative funds are defined as regulated funds under the Investment Company Act that attempt to replicate the strategies of the private fund industry, including use of leverage, derivatives, short selling, and purchase of nontraditional asset classes. Different authors and industry representatives use different definitions from those used in this chapter, including liquid alternatives, unconstrained funds, alternative mutual funds, and synthetic hedge funds (Vanguard 2014). Retail alternative funds combine the structure of a traditional mutual fund (with its attractive liquidity and daily valuation features) with the higher returns and risk mitigation associated with private funds. Because of their portfolio diversification and comparatively high risk-adjusted returns, retail alternative investments have become increasingly popular over the past 20 years and have become an integral part of institutional investor portfolios.[8]

Several studies have applied different methodologies and provide different estimates of the growth of retail alternatives funds over the past several years. According to SEI, investments in retail alternatives have more than doubled since 2008 and represent more than $550 billion in assets as of 2013 (SEI 2013). Similarly, the Investment Company Institute's mutual fund data reveals startling growth in the retail alternatives segment, from 41 billion in 2007 to 170 billion by 2014 (Investment Company Institute 2015). The analysis of ICI data in Figure 13.1 suggests that net assets of mutual funds employing alternative strategies have quadrupled since 2007 (a 27 percent annualized growth rate). The number of funds offering investors alternative strategies grew from 181 in 2007 to 402 in 2014 (Investment Company Institute 2015). Similarly, KPMG/Strategic Insight Simfund claims that total assets in retail alternative funds jumped to nearly $450 billion in 2015 from less than $50 billion in 2008 (KPMG 2016). This growth was not expected to slow: JPMorgan/Strategic Insight estimated that by 2022, 15.8 percent of all mutual fund AUM will be tied up in alternative mutual funds, making it a multitrillion-dollar industry (JPMorgan Investor Services 2013).

Additionally, the author of this chapter recently copublished a study on a subtype of alternative mutual funds called "unconstrained mutual funds," which are fixed income mutual funds that attempt to replicate fixed income hedge fund strategies (Kaal & Anderson 2016). The study not only found significant growth in these funds by launch, but also provided evidence pertaining to the extent to which unconstrained mutual funds differ in trading strategy from traditional mutual funds, with the former using futures, short sales, and derivatives. Even unconstrained mutual fund turnover and fee structure appeared more similar to hedge funds than to traditional fixed income mutual funds.

This substantial growth in retail alternatives can at least partially be explained by growing retail demand for hedge fund strategies that were previously only accessible to accredited investors and large institutions (Investment Company Institute 2015). See Figure 13.1.

---

[8] The mutual fund industry utilized the popularity of private funds as a tool for wealth creation and the private investment advisers' registration obligation with the SEC, supposedly a source of comfort to investors otherwise apprehensive about entrusting capital to unknown managers, to create the liquid alternative product. Although it was an important objective for the mutual fund industry to be able to offer a new product, mutual fund managers were interested because adding one or more subadvisers to the mutual fund simply did not create significant additional regulatory obligations for the mutual fund manager or for the private fund adviser.

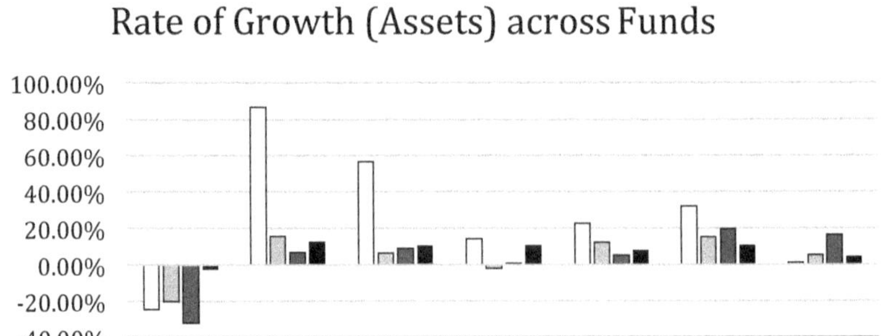

Rate of Growth (Assets) across Funds

	2008 (%)	2009 (%)	2010 (%)	2011 (%)	2012 (%)	2013 (%)	2014 (%)
Alternative Mutual Funds	−24.64	86.46	56.51	13.97	22.58	32.13	1.08
All Mutual Funds	−19.98	15.72	6.48	−1.70	12.21	15.19	5.44
Hedge Funds	−31.77	6.60	9.00	0.95	5.19	19.90	16.31
Private Equity	−2.69	12.57	10.36	10.74	7.95	10.64	4.64

Figure 13.1 ICI data—rate of growth of fund categories 2008 to 2014

3 PERSISTENT DIFFERENCES AND NOMINAL CONFLUENCE

Mutual funds and hedge funds have evolved in different market and regulatory structures. The two asset classes employ different investment strategies, serve largely different classes of investors, and therefore have traditionally occupied distinct segments of the investment market. Mutual funds serve mostly retail and institutional investors. They offer risk mitigation by way of diversification, a limited array of investments and strategies, instant liquidity, and daily valuation. They have traditionally been allowed to advertise. Mutual funds and investment advisers to mutual funds are required to register with the SEC and provide regular disclosures, including funds' holdings.[9] By contrast, private investment fund investments have traditionally have been limited to accredited high net worth and institutional investors. Investors in hedge funds need to be able to fend for themselves,[10] and they are subject to more rigorous verification procedures and contractual requirements (Strachman 2007; McCrary 2002).[11] Private investment fund advisers employ a near unlimited array of investments and strategies, and they are subject to redemption restrictions (Morley 2012). Unlike mutual fund advisers, hedge fund advisers are able to avoid registration with the SEC (Kaal 2016a), provided they comply with certain safe harbors under the securities laws.

---

[9] 15 U.S.C. § 80b–3 (2012) (describing registration of investment advisers).
[10] 17 C.F.R. § 230.501(a) (defining "accredited investor"); S.E.C. v. Ralston Purina Co., 346 U.S. 119 (1953) (private offerings turn on whether the offerees are able to "fend for themselves" and therefore do not need protection under federal securities laws).
[11] 17 C.F.R. § 230.506(c)(ii) (2014) ("Verification of accredited investor status. The issuer shall take reasonable steps to verify that purchasers of securities sold in any offering under paragraph (c) of this section are accredited investors").

Until 2014, private investment fund advisers could not advertise.[12] Unlike mutual funds, hedge funds are typically organized as Delaware LLCs or LPs,[13] and they are not subject to an SEC or other requirement that the fund, for example (among many others), has to: have an independent board;[14] provide daily valuation of fund positions/holdings;[15] provide daily liquidity to investors;[16] report holdings publicly and to investors on a regular basis;[17] adhere to '33 Act and '34 Act disclosure/filing/trading/purchase sale (and so on) requirements (Glazer 2016); use transfer agents and underwriters; comply with Subchapter M of the IRC;[18] or refrain from engaging in certain kinds of transactions that encourage undue leverage.[19] Moreover, the size of the investment in trading and operational technology and in experienced portfolio management, trading, reporting, operations, risk management, and other staffing incurred by a mutual fund adviser is materially larger than that required by a hedge fund manager to operate its business.

Hedge fund managers and advisers to mutual funds face material differences in the context of litigation and other enforcement. Mutual fund advisers are subject to ongoing, high dollar-value, private party litigation initiated by investors in registered mutual funds (Sjostrom 2005; Langevoort 2005). Indeed, many parts of the ICA authorize private rights of action against the mutual fund manager in the event of a violation.[20] Investors and their lawyers are not reluctant to use these provisions. Recent cases include cases brought against mutual fund managers for charging excessive

---

[12] Eliminating the Prohibition against General Solicitation and General Advertising in Rule 506 and Rule 144A Offerings, 78 Fed. Reg. 44,771 (Jul. 24, 2013); Kaal (2011) (pre-Dodd–Frank summary of private fund regulation).

[13] For private funds organized outside of the US, such as in the Caymans (which would be relevant for US tax-exempt investors, for example), there are even fewer requirements relating to governance and reporting to investors than would apply to private funds organized under US (e.g., Delaware) law. Browning, "A Hamptons for Hedge Funds," *New York Times* (2007).

[14] 15 U.S.C. § 80a-10(a) (2012); Kirsch (2015).

[15] 17 C.F.R. § 270.22c-1(b)(1) (2014) ("The current net asset value of any such security shall be computed no less frequently than once daily, Monday through Friday ...").

[16] 15 U.S.C. 80a-22(e) (2012); Revisions of Guidelines to Form N-1A, Investment Company Act Release No. 18612, 57 Fed. Reg. 9,828 (Mar. 20, 1992) (mutual funds can invest no more than 15 percent in illiquid assets).

[17] U.S. SEC. & EXCH. COMM'N, OMB NO. 3235-0307, FORM N-1A (2015), https://goo.gl/0CIImKU.

[18] Subchapter M requires a mutual fund to comply with certain distribution and portfolio diversification requirements in order to avoid being subject to federal income tax on income and capital gains it distributes to shareholders. 26 U.S.C. § 851(b)(2) (2012) (company must derive at least 90 percent of its gross income from dividends, interest, and gains from the sale of securities).

[19] 15 U.S.C. § 80a-12(d) (2012) (limiting margin purchases, short selling securities, or investing more than a small percentage of assets in other investment companies); 18(f) (mutual funds must have 300 percent asset coverage for any borrowings from a bank); Use of Derivatives by Investment Companies Under the Investment Company Act of 1940, Investment Company Act Release No. 29776, 76 Fed. Reg. 55,237 (concept release Sept. 7, 2011) (seeking review of the use of derivatives by mutual funds).

[20] 15 U.S.C. § 80a-35(b) (2012).

fees,[21] which would be unheard of in the hedge fund sphere, as well as several recent cases alleging deviations from investment strategies (for example, the current case against Schwab).[22] By contrast, private party litigation involving hedge fund managers is minimal because of the extent and nature of the disclosures which well-counseled hedge fund managers provide to their investors (who are, in turn, supposed to be sophisticated) and because the statutory regime establishing a hedge fund investor's right is severely limited,[23] almost to the point of nonexistence (both in the US and in jurisdictions such as the Caymans and BVI, where a significant number of hedge funds are chartered) (WalkersGlobal 2015).

The cases brought by the SEC against mutual fund managers and advisers to hedge funds show substantial differences in the scope and number of charges. Given the extensive scope of obligations for mutual fund advisers under the ICA, the '33 Act, and the '34 Act, the SEC may pursue the adviser for a large number of potential rule violations. The string of SEC investigations involving so-called distribution-in-guise payments by mutual fund advisers (SEC Press Release (2015)) provides a sense of the distinction in the nature of regulatory claims that the SEC might bring against mutual fund advisers.[24] Provided that industry standard disclosures are made to hedge fund investors, there is simply no basis for the SEC to bring a distribution-in-guise claim against a hedge fund manager.[25]

The term "nominal confluence" as used herein describes otherwise identical legal requirements for mutual and hedge fund managers that can be materially different in practice. While the applicable statutes and regulations may appear to apply nominally to both mutual and hedge fund managers, the nature of how the investment vehicles are structured and operated, and how they conduct business, can make their application materially different in practice (Zask (2013)). For instance, an investment adviser to a registered mutual fund is subject to the same Investment Advisers Act obligations as an

---

[21] *Redus-Tarchis v. New York Life Inv. Mgmt. LLC*, No. CV 14-7991, 2015 WL 6525894, at *1 (D.N.J. Oct. 28, 2015) (investors alleging excessive management fees taken by manager of four mutual funds); *R.W. Grand Lodge of F. & A.M. of Penn. v. Salomon Bros. All Cap Value Fund*, 425 F. App'x 25 (2d Cir. 2011) (investors brought action against various mutual funds alleging excessive fees in violation of the ICA).

[22] *Northstar Fin. Advisors Inc. v. Schwab Investments*, 779 F.3d 1036 (9th Cir. 2015), *cert. denied*, 136 S. Ct. 240 (2015) (plaintiff alleged that the mutual fund in question violated ICA/state securities laws by deviating from the fund's investment objective by investing in CMOs; 9th Circuit held that the plaintiffs could go forward with breach of contract and breach of fiduciary duty claims against Schwab).

[23] The unique American securities regulation regime creates a distinction between "public" and "private" offerings based on the concept of "accredited investors." Accredited investors (accreditation is a requirement to become an investor in a hedge fund or private equity fund) are theoretically able to "fend for themselves," while small investors need the protection of securities laws. See 15 U.S.C. § 77b (15) (2012) (defining accredited investor); 17 C.F.R. § 230.506 (2014) (safe harbor for private offerings); *SEC v. Ralston Purina Co.*, 346 U.S. 119, 125 (1953) ("[S]hould turn on whether the particular class of persons affected need the protection of the Act. An offering to those who are shown to be able to fend for themselves is a transaction 'not involving any public offering.'").

[24] Grind, "SEC Cranks Up Probe into Fund Firms' Fees," *Wall Street Journal* (2015).

[25] ICA claims can only be made by registered investment companies, such as mutual funds.

investment adviser to a hedge fund (Leonard et al. 2012). The scope of private and mutual fund managers' Investment Advisers Act obligations, however, diverge significantly. Because of the nature of their respective businesses such obligations are far more onerous for mutual fund managers.[26] As the two industries evolve and converge, it seems possible that other regulatory commonalities will emerge that are in fact still only nominally identical, but are practically still subject to differences that will dissipate over time.

Best execution requirements offer a prominent example of nominal confluence. Best execution obligations are similar but practically different for private and mutual fund advisers. In practice, best execution requirements are far more complicated and burdensome for the mutual fund manager than for the hedge fund adviser. Private and mutual fund managers have an obligation to seek to obtain best execution of the trades they direct to brokers.[27] The registered mutual fund manager has to be able to report daily on the fund's operating costs and expenses, including trading-related expenses, and therefore invests significantly in—and operates—technology-based systems to collect and track trading-related expense information with a high degree of precision. Constructing, maintaining, and supervising such a system is costly and subject to a great deal of investor and SEC scrutiny. Mistakes in such a system can lead to significant SEC fines and private party litigation initiated by mutual fund share holders. By contrast, a hedge fund manager trying to satisfy best execution obligations does not have to create the same technology-based system, but can elect to periodically (for example, quarterly) and manually review its internal trade processes and select a reasonable sample of trade data for review. Accordingly, in comparison with the mutual fund manager who is exposed to much higher regulatory and litigation risks, the hedge fund manager incurs minimal time and expense obligations in fulfilling best execution obligations.

4 CONFLUENCE OF PRIVATE AND MUTUAL FUNDS

Market-driven trends in financial markets suggest that traditional distinctions between mutual and hedge funds are eroding. Responding to investor demands for a combination of risk mitigation, liquidity, and the lower fees and absolute returns of hedge funds, investment managers introduced so-called hybrid or alternative funds, including

---

[26] In addition to the best execution differences described in the next paragraph, valuation of fund positions is another example of an area in which private and mutual fund managers are subject to similar legal requirements with very different practical implications. Mainly because a private fund manager is not required to publicly report a daily NAV (or, indeed, any NAV), or to provide daily liquidity to investors, mutual fund managers' valuation obligations are in practice far more complicated. It takes a significant amount of capital to design and implement a system to value, in real time, every position in a trading portfolio—this is the case not just with respect to technology, but also in terms of other infrastructure (e.g., people).

[27] Securities; Brokerage and Research Services, Exchange Act Release No. 34-23170, 51 Fed. Reg. 16,004, 16,006 (Apr. 30, 1986); In re Portfolio Advisory Serv., Investment Advisers Act Release No. 2038, 35 SEC Docket 703, 2002 WL 1343823, at *2 (June 20, 2002).

hedged mutual funds and synthetic hedge funds, and increased side by side management of mutual funds and hedge funds. The growth of hybrid funds and public offerings of alternative asset managers, among other factors, allows retail investors increasing access to hedge fund-like investments. Investor demand for alternative investment products will likely continue to shape the evolution of the two asset classes.

The fundamental reshaping of the regulatory landscape for the hedge fund industry intensifies the market-based assimilation of the private and mutual fund industries. The Dodd–Frank Act and the JOBS Act reframe core regulatory assumptions about the hedge fund industry and support the increasing recognition of hedge funds' critical role in capital formation. These regulatory changes increase the demand for retail alternative funds and may supplement the confluence of the mutual and hedge fund industries.

4.1 Investor Preferences

Market-driven trends in financial markets suggest that the traditional distinction between mutual and hedge funds is dissipating. Starting in the mid-2000s, retail investor demand for absolute returns precipitated public offerings of alternative asset managers (Davidoff 2008; Timmons 2006) and, despite regulatory restrictions,[28] retail investors gained increasing access to hedge fund-like investments through exchange traded funds (ETFs) and ever more sophisticated publicly available trading tools (Davidoff 2008).

The market-driven confluence of mutual and hedge funds is perhaps best illustrated by the rise of retail alternative funds in the early 2010s (Citi Fund Services 2010). Alternative mutual funds are investment vehicles that are legally structured as mutual funds and registered under the 1940 Investment Company Act. Despite different legal obligations and opposing incentives for private and mutual fund managers who operate alternative mutual funds,[29] alternative mutual funds offer the attractive features of mutual funds, such as significant diversification, daily pricing and liquidity, relative stability, and transparency. By offering investors exposure to hedge fund strategies (including going short, investing in illiquid securities, currencies, long–short equity,

---

[28] 17 C.F.R. § 230.506(c)(ii) (2014) ("Verification of accredited investor status. The issuer shall take reasonable steps to verify that purchasers of securities sold in any offering under paragraph (c) of this section are accredited investors.")

[29] Differences persist in the nature and scope of the obligations faced by mutual fund managers and those applicable to the private investment advisers who serve as subadvisers to funds/subfunds/accounts of a mutual fund. Very few substantive obligations exist for private fund managers who agree to subadvise a mutual fund or account. More specifically, none of the mutual fund manager's regulatory obligations (such as daily valuation, public/SEC reporting, independent boards, etc.) apply to the private fund subadviser. Hence, participating as a liquid alternative subadviser may be a great deal for the private fund manager: the private fund adviser gets access to "sticky" capital (i.e., redemption from the "registered fund" may be drawn out, if it occurs), likely in a meaningful quantity (e.g., initially in excess of $25–30 million, which is a good "ticket" in the private fund space), and the manager is able to associate its name with a mutual fund adviser, which has some potentially positive marketing implications. While private fund advisers and mutual fund advisers may share investment strategies via liquid alternative funds, the regulatory obligations of private and mutual fund advisers in a subadvised mutual fund offering are likely to remain dissimilar.

private equity, real estate, commodities, and global macro) and certain asset classes, complex trading techniques, and leverage, retail alternative funds combine mutual fund characteristics with the more aggressive strategies and the corresponding prospect of absolute returns of hedge funds (Kaal & Anderson 2016). Changes to the capital markets precipitated by the financial crisis of 2007–8, investors' post-crisis flight to safety, and a very low interest rate environment, in combination with the enormous growth, increased visibility, and popularity of hedge funds, created and, over time, increased the demand for alternative mutual funds (McKinsey & Company 2014). Alternative funds generally cannot generate the same absolute returns as hedge funds (Hasanhodzic & Lo 2007; McCarthy 2015), which is attributed by some to the lighter touch regulation and better incentives applicable to hedge funds. The increasing availability of alternative funds can have an effect on the overall demand for hedge funds (Stulz 2007) and startup hedge funds (Kaal 2016b).

Retail investors are a core factor for the proliferation of the retail alternative fund market. Starting in the early 2000s, retail investors, traditionally excluded from hedge fund investments, gained access to hedge fund-like investments through ETFs and ever more sophisticated publicly available at-home trading tools (SEI 2013). Alternative funds offered retail investors access to hedge fund strategies and higher returns than mutual funds while paying mutual fund fees, thus increasing demand by retail investors. Because of investment managers' recognition of retail investors' demand for alternative funds, retail investors gained increasing access to a broader array of alternative investment strategies, further increasing demand for alternative investments (McKinsey & Company 2014). Retail investors are driving the overall demand in the alternative investment sector, seeking more than just the prospect of significant performance—they also want risk-adjusted and consistent returns that are not correlated to the market (Citi Fund Services 2010; McKinsey & Company (2014)).

Multimanager series trusts illustrate the consumer demand-driven confluence of mutual and hedge funds. As a proliferating alternative model of mutual fund governance (SEC IM Guidance 2014), multimanager series trusts enhance retail investor access to alternative funds. The traditional mutual fund governance model is characterized by a single group of directors that is typically beholden to the sponsoring investment adviser firm (Morley & Curtis 2010; Roiter 2016; Krug 2013), serving as a single board for multiple discrete funds (Morley & Curtis 2010). The traditional governance model is, thus, subject to significant oversight challenges. By contrast, multimanager series trusts are not centered on the investment adviser but rather on the fund's administrator—a firm that is typically unaffiliated with the sponsoring adviser. Multimanager series trusts create numerous advisers, each managing one or a small number of funds within the group (Securities and Exchange Commission Press Release 2013), providing governance improvements. The growth of the multimanager series trust governance model can be traced back to elevated retail investor demand for alternative investments and the associated increase in investment managers. In particular, growing numbers of smaller investment advisers (by AUM) (Kern 2012), hoping to attract retail investors, benefit from cost efficiencies associated with multimanager series trusts, which further enhances the growth of that governance model. The combination of factors enhancing the growth of this governance model, especially cost efficiencies for a rapidly growing number of smaller investment advisers trying to attract retail investors, elevates the confluence of mutual and hedge funds. The cost savings associated with the multimanager series trust governance model allow the increasing number of smaller hedge fund investment advisers to attract retail investors by setting up a mutual fund.

Finally, investment advisers satisfy investor demand for retail alternative products partially through side by side management of mutual and hedge funds. Side by side management describes the simultaneous management of both a mutual and a hedge fund (Nohel et al. 2010; Cici et al. 2010). Side by side management has been steadily increasing since 2010 and is expected to continue to rise as investment advisers are seeking to offer their clients a combination of hedge fund characteristics with the benefits associated with mutual funds (Cici et al. 2010). An important limiting factor in the steady rise of side by side management is the inherent conflict of interest for the investment manager (SEC 2003; Chen & Chen 2009; Cici et al. 2010). Conflicts of interest can arise in situations where the investment adviser for the retail alternative fund manages both the fund and separate private or proprietary accounts, such as hedge funds (SEI 2013). While the investment adviser does have a fiduciary obligation in this situation, the investment adviser has incentives to give preferential treatment to the hedge fund accounts that are associated with higher compensation (the 2 and 20 model vs. mutual fund fee structure) for the investment adviser.

4.2 Regulation

The mutual and hedge fund industries evolved in different legal settings. Unlike hedge funds, mutual funds have traditionally been subject to a comprehensive system of federal oversight under the Investment Company Act of 1940 (ICA), as amended, including restrictions on compensation structures, numerous reporting requirements, and restrictions on leverage and investments, among others (Riggs et al. 1996; Investment Company Institute 2015). Hedge funds, on the other hand, have been able throughout their history to remain largely exempt from federal regulation, provided that hedge fund advisers and their legal counsel complied with applicable safe harbor requirements. Through applicable exemptions from registering as investment companies, exemptions from registering their securities, and exemptions from registering the investment advisers, hedge funds have traditionally been able to operate in the financial markets without significant regulatory oversight. Without significant regulatory oversight, hedge funds were able to employ more exotic investment strategies involving more leverage to generate absolute returns for their investors.

The fundamental reshaping of the regulatory landscape for the hedge fund industry eradicates many of the legal differences separating the two industries. The Dodd–Frank Act,[30] as well as the JOBS Act,[31] made important contributions to increased recognition of hedge funds' critical role in capital formation and helped transition the hedge fund

---

[30] Dodd–Frank Wall Street Reform and Consumer Protection (Dodd–Frank Act), Pub. L. No. 111-203, §§ 401–16, 124 Stat. 1376, 1571 (2010).

[31] Jumpstart Our Business Startups Act, Pub. L. No. 112-106, § 201(a)(1), 126 Stat. 306, 313–14 (2012).

industry from a secretive association of elite investment managers to a more widely recognized group of investment professionals (White 2013).

The Dodd–Frank Act and the JOBS Acts converged formerly distinct legal rules applicable to the formerly distinct asset classes. The registration and increased disclosure requirements for certain hedge fund advisers under the Dodd–Frank Act subjects investment advisers to hedge funds to similar registration and reporting obligations as mutual fund advisers. Similarly, the removal of advertising restrictions for hedge fund advisers under the JOBS Act and the equal treatment of mutual and hedge funds for FSOC's SIFI designation in effect assimilated the advertising requirements of mutual and hedge funds.

The registration and disclosure requirements for hedge fund advisers under the Dodd–Frank Act illustrate a core point of confluence of the legal regimes applicable to mutual and hedge funds. While the registration and disclosure requirements for hedge fund advisers under the Dodd–Frank Act are significantly less onerous than the registration regime applicable to mutual funds,[32] several core overlaps of the two registration regimes illustrate the confluence of mutual and hedge funds. For the first time in the history of the hedge fund industry, the Dodd–Frank Act required most advisers to hedge funds to register with the SEC. By eliminating previous registration exemptions and requiring investment advisers with AUM of more than $150 million to register with the SEC,[33] the Dodd–Frank Act mandated SEC registration and reporting of information that was hitherto considered proprietary and private.

Hedge funds are becoming more like mutual funds because they are allowed to advertise. A key legal distinction between mutual and hedge funds was their unequal treatment for purposes of advertising. Mutual funds advertised broadly across multiple forms of media while hedge fund advisers were prohibited from advertising.[34] After more than six decades of private offerings with a ban on general solicitation and general advertising (GSGA) that applied when companies or funds make private securities offerings under Rule 506 of Regulation D,[35] with the passing of the JOBS

---

[32] Mutual funds also must disclose use and details of derivatives contracts they trade: *see* Investment Company Reporting Modernization, Investment Company Act Release No. 31610, 80 Fed. Reg. 33,590 (proposed Jun. 12, 2015); *see also* Notice of Filing of Proposed Rule Change Relating to Amendments to NYSE Arca Equities Rule 8.600 to Adopt Generic Listing Standards for Managed Fund Shares, Exchange Act Release No. 34-76486, 80 Fed. Reg. 12,690 (proposed Mar. 10, 2015) (although no limitation on the percentage of an active ETF's portfolio that may be invested in derivatives, ETFs would have to disclose more information about such contracts.).

[33] Dodd–Frank Act §§ 403, 408 and 410 (removing exemptions for private fund investment adviser registration under the Investment Advisers Act of 1940 and mandating investment adviser registration at over $100k AUM).

[34] 15 U.S.C. §§ 80a-3(c)(1) (2006) (the pre-JOBS Act law banning private fund advertising).

[35] Advertising was banned under the previous Rule 506- Revision of Certain Exemptions from Registration for Transactions Involving Limited Offers and Sales, Investment Company Act Release No. 33-6389, 47 Fed. Reg. 11,251 (Mar. 16, 1982). For discussion about why the solicitation ban was likely overinclusive and impeded full regulatory transparency *see* Martin (2014).

Act in 2012,[36] the SEC finally had a mandate to amend Rule 506.[37] The SEC's new proposed Rule 506(c), for the first time, allowed GSGA in a Regulation D offering.[38] The Rule was finalized and published in the Federal Register on June 24, 2013, and became effective on September 23, 2013.[39]

The equal treatment of mutual and hedge funds as nonbank financial institutions for purposes of designating an entity a SIFI supports the identified trend toward legal confluence of these formerly more clearly distinct asset classes. The Dodd–Frank Act created the Financial Stability Oversight Council (FSOC),[40] a council of banking and securities regulators tasked with monitoring systemic risk in US financial markets,[41] as well as correcting perceived regulatory weaknesses that may have contributed to the financial crisis of 2008–9.[42] SIFI designation changes the regulatory burden for a nonbank financial institution substantially,[43] and may require a bolstering of the entity's balance sheet and curtailing of risk. It can impact the respective entity's growth (Elliot 2013). While evidence exists that SIFI designation could have disparate affects on mutual and hedge funds (Stevens Letter 2015), the applicable regulatory framework does not distinguish between the two asset classes.[44] The process applied by FSOC for

---

[36] Jumpstart Our Business Startups Act, Pub. L. No. 112-106, § 201(a)(1), 126 Stat. 306, 313–14 (2012).

[37] Section 201 of the JOBS Act directed the SEC to lift the prohibition against general solicitation or general advertising, allowing a broadening of marketing efforts provided that all purchasers of the securities are accredited investors. Jumpstart Our Business Startups Act, Pub. L. No. 112-106, § 201(a)(1), 126 Stat. 306, 313–14 (2012). Under Section 201(a)(1) of the JOBS Act, the SEC was required to revise Rule 506 not later than 90 days of the enactment of the JOBS Act, i.e., July 4, 2012. However, the SEC Proposing Release was not issued until August 2012 and was finally adopted in October 2013.

[38] Eliminating the Prohibition against General Solicitation and General Advertising in Rule 506 and Rule 144A, Release No. 33-9354, 77 Fed. Reg. 54,469 (proposed Sept. 6, 2012) at 6 [hereinafter Rule 506(c) Proposing Release].

[39] Eliminating the Prohibition against General Solicitation and General Advertising in Rule 506 and Rule 144A Offerings, Securities Act Release No. 33-9415, 78 Fed. Reg. 44,771 (Jul. 24, 2013) (codified as amended at 7 C.F.R. pts. 230, 239, 242). [hereinafter Final 506 Rule], http://www.sec.gov/rules/final/2013/33-9415.pdf.

[40] Dodd–Frank Wall Street Reform and Consumer Protection Act (Dodd–Frank Act), Pub. L. No. 111-203 § 111, 124 Stat. 1376 (2010).

[41] The Dodd–Frank Act defines potential systemic risk posed by U.S. or foreign nonbank financial entities as the "material financial distress at the [company], or the nature, scope, size, scale, concentration, interconnectedness, or mix of the activities of the [company that] could pose a threat to the financial stability of the United States." Dodd–Frank Act § 113(a)(1).

[42] Reporting by Investment Advisers to Private Funds and Certain Commodity Pool Operators and Commodity Trading Advisors on Form PF, Investment Advisor Release No. IA-3308, 76 Fed. Reg. 71,128, 71,129 (Nov. 16, 2011); *see also* Dodd–Frank Act § 112(a)(1)(A)–(C).

[43] Dodd–Frank Act § 115(a)(1) (once designated as a SIFI, the respective entity will be subject to extensive regulation and supervision by the Federal Reserve Board under Title I of the Dodd-Frank Act); *Id.* at § 115(a) (noting that the regulatory standards for nonbank financial firms under Fed supervision are more stringent than the standard for nonbank financial firms outside of Fed supervision); *Id.* at § 115(b)(1).

[44] The latest FSOC solicitation for comment on SIFI designation makes no attempt to separate the two in their designation and risk criteria. Financial Stability Oversight Council,

Confluence of mutual and hedge funds 291

SIFI designation, which has three stages,[45] does not distinguish between mutual and hedge funds.[46] In fact, while Dodd–Frank prescribes several considerations that the Council must take into account in its determination of what entities qualify as SIFIs, the FSOC has some discretion in the systemic risk assessment process.[47]

5 IMPLICATIONS OF CONFLUENCE

The factors of mutual and hedge fund confluence identified in this chapter could, over time, have broad implications in several contexts. First, the confluence factors can affect the evolution of the hedge fund industry and its role in capital formation. Second, confluence has the potential to introduce and facilitate alternative mutual fund governance models that promise to address core governance shortcomings in the mutual fund industry. Third, the factors of confluence can further increase the demand for and proliferation of retail alternatives, which in turn can accelerate confluence of the two asset classes. Finally, the factors of confluence may have a lasting impact on the public/private distinction in federal securities regulation.

The emerging process of confluence of mutual and hedge funds can have unexpected peripheral effects that may themselves reinforce confluence of the two asset classes. I do not claim cause and effect in this context. Nor do I suggest that any of the observed possible effects will have drastic immediate repercussions for market participants. Rather, the discussion of confluence trends observed herein is intended to highlight possible long-term implications and peripheral effects that merit continued monitoring.

5.1 Evolution of the Private Fund Industry

The confluence of private and mutual funds impacts the market position, recognition, and overall evolution of the hedge fund industry. Policymakers and commentators have traditionally excluded the private fund industry from mainstream finance. The high

---

Notice Seeking Comment on Asset Management Products and Activities, 79 Fed. Reg. 77,488 (Dec. 24, 2014).

[45] The numerical thresholds considered by FSOC in stage one, excluding nonbank financial institutions from review if they do not exceed threshold considerations, apply to all nonbank financial institutions and do not distinguish between asset classes. 12 C.F.R. § 1310 app. A(III)(a). Only those nonbank financial institutions that raised systemic concerns in stage one will be subject to more institution-specific and qualitative evaluation in stage two, and thereafter possibly stage three. In stage two, FSOC prioritizes those nonbank financial institutions identified in stage one based on quantitative and qualitative public and regulatory sources of information and initiates the consultation process with the primary financial regulatory agencies. 12 C.F.R. § 1310 app. A(III)(b). In stage three, FSOC contacts each identified nonbank financial institution to collect additional information that was not available in stages one and two. § 1310 app. A(III)(c). The combined information from all three stages is then evaluated.

[46] 12 C.F.R. § 1310 app. A(III) (applying same standards to all nonbank financial companies).

[47] The quantitative systemic risk assessment measures are not specifically codified. FSOC can change thresholds and analysis via the rule making process—Dodd–Frank Act §§ 113(a)(1), (a)(2)(K); 12 C.F.R. § 1310 app. A (2014).

profitability of the private fund industry, in combination with its penchant for secrecy, alienated politicians (Knowles 2015; Sanders 2014; Seretakis 2013) and regularly triggered calls for increased oversight (Christie and Katz 2011). The compensation of hedge fund managers has particularly angered many policy makers and regularly triggers public outcries for increased regulation (Lowenstein 2015; Stevenson 2015; Fleischer 2015). The media regularly accuses the hedge fund industry of excessive speculation (Mills 2003) that impacts commodity markets, the real economy, and consumers (Allen 2010; Jickling & Austin 2011; Elias 2014). In fact, since its inception in the 1940s, the hedge fund industry has been the poster child for reckless investments and high risk-taking in financial markets (Mallaby 2011; Lhabitant 2007). It has often been accused of fostering systemic risk (Lee 2015). Politicians and commentators blamed the hedge fund industry for triggering the financial crisis of 2007–8.[48] Policymakers regularly use the industry as a scapegoat when financial markets experience volatility (Lowenstein 2015; Crutchfield et al. 2009).

Factors associated with the confluence of mutual and hedge funds have helped the hedge fund industry transition from an industry operating at the fringes of finance to one recognized as part of the mainstream finance world (Baghai et al. 2015; Muhtaeb 2012). Hedge funds have been able to proliferate and increasingly attract investors, due in part to the Federal Reserve's policies of the early 2010s and the low interest rates that resulted (Stevenson 2015; Shilling 2012). Unprecedented changes in the rules and regulations pertaining to the hedge fund industry under Title IV of the Dodd–Frank Act and the JOBS Act have allowed increased oversight of the industry and contributed to the increasing recognition of the hedge fund industry as a fully regulated asset class.[49] These changes established the hedge fund industry not only in the eyes of investors but also in the eyes of the SEC. Epitomizing the increasing recognition of the hedge fund industry and its important role in capital formation, in 2013 SEC chairwoman Mary Jo White declared: "Private funds, including hedge funds, play a critical role in capital formation, and are influential participants in the capital markets" (White 2013).

5.2 Mutual Fund Governance

The confluence of mutual and hedge funds can also influence mutual fund governance. The proliferation of multimanager series trusts, for example, established a hitherto nonexistent alternative governance model for mutual funds. Given the proliferation of confluence between mutual and hedge funds, it is possible that other governance models for mutual funds emerge over time. Multimanager series trusts can support mutual fund governance. Unlike the board in a traditional mutual fund governance setting, the board in a multimanager series trust arrangement is largely independent of any advisers within the fund group. Thus independent directors on the board are not subject to conflicts of interest that often exist in traditional mutual fund governance

---

[48] *Hedge Funds and the Financial Market: Hearing Before the H. Comm. on Oversight and Govt. Reform*, 110th Cong. 2 (2008) (statement of Rep. Waxman).
[49] Including mandatory private fund adviser registration and disclosure requirements under the Dodd–Frank Act and general advertising and general solicitation criteria under revised Rule 506 of Regulation D under the Securities Act of 1933.

settings (Roiter 2016; Morley & Curtis 2010) if directors are affiliated with the investment adviser. Apart from its involvement in approving each adviser in a group structure, the board in the trust setting also typically has no involvement in selecting the group's investment advisers, creating fewer incentives for the board to comport with advisers in contradiction of fiduciary obligations. Despite the open issues and possible shortcomings of the multimanager series trust model, the trust model governance structure for mutual funds appears to offer lasting substantive governance improvements for mutual funds.

5.3 Retail Alternative Fund Growth

Factors of mutual and hedge fund confluence increase the demand for retail alternative funds. While the market-driven proliferation of retail alternative funds itself drives confluence, several additional nonmarket confluence factors support the growth of the market for alternative funds. For instance, several provisions in the Dodd–Frank Act revised legal requirements applicable to hedge funds and in effect assimilated the legal requirements of mutual and hedge funds. Merging the regulatory requirements applicable to mutual funds with the formerly more distinct rules applicable to hedge funds creates incentives for private investment managers to set up retail alternative funds. A higher supply of retail alternative funds, in turn, is likely to further increase investor demand for retail alternative funds. A higher demand for retail alternative funds, in turn, precipitates more sustainable market-driven confluence of the mutual and hedge fund industries.

The mandatory investment adviser registration provisions under the Dodd–Frank Act incentivize investment advisers to set up retail alternative funds. Prior to the enactment of the Dodd–Frank Act, the registration of a hedge fund was a significant disincentive for investment managers to enter into the mutual fund sector. Investment advisers to hedge funds disfavored registration with the SEC because they considered the associated disclosures intrusive and feared negative affects on profitability. By eliminating previous registration exemptions and requiring investment advisers with AUM of more than $150 million to register with the SEC,[50] the Dodd–Frank Act mandates SEC registration and reporting of information that was hitherto considered proprietary and private. Hedge fund advisers who are required to register with the SEC have incentives to also manage mutual funds or set up retail alternative funds because the regulatory burden is minimally higher in comparison with preregistration legal requirements. Some registered hedge fund advisers may choose to offer hedge fund strategies in a mutual fund setting, thus increasing the trend toward confluence.

In addition to the restrictions applicable in accordance with the qualified purchaser definition in section 3(c) (7) of the 1940 Investment Company Act, the tightening of accredited investor provisions under the Dodd–Frank Act increases investor demand for

---

[50] Dodd–Frank Act §§ 403, 408, 410 (removing exemptions for private fund investment adviser registration under the Investment Advisers Act of 1940 and mandating investment adviser registration at over $100k AUM).

retail alternative funds. The Dodd–Frank Act increases restrictions on certain individuals and institutions that previously qualified as accredited investors,[51] rendering an increasing number of investors ineligible for hedge fund investments.[52] The Dodd–Frank Act decreases the number of eligible hedge fund investors by raising the minimum net worth requirement for individuals to qualify as "accredited investors."[53] While the number of such investors may be negligible, investors who no longer qualify for retail alternative fund investments under Dodd–Frank qualified investor standards are likely to seek out hybrid funds.

Limitations to bank investments in the hedge fund industry, mandated by the Dodd–Frank Act, incentivize retail alternative fund investments for banks. Banks have traditionally been one of the largest investor groups in the hedge fund industry (Preqin 2012). Despite banks' prominent position as investors in the hedge fund industry, the Dodd–Frank Act, in its Volcker Rule provisions,[54] severely restricts banks' ability to be large investors in hedge funds. Dodd–Frank's Volcker Rule provisions both prohibit banks and bank holding companies from engaging in most proprietary trading activities and investing in or sponsoring private equity and hedge funds.[55] The final regulations prevent bank holding companies from sponsoring or retaining an ownership interest in most hedge funds after July 21, 2015, except in very limited cases.[56] By limiting banks' investments in derivatives and the hedge funds they sponsor,[57] the Dodd–Frank Act limits access to hedge fund investments but incentivizes banks to access hedge fund strategies using a retail alternative fund. Given the prior role of bank investments in the hedge fund industry, the shifting of investments from the hedge fund industry to the retail alternative fund market could be substantial (SEI 2013).

The JOBS Act also creates incentives for investment advisers to set up retail alternative funds. The legal uncertainty of investor verification after the ban on GCGA was lifted, among other reasons such as path dependencies and peer pressure, creates disincentives for private investment managers to advertise. Investment advisers to hedge funds have better incentives to set up retail alternative funds that allow them to offer features that are attractive to retail investors rather than to advertise under the uncertain new regime (Rule 506(c)) in an effort to attract a now smaller pool of qualified investors that are willing to invest in their hedge funds.

---

[51] Dodd–Frank Act § 413 (removing the value of the primary residence from the calculation of net worth for purposes of accredited investor status, reducing the number of accredited investors).

[52] Dodd–Frank Act § 413.

[53] Dodd–Frank Act § 413(b) (the commission also may review the accredited investor standard every four years and make adjustments to protect investors, perhaps opening up a possibility of increasing restrictions to the accredited investor standard in coming years); 17 C.F.R. § 230.501(a) (2014).

[54] Dodd–Frank Act § 619.

[55] Dodd–Frank Act § 619.

[56] Prohibitions and Restrictions on Proprietary Trading and Certain Interest in, and Relationships with, Hedge Funds and Private Equity Funds, 79 Fed. Reg. 5,536, 5,538 (Jan. 31, 2014).

[57] Dodd–Frank Act § 737 (limiting banks' ability to take derivative positions). Dodd–Frank Act § 619 (limiting investment in private funds to no more than 3 percent ownership and no more than 3 percent of investing bank's Tier 1 capital.) Dodd–Frank Act at Title VII (entailing additional capital and margin requirements and limitations on use of derivatives).

Despite the regulatory trends and investor preference trends favoring increasing confluence of mutual and hedge funds, the SEC might counteract some of the confluence drivers. First, the SEC is attempting to curtail the use of some hedge fund strategies, such as derivative trading and short selling, used by retail alternative mutual funds to mimic hedge funds. It issued a concept release in 2011 soliciting comments about the issues raised by derivative use in mutual funds, although so far no final action has been taken.[58] Additionally, the SEC may increase the portfolio reporting by mutual funds, ETFs, and other registered investment companies to include disclosure of the terms of derivative contracts and the counterparty risks posed by these contracts.[59] The SEC also amended Regulation SHO, restricting short selling of stocks that are subject to significant downward price pressure.[60] Investment advisers to mutual funds may not be able to use certain hedging techniques after the amendment of Regulation SHO, making it less likely that investment advisers running mutual funds will be able to attract retail investors who are seeking alternative investment opportunities. Lastly, SEC leaders have indicated in recent years that they will vigorously investigate whether retail alternatives are complying with 1940 Act rules on valuations, leverage, disclosure, and liquidity (Katz 2014; Champ 2014; Marriage 2014). In a recent speech, SEC Commissioner Kara M. Stein called for enhanced regulations to deal with retail alternatives, quoting a colleague's statement that such funds are "bright, new, shiny objects in the marketplace that are also very sharp and fraught with risk" (Stein 2015). Commissioner Stein stated that perhaps the SEC should consider regulating retail alternatives under a different regime than the one applied to traditional, plain vanilla mutual funds (Stein 2015).

5.4 Structure of Federal Securities Law

Mutual and hedge fund confluence contributes to the gradual erosion of the public/private distinction in federal securities regulation. The literature on the public/private distinction in federal securities regulation (Langevoort & Thompson 2013; Sale 2014; Sale 2011) examines factors that contribute to the continuous blurring of the traditional boundary lines between regulated and "private" firms and transactions, including reforms introduced under the JOBS Act, private investment in public equity ("PIPE") transactions, reverse mergers, and the Crowdfunding Act. This chapter adds to that literature by pointing out additional regulatory confluence factors that undermine the traditional public/private distinction in federal securities regulation. In addition to the widely discussed new Rule 506(c), the regulatory confluence exemplified by the

---

[58] Use of Derivatives by Investment Companies Under the Investment Company Act of 1940, Investment Company Act Release No. 29776, 76 Fed. Reg. 55,237 (Aug. 31, 2011).
[59] Investment Company Reporting Modernization, Investment Company Act Release No. 31610, 80 Fed. Reg. 33,590 (proposed Jun. 12, 2015); Notice of Filing of Proposed Rule Change Relating to Amendments to NYSE Arca Equities Rule 8.600 to Adopt Generic Listing Standards for Managed Fund Shares, 80 Fed. Reg. 12,690 (proposed Mar. 10, 2015) (although no limitation on the percentage of an active ETF's portfolio that may be invested in derivatives, ETF would have to disclose more information about such contracts).
[60] Securities and Exchange Commission, Amendments to Regulation SHO, SEC Release No. 34-61595, 75 Fed. Reg. 11,232 (Mar. 10, 2010).

mandatory registration of hedge fund advisers and their heightened reporting obligations in combination with the equal treatment of mutual and hedge funds by FSOC in its SIFI designation processes underscore the perhaps accelerating erosion of the public/private distinction in federal securities law (Kaal & Anderson 2016).

6 CONCLUSION

The evidence presented in this chapter suggests that an increasing number of mutual funds are becoming more like hedge funds as a matter of investment strategy, while hedge funds are becoming more like mutual funds due to the regulatory framework. Such a confluence has several implications. The chapter shows that this confluence of mutual and hedge funds can have implications for the evolution of the hedge fund industry, the governance of the mutual fund industry, the growth of the retail alternative fund market, and the structure of federal securities regulation. The evidence listed herein suggests that the traditional public/private distinctions between mutual and hedge funds are eroding at a rate higher than previously anticipated.

The observed possible effects of confluence are unlikely to precipitate drastic immediate repercussions for market participants, but possible long-term implications and peripheral effects merit continued monitoring and regulatory scrutiny. At the time of this chapter's writing, the author was not aware of any effort to extend the far more onerous regulatory regime pertaining to mutual funds, that is, under the ICA, '33 Act, '34 Act, and so on, to hedge funds, either directly through the SEC enacting regulations or congressional legislation, or indirectly through the SEC's enforcement processes, by which the agency might seek to effect some of that extension. However, while mutual funds have historically used little leverage (or leverage-creating derivatives) and presented little risk, the increasing demand for alternative strategies (Kaal & Anderson 2016) creates incentives for mutual fund managers to seek ways to simulate leverage. Given this trend, it seems at least possible that the mutual fund industry of the future could be subjected to greater risk than the historical averages suggested in the past. Given the comparative size of the mutual fund and hedge fund markets (Managed Funds Association 2015) and the possible systemic implications, this could be a concern that may merit continued monitoring, scholarly evaluation, and regulatory scrutiny.

Proposed SEC Rule 18f-4 constitutes a potential threat for the business model of the alternative mutual fund industry.[61] The proposed rule could undermine alternative mutual fund managers' ability to structure their portfolios in ways that would allow the implementation of their overall investment strategy using derivatives. The SEC warns that the alternative mutual fund industry may be particularly affected by the proposed rule's risk-based portfolio limit. However, the implications of proposed Rule 18f-4 for the policy analysis in this chapter are limited. Proposed Rule 18f-4 is the product of several years of interactions between the industry and the SEC (starting in 2011) over

---

[61] Use of Derivatives by Registered Investment Companies and Business Development Companies, Investment Company Act Release No. 31933, 80 Fed. Reg. 80,883 (proposed Dec. 28, 2015).

a broader issue that is only indirectly related to the analysis of confluence factors in this chapter: whether mutual funds are taking on too much investment risk through derivatives.[62]

REFERENCES

12 C.F.R. § 1310 app. A(III)(a) (2015).
15 U.S.C. § 77b (15) (2012).
15 U.S.C. § 80a–10(a) (2012).
15 U.S.C. § 80a–35(b) (2012).
15 U.S.C. § 80b–3 (2012).
15 U.S.C. §80a-22(e) (2012).
17 C.F.R. § 230.501(a) (2015).
17 C.F.R. § 230.506 (2015).
17 C.F.R. § 270.22c-1(b) (2015).
26 U.S.C. § 851(b)(2) (2012).
Allen, Katie, 2010, Hedge Funds Accused of Gambling with Lives of the Poorest as Food Prices Soar, *The Guardian* (July 18), available at https://perma.cc/HWA8-ZEXQ.
Amendments to Regulation SHO, SEC Release No. 34-61595, 75 Fed. Reg. 11,232 (Mar. 10, 2010).
Baghai, Pooneh, Omar Erzan, and Ju-Hon Kwek, The $64 Trillion Question: Convergence in Asset Management, *McKinsey on Investing*, February 2015, available at https://perma.cc/KS4D-L684.
Browning, Lynnley, 2007, A Hamptons for Hedge Funds, *New York Times* (July 1), available at https://perma.cc/QJ5T-WVJ6.
Cavoli, James G. et al, 2010, The SEC's Mutual Fund Fee Initiative: What to Expect, *Securities Litigation and Regulation* 16, 1–14, available at https://perma.cc/VS9C-MUPD.
Champ, Norm. Remarks to the Practicing Law Institute. Speech presented at the Private Equity Forum, New York, June 30, 2014, available at https://perma.cc/K4FA-T2VP.
Chen, Li-Wen and Fan Chen, 2009, Does Concurrent Management of Mutual and Hedge Funds Create Conflicts of Interest? *Journal of Banking and Finance* 33, 1423–33.
Christie, Rebecca and Ian Katz, 2011, Hedge Funds May Pose Systemic Risk in Crisis, U.S. Report Says, *Bloomberg Business* (February 17), available at https://perma.cc/QSR2-N9WU.
Cici, Gjergji, Scott Gibson, and Rabih Moussawi, 2010, Mutual Fund Performance When Parent Firms Simultaneously Manage Hedge Funds, *Journal of Financial Intermediation* 19, 169–87.
Citi Fund Services, 2010, The Convergence of Traditional and Alternative Investment Products: Regulatory and Operational Considerations, *Investment Lawyer* 17, 1–10.
Davidoff, Steven M., 2008, Black Market Capital, *Columbia Business Law Review* 2008, 172–268.
Deutsche Bank, 2014, *Twelfth Annual Alternative Investment Survey*, available at https://perma.cc/34N5-H2DH.

---

[62] 18f-4 is really the culmination of a longrunning debate on derivatives that the mutual fund industry, the SEC, the Senate and other regulators have been engaging in for several years. For the original SEC concept release, see Use of Derivatives by Investment Companies under the Investment Company Act of 1940, Investment Company Release No. 29776, 76 Fed. Reg. 55,237 (concept release Sept. 7, 2011) ("The Securities and Exchange Commission (the 'Commission') and its staff are reviewing the use of derivatives by management investment companies registered under the Investment Company Act of 1940 (the 'Investment Company Act' or 'Act') and companies that have elected to be treated as business development companies ('BDCs') under the Act (collectively, 'funds'). To assist in this review, the Commission is issuing this concept release and request for comments on a wide range of issues relevant to the use of derivatives by funds, including the potential implications for fund leverage, diversification, exposure to certain securities-related issuers, portfolio concentration, valuation, and related matters.").

Dodd–Frank Wall Street Reform and Consumer Protection, Pub. L. No. 111-203, §§ 401-416, 124 Stat. 1376, 1571 (2010).

Elias, Barry, 2014, "Algorithmic Trading Continues to Disrupt the Market," *NewsMax Finance* (June 20), available at http://goo.gl/3W8vr6.

Eliminating the Prohibition against General Solicitation and General Advertising in Rule 506 and Rule 144A Offerings, 78 Fed. Reg. 44,771 (July 24, 2013) (codified as amended at 7 C.F.R. pts. 230, 239, 242)

Eliminating the Prohibition against General Solicitation and General Adverting in Rule 506 and Rule 144A, Release No. 33-9354, 77 Fed. Reg. 54,469 (proposed Sept. 6, 2012).

Elliot, Douglas J., 2013, Regulating Systemically Important Financial Institutions That Are Not Banks, Brookings Paper, available at https://perma.cc/TYH5-8DMM.

Financial Stability Oversight Council, Financial Stability Oversight Council Makes First Nonbank Financial Company Designations to Address Potential Threats to Financial Stability, news release, July 9, 2013, available at https://perma.cc/XE6V-T96R.

Financial Stability Oversight Council, Notice Seeking Comment on Asset Management Products and Activities, 79 Fed. Reg. 77,488 (Dec. 24, 2014).

Fleischer, Victor, 2015, Stop Universities from Hoarding Money, *New York Times* (August 19), available at http://goo.gl/y2mF81.

Glazer, Michael, 2016, Prospectus Disclosure and Delivery Requirements, in Clifford E. Kirsch, ed., *Mutual Funds and Exchange Traded Funds Regulation*, vol. 1, 3rd ed. (Practicing Law Institute, New York, NY).

Grind, Kirsten, 2015, SEC Cranks Up Probe into Fund Firms' Fees, *Wall Street Journal* (July 16), available at www.wsj.com/articles/sec-cranks-up-probe-into-fund-firms-fees-1437087282.

Hasanhodzic, Jasmina and Andrew W. Lo, 2007, Can Hedge-Fund Returns Be Replicated? The Linear Case, *Journal of Investment Management* 5, 5–45.

Hedge Funds and the Financial Market: Hearing Before the H. Comm. on Oversight and Govt. Reform, 110th Cong. 2 (2008).

Hedge Fund Industry, *BarclayHedge*, accessed September 1, 2015, http://goo.gl/PB3P86.

In re Portfolio Advisory Services, Investment Advisers Act Release No. 2038, 35 SEC Docket 703, 2002 WL 1343823 (June 20, 2002).

Interpretive Release Concerning the Scope of Section 28(e) of the Securities Exchange Act of 1934 and Related Matters, Exchange Act Release No. 34-23170, 51 Fed. Reg. 16,004, 16,006 (Apr. 30, 1986).

Investment Company Institute, 2015, *Investment Company Fact Book*, 55th ed., available at https://perma.cc/EG69-6ZXQ.

Investment Company Reporting Modernization, Investment Company Act Release No. 31610, 80 Fed. Reg. 33,590 (proposed June 12, 2015).

Jickling, Mark and D. Andrew Austin, 2011, Cong. Research Serv., R41902, Hedge Fund Speculation and Oil Prices, available at https://perma.cc/UP7T-GW69.

JPMorgan Investor Services, 2013, *Alternative Strategies in the '40 Act World: Opportunities and Obstacles for Multi-Manager Registered Mutual funds*, available at https://perma.cc/BCW9-ETKE.

Jumpstart Our Business Startups Act, Pub. L. No. 112-106, § 201(a)(1), 126 Stat. 306, 313-14 (2012).

Kaal, Wulf A., 2011, Hedge Fund Regulation via Basel III, *Vanderbilt Journal of Transnational Law* 44, 389–463.

Kaal, Wulf A., 2016a, The Post Dodd-Frank Act Evolution of the Private Fund Industry: Comparative Evidence from 2012 and 2015, *The Business Lawyer*, available at http://papers.ssrn.com/sol3/papers.cfm?abstract_id=2739479.

Kaal, Wulf A., 2016b, What Drives Dodd-Frank Act Compliance Cost for Private Funds?, Journal of Alternative Investments, available at http://papers.ssrn.com/sol3/papers.cfm?abstract_id=2629386.

Kaal, Wulf A. and Bentley J. Anderson, 2016, Unconstrained Mutual Funds and Retail Investor Protection, University of St. Thomas (Minnesota) Legal Studies Research Paper No. 16–18, available at http://papers.ssrn.com/sol3/papers.cfm?abstract_id=2811729.

Katz, Alan, 2014, "SEC Takes Aim at Hedged Mutual Funds' Leverage, Liquidity," *Bloomberg* (April 23), available at https://perma.cc/QDN3-B933.

Kern, Bob, 2012, MSTs Experience Record Growth: How to Meet Regulatory and Legal Administration Requirements of Specialty Investments, *U.S. BanCorp In Focus*, available at https://perma.cc/QD7F-E67Y.

Knowles, David, 2015, Donald Trump Puts "Hedge Fund Guys" on Notice, *Bloomberg Politics* (August 23), available at https://perma.cc/J4AK-5Q8P.

KPMG, 2016, *Taking the Retail Alts Plunge? Considerations Before Launching a Retail Alternative Investment Fund*, available at https://perma.cc/LMN8-HGHW.

Krug, Anita K., 2013, Investment Company as Instrument: The Limitations of the Corporate Governance Regulatory Paradigm, *Southern California Law Review* 86, 263–319.

Langevoort, Donald C., 2005, Private Litigation to Enforce Fiduciary Duties in Mutual Funds: Derivative Suits, Disinterested Directors and the Ideology of Investor Sovereignty, *Washington University Law Quarterly* 83, 1017–44.

Langevoort, Donald C. and Robert B. Thompson, 2013, "Publicness" in Contemporary Securities Regulation after the JOBS Act, *Georgetown Law Journal* 101, 337–86.

Lee, Cecilia C., 2015, Reframing Complexity: Hedge Fund Policy Paradigm for the Way Forward, *Brooklyn Journal of Corporate, Financial and Commercial Law* 9, 478–568.

Leonard, Robert G. et al, 2012, Guide to SEC Investment Adviser Registration for Hedge Fund and Private Equity Fund Managers, *Bingham*, available at https://perma.cc/G4AB-WB2L.

Lhabitant, Francois-Serge, 2007, *Handbook of Hedge Funds* (Wiley & Sons, Hoboken, NJ).

Lowenstein, Roger, 2015, "Hedge Funds' Conspiracy of Mediocrity Keeps Fees High, Returns Low," *Fortune* (May 19), available at http://fortune.com/2015/05/19/hedge-funds-mediocrity.

Mallaby, Sebastian, 2011, *More Money Than God: Hedge Funds and the Making of the New Elite* (Penguin Press, New York).

Managed Funds Association, 2015, *Dodd-Frank at 5: The Role of Alternative Investments in Today's Capital Markets*, available at https://perma.cc/M2DX-597D.

Marriage, Madison, 2014, SEC Widens the Net of Mutual Hedge Fund Review, *Financial Times* (August 24), available at https://perma.cc/D34E-9RTX.

Martin, Cary, 2014, One Step Forward for Hedge Fund Investors: The Removal of the Solicitation Ban and the Challenges That Lie Ahead, *University of Pennsylvania Journal of Business Law* 16, 1143–87.

McCarthy, David F., 2015, Hedge Funds Versus Mutual Funds (2): An Examination of Multialternative Mutual Funds, *Journal of Alternative Investments* 17, 26–42.

McCrary, Stuart A., 2002, *How to Create and Manage a Hedge Fund* (Wiley & Sons, Hoboken, NJ).

McKinsey & Company, 2014, *The Trillion-Dollar Convergence: Capturing the Next Wave of Growth in Alternative Investments*, available at https://perma.cc/E33F-2NAP.

Mills, D. Quinn, 2003, The Problem with Hedge Funds, *Harvard Business School Working Knowledge* (October 6), available at https://perma.cc/3HYY-3QPM.

Morley, John, 2012, Collective Branding and the Origins of Investment Fund Regulation, *Virginia Law and Business Review* 6, 341–401.

Morley, John and Quinn Curtis, 2010, Taking Exit Rights Seriously: Why Governance and Fee Litigation Don't Work in Mutual Funds, *Yale Law Journal* 120, 84–142.

Mutual Fund Directors Forum, 2014, *Report of the Mutual Fund Directors Forum: Board Oversight of Alternative Investments*, available at https://perma.cc/HPA8-MT84.

Nohel, Tom, Z., Jay Wang, and Lu Zheng, 2010, Side-by-Side Management of Hedge Funds and Mutual Funds, *Review of Financial Studies* 23, 2342–73.

Northstar Fin. Advisors Inc. v. Schwab Investments, 779 F.3d 1036 (9th Cir. 2015).

Notice of Filing of Proposed Rule Change Relating to Amendments to NYSE Arca Equities Rule 8.600 to Adopt Generic Listing Standards for Managed Fund Shares, Exchange Act Release No. 34-76486, 80 Fed. Reg. 12,690 (proposed Mar. 10, 2015).

Papagiannis, Nadia, 2013, The World Is Flat: Why the Asset Management World Is Converging, *Alternative Investments Observer* 5, 2–7, available at http://goo.gl/O6GMtQ.

Paul Schott Stevens to Financial Stability Oversight Council, March 25, 2015, available at https://www.ici.org/pdf/15_ici_fsoc_ltr.pdf.

Preqin, 2012, *Preqin Special Report: Banks as Investors in Private Equity*.

Prohibitions and Restrictions on Proprietary Trading and Certain Interest in, and Relationships with, Hedge Funds and Private Equity Funds, 79 Fed. Reg. 5,536, 5,538 (Jan. 31, 2014).

R.W. Grand Lodge of F. & A.M. of Penn. v. Salomon Bros. All Cap Value Fund, 425 F. App'x 25 (2d Cir. 2011).

Redus-Tarchis v. New York Life Inv. Mgmt. LLC, No. CV 14-7991, 2015 WL 6525894, at *1 (D.N.J. Oct. 28, 2015).

Reporting by Investment Advisers to Private Funds and Certain Commodity Pool Operators and Commodity Trading Advisors on Form PF, Investment Advisor Release No. IA-3308, 76 Fed. Reg. 71,128, 71,129 (Nov. 16, 2011).

Revision of Certain Exemptions from Registration for Transactions Involving Limited Offers and Sales, Investment Company Act Release No. 33-6389, 47 Fed. Reg. 11,251 (Mar. 16, 1982).

Revisions of Guidelines to Form N-1A, Investment Company Act Release No. 18612, 57 Fed. Reg. 9,828 (Mar. 20, 1992).

Riggs, David E., Robert C. Rosselot, and Melanie Mayo West, 1996, Securities Regulation of Mutual Funds: A Banker's Primer, *Banking Law Journal* 113, 864–80.

Roiter, Eric D., 2016, Disentangling Mutual Fund Governance from Corporate Governance, *Harvard Business Law Review* 6, 1–82.

S.E.C. v. Ralston Purina Co., 346 U.S. 119 (1953).

Sale, Hillary A., 2011, The New "Public" Corporation, *Law and Contemporary Problems* 74, 137–48.

Sale, Hillary A., 2014, J.P. Morgan: An Anatomy of Corporate Publicness, *Brooklyn Law Review* 79, 1629–55.

Sanders, Bernie, "25 Hedge Fund Managers Made More than 24 Billion, Enough to Pay the Salaries of 425,000 Public School Teachers," *Twitter*, July 21, 2014 (11:06 a.m.), https://twitter.com/sensanders/status/491283067412434946.

SEI, 2013, *The Retail Alternatives Phenomenon: What Enterprising Private Fund Managers Need to Know*.

Seretakis, Alexandros, 2013, Taming the Locusts? Embattled Hedge Funds in the E.U., *New York University Journal of Law and Business* 10, 115–53.

Shilling, Gary, 2012, "Who Loses When Fed Keeps Interest Rates Low?" *BloombergView* (October 30), available at https://perma.cc/D7PP-SF5D.

Sjostrom, William K., Jr., 2005, Tapping the Reservoir: Mutual Fund Litigation Under Section 36(A) of the Investment Company Act of 1940, *University of Kansas Law Review* 54, 251–306.

Stein, Kara M. Mutual Funds—The Next 75 Years. Speech presented at the Brookings Institution, Washington, D.C., June 15, 2015, available at https://perma.cc/PGY5-2UC2.

Stevenson, Alexandra, 2015, For Top 25 Hedge Fund Managers, a Difficult 2014 Still Paid Well, *New York Times Dealbook* (May 5), available at http://goo.gl/z7VwFw.

Strachman, Daniel A., 2007, *The Fundamentals of Hedge Fund Management* (Wiley & Sons, Hoboken, NJ).

Stulz, Rene M., 2007, Hedge Funds: Past, Present, and Future, *Journal of Economic Perspectives* 21, 175–94, available at http://goo.gl/t0NDl8.

Timmons, Heather, 2006, Opening Private Equity's Door, at Least a Crack, to Public Investors, *New York Times* (May 4).

United States Securities and Exchange Commission, SEC Charges Gatekeepers of Two Mutual Funds for Inaccurate Disclosures about Decisions on Behalf of Shareholders, news release, May 2, 2013, http://www.sec.gov/News/PressRelease/Detail/PressRelease/1365171514096.

United States Securities and Exchange Commission, SEC Charges Investment Adviser With Improperly Using Mutual Fund Assets to Pay Distribution Fees, news release, September 21, 2015, https://perma.cc/KG5H-STU9.

United States Securities and Exchange Commission, 2003, *Staff Report: Implications of the Growth of Hedge Funds*, available at https://perma.cc/WAU3-PWPG.

United States Securities and Exchange Commission, 2014, *IM Guidance Update No. 2014-03*, available at https://perma.cc/8JF5-PKT9.

United States Securities and Exchange Commission, OMB No. 3235-0307, Form N-1A, available at https://perma.cc/3M4E-S39Z.

United States Securities and Exchange Commission, Invest Wisely: An Introduction to Mutual Funds, last modified July 2, 2008, accessed August 27, 2015, https://perma.cc/M8UK-94AD.

Use of Derivatives by Investment Companies under the Investment Company Act of 1940, Investment Company Act Release No. 29776, 76 Fed. Reg. 55,237 (Aug. 31, 2011).

Use of Derivatives by Registered Investment Companies and Business Development Companies, Investment Company Act Release No. 31933, 80 Fed. Reg. 80,883 (proposed Dec. 28, 2015).

Vanguard, 2014, *Liquid Alternatives: A Better Mousetrap?* available at https://perma.cc/PE62-ZMYA.

WalkersGlobal, 2015, *Cayman Islands—Guide to Hedge Funds*, available at https://perma.cc/R6C8-7Q5C.

Warren, Russell, 2012, Continuous Innovation in Asset Servicing: The Convergence of Mutual and Hedge Funds, *J.P. Morgan Thought*, available at https://perma.cc/J82J-ZSK8.

White, Mary Jo. "Hedge Funds—A New Era of Transparency and Openness." Speech presented at the Managed Funds Association Outlook 2013 Conference, New York, NY, October 18, 2013, available at https://perma.cc/V7CF-BLHQ.

Zask, Ezra, 2013, *All about Hedge Funds* (McGraw Hill, Columbus, OH).

PART IV

INTERNATIONAL PERSPECTIVES ON INVESTMENT FUNDS

14. The anatomy of European investment fund law
Dirk A. Zetzsche

1 INTRODUCTION

As of December 31, 2017, investment fund managers in the European Union (EU) and the European Economic Area (EEA[1]) managed USD 18.75 trillion, equivalent to 35 percent of worldwide investment fund assets.[2] Among these, USD 11.01 trillion were held by 31,974 Undertakings for Collective Investments in Transferable Securities (UCITS), Europe's most prominent collective investment scheme, with UCITS based in Luxembourg managing 35.9 percent, Ireland 18.8 percent, the UK 12.6 percent, and France 9.0 percent of all UCITS assets. An additional 28,231 non-UCITS collective investment schemes, which European law refers as to as alternative investment funds (AIF),[3] managed an overall USD 7.09 trillion. Germany (28.2 percent), France (17.9 percent), the Netherlands (13.6 percent), and Luxembourg (11.4 percent) headed the list of Europe's AIF locations.

Since outside of Europe little is known about the legal fundamentals underpinning European investment law, this article introduces the principles of such law. Section 2 provides an overview of the relevant sources of law and Section 3 introduces the regulatory objectives. Section 4 explains the pillars of European investment fund law, including the investment triangle, and the joint basis of European manager, depositary, sales, and product regulation. Section 5 offers a discussion of the crucial definitions of and differences between UCITS and AIF. Section 6 unveils the unique features of the UCITSD, and hence the UCITS product, and Section 7 offers an analysis of the future trajectory of European's investment fund law. Section 8 concludes.

2 SOURCES OF LAW

Investment law regulates the activities of asset managers when they are managing the funds of individual clients and pooled (collective) investments of multiple investors. The MiFID framework regulates portfolio management with regard to financial

---

[1] In addition to all EU states, the EEA includes Norway, Iceland, and the Principality of Liechtenstein.
[2] EFAMA, Trends in the European Investment Fund Industry in the Fourth Quarter of 2017 & Results for the Full Year of 2017, EFAMA release March 2018, No. 72; EFAMA, Fact Book, 16th ed. 2017, www.efama.org. Data converted at a rate of EUR 1 = USD 1.2003.
[3] For the distinctive European definition of Alternative Investment Fund (AIF) see *infra* 5.3.

instruments on a discretionary client-by-client basis.[4] An investment activity falls within the scope of MiFID if, according to communications between the asset manager and the client, assets from each client are to be held separately. By contrast, the law of collective investment is regulated by three distinct European Directives: (1) the UCITSD, for indirect investments by the public in financial instruments through diversified funds;[5] (2) a separate framework for pension funds and other occupational retirement systems;[6] and (3) the AIFMD,[7] for all managers of investment funds not regulated by the former two.[8]

Traditional funds marketed to the public and investing in transferable securities and certain other financial instruments based on the principle of risk spreading belong to the domain of the UCITSD. Pension funds are regulated separately since they stand in between asset management and insurance business. Defined benefits schemes where the benefits are guaranteed by the scheme promoter (for example, an industrial company) are closer to the insurance sector. Defined contributions schemes,[9] on the other hand, are in many respects comparable to collective investment schemes under the UCITSD and AIFMD in that they shift market, longevity, and inflation risk to investors and should be regulated accordingly. All managers of collective investment undertakings (CIU) that do not fall within the scope of the UCITSD and the pension fund rules are subject to the AIFMD. For example, the AIFMD regulates entities as diverse as qualified investor funds, where one or a few (institutional) investors negotiate the terms with the fund management company individually, and publicly marketed retail funds in alternative assets (for example, real estate funds).[10]

---

[4] Art. 4(1) No. 8 of the Directive 2014/65/EU ... of 15 May 2014 on markets in financial instruments ... ("MiFID II").

[5] Directive 2009/65/EC ... of 13 July 2009 on the coordination of laws, regulations and administrative provisions relating to undertakings for collective investment in transferable securities (UCITS) (recast), OJ L302/32 (hereafter "UCITSD").

[6] Directive 2003/41/EC ... of 3 June 2003 on the activities and supervision of institutions for occupational retirement provision.

[7] Directive 2011/61/EU ... on Alternative Investment Fund Managers (hereafter "AIFMD").

[8] This article uses the European acronyms as these are not synonymous with US legal terminology. For instance, UCITS is but one diversified type of open-ended fund, while AIF could include both open-ended and closed-ended funds. Speaking about mutual funds would blur the picture. For a detailed view on the terminology see *infra*, at 5.

[9] A defined contribution scheme is a type of retirement scheme in which the amount of the employer's annual contribution is specified. Benefits are based on the amounts credited to these retirement accounts through employer and employee contributions, if applicable, plus any investment earnings on the assets in the account. Defined contribution (DC) schemes do not offer a principal and/or investment guarantee. Only the employer contributions to the account are guaranteed, not the future benefits. Future benefits fluctuate on the basis of investment earnings. Since any defined contribution or defined benefit scheme comes with a lopsided risk structure for one of the stakeholders, intermediate schemes prevail in EU/EEA Member States. For an overview of pension schemes in Europe see EIOPA, Report on risk management rules applicable to IORPs (CEIOPS-OP-22-09), November 6, 2009.

[10] Moreover, while not within the scope of this contribution, unit-linked life insurance and other wrapper products may exhibit economic features similar to investment products.

304 *Research handbook on the regulation of mutual funds*

The European Parliament has adopted a number of variants of the AIFMD, including the European Regulation on Venture Capital Funds (EuVeCaR),[11] the European Regulation on Social Entrepreneurship Funds (EuSEFR),[12] and the European Regulation on Long-Term Investment Funds (ELTIFR).[13] The European Regulation on Money Market Funds (MMFR)[14] applies to both the UCITSD and the AIFMD and addresses the implications of money market funds for MMF investors and the financial system.

Figure 14.1 describes the European regulatory system on a scale ranging from individualism to collectivism.

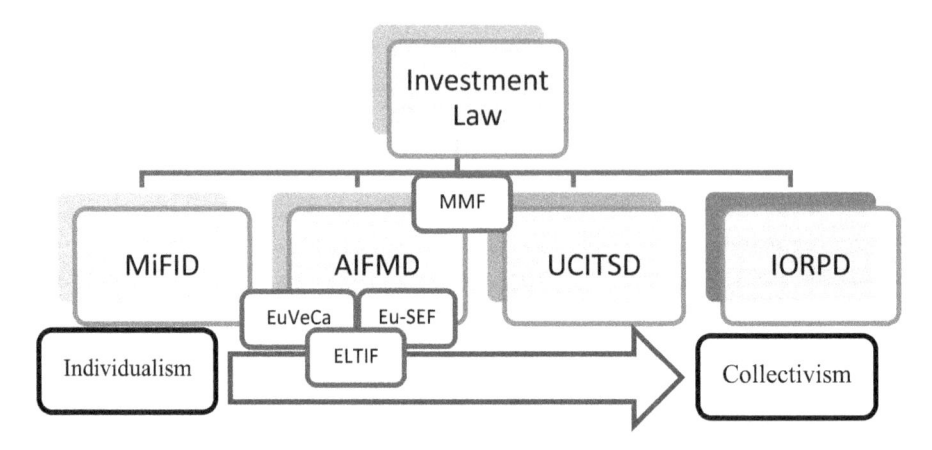

Figure 14.1   European investment law

Together, MiFID, AIFMD, UCITSD, and the pension fund framework ("IORPD") form the basis of European investment law. The AIFMD is also supplemented by three more modern frameworks: the European Venture Capital Fund Regulation (EuVeCaR) and the European Regulation on European Social Entrepreneurship Funds (EuSEFR), which both provide a right to sell fund units across Europe ("European passport"[15]) for certain small-volume AIFs, and the European Regulation on European Long-Term Investment Funds (ELTIFR) for large-volume infrastructure investments, primarily set up as closed-ended funds.

---

[11]   Regulation (EU) No 345/2013 ... of 17 April 2013 on European venture capital funds.
[12]   Regulation (EU) No 346/2013 ... of 17 April 2013 on European social entrepreneurship funds.
[13]   Regulation (EU) 2015/760 ... of 29 April 2015 on European long-term investment funds ("ELTIFR").
[14]   Regulation (EU) 2017/1131 ... of 14 June 2017 on money market funds.
[15]   The European passport refers to a license granting the right to provide financial services crossborder, i.e., in a different country than the regulated entity's home Member State. The concept is crucial for turning several partial autonomous European countries into a single market. For details, see *infra* 2.2.1 and 3.2.

2.1 Historical Development

Given that all legal innovations are built on each other, and then further refined or expanded over the years, European investment law may be best understood from a historical perspective.

2.1.1 UCITS as archetype for the open-ended retail investment fund

The basis for European investment law is the UCITS I Directive of 1985,[16] which came into force on October 1, 1989. Focusing on product regulation only, UCITSD I established a European-wide minimum standard for the authorization and operation of UCITS to meet the two key goals of regulatory harmonization and adequate protection of retail investors.[17]

The initial UCITS Directive instated an authorization requirement with regard to the fund (the "product") as well as minimum standards on the structure of UCITS, the eligible assets, and disclosure requirements. In return, a UCITS authorized in its home Member State could be "passported" to any host Member State within the then European Community (and later the EU and EEA).

While UCITS I provided the foundation for Luxembourg's success as the largest UCITS center in the world,[18] the efficiency of the single market through harmonization was impaired by many Member States imposing stricter requirements which functioned as barriers to the crossborder sale of funds.[19] The strict borrowing and lending limits set by UCITS I were also deemed overly burdensome as they consigned UCITS to the vagaries of the market cycle.

The UCITSD III (Product Directive) of 2001 granted more investment flexibility to UCITS Management Companies ('UCITS ManCos')[20] in response to changing financial market conditions. UCITS III widened the eligibility criteria of investments to include money market instruments, bank deposits, funds of funds, standardized financial futures, options traded on regulated markets, and replication of stock index compositions.[21] For the first time, financial derivatives could be used for investment purposes.[22] UCITS III also raised the thresholds for investing into a single issuer (albeit

---

[16] Directive 85/611/EEC.
[17] Cf. Recitals 1 and 2 of UCITSD I.
[18] Luxembourg provided the first national legislation implementing the UCITSD I, so Luxembourg intermediaries were the first for which the legislation enabling a crossborder license was put in place. While all countries could have taken the same route, most were slow in implementing UCITSD I or added additional rules to the minimum rules required by European law.
[19] See D. Schubauer, *The Inadequacy of the UCITS Directive in a Global Marketplace*, 21:2 New York Law School Journal of International and Comparative Law 323, 324 (2002); N. Moloney, *EU Securities and Financial Markets Regulation*, 3rd ed. (Oxford: Oxford University Press, 2014), at 200.
[20] Directive 2001/108/EC.
[21] Cf. Recital 10 of UCITS III.
[22] With regards to the details on UCITS entering into over-the-counter financial derivatives, see ESMA/2012/832, Guidelines on ETFs and other UCITS issues.

in different securities) to 20 percent and for investments in non-UCITS funds to 30 percent as long as they were sufficiently liquid.[23]

In return for the expanded product range,[24] the UCITS III (Management) Directive of 2001 raised the requirements for the UCITS ManCos by demanding a greater level of sophisticiation to handle more sophisticated financial instruments.[25] Both directives mark a change from product-only regulation to product and manager regulation: with the UCITS III (Product Directive) enabling more and more complex products, regulators deemed product regulation alone insufficient to protect investors; additional rules requiring managers' fitness and properness were planned to ensure that the newly granted freedoms were not abused by fund managing companies. The management passport was introduced concurrently, which for the first time entitled the UCITS ManCos to manage UCITS established in different EU countries.

In order to mitigate the controversy regarding the exact limits of the new eligible asset definitions, the UCITS EAD from 2007,[26] and the accompanying Level 3 guidelines issued by CESR,[27] the predecessor of the European Securities & Markets Authority ("ESMA"),[28] sought to restrict techniques (typically using derivatives) that had been developed by some UCITS ManCos to circumvent the liquidity criteria. However, the UCITS EAD also deemed certain closed-ended funds, asset-backed securities, commercial paper denominated in EUR, index-based derivatives, and credit derivatives to be eligible.

The UCITS IV Directive of 2009 (here "UCITSD")[29] consolidated the status quo. It further introduced some structural features aimed at enhancing fund size, including harmonized rules for master-feeder structures and fund mergers. The simplified prospectus—which did not deserve its name since it was neither simple nor short in practice—was replaced by the UCITS Key Investor Document, a two-page (for

---

[23] UCITS III, Recital 2.
[24] Cf. N. Moloney, *EU Securities and Financial Markets Regulation*, 3rd ed. (Oxford: Oxford University Press, 2014), 236.
[25] Directive 2001/107/EC.
[26] See Commission Directive 2007/16/EC of 19 March 2007 implementing Council Directive 85/611/EEC on the coordination of laws, regulations and administrative provisions relating to undertakings for collective investment in transferable securities (UCITS) as regards the clarification of certain definitions, OJ L79/11 of 20.3.2007('UCITS EAD'); see also CESR, *Advice on Clarification of Definitions concerning Eligible Assets for Investments of UCITS: Consultation Paper*, 05-064b (2005); CESR, *Draft Advice on Clarification of Definitions concerning Eligible Assets for Investments of UCITS: 2nd Consultation Paper*, 05-490b (2005); CESR, *Advice to the European Commission on clarification of definitions concerning eligible assets for investments of UCITS*, 06-005(2006).
[27] See CESR, *CESR's Guidelines Concerning Eligible Assets for Investment by UCITS*, 07-044(2007).
[28] ESMA coordinates financial supervision by the national competent authorities appointed by the EU/EEA Member States and has certain rulemaking, interpreting, and advisory powers regarding European investment fund legislation.
[29] Cf. N. Moloney, *EU Securities and Financial Markets Regulation*, 3rd ed. (Oxford: Oxford University Press, 2014), 200; I. Riassetto & M. Storck, *Les organismes de placement collectif*, 2nd ed. (Joly editions: Issy-les-Moulineaux, 2016), ¶16, 20; D. Zetzsche, *Prinzipien der kollektiven Vermögensanlage* (Tübingen: Mohr Siebeck, 2015), 367–70.

noncomplex funds) or three-page (for complex funds) form setting out investor information. Further rules on market timing and other insider deals working against the funds were added in response to US experiences.

The financial crisis, which brought about CESR's replacement by ESMA,[30] marks the turning point at which a liberal approach toward UCITS became more restrictive. Evidence includes ESMA's strict approach toward the so-called 'trash quota' (see Section 6.2.2) and the post-GFC regulation of money market funds,[31] despite the fact that the former are subject to the UCITSD and the AIFMD. The latter was initiated as a precautionary measure in response to the US experience; European money market funds were remarkably resilient during the financial crisis.

2.1.2 The postcrisis expansion

Funds outside of the scope of the UCITSD (today referred to as AIFs) were not subject to European legislation prior to the adoption of the AIFMD in 2011. While some managers of these funds were subjected to MiFID in relation to their portfolio management and investment activities, and the distribution of fund units that qualified as securities became subject to the Prospectus Directive,[32] private equity and real estate fund managers in particular were able to avoid any regulation in some Member States (notably Germany).

Member States' fund legislation remained fragmented and inconsistent. Ireland, for example, established a regime for product-only qualified investor funds. Germany, by contrast, implemented a form of sophisticated manager regulation limited to open-ended investment funds; open-ended "special" funds for institutional investors were liberated from any significant product rules since the management company was subject to regulation. Closed-ended funds remained unregulated. Luxembourg issued specific laws for specific products (including Partie II for retail funds, SICARs for private equity and venture capital funds, and SIFs for special funds), with either a greater or lesser degree of manager and product regulation. Some type of fund regulation was applied throughout virtually all European jurisdictions—and beyond.[33]

In light of this, the non-UCITS domain was a natural candidate for European harmonization. But as a postcrisis directive the Directive on Alternative Investment Fund Managers of 2011 went well beyond harmonization. The most prominent of crisis-inspired measures included:

- a focus on systemic risk and strong risk oversight by the Competent Authorities;
- enhancing intermediary-specific risk oversight by rending risk management a core activity and imposing oversight obligations upon depositaries;

---

[30] Cf. N. Moloney, *EU Securities and Financial Markets Regulation*, 3rd ed. (Oxford: Oxford University Press, 2014), 938.

[31] *Supra*, n. 14.

[32] Directive 2003/71/EC on the prospectus to be published when securities are offered to the public or admitted to trading and amending Directive 2001/34/EC, OJ L345/64, as amended.

[33] See D. Zetzsche, *Prinzipien der kollektiven Vermögensanlage* (Tübingen: Mohr Siebeck, 2015), at 410–25.

- disincentivizing excessive risk-taking by imposing cross-sectoral rules developed for all financial intermediaries on remuneration and governance;[34]
- scrutinizing the use of leverage;
- mandatory investor protection for professional investors;
- close cooperation between all Competent Authorities and ESMA;
- putting ESMA at the centre of European supervisory activities; and
- considering stakeholder governance as a regulatory objective in addition to investor and market governance.[35]

In the context of the four European investment law directives (see Section 2.1), the AIFMD played a vital role in defining the future trajectory of European investment law. This particularly concerned the following regulatory innovations:

- the enhanced depositary framework (imposing strict liability for lost assets) as a consequence of the Madoff scandal and the Lehmann insolvency;[36]
- the rules on manager governance, especially with respect to remuneration of the manager as a reaction to some of the excesses associated with the bankers' pay;[37] and
- a high degree of supervisory cooperation under the auspices of ESMA in order to mitigate the effect of national borders on the intensity of supervisory scrutiny (see Section 2.2.3).

All three aspects influenced the succeeding reforms of European investment law, as will be pointed out in detail with regard to the UCITS framework in Section 6.

The AIFMD also influenced the banking directives, in particular the Capital Requirement Directives. This is because (1) many banks function as distribution channels for AIFs and (2) credit institutions often provide depositary functions to AIFs.

---

[34] See European Commission, *Commission Staff Working Document: Corporate Governance in Financial Institutions: Lessons to be Drawn from the Current Financial Crisis, Best Practices; Accompanying Document to the Green Paper Corporate Governance in Financial Institutions and Remuneration Policies*, SEC (2010) 669, June 2, 2010.

[35] D. Zetzsche, Investment Law as Financial Law: From Fund Governance over Market Governance to Stakeholder Governance? 337 in *The European Financial Markets in Transition* (H.S. Birkmose, M. Neville, & K.E. Sorensen eds, Alphen aan den Rijn: Wolters Kluwer Law, 2012); the CSR dimension is examined by D. Zetzsche & C. Preiner, CSR, Responsible Investments and the AIFMD, 167–92 in *The Alternative Investment Fund Managers' Directive: European Regulation of Alternative Investment Funds* (D. Zetzsche ed., 2nd ed. Alphen aan den Rijn: Wolters Kluwer 2015). For details, see *infra* 3.3.

[36] For details see S. Hooghiemstra, Depositary Regulation, 479–520; C. Clerc, The AIF Depositary's Liability for Lost Assets, 521–30. 18; and J. Siena, Depositary Liability—A Fine Mess and How to Get Out of It, 531–72, in *The Alternative Investment Fund Managers' Directive: European Regulation of Alternative Investment Funds* (D. Zetzsche ed., 2nd ed., Alphen aan den Rijn: Wolters Kluwer 2015). See also *infra* at 5.1 for details.

[37] For details see P. Câmara, The AIFM's Governance and Remuneration Committees: The Impact of the AIFMD, 293–310, in *The Alternative Investment Fund Managers' Directive: European Regulation of Alternative Investment Funds* (D. Zetzsche ed., Alphen aan den Rijn: Wolters Kluwer 2015).

For both, credit institutions will need to meet capital requirements for covering operational and off-balance sheet risk. The potential liability of depositaries has raised concerns in the industry that either the depositary business will not be viable from an economic perspective or that investments will not bear reasonable returns due to enhanced costs for depositaries.

The AIFMD's systemic risk perspective has been accompanied by two additional pieces of regulation: the Regulation on Securities Financing Transactions (SFTR)[38] and the Regulation Securitization (STSR).[39] The SFTR adds disclosure requirements to European investment law for investment funds actively investing in derivatives and capital markets techniques while the STSR provides a more extensive general regulatory framework for securitization.[40]

2.1.3 From risk management to growth: capital market union

The AIFMD's spinoffs—the European regulations on venture capital, social entrepreneurship, and long-term investment funds—do not take the same stringent approach. While the AIFMD's function is to primarily limit risks in the financial system, the European Parliament adopted the three other pieces of legislation in order to promote specific socioeconomic objectives in the public interest. EuVeCaR is supposed to provide assistance to innovative startups by closing the early stage gap of young, innovative firms; EuSEFR should support companies which forgo maximum profits for the social good; and ELTIFR is supposed to increase the amount of investment in European infrastructure.

Little has been done to practically implement these three pieces of legislation. The European Commission's Capital Market Union (CMU) workplan is therefore currently seeking to further liberalize European investment law in certain sectors,[41] and a reform proposal for the EuVeCaR and EuSEFR has recently been adopted.[42]

2.2 Degree of Harmonization

With regard to potential regulatory competition and the efficiency of the single market within the EU and the EEA, it is crucial to understand from a legal perspective the level of discretion which Member States can deploy when implementing and applying

---

[38] See Regulation (EU) 2015/2365 ... of 25 November 2015 on transparency of securities financing transactions and of reuse and amending Regulation (EU) No 648/2012, OJ L 337/1.

[39] See Regulation (EU) 2017/2402 ... of 12 December 2017 laying down a general framework for securitization and creating a specific framework for simple, transparent and standardized securitization (...).

[40] For a US–EU comparison see Steven L. Schwarcz, Securitization and Post-Crisis Financial Regulation, 101 *Cornell Law Review* 115 (2016).

[41] European Commission, Action Plan on Building a Capital Markets Union, 30.9.2015, COM(2015) 468 final.

[42] Cf. European Commission, Proposal for a Regulation amending Regulation (EU) No 345/2013 on European venture capital funds (EuVECA) and Regulation (EU) No 346/2013 on European social entrepreneurship funds (EuSEF)—14.07.2016, COM(2016) 461 final.

European investment law. In a world where Member States benefit from the establishment of investment funds and fund managers within their territories while the harm created by financial intermediaries is borne by the distribution countries, harmonization of legislation and supervision provides the counterweight to national egotism.

2.2.1 Legislation

While a directive—in particular the UCITSD or the AIFMD—requires implementation and adoption by the Member States in order to come into force, regulation—such as the EuVeCaR, ELTIFR, MMFR, and EuSEFR—takes effect immediately upon the date it comes into force.

Directives are deemed legal acts requiring implementation at the discretion of individual Member States. Regulations, by contrast, must be enacted in the same way throughout the Member States. In practice, however, the distinction between the two in relation to harmonized application is slight. Many regulatory ordinances issued by the European Securities & Markets Authority, for instance, limit Member State discretion when implementing a directive while the wording of regulations remains fragmentary in practice. This leaves many questions open for the Member States. The EuVeCaR, EuSEFR, and ELTIFR European investment fund regulations refer implicitly to national investment fund legislation rather than issuing a statute on the formation and establishment of the investment fund.

The UCITSD and the AIFMD define the level of harmonization. With regard to manager regulation (see Section 5.2), full harmonization applies, meaning that Member States shall neither add to nor water down requirements set by European law.[43] With regard to product regulation (see Section 5.5), Member States may be prevented from reducing requirements, although they may add requirements. Generally speaking, the UCITSD limits the maximum exposure of a UCITS to one security to 5 percent of the fund's assets under management,[44] although Member States may set the limit at 3 percent. The AIFMD also refrains from prescribing investment strategies for AIFs, although Member States may add product-related rules. In practice, Member States set additional rules for certain retail funds while they take a more liberal stance with regard to funds for sophisticated investors.

2.2.2 Level of detail: the AIFMD

The AIFM framework consists of several legislative acts. The AIFMD constitutes the basis that must be implemented as a national bill by Member States. Since the AIFMD's principles are rather vague, many provisions of the AIFMD allow many legislative acts to be delegated to the European Commission.[45] These so-called Level 2 measures consist of the AIFMD (Commission) Regulation as the main body of

---

[43] See Recitals 6–10 and Art. 43 AIFMD (arg ex); re UCITS see, inter alia, the entitlements granted to ESMA under Art. 7(6) UCITSD (detailing the conditions for authorization) as well as the Commission's power to issue delegated acts in Ch. III, Section III "Operating Conditions."
[44] Cf. Art. 51(1) lit. UCITSD.
[45] See Arts 3, 4, 9, 12, 14–25, 34–7, 40, 42, 53, 67, and 68 AIFMD.

implementing legislation,[46] and three smaller regulations. These measures deal with the extent to which fund managers opt into the AIFMD, the determination of a third country ("TC") AIFM's Member State of Reference, the Memorandum of Understanding which the authorities participating in ESMA sign with national regulators of third countries, and clarification on the types of AIFM to which the AIFMD refers.[47] Level 3 ESMA guidelines deal with the scope of the AIFMD pertaining to the definition of AIF, the reporting obligations of "small" AIFM and fully authorized AIFM, and the remuneration system of the AIF manager.[48] Future guidelines are expected on the asset segregation requirements that depositaries have to meet.[49]

The AIFMD (Commission) Regulation takes direct effect in EU and EEA Member States pursuant to the "Lamfalussy" approach.[50] The European Commission may adopt measures as binding technical standards which are "implementing technical standards"[51] and "regulatory technical standards."[52] Regulatory technical standards are "delegated acts." The European Parliament and Council may raise objections to the delegated act and therefore prevent the act from entering into force.[53] Conversely, neither the Parliament nor Council can overturn the implementation of technical

---

[46] See Commission Delegated Regulation (EU) No 231/2013 of 19 December 2012 supplementing Directive 2011/61/EU ... with regard to exemptions, general operating conditions, depositaries, leverage, transparency and supervision.

[47] See Commission Implementing Regulation (EU) No 447/2013 of 15 May 2013 establishing the procedure for AIFMs which choose to opt in under Directive 2011/61/EU (...); Commission Implementing Regulation (EU) No 448/2013 of 15 May 2013 establishing a procedure for determining the Member State of reference of a non-EU AIFM (...); Commission Delegated Regulation (EU) No 694/2014 of 17 December 2013 ... with regard to regulatory technical standards determining types of alternative investment fund managers.

[48] See *Guidelines on Reporting Obligations under Art. s 3(3)(d) and 24(1), (2) and (4) of the AIFMD*, ESMA/2014/869; *Guidelines on the model MoU concerning consultation, cooperation and the exchange of information related to the supervision of AIFMD entities*, ESMA/2013/998; *Guidelines on sound remuneration policies under the AIFMD*, ESMA/2013/232; ESMA/2016/411, *Guidelines on sound remuneration policies under the UCITS Directive*, ESMA/2016/575; *Guidelines on sound remuneration policies under the AIFMD*, ESMA/2016/579; *Guidelines on sound remuneration policies under the UCITS Directive and AIFMD*, ESMA, *Guidelines on key concepts of the AIFMD*, ESMA/2013/600 (May 24, 2013).

[49] See ESMA, *Consultation Paper: Guidelines on Asset Segregation under the AIFMD*, ESMA/2014/1326; ESMA/2016/1137, Call for evidence: Asset segregation and custody services.

[50] The Lamfalussy process is an approach to the development of financial law used by the European Union that is named after the chair of the EU advisory committee that created it, Baron Alexandre Lamfalussy. It is composed of four "levels," each focusing on a specific stage of the implementation of legislation, ranging from material decisions vested in Parliament to technical details being implemented by the European Commission, guidelines drawn up by the European Supervisory Authorities, and mere factual coordination among the national competent authorities of Member States at the lowest level. See Alexander Schaub, The Lamfalussy Process Four Years On, 13:2 *Journal of Financial Regulation & Compliance* 110–20 (2005). The Lamfalussy process was reformed after the GFC to reflect the establishment of the three European supervisory authorities, ESMA, EBA, and EIOPA, for the securities, banking, and insurance/pension sectors respectively, and to achieve more harmonization and better enforcement.

[51] "Implementing acts" pursuant to Art. 291 TFEU.

[52] "Delegated acts" pursuant to Art. 290 TFEU.

[53] And may also revoke the delegation: see Arts 57 and 58 AIFMD.

standards. ESMA is authorized to draft both kinds of binding technical standards that the Commission may subsequently adopt.[54]

The AIFMD entitles ESMA to issue guidelines with advisory, sometime even binding effect upon the supervisory authorities within the EU.[55] The legal character of these guidelines is far from clear.[56] Questions relating to these guidelines include (1) how these guidelines can be justified from a constitutional perspective that upholds the principle of sovereign legislative power,[57] (2) whether these guidelines have a binding effect on private law relations between the manager, the depositary, the AIF, and its investors,[58] and (3) the way in which persons, entities, or supervisory authorities may effectively appeal in cases where they deem a guideline inappropriate or even illegal.[59]

Notwithstanding the high level of detail provided by European law, some questions remain in Member State jurisdiction. Member State jurisdiction pertains to (1) the type of AIF (in contrast to the UCITSD, the AIFMD does not regulate the AIF's investment strategy),[60] (2) the contract, trust, corporate, and partnership law which forms the legal basis for the fund establishment, (3) product and distribution rules aimed at the protection of retail investors, and (4) national requirements for subthreshold AIFs exempted from the AIFMD (so-called "small" AIFMs[61]).

2.2.3 Supervision

Despite the existence of a European Securities & Market Authority (ESMA), national financial regulators (referred to as National Competent Authorities—NCAs) supervise European investment funds and their managers. A reference point for supervision may either be the manager, the product (that is, the fund itself) or the distribution/sales disclosure and conduct (see Section 4.4).

---

[54] See D. Weber-Rey & C. Baltzer, Verlautbarungen der EU und der BaFin zur internen Governance von Banken: 1. Lamfalussy-Verfahren, in *Handbuch Corporate Governance von Banken* (K.J. Hopt & G. Wohlmann-Stetter eds, Munich: Vahlen/C.H. Beck 2011), p. 371 et seq., providing further details on the Lamfalussy process in financial law.
[55] See Arts 34 to 38, 40, 42, and 47 AIFMD.
[56] See E. Wymeersch, Europe's Financial Regulatory Bodies, 337–56 in *The European Financial Markets in Transition* (H.S. Birkmose, M. Neville, & K.E. Sorensen eds, Alphen aan den Rijn: Wolters Kluwer Law, 2012); N. Moloney, *The European Securities and Markets Authority and Institutional Design for the EU Financial Market—A Tale of Two Competences: Part (2) Rules in Action*, 12 European Business Organisation Law Review 177–225 (2011).
[57] See K. Langenbucher, *Zur Zulässigkeit parlamentsersetzender Normgebungsverfahren im Europarecht*, 10 Zeitschrift fur Europäisches Privatrecht 265 (2002).
[58] See J.A. Kämmerer, *Das neue Europäische Finanzaufsichtssystem (ESFS)—Modell für eine europäisierte Verwaltungsarchitektur?* Neue Zeitschrift für Verwaltungsrecht 1281–8 (2011).
[59] See N. Sonder, *Rechtsschutz gegen Maßnahmen der neuen europäischen Finanzaufsichtsagenturen*, Bank und Kapitalmarktrecht 8 (2012); M. Lehmann, C. Manger-Nestler, *Die Vorschläge zur neuen Architektur der europäischen Finanzaufsicht*, 91 Europäische Zeitschrift für Wirtschaftsrecht 87–92 (2010).
[60] Recital 10 AIFMD.
[61] Cf. Art. 3(2) AIFMD.

However, the crisis revealed significant weaknesses in the sketchy European enforcement landscape. In particular, not all Member States' financial regulators were equally equipped to enforce, and equally strict in enforcing, European minimum standards enabling intermediaries' shopping for arbitrage. In light of this, the AIFMD touched upon new territory when it made the supervisory cooperation and mediation process under the auspices of ESMA a requirement.[62] Given the crossborder dimension and impact of the AIFMD along with the tendency to champion national industries, the harmonization of supervision by ESMA is a more than welcome addition. However, ESMA still relies on national expertise for its various expert circles. Since the larger Member States focus on the sales dimension, rather than the intermediary ('production') dimension of the fund industry, I expect an intermediary-hostile rather than a sensible, middle-of-the-road approach.[63] The AIFMD's approach has been mirrored by the AIFMD's spinoffs as well as the UCITSD V reform that came into force in 2016.[64]

Today, European investment law is characterized by cross-sectoral consistency concerning the instruments that NCAs may put to use,[65] the level of information exchange among NCAS, and the available sanctions.[66] On this matter, it is not only cross-sector consistency, but also the efficient enforcement of European financial law that drives developments.

2.3 Investor Type

If sorted by investor type, the UCITS stands in the retail domain while the AIFMD provides manager regulation that forms, at its core, the basis for funds marketed to professional investors. At the same time, the AIFMD's standard for professional investors functions as a minimum standard for fund managers that manage funds marketed to retail investors. For this reason, and despite their history, the AIFMD may be deemed the basic law and the UCITSD the *lex specialis* to the AIFMD. European

---

[62] See Arts 47 and 50 AIFMD.

[63] See D. Zetzsche, Competitiveness of Financial Centers in Light of Financial and Tax Law Equivalence Requirements at 390 in *Rethinking Global Financial Law and its Regulation* (R. Buckley, D. Arner, & E. Avgouleas eds, Cambridge: Cambridge University Press 2016).

[64] Cf. Art. 101 UCITSD, as amended by Directive 2014/91/EU ... of 23 July 2014 amending Directive 2009/65/EC on the coordination of laws, regulations and administrative provisions relating to undertakings for collective investment in transferable securities (UCITS) as regards depositary functions, remuneration policies and sanctions ("UCITS V"), OJ L257/186-213.

[65] Cross-sectoral consistency refers to the objective of having the same principles embedded in all pieces of European investment legislation regardless of whether an entity is licensed under the UCITSD, the AIFMD, the MiFID, or the respective satellites of the former, such as the MMFR, EuVeCaR, EuSEFR, and ELTIFR.

[66] Cf. Ch. XII Provisions concerning the authorities responsible for authorization and supervision, as amended by UCITS V. The AIFMD (in Ch. IX "Competent Authorities") and the EuVeCaR and EuSEFR (both in Ch. III "Supervision and Administrative Cooperation") harmonize supervisory instruments and information exchange; while refraining from harmonizing sanctions, the European Commission is to ensure that the administrative penalties and other measures provided for shall be effective, proportionate, and dissuasive. See Art. 48 AIFMD and Arts 20, 26(1) EuVeCar and EuSEFR.

314   *Research handbook on the regulation of mutual funds*

legislation for venture capital and social entrepreneurship funds (EuVeCaR, EuSEFR) also addresses the AIFMD's professional audience, adding that high net worth individuals (HNWis) qualify as investors for those funds. The legislation for long-term investment funds (ELTIFR) provides product regulation that modifies and expands the AIFMD's manager regulation to enable retail investors to invest. Only retail investors that have financial assets of at least EUR 100,000 may invest in ELTIFs.

Similarly, the Money Market Fund Regulation straddles the UCITSD and the AIFMD,[67] meaning money market funds can be structured as UCITS for retail investors or AIFs for (primarily) professional investors.

Figure 14.2 shows the resulting structure of European investment fund law by investor type.

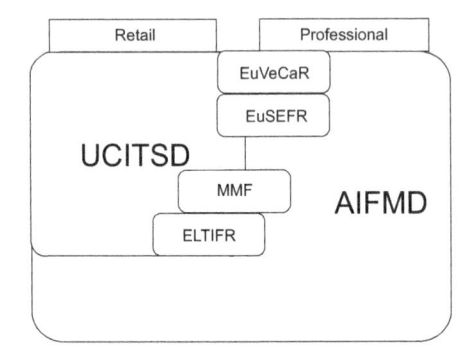

Figure 14.2   European investment fund law by investor type

2.4   Category of Regulation: Manager, Depositary, Product, and Sales Regulation

All investment law may be categorized according to its regulatory topic. This includes the regulation of investment fund managers, depositaries, the product (that is, the fund), and its marketing/distribution to investors.

Today, the UCITSD is the sole European investment fund legislation that covers all categories. As a product and sales regulation that originally provided some depositary regulation, it was supplemented by the full-fledged regulation of the UCITS ManCo with UCITS III (parallel to an expansion of the product range). When UCITS IV expanded the sales and manager regulation, the product regulation was supplemented with master-feeder and fund merger rules. UCITS V's expansion of the depositary and manager regulation marks the latest regulatory development.

The AIFMD focuses on manager and depositary regulation. It provides marketing rules regarding professional investors only and refrains from product rules altogether. The ELTIFR builds on the AIFMD, providing additional depositary, sales, and—for the most part—product regulation that allows the AIFMD passport to expand into the retail domain. The Money Market Funds Regulation,[68] relying on both the AIFMD's and

---

[67]   *Supra*, n. 15.
[68]   *Supra*, n. 15.

UCITSD's manager regulation, focuses on product regulation but also adds obligations for the manager with regard to valuation, liquidity management, and stress testing as well as additional Know Your Customer requirements. The latter shall not protect the investors; rather, they shall prevent concurrent redemptions by several investors creating liquidity stress on the side of the fund.

By contrast, the EuVeCaR and EuSEFR provide for some low-key manager regulation as well as some product regulation; the sales and depositary dimension has not been addressed (see Table 14.1).

Table 14.1 European investment fund law by regulatory content

	Manager	Depositary	Product	Sales
UCITSD	X	X	X	X
AIFMD	X	X	(–)	(x) [professional investors]
MMFR	X	(–)	X	(x)
ELTIFR	(x)	(x)	X	(x)
EuVeCaR	(x)	(–)	X	(x)
EuSEF	(x)	(–)	X	(x)

2.5 Public or Private Law Dimension

European investment law may also be categorized according to its effects on private law. While some rules almost certainly address supervisory institutions only (such as cooperation and information exchange rules), to the extent of this writer's knowledge, the marketing rules have consequences on private law in all EU/EEA Member States in that wrongful disclosure leads to liability. Similarly, a violation of product rules (for instance, investment limits) prompts liability if the violation causes harm and the claimant may prove at least negligence.

The extent to which the manager and depositary regulation apportions manager or depositary liability is uncertain at best. Parliament answered the question in ruling that the depositary carries strict liability for lost assets and negligence-based liability for other violations in the AIFMD's and UCITS V's depositary section.[69] Thus the question remains open only for the manager regulation, including risk and liquidity management requirements, rules on the fund manager's personal compensation, and conduct of business rules, for example regarding conflicts of interest. Since fund management is a fiduciary relationship vis-à-vis the fund and its investors, on a general basis manager regulation prompts private law effects and may be enforced by investor suits and class actions where available.

---

[69] Cf. Art. 24 UCITSD; Art. 21 AIFMD.

3 REGULATORY OBJECTIVES

In addition to the traditional dualism of investor and market protection European investment law is concerned with two more objectives: building a single European market for capital and financial services and the protection of certain stakeholders including the public interest.

3.1 Traditional Dualism of Investor and Market Protection

Financial law serves to protect investors and the financial markets.[70] The law of investor protection looks after the interests of the investing public and/or individual investors. It does this by attempting to reduce or limit transaction costs such as intermediary fees and indirect benefits from inducements and by enhancing the stability of financial intermediaries through measures such as the fit and proper test for its directors, minimum capitalization, and organizational requirements.

In contrast, financial law protects financial markets or the financial system, respectively, as a whole by taking a macroeconomic perspective. Legislation refers to this function when it tries to protect market integrity and the stability of the financial system. This objective reflects the overall desirability of a well-functioning financial market from a welfare economics point of view and strives for circumstances in which markets and financial intermediaries function best. For example, insider trading and disclosure rules seek to protect investors' faith in the fairness of capital markets. Maintaining trust in the market is a way to reduce transaction costs, enhance liquidity, and let markets perform their pricing and liquidity functions efficiently.

In addition to financial markets, financial law stabilizes financial institutions because they constitute a necessary link to financial markets. Financial intermediaries facilitate investors' access to information, financial markets, and assets. One of the most important aspects of their intermediating function is their tailoring of cash flows to time, liquidity, and risk level according to investor and operating business demands. Financial intermediaries guide cashflow streams to their most productive use by taking monies from where there is a surplus and channeling it to where there is demand and—at the same time—the paying of risk-adequate returns. Efficient financial intermediation and dynamic growth go hand in hand.[71] If this causal relationship is

---

[70] D. Zetzsche, Investment Law as Financial Law: From Fund Governance over Market Governance to Stakeholder Governance? at 341–5 in *The European Financial Markets in Transition* (H. S. Birkmose, M. Neville, & K. E. Sorensen eds, Alphen aan den Rijn: Wolters Kluwer Law, 2012).

[71] See R.W. Goldsmith, *Financial Structure and Development* (New Haven and London: Yale University Press 1969), at 48; J. Greenwood & B. Jovanovic, Financial Development, Growth and the Distribution of Income, 98:5 *Journal of Political Economy* 1076 (1990); G.S. Paul, Technological Choice, Financial Markets, and Economic Development, 36 *European Economic Review* 763 (1992); V.R. Bencivenga & B.D. Smith, Financial Intermediation and Endogenous Growth, 58 *Review of Economic Studies* 195 (1991).

accepted, there is no need to pursue a futile discussion on whether financial infrastructure is a precondition for growth,[72] or whether markets-based (intermediated) financing is superior to bank-based (relationship) finance.[73]

3.1.1 The past: investor protection

The history of investment law prior to European harmonization shows the key role played by investor protection concerns. The first fund legislation on the European continent (for instance, that in Germany in the 1950s) had a vital interest in furthering investment, given the scarcity of capital for entrepreneurial purposes following World War II. The laws finally put in place were in many respects modeled on the US ICA 1940, whose key objective was investor protection.

The first generation of European investment law—the UCITSD 85/611 and the Investment Services Directive 93/22—were followed by a second generation of laws that included the MIFID, three UCITSDs (2001/108, 2001/109, and 2009/65(recast)), and the pension fund rules ("IORPD"). Albeit not the exclusive focus of these directives, investor protection was dominant in the first and second generations of European investment law.

3.1.2 The present: investor and market protection from the systemic risk perspective

The third generation of European investment regulation was strongly influenced by the financial crisis of the late 2000s. This is in addition to an investment industry that has seen its operating environment undergo significant changes.

One of the most striking changes of the past 30 years is the investment industry's progression from a niche player in the financial system to one of its fundamental pillars. This growth can be attributed on the one hand to an increasingly wealthy and aging society that depends on savings and retirement income, and on the other to the general tendency to choose not a state-backed pension system but a capital-based one with a greater private component. Given that professional investors constitute a fundamental pillar of today's financial system, it should be ensured that they are effectively regulated. If investment regulation is deficient, the greater the investment, the more detrimental its effects on financial markets and the public. As these institutional holdings grow in importance, their collective power can also distort market valuations and unbalance a state's financial sector. Regulators and policymakers may see themselves pressed to interfere in the investment market due to the sheer size of professionally managed funds. But they should also keep in mind that few of these institutions are "too big to fail," while they are collectively "too big to systematically do wrong." It comes as no surprise, then, that the risks associated with professional

---

[72] For the existence of financial infrastructure as a precondition of growth see J.A. Schumpeter, *Theorie der Wirtschaftlichen Entwicklung* (Berlin: Dunchker & Humblot, 1911) 193; R. Sylla, Financial Systems and Economic Modernization, 62 *Journal of Economic History* 281 (2002).

[73] Cf. L. Deidda & B. Fattouh, Banks, Financial Markets and Growth, 17:1 *Journal of Financial Intermediation* 6 (2008) (change from relationship banking to financial markets-based finance does not necessarily enhance growth); *contra* R. Levine, Bank-Based or Market-Based Financial Systems: Which Is Better? 11:4 *Journal of Financial Intermediation* (2002), 398–428.

investments received the same level of parliamentary attention as capital markets crises' impact on the public.

3.1.3 Progenitors of market governance

Recent investment law legislation represents a shift from an approach based on fund investor protection—mixed with the probusiness attitude of some early European fund laws—to one where a balance is maintained between investor protection and market governance. Three regulatory changes embody this shift: (1) limits on leverage;[74] (2) regulating remuneration policies;[75] and (3) the regulatory approach toward risk management, in particular that risk management should not only assist in identifying and controlling typical risks to investors or the companies but also reduce risks that may impact markets. Risk-based supervision is a principle and legal obligation found in all branches of modern European investment law.[76]

The dualism of fund and market governance is sound for the most part. This is due to the basic idea that both institutions—investors and markets—depend on each other. Without investors there are no markets, and without fair and efficient markets investors are likely to leave as they cannot expect fair treatment or a fair pricing function. Without liquid markets, asset managers cannot sell the assets on investors' demand.

The pricing and liquidity service provided by well-functioning capital markets is not at odds with investor protection, but in line with it. All financial actors are interconnected in advanced capital markets. For example, money market funds provide short-term liquidity for banks and commercial entities. During the financial crisis of the late 2000s one US money market fund collapsed, several suffered runs, and all US funds were deeply threatened by systemic instability.[77] Investors consequently suffered to the same extent as banks and commercial entities that could not refinance themselves and businesses that depended on bank lending. To a certain extent, recent developments have brought back to the forefront of the public and regulators' collective consciousness the principle that market governance is just the flip side of fund governance. Investor and market protection go hand in hand.

However, some aspects of these two objectives are incompatible. One conflict results from excessive use of leverage. Enhancing leverage can further investors' goals, as the

---

[74] Cf. Art. 25 AIFMD. For details, see R. Wilhelmi & M. Bassler, AIFMD, Systemic Risk and the Financial Crisis, 23–48, and F. Dornseifer, Hedge Funds and Systemic Risk Reporting, 627–48, in *The Alternative Investment Fund Managers' Directive: European Regulation of Alternative Investment* Funds (D. Zetzsche ed., 2nd ed., Alphen aan den Rijn: Wolters Kluwer 2015).

[75] Art. 13, Annex II AIFMD, Arts 14–14b UCITS V. For details, see P. Câmara, *The AIFM's Governance and Remuneration Committees: The Impact of the AIFMD*, at 293, in *The Alternative Investment Fund Managers' Directive: European Regulation of Alternative Investment Funds* (D. Zetzsche ed., 2nd ed., Alphen aan den Rijn: Wolters Kluwer 2015).

[76] See, in particular, the implementing provisions to the UCITSD in Art. 12, 38-45 Commission Directive 2010/43/EU; Recitals 21, 24, 81, 89 and Arts. 13(1) and 15–16 AIFMD ("The single AIFM to be appointed pursuant to this Directive should never be authorized to provide portfolio management without also providing risk management or vice versa").

[77] See William A. Birdthistle, Breaking Bucks in Money Market Funds, 5 *Wisconsin Law Review* 1155 (2010); see also Jill E. Fisch, Tales from the dark side: money market funds and the shadow banking debate, in this book, *supra*, at pp. 228 et seq.

returns are potentially unlimited while losses are limited by virtue of the limited liability which comes along with collective investments. The market may prove unfit to assume the risks that are a consequence of leverage. While margin requirements protect the market against financial hazards, a liquidity crisis may render inefficient margin as a market-inherent safeguard. Margin requirements are useless when assets cannot be sold at the price used for calculating the margin requirement. In such a state, legal limits on leverage may provide alternative protection for the counterparties,[78] as they limit the maximum loss that their counterparty must bear in case of default. For example, if the AIFM is entitled to take on debt limited at 300 percent of the AIF's assets, the maximum loss to the market (as the combined counterparties to the AIF in question) is three times the amount of the AIF's assets at the time the AIFM entered into the contract.

Another point needs emphasis: moral hazard is not specific to financial institutions. Nonfinancial institutions may manipulate the system to the same extent as financial institutions. Safeguards protecting the market from moral hazard need to be imposed on all participants, not just investment market participants. Exemptions from rules that are deemed important should thus be carefully scrutinized.

While inconsistencies appear whenever the law promotes more than one policy objective—no man can serve two masters—legal objectives' conflicts between protecting investors and protecting the markets are limited to specific circumstances and have a minor impact in relative terms.

3.2 Furthering the Single Capital Market

Other objectives of European investment law include the single market ideal, according to which enhancing the size and competitiveness of the common market will enhance crossborder market efficiency.[79]

3.2.1 European passports

3.2.1.1 Foundation in European constitutional law The European Union was established as economic union under the premise of a free, borderless single market. The Treaty on the Functioning of the European Union defines integration into a single market as the main goal of EU policy.[80]

---

[78] Cf. Art. 25(3), (7), (8) AIFMD.
[79] For the first generation see Recitals 1 UCITSD 85/611("Whereas national laws governing collective investment undertakings should be coordinated with a view to approximating the conditions of competition between those undertakings at Community level, while at the same time ensuring more effective and more uniform protection for unit-holders"). For the second generation see Recitals 4, 88, and 90, and Art. 67(6) of AIFMD (listing the objectives of the AIFMD with "the internal market, investor protection and the effective monitoring of systemic risk"; Recitals 27, 51, and 52 UCITSD ("In order to facilitate the effective operation of the internal market and to ensure the same level of investor protection throughout the Community, master-feeder structures should be allowed").
[80] Cf. Art. 26 TFEU.

3.2.1.2 Rationale The rationale underlying the single market objective is that larger markets lead to lower costs, or an enhanced product range. Take Luxembourg, with its slightly fewer than 600,000 inhabitants, as an example. A Luxembourg UCITS comes along with setup costs of at least EUR 100,000. If UCITS fund units can be sold only to investors in Luxembourg, very few UCITS, if any, will be established. In turn, very few investment strategies would be applied by fund managers, limiting investor choice. Investors would be forced to buy the handful or so products available under these conditions.

On the upside, the borderless market for investment funds enhances market efficiency and makes a large variety of products available to inhabitants and businesses of small EU countries. At the same time, larger countries benefit from the increased competition, either through lower prices, greater product variety, or the financial innovation provided by intermediaries based in other EU countries.

On the downside, crossborder access may facilitate regulatory arbitrage. The risk of regulatory arbitrage is low as long as the home and host countries' financial services attach the same level of importance to investor protection and systemic risk prevention. Whether this is the case depends on the demand for and supply of financial services within the home and host countries. For example, in some financial centers, supply and demand of financial services might be equally high,[81] while the intermediaries in other countries primarily provide supply-side financial services (hereafter referred to as a production country) or demand-side services (referred to as a distribution country). Where demand and supply are equal we expect balanced regulation and supervision which takes the needs of both intermediaries and investors/clients into account.

However, if either the production or the distribution component of financial services is of greater importance, the government and the regulators have incentives to overly protect intermediaries in production countries or investors in distribution countries. In the latter case, which constitutes an imbalance in supply and demand within one country, an intermediary from a production country is likely to be subject to laxer laws and enforcement than intermediaries in the distribution countries.

European investment law counters regulatory arbitrage and race-to-the-bottom-style competition with harmonization.[82] In fact, a race to the bottom is most likely to occur when externalities exist, that is, when upsides can be concentrated in one country and downsides (such as investor damages) can be allocated to other countries. European law, however, requires home country regulators and enforcement agencies to adopt rules and enforcement that is similar, if not identical, to the laws and regulation of the host country. Close cooperation between regulators ensures that misconduct in a host country will be sanctioned in the intermediary's home country. In order to ensure a regulator's grip on an intermediary, the statutory seat and the head office of an

---

[81] For instance, Liechtenstein intermediaries offer services to thousands of trusts and foundations. Both demand (by foundations and trusts) and supply (by intermediaries) are important for Liechtenstein regulators.

[82] See, on the US, J. Adler, Interstate Competition and the Race to the Top, 35 *Harvard Journal of Law & Public Policy* 89 (2011).

authorized intermediary must be located in the same domicile.[83] In light of this observation, the harmonizing of investment fund regulation across Europe (and partly beyond) has become a policy goal in itself, as the harmonization partly mitigates the procompetition effect triggered by the European passport. In turn, some of the most successful modern financial centers, such as Luxembourg and Ireland, have well-developed rulebooks for investment funds. These rules, in addition to market mechanisms, have contributed to an "arms race" to the *best*, rather than the bottom or top, regulatory environment for intermediaries *and* investors.

One of the political objectives of the AIFMD and UCITSD is granting access to the markets of all Member States subject to strict requirements. If the fund managers meet these requirements, they may provide crossborder fund management to investment funds domiciled in other Member States or market their fund units to investors all over the EU and the EEA as if the host countries were its home market. These requirements prevent the host Member States from being exposed to externalities that stem from profits materializing in the fund manager's home Member State and losses showing on the balance sheets of the investor or counterparty in the host Member State.[84]

3.2.1.3 Implementation The European passporting rules for crossborder sales are virtually identical across all European investment law. The passport is typically granted to the fund manager (UCITS ManCo, AIFM) from which the right to either sell fund units or manage investment funds on a crossborder basis is derived.

Example 1: A Luxembourg UCITS is managed by a Luxembourg UCITS ManCo. The European – at least until 2019 – marketing passport entitles the ManCo to sell UCITS units in Germany, France, and Britain.

Example 2: A Liechtenstein UCITS ManCo seeks to manage a Luxembourg UCITS. The European management passport entitles the ManCo to do so.

In order to obtain the European marketing passport, European investment law requires:[85]

- an application on the part of the intermediary;
- a review of the European provisions by the NCA;
- a notification of the NCA to the authorities of the host state; and
- a few days' minimum waiting period before the intermediary provides services in the host state.

---

[83] For details, see D. Zetzsche & T. Marte, The AIFMD's Cross-Border Dimension, Third-Country Rules and the Equivalence Concept at 433–80 in *The Alternative Investment Fund Managers' Directive: European Regulation of Alternative Investment Funds* (D. Zetzsche ed., 2nd ed., Alphen aan den Rijn: Wolters Kluwer 2015).

[84] See D. Zetzsche, Competitiveness of Financial Centers in Light of Financial and Tax Law Equivalence Requirements at 390 in *Rethinking Global Financial Law and Its Regulation* (R. Buckley, D. Arner, & E. Avgouleas eds, Cambridge: Cambridge University Press 2016).

[85] Cf. S. 4 "Freedom of establishment and freedom to provide services," Arts 16–20 UCITSD, Arts 32–33 AIFMD, Arts 5–7 and 26–31 ELTIFR (partly referring to AIFMD, partly setting additional requirements); Arts 14–16 EuVeCAR, Arts 14–16 EuSEFR.

In addition, the European management passport under UCITSD and AIFMD requires an entity in the host state which may be managed, and a distinction between the functions that are subject to the intermediary and those which are subject to the entity (the CIS) laws and regulations.

An expanded version of the European passport also enables the establishment of a branch in a host state that may be run on the license granted to the fund management company in its home state. Despite the fact that the branch may establish significant operational resources in the host state, no second license in the host state is required in this case. In addition to the above requirements for the European marketing passport, in order to establish a branch the intermediary must:[86]

- show that it meets the organizational requirements to abide to the business rules in the host state; and
- subject itself to supervision within a limited scope in the host state.

For instance, based on the UCITSD's crossborder management passport, the UCITS (that is, the fund) and its manager (that is, the UCITS ManCo) can be located in different Member States.[87] In this case the National Competent Authority ("NCA") of the UCITS home Member State decides upon the application of the UCITS ManCos. As an antiexternality measure, UCITS must not be licensed by their home NCA if the UCITS is legally prevented from marketing fund units in its home Member State.[88] This rule counters externalities by ensuring that any risk imposed on foreign investors in other EU Member States is also shared by the retail investors in the UCITS home Member State.

All in all, the management passport allows for both a greater degree of competition and the specialization of fund centers. For instance, Luxembourg's strength in depositary services makes it a natural location for the fund. UCITS ManCos from other jurisdictions could make use of the strong depositary network by managing Luxembourg UCITS from their home country. This enables the latter to compete without first building an extensive depositary network.

European legislature deemed the depositary's control of the manager's conduct an impossible undertaking if the investment fund and depositary are established in different countries. Hence, regulators refrained from enabling a depositary passport under the UCITSD. However, the AIFMD has enabled a depositary passport through the backdoor through which the AIFM can name a depositary in its home state if the AIF is in a non-European country.[89]

---

[86] Cf. Arts 19–20 UCITSD, Arts 32–33 AIFMD.
[87] Art. 5(3) UCITSD.
[88] Art. 5(5) UCITSD.
[89] See S. Hooghiemstra, Depositary Regulation, in *The Alternative Investment Fund Managers' Directive: European Regulation of Alternative Investment Funds* (D. Zetzsche ed., 2nd ed., Alphen aan den Rijn: Wolters Kluwer 2015)

3.2.2 Third countries

For the most part, third country relationships are part of each Member State's jurisdiction. European law imposes a nondiscrimination rule and the right of third country entities to enter the European market by establishing subsidiaries.

In the few cases where European investment law adopts a supraterritorial approach,[90] the principles follow the line that third country passports are available (under the AIFMD and MiFID II) only if services are provided to professional investors. This may have two dimensions.

First, the AIFMD allows for a national placement regime based on a country-by-country authorization scheme for third country entities known as NPPR—national private placement regimes. In some Member States, in particular Britain, the NPPR continued to be available to TC-AIFMs marketing AIFs and EEA-AIFMs marketing TC-AIFs at the discretion of Member States after the AIFMD entered into force. However, following a review by ESMA due October 22, 2018, the European Commission will have to decide whether to phase out the national private placement regime.[91]

Second, under the AIFMD and MiFID, European AIFMs and TC-AIFMs may obtain a European passport which allows them to manage both EU-AIFs and TC-AIFs and market them to professional investors across the EEA. While the European passport has been available to EU-AIFMs managing or marketing EEA-AIFs since the AIFMD's transposition into domestic law,[92] the European passport available to TC-AIFMs or EU-AIFMs managing or marketing TC-AIFs is subject to a lengthy approval procedure involving ESMA,[93] the European Commission, the Council, and the Parliament.[94] Since the UCITSD and ELTIFR focus on retail investors, the third country passport is available solely under the AIFMD. In fact it is here that, for the first time in European law, the passporting regime for third countries and its fundamentals have been developed, although applicability has been postponed until the third country regime has been adopted by the European Commission in accordance with the European Council and the European Parliament.

The expansion of the European passport follows the risk symmetry rationale mentioned above. Equivalent standards prevent a race to the bottom and, in the absence of equivalence restricted by (overly) strict and costly investor protection requirements, intermediaries from distribution countries are deemed unfit to compete with intermediaries from production countries. Apart from the risk asymmetry argument, equivalence also adds to the competitiveness of distribution countries. This double

---

[90] D. Zetzsche & T. Marte, The AIFMD's Cross-Border Dimension, Third-Country Rules and the Equivalence Concept at 433–80 in *The Alternative Investment Fund Managers' Directive: European Regulation of Alternative Investment Funds* (D. Zetzsche ed., 2nd ed., Alphen aan den Rijn: Wolters Kluwer 2015) at 431.
[91] Art. 68(6) AIFMD.
[92] Art. 66(1) AIFMD.
[93] Cf. ESMA/2016/1140, Advice to the European Parliament, the Council and the Commission on the application of the AIFMD passport to non-EU AIFMs and AIFs (July 18, 2016).
[94] See Art. 68(4) AIFMD.

impact explains the appeal of equivalence for governments from distribution countries and maintains the benefit of an enhanced market size.

For these reasons, Articles 36–42 AIFMD provide full-fledged regulation for third country managers and third country investment funds based on the equivalence principle.[95] Similarly, the MiFID framework which governs asset management services provided by third country asset managers to European investment funds and their fund managers introduces a third country passport; a third country company must not provide investment services to eligible counterparties and professional clients unless they are registered as equivalent third country companies.[96]

The core element of the European equivalence test is the duality of equivalent substantive law and equivalent enforcement by the third country authorities.[97] In particular, European law necessitates that the financial intermediary is subject to legally binding rules which are equivalent to those set out in European law, and that the intermediary is subject to (1) authorization or registration and (2) effective supervision and enforcement on an ongoing basis.

In addition, cooperation agreements must ensure that European authorities or NCAs of the Member States rely on the information gathered by the (effective) supervision in the third country.[98] These agreements must specify "(a) the mechanism for the exchange of information between [the ESAs] and the relevant supervisory authorities of the third countries concerned; and (b) the procedures concerning the coordination of supervisory activities."[99] Furthermore, the data exchanged must be subject to professional secrecy rules as well as adequate data protection.[100] Hence, equivalence counts for nothing if not paired with formal supervisory cooperation with European authorities. The latter is negotiated centrally on behalf of all EU/EEA states by the European Commission and the ESAs.

Here, again, the European legislature may have feared externalities. Though not provided for in the recitals, another objective may have been the protection of the highly regulated, AIFMD-compliant European fund industry from less regulated competitors in third countries.

---

[95] See D. Zetzsche, Competitiveness of Financial Centers in Light of Financial and Tax Law Equivalence Requirements at 390 in *Rethinking Global Financial Law and Its Regulation* (R. Buckley, D. Arner, & E. Avgouleas eds, Cambridge: Cambridge University Press 2016).

[96] See Recital 42 and Art. 46 MIFIR.

[97] See Art. 102(1) UCITSD; Art. 21(6), 37(2) AIFMD; Art. 28(4), 47(1) MiFIR. For details, see D. Zetzsche & T. Marte, The AIFMD's Cross-Border Dimension, Third-Country Rules and the Equivalence Concept, 433–80 in *The Alternative Investment Fund Managers' Directive: European Regulation of Alternative Investment Funds* (D. Zetzsche ed., 2nd ed., Alphen aan den Rijn: Wolters Kluwer 2015), at 431.

[98] See Recital 17 and Art. 5(6) Rating Regulation; Art. 25(4)(c) and (10) of CSD Regulation; Art. 55–57, 115 CRD IV; Art. 68 Solvency II; Art. 76 EMIR; Art. 88 MiFID II; Art. 47(2) MiFIR; Recital 39, Art. 38 Short Selling Regulation; Recital 69, Art. 26 Market Abuse Regulation; Recital 63, 69, 74, Art. 34(2)(b), 35(2)(a), 36(1)(b), 37(7)(d), 40(2)(a), 42(1)(b) AIFMD.

[99] Recital 17 and Art. 5(6) Rating Regulation.

[100] For example, Art. 63 MiFID.

3.3 Stakeholder Protection/Public Interest

Since the crisis that began late in the first decade of the 2000s, European institutions have shown a desire to add other stakeholder interests (including labor and local incumbents) to the established dualism of investor and market protection as a third objective of investment law. The (not so) hidden agenda of employing investment law to further stakeholder interests rather than those of investors is introduced by: (1) the prohibition of asset stripping imposed on managers of AIF; (2) the prerequisites for third country equivalence for the purposes of granting a passport; and (3) making responsible investment a requirement of investment law.

3.3.1 AIFMD private equity rules

The AIFMD private equity rules are a prominent example of stakeholder governance finding its way into legislation. The fund manager needs to inform employees of a nonlisted company about significant shareholdings it acquires in the company, as well as its plans to restructure the undertaking. Further, European law limits asset stripping for a period of two years following the acquisition.[101] In both cases, managers are prevented from furthering investor interests when these interests collide with stakeholder interests. Both of these aspects also contradict the market governance perspective, as they increase transaction costs for private equity funds and help managers of failing companies to hold onto their positions.

3.3.2 Third country equivalence prerequisites

Both AIFMD and MiFID supplement the equivalence test necessary to obtain a third country passport with two wider policy goals: combating money laundering, on one hand,[102] and tax avoidance, on the other, by requiring a tax information exchange agreement as a precondition for market access.[103] These additional requirements reflect a stakeholder perspective on a financial system that exceeds the common duality of protecting both investors/clients and so on, while maintaining financial stability.[104]

The fact that access to the single market is bundled with tax information exchange may, in addition to pan-European interests, signal the fiscal interests of Member States

---

[101] Pursuant to ss. 26–30 AIFMD. For details, see C. Clerc, The AIFM'S Duties upon the Acquisition of Non-Listed Firms at 649–66 in *The Alternative Investment Fund Managers' Directive: European Regulation of Alternative Investment Funds* (D. Zetzsche ed., 2nd ed., Alphen aan den Rijn: Wolters Kluwer 2015).

[102] For example, Art. 36(1)(c), 42(1)(c) AIFMD; Art. 39(2) MiFID II.

[103] For example, Art. 21(6)(d), 35(2)(c), 37(2)(f) AIFMD, Art. 39(2)(e) MiFID II. For details, see D. Zetzsche & T. Marte, The AIFMD's Cross-Border Dimension, Third-Country Rules and the Equivalence Concept, 433–80 in *The Alternative Investment Fund Managers' Directive: European Regulation of Alternative Investment Funds* (D. Zetzsche ed., 2nd ed., Alphen aan den Rijn: Wolters Kluwer 2015), at 431.

[104] See on the stakeholder orientation of European financial law D. Zetzsche, Investment Law as Financial Law: From Fund Governance over Market Governance to Stakeholder Governance? at 337–56 in *The European Financial Markets in Transition* (H.S. Birkmose, M. Neville, & K.E. Sorensen eds, Alphen aan den Rijn: Wolters Kluwer Law, 2012). On competition on the merits, see OECD, What Is Competition on the Merits? Policy Brief (June 2006), online www.oecd.org/competition/mergers/37082099.pdf (last accessed May 14, 2017).

and increase the pressure on offshore domicile. However, to the same extent that tax matters become less important, this novel move unlocks the efficiency enhancing potential for true competition of financial regulation and financial *regulators* "on the merits."[105] Under the AIFMD the regulators' expertise and service orientation are likely to become the prime features for fund center success.

3.3.3 Stakeholder concerns and stewardship codes

The AIMFD rules are part of a broader policy agenda that seeks to make stakeholder governance a pillar of investment law. Following the great financial crisis, the European Commission committed itself to ensuring that the interests of consumers and other stakeholders are better taken into account, businesses are managed in a more sustainable way, and bankruptcy risks are reduced in the longer term.[106] The Commission implemented this approach in the governance requirements of the AIFMD and the UCITS V for AIFMs and UCITS ManCos.[107] The discussion on legally embedding responsible investment is taking place along the same lines. The reform of the Shareholder Rights Directive adopted in 2017 presents pro-stakeholder concerns clothed in the apparent interests of long-term shareholders/beneficiaries.[108] In all cases the dualism of fund and market governance as objectives of investment law would become a triple agenda of furthering fund, market, and stakeholder governance simultaneously.

4 THE FUNDAMENTALS OF EUROPEAN INVESTMENT FUND LAW

The unique feature of European investment law from a comparative perspective is the division of labor between the fund management company and the depositary. European investment law lays down more or less similar rules for the authorization, ongoing

---

[105] See D. Zetzsche, Investment Law as Financial Law: From Fund Governance over Market Governance to Stakeholder Governance? at 341–5 in *The European Financial Markets in Transition* (H.S. Birkmose, M. Neville, & K.E. Sorensen eds, Alphen aan den Rijn: Wolters Kluwer Law, 2012).

[106] See European Commission, The EU Corporate Governance Framework 9, COM(2011) 164 final.

[107] Arts 12–13 AIFMD, Arts 14–14b UCITSD. For details, see ESMA/2016/411, Guidelines on sound remuneration policies under the UCITS Directive and AIFMD; P. Câmara, *The AIFM's Governance and Remuneration Committees: The Impact of the AIFMD*, at 293–310, in *The Alternative Investment Fund Managers' Directive: European Regulation of Alternative Investment Funds* (D. Zetzsche ed., 2nd ed., Alphen aan den Rijn: Wolters Kluwer 2015); and D. Zetzsche & D. Eckner, Appointment, Authorization and Organization of the AIFM at 193–242 in *The Alternative Investment Fund Managers' Directive: European Regulation of Alternative Investment Funds* (D. Zetzsche ed., 2nd ed., Alphen aan den Rijn: Wolters Kluwer 2015).

[108] See Directive (EU) 2017/828 … of 17 May 2017 amending Directive 2007/36/EC as regards the encouragement of long-term shareholder engagement.

operation, and reporting to NCAs of fund management companies (referred to as manager regulation); the authorization, operations, and reporting of depositaries (referred to as depositary regulation); product rules, including investment limits and techniques; and sales regulation, including mandatory disclosure to investors.

4.1 Investment Triangle

European investment fund law builds on the so-called investment triangle first implemented by the UCITSD in 1985 for retail investment funds that invest according to the principle of risk spreading in transferable securities.[109] Both the UCITSD and the AIFMD require a general structure of investment activities which can legally be characterized as a triangle, the three corners of which constitute: (1) the investor; (2) the asset manager/AIFM; and (3) the depositary/custodian. The fund(s) is/are at the center of this arrangement. This holds true even when, in practice, many services are delegated to specialized service providers, or when funds are set up as an investment company which is available in corporate or partnership form.

4.1.1 Regulatory implementation

The UCITS ManCo or AIFM make the investment decisions and the depositary,[110] holds the assets on behalf of the fund in custody (see Fig. 16.3). The depositary functions as the point of contact for money flowing to and from the investor, as asset separation rules seek to reduce the manager's access to the client's monies and assets. Both intermediaries—the AIFM and depositary—oversee each other's activities.[111]

This investment triangle is not an innovation of the European legislature, nor was it first established by European financial law. It can be traced back to the golden age of the first Dutch investment funds in the eighteenth century.[112] The triangle has only changed in minor ways over the centuries, during its development within Swiss contractual funds and British Income Trusts in the nineteenth century, with the advent of French and Luxembourgish Organismes de Placement Collectif and German *Investmentfonds* and UCITS in the twentieth century, and with the AIFs of the AIFMD of the early twenty-first century. If an organizational structure has survived for such a long time with no significant changes (and at first without mandatory law), despite the

---

[109] For a comparison of the UCITSD and the AIFMD, see U. Klebeck, Interplay between the AIFMD and the UCITSD, 95–118 in *The Alternative Investment Fund Managers' Directive: European Regulation of Alternative Investment Funds* (D. Zetzsche ed., 2nd ed., Alphen aan den Rijn: Wolters Kluwer 2015).

[110] For details on the depositary function see *infra*, at 5.

[111] Cf. Arts 22 et seq. UCITSD and Commission Delegated Regulation (EU) 2016/438 of 17 December 2015 supplementing Directive 2009/65/EC ... with regard to obligations of depositaries, OJ L 78/11, 24.3.2016; Art. 21 AIFMD and Ch. IV "Depositary") Regulation No 231/2013.

[112] Cf. W.H. Berghuis, *Ontstaan en Ontwikkeling van de Nederlandse Beleggingsfondsen tot 1914 46* (Van Gorcum & Comp 1967); for a detailed account of investment funds history see D. Zetzsche, *Prinzipien der kollektiven Vermögensanlage* (Tübingen: Mohr Siebeck, 2015), at 275.

significant bargaining power of sophisticated investors, it can provide an effective balance between the interests of intermediaries and investors.

Today, the investment triangle is part of European legislation for both retail and institutional fund managers.[113] However, the AIFMD's adoption of the triangle structure necessitated some changes to the structure of AIFs in some countries.[114]

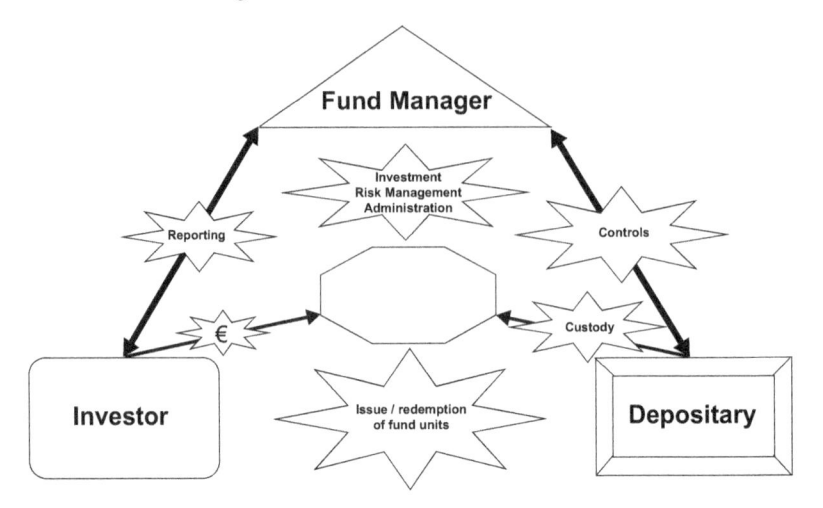

Figure 14.3   Investment triangle

4.1.2   Economic rationale

The rationale behind the investment triangle becomes obvious when taking into account the managers' and depositaries' capital requirements and returns from engagement in a collective investment scheme. The manager's own investment in the fund is low, in relative terms, although the returns may be quite large. For instance, a carried interest or performance premium could result in a very large return for the manager's key staff, while investors suffer solely when fund management results in losses. Further, due to information asymmetry, investors may face difficulties in taking legal action against fund managers.

By contrast, depositaries under European law are not allowed to benefit from the fund's performance, as this creates a conflict of interest with its safekeeping and control obligations. The depositaries are subject to (quite high) bank capital requirements and can gain at best a low but stable return. If the fund investment fails, investors are inclined to pursue the bank with the higher likelihood of having their losses reimbursed. Depositaries aware of their position seek to intensify controls and make sure that fund managers act in line with the obligations laid down in the fund's constituting documents. While there are limits to the depositaries' liabilities under

---

[113]   Cf. Art. 22 et seq. UCITSD; Art. 21 AIFMD.
[114]   See, in particular, J. Siena, Depositary Liability, 531 and D. Zetzsche, (Prime) Brokerage at 531–72 in *The Alternative Investment Fund Managers' Directive: European Regulation of Alternative Investment Funds* (D. Zetzsche ed., 2nd ed., Alphen aan den Rijn: Wolters Kluwer 2015).

European law, the prospect of yearlong legal proceedings pushes depositaries toward a careful approach whenever risks are involved. This risk-averse depositary functions as a counterweight to the fund manager's appetite for risk.[115]

The above is subject to two qualifications, however. First, some fund managers focus on the fund's administration and asset management only while the asset management and its positive potential is outsourced to external risk managers. In this case the fund manager's incentive structure is similar to that of the depositary; depositaries and administrator-fund managers together keep tight control over the asset manager's activities. Second, the depositary triangle is ineffective at controlling the fund manager's activities when depositary and fund manager collude. For this reason, regulation was put in place to deal with conflicts in the case that the fund manager and depositary belong to the same group of companies.[116]

4.1.3 Contractual explanation of the investment triangle

While European regulation mandates the division of labor between the fund manager and the depositary, liability reinforces the effect of regulation. For instance, while the contract between the fund, the fund manager, and the depositary is signed by the fund manager and the depositary—and, in the case of investment companies, the company's board as well—European regulation grants investors standing in relation to legal action against the fund manager and the depositary.[117] While this issue has been widely discussed in relation to Member States' private law systems, a contractual explanation that includes the investors as natural beneficiaries of any service contract within the investment triangle is the most convincing approach to clarifying the unique setup of the fund under European law.[118]

While the standing granted under European law enables investors to bring suits, whether they win the suits depends on the circumstances. Very few generalizations can be made. For instance, frequent litigation on wrongful disclosure by German closed-ended funds has led to multiple judgments against fund sponsors and their sales representatives. To a lesser extent, sophisticated investors take cases to court. On Luxembourg UCITS a lot of litigation occurred in the aftermath of the Madoff scandal alleging that the use of subdepositaries linked to the Madoff empire amounted to negligent conduct on the side of the depositary. Most of these cases were settled out of court, with Luxembourg depositaries making up for investors' losses despite claiming that no legal obligation to do so exists

---

[115] See D. Zetzsche, *Prinzipien der kollektiven Vermögensanlage* (Tübingen: Mohr Siebeck, 2015), at 507–35.

[116] See Art. 23, 24 Regulation 2016/438.

[117] See Art. 24(5) UCITSD ("Unit-holders in the UCITS may invoke the liability of the depositary directly or indirectly through the management company or the investment company provided that this does not lead to a duplication of redress or to unequal treatment of the unit-holders"); Art. 21(15) AIFMD ("Liability to the investors of the AIF may be invoked directly or indirectly through the AIFM, depending on the legal nature of the relationship between the depositary, the AIFM and the investors").

[118] See D. Zetzsche, *Klagebefugnis im Investment-Drei- und -Viereck* (FS Johannes Köndgen, Cologne, RWS Verlag: 2016), 677–700; I. Riassetto & M. Storck, *Les organismes de placement collectif*, 2nd ed. (Joly Editions, 2016), ¶1073.

4.2 Manager Regulation

All European investment law provides an extensive framework for UCI managers. Among these frameworks, that provided by the UCITSD (which also applies in part to MMFs regulated by the MMFR) is the most stringent, given that UCITS raise capital from the public purse, and are trailed by the AIFMD for AIFs (which also forms the basis of the framework for long-term investment funds (ELTIFR) and the MiFID for portfolio managers and investment advisers). The manager regulation of the regulations on venture capital and social entrepreneurship funds (EuVeCaR, EuSEFR) is liberal by comparison, which is best understood by considering the legislation's probusiness attitude (see Section 2.1.3). Notwithstanding the differences, cross-sectoral consistency is an explicit policy goal of the European legislature.[119] This is important since entities usually hold licenses under more than one regulatory regime. For instance, a fund management company may be licensed under the UCITSD, the AIFMD, and the EuVeCaR; manage MMFs authorized under MMFR; and function as a delegated asset manager to a different fund company, in which case MiFID applies.

4.2.1 Licensing requirements

Managers are subject to a general prohibition under all investment legislation which is lifted when the manager is authorized by the NCA.[120] The licensing requirement is a response by European investment law to the G20 commitment from spring 2009 that relevant financial asset pools and their managers should be subject to regulation and external supervision in order to allow for better assessment of financial systemic risks and better monitoring of the suitability of risk management techniques applied to these pools.[121]

The most important licensing requirements include a fit and proper test for senior management,[122] including a review of management's financial competence and experience in leading regulated entities; minimum capital requirements of at least EUR 125,000 and up to EUR 10 million;[123] a viable business plan; adequate risk and business organization; reliable significant shareholders and third country relationships,

---

[119] Cf. D. Zetzsche & D. Eckner, *Risk Management*, 325–92; D. Zetzsche & D. Eckner, *Securitizations*, 609–28; P. Câmara, *The AIFM's Governance and Remuneration Committees: The Impact of the AIFMD*, at 293, and D. Zetzsche & D. Eckner, Appointment at 195–244 in *The Alternative Investment Fund Managers' Directive: European Regulation of Alternative Investment Funds* (D. Zetzsche ed., 2nd ed., Alphen aan den Rijn: Wolters Kluwer 2015).

[120] See Art. 5(1) and 6 UCITSD; Art. 6(1) AIFMD; Art. 14 EuVeCaR (registration); Art. 14 EuSEFR (registration); Art. 5, 6 ELTIFR; Art. 5(1) MMFR.

[121] See G20 Leaders Statement: The Pittsburgh Summit, September 24–25, 2009, ¶13 ("All firms whose failure could pose a risk to financial stability must be subject to consistent, consolidated supervision and regulation with high standards").

[122] See Arts 6–7 UCITSD, Arts 6–10 AIFMD; Arts 7–10, 12–14 EuVeCaR; Arts 7–10, 12–14 EuSEFR; Art. 7 ELTIFR (referring to AIFMD); Arts 5–6 MMFR (referring to UCITSD and AIFMD).

[123] In addition, managers must provide liability insurance covering operational risks in correlation to their asset size.

if any; and a mandatory withdrawal of the license if the intermediary no longer meets the requirements of the applicable directive.

4.2.2 Operating conditions

The standardization of operating conditions has gained momentum with the EC's statements on the governance of financial institutions.[124] The most important rules governing the manager's operations include, *inter alia*:[125]

- commitments to fairness, honesty, and the investor's best interests—an aspect of this is the anti-market timing rules and other bans on insider trading against the fund or its investors;
- conflict of interest rules;
- best execution rules;
- rules on the intermediary's remuneration;
- the prohibition of letterbox entities/shell companies;
- valuation rule;
- extensive reporting to NCAs especially with regard to the use of securities financing techniques; and
- limits on leverage; in the case of UCITS these limits are implicit in the UCITS investment strategy (see Section 6.2.3), while AIFM's leverage may be limited by either NCAs or ESMA.

4.2.3 Risk and liquidity management

Modern European risk management rules are driven by developments in risk management methodology introduced via the banking sector.[126] Since cross-sectoral consistency is an announced policy goal, I deem the tripartite distinction between institutional risk management (risk organization), operational risk management (risk procedures), and quantitative risk management (risk measurement) a common feature of European risk management law.[127] In particular, the substantive rules on risk management show remarkable similarities. These include:[128]

---

[124] See P. Câmara, The AIFM's Governance and Remuneration Committees: The Impact of the AIFMD at 293 in *The Alternative Investment Fund Managers' Directive: European Regulation of Alternative Investment Funds* (D. Zetzsche ed., 2nd ed., Alphen aan den Rijn: Wolters Kluwer 2015) 3; European Commission, Corporate Governance in Financial Institutions: Lessons to be Drawn from the Current Financial Crisis, Best Practices; SEC (2010) 669, June 2 2010.

[125] See Arts 10–15 UCITSD, Arts 12–19 AIFMD; Arts 7, 10–13 EuVeCaR, Arts 7, 10–13 EuSEFR; Art. 7, ELTIFR (referring to AIFMD); Arts 7, 21–22, 29–33 MMFR.

[126] See D. Zetzsche & D. Eckner, Risk Management, at 323 in *The Alternative Investment Fund Managers' Directive: European Regulation of Alternative Investment Funds* (D. Zetzsche ed., 2nd ed., Alphen aan den Rijn: Wolters Kluwer 2015).

[127] *Ibid.*

[128] See Art. 51(1) UCITSD; Art. 15, 16 AIFMD; Art. 7 ELTIFR (referring to AIFMD) with additional rules in Art. 5(2) and 23(6) ELTIFR; Art. 5(2), 17(4)-(6), 20, 23, 28, 34, 37 MMFR (EuVeCaR and EuSEFR as low key regulation do not provide explicitly for risk management).

- the types of risks to be considered;
- as a result of the crisis, an upgrade of operational risks to the same level as financial risks;
- the measurement methodologies;
- risk measurement across sectors relies on the commitment approach, VaR or company-specific models; and
- risk limits which are either mandatory as part of the fund type chosen,[129] or contractually agreed upon in the fund's constituting documents.

The cross-sectoral consistency is welcome at the level of intermediaries, who (until now) have had to base business decisions/transactions on a paucity of risk management expertise. However, consistency may also pose a threat to the stability of the financial markets if the underlying models do not reflect reality due to the joint misapplication of risk management tools.

There is one difference with regard to the regulatory treatment of risk management within European investment law. While risk management is an operating condition for licensed intermediaries under the remaining European investment law, it is a core activity for AIFMs licensed under AIFMD. It opens the AIFM license and passport for entities focusing on risk management, administration, and sales that outsource portfolio management to authorized asset managers.[130]

4.2.4 Securitization

A new part of European asset management law added in the aftermath of the financial crisis requires that all financial intermediaries be subject to the same restrictions when investing in securitization positions. The most important common aspects of European securitization law include a mandatory 5 percent equity retainer, conflict of interest rules and due diligence requirements imposed on all professional investors in securitization products.[131] These rules, which were primarily adopted from the CRD,[132] also form the basis of the Securitization Transactions Regulation (STSR).[133] For details, see Section 5.4.

4.3 Depositary Regulation

Consistency is still a work in progress at the depositary level. While AIFMD and UCITSD V have created a level playing field in the collective investment world, there is a lack of consistency between collective investment schemes and individual portfolio managers governed by MiFID. The EuVeCaR and the EuSEFR also refrain from setting

---

[129] See for UCITS Art. 51(3) UCITSD.
[130] Cf. D. Zetzsche & D. Eckner, Risk Management, at 323 in *The Alternative Investment Fund Managers' Directive: European Regulation of Alternative Investment Funds* (D. Zetzsche ed., 2nd ed., Alphen aan den Rijn: Wolters Kluwer 2015).
[131] Cf. Art. 50a UCITSD; Art. 17 AIFMD and Arts 50-56 Regulation No 231/2013 (n. 47).
[132] See D. Zetzsche & D. Eckner, *Securitizations*, at 607 in *The Alternative Investment Fund Managers' Directive: European Regulation of Alternative Investment Funds* (D. Zetzsche ed., 2nd ed., Alphen aan den Rijn: Wolters Kluwer 2015).
[133] See *supra*, n. 39.

a depositary requirement, which may be explained by cost considerations for funds tailored to invest in SMEs.

Where there is a depositary requirement, European investment law governs:[134]

- the appointment of a depositary which must be either a credit institution governed by the Capital Requirements Directive and Regulation,[135] or a MiFID-licensed investment company—professional trustees may function as depositaries for AIF assets;
- a mandatory safekeeping function with by and large strict liability for lost assets;
- a mandatory control function that includes a legal oversight of managers' investment decisions; and
- investors' standing regarding legal action against the depositary.

The licensing and capital requirements for credit institutions and investment firms acting as depositaries are for the most part governed by CRD IV and MiFID, while the operating conditions are separately regulated in remarkable detail for both UCITS depositories, on the one hand,[136] and AIF depositaries, on the other.[137] For details on the UCITS depositaries see Section 6.1.

4.4 Sales Regulation/Disclosure to Investors

European investment law demands initial disclosure prior to investors entering into the investment, and ongoing periodical disclosure. Periodical disclosure may be supplemented by ad hoc disclosure in case of material changes. The intensity of disclosure varies depending on whether the fund units are distributed to professional or retail investors.

Notwithstanding further contractual obligations, professional investors receive:[138]

- a basic initial disclosure, which in practice often looks like a long-form prospectus;
- annual accounts, and
- information on material changes.

With regard to retail investors, fund managers must disclose:[139]

---

[134] See Art. Ch. IV "Obligations regarding the depositary" of the UCITSD; Art. 21 AIFMD; Art. 29 ELTIFR; Art. 4(2)(c), 5(1), 92) MMFR.
[135] Cf. Directive 2013/36/EU ... of 26 June 2013 on access to the activity of credit institutions and the prudential supervision of credit institutions and investment firms ("CRD IV"), OJ L176/338, and Regulation (EU) No 575/2013 on prudential requirements for credit institutions and investment firms ("CRR"), OJ L 176/1.
[136] Cf. Regulation 2016/438.
[137] Cf. Art. IV "Depositary" Regulation No. 231/2013.
[138] See Arts 22–23 AIFMD.
[139] See Art. Ch. IX "Obligations concerning information to be provided to investors" of UCITSD; Arts 5 et seq. Regulation (EU) No. 1286/2014 of the European Parliament and of the

- the key investor information document required by the UCITSD and PRIIPSR,[140] with a focus on the fund unit's volatility and costs;
- the long-form prospectus required by the UCITSD, or, in the case of AIFs, the Prospectus Directive (unless the manager relies on a private placement exemption);
- the intermediaries' obligation to submit some mid-term information in addition to the annual report as required by the UCITSD or AIFMD—priority is given to the fund's performance and the costs; and
- ad hoc information in case of material changes.

4.5 Product Regulation (for Retail Funds Only)

For funds marketed solely to professional investors, European law only relies on the manager's regulation, allowing for freedom on the details of the investment strategy within the contract. This approach is based on the insight that product innovation rapidly evolves and that any regulation lags behind and hampers it.

With regard to retail funds, regulators tend to rely more extensively on product regulation in order to avoid mismarketing and misselling. *European* product regulation is limited to UCITS, AIFs qualifying as ELTIFs, UCITS and AIFs qualifying as money market funds,[141] and subthreshold AIFs that want to market the fund units under the EuVeCaF and EuSEF label. This European product regulation includes:

- investment limits calculated as a percentage of NAV;
- issuer limits; and
- minimum and maximum valuation/net asset value ("NAV") calculation periods.

A further separate regime governing debt funds was proposed by ESMA.[142] Both the MMFR and the proposed debt fund regulation address systemic risk, so they could result in new/alternative options in the regulatory toolbox.

With regard to national product regulation, Member States differ with regard to level of detail, ranging from very liberal, disclosure-based approaches in the Netherlands and Liechtenstein to stringent approaches for retail funds in France and Germany.[143]

Council of 26 November 2014 on key information documents for packaged retail and insurance-based investment products (PRIIPs), OJ L352/1; Art. 3(1) Directive 2003/71/EC.

[140] Regulation (EU) No. 1286/2014 (n. 137).

[141] See Arts 9–18 MMFR.

[142] See ESMA/2016/596, Opinion: Key principles for a European framework on loan origination by funds.

[143] For details, see the country overviews in D. Zetzsche (ed.) *The Alternative Investment Fund Managers' Directive: European Regulation of Alternative Investment Funds* (2nd ed., Alphen aan den Rijn: Wolters Kluwer 2015) (Wolters Kluwer, 2015), at 719–847.

5 DELINEATING THE SCOPE

In order to fall within the purview of European investment fund law, a vehicle must fulfill the definition for undertakings for collective investments (UCI). Further European law differentiates between two types of investment funds: (1) undertakings for collective investment in transferable securities (UCITS); and (2) alternative investment funds (AIFs).

5.1 Undertaking for Collective Investments

The "undertaking for collective investment" (UCI) or "collective investment undertaking" is a central concept of European investment fund law.[144] The term has been used since the 1970s to describe a range of exceptions from the company law directives and the European law on financial services for investment funds.[145] As a result, certain directives—some company,[146] some capital market law[147]—do not apply to (certain types of) UCI.

Despite its importance, the European UCI has no clear definition.[148] ESMA only goes so far as to point out that the UCI focuses on achieving profits by selling assets for the benefit of its investors. Conversely, a unit is not an undertaking if it creates a profit by managing the underlying assets over the lifetime of the company for its own account. However, there are undertakings of collective investment that take the shape of legal entities which—at first hand—hold assets on their own account, and from which investors benefit only indirectly.[149] In any case, it is unclear at which point a company acts for its own benefit and at which point it acts on behalf of its shareholders, as the shareholders/investors seek to profit in both cases.

Similarly, literature on UCIs is scarce.[150] Similarities do exist between CIUs under European law and the collective investment schemes regulated under the Swiss

---

[144] Cf. Art. 1(1) UCITSD, Art. 4(1)(a) AIFMD, Art. 4(1) ELTIFR, Art. 3(a) EuVeCaR, Art. 3(a) EuSEFR.

[145] Cf. D. Zetzsche, *Prinzipien der kollektiven Vermögensanlage* (Tübingen: Mohr Siebeck, 2015), at 354.

[146] See Art. 1(2) Directive 2012/30/EU for the protection of the interests of members and others, OJ L 315, 14.11.2012, 74.

[147] See for example Art. 1(2) Directive 2004/25/EC ... of 21 April 2004 on takeover bids, OJ L 142, 30 April 2004, 12. Art. 1(2) Directive 2004/109/EC ... of 15 December 2004 on the harmonisation of transparency requirements in relation to information about issuers whose securities are admitted to trading on a regulated market and amending Directive 2001/34/EC; Art. 1(2) Directive 2010/73/EU ... of 24 November 2010 amending Directives 2003/71/EC, OJ L 327, 11.12.2010, 1.

[148] The definition contained in Art. 3(a) EuVeCaR and in Art. 3(a) EuSEFR is identical to the definition of AIF contained in the AIFMD and therefore does not provide further clarification. The term is used but remains undefined in Art. 4(1) ELTIFR.

[149] See e.g. closed-ended investment corporations.

[150] See D. Zetzsche, *Prinzipien der kollektiven Vermögensanlage* (Tübingen: Mohr Siebeck, 2015) on Luxembourg, Germany, France, UK, Switzerland, Liechtenstein, and others; I. Riassetto & M. Storck, *Les organismes de placement collectif*, 2nd éd. (Joly Editions, 2016);

Collective Investment Law,[151] or "pooled investment vehicles" of US securities regulation.[152] Semantic and historical interpretations and a comprehensive survey of European legal sources allow us to distinguish four distinct features common to investment vehicles.[153]

5.1.1 Investment vs. operating company

The word *investment* distinguishes investment schemes from operating companies that pursue a commercial activity. This distinction raises difficulties in practice, particularly when it comes to distinguishing separate holding companies which are defined by Article 4(1)(o) AIFMD and subject to an exemption by Article 2(3)(a) AIFMD from investment schemes.[154] In contrast to the 40 percent threshold for investment in other companies in the United States, no fixed threshold applies for distinguishing between investment and operating company. Instead, NCAs apply a form of case-by-case review, considering multiple factors, with little certainty.

5.1.2 Collective

UCIs are *collective* investments, meaning that two or more investors hold shares. There are no guidelines/rules on the minimum quantity of shares, but all parties as investors must bear the residual investment risk. In order to avoid circumvention it is necessary to deny the collective criterion where a secondary participation is merely held in trust on behalf of the other investor. By making "a number of investors" a requirement, the AIFMD sets an additional criterion for AIF, which is dealt with in that context (see Section 5.3).

5.1.3 Pooling

To qualify as an UCI, all assets—from a legal perspective—must be pooled. The criterion distinguishes collective from individual investments governed by MiFID. Pooling means that the assets belong to a single body, which is called the "fund," and

---

Claude Kremer and Isabelle Lebbe,, *Collective Investment Schemes in Luxembourg—Law and Practice*, 2nd ed., Oxford: Oxford University Press, 2014.

[151] Art. 7 Abs. 1 S. 1 KAG; M. Courvoisier & R. Schmitz, Grenzfälle kollektiver Kapitalanlagen, *Schweizerische Zeitschrift für Wirtschafts- und Finanzmarktrecht* 407 (2006); S. Schären, *Unterstellungsfragen im Rahmen der Genehmigungs- und Bewilligungspflicht gemäss Kollektivanlagengesetz: unter vergleichender Berücksichtigung des Rechts der EG, Luxemburgs und Liechtensteins* (Zürich: Schulthess 2011).

[152] Cf. par. 275.206(4)-8(b) C.F.R. (US): "For purposes of this section 'pooled investment vehicles' means any investment company as defined in section 3(a) of the Investment Company Act of 1930 (15. U.S.C. 80a-3(a)) or any company that would be an investment company under section 3(a) of that Act but for the exclusion provided from that definition by either section 3(c)(1) or section (7) of that Act (15 U.S.C. 80a-3(c)(1) or (7))." See H.E. Bines & S. Thel, *Investment Management Arrangements and the Federal Securities Laws*, 58 *Ohio State Law Journal* 459, 469 n. 49 (1997–8).

[153] Cf. D. Zetzsche, *Prinzipien der kollektiven Vermögensanlage* (Tübingen: Mohr Siebeck, 2015), at 57.

[154] For details, see D. Zetzsche & C. Preiner, Scope of the AIFMD, 39–84 in D. Zetzsche (ed.) *The Alternative Investment Fund Managers' Directive: European Regulation of Alternative Investment Funds* (2nd ed., Alphen aan den Rijn: Wolters Kluwer 2015).

which may or may not have the status of a legal person. Pooling does not require a corporate or partnership-type structure. Rather, this is understood to include any legal device through which the investors' contribution may be pooled, for example, the law of contracts, trusts, companies and partnerships. Any kind of structure which allows this basket or bucket to function as a "pool" will suffice.[155]

The requirement to pool assets excludes managed accounts where assets are segregated and assets that are held and managed in a joint account without being part of a joint corporate, partnership, contractual, or trust body.[156] The lack of a "fund" has previously led to the view that managed accounts lie beyond the AIFMD's scope. I consider this qualification inaccurate given that AIFs can be structured in any legal form. A "fund" can exist if one account over which all assets are managed is deemed a trust fund on behalf of all investors. The AIFMD's policy rationale, in particular the risk for investors in the case of bank insolvency and the systemic risk which is imposed on financial markets, warrants this interpretation. Thus, the separate or collective treatment according to insolvency law ultimately determines the pooling requirement.

5.1.4 Third party investment management

The fourth criterion of third party investment management excludes from the scope of undertakings of collective investments funds self-managed by investors and investment clubs whose investors participate in the making of investment decisions.[157] In practice, there are many variations on the examples above. The scale ranges from a general right of investors to decide upon investments collectively, to the investors' right to veto investment decisions. In some cases investor representatives decide upon exposure limits while the investment decisions remain in the hands of the manager; in others, a predefined investment and payout plan is executed with very little discretion on the side of the manager ("autopilot").[158]

In order to rely on the self-management exclusion criterion it is crucial that the investment decision is made by the investors themselves.[159] Investor-managed funds

---

[155] *Ibid.*, at 49.

[156] This refers to Swiss and Liechtenstein "*bankinterne Sondervermögen*" and the "collective savings funds" of Luxembourg. D. Zetzsche & C. Preiner, 'Was ist ein AIF?', *Wertpapiermitteilungen* 2103 (2013); K. Loritz & B. Rickmers, Unternehmensfinanzierung im Kapitalmarkt und Kapitalanlagegesetzbuch bei operativ tätigen Unternehmen, NZG 2014, 1241, 1248 et seq; FSA, Consultation Paper: Implementation of the Alternative Investment Fund Managers Directive, Part 2, CP 13/9, 180.

[157] The criterion of third party management is also applied by the ESMA in order to define the AIF, deriving it from the position of AIFM. See ESMA/2012/117, No. 34: "The AIFM or internally managed AIF must have responsibility for the management of the AIF's assets. Investors have day-to-day no discretion or control over these assets."

[158] For details, see D. Zetzsche & C. Preiner, Scope of the AIFMD at 49 in D. Zetzsche (ed.) *The Alternative Investment Fund Managers' Directive: European Regulation of Alternative Investment Funds* (2nd ed., Alphen aan den Rijn: Wolters Kluwer 2015).

[159] ESMA draws the line at direct day-to-day discretion or control over the assets, whether exercised or not. The power must exceed the ordinary exercise of voting rights at shareholder meetings, see ESMA/2013/600, *Key concepts of the AIFMD* (May 24, 2013), at 3, 5. See also A. Hudson, *Collective Investment Schemes, the Law and Regulation of Finance* (2nd ed., London: Sweet & Maxwell 2013), 1460.

338   *Research handbook on the regulation of mutual funds*

differ from AIFs in that investors have objective, unlimited decisional authority with respect to the selection of assets. In practice, however, what is laid down in the constituting documents may differ from what is practiced in daily operations; in order to avoid circumvention of investor protection rules, I hold that practice is relevant here.

An advisory relationship between the self-managed investment vehicle and an investment adviser does not run counter to the investors' decisional authority.[160] Advice from an adviser crosses the asset management line if investment decisions are based on that advice without prior competent and diligent review of investors, resulting in advice that is followed more or less blindly.

5.2   Additional UCITS features

The UCITS definition contains six criteria.

5.2.1   Capital raised from the public
First, UCITS raise capital from the public.[161] Those that raise capital without promoting the sale of their units to the public within the EU are not subject to the UCITSD.[162] "Public" refers to an anonymous, potentially unlimited audience, including but not limited to retail investors. "Raising of capital" assists in differentiating between cases where wealth that exists in a certain form is managed and invested, and cases where wealth provided in smaller amounts by a number of investors is accumulated and pooled by an intermediary prior to investing it. While the feature leads to the nonapplication of UCITS sales rules in case of private placements, the characteristic has become important in the AIF domain, where it leads to an exemption for family offices (see Section 5.3.2).

The assumption that UCITS are distributed to the public is the rationale underlying (1) the manager regulation that deems distribution a core activity and (2) the extensive disclosure requirements of Ch. IX UCITSD.

5.2.2   Principle of risk spreading
Second, UCITS operate on the principle of risk spreading.[163] Diversification is the result of the investment limits set out in Ch. VII UCITSD. Under those limitations, UCITS must not invest more than 5 percent of its assets in one security; with certain exemptions taken into account, UCITS must hold at least 17 different securities. The investment limits prevent UCITS ManCos from creating portfolios composed of illiquid securities, as illiquidity would put the investors' redemption right at risk.

However, the risk-spreading requirement goes beyond meeting the formal investment limits. In fact, it adds an economic view to the precise formal investment limits set out

---

[160]   Regarding financial instruments, this refers to investment advice which is subject to authorization pursuant to Arts 1, 3(1) MiFID; advice concerning other assets as financial instruments (such as real estate or shares in ship vessels) is not subject to authorization under MiFID.
[161]   Art. 1(2) UCITSD.
[162]   Art. 3 UCITSD.
[163]   Art. 1(2)(a) UCITSD.

in Ch. VII UCITSD. For example, due to the risk-spreading principle it would be illegal for a UCITS to invest in 20 securities whose issuers invest exclusively in the same security even though the 5 percent maximum threshold is met.

In the view of some supervisory authorities, the risk-spreading principle applies only where there is risk, with risk being defined as the mathematical likelihood of a default. If the likelihood of default is deemed extremely low (such as indicated by AAA ratings), the risk-spreading prerequisite does not apply.

5.2.3 Open-ended

Third, UCITS issue "units which are, at the request of holders, repurchased or redeemed, directly or indirectly, out of those undertakings' assets."[164] Article 84 UCITSD stipulates further details. For instance, a UCITS must publish the price at which it redeems its units at least twice a month.[165] Member States may reduce that obligation to a monthly redemption if all investors are treated equally.[166]

The open-ended type encourages discipline on behalf of the fund manager. Since most European fund units do not offer voting rights, the investors' redemption right ensures that they can exit their investments if they need the funds or if they are dissatisfied with the manager. In the latter case the manager will be penalized by income loss, since most funds charge fees subject to the funds' assets under management. If the fund shrinks, so does the fund manager's income.

The redemption right requires the manager to maintain a certain minimum liquidity. The further requirements to invest solely in liquid assets that can be easily sold on public markets (see Section 6.2.2) assist in meeting investors' redemption requests.

The fund manager is entitled to substitute for redemption rights with a listing of fund units at a recognized stock exchange and engage a third party liquidity provider to ensure that the listing price does not significantly vary from the UCITS' net asset value.

5.2.4 Transferable securities or other liquid financial assets

Fourth, the UCITS portfolio selection is limited to transferable securities,[167] and also other liquid financial instruments.[168] The meaning of "other liquid financial instruments" is expressed in a lengthy list in Article 50(1) UCITSD. The latter includes money market instruments and certain derivatives. The UCITS Eligible Assets Directive stipulates further details.[169]

The common feature of all UCITS qualifying assets is a high degree of liquidity. The liquidity management device implicit in these investment restrictions correlates with the investors' redemption right and assists in meeting the legal requirement (for details, see Section 6.2.3).

---

[164] Art. 1(2)(b) UCITSD.
[165] Cf. Art. 76 UCITSD.
[166] Cf. Art. 76 UCITSD.
[167] Pursuant to Art. 2(1)(n) UCITSD, "transferable securities" means: (1) shares in companies and other securities equivalent to shares in companies (shares); (2) bonds and other forms of securitized debt (debt securities); (3) any other negotiable securities which carry the right to acquire any such transferable securities by subscription or exchange.
[168] Art. 1(2)(a) UCITSD.
[169] *Supra*, note 26.

5.2.5 Legal form

Fifth, in contrast to the AIFMD, UCITSD is at its core a product regulation. This explains why Article 1(3) UCITSD limits the setup of UCITS to entities in accordance with:

- contract law (as common funds managed by management companies);
- trust law (as unit trusts); and
- statute (as investment companies).

At first glance, this list seems to exclude partnerships and other legal entity types (such as foundations). However, the English term "company" in the context of UCIs is not a technical term referring to "corporations" but—similar to the US investment company—a reference to any legal entity used for investment purposes. Both partnerships and foundations derive their legal entity status from the law. I see no factual reason to exclude partnerships and foundations from functioning as fund-carrying entities, since all investor concerns are covered by mandatory fund regulation. This is all the more true since foundations are the functional equivalent of the trust on the European continent.

Member States may allow UCITS to consist of several investment compartments. In contrast to unit classes (in which all invest into the same asset pool, although the economic characteristic may be amended by virtue of derivatives), compartments include funds that invest in different asset pools. Each compartment is deemed a UCITS and requires its own authorization, and so on.[170]

5.2.6 Established in Member States

Finally, only UCIs established in a EU or EEA Member State meet the UCITS definition.[171] Funds from third countries are prevented from qualifying as UCITS. Marketing third country funds as UCITS within the EU or EEA would be deemed illegal misselling.

5.3 Alternative Investment Funds

The central concept that determines the AIFMD's scope is the AIF.[172] The term "alternative investment fund" is industry jargon,[173] referring to hedge funds and private

---

[170] Cf. Art. 49 UCITSD.

[171] Art. 1(1) UCITSD.

[172] Pursuant to Arts 1, 5 AIFMD the "management" and "sales" of "alternative investment funds" is an occupation subject to authorization, if it is conducted as a regular business activity. See on management, sales, and activity on a commercial basis see D. Zetzsche & D. Eckner, Appointment at 195 in *The Alternative Investment Fund Managers' Directive: European Regulation of Alternative Investment Funds* (D. Zetzsche ed., 2nd ed., Alphen aan den Rijn: Wolters Kluwer 2015) (n. 104).

[173] See final report of the alternative investment expert group set up by the European Commission, *Report of the Alternative Investment Expert Group: Managing, Servicing and Marketing Hedge Funds in Europe*, http://ec.europa.eu/finance/investment/docs/other_docs/reports/hedgefunds_en.pdf (accessed May 14, 2017); and *Report of the Alternative Investment*

equity funds as alternatives to the traditional investment funds that invest in liquid securities. The success of traditional (investment) funds is measured by comparing the funds' performance with the overall development of a reference market (so-called beta strategies). Alternative funds seek to generate positive returns that are independent of the volatility of capital markets, or which at least do not correlate too strongly with them (the so-called alpha strategy).[174] The AIFMD uses the term "alternative" in a different, and perhaps somewhat misleading, way to include all investment funds that are *not* governed by the UCITSD.[175] In particular, any open-ended retail fund less diversified than a UCITS or investing in other assets than tradable securities (including real estate, airplanes, ships, and commodities) is an AIF under the European definition.

The AIFMD sharpens the understanding of the AIF in three ways. First, it introduces additional explanatory elements expressed in its binding text as well as its recitals. These are understood to be the AIF characteristics. Second, it contains a permanent exclusion catalogue of activities that lead to the nonapplication of the Directive (safe harbor rule). Third, this scope is further substantiated by guidelines, set out by ESMA,[176] on the scope of the AIFMD,[177] as well as by a Q&A published by the European Commission.[178] As this is not the place to consider all the details,[179] I will focus on the AIF characteristics only.

5.3.1 AIF characteristics

5.3.1.1 Raising capital The seventh recital of the AIFMD states that investment undertakings such as family office vehicles, which invest the private wealth of investors without raising external capital,[180] are not AIFs. Due to the AIF's potentially unlimited investment strategy, the "raising of capital" test from the UCITSD (see Section 5.2.1) requires some modifications. For instance, since the AIFMD does not limit the investment strategies or the assets held by an AIF, the rationale of the AIFMD covers

---

Expert Group: Developing European Private Equity, http://ec.europa.eu/internal_market/investment/docs/other_docs/reports/equity_en.pdf (accessed May 14, 2017).

[174] See e.g. J.M. Longo, *Hedge Funds: Overview, Strategies, and Trends in Encyclopedia of Finance* in Encyclopedia of Finance (C.F. Lee & A.C. Lee eds, Springer Science and Business 2013), 621–32.

[175] Art. 4(1)(a) AIFMD.; for a criticism on the broad scope see P. Athanassiou & T. Bullman, The EU's AIFM Directive and Its Impact—An Overview in *Research Handbook on Hedge Funds, Private Equity and Alternative Investments* (P. Athanassiou ed., Cheltenham: Edward Elgar, 2012), 445 and D. Busch & L. van Setten, *The Alternative Investment Fund Managers Directive* in Alternative Investment Funds in Europe (L. van Setten & D. Busch eds, Oxford: Oxford University Press 2014) 8.

[176] ESMA/2013/600, *Key Concepts of the AIFMD* (May 24, 2013).

[177] Delegated Regulation (EU) No. 694/2014 determining types of alternative investment fund managers.

[178] European Commission, *Questions on Single Market Legislation* (Q&A), http://ec.europa.eu/finance/koel/ (accessed 5 October 2016).

[179] Cf. D. Zetzsche & C. Preiner, Scope of the AIFMD, 49 in D. Zetzsche (ed.) *The Alternative Investment Fund Managers' Directive: European Regulation of Alternative Investment Funds* (2nd ed., Alphen aan den Rijn: Wolters Kluwer 2015).

[180] Recital 7 AIFMD.

the provision of all types of capital, regardless of its form (cash, securities, real estate, or commodities), when it is included in an AIF. Any cashflow-bearing item eligible under the AIF's investment strategy will suffice.

ESMA considers that the raising of capital must take place together with a *commercial communication, directed at the investor.* Raising capital does not necessarily coincide with "marketing" or "sales" in the sense of the AIFMD.[181] It is also irrelevant whether the communication occurs uniquely (as with closed-ended funds) or permanently (as with open-ended funds).[182] On the other hand, it is possible to gain AIF status if an AIF which previously collected external capital is liquidated and its previous assets constitute the startup capital of the new unit.[183]

The criterion added by ESMA regarding an investor-oriented communication is not established in the AIFMD's text. It is also unclear and misleading as it raises the question of whether capital is raised when several investors (for example, several families) seek the same AIFM of their own accord for setting up a fund and for wealth-structuring purposes. This usually happens because of an AIFM's reputation, but it does not necessarily require investor-oriented communication. Further questions discussed within the "raising of capital" test include the treatment of self-used investments and the regulatory treatment of family offices as well as the discussion on whether other preexisting groups are exempted from the AIFMD.[184]

5.3.1.2 Number of investors While it follows from the UCI term that an investment is collective when at least two investors hold shares, single investor funds ("special funds") are recognized as AIFs. In fact, in some Member States, such as Germany, single investor funds set up by insurance undertakings and pension plans represent the majority of AIF assets. Accordingly, in ESMA's liberal view, there are two cases where the assumption must be made that single investor funds are AIFs.[185]

- *Potential two-party investor funds:* One investor holds all of the funds' shares but, subject to the constitutive documents of the fund, another investor can acquire units of the fund; and

---

[181] Cf. D. Zetzsche & T. Marte, The AIFMD's Cross-Border Dimension, Third-Country Rules and the Equivalence Concept at 433–80 in *The Alternative Investment Fund Managers' Directive: European Regulation of Alternative Investment Funds* (D. Zetzsche ed., 2nd ed., Alphen aan den Rijn: Wolters Kluwer 2015) Zetzsche & Marte, *The AIFMD's Cross-Border Dimension* (n. 83), at 431.

[182] ESMA/2013/600, *Key Concepts of the AIFMD* (24 May 2013), No. 14.

[183] One could also argue that in such a case the capital does not come from investors, but from the previous fund, in which case the follow-up "fund" would not be deemed a fund. This, however, opens the door for circumventive schemes and structures set up exclusively for liquidation.

[184] See D. Zetzsche & C. Preiner, Scope of the AIFMD, at 49 in D. Zetzsche (ed.) *The Alternative Investment Fund Managers' Directive: European Regulation of Alternative Investment Funds* (2nd ed., Alphen aan den Rijn: Wolters Kluwer 2015).

[185] ESMA/2013/600, *Key Concepts of the AIFMD* (24 May 2013), No. 17. This interpretation corresponds to the German definition of the investment fund prior to implementing the AIFMD: see also D. Zetzsche, *Prinzipien der kollektiven Vermögensanlage* (Tübingen: Mohr Siebeck, 2015), at 68.

- *Single investor funds which, when applying the transparency hypothesis, act on behalf of several investors:* Only one investor holds all of the fund's shares but this investor represents a variety of other investors who are thus indirectly associated with the fund. Examples include feeder funds, trust funds or funds for insurance undertakings, or pension funds which hold investment entities for a variety of policy holders or pensioners.

5.3.1.3 Investment in accordance with a defined investment policy The AIFMD applies to all types of assets and investment strategies. While this is not explicitly specified in the Directive,[186] the application to all investment strategies follows from Article 4(1)(a) AIFMD, which does not foreclose the AIFMD's application to certain investment strategies. The AIFMD must therefore bridge the gap between a broad range of asset classes, including funds investing in securities, commodities, art, wine, patents/intellectual property, private equity and venture capital investments, ships, airplanes, real estate, and derivatives.[187]

It is also irrelevant whether or not a concentrated or diversified investment strategy is pursued. Similarly, the number of assets does not matter. Single asset companies which are common for ship, airplane, energy, and real estate funds therefore also fall within the Directive's scope. These are treated independently of their fiscal classification as investment management or coentrepreneurships.[188]

The lack of clarity has led to ESMA compiling a catalogue of indicative, non-exhaustive criteria which can help establish an investment strategy as a "defined investment policy."[189] The investment strategy:

- is fixed at the point of time at which the investor declares his disposition to invest—later amendments are not opposed by this criterion;
- is determined in the constituting documents of the AIF and is combined with these accordingly (for example, via a reference to another document, included therein);
- is legally binding (subject to a later amendment); and
- includes certain investment specifications, especially guidelines or constraints regarding the eligible assets and regions, applicable strategies (for example, quantitative models), holding periods, and investment limits.

If construed narrowly, investing in assets without any investment guideline (so-called blind pools or black boxes) would not qualify as an AIF. This contradicts the intention of the AIFMD, which warrants a certain measure of protection for the investor, because

---

[186] The Recitals refer to hedge funds, private equity, and venture capital funds as well as real estate funds.

[187] ESMA names six categories of investment strategies, the last one being a fallback provision: see ESMA 2012/117, No. 31.

[188] A. Mann, *AIFM-StAnpG* in *KAGB*, W. Weitnauer, L. Boxberger, & D. Anders eds. (Munich: C.H. Beck 2014); R. Stadler & T. Elser, *Einschneidende Änderungen der Investmentbesteuerung nach dem nunmehr in Kraft getretenen AIFM-Steuer-Anpassungsgesetz*, DStR 2014, 233.

[189] ESMA/2013/600, *Key Concepts of the AIFMD* (May 24, 2013), No. 20.

investors require vastly more protection if there are no investment guidelines. Furthermore, this construction does facilitate the creation of loopholes. One should therefore include blind pools in the AIFMD's scope by deeming completely discretionary investments an investment strategy.[190]

5.3.1.4 For the benefit of these investors   The fund must operate for the benefit of its investors. The beneficiary test separates AIFs from ordinary trusts and foundations. If the income of the trust or foundation benefits persons other than the founder, the trust is not an AIF. Structures which involve circumventions are still regarded as AIFs, as the legal form of the AIF is not determinant.[191]

While the investment must benefit the investor, the AIFMD is not limited to funds that are "profitable" for investors. Tax-efficient vehicles which allocate losses in a first investment stage, while allocating profits in a second stage, are still deemed beneficial to investors, as the losses may be part of a tax-driven investment strategy.

5.3.2   Investment strategies

The following section lists some AIF types by importance.

5.3.2.1 Qualified investor funds   Qualified investor funds ("QIF"), referred to in Germany (the largest QIF market) as special funds,[192] are created for investors with a special set of needs. Two types of QIF are particularly important.

First is QIF for professional investors,[193] such as pension funds, insurance companies, or companies seeking an adequate form of investment for their excess cash. These investors may deem the fund structure an adequate way of dealing with the valuation issue of illiquid assets, enjoy the standardized disclosures and investor protection benefits stemming from the AIFMD, and at the same time optimize their regulatory capital requirements.

Second is funds tailored to the needs of high net worth individuals (HNWi funds or billionaires' funds). Family offices often invest in HNWi funds. HNWis tend to look for coinvestments that are professionally managed, and employ sophisticated strategies or invest large stakes in illiquid assets while regarding the protection that retail investors experience when investing in these asset classes as overly burdensome.

---

[190]   Cf. D. Zetzsche, *Prinzipien der kollektiven Vermögensanlage* (Tübingen: Mohr Siebeck, 2015), at 91; T. Eckhold & P. Balzer, § 22 *Handbuch des Kapitalanlagerechts* (4th ed., H. Assmann & R. Schütze eds), margin 19 (Munich: C.H. Beck 2015); ESMA/2013/600, *Key Concepts of the AIFMD* (May 24, 2013), No. 22 says "Leaving full discretion to make investment decisions to the legal person managing an undertaking should not be used as a mean to circumvent the provisions of the AIFMD."

[191]   Art. 2(2)(b) AIFMD.

[192]   See D. Zetzsche, *Prinzipien der kollektiven Vermögensanlage* (Tübingen: Mohr Siebeck, 2015), at 140.

[193]   See on the AIFMD's definition of professional investors, D. Zetzsche & D. Eckner, *Transparency & Reporting*, chapter 14 in D. Zetzsche (ed.) *The Alternative Investment Fund Managers' Directive: European Regulation of Alternative Investment Funds* (2nd ed., Alphen aan den Rijn: Wolters Kluwer 2015).

5.3.2.2 Private equity Private equity funds include a full spectrum of investment strategies.[194] Some companies specialize in (leveraged) buyouts of listed companies. Others focus on noncontrolling stakes and syndicated structures. The common denominator for these funds is the creation of value using nonlisted (private) firms.

5.3.2.3 Real estate and infrastructure Real estate funds invest in real estate or real estate holding companies. They seek to provide investors with exposure to real estate markets with a regional or international focus. Real estate is often deemed a "safe" product, although the safety vanishes when (1) debt is loaded on the fund or (2) a macroeconomy downswing makes meeting rent payments untenable. Another issue for investment funds is the combination of illiquid assets with the open-ended fund structure, as redemptions of a major fraction of fund units may tip the fund into a liquidity crisis.[195]

A variant of real estate investments involves infrastructure funds which cater to the needs of very long-term investors such as pension funds and insurance companies. These strategies are also the target of the regulation on long-term investment funds (ELTIFR) that aims at unlocking the potential of retail investors in financing the European economy (see Section 2.1.3).

5.3.2.4 Hedge funds Although some laws attempt a definition,[196] "hedge fund"[197] is not a technical term. Rather it refers to investment policies that employ a higher-than-average level of leverage and derivatives for adjusting and often increasing exposure. Due to definitional issues, their low number of sophisticated investors, and their international setup, hedge fund managers have for a long time escaped meaningful regulation. While some see hedge funds as a threat to the stability of the financial markets,[198] as these "have the potential to create financial shock and disrupt the stable functioning of the financial markets more than other financial products because they involve greater leverage and risks,"[199] others emphasize their proinnovative approach

---

[194] See N. Gabrysch, § 2 *Wachstumsfinanzierung*, in *Kompendium Gesellschaftsrecht* Rn 60 (J. Breithaupt & J.H. Ottersbach eds, C.H. Beck/Vahlen 2010); P. Gompers & J. Lerner, *The Venture Capital Cycle* (2nd ed., Cambridge, MA: MIT Press 2006).

[195] See on real estate funds: W. Bals, *Die ökonomische Position von Anteilinhabern offener Immobilienfonds: eine Analyse* (Frankfurt: Peter Lang 1994), B. Abromeit-Kremser, *Offene Immobilienfonds. Betriebswirtschaftliche Aspekte ihres Managements* (Wien: Springer 1986).

[196] See s. 283(1) German Kapitalanlagegesetzbuch.

[197] See on hedge funds M. Kahan & E.B. Rock, Hedge Funds in Corporate Governance and Corporate Control, 155 *University of Pennsylvania Law Review* 1021 (2007); Zetzsche, 'Die Europäische Regulierung'; see also M. Ricke, *Stichwort: Hedge Fonds*, Zeitschrift für Bank und Kapitalmarktrecht 60–65 (2004).

[198] See R. Wilhelmi & M. Bassler, *AIFMD, Systemic Risk and the Financial Crisis*, chapter 2 in D. Zetzsche (ed.) *The Alternative Investment Fund Managers' Directive: European Regulation of Alternative Investment Funds* (2nd ed., Alphen aan den Rijn: Wolters Kluwer 2015).

[199] Pearson and Pearson, Protecting Global Financial Market Stability and Integrity: Strengthening SEC Regulation of Hedge Funds, 33(1) *North Carolina Journal of International Law and Commercial Regulation* 1, 32 (2007).

and liquidity provider function.[200] Notwithstanding the former and the manager regulation imposed by AIFMD, financial stability concerns have led European regulators to impose additional disclosure requirements on UCIs and capital requirements on their counterparties imposing indirect limits on the hedge fund leverage.[201]

5.3.2.5 AIFMD application threshold In addition to the AIF definition, a size-based threshold defines the AIFMD's scope, which is subject to managers' total assets under management. While managers of AIF who manage assets below certain thresholds are not subject to the AIFMD, they are still subject to a registration requirement.[202]

To qualify for the size-based exemption from the AIFMD, total assets under management must not exceed EUR100 million if the AIFM manages open-ended funds or funds which employ leverage (for example, applying credits or derivatives for the purpose of growth and profit increase). In the event that the AIFM manages only closed-ended funds and renounces any type of leverage,[203] the limit is set to a maximum of EUR500 million.[204] The AIFM must fully comply with the AIFMD in the event that the limit is exceeded over three months. Once this happens the fund manager must inform the NCAs immediately.[205]

5.4 Treatment of "Out of Scope" Structures

The wide scope of the AIFMD prompts discussion as to whether the AIFMD fulfills a "basket function," in that it covers all types of investment fund which are not regulated by other acts of European investment law.[206] Certain UCIs are exempted from the Directive's scope.[207] However, these exemptions take place in a rather concealed way due to the fact that the AIF definition draws on the term "UCI" and adds additional criteria whose meanings are vague.

This raises the question as to whether the AIFMD does indeed reflect the principles of all investment undertakings. Due to its high-level principles, the AIFMD is *suitable*

---

[200] Cf. T. Frankel, Private Investment Funds: Hedge Funds' Regulation by Size, 39 *Rutgers Law Journal* 657, 659 (2007–8); T. Bullman, Hedge Funds and the Definition Challenge—Part 1, 15 *Commercial Law Practitioner* 14 (2008).
[201] *Supra* n. 38.
[202] Art. 3(2)–(4) AIFMD.
[203] For a definition of leverage see Arts 4(1)(v) AIFMD and Arts 6 et seq. Regulation No 231/2013. See also F. Dornseifer, Hedge Funds and Systemic Risk Reporting, chapter 22 in D. Zetzsche (ed.) *The Alternative Investment Fund Managers' Directive: European Regulation of Alternative Investment Funds* (2nd ed., Alphen aan den Rijn: Wolters Kluwer 2015); N. Moloney, *EU Securities and Financial Markets Regulation* 301 (Oxford: Oxford University Press, 3rd ed., 2014).
[204] The calculation of the threshold value is subject to Arts 2 et seq. AIFMD (Commission) Regulation.
[205] Art. 4 Regulation No 231/2013.
[206] See also D. Zetzsche, The AIFMD and the Joint Principles of European Asset Management Law, 863–70 in D. Zetzsche (ed.) *The Alternative Investment Fund Managers' Directive: European Regulation of Alternative Investment Funds* (2nd ed., Alphen aan den Rijn: Wolters Kluwer 2015).
[207] Cf. Art. 2(3) AIFMD.

as a kind of general law for collective investments. As such, it may function as a general role model for the regulation of UCIs as well as AIFs. However, the AIFMD's scope is limited by the additional AIF features (see Section 5.3), as can be demonstrated by taking the example of sovereign wealth funds and black pools, which are UCIs without *any* investment strategy. Beyond UCITS and AIF, it is worth mentioning that "holding funds," "single investor funds," "self-managed funds," and "family office funds" all omit at least one of the four UCI criteria. The originators of these structures aim at one or more privileges granted to UCIs, for instance in terms of crossborder recognition, private law structuring options, or tax. It is inadequate to grant these privileges if investor and market concerns are put at risk, that is, if these structures are not subjected to the AIFMD or a similar European investment regulation.

6 UNIQUE FEATURES OF THE UCITSD

While the UCITS manager and sales regulation is generally in line with the principle set out in Section 5.2, the UCITSD's depositary and product regulations are more stringent than those set out by the AIFMD. The UCITSD's regulation of investment companies also includes interesting modifications of the U.S. investment company concept.

6.1 Depositary Regulation

An investment company and, for each of the common funds that it manages, a UCITS ManCo must ensure that a single depositary is appointed.[208] The appointment takes place by virtue of a written depositary contract. The depositary contract regulates, in particular, the flow of information that is necessary to allow the depositary to perform its functions as UCITS depositary.[209]

6.1.1 Safekeeping vs. control
The UCITS depositary has two functions: the safekeeping of assets (custody) and certain control functions vis-à-vis the ManCo.

6.1.1.1 Safekeeping of assets The UCITSD requires financial instruments that may be held in custody to be booked on accounts in the name or on behalf of the UCITS, and in such a manner that they are segregated and clearly identifiable as assets of the UCITS at all times. This requires an up-to-date registry. The segregation requirement raises difficulties at the subdepositary level, to which the same segregation principle applies *mutatis mutandis*. For assets that cannot be held in custody (for instance, certain commodities), the depositary must verify the UCITS' ownership at all times and maintain up-to-date records.[210]

---

[208] Cf. Art. 5, 22(1) UCITSD.
[209] Art. 22(2) UCITSD.
[210] Art. 22(5) UCITSD.

All UCITS assets—regardless of whether these are held by the depositary or whether custody is delegated to third parties ("subdepositaries")—must be ringfenced in order to protect investors in case of the depositary's insolvency. All assets must be kept separately from the (sub)depositary's own assets, and earmarked as the fund's assets.[211] As the UCITSD only applies on European soil, the UCITS depositary is obliged to ensure that ringfencing also takes places in non-EU/EEA countries, for instance, contractually or according to additional segregation requirements.[212]

The assets held in custody must not be reused to the depositary's or the ManCo's benefit, regardless of whether these assets are held by the depositary or by any third party to which the custody function has been delegated. Hence, reuse must not take place at the subdepositary level. Reuse is allowed only where: (1) the reuse of the assets is executed for the account of the UCITS; (2) the depositary is carrying out the instructions of the management company on behalf of the UCITS; (3) the reuse is for the benefit of the UCITS and in the interest of the unitholders; and (4) the transaction is covered by high-quality and liquid collateral received by the UCITS under a title transfer arrangement. The market value of the collateral shall at all times amount to at least the market value of the reused assets plus a premium.[213]

This ban on reuse prompts the question as to whether UCITS assets may be reused by prime brokers financing the UCITS' use of derivatives. The answer depends on how the prime brokers are included in the depositary chain. If the prime broker is a subdepositary, the prime broker will be subject to the reuse ban as well. For this reason, prime brokers tend to avoid the subdepositary position.[214] The collateral requirements, in particular the fact that collateral *plus a premium* shall be granted to the depositary in return for the reuse of UCITS assets,[215] render the reuse of UCITS assets unlikely. Likewise, UCITS rarely short stock they hold unless they deal with derivatives.

6.1.1.2 Controlling the ManCo Article 22(3)–(4) UCITSD imposes a number of control functions upon depositaries, which can be divided into a compliance/supervisory function and a cash custody function.

In the former, the depositary must ensure that (1) the sale, issue, repurchase, redemption, and cancellation of units of the UCITS are carried out in accordance with the applicable national law and the fund rules or instruments of incorporation, and (2) the value of the units of the UCITS is calculated in accordance with the applicable national law and the fund rules or the instruments of incorporation.[216]

---

[211] On earmarking and asset segregation, see, n. 49. The UCITSD does not explicitly require that the assets of each UCITS must be booked in a separate sublevel account. Rather it suffices to book all UCITS and AIF assets together in a separate sublevel account.

[212] For details, see Arts 12–16 Regulation 2016/438.

[213] Art. 22(7) UCITSD.

[214] Cf. the nine prime broker models available under AIFMD see D. Zetzsche, (Prime) Brokerage at 573 in *The Alternative Investment Fund Managers' Directive: European Regulation of Alternative Investment Funds* (D. Zetzsche ed., 2nd ed., Alphen aan den Rijn: Wolters Kluwer 2015).

[215] Art. 22(7) UCITSD.

[216] For details, see Art. 5 Regulation 2016/438.

The depositary must carry out the instructions of the management company unless they conflict with the applicable national law or the fund rules. The practical emphasis is on the subclause ("unless ..."). The duty to carry out instructions that only comply with the law and the fund rules places the onus upon the depositary to review all investment decisions, with a special view of regional diversification and asset class-related investment restrictions.[217]

In its cash custody function,[218] the UCITS depositary needs to ensure that: (1) in transactions involving the UCITS' assets, any consideration is remitted to the UCITS within the usual time limits; (2) the income of the UCITS is applied in accordance with the applicable national law and the fund rules or the instruments of incorporation. As a consequence, the fund manager or his/her staff should never have direct access to the UCITS' cash. All cash transfers are handled by the depositary.

The UCITS depositary ensures that the cash flows of the UCITS are properly monitored (which means that the depositary must engage in monitoring). Monitoring particularly includes all payments made by investors upon the subscription of fund units that have been received by the depositary, and ensuring that all cash has been booked in cash accounts opened in the name of or on behalf of the UCITS in such a manner that the cash is ringfenced in the case of bank insolvency. The UCITS' cash must not be mixed with the respective personal accounts of the ManCo or the depositary.

The depositary is required to provide the ManCo with a comprehensive inventory as additional services to the ManCo. This inventory does not substitute the ManCo's own bookkeeping. It merely serves as an additional check.[219]

6.1.1.3 Extraordinary strong position The UCITS depositary is the UCITS custodian, payment institution, and transfer agent, as well as the supercompliance officer in one entity. The extraordinary strong position of the UCITS depositary is deeply ingrained in the European history of investment funds and can be tracked back to the sixteenth century. It is one of the most characteristic features of the UCITS brand worldwide and distinguishes the UCITS depositary from US-style custodians.[220]

6.1.2 Eligible entities

Depositaries must be independent entities separate from the ManCo and located in the UCITS' home Member State.[221] Only national central banks, credit institutions licensed under CRD IV, and certain nationally governed institutions with capital requirements, organization, and supervision similar to credit institutions are eligible as UCITS depositaries.[222] In the context of their respective roles, the management company and the depositary act independently and solely in the interest of the unitholders.[223]

---

[217] Cf. Art. 22(3) UCITSD, Art. 6 Regulation 2016/438.
[218] For Art. 22(4) UCITSD, Arts 9–10 Regulation 2016/438.
[219] See Art. 22(6) UCITSD, Art. 14(2) Regulation 2016/438.
[220] For a discussion regarding the economic rationale, see *supra*, at 4.1.
[221] Art. 23(1) UCITSD.
[222] See Art. 23(1) UCITSD and Art. 10(1) Regulation 2016/438.
[223] Art. 25 UCITSD.

European law allows that the depositary and ManCo belong to the same group of companies. The obvious conflicts here have prompted some criticism. However, reputational effects created by the joint group membership have proven valuable in restructuring ailing funds. These positive reputational effects are likely to find their limits when the harm is sufficiently large and a threat to the depositary's continued existence. In addition, European law requires transparency, awareness, and conflict management in these cases.[224]

Depositaries provide a crucial guarantor function to the fund. For this reason the fund rules must set out the conditions under which the depositary (and the ManCo) may be replaced in line with the overarching objective of investor protection.[225] The depositary also functions as an informational intermediary for the UCITS home NCAs. The depositary requires all information from the fund management company in order to meet its obligations.[226]

While the control functions must not be delegated to third parties,[227] the depositaries may rely on third parties for safekeeping.[228] The depositary remains liable for any lost assets under the conditions of Article 24 UCITSD regardless of whether the depositary safekeeps the assets itself or delegates safekeeping to third parties.

As third party custody is the norm in a global custodian chain and depositary safekeeping is the rare exception, UCITS depositaries bear enormous liability risks. In turn, a UCITS depositary will carefully select its subdepositaries, ensuring an enhanced level of diligence along the depositary chain.

6.1.3 Depositary's liability

6.1.3.1 Strict liability for lost assets Depositaries are strictly liable for the loss of financial instruments held in custody.[229] The depositary is liable regardless of whether it held the assets or delegated custody to a subdepositary. The depositary is mandated to return an instrument of an identical type or the corresponding amount to the UCITS without undue delay for each financial instrument lost.[230]

The liability must neither be excluded nor limited by contract. Any agreement to the contrary is void. The only way the depositary may limit its liability is by proving that the loss has arisen as a result of an external event beyond its reasonable control, the consequences of which would have been unavoidable despite all reasonable efforts to the contrary. This force majeure clause, further specified in implementing legislation, applies in very rare cases.[231]

6.1.3.2 Liability for other violations With regard to harm caused to investors beyond lost assets, the depositary is liable for its negligent or intentional failure to properly

---

[224] Art. 23–24 Regulation 2016/438.
[225] See Art. 26 UCITSD and Art. 22 Regulation 2016/438.
[226] Art. 26a UCITSD.
[227] Art. 22a(1) UCITSD.
[228] See Arts 22(5), 22a(2)–(4) and 24 UCITSD and Arts 18–19 Regulation 2016/438.
[229] Art. 24(1)–(4) UCITSD.
[230] See Art. 24 UCITSD.
[231] See Art. 19 Regulation 2016/438.

fulfill its obligations. This fault-based liability particularly applies to violations of the depositaries' cash monitoring and oversight duties, as well as to the registration requirement applicable to assets that cannot be held in custody.[232]

6.1.3.3 Investors' standing in relation to legal recourse   UCITS investors may invoke the depositary's liability directly or indirectly through the management company or the investment company. The standing is subject to the condition that it does not lead to a duplication of redress or to unequal treatment of the unitholders.[233] Member States implement this confusing standing clause in two ways: either they give the investors a right to demand action against the depositary from the ManCo, or national laws directly grant investors the right to sue, with the ManCo joining the procedures initiated by investors against the ManCo on behalf of the passive (that is, not suing) investors.

6.2 Product Regulation

No UCITS shall pursue activities unless it has been authorized in accordance with the UCITSD. Such authorization is valid for all Member States.[234] The authorization signals the pan-EU/EEA approach of the UCITSD which is the basis for the European passport. The authorization is based on adequate documents and a UCITS set up in accordance with the UCITSD, including the appointment of a qualified depositary and an investment policy complying with the following eligibility criteria.[235]

6.2.1 Eligible assets

The UCITS investment strategy specified in Articles 50–57 UCITSD focuses on liquid assets due to its open-ended type. Liquidity is achieved, first, with a list of assets which should be liquid, by definition.

UCITS investments exclusively comprise:

- transferable securities and money market instruments traded on regulated capital markets;[236]
- units of other UCITS or UCITS-equivalent open-ended funds up to 10 percent of the fund's assets;[237]
- deposits with credit institutions repayable on demand or ready for withdrawal within the next 12 months;[238]
- certain financial derivative instruments traded at regulated capital markets;[239] and
- untraded money market instruments backed by trustworthy private and public institutions subject to approval by the NCAs.[240]

---

[232] See Art. 22(5)(b) UCITSD and Art. 14 Regulation 2016/438.
[233] Art. 22a (5) UCITSD.
[234] Art. 5(1) UCITSD.
[235] Art. 5(2) (4) UCITSD.
[236] Art. 50(1)(a)–(d) UCITSD.
[237] Art. 50(1)(e) UCITSD.
[238] Art. 50(1)(f) UCITSD.
[239] Art. 50(1)(g) UCITSD.
[240] Art. 50(1)(h) UCITSD.

Article 50(2)(b) UCITSD prohibits the acquisition of precious metals, or certificates representing them, and real estate for investment purposes.

A UCITS shall not invest more than 10 percent of its assets in transferable securities or money market instruments other than those being defined as eligible assets. This 10 percent threshold of Article 50(2)(a) UCITSD is pejoratively referred to as a "trash quota." While the Central Bank of Ireland, the Luxembourg CSSF, and the Liechtenstein FMA have deemed it permissible for UCITS ManCos to invest in unregulated open-ended investment funds, including hedge funds provided that the investment complies with the eligibility criteria for UCITS, ESMA holds that Article 50(2)(a) UCITSD allows only for investments in transferable securities and money market instruments other than UCI units.[241]

6.2.2 Investment limits

Anticoncentration rules shall maintain liquidity even in periods of market stress. As a principle, a UCITS shall:

- invest no more than 5 percent of its assets in transferable securities or money market instruments issued by the same body;
- invest no more than 20 percent of its assets in deposits made with the same body; and
- not invest in derivatives that exceed a certain risk exposure level, which is 10 percent of its assets when the counterparty is a credit institution and 5 percent of its assets in other cases.[242]

Notwithstanding the individual limits above, a UCITS shall never combine, in cases where this would lead to investment of more than 20 percent of its assets in a single body:

- investments in transferable securities or money market instruments issued by that body;
- deposits made with that body; and
- exposures arising from OTC derivative transactions undertaken with that body.

These rules are subject to a number of exemptions detailed in Articles 52–55, subject to Member State discretion. For instance, Member States could raise the 5 percent limit to a maximum of 10 percent. If they do so, however, the total value of the transferable securities and the money market instruments held by the UCITS in the issuing bodies in each of which it invests more than 5 percent of its assets shall not exceed 40 percent of the value of its assets. That limitation shall not apply to deposits or OTC derivative transactions made with financial institutions subject to prudential supervision. The 5 percent limit may be raised to 25 percent where bonds are issued by a credit institution which has its registered office in a Member State and is subject by law to special public supervision designed to protect bondholders. In particular, sums deriving

---

[241] ESMA/2012/721, Opinion: Article 50(2)(a) of Directive 2009/65/EC.
[242] Art. 52 UCITSD.

from the issue of those bonds shall be invested in accordance with the law in assets which, during the whole period of validity of the bonds, are capable of covering claims attached to the bonds and which, in the event of failure of the issuer, would be used on a priority basis for the reimbursement of the principal and payment of the accrued interest. Where a UCITS invests more than 5 percent of its assets in these bonds issued by a single issuer, the total value of these investments shall not exceed 80 percent of the UCITS' value. Member States must not combine these exemptions.[243]

Further exemptions apply to certain index funds, public issuers, and funds of funds.[244] In practice most Member States exercise maximum discretion, since the UCITS from other EU/EEA countries that could rely on the wider investment limits could sell their UCITS via the European passport to investors in all other EU/EEA states.

6.2.3 Control ban

As another anticoncentration rule, UCITS must not exercise significant influence upon or even control issuers.[245] The control ban should ensure that the UCITS ManCo focuses on investment rather than operating business. This is due to the fact that additional legal obligations are prompted once the investment passes the "control" threshold; for instance, under European takeover law, "control" triggers the obligation to issue a takeover bid to the other shareholders. Controlling stakes also reduce the ability to liquidate the UCITS' assets when necessary. A controlling stake is hard to sell in distressed times and is almost always offered with some discount. Controlling stakes reduce the ability to liquidate the UCITS' assets when necessary.

Beyond the general control ban, notwithstanding the time of acquisition, a UCITS may acquire no more than:

- 10 percent of the nonvoting shares of a single issuing body;
- 10 percent of the debt securities of a single issuing body;
- 25 percent of the units of a single UCI; and
- 10 percent of the money market instruments of a single issuing body.

Member States may waive the control ban as well as the specific limits for public issuers, certain SPVs, and subsidiaries engaged in investment management.[246]

Again, these formal limits aim at securing the liquidity of the UCITS' assets. While several regulatory approaches exist worldwide to achieve the same objective, the great level of detail has led to significant certainty, which is crucial in light of the harmonization rationale of European investment law (see Sections 2.3 and 3.2). Moreover, the UCITS limits worked well in practice; in the more than 25 years during which the UCITS framework has operated, no liquidity crisis has been reported in the UCITS core assets. Liquidity pressure resulted, however, from noncore assets (the

---

[243] Art. 52(5) UCITSD.
[244] For details, see Dirk A., Zetzsche The Anatomy of European Investment Fund Law (April 12, 2017). Available at SSRN: https://ssrn.com/abstract=2951681, at VI.2.c.
[245] Art. 56(1) UCITSD.
[246] Art. 56(4) UCITSD.

so-called trash quota), as well as from low-volume index products which are eligible as UCITS assets under certain circumstances.

6.2.4 Violation of investment limits

Under certain conditions, UCITS may deviate from the aforementioned limits for a limited period of time in cases where the passing of the threshold is the result not of a willfully taken investment decision, but of external events. These cases include:[247]

- the period up to six months after the UCITS' initial authorization. While UCITS must also observe the principle of risk spreading in this stage, the hard investment limits do not apply;
- the exercise of subscription rights; and
- events beyond the control of the UCITS ManCo.

In the second two of these cases, UCITS shall prioritize the sale of the assets that exceed the investment limits to remedy the situation. However, the interests of the unitholders need to be taken into account. This could justify a delay. Interestingly, the UCITSD refrains from stipulating rules if the asset manager breaches investment restrictions willfully. In this case, the same rationale, which is investor protection, applies. This means the UCITSD does not mandate a fire sale; rather, a smooth reduction of excess position is of the essence.

6.3 The Secret of the UCITS' Success

With regard to legislation, this author believes that clearcut product regulation paired with the interlocking control functions of the UCITS ManCo and the depositary (which I referred to as the investment triangle) are important factors that reduce the likelihood of fund managers violating investment rules. The investment triangle is, however, unlikely to prevent losses from lawful investments. Since the 1990s, when the UCITS brand was introduced, stock markets have on average been on the rise, despite the financial crisis that began in 2007.

A second aspect catering to the UCITS success is flexibility. UCITS today can be modified to respond to any investment trend. For instance, UCITS are open to function as exchange traded funds, 130/30 funds, money market funds, pure equity, and bond funds. They will also be open to automatization, regardless of the strategy that the fund manager applies.

Third, the UCITS brand has kept out of trouble and away from worldwide scandals for the better part of its 25-year existence. This may have contributed to its legendary status. While money market funds failed in the US, European money market funds were not marketed to investors as a cash substitute. Investors in turn deemed money market funds an investment rather than cash. Where scandals occurred (as in the response to the Madoff scandals), for the main part financial intermediaries covered

---

[247] Art. 57(1) UCITSD.

the investors' losses on a voluntary basis.[248] I assume that the community of financial centers that thrive on the success of UCITS (including Luxembourg and Ireland), and where most international distribution takes place, exerts additional discipline on market participants. This has encouraged intermediaries to act responsibly vis-à-vis their investors rather than letting them bear losses when this was opportune from a short-term perspective. This exertion of control is due to the insight that any scandal will lead to restrictions of crossborder distribution, which is harmful to the financial center. In the worst case it could lead to a repeal of European passports granted by an EU Member State, or the entire abolition of the European passport. These centers are expected to rely on gatekeepers (such as established law firms) and additional nonlegal means (including peer pressure and subordination to strong depositaries) to restrict intermediaries' conduct in the centers' collective interests.[249]

Finally, the fact that UCITS are harmonized EU/EEA-wide has facilitated their recognition as a flowthrough vehicle from a tax law perspective. The judicature of the European Court of Justice,[250] considering the freedom of capital,[251] prevents Member States from discriminating against UCITS established in other Member States and similarly structured funds from third countries (including the US). The ECJ holds that there is an undue restriction of the freedom of capital where, under the tax legislation of a Member State, the dividends paid by companies established in that Member State to an investment fund established in a different or a non-Member State do not qualify for a tax exemption, whereas investment funds established in that Member State do receive such an exemption. This judicature presses for forgoing withholding taxes entirely, or reimbursement of withholding taxes to the fund with an administrative

---

[248] This could not stop the European Commission from initiating a more harmonized approach. Cf. European Commission, Consultation Paper on the UCITS Depositary Function (July 2009); Summary of Responses to UCITS Depositaries Consultation Paper—Feedback Statement; Consultation Paper on the UCITS Depositary Function and on the UCITS Managers' Remuneration (December 2010); Feedback on public consultation on the UCITS V (February 2011) (revealing significant differences among Member States).

[249] This assumption of better joint coordination is in line with what financial centers are expected to do in a compliant world without tax evasion. See D. Zetzsche, Competitiveness of Financial Centers in Light of Financial and Tax Law Equivalence Requirements at 64, in *Rethinking Global Financial Law and Its Regulation* (R. Buckley, D. Arner, & F. Avgouleas eds, Cambridge: Cambridge University Press 2016).

[250] See, for instance, ECJ of 10 May 2012, Case C-338/11 *Santander Asset Management SGIIC SA v Directeur des résidents à l'étranger et des services généraux* and C-339/11 to C-347/11 *Santander Asset Management SGIIC SA and Others v Ministre du Budget* ... (holding that EU law precludes French legislation establishing different tax rules for nationally sourced dividends received by resident and non-resident UCITS); ECJ of 16 April 2014, Case C-190/12, *Emerging Markets Series of DFA Investment Trust Company v Dyrektor Izby Skarbowej w Bydgoszczy*, ECLI:EU:C:2014:249 (holding that Polish tax rules exempting dividend payments to domestic investment funds, but taxing dividend payments to comparable non-EU funds restrict the free movement of capital). For a discussion see D. Zetzsche, *Analoge Anwendung von § 11 InvStG auf ausländische Investmentfonds wegen ungleichen Quellensteuerabzugs auf inländische Dividenden!*, ISTR 2015, 8.

[251] Art. 63 TFEU.

burden as low as possible. Although far from easy, tax law may have contributed to UCITS' success.

7 THE FUTURE OF EUROPEAN INVESTMENT LAW

The future path of European investment law depends on the answers to a handful of questions.

7.1 Rules vs. Principles

While the UCITSD and the AIFMD provide the regulatory fundament for professional investor funds, this author sees more and more product rules interfering with this clear distinction. The Money Market Fund Regulation subjects, for the first time, manages under both the UCITSD and the AIFMD to product regulation for money market funds, in the case of UCITS in addition to UCITS product regulation. Further potential product regulations include debt funds.

While an enormous amount of product regulation exists, for example in France, important fund jurisdictions have become successful with a simpler distinction between retail and professional funds.

7.2 Harmonization vs. Openness to Innovation

Another issue is whether a higher degree of harmonization is desirable or whether European investment law should retain some openness to innovation. Harmonization could be warranted if there is evidence of significant regulatory arbitrage. However, few sectors still have room for arbitrage. Market differentiation remains, however, with regard to the speed with which regulators respond to new developments. The established financial centers respond quickly and effectively; the large distribution states generally take a slow and heavyhanded approach.

In light of the substantial degree of harmonization and the far-reaching arm of ESMA, it is preferable to retain some openness for innovation, especially in order to be able to compete with fund managers from non-EU/EEA jurisdictions. If the European fund centers lose competitiveness, the whole of Europe will lose out.

7.3 Investor Protection vs. Systemic Risk

Another regulatory divide is the extent to which investor protection or systemic risk concerns should determine the future of regulation. Europe is unique in already protecting professional investors with the AIFMD. For reasons of competitiveness, it is not desirable to pursue investor protection any further. A future field for investor protection may include certain fund types on the national level, in particular closed-ended funds.

Systemic risk concerns have ruled European regulation for almost a decade. European legislators have:

- implemented risk management requirements and supervisory powers to impose leverage limits for all AIF through AIFMD;[252]
- mandated fund managers to substitute the blind adoption of ratings with professional rating agencies using their own assessments;[253]
- enhanced transparency regarding the use of counterparties when entering into derivative contracts not traded at regulated markets;[254]
- added disclosure and transparency requirements regarding securities financing transactions;[255]
- developed rules for money market funds;[256] and
- developed a framework for securitization in general, as well as investments in securitization positions by professional investors.[257]

All of these steps have increased transaction costs for some or all investors engaging in transactions that European regulators view as sufficiently suspicious to add a layer of new legislation to. The beneficiaries of professional investors (such as pensioners) will feel the additional costs in their investment returns, while the benefits from a systemic risk perspective are uncertain and (too) hard to measure. The uncertain benefits of systemic risk regulation coalesce around increasing discomfort regarding the application of these rules. As discussed here, the delineation between European investment fund law and the new European securitization framework is less than certain.[258]

We see both supervisors and financial intermediaries overwhelmed by the sheer mass of new rules. Before an additional set of rules is put in place, it is surely advisable to wait and see what the effects of the rules already implemented will be. Proportionality suggests exempting all small financial intermediaries from all rules based on the systemic risk rationale. While there is agreement that the cost of regulation needs to be reduced, the means of achieving this also touch upon the interests of large, well-organized intermediaries seeking to retain their competitiveness.

7.4 Fee Reduction

In the past, European regulators were concerned with enhancing the fund size of UCITS. This was because Europe was characterized by many undersized UCITS, which made UCITS investment unprofitable in many cases due to overly high fees. The fragmentation was due to the home bias of many UCITS ManCos and the low level of interest on behalf of UCITS investors in foreign UCITS (that is, UCITS set up in other Member States).

---

[252] See Arts 15–16, 24 AIFMD.
[253] See Directive 2013/14/EU ... amending Directive 2009/65/EC ... and Directive 2011/61/EU ... in respect of the excessive reliance on credit ratings, OJ L145/1.
[254] See Regulation (EU) No 648/2012 ... of 4 July 2012 on OTC derivatives, central counterparties and trade repositories, OJ L201/1.
[255] *Supra*, n. 38.
[256] *Supra*, n. 14.
[257] See Art. 50a UCITSD, Art. 17 AIFMD.
[258] *Supra*, at 5.4.

The concern is even more warranted today in light of record low interest rates. While legislators have since taken steps to enhance fund sizes, including uniform rules on UCITS mergers and master-feeder structures,[259] the positive impact of crossborder fund distribution on costs is mitigated by increasing legal, compliance, and IT costs following the financial crisis. However, these costs are, for the most part, fixed costs and as such contribute to market concentration, which may constitute an issue from a systemic perspective in the long term, but contributes to cost cutting in the short term. The increased level of automation, including robot advisory and other FinTech applications, is likely to drive fees further down. The concentration of fund business in some European fund centers—3 out of 31 EU/EEA Member States hold a share of more than 66 percent of the European UCITS market (Luxembourg alone holds 36 percent); four EU/EEA Member States together hold more than 71 percent of the AIF assets—is likely to speed up the development of larger funds and lower fees even further. As products become more comparable, investors may choose lower fee funds.

All of the mentioned factors are meaningless unless investors choose low-cost funds over high-cost ones. European legislation has been facilitating investor choice since 2011 (for UCITS) and 2016 (for AIF) with short key investor documents that assist investors in comparing fund costs with very little effort and insight required on the investor side. The longer these instruments are at work, the more their cost-reducing effects become apparent.[260] Although the end of history is still far away, with regard to fund size and fund fees, European investment law is on the right track. (That statement should not preclude *some* reform of the key investor document rules. For instance, drawing on the economic presumption that all other factors are reflected in volatility, profitability is underweighted while volatility is overrated as a factor for investors. Retail investors have a hard time following this logic.)

The flood of regulation following the financial crisis has been anything but helpful for cost reduction, as implementing legislation is first and foremost a cost to investors, who need to pay fund managers and depositaries for additional compliance. The opinion that costs and benefits of regulation must be carefully assessed prior to legislation is therefore more warranted today than ever before.

7.5 Impact of Brexit

Brexit—the UK's departure from the European Union—is likely to impact European investment fund law in various ways. Areas that are most likely to be affected are the cross-border activity of institutions generated through foreign branches, the rules on outsourcing portions of fund management to third parties, the definition of reverse solicitation and the minimum requirements for setting up a fund management

---

[259] See Chs VI and VIII UCITSD. In turn, between 2004 and 2014, crossborder fund distribution (including round trips) rose from 29 percent to 42 percent, see EFAMA, annual report 2015, p. 8.

[260] See Deloitte & Fundsquare, Europa's Fund Expenses at a Crossroads (2015), www2.deloitte.com/lu/en/pages/investment-management/articles/europe-cross-border-fund-industry-pr.html (arguing declining overall cost ratios for UCITS 2002–2012, with passively managed funds showing the most rapid decline, and further cost-cutting potential of up to 70 percent in terms of distribution chain costs).

company/AIFM in a Member State (i.e., details on the letter box prohibition). While the principles presented in this chapter are likely to remain as they are now, we expect ESMA to harmonize and to clarify the rules in these areas because European law is not yet harmonized in this space, and further harmonization is necessary to avoid a race to the bottom among Member States in their efforts to attract fund management business from the UK.

8 CONCLUSION

With the UCITS and AIF legislation, European investment law provides a strongly developed, widely harmonized framework, with few opportunities for regulatory arbitrage to harm investors, while at present still retaining some openness to innovation. The level of harmonization has led to competition "on the merits" among specialized fund centers which seek to develop—and protect—"their" UCITS brands.

A number of factors will determine the future path of European investment fund law. Regarding the form of legislation, either a focus on the UCITSD and AIFMD and a principal-style regulation, or rule-based regulation with many different product types written into European law, will prevail. (Brexit may tip the tide in the second direction, as fund-type regulation is excessively developed in France, and well developed in Germany.) The more rules and the stronger the degree of harmonization, the less openness to innovation there will be. After a decade of regulatory activity, investor protection, systemic risk or stakeholder concerns hardly provide ground for an additional layer of regulation.

Another ever topical issue is fees. While the European legislature have implemented a wide range of initiatives, ranging from a simplified fund merger scheme over master-feeder structures to short key investor documents to enhance pressure on the distribution chain, and the increasing appeal of passively managed funds drives fees down further, increasing compliance costs prompted by excessive regulation create a challenge in a zero interest environment. While FinTech, RegTech and further market concentration provide solutions to the cost problem, I speculate that the intense competition for investors' capital in Europe will keep the downward trend for fees intact[261]—to the benefit of investors.

---

[261] See J.B. Beckett, *New Fund Order—A Digital Death for Fund Selection?*, at 75, 171 (Blurb, 2016).

15. Governance aspects of mutual funds in Ireland
Blanaid Clarke and Mark White

1 INTRODUCTION

Mutual funds are investment vehicles designed to facilitate the collection of assets from a number of investors and the investment of those assets in a diversified pool of assets. This structure allows small investors to acquire exposure to a professionally managed and typically diversified basket of assets. Efficiencies can be achieved by spreading costs over a pool of investors and by investors gaining exposure to a diversified portfolio of assets which might not otherwise be possible to access if the investors were required to purchase and hold the securities directly. It is also a means by which institutional investors can gain access to a diversified portfolio of assets within a well-regulated environment, and this has become particularly important for investors such as pension funds and insurance companies post-Madoff and the Lehman collapse.

There are two broad categories of mutual funds in Ireland,[1] which are regulated (or the management of which is regulated) at European Union level through the introduction of specific legislative instruments:[2] undertakings for collective investment in transferable securities ("UCITS") within the scope of the UCITS Directive,[3] and alternative investment funds ("AIFs") falling under the Alternative Investment Fund Managers Directive.[4] As is described in Section 2 of this chapter, the two categories differ in their regulatory framework, their investment policies, and the manner in which they are marketed to investors. The Central Bank of Ireland, as the sole financial markets regulator in Ireland, is the competent authority for the authorization and supervision of mutual funds in Ireland. Section 3 of the chapter explores the choices of fund structure for mutual funds, focusing on investment companies and Irish Collective Asset-Management Vehicles. Section 4 examines the role of the key parties in mutual fund governance. Finally, Section 5 of the chapter considers the legal and regulatory framework which imposes standards relating to fiduciary obligations, operations, transparency, conflicts of interest, and financial reporting.

In 1987, in order to stimulate the Irish economy and increase employment, a designated site in the heart of Dublin, the International Financial Services Centre, was identified and financial services firms establishing themselves there were offered

---

[1] References in this chapter to Ireland are to the Republic of Ireland and do not include Northern Ireland.
[2] By setting out the rules for these funds in the form of a Directive, the EU ensures that its goals are met while enabling the implementing provisions to be adjusted to the specificities of the particular market and legal system in each member state.
[3] Directive 2009/65/EC (referred to as "the UCITS IV Directive") as amended by Directive 2014/91/EU ("referred to as the UCITS V Directive") is now the main regulatory instrument.
[4] Directive 2011/61/EU.

financial incentives including lower rates of tax.[5] This marked a turning point in the development of Ireland as a global hub for financial services entities. The international funds industry became a core component of this following the implementation of the first UCITS Directive in 1989.[6] This Directive sought to coordinate disparate national laws governing collective investment undertakings in order to: avoid distorting the conditions of competition between those undertakings; ensure equivalent protection for unit-holders; and facilitate undertakings situated in one Member State marketing their units in other Member States. In order to do this, common basic rules needed to be established for the authorization, supervision, structure, and activities of undertakings and the mandatory information to be published. More than 75 percent of the assets of Irish-domiciled funds are held in UCITS with a value of €1.8 trillion, with more than €4.4 trillion in assets under administration for both domiciled and nondomiciled funds.[7] The Irish stock exchange trading under the name Euronext Dublin boasts of its reputation as the world leader for the listing of investment funds, including hedge funds, exchange traded funds (ETFs), private equity funds, multimanager funds, property funds, venture capital funds, emerging market funds, derivative funds, and funds of funds. It has a set of rules for listing investment funds, and applications to Euronext Dublin for listing Irish-domiciled funds generally run parallel to applications to the Central Bank for authorization. Euronext Dublin has 365 funds and 986 subfunds currently listed.[8] ETFs in the form of UCITS established as investment companies are particularly attractive as they are traded like a common stock on the exchange, allowing investors to diversify a single investment over an entire sector or market segment. In total, 54 percent of all European domiciled ETFs are based in Ireland. In advertising its listing services, Euronext Dublin emphasizes the particular benefits it offers as including: competitive fees applied per fund rather than per class;[9] guaranteed listing review times of 2–5 days; increased visibility; enhanced transparency; an ability to meet investor requirements; increased tax efficiency; the benefit of third party oversight; and access to ETF trading.

More broadly, Ireland is an attractive domicile for funds and asset managers for a number of reasons over and above the benefits which compliance with EU regulations afford to all Member States. One of the key drivers for ETFs being domiciled in Ireland is the infrastructure, technology, and expertise in servicing ETFs which has been developed in the country over the years. As the servicing of ETFs is very systems-based and technology-driven, Irish service providers have invested more heavily, and developed more experience, in servicing ETFs than any other EU jurisdiction. Another key attraction for funds more generally is that the Irish legal system is a common law

---

[5] The special IFSC rate was abolished as and from 2006 in accordance with agreements between Ireland and the EU on state aid rules.

[6] Directive 85/611/EC.

[7] Irish Funds Industry Association figures as at end December 2017. See www.irishfunds.ie/facts-figures.

[8] See ISE Monthly Report (April 2018) available at www.ise.ie/Market-Data-Announcements/Statistical-Reports/.

[9] At the time of writing, the annual listing fee for an EU fund was €2,000 and for an offshore fund it was €2,180. See www.ise.ie/Products-Services/Investment%20Funds/List-a-Fund/.

system, as opposed to the civil law system which operates, for example, in Luxembourg, a main competitor. Well-developed common law rules of contract law thus apply which lead to comprehensive, detailed, and accessible contracts setting out the rights and obligations of all parties. Ireland is also a party to a number of conventions, including the Hague Convention on Choice of Court Agreements and the Recast Brussels Regulation on the recognition and enforcement of certain choice of court agreements. All this contributes to making the agreements easier for parties to navigate, to understand, and to enforce. The resulting increase in legal certainty, together with the technical expertise and experience of practitioners and the efficient court system, constitutes a strong draw. Ireland offers a corporate tax rate of 12.5 percent and no taxes on funds or investors. In terms of broad business environment, Ireland is generally perceived as a good place to do business with Forbes annual rankings listing it in eighth place in 2018.[10] It is a member of the OECD and benefits from an educated, English-speaking workforce,[11] low incidences of corruption, anti-money laundering regulation, a good technological infrastructure, and a strong track record in inward investment.

2 UCITS AND NON-UCITS

2.1 UCITS

UCITS are open-ended investment units and benefit from a so-called "passporting regime" which means that once authorized in one Member State, they may be marketed throughout the EU without further authorization, subject only to complying with a relatively straightforward passporting procedure. This means that fund promoters can create a single fund product for the entire EU rather than having to establish a product on a jurisdiction by jurisdiction basis. It is estimated that UCITS account for approximately 75 percent of all collective investments by small investors in Europe.[12] However, although UCITS funds, by their nature, are designed as retail funds, a significant amount of investor money is institutional money.

In most circumstances, the UCITS Directive applies in the same way in all Member States and uniform rules thus apply. However, in a small number of areas, Member States are afforded limited discretion to deviate and thus the Irish rules may differ from their EU counterparts. The UCITS Directive as implemented in Ireland by the European Communities (Undertakings for Collective Investment in Transferable Securities) Regulations 2011 ("the UCITS Regulations")[13] imposes a number of requirements on UCITS investment funds, and also on their management companies and UCITS depositaries. The most recent amendment of the UCITS Directive was made by Directive 2014/91/EU, which is colloquially referred to as UCITS V. The latter was

---

[10] www.forbes.com/places/ireland/.
[11] The IMD World Competitiveness Yearbook 2017 rated Ireland as sixth overall and third in terms of business efficiency.
[12] http://ec.europa.eu/finance/investment/ucits-directive/index_en.htm.
[13] S.I. No. 352 of 2011.

transposed into Irish law by the European Union (Undertakings for Collective Investment in Transferable Securities) (Amendment) Regulations 2016, which amended the UCITS Regulations.[14] In addition, the Central Bank UCITS Regulations consolidate all of the requirements which the Central Bank imposes on UCITS, UCITS management companies and depositaries of UCITS.[15] They both supplement rules contained in the UCITS Directive and regulate areas outside the scope of the UCITS Directive, such as dealings with connected persons. Guidance is also provided by the Central Bank on a number of topics including marketing requirements.[16]

As UCITS are available for subscription by retail investors on a pan-European basis through the UCITS passport, UCITS are subject to more stringent investment restrictions, asset eligibility criteria, and liquidity requirements than non-UCITS and consequently offer greater investment protection measures. For example, UCITS funds must deal at least on a fortnightly basis, with no minimum holding periods; they will often have weekly and even daily liquidity; and redemption settlement periods must be fewer than 14 days. As mentioned above, institutions, such as insurance companies and pension funds, are increasingly seeking highly regulated, diversified, and liquid investment vehicles in which to invest their money post-Madoff and the financial crisis of 2008. UCITS funds offer these safeguards to those types of institutional investors.

While UCITS are limited in their investment options, the range of permissible investments has increased over time,[17] and includes listed equities, corporate and sovereign bonds, bank deposits, money market instruments, and certain types of derivatives. This has facilitated the establishment of a greater number and variety of funds. Investment restrictions include a prohibition on investing more than 10 percent of a fund's net assets in unlisted securities or in any one issuer and a prohibition on acquiring units carrying voting rights which would enable a fund to exercise a significant influence over the management of any issuer. There is no restriction on investing in European assets, however, and assets can be located in most countries around the world provided they comply with the UCITS Directive.

2.2 AIFs

Mutual funds which are not authorized under the UCITS Directive are termed non-UCITS or "alternative investment funds" ("AIFs"). AIFs are not themselves regulated, but each AIF must appoint an Alternative Investment Fund Manager ("AIFM") and those AIFMs and their activities are regulated under the Alternative Investment Fund Managers Directive ("AIFMD"), which was implemented in Ireland

---

[14] S.I. No. 143 of 2016.
[15] The Central Bank (Supervision and Enforcement) Act 2013 (Section 48(1)) (Undertakings for Collective Investment in Transferable Securities) Regulations 2015 (S.I. No. 420 of 2015) as amended by the Central Bank (Supervision and Enforcement) Act 2013 (Section 48(1)) (Undertakings for Collective Investment in Transferable Securities) (Amendment) Regulations 2016 (S.I. No. 307 of 2016).
[16] Available at www.centralbank.ie/regulation/industry-market-sectors/funds/ucits/guidance.
[17] Directive 2001/107/EC (the "Management Company Directive") and Directive 2001/108/EC (the "Product Directive") colloquially referred to as UCITS III.

by the European Union (Alternative Investment Fund Managers) Regulations 2013.[18] This sets out a common regulatory regime for AIFMs within the EU. The Central Bank has always regulated AIFs and it is on the basis of this Central Bank authorization that Irish funds are tax exempt. The Central Bank has published an AIF Rulebook which sets out the conditions to be imposed on AIFs, their AIFMs, and service providers such as the depositary and the fund administrator. Each AIF is required to have a single AIFM who is responsible for compliance with the regulatory requirements.[19] This may be an external manager appointed by or on behalf of the AIF to manage it. Alternatively, the board of a corporate AIF with an internal management may choose to manage itself. In the latter case, it will then be authorized as the AIFM.

AIFs may be open- or closed-ended, and different investment restrictions and investor protection measures apply depending on whether the fund is established for retail investors, professional investors,[20] or qualifying investors. A qualifying investor alternative fund ("QIAIF") is allowed to avoid a number of the restrictions which apply to retail investor alternative funds ("RIAIF") because of the more sophisticated nature of the investors. To benefit from this regime, a QIAIF must require a minimum initial subscription of €100,000 and be open to professional clients as defined by MiFID:[21] investors certified by an EU credit institution, a MiFID firm, or a UCITS management company as having appropriate expertise, experience, and knowledge to understand the investment or investors who certify that they are informed investors. In Ireland, the QIAIF is by far the most popular form of alternative investment fund, due to the nature of the greater investment flexibility it enjoys over a RIAIF. Once an AIFM has been authorized in one Member State in accordance with the full AIFMD regime, EU AIFs to which that AIFM has been appointed may be marketed throughout the EU without further authorization. Note, however, that unlike the UCITS regime, which has a retail passport, the passport under AIFMD extends only to professional clients under MiFID. This means that, typically, it will not be possible to sell a QIAIF to high net worth individuals outside Ireland unless the relevant country into which the QIAIF is being marketed has a private placement regime that permits such a sale to take place. For example, the UK, Switzerland, and the Scandinavian countries all have clearly defined private placement regimes and an active high net worth private banking business. Since the AIFMD is concerned with regulating the AIFM, not the AIF (in contrast to the UCITS Directive which regulates not only the UCITS manager but also the UCITS fund itself), the AIFMD passport attaches to the AIFM, not the AIF. In addition to the passport to market the AIF's units to professional investors on a pan-European basis, an authorized AIFM has a second passport which allows the AIFM to provide AIFM

---

[18] See also the Commission Delegated Regulation of 19 December 2012.
[19] Regulation 6(1).
[20] Professional investor funds are a legacy of the old non-UCITS regime that applied prior to the introduction of AIFMD and the AIF Rulebook. No new professional investor funds may be established under the AIF regime and so all new Irish-regulated AIFs will be authorized as either QIAIFs or RIAIFs.
[21] Markets in Financial Instruments Directive 2014/65/EU. It and the Markets in Financial Instruments Regulation (Regulation (EU) No. 600/2014) are collectively referred to as "MiFID II." The European Union (Markets in Financial Instruments) Regulations 2017 transpose the Directive into Irish law.

services on a crossborder basis to AIFs in other EU jurisdictions. What this means is that an Irish AIFM may act as the designated AIFM to a Luxembourg AIF (and vice versa) provided the AIFM notifies its home regulator that it intends to offer its services on a crossborder basis to entities in other EU Member States. This so-called management passport of AIFM services is very similar to the MiFID passport that allows MiFID firms to provide investment services throughout the EU on a crossborder basis.

3 FUND STRUCTURE

In Ireland, UCITS and AIFs may be established as investment companies, Irish Collective Asset-Management Vehicles ("ICAVs"), unit trusts,[22] or a common contractual fund ("CCF").[23] AIFs may also be established as investment limited partnerships ("ILPs"),[24] although this structure is very rare. This chapter will focus on the two forms likely to be the most common in the future: investment companies and ICAVs.

Until the introduction of the ICAV regime (see further below), the variable capital investment company was the most popular form of structure for new funds in Ireland. Approximately 86 percent of ETFs are currently investment companies.[25] Such a company can be established pursuant to the provisions of Part 24 of the Companies Act, 2014 ("the 2014 Act") for AIFs or the UCITS Regulations for UCITS funds. Investment companies under the 2014 Act must be authorized by the Central Bank before they are entitled to carry on business in Ireland.[26] This entity has a separate legal personality distinct from its shareholders and offers its shareholders limited liability. An AIF investment company may only be formed and registered if it is clear that the company, when registered, will carry on its collective investment activity in Ireland.[27] For UCITS investment companies, Central Bank authorization is also required and may only be given if the Central Bank has approved its articles,[28] the choice of trustee, and the application of the designated management company, if applicable.[29] It must also be satisfied that it complies with the statutory obligations regarding investment companies set out in Part 6 of the Regulations. All investment companies, whether UCITS or AIFs,

---

[22] A unit trust is constituted by trust deed which sets out the rules of the fund and the rights of the unit holders. They are regulated pursuant to the Unit Trusts Act, 1990.
[23] A common contractual fund is an unincorporated entity constituted by a contract between investors pursuant to the Investment Funds, Companies and Miscellaneous Provisions Act, 2005.
[24] An investment limited partnership is constituted by means of a limited partnership agreement pursuant to the Investment Limited Partnership Act 1994.
[25] See ISE Monthly Report (April 2018) available at www.ise.ie/Market-Data-Announcements/Statistical-Reports/.
[26] Companies Act 2014, s.1395.
[27] Companies Act 2014, s.1391.
[28] The Central Bank would not approve, for example, articles which did not meet the informational and other requirements of the UCITS Regulations.
[29] The European Communities (Undertakings for Collective Investment in Transferable Securities) Regulations 2011, reg. 8(2).

are subject to the various statutory requirements set out in the 2014 Act on governance discussed in Section 5 of this chapter.

An option open to promoters since 2015 is an ICAV, which is a purpose-built corporate structure for investment funds established pursuant to the Irish Collective Asset-Management Vehicles Act 2015 ("the 2015 Act"). The ICAV is the legal vehicle of choice for new fund establishments in Ireland and comprises more than 3 per cent of ETFs. It is modeled on the European *société d'investissement à capital variable* structure and resembles an open-ended US mutual fund. It is not a company for the purposes of the 2014 Act and it is not subject to the onerous rules applicable to ordinary companies. However, it is a corporate entity with separate legal personality and its own board of directors. It can contract on its own behalf and in its own name (unlike a unit trust, a CCF, or an ILP). The Central Bank is responsible for the incorporation, authorization, and ongoing supervision of ICAVs. The 2015 Act prescribes the appointment and approval of the depositary and management company. It also sets out a number of distinct governance requirements, described in Section 5 of this chapter. Importantly, under US tax law, Irish investment companies, by virtue of their legal structure as a plc, are treated as "per se" corporations and are not permitted to "check the box" in order to be treated as transparent entities for US tax purposes. By contrast, the ICAV may elect to be treated as a partnership, which brings positive benefits for investors. This structure is expected to become the most popular form for new funds in the future, particularly for funds that wish to target US investors.

A board of directors exists for corporate funds in the form of investment companies and ICAVs. In the case of a unit trust, a CCF or an investment limited partnership, there is no board of the fund, as such, since those fund structures do not have separate legal personality.

3.1 Umbrella Funds

3.1.1 Umbrella fund or standalone fund?

An umbrella fund is a collective investment scheme which is divided into a number of subfunds. Generally, the subfunds pursue different investment strategies and each subfund has a separate pool of assets.

All investment funds constituted as an umbrella fund must provide for segregation of liability between subfunds. Constitutional documents for umbrella funds are required to provide that the assets and liabilities of each individual subfund are kept separate from all other subfunds and that separate books and records are maintained for each. The subfunds are not separate legal entities in their own right so there are no individual boards for each subfund. Instead, for corporate funds there is a single board which operates at umbrella level.

There are significant benefits to promoters/investment managers establishing fund products within an umbrella structure, as it means that each time the promoter wishes to launch a new strategy, it can leverage off the existing umbrella structure and from a documentation perspective. All that is typically required as part of a new subfund approval process is the preparation and filing of a supplemental prospectus for that new subfund with the Central Bank. Significant efficiencies arise, therefore, in using an umbrella fund structure. The fact that Irish law provides for segregated liability between subfunds gives investors comfort that the assets of their subfund cannot be used to meet a shortfall in another subfund of the same umbrella structure.

In addition to being able to establish different subfunds within an umbrella scheme, an Irish fund may also provide for the establishment of different classes of shares or units within a fund, or, in the case of an umbrella fund, within each subfund of the fund. Such classes may, for example, provide for different charging structures or different currencies. Unlike subfunds, a separate pool of assets is not maintained for each class of share/unit.

4 KEY PARTIES IN MUTUAL FUND GOVERNANCE

At the outset, it should be noted that all providers of financial services must be authorized and supervised by the Irish Central Bank, though it may be possible for a non-Irish firm to offer services in Ireland on the basis of an authorization in its home Member State subject to compliance with Central Bank notifications.

Investors in funds are in a different position to shareholders in an ordinary company. Eric Roiter has described investors in mutual funds as both customers of the investment adviser in relation to the product that is the fund and shareholders of the legal entity that is the fund.[30] The International Organization of Securities Commissions ("IOSCO"), the representative body for national securities regulators, describes the fundamental rights of fund investors as including: the operation of the fund for their benefit; entitlement to certain information about the fund; rights to exit the fund; and possibly the right to vote on certain matters.[31] Shareholders in Irish companies may not take personal actions against directors for breach of any of their fiduciary duties to the company, and only in very limited cases are they entitled to launch derivative actions. They are entitled, however, to bring a claim for minority oppression on the basis that the affairs of the company are being conducted in a manner oppressive to members, or in disregard of their interests.[32] Generally, investors in Irish funds do not tend to be activist in nature. Since most of the Irish funds (and all UCITS) offer significant liquidity options, disgruntled investors tend to "vote with their feet" and redeem from the fund instead of agitating for changes to the board of directors of a fund or investment manager. Where more serious concerns for investors arise is in relation to illiquid AIFs such as property or private equity funds, where the option to simply redeem is not available. In such cases, there is a greater incentive to take a more active role in fund governance. It should be noted, however, that a significant amount of the money invested in funds is not derived from Irish investors but rather from international investors who, for the reasons explained above, choose to invest in Irish funds and to use Ireland as a domicile to establish a fund.

---

[30] E. Roiter, "Disentangling Mutual Fund Governance from Corporate Governance" 6 *Harvard Business Law Review* 1 (2016).

[31] IOSCO, Examination of Governance for Collective Investment Schemes, Final Report Part I (2007), p. 2.

[32] Companies Act 2014, s.212.

368 *Research handbook on the regulation of mutual funds*

The board is the focal point of the governance framework for funds which have a corporate form. The Investment Company Institute has noted that:

> Because a fund has no employees and relies on the advisor and other service providers to carry out the fund's day-to-day operations, the board focuses on the performance of these entities under their respective contracts and monitors the potential conflicts of interest that can arise between them and the fund.[33]

Although the investment manager is primarily responsible for establishing the fund (and would therefore have significant involvement in selecting the directors of the fund), the board of the fund and the investment manager operate quite separately once the fund is authorized by the Central Bank. The board has full responsibility for the management, oversight and governance of the fund. Whereas it may delegate the day to day investment management function to the investment manager, the investment manager is simply a delegate, much like the depositary or the fund administrator, and the board of the fund still retains full responsibility for the management of the fund. It can remove (and must have the ability to remove) the investment manager if it is in the best interests of the fund's shareholders to do so. In December 2016, the Central Bank produced guidance for boards of directors of investment companies, UCITS management companies, AIFMs, and AIF management companies incorporated and authorized in Ireland which places additional independent responsibilities on the boards.[34] This guidance, discussed below, focuses on the role of boards where significant tasks are delegated externally. AIFMs and UCITS management companies are prohibited from delegating to the extent that they become letterbox entities.[35] This is in order to safeguard the protection of investors. The composition and role of the board is described in greater detail in Section 5 of this chapter.

The management company is responsible for managing mutual funds which have been established as unit trusts or CCFs. Investment companies and ICAVs may also choose to delegate the management of the fund to a third party management company rather than being self-managed. One negative consequence of this is that it may give rise to a degree of ambiguity in the role of the investment company board versus the role of the fund management board.[36] If an investment company chooses to manage itself, it must have a minimum level of paid-up share capital in place and satisfy certain other conditions. The management company will normally delegate its main functions to service providers but it retains responsibility for oversight and control. Ireland is a leading choice of domicile for UCITS management companies. A passporting regime

---

[33] Investment Company Institute, "Director Issues: Overview of Mutual Fund Governance" available at www.idc.org/idc/issues/governance/overview_fund_gov_idc.

[34] Central Bank, Fund Management Companies—Guidance (December 2016) available at www.centralbank.ie/docs/default-source/Regulation/industry-market-sectors/Funds/UCITS/Guidance/fund-management-company-guidanceb34cc0134644629bacc1ff0000269695.pdf?sfvrsn=2.

[35] Regulation 23(2) of the UCITS Regulations and Regulation 21(4) of AIFM Regulations 2013.

[36] UCD Centre for Corporate Governance, Response to CP 86 at p. 3. Available at www.centralbank.ie/REGULATION/POLDOCS/CONSULTATION-PAPERS/Pages/closed.aspx?PagingID=2.

for UCITS management companies allows UCITS funds to be managed on a cross-border basis so that a management company located in Ireland (or any other EEA country) may manage UCITS established in other Member States. As mentioned earlier, a similar passporting regime exists for AIFMs. The statutory obligations for management companies, which differ depending on whether the underlying fund is a UCITS or an AIF, are set out in Part 4 of the UCITS Regulations and the 2014 Act Part 24, respectively, and in the AIFMD/AIF Rulebook (for AIFMs). UCITS V and AIFMD permit dual authorization such that a UCITS management company may be authorized to hold an AIFM license and vice versa. The governance requirements of a management company are set out in Section 5 of this chapter. The global financial crisis highlighted the dangers of remuneration policies which encourage excessive risk taking, and UCITS V and the AIFMD require management companies to maintain remuneration policies and practices which are consistent with sound and effective risk management for staff who have a material impact on the risk profile of the funds they manage.

Once a fund has been launched, the investment manager implements the fund's investment strategy by taking the day to day investment decisions. This system gives the investment manager a significant degree of discretion and influence and control over the fund's core business—investing in securities—although, as will be set out below, legal responsibility for the fund lies with the board of the investment company. As previously noted, the investment manager may also have played an earlier role as promoter of the fund and had sizable input into determining that strategy. Investment managers located in Ireland must be authorized by the Central Bank.[37] If they are located outside Ireland (which most of them are, with the EU and America being the most common locations),[38] the Central Bank will seek to satisfy itself that the firm is authorized and subject to ongoing supervision in its home state and that such local supervision is equivalent to the MiFID regime. It will also require sufficient information to satisfy itself as to the firm's expertise, integrity, and adequacy of financial resources. This information should include details of shareholders, audited accounts, and any foreign regulatory status. If the fund promoter will also act as the investment manager, it is not necessary to obtain a separate approval for the investment manager. A fund may also choose to retain the services of an investment adviser. If the adviser has discretionary powers, it is treated by the Central Bank as an investment manager. If it has no such powers, it does not need to be approved by the Central Bank.

A depositary or trustee is the custodian of the fund's assets and plays a vital role as the supervisor or the "legal conscience" of the fund. State Street Custodial Services, BNY Mellon Trust Company, Northern Trust, Brown Brothers Harriman, Citi, JPMorgan, and BNP Paribas all have very significant presences in Ireland (typically, it acts as their European headquarters) and all of the other major providers of custodial services have a presence in Ireland. The depositary of an Irish-authorized fund must be a credit institution authorized in Ireland, the Irish branch of an EU credit institution, or an Irish incorporated wholly owned subsidiary of an EU credit institution or equivalent in a

---

[37] Markets in Financial Instruments Directive 2004/39/EC.
[38] See Irish Funds, "Ireland: A Guide To International Fund Distribution" available at http://files.irishfunds.ie/1466433382-IF_Distribution_Brochure_2016_web.pdf.

non-EU jurisdiction which guarantees the subsidiaries' liabilities. To avoid conflicts, depositaries are required to be independent from the fund, the fund manager, or any counterparties. Their responsibilities are set out by the Central Bank together with other conditions and include: holding the fund assets in safekeeping;[39] overseeing certain fund transactions, such as redemptions and investor payments to the fund; checking compliance with the relevant law; and enquiring into the conduct of the fund during the financial year and reporting this to investors. The latter reporting function is an essential part of the investor protection regime ensuring complete transparency for investors. Depositaries are required to act honestly, fairly, professionally, independently, and in the interest of the fund and its investors. They cannot undertake potentially conflicting activities with regard to a fund unless there is functional and hierarchical separation between these activities and the depositary functions. In addition, these potential conflicts must be managed, monitored, and disclosed to investors.

A fund administrator provides services including the maintenance of the investor register, issue of subscription and redemption documents, net asset valuations, and fund accounting in respect to funds. An estimated 40 percent of the world's AIF assets are administered in Ireland, with Luxembourg being its major competitor. The entities which provide the depositary services referred to above all have very significant fund administration operations in Ireland. Fund administration is a regulated activity,[40] and Central Bank authorization is required. The administrator of an Irish-authorized fund must be incorporated in Ireland. Where certain of its activities are outsourced to a third party, strict requirements are in place to ensure sufficient oversight over the service providers.

5 GOVERNANCE OF INVESTMENT COMPANIES AND MANAGEMENT COMPANIES

It is generally acknowledged that the structure and purpose of mutual funds mean that fund governance is different to corporate governance. A separation of the ownership of the funds from control is necessary in order to take advantage of the pooling of the funds. IOSCO, which provides guidance to its members and promotes best practice standards, has described mutual fund governance as "A framework for the organization and operation of [funds] that seeks to ensure that [funds] are organized and operated efficiently and exclusively in the interests of [fund] investors, and not in the interests of [fund] insiders."[41]

This definition emphasizes one of the core aspects of fund governance—ensuring that the conflict of interests which arises is managed so as to protect fund investors. This conflict arises because of the potential for the interests of those who organize and

---

[39] Assets which by nature cannot be held in custody are subject to a recordkeeping obligation.
[40] Investment Intermediaries Act as amended.
[41] IOSCO, Examination of Governance for Collective Investment Schemes, Final Report Part I (2007), p. 3.

operate funds to diverge from those of the fund investors.[42] IOSCO explained that a robust governance framework:

> should seek to protect, through oversight and review, the [funds] assets from loss due to malfeasance or negligence on the part of those that organize or operate the [funds] and should strive to ensure that investors are adequately informed of the risks involved in their investment and the rewards they can obtain, and above all that the [funds] is operated in the investors' best interests at all times.[43]

As indicated previously, apart from the depositary, the board of the mutual fund or, in the case of the noncorporate mutual fund or a corporate entity which has delegated management, the board of the management company is the focal point for fund governance. The various regulatory sources which support this framework are described in what follows. In addition, market forces will exert a degree of control as funds and their promoters compete on the basis of both performance and firm reputation.

5.1 Companies Act 2014

Where the investment companies and management companies are companies incorporated in Ireland, the Companies Act 2014 ("the 2014 Act") will apply. Because all UCITS funds and a large number of AIFs are marketed to the public, most companies were set up as public limited companies. Parts 1–14 of the 2014 Act set out the general rules for all limited companies except to the extent that the 2014 Act or the UCITS Regulations expressly provide that they do not apply, or disapply or amend them. Part 24 of the 2014 Act deals specifically with non-UCITS investment companies and Part 17 deals with public limited companies other than non-UCITS investment companies.[44]

Management companies may be established as private companies limited by shares or designated activity companies. Parts 1–14 of the 2014 Act apply to both categories except to the extent that they are disapplied or amended by Part 16, which deals specifically with designated activity companies.[45] The main distinguishing feature between the two is that the designated activity company will have both a memorandum and articles of association, whereas the private company limited by shares will have a single constitutional document which will not have an objects clause. Private companies limited by shares have full and unlimited capacity to carry on and undertake any business or activity, to do any act, or to enter into any transaction.[46] The establishment of such a company takes approximately two weeks and this period runs concurrently with the CBI's authorization process for a fund management company.

---

[42] IOSCO, Conflicts of Interest of CIS Operators (2000).
[43] IOSCO, Examination of Governance for Collective Investment Schemes, Final Report Part I (2007), p. 4.
[44] Although non-UCITS investment companies are also public limited companies, s.1001(2) disapplies Part 17 of the Companies Act 2014 to them.
[45] A designated activity company is a specific type of private company regulated under the Companies Act 2014 whose capacity is limited to the objects clause in its memorandum of association.
[46] Companies Act 2014, s.38. In general, they may also dispense with the obligation to hold an AGM and they may operate with only one director.

Under the 2014 Act, all corporate directors must be natural persons, and there is no provision for corporate directors.[47] At least one of the directors must be resident in the EEA. However, the Central Bank currently requires there to be a minimum of two Irish resident directors on the Board of any regulated corporate investment fund or management company (UCITS management company or AIFM) regulated by them. If the securities of the investment company are listed or traded on a market, the company must publish in its annual report a corporate governance statement including disclosures regarding the main features of the company's internal control and risk management systems. Investment companies are exempt from the requirements under the 2014 Act to include a directors' compliance statement in their Directors' Report acknowledging their responsibility for securing the company's compliance with certain specified "relevant obligations" and confirming certain other matters. However, management companies are not exempt from this requirement and those exceeding certain thresholds will have to prepare compliance statements. Investment companies are also exempted from the requirement to form audit committees. The 2014 Act also contains a statutory statement of directors' fiduciary duties. These include duties: to act in good faith in the interests of the company; to act honestly and responsibly in relation to the conduct of the affairs of the company; to avoid any conflict of interest; and to exercise care, skill, and diligence.[48] These duties are owed by the directors to the company rather than to the investors and, save in the most exceptional cases, only the directors are entitled to enforce these rights.

5.2 The Irish Collective Asset-Management Vehicles Act 2015

The 2015 Act requires that the ICAV must have its registered office in Ireland and have a board of directors, consisting of at least two directors. The duties of these directors are set out in the act and are the same statutory duties owed by directors under the 2014 Act.[49] A minimum of two shareholders are required and their liability will be limited to the amount unpaid on their shares. The ICAV will be constituted by a single instrument of incorporation, which may be amended without investor approval subject to certification from the depositary that the change is not detrimental to investors.

5.3 UCITS Regulations and AIFM Regulations

The Central Bank may not authorize a management company for a UCITS fund unless the persons who effectively conduct the business of the management company are of sufficiently good repute,[50] and are sufficiently experienced in relation to the type of UCITS to be managed by the management company.[51] Where close links exist between a management company and other natural or legal persons, the Central Bank may grant

---

[47] Companies Act 2014, s.130.
[48] Companies Act 2014, s.228.
[49] The Irish Collective Asset-Management Vehicles Act 2015, s.79(1).
[50] The Regulations define this term as follows: "'management company' means a company the regular business of which is the management of UCITS in the form of unit trusts, common contractual funds or investment companies."
[51] UCITS Regulations, reg. 17(1)(c).

authorization only if those links do not prevent the effective exercise of its supervisory functions.[52] Authorization also depends on satisfying the Central Bank as to "the probity and competence of each of its directors and managers," "the suitability of each of its qualifying shareholders," and "the organisational structure and management skills of the company."[53] Under the UCITS Regulations, the Central Bank is required to draw up rules of conduct which authorized management companies shall observe at all times. Such rules shall implement at least the following principles ensuring that a management company: (1) acts honestly and fairly in conducting its business activities in the best interests of the UCITS it manages and the integrity of the market; (2) acts with due skill, care, and diligence, in the best interests of the UCITS it manages and the integrity of the market; (3) has and employs effectively the resources and procedures that are necessary for the proper performance of its business activities; (4) tries to avoid conflicts of interest and, when they cannot be avoided, ensures that the UCITS it manages are fairly treated; and (5) complies with all regulatory requirements applicable to the conduct of its business activities so as to promote the best interests of its investors and the integrity of the market.[54]

The AIFM Regulations similarly prohibit the Central Bank authorizing an AIFM unless the persons who effectively conduct the business of the AIFM are of sufficiently good repute and are sufficiently experienced also in relation to the investment strategies pursued by each AIF managed by the AIFM.[55] The shareholders of the AIFM who have qualifying holdings must also be deemed suitable taking into account the need to ensure the sound and prudent management of the AIFM.[56] Regulation 13(1) requires the AIFM at all times to: (1) act honestly, with due skill, care, and diligence, and fairly in conducting its activities; (2) act in the best interests of each AIF or the investors of each AIF it manages and the integrity of the market; (3) have and employ effectively the resources and procedures that are necessary for the proper performance of its business activities; (4) take all reasonable steps to avoid conflicts of interest and, when they cannot be avoided, to identify, manage, monitor and, where applicable, disclose those conflicts of interest in order to prevent them from adversely affecting the interests of each AIF and its investors and to ensure that each AIF it manages is fairly treated; (5) comply with all regulatory requirements applicable to the conduct of its business activities so as to promote the best interests of each AIF or the investors of each AIF it manages and the integrity of the market; (6) treat all AIF investors fairly.

5.4 Central Bank Regulation

As mentioned above, the Central Bank of Ireland is the sole regulatory authority in Ireland responsible for authorizing and regulating Irish investment funds. The duties of the Central Bank include: approval of an investment manager and AIFM/management company; approval of directors appointed to an investment company/management

---

[52] UCITS Regulations, reg. 17(2)(a).
[53] UCITS Regulations, reg. 18(2).
[54] UCITS Regulations, reg. 24(1).
[55] AIFM Regulations, reg. 9(1)(a)(iii).
[56] AIFM Regulations, reg. 9(1)(a)(iv).

company—such directors must meet the Fitness & Probity Standards imposed by the Central Bank (discussed later); approval of a fund administrator and custodian/depository; authorization and ongoing supervision of Irish funds; approval for marketing in Ireland of non-Irish investment funds; and enforcement of anti-money laundering regulations under the Criminal Justice (Money Laundering and Terrorist Financing) Act 2010 and the Criminal Justice Act.

Every investment fund established in Ireland must be authorized by the Central Bank in accordance with the requirements set out in the Central Bank UCITS Regulations or the AIF Rulebook. These set out detailed regulations and policies for all categories of funds, including investment and borrowing restrictions, covering both initial authorization and ongoing supervision. They also cover issues such as the content of prospectuses, the administrative activities which must be carried out in Ireland, the duties of fund administrators and depositaries, and the ongoing reporting obligations of authorized funds.

5.4.1 Process and timing

The Central Bank has made a general commitment to authorize funds, such as UCITS and RIAIFs, within six to eight weeks from the date of submission of an application, provided the application is complete. The fund application involves submission, by the legal advisers to the fund, of certain fund documentation (in particular, the prospectus and custody agreement) together with various Central Bank application forms and letters. The approval process is primarily concerned with addressing the comments that the Central Bank issues on the fund documentation.

5.4.2 One-day authorization process for QIAIFs

Provided the Central Bank receives a complete application for the authorization of a QIAIF before 3.00pm on a particular day, a letter of authorization for that QIAIF can be issued on the following business day. A prerequisite to the new procedure being available in a particular case is that the promoter, investment manager, depositary, administrator, and all of the directors of the QIAIF must be approved in advance by the Central Bank. Furthermore, any policy issues relating to the QIAIF must be cleared in advance with the Central Bank.

As part of the one-day QIAIF authorization process, the investment company or management company (as appropriate) is required to certify that all of the fund documentation complies, in all material respects, with the AIF Rulebook. In addition, the depositary of the QIAIF must provide a similar confirmation in relation to the provisions of the custodian/depositary agreement or trust deed.

As noted above, the UCITS Directive and the AIFM Directive allow the Central Bank to impose additional requirements on investment companies and management companies, and these are set out in the Central Bank UCITS Regulations, NU Notices for Non-UCITS,[57] and AIFM Rulebook. The Central Bank conducts thematic inspections to examine the manner in which these requirements are applied in practice. The

---

[57] Notice NU 4 sets out information and document requirements of the Central Bank of Ireland in support of an application for authorization as a unit trust, investment company, investment limited partnership, or common contractual fund.

Notices and Rulebook also allow the Central Bank to explain and clarify various aspects of the UCITS and AIFM Regulations. In addition, the Central Bank provides further guidance material, including, for example, Guidance Note 4/07—Undertakings for Collective Investment in Transferable Securities (UCITS)—Organisation of Management Companies and Guidance Note 2/96 Promoters of collective investment schemes.

A new Fitness and Probity Regime came into effect on December 1, 2011. This requires persons performing specified controlled functions or preapproval controlled functions in regulated financial service providers to meet the Central Bank's Standards of Fitness and Probity Code.[58] This Code requires these persons: to be competent and capable; to be honest and ethical; to act with integrity; and to be financially sound. In the case of persons performing preapproval controlled functions, they cannot be appointed until they have filled in a questionnaire and completed an approval process with the Central Bank. A directorship of an investment company or fund management company would constitute a preapproval controlled function. This regime should ensure that all fund directors, including those that have been appointed perhaps solely to meet the aforementioned requirement for two Irish residents, are aware of their responsibilities and willing to make an appropriate commitment. The Irish courts are not sympathetic to an argument that "passive directors" should be subject to less onerous standards.[59]

The Central Bank has affirmed its commitment to encouraging and supporting the continuous improvement of management company effectiveness by having a good organization and governance structure.[60] Responses to a series of consultations (CP 86)[61] led to the Central Bank's publication of *Fund Management Companies— Guidance* (2016), containing sections on delegate oversight, organizational effectiveness, directors' time commitments, managerial functions, operational issues, and procedural matters. As noted above, the Guidance applies to the boards of directors of investment companies, UCITS management companies, AIFMs, and AIF management companies incorporated and authorized in Ireland. In addition, the new rules were included in the Central Bank (Supervision and Enforcement) Act 2013 (Section 48(1)) (Undertakings for Collective Investment in Transferable Securities) (Amendment) Regulations 2017. In terms of delegate oversight, the Guidance focuses on the role of boards where significant tasks are delegated externally. In such cases, the board is still expected to retain and exercise overall control of the relevant company's management.

---

[58] Available at www.centralbank.ie/regulation/processes/fandp/serviceproviders/Documents/Fitness%20and%20Probity%20Standards%202014.pdf.

[59] Office of the Director of Corporate Enforcement v Walsh [2016] IECA 2.

[60] Speech Gerry Cross to Independent Fund Directors at Central Bank Breakfast Briefing, July 7, 2015. Available at www.centralbank.ie/press-area/speeches/Pages/AddressbyDirectorofPolicyandRiskGerryCrosstoIndependentFundDirectorson7July2015.aspx.

[61] Consultation Paper 86, *Consultation on Fund Management Company Effectiveness— Delegate Oversight* (2014); *Fund Management Company Boards—Feedback Statement on CP86, Consultation on Delegate Oversight Guidance, and Publication of Guidance on Organisational Effectiveness and Directors' Time Commitments* (2015); and *Consultation on Fund Management Company Effectiveness—Managerial Functions, Operational Issues and Procedural Matters* (2016).

The Central Bank noted that guidance on other aspects of a board's work was not considered necessary at this time but that "boards are recommended to exercise prudent judgement having regard to, but not necessarily confining themselves to, widely accepted standards of good governance and to have regard to the particular challenges of the relevant company."[62]

The Guidance introduces a new organizational effectiveness role for an independent director on the board of an investment company or fund management company who is tasked with monitoring the way that it is organized and suggesting improvements for consideration by the board. This independent director will be expected to provide an outside perspective on the organization in order to protect fund investors. The Central Bank has identified six managerial functions for fund management companies: investment management, fund risk management, operational risk management, distribution, regulatory compliance, and capital and financial management. Persons who are appointed to be responsible for these functions are described as "a fund management company's line of management that lies between the board of directors and delegates" and must ensure compliance with the strategies, policies, and directions issued by the board.[63]

The Central Bank has also introduced a new location requirement. According to that rule, each fund management company must have at least half of its directors and half of its managerial functions performed by at least two designated persons resident in the EEA or some other specified country. In addition, a low-risk management company must have at least two directors resident in Ireland, while higher-risk management companies must have at least three directors resident in Ireland, or two directors and one designated person.

In parallel with its CP86 consultation, the Central Bank conducted a thematic review of directors' time commitments on the boards of investment funds and fund management companies. It subsequently expressed concern that a large aggregate professional time commitment and excessive concentration at board level would undermine fund governance standards on relevant boards. In light of the increased complexity of investment strategies and the additional obligations under AIFMD and UCITS regimes, the Central Bank opined that the directorships require a greater time commitment than may have previously been the case.[64] To address this issue, the Guidance states that directors should satisfy themselves, and their boards, that they have sufficient time to fully discharge their duties. The Central Bank will monitor individual directors' commitments and has indicated its intention to treat levels of directorships above 20 in number, combined with aggregate levels of annual professional time commitments in excess of 2,000 hours, as a risk indicator.

---

[62] Central Bank, Fund Management Companies—Guidance (2016) p. 2.
[63] Central Bank, Fund Management Companies—Guidance (2016) p. 30.
[64] Address by Director of Market Supervision, Gareth Murphy, at the Irish Funds Annual Conference, June 11, 2015, www.centralbank.ie/press-area/speeches/Pages/AddressbyDirectorofMarketSupervisionGarethMurphyattheIrishFundsAnnualConference.aspx

5.5 Tax Regime

5.5.1 Tax

As noted above, Ireland's international reputation as an open and tax-efficient jurisdiction plays a large part in its preeminence in the investment funds industry. It has one of the most developed and most favorable tax treaty networks in the world, including double taxation treaties with 72 countries. It is also the only international funds center to have been listed on the original OECD whitelist of countries that are in compliance with internationally agreed tax standards.

All Irish investment funds authorized by the Central Bank that are available to the public are exempt from tax on their income and gains, irrespective of where their investors are resident. In addition, no withholding tax applies on payments by a fund to non-Irish resident investors and certain Irish resident investors once certain declarations have been put in place, or the fund has received approval in respect of "equivalent measures."

No Irish stamp, capital, or other duties apply on the issue, transfer, or redemption of shares/units in an Irish-authorized fund.

Funds set up as an ICAV may elect to be treated as "passthrough" entities for US federal tax income purposes, and as such the income and gains of an ICAV are treated as if they directly accrue to the investors from the underlying assets. CCFs are tax transparent, as are, in some instances, Irish unit trusts and investment limited partnerships.

5.5.2 VAT

Certain services supplied to a fund are VAT-exempt activities. The principal exemptions relate to discretionary investment management services, administration services (including corporate administration), and marketing services. Custodial services are also generally exempt from VAT. Other services provided to a fund may create a VAT cost. VAT recovery is, however, generally available to the extent that the fund has either non-EU assets or non-EU investors.

The beneficial tax regime afforded to Irish-regulated funds is one of the significant benefits of Ireland as a domicile for investment funds.

6 CORPORATE GOVERNANCE CODE FOR THE COLLECTIVE INVESTMENT SCHEMES AND MANAGEMENT COMPANIES (2011)

The Irish Funds Industry Association (IFIA) is the representative trade body for the international investment fund community in Ireland. At the encouragement of the Central Bank, it produced a Corporate Governance Code for the Collective Investment Schemes and Management Companies ("the Code") in 2011 in order to promote strong and effective governance.[65] The Code is a voluntary code which management companies and Irish-authorized funds structured as investment companies are invited to apply on a "comply or explain basis." This means that if the board of directors of one of these companies agrees to adopt the Code but decides not to apply any provision of it, it should explain its reasons for noncompliance in the Directors' Report which accompanies its annual audited accounts.

The board of an investment company is made responsible for compliance with the Code if it is adopted. The IFIA recommends that a board which adopts the Code should explain any areas of noncompliance with its provisions in the Directors' Report accompanying the annual report or in a publicly available medium referred to in the annual report. The Code contains provisions on good governance which are based on principles of good practice and common to other governance codes such as the OECD Principles of Corporate Governance, the UK Corporate Governance Code, and the Central Bank's Corporate Governance Code for Credit Institutions and Insurance Undertakings. The Code contains rules on the composition of the board, the chairman, independent directors, the role of the board, board appointments, board meetings, reserved powers of the board, board committees, compliance, delegates, risk management, audit, and control and compliance. It provides that the board should retain "primary responsibility" for corporate governance of the investment company at all times and that the governance structure should be "sufficiently sophisticated to ensure that there is effective oversight of the activities of the company taking into consideration the nature, scale, complexity and outsourcing arrangements of the activities being conducted." The board is responsible for "effective and prudent oversight" and for strategic decision making. It is clear that the board can delegate its authority but not its responsibilities. A useful provision which will focus the minds of the directors is that "the Board should be in a position to explain its decisions to the Central Bank."[66]

As noted above, the ability to manage the conflicts of interest issue is at the core of fund governance and the Code emphasizes the importance of strong boards of sufficient size (at least three directors) and expertise to oversee operations. It provides that the board should be composed of a majority of nonexecutive directors including at least one independent director who would not be an employee, partner, significant shareholder, or director of a service provider firm, or provider personally of services receiving professional fees from the investment company. It should be chaired by a nonexecutive director. The importance of this is to ensure that a nominee of the promoter or investment manager is not in a position to control the meeting. The board is required to document its procedures for dealing with any possible conflicts of interest. Conflicts in respect of any matters being considered by the board must be disclosed to the board. In addition, the board must not have directors in common with the board of directors of the depositary/trustee.

---

[65] In 2014, the Irish Funds Industry Association also introduced a Corporate Governance Code for Fund Service Providers.

[66] IFIA, Corporate Governance Code for the Collective Investment Schemes and Management Companies para. 7.4.

The Code provides that while all directors have a legal duty to act independently, having regard to the interests of the company and its investors collectively, "independent directors represent an additional layer of oversight of the activities" of the company.[67] They must understand the investment objectives, the regulatory environment, policies, and outsourcing arrangements. In order to obtain a balance of skills and expertise, it is also recommended that at least one director be an employee, partner, or director of the promoter or investment manager. At least two of the directors must be Irish residents and at least two of the directors (including an independent nonexecutive director) must be available to meet the Central Bank at short notice if required. As noted above, directors must meet the Central Bank's fitness and probity standards and the Code provides that the board must be satisfied that the person meets these standards before they appoint a director.

The issue of commitment is a strong element running through the Code, and in particular the need for the board to ensure that directors can devote sufficient time to their roles. The time commitment expected from each director must be documented by the investment company and directors are required to disclose their other time commitments, including foreign directorships. There is also a limitation on the holding of directorships, in the sense that there is a presumption that a maximum of eight non-fund directorships may be held without negatively impacting a director's available time commitment,[68] but that any more would need explanation in its annual compliance statement. The Code acknowledges that the Board may delegate all or part of the management of an investment firm to a third party, but in the event it does so, it must have mechanisms in place for monitoring the exercise of such delegated functions. It states clearly that "the Board cannot abrogate its overall responsibility."[69] The Board is also responsible for the appointment of delegate service providers and for monitoring their performance of its delegate service providers, including, inter alia, the monitoring of investment performance. As noted above, the Central Bank has recently indicated that the Code's provisions in these areas have not been fully effective in this regard and further guidance is being provided.

Responsibility for ensuring that all applicable risks pertaining to the fund can be identified, monitored and managed at all times also lies with the Board. It is also responsible for maintenance of accounting information and financial reporting, compliance with the relevant legislation and applicable regulatory requirements, and compliance with provisions of the fund's prospectus and constitutional documents.

---

[67] IFIA, Corporate Governance Code for the Collective Investment Schemes and Management Companies, para. 1.

[68] A number of exemptions are set out, including directorships in group companies, public interest entities, and any company, subsidiary, or entity established or promoted by a promoter of the Irish and/or Foreign CIS, or any affiliated company of a promoter of Irish and/or Foreign CIS.

[69] IFIA, Corporate Governance Code for the Collective Investment Schemes and Management Companies, para. 14.2.

7 FINAL REMARKS

Enormous uncertainty exists as to the implications of the Brexit referendum in June 2016 and the triggering of Article 50 indicating the UK's intention to withdraw from the European Union. One of the areas which will change significantly will be the financial services sector, and it is not yet clear what arrangements will be put in place to protect the UK's financial services industry. What is clear is that if the UK becomes a "third country," that is, outside the EU and European Economic Area, a UK UCITS will become an AIF after March 29, 2019. UK-domiciled investment funds and UK-authorized management companies would no longer be able to use the EU marketing passport. Ireland is seen as a natural home for UK investment managers seeking to continue to use UCITS and AIFMD passports post-Brexit and to retain the right to distribute into EEA markets. As noted above, Ireland has long had an excellent reputation as a location for robust and efficient regulation which facilitates market and product developments while protecting investor interests. This factor, together with its tax benefits, its probusiness environment, and its proven expertise, may be considered to give it a strong competitive advantage in persuading funds and companies to move across the Irish Sea. From the perspective of Irish investment managers, Irish UCITS management companies and AIFMs may delegate the day to day portfolio management function to an investment manager located outside of Ireland (either within or outside the EU) if the latter is subject to a comparative level of prudential supervision as that which would exist under the MiFID regime.

At the time of writing, a number of regulatory changes were in the pipeline at the European Union level. In late 2017, the European Commission proposed a number of amendments to the supervisory powers of the ESMA as well as to its governance structure and funding arrangements.[70] If adopted, this will give ESMA a greater role in coordinating supervisory action in respect of elements of MiFID and certain collective investment funds both at the time that an undertaking is being authorized by the national competent authority and as part of an ongoing review of supervisory practices. In 2018, the European Commission adopted a proposal for a Regulation on facilitating crossborder distribution of collective investment funds and a proposal for a Directive amending the UCITS Directive and the AIFMD. The stated aim of these proposals is to "improve the transparency of national requirements, remove burdensome requirements and harmonise diverging national rules."[71]

---

[70] COM(2017)536/948972 available at https://ec.europa.eu/info/law/better-regulation/initiatives/com-2017-536_en.

[71] Proposal for a Regulation on facilitating cross-border distribution of collective investment funds and amending Regulations (EU) No 345/2013 and (EU) No 346/2013 (COM(2018)110) and Proposal for a Directive amending Directive 2009/65/EC of the European Parliament and of the Council and Directive 2011/61/EU of the European Parliament and of the Council with regard to cross-border distribution of collective investment funds (COM(2018)92).

BIBLIOGRAPHY

Central Bank, 2014, Consultation Paper 86: Consultation on Fund Management Company Effectiveness—Delegate Oversight.

Central Bank, 2015, Fund Management Company Boards; Feedback Statement on CP86; Consultation on Delegate Oversight/Guidance; Publication of Guidance—Organisational effectiveness; and Directors' Time Commitments (December 12). Available at www.centralbank.ie/regulation/poldocs/consultation-papers/Pages/closed.aspx?PagingID=2.

Central Bank, Consultation on Fund Management Company Effectiveness—Managerial Functions, Operational Issues and Procedural Matters (2016). Available at https://www.centralbank.ie/docs/default-source/publications/Consultation-Papers/cp86/161219_cp86-feedback-statement_third-consult_final_rhd.pdf?sfvrsn=4.

Central Bank of Fund Management Companies—Guidance (2016). Available at www.centralbank.ie/docs/default-source/Regulation/industry-market-sectors/Funds/UCITS/Guidance/fund-management-company-guidanceb34cc0134644629bacc1ff0000269695.pdf?sfvrsn=2.

Cross, Gerry, 2015, Presentation to the Independent Fund Directors at Central Bank Breakfast Briefing (July 7). Available at www.centralbank.ie/press-area/speeches/Pages/AddressbyDirectorofPolicyandRiskGerryCrosstoIndependentFundDirectorson7July2015.aspx.

International Organization of Securities Commissions, 2000, Conflicts of Interest of CIS Operators.

International Organization of Securities Commissions, 2007, Examination of Governance for Collective Investment Schemes, Final Report Part I.

Investment Company Institute Director Issues: Overview of Mutual Fund Governance. Available at www.idc.org/idc/issues/governance/overview_fund_gov_idc accessed August 29, 2016.

Irish Funds, 2016, Ireland: A Guide To International Fund Distribution. Available at http://files.irishfunds.ie/1466433382-IF_Distribution_Brochure_2016_web.pdf.

Irish Funds Industry Association, 2011, Corporate Governance Code for the Collective Investment Schemes and Management Companies.

Irish Funds Industry Association, 2014, Corporate Governance Code for Fund Service Providers.

Irish Funds Industry Association, Facts and Figures, 2018. Available at www.irishfunds.ie/facts-figures.

Irish Stock Exchange, 2017 Monthly Report (March). Available at www.ise.ie/market-data-announcements/statistical-reports/ise-monthly-report-march-2017.pdf.

McCann FitzGerald, 2016, Irish Qualifying Investor Alternative Investment Funds (July). Available at www.mccannfitzgerald.com/knowledge/client-briefings/item/6555/irish-qualifying-investor-alternative-investm.aspx.

McCann FitzGerald, 2017, Brexit: Establishing a Fund Management Company in Ireland. Available at www.mccannfitzgerald.com/knowledge/brexit/brexit-establishing-a-fund-management-company-in-ireland.

McCann FitzGerald, 2017, Investment Funds in Ireland (August). Available at www.mccannfitzgerald.com/uploads/1679_Guide_To_Investment_Funds_in_Ireland.pdf.

Murphy, Gareth, 2015, Presentation to the Irish Funds Annual Conference (June 11). Available at www.centralbank.ie/press-area/speeches/Pages/AddressbyDirectorofMarketSupervisionGarethMurphyattheIrishFundsAnnualConference.aspx.

Roiter, Eric, 2016, "Disentangling Mutual Fund Governance from Corporate Governance" 6 Harvard Business Law Review 1. Available at SSRN: http://ssrn.com/abstract=2568392.

UCD Centre for Corporate Governance, 2014, Response to Central Bank Consultation Paper 86 (December 12). Available at www.centralbank.ie/regulation/poldocs/consultation-papers/Pages/closed.aspx?PagingID=2.

16. Regulating collective retail investment funds in the United Kingdom with the objective of investor protection, and some implications
*Iris H-Y Chiu**

1 INTRODUCTION

Collective retail investing is a growing industry in the United Kingdom, as consumer interest in nonbank-based saving products is supported by sustained low interest rates and an increasingly proconsumer regulatory environment in investment regulation. Unlike in the United States, pension savings are not necessarily a source of capital for the retail collective investment schemes to be discussed in this chapter. In the European Union, pension schemes are subject to rather different and fragmented national regulations governing defined contribution and benefit schemes, and defined contribution schemes are not channeled into and do not necessarily invest in the retail collective investment schemes known as UCITS (Undertakings in Collective Investments in Transferable Securities).[1] The UK has its own regulatory frameworks for occupational and personal defined contribution schemes, governed separately from the regulatory regime for collective investment schemes (or mutual funds). Retail collective investment schemes in the UK cater for voluntary private savings needs.

The growth of retail collective investment schemes in the UK is supported in no small part by harmonized European legislation that provides funds and their managers the right to access the European Union market. This legislative regime establishes relatively high standards of investor protection to inspire consumer confidence. In the aftermath of the UK's "Brexit" referendum vote of June 23, 2016, the rights of UK-based funds and fund managers to access the European Union market will be uncertain until trade negotiations between the UK and EU can clarify the situation.[2] However, in anticipation of (1) the desire on the part of the UK financial services sector to maintain equivalencies (in order to maintain access) and (2) the importance of the objectives of consumer protection to which the UK regulator, the Financial Conduct

---

  * I am indebted to the editors, William Birdthistle and John Morley, for comments on and edits to an earlier draft. All errors and omissions are mine.

  [1] For example, the different markets are reflected in "Warning over Using UCITS for Pensions," *Financial Times* (July 25, 2010).

  [2] In this regard, plenty of speculation on the options for access is canvassed in various blogs, newspapers and academic literature. See *Special Issue on the UK's Referendum Vote of 23 June 2016 and Implications for Business Law Widely Defined* (European Business Law Review, 2016); discussions by MacFarlanes, Eversheds, Linklaters, and others on the Oxford Business Law Blog; and "Three Scenarios for the City after Brexit," *Financial Times* (July 27, 2016).

Authority, is firmly committed, it is unlikely that the regulatory framework will change significantly.

This chapter, in discussing the UK retail collective investment schemes market and the regulatory framework, will argue that the regulatory framework has been shaped largely by European market integration and the need to brand pan-European collective investment retail products (UCITS). The regulatory framework is arguably constitutive of the UCITS market which has come to dominate the UK and European markets in retail collective investment schemes.[3] Although the UCITS brand is now a strong one associated with robust investor protection (which was further strengthened in the post-global financial crisis reforms), this chapter considers the implications of strong investor protections in regulation in terms of their tradeoffs.

Non-UCITS collective investment funds are also available in the UK and are regulated by the Financial Conduct Authority.[4] This chapter first surveys the market for collective retail investing in the UK, and observes that UCITS products dominate the scene. The popularity and success of UCITS products is important in the larger context of European policymaking. The promotion of private sector savings is important in the EU, given the retreat of state welfare in financial provision for individuals. The success of UCITS products is largely due to the branding effects achieved by harmonized European legislation, which facilitate the freedom of movement of such products. This chapter will argue that although harmonized European legislation provided only a veneer of investor protection in its early stages, consumer confidence and demand responded robustly. The level of investor protection has ramped up since the global financial crisis of 2008-9, although collective retail investment funds did not experience any major scandals. Investor protection is a strong underlying objective of European legislative harmonization and this has influenced the UK regulatory framework in general even for non-UCITS products.

This chapter critically queries the ramifications of the regulatory emphasis on investor protection. The needs of investor protection, such as in the areas of liquidity, transparency, and cost effectiveness, are crucial to shaping the regulatory regimes in the EU and UK and the design of collective investment products. We query whether the regulatory objective of investor protection shapes consumer choices in mutual fund investing toward a limited range of preferences in investment. For example, some dominant trends are toward passive investing and exchange-traded products. This chapter considers the consequences for the allocation functions of retail collective investment funds and suggests that the regulatory emphasis on investor protection creates a bias toward certain product features. Such a bias results in wider economic effects in terms of limiting the growth of unconventional product markets, which are important for financing a wide range of economic activities and investment. The

---

[3] Directive 2009/65/EC of the European Parliament and of the Council of 13 July 2009 on the coordination of laws, regulations and administrative provisions relating to undertakings for collective investment in transferable securities (UCITS) (recast) (aka UCITS III, superseding the first and second UCITS legislative initiatives in 1985 and 2001).

[4] The Financial Conduct Authority, or FCA, is the UK financial services regulator for banks, insurance companies, investment firms, and collective investment schemes in respect of conduct of business. It is established by the Financial Services Act 2012 amending the Financial Services and Markets Act 2000. See www.fca.org.uk.

chapter reflects on the need for a coherent regulatory framework for non-UCITS and unconventional retail collective investment schemes that provide investor choice and financing options in terms of different forms of liquidity and maturity profiles. This is particularly important in the wake of the UK's Brexit vote, which is likely to entail great uncertainties and have a major impact on its UCITS sector.

2 THE ROLE OF REGULATION IN SHAPING THE RETAIL COLLECTIVE INVESTMENT MARKET IN THE UK

The operation of collective investment schemes is a regulated activity in the UK:[5] that is, it is unlawful to operate a collective investment scheme without securing the approval of the Financial Conduct Authority (FCA). A collective investment scheme is defined by the Financial Services and Markets Act 2000 as

> any arrangements with respect to property of any description, including money, the purpose or effect of which is to enable persons taking part in the arrangements (whether by becoming owners of the property or any part of it or otherwise) to participate in or receive profits or income arising from the acquisition, holding, management or disposal of the property or sums paid out of such profits or income.

In essence, the arrangements include pooling of participants' contributions and must be controlled on a day to day basis by persons who *manage* the property,[6] as delegated by the participants.

In the UK, the retail collective investment scheme market is dominated by a type of product that is also marketable in the EU, known as UCITS.[7] Non-UCITS schemes are also marketed in the UK, and may relate to investments made in asset classes not permitted in UCITS, such as real estate. These schemes are known as NURs (non-UCITS retail schemes), and they can be established in the UK or in a third country subsequently attaining recognized investment scheme status in the UK.[8] The regulatory framework for retail collective investment schemes in the UK has become dominated by UCITS regulation, and this has shaped the regulation of NURs as well. Many equivalent regulatory standards now apply to UCITS and NURs, although NURs are by comparison subject to an overall less prescriptive regulatory framework.[9]

A wide interpretation of what may be regarded as "collective investment schemes" has been adopted by the FCA as well as by courts in order to secure a high level of protection for retail investors entering into arrangements of such nature. A consequence of this is that relatively exotic arrangements not authorized by the FCA are often

---

[5] Section 19, Financial Services and Markets Act 2000, read with Schedule 2.
[6] Section 235, Financial Services and Markets Act 2000.
[7] Council Directive 85/611/EEC of 20 December 1985 on the coordination of laws, regulations and administrative provisions relating to undertakings for collective investment in transferable securities (UCITS).
[8] Sections 264, 270, 272, Financial Services and Markets Act 2000.
[9] For example, FCA Handbook COLL 6A, which applies largely to UCITS fund managers, does not apply to NURS.

regarded as illegal collective investment schemes and forced to shut down. The dominance of the UCITS regulatory framework has perhaps marginalized the FCA's development of regulatory thinking for non-UCITS and unconventional retail collective investment products.[10] This has also had an impact on the market in terms of encouraging investors' bias toward UCITS products. We will return to this point again later, in urging the FCA to consider developing a more coherent and different regulatory framework for regulating retail collective investment schemes of an unconventional nature, taking into account of the patchwork nature of existing non-UCITS regulation, and becoming more open to the growth of nonconventional products.

Over the years, various arrangements that may be perceived as "borderline" have been held to fall within the scope of collective investment schemes, thus requiring authorization and oversight. They include purchases of real estate interests by individuals under an understanding that there would be a centrally managed process to secure planning and development permission over the plot;[11] purchases of sublease interests in foreign real estate for the purposes of securing income generated by the land in terms of agricultural or carbon credit income;[12] services organized to place horse-racing bets on behalf of subscribers;[13] collective financing of a film venture;[14] and collective financing to acquire patent rights.[15] In other words, most forms of collective financing that are subject to a form of centrally managed process would fall within the definition of the collective investment scheme. The FCA has relentlessly carried out enforcement activities against unauthorized exotic arrangements, and this has inevitably shaped (and narrowed) the market for legitimate products.

Nevertheless, the role of European legislation has played a more important role in shaping the market for retail collective investment schemes. On the one hand, the FCA's ruthless enforcement defines what products are not permitted; on the other, it is EU legislation that has supported the market for a type of retail collective investment product that is seen as "safe" and "liquid," making such products explosively popular in the UK and EU.

---

[10] Arguably the regulatory framework for NURS, including property fund-type products such as real estate investment trusts (REITs), is slightly different from the regulatory framework for UCITS; even "lighter" regulation has been developed for online crowdfunding and P2P lending platforms, which will be returned to later in this chapter. However, there seems to be a general lack of synthesized thinking for regulating unconventional and non-UCITS products in general.

[11] *In re Sky Land Consultants Plc* [2010] EWHC 399 (Ch); *FSA v Asset LI Inc* [2014] EWCA Civ 435.

[12] *FCA v Capital Alternatives Ltd and Ors* [2014] EWHC 144 (Ch); [2015] EWCA Civ 284.

[13] *Financial Services Authority v Fradley* [2005] EWCA Civ 1183 CA.

[14] *Raymond Bieber v Teathers Ltd (in liquidation)* [2012] EWHC 190 (Ch).

[15] *Brown 7 Ors v Innovator One Plc and Ors* [2012] EWHC 1321.

2.1 European Harmonization and Its Impact on the UK Retail Collective Investment Market: The Growth of UCITS as a Popular Brand

Since 1985, European legislation has introduced a form of retail collective investment fund that could be marketed across the European Economic Area, based on harmonized rules regarding the composition and authorization of such funds, known as UCITS.[16] These "safe" retail collective investment funds, open-ended in nature, became the most popular and dominant retail fund product across the European Economic Area.

The 1985 UCITS legislation provided that a retail collective investment fund investing in transferable securities products and money market instruments on a liquid market that is authorized in one Member State could be marketed to the retail sector in other Member States without further national obstruction from host Member States. Such a fund would have to comply with the composition requirements in the 1985 Directive, as well as investor protection requirements such as disclosure via a prospectus. The composition requirements are based on portfolio diversification, such as limiting maximum investments in securities issued by a single issuer to 5 percent. Further, the composition requirements comprise prescriptive prudential regulation to make UCITS products "safe." The UCITS Directive 1985 provides for mandatory prudential risk management in terms of capital adequacy (initial capital at 125,000 euros and own funds at 0.02 percent of assets under management) and the avoidance of exotic and potentially illiquid assets such as real estate, commodities, and precious metals, as well as leverage. These regulatory attributes have fashioned the UCITS fund as a relatively safe and retail-friendly collective investment fund product that is appealing to savers, and the market for the UCITS fund has grown in Europe and beyond.[17]

The "safety" appeal of UCITS products made them highly popular in the consumer market. However, investor protection in the UCITS regime, such as in presale or postsale conduct, was in fact rather skeletal. In introducing the 1985 legislation, European policymakers were more interested in supply-side reforms that would create an integrated and robust mutual fund market across the EU, and hence legislative reforms focused on market creation and liberating the potential of retail collective investment funds. The 2001 amendment to the UCITS Directive, which will be discussed shortly, may be understood in that light.

The UCITS market has grown phenomenally since the introduction of the 1985 legislation. There has been a growing concentration in Dublin and Luxembourg as the originating jurisdictions for authorized funds, followed by systematic marketing cascades across the rest of the European Economic Area. The growth of Dublin and Luxembourg as major UCITS originating jurisdictions is due to favorable company law and tax regimes, as well as increasing regulatory expertise in providing a smooth and

---

[16] Council Directive 85/611/EEC of 20 December 1985 on the coordination of laws, regulations and administrative provisions relating to undertakings for collective investment in transferable securities (UCITS).

[17] Douglas Cumming, Gael Imad'Eddine and Armin Schwienbacher, "Harmonized Regulatory Standards, International Distribution of Investment Funds and the Recent Financial Crisis" (2011) 18 European Journal of Finance 261.

reliable authorization procedure.[18] However, until 2001, crossborder marketing of the UCITS product was affected by fragmented national laws that imposed different requirements in terms of the management of the funds. This was addressed by an amendment to the Directive (frequently known as UCITS II)[19] that allowed management companies appointed to manage UCITS funds the freedom to operate in any Member State in the European Economic Area upon receiving authorization in a home Member State. Although national distribution channels remain different in different European jurisdictions,[20] as can be seen in such areas as the dominance of bank-based distribution in many parts of Continental Europe as opposed to the more independent channels of intermediary distribution in the UK, the crossborder proliferation of UCITS funds has by and large created a successful and popular brand among retail savers. The UCITS market has become a highly integrated market, with pan-European funds and managers offering myriad choices to savers outside of the pensions market.[21]

The growth in assets under UCITS management reflects the need, on the part of retail savers in Europe, for yield as well as long-term saving, and this matches up well with the European policy interest in developing the capital markets of Europe,[22] which remain relatively underdeveloped due to the dominance of bank-based finance. The development of UCITS funds as a trusted and still growing retail saving industry is not only about improving consumer choice and responsibilizing consumers to save in an era of state retreat in providing individual welfare; the swelling assets under UCITS management also allow such capital to become a significant source of finance as an alternative to bank-based finance in different parts of the European economy. UCITS funds can invest in corporate equities, improving the corporate finance options for European companies. In 2001, European policymakers further liberalized the asset classes for UCITS investment.

The 2001 amendment Directive provided for a liberation of the classes of financial instruments in which UCITS funds could invest, albeit maintaining the portfolio diversification and prudential management principles in the 1985 Directive. The 2001 Directive permits UCITS funds to invest in bank deposits; a wide range of wholesale

---

[18] Friedrich Heinemann, "The Benefits of Creating an Integrated EU Market for Investment Funds" (2002) at http://ssrn.com/abstract=309099; Elias Bengtsson and Bernard Delbeque, "Revisiting the European Asset Management Industry" (2011) 20 Financial Markets, Institutions and Instruments 163.

[19] Directive 2001/107/EC of the European Parliament and of the Council of 21 January 2002 amending Council Directive 85/611/EEC on the coordination of laws, regulations and administrative provisions relating to undertakings for collective investment in transferable securities (UCITS) with a view to regulating management companies and simplified prospectuses.

[20] Elias Bengtsson and Bernard Delbeque, "Revisiting the European Asset Management Industry" (2011) 20 Financial Markets, Institutions and Instruments 163.

[21] Pensions products are not discussed in the chapter, as defined contribution products are largely employer-established schemes and are governed by substantially different national legislation.

[22] European Commission, "Financial Services Action Plan: Implementing the Framework for Financial Markets" (Communication) COM (1999) 232.

money market instruments, such as treasury and local authority bills, certificates of deposit, commercial paper, medium-term notes, and bankers; acceptances; other UCITS schemes; and even non-UCITS collective investment schemes which invest in a range of exotic assets such as real estate, foreign assets, and so on.[23] UCITS funds are also permitted to trade in derivative products, including over-the-counter derivatives, envisaged for hedging purposes. They may also be structured as index-based or index-replicating products. The expansion in the eligible assets for UCITS investment is consistent with portfolio diversification, but it is important to note that such an expansion also increases the risk profile of UCITS products.[24] It may be argued that European policymakers' willingness to raise the risk profile of UCITS products is aimed more at wider deployment of capital in the assets under UCITS management than at simply improving consumer choice.

By the early 2000s, the UCITS fund had been established as a relatively "safe," diversified and liquid collective investment product with a credible level of investor protection. Besides mandatory portfolio diversification and prudential risk management requirements that entail the perception of safety, regulation provides for investor-friendly features such as the open-ended nature of UCITS and the minimum requirement of publication of net asset values at least twice a month in order to facilitate redemptions. In terms of disclosure, investors are entitled to a UCITS fund prospectus as presale information. Such prospectuses are often lengthy and technical in terms of the financial information provided and are not readily accessible to many retail investors. The ongoing disclosure documents—in the form of an annual long report and a half-yearly short report—are also populated with financial and technical information. The disclosure regime is arguably comprehensive, but on the whole not highly accessible to investors.[25]

The conduct of relations between funds and their investors is not highly regulated, this area being very much left to corporate governance mechanisms in the fund company.[26] Management companies, if regulated in their conduct of business (either in

---

[23] Directive 2001/108/EC of the European Parliament and of the Council of 21 January 2002 amending Council Directive 85/611/EEC on the coordination of laws, regulations and administrative provisions relating to undertakings for collective investment in transferable securities (UCITS), with regard to investments of UCITS.

[24] Christian Szylar, "UCITS TO UCITS III/IV" in Christian Szylar, *Risk Management under UCITS III/IV* (Chichester: John Wiley & Sons 2010), pp. 1–32.

[25] Problems regarding information overload and lack of accessibility in investment disclosure have been discussed generally see for example Troy A. Paredes, "Blinded by the Light: Information Overload and its Consequences for Securities Regulation" (2003) 81 Washington University Law Quarterly 417 at pp. 431–62.

[26] Problems may occur in this area, especially given that fund companies may appoint token directors to the Board and such token directors may sit on numerous fund companies: see the "jumbo directors" problem with Cayman hedge fund companies. "Finance: Buried Treasure," *Financial Times* (February 8, 2013). Jumbo directors may be less of a problem in Ireland, which limits the number of specialist directorships an individual can hold. Luxembourg fund Boards also tend to be small but are often populated with cross-directorships from management companies, and so issues of the lack of independence remain a work in progress. See PricewaterhouseCoopers, *Luxembourg Fund Governance Survey 2014* at www.pwc.lu/en/asset-management/docs/pwc-fund-governance-survey.pdf.

Regulating collective retail investment funds in the United Kingdom 389

national law or subsequently under the Markets in Financial Instruments Directive 2004), would only be accountable to their direct clients, the fund companies.[27] There were also no regulatory mechanisms relating to how processes of valuation for redemption should be carried out, with the determination of how valuation should be done left largely to funds. Further, there was also no depositary regulation in relation to the safeguarding of UCITS assets and client moneys. In sum, the investor protection regime for UCITS fund investors was actually rather skeletal. However, the strength of the UCITS brand was carried through legislative reforms that provided a supply-side boost. Supply side-led expansion of the UCITS industry, responding to the liberalization initiatives in the 2001 UCITS II Directives, was able to sustain the growth of the industry and attract significant saver demand in Europe and beyond, increasing assets under management in spite of the rather minimalist investor protection regime underlying the UCITS brand.

2.2 Acceleration in Investor Protection in the Post-Global Financial Crisis Climate

The global financial crisis of 2007–9 engulfed a number of large multinational banks in the US and EU. While there was a run on certain US money market funds which "broke the buck,"[28] and a number of scandals involving hedge fund fraud,[29] the UK retail fund industry did not experience any scandal. Mintel reports on collective investment schemes in the EU showed that there nevertheless seemed to be a dip in consumer demand for UCITS products in 2009, but by 2014 consumer demand was again on the rise.[30] The general climate of decline in market confidence probably accounted for the temporary decrease in consumer demand for UCITS products in 2009, in the midst of the global financial crisis. However, in light of sustained low interest rates in the US and EU, and the continuous search for yields by funds with

---

[27] The extent of conduct-of-business regulation imposed on intermediaries serving sophisticated clients such as financial institutions and fund companies is relatively small: see Articles 35–7 of the Commission Directive 2006/73/EC of 10 August 2006 implementing Directive 2004/39/EC of the European Parliament and of the Council as regards organisational requirements and operating conditions for investment firms and defined terms for the purposes of that Directive [Official Journal L 241 of 2.9.2006]. The position remains under Articles 25 and 27 of the recast Markets in Financial Instruments Directive 2014, Directive 2014/65/EU of the European Parliament and of the Council of 15 May 2014 on markets in financial instruments and amending Directive 2002/92/EC and Directive 2011/61/EU.

[28] Discussed in The Squam Lake Group, Martin Baily et al., "Reforming Money Market Funds" (2011) at http://ssrn.com/abstract=1740663.

[29] For example, the fraudulent ponzi hedge fund run by Bernard Madoff, which was ultimately brought to light when Madoff turned himself in; see "Bernard Madoff: How the Scandal Worked," *The Telegraph* (Jan. 19, 2009); also see the fraudulent ponzi hedge fund scheme ran by Allen Stanford, discussed in "Five Years after Stanford Scandal, Many Victims Penniless," *CNBC News* (February 15, 2014).

[30] Mintel, *Collective Investments—UK* (July 2009 and July 2014).

swelling assets under management,[31] demand for retail collective investment products such as UCITS funds continues to be strong.

Investor protection regulation has accelerated in the aftermath of the global financial crisis to support market confidence in UCITS funds. This section will discuss reforms to investor disclosure, conduct of business regulation imposed on management companies of UCITS funds,[32] and enhanced protection of client proprietary rights through custodial regulation. Such enhanced investor protection has been driven by a number of factors. While there was no scandal in relation to retail collective investment schemes in the UK and EU, a number of factors drove this enhanced investor protection.

First, investor protection has accelerated due to the perception that there is a link between investor protection and policy concerns regarding the prudential management of financial institutions. A lack of prudential management on the part of a large number of banks has been regarded as the primary cause of a number of bank near-failures in the global financial crisis. Banks that had attained a false sense of security in distributing and holding securitized products based on consumer-type assets such as mortgage-backed securities, in particular subprime mortgage-backed securities, suffered enormous losses on their balance sheets.[33] Hence, policymakers have become more attuned to risks originating in the consumer sector, as such risks could be transmitted and amplified in the wholesale sector through risk and credit transformations in the intermediation process. In this way, consumer or investor protection in the retail sector is seen as a necessary support to prudential management by financial institutions at the wholesale level. Consumer or investor protection is designed not only to protect the retail investor, but also to facilitate better risk management by wholesale-level financial institutions at every level of intermediation.

Commentators also regard increased investor protection as having been swept up in the general momentum in financial regulation reform, particularly in terms of prudential regulation. It is argued that regulatory intervention in investor protection is an attractive option for policymakers who wish to be seen to be doing something

---

[31] The PricewaterhouseCoopers survey of asset management reported that global assets under management stood at about USD$64 trillion at the end of 2013. That related to assets managed by professional asset managers and did not include those managed in-house. PwC, *Asset Management 2020: A Brave New World* (2013) at www.pwc.com/gx/en/asset-management/publications/asset-management-2020-a-brave-new-world.jhtml. In 2014, Haldane estimated the figure of total global assets managed by insurance companies, pension funds, mutual funds, and others at about USD$87 trillion, representing about twice the size of global gross domestic product: www.bankofengland.co.uk/publications/Documents/speeches/2014/speech723.pdf.

[32] Also see Christopher Buttgieg, "The 2009 UCITS IV Directive: A Critical Examination of the Framework for the Creation of a Broader and More Efficient Internal Market for UCITS" (2012) 6 Journal of Business Law 453.

[33] Richard E. Mendales, "Collateralized Explosive Devices: Why Securities Regulation Failed to Prevent the CDO Meltdown, and How to Fix it" [2009] University of Illinois Law Review 1359; Robert J. Shiller, *The Sub-Prime Solution* (Princeton, NJ: Princeton University Press 2008) generally; Andrew Farlow, *Crash and Beyond* (Oxford: Oxford University Press 2011).

important to redress the crisis,[34] even if investor protection may not be directly relevant to the causes of the crisis. Moloney,[35] a key academic commentator in EU financial regulation and one of the first academic appointees to the European Securities and Markets Authority's Stakeholder Panel, sees investor protection reforms that are apparently unrelated to the financial stability-inspired reforms in the immediate aftermath of the global financial crisis as a second wave, or as caught up in the 'backwash' of financial stability-inspired reforms. Reforms aimed at consumer and investor protection have thus become more paternalistic in nature,[36] justified by the general tenor relating to more prescriptive prudential regulation. Further, the wave of conduct scandals in the UK has also created impetus for enhanced investor protection in general, not just in relation to collective investment schemes. Such conduct scandals include the longrunning mis-selling of payment protection insurance,[37] credit card identity theft protection,[38] consumer add-ons,[39] and derivative products.[40] The heightened social aversion to misdemeanor in the mis-selling of financial products (albeit that this is a longrunning problem not unique to these times) has given rise to media and academic articulation of public interest narratives underlying investor protection in financial regulation.[41] As such, the tenor of investor protection reforms has changed from merely dealing with market access or market failures to take a more protective

---

[34] David S. Evans, "Why Now Is Not the Right Time to Revamp Consumer Financial Protection" (January 2010) http://ssrn.com/abstract=1538005 accessed January 6, 2013.

[35] Niamh Moloney, "The Legacy Effects of the Financial Crisis upon Regulatory Design in the EU" in Eilis Ferran, Niamh Moloney, Jennifer G. Hill and John C. Coffee Jnr, *The Regulatory Aftermath of the Global Financial Crisis* (Cambridge: Cambridge University Press, 2012), 111, 112.

[36] See chapter 8, Mads Andenas and Iris H-Y Chiu, *The Foundations and Future of Financial Regulation* (Oxford: Routledge, 2014).

[37] FSA, "The Assessment and Redress of Payment Protection Insurance Complaints: Feedback on the Further Consultation in CP10/6 and Final Handbook Text" (August 2010) PS10/12, www.fsa.gov.uk/pubs/policy/ps10_12.pdf accessed January 8, 2013. See Eilis Ferran, "Regulatory Lessons from the Payment Protection Insurance Mis-Selling Scandal in the UK" (2012) 13 European Business Organisation Law Review 248.

[38] For example, the FCA set up a credit card protection misselling redress scheme involving a large number of banks that had missold card protection insurance to persons who were already protected, under legislation, against card and identity theft.

[39] "FCA Fines Swinton Group Limited £7.38 Million for Mis-Selling Monthly Add-On Insurance Policies" (September 17, 2013).

[40] FSA, "FSA Confirms Full Review of Interest Rate Swap Misselling" (January 31, 2013) at www.fsa.gov.uk/library/other_publications/interest-rate-swaps; *Bailey v Barclays Bank* [2014] EWHC 2882 (QB).

[41] Eric S. Belsky and Susan S. Wachter, "The Public Interest In Consumer and Mortgage Credit Markets" (2010) at http://papers.ssrn.com/sol3/papers.cfm?abstract_id=1582947; Folarin Akinbami, "Retail Financial Products in the Global Financial Crisis" (2012) at http://papers.ssrn.com/sol3/papers.cfm?abstract_id=2087548.

392 *Research handbook on the regulation of mutual funds*

stance. New investor protection reforms include powers of product intervention,[42] and regulation of investment advice.[43]

Further, European reforms have also put the investor protection mandate much more prominently on the agenda. In 2009, the de Larosière Report to the European Commission provided a comprehensive analysis of the weaknesses in the financial sector in the EU and recommended stronger regulatory governance and reform. The Report recommended the institution of a European system of financial supervision (ESFS) in order to provide more robust regulation and supervision of the internal market for financial services. The ESFS comprises three pan-European financial regulators (the European Banking Authority, or EBA;[44] the European Securities and Markets Authority, or ESMA;[45] and the European Insurance and Occupational Pensions Authority, or EIOPA[46]); a Joint Committee of the European Supervisory Authorities and national regulators; and a pan-European macroprudential supervisor (the European

---

[42] Product intervention allows regulators to ban products completely, or place limits upon distribution or compel redesign where regulators are sceptical of their intended purpose or risks. Financial Services Act 2012, inserting sections 1H and 107 into the Financial Services and Markets Act. See also FSA, "The FCA's Use of Temporary Product Intervention Rules" (March 2013) at www.fsa.gov.uk/static/pubs/policy/ps13-03.pdf; ESMA also has such powers: see European Parliament and Council Regulation (EU) 1095/2010 of 24 November 2010 establishing a European Supervisory Authority (European Securities and Markets Authority), amending Decision No 716/2009/EC and repealing Commission Decision 2009/77/EC [2010] OJ L331/84 (ESMA Regulation 2010), Art. 9(3).

[43] This was undertaken first in the UK, in the form of banning product provider commissions for investment advisers. Advisers also have to label themselves as independent or restricted and be remunerated by their clients, therefore removing conflicts of interest and aligning their interests with their clients'. See FSA, "Distribution of Retail Investments: Delivering the RDR—Feedback to CP09/18 and Final Rules" (March 2010) PS10/6 www.fsa.gov.uk/pubs/policy/ps10_06.pdf; FCA Handbook COBS 6.1A generally; and reviews by the regulator, see FSA, *Assessing the Quality of Investment Advice in the Retail Banking Sector: A Mystery Shopping Review* (February 2013); and new launch of the FCA's *Financial Advice Market Review* (August 3, 2015). European legislation does not go this far but imposes a duty on dependent advisers to survey the whole market before offering advice: see Art. 24(7) Directive 2014/65/EU of the European Parliament and of the Council of 15 May 2014 on markets in financial instruments and amending Directive 2002/92/EC and Directive 2011/61/EU (recast).

[44] European Parliament and Council Regulation (EU) 1093/2010 of 24 November 2010 establishing a European Supervisory Authority (European Banking Authority), amending Decision No 716/2009/EC and repealing Commission Decision 2009/78/EC [2010] OJ L331/12 (EBA Regulation 2010).

[45] European Parliament and Council Regulation (EU) 1095/2010 of 24 November 2010 establishing a European Supervisory Authority (European Securities and Markets Authority), amending Decision No 716/2009/EC and repealing Commission Decision 2009/77/EC [2010] OJ L331/84 (ESMA Regulation 2010).

[46] European Parliament and Council Regulation (EU) 1094/2010 of 24 November 2010 establishing a European Supervisory Authority (European Insurance and Occupational Pensions Authority), amending Decision No 716/2009/EC and repealing Commission Decision 2009/79/EC [2010] OJ L331/48 (EIOPA Regulation 2010).

Systemic Risk Board, or ESRB),[47] formed under the auspices of the European Central Bank. The EBA, ESMA, and EIOPA are tasked with the continuing mandate of market integration and legal convergence, but they are also asked to develop policy and a single rulebook on issues relating to systemic stability and investor protection. As such, investor protection regulation has moved up the agenda. I have elsewhere argued that seizing on the investor protection agenda has also helped to consolidate the new European authorities' stature and profile in financial markets regulation.[48] From the perspective of the European authorities, the consolidation of power and authority is particularly important given the fragmented regulatory architecture for financial services in the EU, comprising of EU-level institutions including the European Central Bank and national level regulators, some of which are rather powerful in their own right.

Against this context of generally enhanced consumer and investor protection in the EU, stronger investor protection reforms have been introduced for the UCITS regime. These have been transposed in the UK and the enduring influence upon the UK's NURs regime will also be discussed. Three key aspects will be discussed: investor disclosure, conduct of business by management companies, and depositary regulation.

2.2.1 Improved investor disclosure: Key Investor Information Document

The key pillar for investor protection in the first UCITS Directive in 1985 is a harmonized regime for investor disclosure. The Directive requires the publication of a prospectus that can be used for marketing across the European Economic Area. The prospectus is prescribed to a certain extent in terms of content and should contain all information that a reasonable investor would expect to find. As prospectuses often contain detailed, comprehensive, and highly technical information in terms of financial information, the retail investor may not find such disclosure documents to be particularly accessible. UCITS funds are regarded as noncomplex products that can be sold in the UK and Europe without investment advice, thus it is imperative that the investor disclosure document is fit for purpose and assists investors in making an informed decision. In 2001,[49] the European Commission introduced an accompanying "simplified prospectus" to help retail investors. The "simplified prospectus" must contain a summary of the information in the full prospectus in such a way as to be readily comprehensible, and must include information pertaining to the UCITS management company, depositary, and auditors; the UCITS' objectives, risk profile, historical information, and typical investor profile; and information regarding the

---

[47] European Parliament and Council Regulation (EU) 1092/2010 of 24 November 2010 on European Union macro-prudential oversight of the financial system and establishing a European Systemic Risk Board [2010] OJ L331/1 (ESRB Regulation 2010).

[48] Iris H-Y Chiu, "Power and Accountability in the EU Financial Regulatory Architecture: Examining Inter-Agency Relations, Agency Independence and Accountability" (2015) 8 European Journal of Legal Studies 68.

[49] Art. 27(1), Directive 2001/107/EC of the European Parliament and of the Council of 21 January 2002 amending Council Directive 85/611/EEC on the coordination of laws, regulations and administrative provisions relating to undertakings for collective investment in transferable securities (UCITS) with a view to regulating management companies and simplified prospectuses.

applicable tax regime, relevant commissions, charges and fees, how to buy units and redemption information, frequency of publication of unit prices, and dividend distribution policies. It was envisaged that the "simplified prospectus" would present the most salient information to investors in a more accessible document.

In 2010, the European Commission decided to improve the UCITS investor disclosure regime by further simplifying and prescribing the format of the shorter document accompanying the full-length prospectus. The "Key Investor Information Document" (KIID) was introduced to replace the simplified prospectus.[50] The KIID is a short document, two A4 pages in length, that contains five key sections whose presentation and format is highly prescribed. The prescribed format was developed as a result of empirical research with consumers in order to establish the optimal presentation formats for information delivery to consumers.[51]

The KIID comprises sections on investment objectives, fees and charges, risk and reward, past performance, and practical information. Funds are required to disclose the objects of investment and main asset categories, particular targets in terms of geographical location or specific asset classes, redemption information, dividend distribution policies, and whether the fund is constituted based on an index.[52] Next, funds need to disclose through narrative explanation the main risks of the fund and how the risk/reward indicator works. The indicator is to be constructed on a numerical scale (prescribed as 1–7) in ascending order of riskiness, and the risk/reward profile of the fund should be indicated along the scale, accompanied by prescribed narrative information.[53] Funds then need to disclose all fees and charges in a tabular format, showing a percentage figure for entry and exit charges and a single total figure for all other charges.[54] This will be accompanied by narrative explanations of the charges and charging structure. Further, past performance of the fund has to be presented in a bar chart covering a period of up to ten years previously, and use of simulated data will be severely limited.[55] Finally, the KIID must provide a section on practical information that identifies the tax regime for the fund, the depositary, where to obtain copies of the prospectus, and latest unit prices, and must give a prominent reminder to investors that the KIID cannot give rise to civil liability unless read together with the prospectus as a whole, therefore encouraging investors not to neglect the full prospectus.[56] Specific prescriptions also apply to special funds such as feeder funds that invest only in other UCITS funds, structured funds, or funds with different classes of shares.

The KIID, a highly prescribed document that contains both visual representations and narrative disclosures, is intended to be an investor-friendly document that can be

---

[50] Commission Regulation (EU) No 583/2010 of 1 July 2010 implementing Directive 2009/65/EC of the European Parliament and of the Council as regards key investor information and conditions to be met when providing key investor information or the prospectus in a durable medium other than paper or by means of a website (Commission Regulation 2010).
[51] IFF Research and YouGov, "UCITS Disclosure Testing Research Report" (June 2009) at http://ec.europa.eu/internal_market/investment/docs/other_docs/research_report_en.pdf.
[52] Art. 7, Commission Regulation 2010.
[53] Art. 8, Commission Regulation 2010.
[54] Arts 10–11, Commission Regulation 2010.
[55] Arts 15–19, Commission Regulation 2010.
[56] Art. 20, Commission Regulation 2010.

read and used. It is to be written in a fair, clear and not misleading manner, in nontechnical and accessible language.[57] The KIID has been regarded as a milestone of achievement in disclosure regulation as it seeks to mitigate the irrelevance of bloated and neglected documents that no longer serve the purpose of helping investors make an informed decision. The KIID format is to be adopted for other retail financial products, such as packaged investment products.[58] The UK has also adopted the KIID for its NURs regime,[59] and will be implementing the KIID in its packaged products regime.[60] However, investors need to be mindful that the KIID does not of itself give rise to civil liability for misdisclosure or omission unless read with the full prospectus. In this sense, the KIID may be seen as a measure that boosts the supply rather than the demand side, as it seeks to make UCITS products more appealing and understandable to investors, but does not make investor enforcement any easier.

2.2.2 Conduct of business regulation

In 2010, the European Commission also introduced an initiative to improve investor protection by imposing conduct of business obligations on management companies of UCITS funds.[61] In the absence of such regulation, management companies are appointed by the board of the UCITS fund and are thus only accountable to the board. The duties imposed on management companies would be by way of contract and funds could carry out private enforcement against management companies for breaches of duty, although this is rare. In Luxembourg in particular, it has been identified that many directors of fund boards are also directors of the appointed management companies,[62] and hence private avenues of accountability may be weak. Management companies have not hitherto had direct relationships with the unitholders in funds and have not owed any duties to the ultimate investors.

The Commission Directive of 2010 arguably overcomes a potential enforcement deficit against management companies by subjecting them to regulatory duties. Besides regulatory enforcement, such regulatory duties could also form the basis of unitholder/investor civil actions against the management company for a breach of statutory duties.[63] This regime has been transposed in the UK to govern UCITS fund management

---

[57] Arts 3, 5, Commission Regulation 2010.

[58] Regulation (EU) No 1286/2014 of the European Parliament and of the Council of 26 November 2014 on key information documents for packaged retail and insurance-based investment products (PRIIPs).

[59] FCA Handbook COLL 4 applying all pre and postsale disclosure requirements to UCITS and NURS equally, absorbing the UCITS regulatory standards for NURS.

[60] FCA, *Changes to Disclosure Rules in the FCA Handbook to Reflect the Direct Application of the PRIIPS Regulation: A Consultation Paper* (July 18, 2016) at http://fca.org.uk/news/cp16-18-changes-to-disclosure-rules-for-priips-regulation.

[61] Commission Directive 2010/43/EU of 1 July 2010 implementing Directive 2009/65/EC of the European Parliament and of the Council as regards organisational requirements, conflicts of interest, conduct of business, risk management and content of the agreement between a depositary and a management company (Commission Directive 2010).

[62] PricewaterhouseCoopers, *Luxembourg Fund Management Survey 2014* at www.pwc.lu/en/asset-management/docs/pwc-fund-governance-survey.pdf.

[63] Section 150, UK Financial Services and Markets Act 2000.

companies, but is not applied equally to NURs.[64] This is explicable as many of the regulatory provisions are in relation to liquid portfolios and investments in securities products, whereas NURs are usually invested in different asset classes. However, the ramping up of investor protection for UCITS products through these regulatory reforms may create the impression of differing levels of investor protection between UCITS products and NURs, and this could create biases against the NURs markets. Further, there is a lack of development in regulatory thinking for the NURs market,[65] as indicated by the emergency responses undertaken by some UK real estate funds after the Brexit vote.[66] This is an area in need of regulatory development, as the gaps in NURs regulation reveal the extent to which UCITS regulation has excessively dominated the regulation of retail collective investment schemes in general, creating lacunae in regulatory thinking for managing fund–investor relations in less liquid or longer term products.

Returning to the Commission Directive, it first requires management companies to be robustly and prudently organized, in order to ensure compliance with prudential regulation, as well as to ensure that the management company is set up to achieve regulatory compliance. For example, the Directive requires the management company to ensure that sound internal control mechanisms are instituted, including permanent and effective compliance, risk management, and internal audit functions.[67] Further, senior management is to be responsible for developing and reviewing investment policies and strategies and for having oversight of all internal control functions.[68] The Directive also goes into significant detail as to how risk management policies are to be developed and the aspects of risk and exposure that need to be managed.[69] The prudential management of UCITS funds was further flanked by legislative amendments in 2014,[70] prescribing that the remuneration policies of management companies should be in line with sound risk management and should not provide incentives for excessive risktaking.

Next, the Directive provides for proscriptive duties. Management companies need to effectively prevent personnel from engaging in personal transactions that may compromise funds' interests or make illegitimate use of confidential information.[71] Management companies also need to develop conflict of interest policies that will help identify areas of conflict of interest, and specify how those will be effectively managed and

---

[64] FCA Handbook; see COLL6.6Aff.
[65] More to be discussed shortly.
[66] The gating of redemptions—for example, Standard Life suspended redemptions from its property fund after the Brexit vote, followed by a few others: see "Brexit Fears Hit More UK Property Funds," *Financial Times* (July 5, 2016).
[67] Arts 4 and 10–12, Commission Directive 2010.
[68] Art. 9, Commission Directive 2010.
[69] Art. 38ff, Commission Directive 2010.
[70] Directive 2014/91/EU of the European Parliament and of the Council of 23 July 2014 amending Directive 2009/65/EC on the coordination of laws, regulations and administrative provisions relating to undertakings for collective investment in transferable securities (UCITS) as regards depositary functions, remuneration policies and sanctions, Arts 14a and 14b (UCITS Directive 2014).
[71] Art. 13, Commission Directive 2010.

disclosed.[72] Conflicts of interest need to be stringently recorded and detrimental impact to unitholders in funds needs to be avoided.[73] Management companies also need to ensure that any inducements, that is, payments received by or paid by them from or to third parties, do not compromise the best interests of the fund and must be designed to enhance the quality of the service provided to the funds.[74] Examples of inducements include payment for research made by the management company to the broker whose research charge is bundled in trading commissions. Although management companies benefit from broker research, and this could ultimately benefit the funds, such inducements may also be collusive arrangements between broker and manager and add little value to the funds. The reforms under the Markets in Financial Instruments Directive 2014 are targeted at making research charges more transparent and subject to client consent.[75] This area of reform may become standard for UCITS management in due course.

Further, certain duties are imposed on management companies in order to secure the best interests of investors in funds. Management companies are to develop policies as to how their voting rights in investee companies should be exercised for the benefit of the funds. Management companies are also to consider how forms of shareholder engagement or activism may be carried out in order to secure the best interests of the funds.[76] Management companies are to develop fair and transparent pricing models for asset valuation, and to treat all fund unitholders fairly and equally.[77] Management companies are subject to extensive information recording duties for subscriptions and redemptions and have to ensure that subscriptions and redemptions are dealt with fairly and in an accountable manner.[78] Management companies are subject to detailed recording duties relating to their portfolios and all portfolio transactions have to be recorded in a prescribed manner.[79] Such information recording is used to underpin the duty imposed on management companies to undertake all due diligence in monitoring their portfolios and performance and to ensure that the portfolios are managed within the investment limits and risk appetite of funds.[80] Further, management companies are also subject to a duty of best execution when dealing with execution decisions on behalf of funds.[81] The duty requires management companies to consider how the optimal execution for any trade should be carried out in terms of choice of execution venue, nature of counterparty, size of trade, price and costs, and any other relevant consideration.

The extensive conduct of business regulation of UCITS management companies is intended to secure investor protection at a high level and consolidates the UCITS brand as a premium investor-friendly brand. It is to be noted that, although there are no civil

---

[72] Arts 17–18, Commission Directive 2010.
[73] Art. 20, Commission Directive 2010.
[74] Art. 29, Commission Directive 2010.
[75] Art. 24(8) and (9), MiFID II Directive 2014.
[76] Art. 21, Commission Directive 2010.
[77] Art. 22, Commission Directive 2010.
[78] Art. 15, Commission Directive 2010.
[79] Art. 14, 24, Commission Directive 2010.
[80] Art. 23, Commission Directive 2010.
[81] Art. 25, Commission Directive 2010.

actions to date, regulatory enforcement has been undertaken in the UK against Invesco Perpetual for managing its UCITS fund in breach of disclosed leverage levels and investment limits.[82] The real threat of regulatory enforcement seems to underpin the effectiveness of the conduct of business regulation of UCITS management companies.

2.2.3 Depositary regulation

Investor protection is also supported by regulatory provisions aimed at separating the depositary from the UCITS management companies.[83] UCITS management companies have to appoint independent depositaries to provide oversight of money flows, reconciliation functions, and valuation and redemption processes. These provisions, introduced in the 2014 EU legislative amendments, closely mirror those enacted in 2011 in respect of alternative investment fund managers.[84] These reforms are part of the broader agenda in consolidating harmonized rules in financial services that serve functionally similar purposes.

EU legislation now requires that the UCITS management company appoint a single depositary for each UCITS fund it manages, and such appointments are to be on terms prescribed by supplementary legislation issued by the Commission.[85] The depositary will focus on custodial functions and effective reconciliation of accounts and registers. Under Article 22, the depositary has a cash flow monitoring function, a custodial function over financial instruments, a function to verify ownership of assets by the UCITS fund, a function to ensure that subscription and redemption orders are duly reconciled, a function to ensure valuation procedures are implemented by the management company in compliance with laws and regulations, a function to ensure that any reuse of the assets of the UCITS fund is carried out is in the interest of unitholders and covered by high quality and liquid collateral, and a duty of diligence to oversee any third parties to whom the depositary delegates any functions.[86] Such oversight duties may elevate depositaries' functions to the status of an independent gatekeeper that secures the protection of unitholders' interests in the key areas of valuation, subscription and redemption, generation of income through securities lending, and safe custody of money and assets.

It is also expressly stated that the separate depositary should "act honestly, fairly, professionally, independently and solely in the interest of the UCITS and the investors of the UCITS."[87] Hence, the contractual limitations that would have prevented unitholders from holding depositaries to account are now overcome by regulation. Regulatory duties are now imposed directly on depositaries to take care of unitholder interests, and arguably, this changes the relational construct between depositaries and

---

[82] FCA, "Invesco Perpetual Fined £18.6 Million for Failings in Fund Management" (April 28, 2014) at www.fca.org.uk/news/invesco-perpetual-fined-186-million-for-failings-in-fund-management.
[83] Art. 25, UCITS Directive 2014.
[84] Directive 2011/61/EU of the European Parliament and of the Council of 8 June 2011 on Alternative Investment Fund Managers and amending Directives 2003/41/EC and 2009/65/EC and Regulations (EC) No 1060/2009 and (EU) No 1095/2010, Art. 21.
[85] Art. 22, UCITS Directive 2014.
[86] Art. 22a, UCITS Directive 2014.
[87] Art. 25, UCITS Directive 2014.

UCITS management companies from one of contract to one of gatekeeping or oversight. Where depositaries previously owed contractual duties only to the management company by virtue of the terms of appointment, the private relational construct between depositaries and management is now to an extent overwritten by regulatory prescription, and depositaries owe regulatory duties to unitholders directly. The relational construct between depositaries and unitholders imposed by regulation now incentivizes depositaries to monitor and oversee aspects of management company practices that are within the scope of their responsibilities for the benefit of unitholders.

The depositary is incentivized to perform the abovementioned functions in a diligent and uncompromising manner because civil liability may be incurred as a result of the loss of financial instruments in its custody or in the custody of a delegate institution, where there is negligent or intentional failure in complying with regulatory duties.[88] Civil liability in respect of losses of financial instruments held in the custody of a delegate institution of the depositary seems to be a form of strict liability, subject to the defense of proving that "the loss has arisen as a result of an external event beyond [the depositary's] reasonable control, the consequences of which would have been unavoidable despite all reasonable efforts to the contrary."[89] As depositary duties are by nature statutory duties, they are *prima facie* enforceable by the regulator. In terms of enforcement in private litigation, the management company would have a right of enforcement under contract and it could be argued that the statutory duties are likely implied into the contract if they are not expressly provided for. But do investors in the UCITS have a direct right of action? The UCITS recast Directive of 2009 which carried over the relevant provision from the 1985 Directive did state clearly that the depositary could be liable to the management company and unitholders. Case law in Luxembourg has interpreted this to mean that although the depositary may be liable to the fund and thus to unitholders as a whole,[90] enforcement should be carried out by the management company and a direct right of action is not available to investors unless the jurisdiction's national law permits it.[91] It is arguable that this position has changed, as Article 24 now allows investors to invoke the liability of the depositary directly or indirectly through a management company action as long as the depositary is not subject to double jeopardy.

In sum, UCITS regulation has significantly enhanced the regime for investor protection in the EU and UK. However, this chapter argues that excessive emphasis on investor protection and the securing of regulatory features that are appealing to investors entails certain consequences for the retail collective investment markets. First, in the UK, the regulatory regimes for NURs and unconventional products regimes are relatively underdeveloped, and this creates distortions for investor choice. Second, it is imperative to stimulate a competitive and well-regarded NURs and unconventional products market in the UK to expand investor choice and financing channels for less

---

[88] Art. 24, UCITS Directive 2014.
[89] Art. 24, UCITS Directive 2011.
[90] Vincent Naveaux and Renaud Graas, "Direct Action by Investors against a UCITS Depositary—A Short-Lived Landmark Ruling?" (2012) 7 Capital Markets Law Journal 455.
[91] Or unless there is a direct action in tort due to the individual harm done to the specific investor in question.

conventional investment opportunities. This is especially important in the light of uncertainties surrounding Brexit and its impact on the UCITS sector in the UK.

3 IMPACT OF REGULATION: DISTORTIONS IN THE RETAIL COLLECTIVE INVESTMENT FUNDS MARKET

The high standards of investor protection discussed in Section 1 of this chapter have been crucial to growing investor confidence in the pan-European UCITS markets. This section argues, however, that such high standards cater to certain investor preferences, concentrating such capital upon certain asset classes in the investment markets. This may entail a distortive effect upon the appeal of other asset classes, and has in no small part marginalized regulatory development in the UK for NURs and unconventional collective investment products.

3.1 Investor Preference for Liquidity

In this age of short-termism,[92] even if an investor's investment horizon is not particularly short, an investor may prefer to be able to cash out of an investment at short notice. The availability of liquidity induces a sense of safety. Many mainstream economists view liquidity as a mainstay of financial stability, that is, the availability of liquidity allows risk intermediation and prevents crises.[93] However, one could also view the role of liquidity as being that of a self-fulfilling prophecy—that its availability and increased reliance on it perpetuates short-termist behavior that is susceptible to panic, inducing market volatility and potential crises.[94] Further, investors' preference for liquidity may be attributed to the appeal of potential ease in reallocating capital in this age of choice in global investment opportunities.[95] Whether we characterize investors'

---

[92] Aspen Institute, *Overcoming Short-Termism: A Call for a More Responsible Approach to Investment and Business Management* (2009). But see "The Tyranny of the Long Term: Let's Not Get Carried Away in Bashing Short-Termism", *The Economist* (November 22, 2014).

[93] Franklin Allen and Douglas Gale, "Financial Fragility, Liquidity and Asset Prices" (2004) 2 Journal of European Economic Association 1015 at http://finance.wharton.upenn.edu/~allenf/download/Vita/finfragfinal.pdf; Andrew Crockett, "Market Liquidity and Financial Stability" (Banque de France Financial Stability Review, 2008) at www.banque-france.fr/fileadmin/user_upload/banque_de_france/publications/Revue_de_la_stabilite_financiere/etud3_0208.pdf.

[94] David Roche and Bob McKee, *New Monetarism* (Independent Strategy, 2007).

[95] However, many commentators urge a nuanced understanding of global mobility of capital. For example, Williams argues that geographical limitations to such mobility may still occur due to market preferences such as home bias or political economy contexts: Colin C. Williams, "A Borderless World Of Hypermobile and Homeless Money?" (2004) 2 Industrial Geographer 144. Further, journalistic evidence seems to bear out preferences for greater mobility during boom times and withdrawal during uncertain times: see "Emerging Markets in Retreat," edited by the *Financial Times* (February 1, 2015); Suxiao Li, Jakob de Haan, Bert Scholtens, and Haizhen Yang, "Are International Fund Flows Pro- or Counter-Cyclical?" (2015) 22 Applied Economics Letters 378. Watson also argues that mobility of capital need not mean spatial mobility, but could be fungible mobility, that is, the transformation of capital into different risk forms due to the possibilities of financial innovation in hedging and chasing returns: see

preference for liquidity as being short-sighted and lacking in loyalty or as being hypermobile, necessarily transient, and efficient, the need for liquidity has fed into product design for retail collective investing as a response to market demand. The UCITS-based regulatory framework clearly supports the importance of liquidity and perceived safety. This section highlights the aspects of the regulatory framework that panders to investors' preference for liquidity and argues that these aspects reinforce certain adverse features of fund management that are generally deleterious for longer term and broader economic needs.

First, asset allocation by funds and asset managers caters for investors' preference for liquidity. A European Fund and Asset Management Association survey shows that more than 75 percent of fund assets are allocated to liquid and tradable assets such as equities, corporate and sovereign bonds, and money market instruments.[96] Even if the balance among the three classes differs among different European markets, as in the French market preferring bond and money market instruments over equities, which are favored by the UK market, the overall picture is a preference for liquid and tradable assets. Such a market preference is arguably reflected in the legislative design for UCITS funds, which focuses on transferable securities instruments. The regulatory framework has reinforced investor preference for liquidity by branding as "safe" retail investment products that cater for this preference, and by providing for funds' obligations to meet these liquidity needs. The obligations pertain to regular publication of prices for redemption, and ensuring the robustness of redemption processes. In sum, regulation has reinforced investors' liquidity needs by ensuring the smoothness of exit, achieving the effect of synonymizing investor protection and meeting liquidity needs.

Although promoting retail collective investment in liquid assets does not prevent yieldseekers from looking at alternative assets, assets that are relatively illiquid and long-term would inevitably be regarded as nonmainstream and not in the majority. The less popular asset classes such as inflows into private equity, hedge funds, and real estate remain viable,[97] but non-UCITS funds are in the minority compared to UCITS funds. Further, the lack of recognition for unconventional investments such as those referred to in Section 1 relating to land development, foreign agricultural land, patent rights, and so on could be due to a biased perception toward the relative illiquidity of these asset classes. The FCA, instead of developing a regulatory framework for unconventional asset classes, has instead chosen to regard asset classes lacking in conventional attributes such as liquidity as being "unsafe," and thus prohibited.

Arguably, the potential of channeling retail savings toward a variety of maturity and risk transformations is limited by investor preferences that have been reinforced by regulation, rightly or otherwise. The European Commission has become concerned about the viability of long-term finance in Europe, as bank-based finance has shrunk in the wake of the global financial crisis and there is a need to consider how viable and continuous sources of finance may be channeled into infrastructure, small and

---

Matthew Watson, *The Political Economy of International Capital Mobility* (Basingstoke: Palgrave Macmillan 2007) at chapters 2 and 3.
  [96] Efama, *Asset Management in Europe: Facts and Figures* (June 2014) at pp. 23–6.
  [97] *Lipper European Fund Market Review 2013* (London: Thomson Reuters, 2013).

medium-sized enterprises, and development.[98] Institutions such as pension funds and insurance companies are asked to invest in a wider range of assets over the long term and steps are taken to develop the nonmainstream assets in high-quality securitization,[99] privately placed securities, long-term bonds, and funds with alternative emphases such as the Venture Capital Fund, the Social Entrepreneurship Fund,[100] or the long-term investment fund.[101] However, it remains to be seen how far these measures could encourage growth in less liquid investments and channel financial resources to more diversified uses. It is arguable that the European frameworks for crossborder marketing of social entrepreneurship, venture capital, or long-term funds would not of themselves create incentives to attract investors to these funds. The emphasis on investor protection that reverberates in the regulatory framework for collective investment reinforces investor preferences, and perhaps it would be in the taxation regime that incentives can be created for longer term investments.[102]

Investor preference for liquidity results in investment fund concentration in the liquid and tradable asset classes mentioned above, reinforcing the lesser popularity of marginalized areas where liquidity is already relatively thin. Further, it may be argued that investor preference for liquidity has created an asset management environment that is highly reliant on trading,[103] instead of productive deployment of capital for long term and "patient" returns. Many commentators have opined that investment gains are not generated by putting capital to work in generating real productivity gains, but are made in the relatively easier manner of value arbitrage in trading assets.[104] Such investor preference gives rise to financial intermediation and allocation patterns that become

---

[98] European Commission: *Green Paper: Long Term Financing of the European Economy* (March 2014) at http://eur-lex.europa.eu/legal-content/EN/TXT/?uri=CELEX:52013DC0150; European Commission, *Green Paper: Capital Markets Union* (February 18, 2015) at http://ec.europa.eu/finance/consultations/2015/capital-markets-union/docs/green-paper_en.pdf.

[99] See European legislative initiative to promote standardised and simple securitised products that can be marketed across the EU, in Regulation (EU) 2017/2402 of the European Parliament and of the Council of 12 December 2017 laying down a general framework for securitisation and creating a specific framework for simple, transparent and standardised securitisation, and amending Directives 2009/65/EC, 2009/138/EC and 2011/61/EU and Regulations (EC) No 1060/2009 and (EU) No 648/2012.

[100] Regulation (EU) No 345/2013 of the European Parliament and of the Council on European venture capital funds; Regulation (EU) No 346/2013 of the European Parliament and of the Council of 17 April 2013 on European social entrepreneurship funds.

[101] Regulation (EU) 2015/760 of the European Parliament and of the Council of 29 April 2015 on European long-term investment funds.

[102] Mentioned in European Commission, *Green Paper: Capital Markets Union* (February 18, 2015) at http://ec.europa.eu/finance/consultations/2015/capital-markets-union/docs/green-paper_en.pdf.

[103] Lynne Dallas, "Short-Termism, the Financial Crisis, and Corporate Governance" (2012) 37 Journal of Corporation Law 265.

[104] Branka Mraović, "A Free Market Capitalism or a Speculative Market Capitalism?" (2011) 7 Social Responsibility Journal 578; Stephan Schulmeister, "On the Manic-Depressive Fluctuation of Speculative Prices" in Eckhard Hein, Torsten Niechoj, Peter Spahn, and Achim Truger (eds), *Finance-Led Capitalism: Macro-Economic Effects of Changes in the Financial Sector* (Marburg: Metropolis Verlag 2009) at 309; Roger Bootle, *The Trouble with Markets: Saving Capitalism from Itself* (London: Nicholas Brealey Publishing, 2009, 2012).

irrelevant to and disengaged from real productivity and sustainable development.[105] Even though the UCITS Directives have over the years liberalized the investment parameters of UCITS funds, such liberalization tends to support trading and hedging instruments—the foregoing sections of this chapter have already discussed UCITS liberalization in relation to derivatives and the creation of synthetic indices. The emphasis on trading to produce investment returns contributes to a trading culture that generates certain undesirable ramifications for the modern economy, such as asset price bubbles in securities markets,[106] and short-termism.[107] It has been observed that asset management in general, including where UCITS funds are concerned, is predominantly short-termist.[108]

Another problem regarding "mimicking liquidity" could be created due to investor preference for liquidity. Non-UCITS funds, under competitive pressure from UCITS funds, have been compelled to adopt similar investor protection practices in order to avoid marginalization by the UCITS funds.[109] Funds with exotic features are increasingly trying to latch onto the UCITS brand by naming themselves "alternative" UCITS rather than non-UCITS funds,[110] subscribing to the tenets of investor protection in the UCITS brand. These developments create the problem of trying to mimic a liquidity appeal when liquidity in the alternative UCITS funds may be more limited. Towers Watson, a prominent investment consultant in the UK, warns that "managers could creep into instruments that become less liquid" while maintaining an overall UCITS brand of perceived liquidity.[111] If the liquidity of the fund were tested in a market shock, investors could find their expectations of liquidity are not met, and funds could also take drastic action such as suspending redemptions to prevent massive runs. The impact on market confidence and volatility could be severe. This problem has already arisen in light of money market funds.

---

[105] "Financial Markets and Sustainable Development," *The Guardian* (September 28, 2014).
[106] Michael Hudson, *Finance Capitalism and its Discontents* (Dresden: Islet Verlag, 2012), at pp. 5, 19, 23.
[107] Paddy Ireland, "The Financialization of Corporate Governance" (2009) at http://ssrn.com/abstract=2068478; Engelbert Stockhammer, "Financialization and the Slowdown of Accumulation" in Ismail Erturk, Julie Froud, Sukhdev Johal, Adam Leaver, and Karel Williams (eds), *Financialization at Work: Key Tests and Commentary* (Oxford: Routledge, 2008), pp. 209–22; James Crotty, "The Neoliberal Paradox: The Impact of Destructive Product Market Competition and 'Modern' Financial Markets on Nonfinancial Corporation Performance in the Neoliberal Era" in Gerald A. Epstein (ed.), *Financialization and the World Economy* (Cheltenham: Edward Elgar, 2005) at 77.
[108] For example, BIS, *The Kay Review of UK Equity Markets and Long-Term Decision Making* (Final Report, July 23, 2012); Sir George Cox, *Overcoming Short-Termism* (2012) at www.policyforum.labour.org.uk/uploads/editor/files/Overcoming_Short-termism.pdf; Robert C Pozen, "Curbing Short-Termism in Corporate America" (May 2014) at www.brookings.edu/~/media/research/files/papers/2014/05/06%20pozen/brookings_shorttermismfinal_may2014.pdf.
[109] For example, the UK FCA has imposed similar disclosure regulation in the form of the Key Investor Information Document for non-UCITS retail schemes (NURS): see www.fca.org.uk/firms/firm-types/fund-authorisation-and-supervision/kiid-nurs-kii-requirements.
[110] Towers Watson, *The Alternative UCITS Market: The Power of Perception?* (2014).
[111] Above at p. 15.

Money market funds are funds that invest in short-term wholesale money market instruments such as short-term treasury bills, certificates of deposit, and municipal and corporate debt securities, which cannot be directly accessed by the retail market. The funds create a bridge between the swelling volumes of retail saving and opportunities in short-term financing and liquidity transformation in the wholesale markets.[112] UCITS funds can be invested in money market instruments. As money market funds trade in highly short-term and liquid instruments, they are able to perpetuate an impression of safety which is reinforced by the adoption of a constant net asset value. Investor redemptions are thus guaranteed to be principal-safe and this strongly appeals to investor preferences for safety and liquidity.

However, the truth is that not all money market instruments are that liquid, and market volatility can affect the net asset value in funds. Hence, during the global financial crisis in September 2008, investors were skeptical that a number of money market funds could actually maintain a net asset value of USD$1 and started to withdraw from the funds in droves. The massive run on money market funds caused a high-profile fund, the Reserve Primary, to "break the buck" and resile from its promise to maintain net asset value at USD$1.[113] The fund froze redemptions and at the peak of its crisis was valued at 97 cents on the dollar. The money market fund crisis showed the dilemma between maintaining an appearance of liquidity for investor appeal and the challenges of investment intermediation in volatile markets.

Reforms have been introduced in the US to address the "liquidity mimicking" problem by forcing money market funds to adopt a floating net asset value, and to have the power to erect redemption gates, so that investors would not be misled into excessive expectations regarding the fund's safety.[114] However, commentators have pointed out that although such reforms intend to play down the "liquidity mimicking" effect of funds and force investors to come to terms with more realistic impressions of liquidity and safety,[115] these reforms may not change investors' behavior or their liquidity preferences.[116]

On a broader level, investors' preference for liquidity could entail certain overall destabilizing consequences. If investors crowd into the more popular and liquid quarters of the market, such "groupthink" behavior has the potential to pose systemic

---

[112] S. Manjesh Roy, "Money Market Mutual Funds: A Macro Perspective" (2005) 40 Money, Banking and Finance 1254; Marcin Kacperczyk and Philipp Schnabl, "How Safe are Money Market Funds?" (2013) 128 Quarterly Journal of Economics 1073.

[113] "Reserve Primary Money Fund Falls Below $1 a Share", *Bloomberg* (September 16, 2008).

[114] "SEC Adopts Money Market Reform Rules" (July 23, 2014) at www.sec.gov/News/PressRelease/Detail/PressRelease/1370542347679#.VOH54fmsWSo. The European Commission has proposed a Regulation to prescribe a floating net asset value for money market funds as well as prudential requirements in the form of capital adequacy: see European Commission, Proposal for a Regulation of the European Parliament and of the Council on Money Market Funds/* COM/2013/0615 final – 2013/0306 (COD) */ (September 2013).

[115] The Squam Lake Group, Martin Baily et al, "Reforming Money Market Funds" (2011) at http://ssrn.com/abstract=1740663.

[116] "All Money Market Funds are Created Equal, says Moody's," *Financial Times* (April 12, 2015).

risk problems in the markets—for example, by massive sell-off actions.[117] Such behavioral tendencies, which are based on loss aversion and herding,[118] are arguably nurtured in liquid environments that pander to such investor preferences. Hence, investor protection frameworks that give in to such preferences are unable to reconcile with the more macro needs of systemic stability and the need for wider allocational distribution for capital formation.

Further, investors, used to regulatory frameworks that protect their liquidity needs, may impose this preference upon investments in other asset classes of a less liquid nature, therefore exerting undue pressure on these asset classes in times of stress. For example, in the immediate aftermath of the UK's Brexit vote, the prospects for commercial property in London generally looked bleak as businesses anticipated less economic activity following withdrawal from the European Union. Investors started to withdraw from property funds (mostly NURs) in droves,[119] causing some funds to erect redemption gates to stem outflows. These gates were necessary to prevent the funds from having to liquidate their illiquid holdings through fire sales, and to stabilize the funds. The regulatory framework in the UK for NURs, having largely drawn from UCITS legislation, adheres to the same tenets of investor protection in terms of liquidity needs and redemptions. UK regulation provides that for less liquid funds, appropriate limited redemption arrangements may be in place, and in any case a redemption request should be met within 185 days of such a request.[120] Although the FCA recognizes that NURs are different, the NURs framework has been dominated by investor protection thinking underlying UCITS funds and is arguably underdeveloped to govern funds' and investors' needs. In view of the flood of redemption requests, the FCA urged property funds to bear in mind the importance of investor protection and to resume redemptions where possible.[121] Such a response shows an entrenched bias toward investor liquidity preferences even where such preferences may be misplaced. There is room to consider whether the development of a different regulatory regime for less conventional non-UCITS products is warranted in order to condition investors' expectations and educate investors as to the nature of their investments.

The next section turns to the investor demand for yield and safety. It will discuss how the regulatory framework panders to that demand and its ramifications.

3.2 Investor Preference for Low Cost: Regulation and Market Developments

Investors would, in the ideal world, chase yields while maintaining the safety of capital. This balance is, of course, difficult to meet, as higher yields are often related to taking on higher risk. While UCITS and non-UCITS products for the retail market have to be

---

[117] John Authers, "Fund Management Reform Will Help Avert Groupthink," *Financial Times* (November 24, 2013); Elias Bengtsson, "Fund Management and Systemic Risk—Lessons from the Global Financial Crisis" (2014) 23 Financial Markets, Institutions and Instruments 101.

[118] Discussed in Robert Prentice, "Whither Securities Regulation?" (2002) 51 Duke Law Journal 1397.

[119] "Brexit Fears Hit More UK Property Funds," *Financial Times* (July 5, 2016).

[120] FCA Handbook COLL 6.2.17.

[121] FCA, "Guidance on Fund Suspensions" (July 8, 2016) at www.fca.org.uk/news/guidance-fund-suspensions.

labeled according to their risk/reward profile,[122] the regulatory framework has actively intervened to maintain investors' yield expectations by more robustly controlling how cost to investors may be incurred in the process of investment management. There is a marked regulatory push toward fee/expenses transparency and the moderation of investment management cost. However, it may also be argued that fees and charges have become a battleground between funds and managers, particularly because the investment environment is not favorable for high yields. In this context, the investment markets have responded by introducing a greater number of low-cost products for investors. These have certain ramifications for investor choice and the development of markets for less conventional asset classes.

3.2.1 The push for greater transparency and moderation in management fees and charges

Investment management cost is not always easy to understand. Management fees may be expressed as a percentage of investment, as managers are often remunerated based on assets under management. In addition, there are other operating costs and charges such as execution charges payable for services in connection with fund management. The cost of investment management may be a complex and opaque matter to investors. Regulators have sought to improve this area of investor protection for more than a decade, and the UK and EU have now embarked on regulatory developments to make fund managers further demystify and arguably justify their costs,[123] perhaps with a view to overall cost moderation for the benefit of fund clients. Complaints from funds regarding how cost affects yield are growing ever louder.[124] Regulators have thus embarked on initiatives that target cost transparency and moderation, as this will arguably have an impact upon improving yields.

In 2004 the EU Markets in Financial Instruments Directive introduced a prohibition against third party inducements,[125] unless the portfolio manager demonstrates that the service to the client is not impaired but enhanced. Third party inducements create conflicts of interest and may result in investment decisions that compromise investor interests. Such inducements, if paid out to third parties, could also result in the bulging of cost charged to investors, therefore affecting yield. As inducements are not prohibited per se, and clients find it hard to scrutinize them due to their being bundled in costs and charges, fund managers have been able to pass on charges to clients for

---

[122] The key investor information document.
[123] "Watchdog Urges Clarity on Fund Fees," *Financial Times* (May 13, 2014); "Pressure Grows over Fund Fee Transparency," *Financial Times* (August 22, 2014) in which the Investment Management Association is reported to be leading the push for better fund fee and charges disclosure.
[124] "End 'Heads We Win, Tails You Lose' Fees", *Financial Times* (November 16, 2014). See also John Authers, "Fees Matter More than Asset Allocation", *Financial Times* (March 6, 2015) quoting Mebine Faber, *Global Asset Allocation: A Survey of the World's Top Asset Allocation Strategies* (2014) at http://mebfaber.com/2014/12/03/global-asset-allocation-white-paper/.
[125] This refers to payments to or received from third parties that may result in a conflict of interest. One example is payment for research by brokers through dealing commissions charged by portfolio managers to clients. See FCA Handbook, COBS 11.6; MiFID II Directive 2014, Art. 24(8).

borderline practices such as payments for corporate access, now outlawed in the UK.[126] In dealing with opaque and bundled charges, introducing more accountability for fund managers is a sound development, and the recast MiFID II Directive 2014 and its supplemental legislation demand greater transparency in terms of the breakdown of third party inducements such as brokers' research charges,[127] providing clients with the opportunity to scrutinize them and exert negotiating power upon their fund managers to effect desired changes. However, fund managers warn that clients are naturally disinclined to pay for "common good" services such as brokers' research as it is not always immediately apparent how such research benefits any particular client or transaction. The impact of regulation could cause "common good" services such as research to become undersubsidized and marginalized, resulting in a tragedy of the commons.[128] Some funds have openly declared that they will no longer pass on research costs to investors,[129] but this has not been universally adopted. In particular, research on smaller and less liquid corporate securities may be marginalized, and this would have an adverse knock-on impact upon the corporate finance prospects of these companies, as investors are less likely to give attention to these opportunities if coverage dries up.

The key problem is that investor protection measures that attack costs and charges in order to release more yield may produce the knock-on effect of distorting the market so that less popular or liquid opportunities could be neglected. In particular, investors are switching in droves to passive investment or exchange-traded products due to their low cost. These products are concentrated in the most liquid quarters of the securities market, however, and hence the general reinforcement of investor preferences toward low cost is likely to create biases against less conventional fund products.

Many UCITS are actively managed funds, with managers picking and trading securities in order to generate the highest possible returns. Passively managed funds usually track an existing index and replicate the index composition in their portfolios. Passively managed funds are lower cost in nature,[130] as they involve less management effort. There are ongoing debates as to whether active or passive management outperforms in the long term,[131] but passive products are becoming attractive to

---

[126] FCA, *Changes to the Use of Dealing Commission Rules: Feedback to CP13/17 and Final Rules* (May 2014); "Six Fund Groups Misused Cash for Access," *Financial Times* (January 26, 2014).

[127] Commission Delegated Directive (EU) 2017/593 of 7 April 2016 supplementing Directive 2014/65/EU of the European Parliament and of the Council with regard to safeguarding of financial instruments and funds belonging to clients, product governance obligations and the rules applicable to the provision or reception of fees, commissions or any monetary or non-monetary benefits, Art. 13.

[128] "EU Toughens Up Research Fee Rules," *Financial Times* (December 17, 2014); "The Old Model of Stockmarket Research Is Changing," *The Economist* (September 21, 2013).

[129] For example, "Neil Woodford Stops Charging for Research," *Financial Times* (April 2, 2016).

[130] Lodewijk van Setten, *The Law of Institutional Investment Management* (Oxford: Oxford University Press 2009) at para. 4.48ff; 4.86ff.

[131] Kevin R. James, "The Price of Retail Investing in the UK" (FSA Occasional Paper 2000), arguing that passive investing works out better for investors as cost is low and eats less into yield. Although active management delivers, cost is generally too high and affects yield: Larry E.

investors due to the desire to keep costs down. Passively managed products do cater for investor protection in a number of ways, as their mandate is clear, the investment strategy is more transparent, and yields have been predictable and consistent over the long term, therefore meeting retail investors' safety and returns needs. However, concentrating on passive products usually means concentrating on the quarter of the market that is most liquid and popular (and hence featured in index compositions). Such an approach to investing would cause crowding into a section of the market, and could distort the financing options for other asset classes.

Further, regulators are stepping up efforts to expose active managers who are closet "index huggers" in an effort to bring fee abuse under control.[132] Although such enforcement is in principle sound, there is a danger of overly tainting the actively managed funds market and subjecting them to blanket condemnation. Actively managed funds are more likely to delve into more diverse asset classes while generating superior returns in some cases.[133] The danger in marginalizing active management of

---

Swedroe, "Active versus Passive Investing," chapter 6 in John D. Haslem (ed.), *Mutual Funds: Portfolio Structures, Analysis, Management, and Stewardship* (Chichester: John Wiley & Sons 2010); "Active Share Revealed to Have Feet of Clay," *Financial Times* (where Nomura research doubts the benefits of active investing (January 25, 2015). See also Hymans Robertson, *LGPS Structure Analysis* (December 2013); Department for Communities and Local Government, *Local Government Pension Scheme: Opportunities for Collaboration, Cost Savings and Efficiencies* (May 2014), applying to pension funds; "Vanguard's Record Inflows Prove Passive is Massive," *Financial Times* (January 11, 2014); but see a more nuanced assessment in Edward D. Tower, "Performance of Actively Managed versus Index Funds: The Vanguard Case," chapter 12 in John D. Haslem (ed.), *Mutual Funds: Portfolio Structures, Analysis, Management, and Stewardship* (Chichester: John Wiley & Sons 2010), and also see generally warnings against making active or passive a binary choice, as performance determinations are based on certain assumptions: in particular here Michael W. Crook, "A Stochastic Portfolio Perspective on Utilizing Active and Passive Fund Management" (2012) at http://ssrn.com/abstract=2170776. The outperformance of passive funds is largely due to efficient markets in many parts of the world, making it difficult for active managers to beat the market: see Burton G. Malkiel, "Efficient Markets and Mutual Fund Investing: The Advantages of Index Funds," chapter 7 in John D. Haslem (ed.), *Mutual Funds: Portfolio Structures, Analysis, Management, and Stewardship* (Chichester: John Wiley & Sons 2010). But there is also research affirming the superior performance of real active managers: see "Almost 90% of UK Active Managers Beat the Stock Market," *Financial Times* (August 3, 2014); Robert C. Jones, "Active Management in Mostly Efficient Markets" (2011) 67 Financial Analysts Journal 29; Valery Polkovnichenko, Kelsey Wei, and Feng Zhao, "Cautious Risk-Takers: Investor Preferences and Demand for Active Management" (2012) at http://ssrn.com/abstract=2022416; Lubos Pastor, Robert F. Stambaugh, and Lucian A. Taylor, "Scale and Skill in Active Management" (January 2014) at http://ssrn.com/abstract=2390285, arguing that small specialist funds can add value, although that value may be eroded with fund scale. See also reports that boutique fund managers can add significant value through active investing: "Fund Investors Find Small Is Beautiful," *Financial Times* (February 27, 2014).

[132] John Authers, "Active Fund Managers Are Closet Index Huggers," *Financial Times* (March 12, 2014); "European Markets Watchdog Examines Closet Trackers," *Financial Times* (November 23, 2014).

[133] Robert C. Jones, "Active Management in Mostly Efficient Markets" (2011) 67 Financial Analysts Journal 29; Valery Polkovnichenko, Kelsey Wei, and Feng Zhao, "Cautious Risk-Takers: Investor Preferences and Demand for Active Management" (2012) at http://ssrn.com/

funds is that there will be fewer and fewer financial intermediaries to take on the role of price discovery for capital formation over a diverse range of opportunities.[134]

The regulatory push toward cost transparency and moderation is likely to put more pressure on actively managed funds and could make active management more costly due to regulatory burdens, as well as exacerbating such funds' dwindling popularity, which is already under attack.[135] Although it is sound to ask active managers to be more accountable to investors, it is also desirable to promote diversity in investment approaches, choice, and competition. However, it may also be argued that we need not be excessively concerned about concentration in passive investment. Overcrowding in such an approach would also produce diminishing marginal returns. Asset managers would again innovate and hark back to active forms of management to distinguish themselves among the competition.

3.2.2 The growth of exchange-traded funds

The growth of the market for exchange-traded funds is another manifestation of how the market caters for investor needs in keeping cost low. The growth of this market reinforces some of the ramifications discussed earlier in relation to the growth of passively managed funds.

An exchange-traded fund is a portfolio of assets that can be traded on an exchange.[136] The portfolio may comprise assets in equity securities, currencies, commodities, fixed income, and real estate.[137] The portfolio can be constructed to passively hug an index or be actively managed. Index-hugging portfolios can be actively managed, such as via a basket of assets with correlation to indexed securities or via derivatives. Investors can trade in and out of the entire portfolio and the fund has to ensure that the underlying assets are maintained in fungibility and in proportion to investors' trades throughout the day.[138] In the UK, listed exchange-traded funds have to comply with the Listing Authority's Listing Rules, which requires that the funds be UCITS-compliant.[139] This means that the underlying portfolios must comprise liquid securities assets, although it was earlier mentioned that a broad range of securities are

---

abstract=2022416; Lubos Pastor, Robert F. Stambaugh, and Lucian A. Taylor, "Scale and Skill in Active Management" (January 2014) at http://ssrn.com/abstract=2390285.

[134] John Authers, "The Active Fund Management Model Is Not Fit for Purpose," *Financial Times* (February 20, 2015).

[135] The passively managed industry accounts for 23 percent of the market and is growing: see *Asset Management Survey (2014–15)* at www.theinvestmentassociation.org/investment-industry-information/research-and-publications/asset-management-survey/investment-trends.html.

[136] David J. Abner, *The ETF Handbook: How to Value and Trade Exchange-Traded Funds* (Chichester: John Wiley & Sons, 2010) at chapter 2; Gary L. Gastineau, "Mutual Funds versus Exchange-Traded Funds," chapter 14 in John D. Haslem (ed.), *Mutual Funds: Portfolio Structures, Analysis, Management, and Stewardship* (Chichester: John Wiley & Sons 2010).

[137] David J. Abner, *The ETF Handbook: How to Value and Trade Exchange-Traded Funds* (Chichester: John Wiley & Sons, 2010) at chapter 1.

[138] David J. Abner, *The ETF Handbook: How to Value and Trade Exchange-Traded Funds* (Chicester: John Wiley & Sons, 2010) at chapters 2 and 10.

[139] London Stock Exchange, *Exchange-Traded Funds: Introducing and Operating ETFs in the UK* at www.londonstockexchange.com/specialist-issuers/etfs/how-to-issue-etfs/listingand admissionguide.pdf.

now covered under the UCITS Directives. The Listing Rules allow ETFs to be constructed synthetically, that is, swap-based and not actually holding the assets in the benchmark that the ETF is based on, provided that the underlying assets are still UCITS-compliant.[140] Hence it would appear that the London Stock Exchange does not permit actively managed ETFs that may hold illiquid assets.[141]

Exchange-traded funds have been developed as a hedging device for institutions, so that an entire portfolio can be hedged.[142] Hence, commentators see them as useful hedging tools for exotic and relatively illiquid assets.[143] However, the exchange-traded fund structure has become appealing to retail investors as the fund is listed and benefits from the transparency requirements imposed on listed entities. Further, the fund can be traded at any time during the trading day, and such intraday liquidity is highly desired by investors, as compared with mutual funds that allow daily redemptions with one published price every day.[144] Where the exchange-traded fund is based on an index and is passively managed, the liquidity and transparency features seem to be superior to mutual funds that are index-hugging and passively managed too. Exchange-traded funds have also been able to charge lower fees than passively managed mutual funds,[145] thus ensuring that yield is not taken up by fees.

Investors have become attracted to exchange-traded funds and the market has grown phenomenally in the UK.[146] This now seems to be a safe investment option,[147] although it would be difficult for the fund to be trading above its NAV in the market for highly

---

[140] See Eddy Wymeersch, "The Regulatory Regime for Exchange-Traded Funds in the EU" (2011) at http://ssrn.com/abstract=1986852.

[141] This area is subject to huge debate in terms of whether the apparent safety of ETFs is compromised by active management, but the number of active managers in ETFs is increasing due to the difficulty of generating superior returns otherwise: see Michael R. Rosella and Domenick Pugliese, "The Evolution of the Exchange-Traded Fund: Is Active Management on the Horizon?" (2006) 7 Journal of Investment Compliance 44.

[142] Gary L. Gastineau, "Mutual Funds versus Exchange-Traded Funds," chapter 14 in John D. Haslem (ed.), *Mutual Funds: Portfolio Structures, Analysis, Management, and Stewardship* (Chichester: John Wiley & Sons 2010).

[143] Ilan Guedj and Jennifer Huang, "Are ETFs Replacing Index Mutual Funds?" (2009) at http://ssrn.com/abstract=1108728.

[144] Gary L. Gastineau, *The Exchange-Traded Funds Manual* (Chichester: John Wiley & Sons 2010) at chapter 1. But empirical research has also found that exchange-traded funds do not consistently outperform passively managed mutual funds: see Mohamed Sharifzadeh and Simin Hojat, "An Analytical Performance Comparison of Exchange-Traded Funds with Index Funds: 2002–2010" (2012) 13 Journal of Asset Management 196–209; Adam Turner, "Exchange-Traded Funds vs. UK Investment Trusts: A Comparison of Performance" (2010) at http://papers.ssrn.com/sol3/papers.cfm?abstract_id=1689534.

[145] Forbes.com, "What's the Difference? Mutual Funds and Exchange-Traded Funds Explained" (July 2013) at www.forbes.com/sites/feeonlyplanner/2013/07/18/whats-the-difference-mutual-funds-and-exchange-traded-funds-explained/.

[146] "Rapid Expansion across UK Exchange Traded Funds Industry," *Financial Times* (February 22, 2011); globally, see "Exchange Traded Funds Make Strongest Ever Start to a Year," *Financial Times* (April 12, 2015).

[147] But underlying securities can be volatile—see the episode involving BlackRock and Vanguard's exposure to HK-listed securities in their ETFs: "ETFs Endure Goldin-Hanergy Rollercoaster," *Financial Times* (May 26, 2015).

liquid securities that are included in an index. There is potential for greater returns for the actively managed exchange-traded fund, but investors would actually get less transparency regarding the underlying assets, their liquidity, and their fungibility, and would risk tracking error and other forms of deviation and arbitrage by the fund.[148]

The growth of the retail exchange-traded fund market reflects investor preferences for liquidity and low cost, but such preferences have certain implications. As exchange-traded funds are largely based on indices of UCITS-compliant securities, this quarter of the market relates to highly liquid and popular securities. Retail savings channeled into this quarter again reinforce the imbalance of financing for already highly popular and liquid markets as opposed to more diverse, long-term, and illiquid opportunities. This is unless exchange-traded funds are allowed to be developed as a saving or hedging structure for illiquid forms of finance in the UK and EU. This chapter also suggests that trading in exchange-traded funds allows investors to be one step removed from engagement as equity investors in corporate finance. Investors buy into a fund portfolio and are distanced from each corporate security in the basket. They are thus disengaged from being "investors" in firms and behave more like traders in whole portfolios. It is arguable that exchange-traded fund investors are largely attracted to the trading freedoms and this reinforces a trading and short-termist culture rather than an investing culture with retail savers.

This section of the chapter has pointed out how investor preferences have moved both the markets and regulatory regimes toward certain product designs and regulatory structures for investor protection. It is argued that although many investor protection aims are sound and mitigate the principal–agent problems between fund management and investors, the convergence toward certain product designs that emphasize liquidity, low costs, and index-hugging could result in biases against other more exotic, illiquid, and long-term opportunities, marginalizing these markets for retail participation.[149] Prominent UK economist John Kay warns that convergence of investment strategies would only result in less overall performance for every investor and lack of growth in the underlying assets.[150] The trends discussed above could potentially inhibit the deployment of retail savings across a wide range of diverse investment opportunities—an issue that relates to investor choice as well as allocative efficiency.

4 CONCLUSION

This chapter has observed that the market for retail collective investment funds in the UK is largely dominated by UCITS, the European retail collective investment structure

---

[148] Lucy F. Ackert and Yisong S. Tian, "Arbitrage, Liquidity, and the Valuation of Exchange Traded Funds" (2008) 17 Financial Institutions, Instruments and Markets 331; Si Cheng, Massimo Massa, and Hong Zhang, "The Dark Side of ETF Investing: A World-Wide Analysis" (2011) at http://papers.ssrn.com/sol3/papers.cfm?abstract_id=2224424.

[149] Of course the different risk profiles may not appeal to all retail investors, and it remains important that risks be communicated clearly.

[150] John Kay, "No Investor Wins If All Investors Are the Same," *Financial Times* (June 2, 2015).

that can be marketed throughout the EU. The growth and now preeminence of the UCITS product in the UK is in no small part due to deliberate policy and lawmaking at the EU to promote the UCITS markets. The regulatory framework is purported to be based on high standards of investor protection, and although these standards took time to evolve from the first Directive of 1985, retail investors have bought into the appeal of UCITS funds. In the UK, even NURs closely follow the UCITS investor protection regime in order to achieve an appropriate branding appeal. This chapter has highlighted the key areas of investor protection that cater to investor preferences: comprehensible disclosure; portfolio composition rules that cater to safety and liquidity needs; and conduct of business regulation based on European "gold standards" that have been replicated throughout functionally similar regulation.[151]

The chapter highlights, however, that the regulatory framework and market developments have all rallied round investors' preferences for liquidity, safety, and low management cost (therefore boosting yields). These emphases have resulted in the relative underdevelopment of regulation in the UK for non-UCITS products which have different attributes, such as relative illiquidity and long-termism, and which require a different investor protection framework. This may reinforce investor perceptions that UCITS product attributes are more "ideal" or "optimal" and could result in the marginalization of the market for other collective investment funds that are invested in exotic or unconventional asset classes with different attributes. The bulk of retail savings in the UK and EU are arguably put to work in a narrow and crowded section of the highly tradable market, chasing already low and competitive yields. This chapter raised the question whether there is a trade-off between investor protection and the more diverse deployment of capital from the retail savings sector. It urges the FCA to consider developing more comprehensive regulatory thinking for non-UCITS retail funds so that those markets can benefit from more appropriate regulation and investors can be educated about, and become less risk-averse regarding, these diverse and unconventional opportunities.

SELECT BIBLIOGRAPHY

Abner, David J., *The ETF Handbook: How to Value and Trade Exchange-Traded Funds* (Chichester: John Wiley & Sons, 2010).
Andenas, Mads and Iris H-Y. Chiu, *The Foundations and Future of Financial Regulation* (Oxford: Routledge, 2014).
Bengtsson, Elias and Bernard Delbeque, "Revisiting the European Asset Management Industry" (2011) 20 Financial Markets, Institutions and Instruments 163.
Bootle, Roger, *The Trouble with Markets: Saving Capitalism from Itself* (London: Nicholas Brealey Publishing, 2009, 2012).
Business, Innovation and Skills, *The Kay Review of UK Equity Markets and Long-Term Decision Making* (Final Report, July 23, 2012).
Buttgieg, Christopher, "The 2009 UCITS IV Directive: A Critical Examination of the Framework for the Creation of a Broader and More Efficient Internal Market for UCITS" (2012) 6 Journal of Business Law 453.

---

[151] The Markets in Financial Instruments Directive II 2014; The Alternative Investment Fund Managers Directive 2011.

Crook, Michael W., "A Stochastic Portfolio Perspective on Utilizing Active and Passive Fund Management" (2012) at http://ssrn.com/abstract=2170776

Cumming, Douglas, Gael Imad'Eddine, and Armin Schwienbacher, "Harmonized Regulatory Standards, International Distribution of Investment Funds and the Recent Financial Crisis" (2011) 18 European Journal of Finance 261.

Dallas, Lynne, "Short-Termism, the Financial Crisis, and Corporate Governance" (2012) 37 Journal of Corporation Law 265.

Epstein, Gerald A. (ed.), *Financialization and the World Economy* (Cheltenham: Edward Elgar, 2005).

Erturk, Ismail, Julie Froud, Sukhdev Johal, Adam Leaver, and Karel Williams (eds), *Financialization at Work: Key Tests and Commentary* (Oxford: Routledge, 2008).

Ferran, Eilis, Niamh Moloney, Jennifer G. Hill, and John C. Coffee Jnr, *The Regulatory Aftermath of the Global Financial Crisis* (Cambridge: Cambridge University Press, 2012).

Gastineau, Gary L., *The Exchange-Traded Funds Manual* (Chichester: John Wiley & Sons 2010).

Guedj, Ilan and Jennifer Huang, "Are ETFs Replacing Index Mutual Funds?" (2009) at http://ssrn.com/abstract=1108728

Haslem, John D. (ed.), *Mutual Funds: Portfolio Structures, Analysis, Management, and Stewardship* (Chichester: John Wiley & Sons 2010).

Hein, Eckhard, Torsten Niechoj, Peter Spahn, and Achim Truger (eds), *Finance-led Capitalism: Macro-Economic Effects of Changes in the Financial Sector* (Marburg: Metropolis Verlag 2009).

Heinemann, Friedrich, "The Benefits of Creating an Integrated EU Market for Investment Funds" (2002) at http://ssrn.com/abstract=309099

IFF Research and YouGov, "UCITS Disclosure Testing Research Report" (June 2009) at http://ec.europa.eu/internal_market/investment/docs/other_docs/research_report_en.pdf

Jones, Robert C., "Active Management in Mostly Efficient Markets" (2011) 67 Financial Analysts Journal 29.

Kacperczyk, Marcin and Philipp Schnabl, "How Safe Are Money Market Funds?" (2013) Quarterly Journal of Economics 1073.

Naveaux, Vincent and Renaud Graas, "Direct Action by Investors against a UCITS Depositary—A Short Lived Landmark Ruling?" (2012) 7 Capital Markets Law Journal 455.

Pastor, Lubos, Robert F. Stambaugh, and Lucian A. Taylor, "Scale and Skill in Active Management" (Jan 2014) at http://ssrn.com/abstract=2390285

Polkovnichenko, Valery, Kelsey Wei, and Feng Zhao, "Cautious Risk-Takers: Investor Preferences and Demand for Active Management" (2012) at http://ssrn.com/abstract=2022416

Pozen, Robert C., "Curbing Short-Termism in Corporate America" (May 2014) at www.brookings.edu/~/media/research/files/papers/2014/05/06%20pozen/brookings_shorttermismfinal_may2014.pdf

PricewaterhouseCoopers, *Asset Management 2020: A Brave New World* (2013) at www.pwc.com/gx/en/asset-management/publications/asset-management-2020-a-brave-new-world.jhtml.

PricewaterhouseCoopers, *Luxembourg Fund Governance Survey 2014* at www.pwc.lu/en/asset-management/docs/pwc-fund-governance-survey.pdf

Roche, David and Bob McKee, *New Monetarism* (London: Independent Strategy, 2007).

Rosella, Michael R. and Domenick Pugliese, "The Evolution of the Exchange-Traded Fund: Is Active Management on the Horizon?" (2006) 7 Journal of Investment Compliance 44.

Roy, S. Manjesh, "Money Market Mutual Funds: A Macro Perspective" (2005) 40 Money, Banking and Finance 1254.

Sharifzadeh, Mohamed and Simin Hojat, "An Analytical Performance Comparison of Exchange-Traded Funds with Index Funds: 2002–2010" (2012) 13 Journal of Asset Management 196–209.

Szylar, Christian, *Risk Management under UCITS III/IV* (Chichester: John Wiley & Sons 2010).

The Squam Lake Group, Martin Baily et al, "Reforming Money Market Funds" (2011) at http://ssrn.com/abstract=1740663

Towers Watson, *The Alternative UCITS Market: The Power of Perception?* (2014).

Turner, Adam, "Exchange-Traded Funds vs. UK Investment Trusts: A Comparison of Performance" (2010) at http://papers.ssrn.com/sol3/papers.cfm?abstract_id=1689534

van Setten, Lodewijk, *The Law of Institutional Investment Management* (Oxford: Oxford University Press 2009).

Wymeersch, Eddy, "The Regulatory Regime for Exchange-Traded Funds in the EU" (2011) at http://ssrn.com/abstract=1986852.

17. Regulation of mutual funds in Australia
Pamela Hanrahan and Ian Ramsay*

1 INTRODUCTION

This *Handbook* brings together a range of perspectives on mutual funds, including international ones. Mutual funds are present in most developed markets, and in most jurisdictions have common commercial features that are easy to recognize. However, they adopt a range of legal forms.

In most markets, including Australia, a mutual fund is initiated by a financial firm (such as a bank, insurance company, broker, or other financial intermediary) that offers to accept and aggregate contributions from retail investors. The intention is that these contributions will be held as a discrete fund and managed collectively by the firm for the benefit of those investors, pursuant to the fund's published mandate. That mandate will usually contemplate the active or passive investment of the fund in some mix of transferable securities and money market instruments.[1] Mutual funds are "open-end," in that the firm allows investors to withdraw their investment by redeeming their share of the fund on request, at a price that reflects in some way the value of a pro rata interest in the fund at the relevant time. Unlike their close cousin the exchange-traded fund, interests in mutual funds are not listed or traded in organized securities markets.

Wherever they arise, mutual funds exist for a reason. The investor hopes that, by pooling his or her contributions with others and utilizing the professional skills, purchasing power, and resources of the financial firm, the investor can achieve better investment outcomes (including through diversification or through access to investment opportunities that are not directly available to small investors) than would otherwise be possible. The financial firm hopes and expects to be paid for its services—often in the form of a management fee that may or may not be calculated by reference to the performance of the fund. In most cases, the firm will operate several different funds. Although sometimes the financial firm is itself owned by the fund investors,[2] this not the dominant model and generally the firm has a quite different group of stakeholders in its business operations.

---

[*] The authors thank Joseph Horbec for his assistance in collecting the data referred to in section 2.

[1] Mutual funds that invest predominantly in transferable securities and money market instruments are the focus of this *Handbook*. However in Australia the legal form of the registered "managed investment scheme" is also routinely used for a number of different collective investment arrangements, described below.

[2] An example is the Vanguard model. This type of structure (sometimes referred to as internalized management) is often used in exchange-traded Australian Real Estate Investment Trusts (A-REITS) but is not common in the Australian mutual funds market.

The mutual fund has been a highly effective and (at least for the financial firms involved) lucrative vehicle for the provision of this type of investment service to retail clients. Recent industry data put the worldwide total net assets of mutual funds in 2017 at USD 49.29 trillion,[3] a more than tenfold increase on the estimated USD 4 trillion in funds under management 20 years earlier.[4] Relative to population, Australia is one of the world's larger mutual fund markets,[5] and about 10 percent of Australians own shares indirectly through an unlisted mutual fund.[6] The majority of these funds have been promoted and operated by financial firms affiliated with the major Australian retail banks and life insurance companies, although this vertically integrated model is now under challenge.[7]

All mutual funds tend to exhibit three common characteristics. First, they exist for the reason and behave in the manner that we have described. Second, they therefore necessarily involve the "separation of funds and managers," a feature that, as John Morley points out, "runs so deep in the DNA of the investment management industry that its significance has tended to be felt implicitly rather than identified expressly."[8] Third, this separation gives rise to certain emergent ordering or organizational issues that it falls to law or regulation to resolve.

This third characteristic is a large part of the reason why mutual funds are so interesting for comparative legal scholars. While mutual funds in different jurisdictions have similar economic and functional characteristics, and all exhibit this separation, there remain significant differences in legal form.[9] In other words, despite the fact that many funds' management firms operate globally, different legal and regulatory systems continue to resolve the issues arising from this separation of funds and managers differently.

Australia, appropriately for the home of the platypus, has taken a unique approach to resolving those issues. This chapter provides some insights into that approach. We structure it as follows. Section 2 introduces the Australian mutual fund market. Section 3 explains, in broad terms, the legal and regulatory architecture within which Australian mutual funds operate. If the different legal forms adopted by mutual funds can be grouped into three broad genera—corporate, trust-based, or contract-based—Australian

---

[3] ICI, *Worldwide Regulated Open-End Fund Assets and Flows, Fourth Quarter 2017*. Available at www.ici.org/research.

[4] ICI Global, *2014 Annual Report to Members* (2014) 15.

[5] For an overview of the Australian mutual funds market, see Commonwealth of Australia, Australian Trade and Investment Commission, *Australia's Managed Funds 2017 Update—Trade and Investment Note* (April 2017).

[6] Australian Securities Exchange *ASX Australian Investor Study* (2017) 48.

[7] Section 2 below contains a more detailed description of the Australian mutual funds market, and how it fits within the broader investment management industry (including Australia's large superannuation (pension) fund market).

[8] J. Morley, "The separation of funds and managers: A theory of investment structure and regulation" (2014) *The Yale Law Journal* 123:1228, 1236.

[9] There is far less convergence in the legal forms used for CIS in different jurisdictions than for ordinary trading businesses, which in most jurisdictions utilize some recognizable form of the limited liability corporation as the vehicle for aggregating capital and carrying on business.

funds to date have been trust-based vehicles.[10] However, within the trust genus they are unusual internationally because there is no mandated separation between the roles of trustee and manager, which are merged in a single "responsible entity." Funds that are open to retail investors must be registered with the Australian Securities and Investments Commission (ASIC) and the responsible entities that operate them must be licensed by ASIC under the Australian Financial Services (AFS) licensing regime.

The legislation governing the structure and operation of mutual funds and other noncorporate collective investment schemes—Chapter 5C of the Corporations Act 2001 (Cth) (Corporations Act)—contains few, if any, restrictions on the commercial features of the fund. For example, the fund can include any combination of assets and can add to the funds under management by borrowing. Instead, the legislation imposes onerous fiduciary-type obligations on the responsible entity and its officers, and confers certain control rights on fund investors (including voting rights). However, again unusually, these do not include an unqualified right in investors to redeem their investment on demand.

In what follows, we look in some more depth at how the Australian system resolves certain of the emergent issues resulting from the separation of funds and managers in mutual funds. We then consider the fiduciary-type duties imposed by Australian law on responsible entities and their officers. After this, we look at the (again, unusually) limited role of any kind of independent oversight of the activities of responsible entities in the Australian framework. We move on to consider the rights conferred on investors, including information rights, voting rights (including a right to remove and replace the responsible entity), enforcement rights, and withdrawal rights. The final section offers our conclusions.

2 MUTUAL FUNDS IN AUSTRALIA

Australian mutual funds have an unusual structure by global standards. Mutual funds in Australia are constituted as unit trusts,[11] rather than as corporations. Investors in the fund acquire and hold a proportionate but undivided beneficial interest in the fund's assets, rather than shares in a corporation.[12] Of course, the fact that the Australian

---

[10] The different legal forms and structures adopted by mutual funds in IOSCO member jurisdictions are identified in the Consultation Report of the Technical Committee of the International Organization of Securities Commissions, *Examination of the Governance of Collective Investment Scheme* (February 2005). In 2018, the Australian government introduced new legislation to provide for a corporate-form collective investment vehicle (CCIV) and limited partnership collective investment vehicle (LPCIV) as part of its commitment to the Asia Region Funds Passport (ARFP) multilateral initiative. The ARFP aims to provide a multilaterally agreed framework to facilitate the crossborder marketing of managed funds across participating economies in the Asia region. The first Australian CCIVs are expected to be launched late in 2018 or in 2019. CCIVs are discussed briefly in the Conclusion.

[11] A "unit trust" is a trust that divides the beneficial interest in the trust fund into a number of equivalent and fungible units.

[12] There are some existing examples of corporate collective investment vehicles in Australia, including several large closed-end, listed investment companies (LICs). In very broad

mutual funds are structured as trusts is not unique,[13] but what is unusual is that, in Australia, the role of trustee and that of the fund adviser and sponsor are combined in a single "responsible entity." The legal and regulatory framework, explained in Section 3 of this chapter, does not attempt to address the consequences of the separation of funds and managers by interposing some external or independent monitor, such as a trustee or depository or independent fund board, to supervise or control the activities of the fund adviser on behalf of investors. Instead the emphasis is on using a combination of statutory obligations, private litigation rights, public sanctions, and market forces to ensure that the responsible entity conducts the affairs of the fund in a manner consistent with a high level of fiduciary accountability.

2.1 Managed Investment Schemes

Mutual funds are one of a number of different types of collective investments in Australia that are subject to governmental regulation as "managed investment schemes."[14] "Managed investment scheme" is a term of art defined in the Corporations Act to capture most forms of collective investments that are neither structured as corporations nor prudentially regulated.[15] The definition does not include superannuation (that is, pension) funds, which are separately dealt with in the Australian system.[16] The eight main types of managed investment schemes available in the

---

terms, trusts are the generally preferred structure in Australia because they allow for flow-through tax treatment (which at present is not an option for Australian companies—they are always subject to entity-level taxation) and because the trust can be open-end (overcoming the restrictions on Australian companies reducing their capital). The CCIV changes proposed for 2018 will alter this position. Interestingly, while LICs are required to hold an AFS licence and prepare a prospectus for any new share issues, they are not subject to the structure and governance rules that apply to (noncorporate) managed investment schemes under Chapter 5C of the Corporations Act, explained in section 3.

[13] Unit trusts are also the most common form of mutual fund in the United Kingdom and a number of Asian jurisdictions.

[14] The statutory definition of a managed investment scheme appears in section 9 of the Corporations Act.

[15] Prudentially regulated entities are regulated by the Australian Prudential Regulation Authority (APRA). APRA regulates authorized deposit-taking institutions (ADIs) such as banks, building societies, and friendly societies; insurance companies; and the trustees of public offer superannuation entities.

[16] Australia has a very large and robust superannuation system, with the total value of superannuation assets as at December 2017 at AUD 2.6 trillion (about USD 1.95 trillion) and growing at over 10 percent per annum: www.apra.gov.au and www.superannuation.asn.au. The defining feature of the Australian superannuation system is that employers are required by law to contribute a set percentage (currently 9.5 percent) of each employee's wage or salary into one of a range of approved types of investment vehicles, to accumulate for their retirement. The funds accumulated must remain in the person's superannuation account until they reach the prescribed retirement age. In return, the government provides generous taxation concessions on fund contributions and earnings. Most superannuation vehicles in Australia operate as defined contribution, rather than defined benefit, schemes. The three main types of vehicle, each of which has about one third of the overall market, are known as industry funds (which are operated by nonprofit trustee companies many of which were originally affiliated with trade

Australian market are: unlisted managed funds; listed managed investments (constituted either as exchange-traded funds (ETFs) or listed investment trusts); Australian listed real estate investment trusts (known as A-REITs); unlisted real property schemes; mortgage schemes; infrastructure schemes; agribusiness schemes; and timeshare and serviced strata schemes.[17] Here we are concerned only with the first category, which is also the largest by both number of registered funds and total funds under management.

2.2 Registrable Schemes

Like many other jurisdictions, Australia distinguishes between public and private funds, with the former category being subject to more intensive regulation than the latter. What is generally described elsewhere as a public fund corresponds roughly to the Australian notion of a registerable managed investment scheme. If a mutual fund is open for investment to "retail clients" as defined in the Corporations Act,[18] the fund must be registered with ASIC if it has more than 20 members or is promoted by a person or group in the business of promoting such schemes.[19]

Significantly, there is no restriction imposed in Australia on the kinds or the concentration of assets in which a registered scheme may invest, or on its borrowings or other commercial features. Alternative investment funds, including private equity and venture capital funds, hedge funds, and special strategy funds are all eligible to be registered and, once registered, to be offered for sale to the retail market.

---

unions), retail funds (which are operated by for-profit trustee companies, often affiliated with one of the five largest Australian financial conglomerates—four of which are predominantly trading banks and the other of which is a life insurer) and "self-managed superannuation funds" or SMSFs, in which the (up to five) trustees or trustee company directors are also the members of the fund. SMSFs are a popular self-directed vehicle for higher net worth individuals.

[17] ASIC, *Regulation Impact Statement: Holding Scheme Property and Other Assets— Update to RG 133* (November 2013) at [19]. ASIC notes that in November 2013 there were approximately 3,600 managed funds, the main categories of which are cash, cash-enhanced, equities, specialist equities, bonds, yield, alternative, and multisector. There were also 62 A-REITS (that is, exchange-traded real estate trusts), 650 unlisted property schemes, 124 pooled mortgage schemes, 44 contributory mortgage schemes, 22 listed infrastructure funds, 410 agribusiness schemes and 40 timeshare and serviced strata schemes. While the number of registered agribusiness schemes is recorded as 410, ASIC goes on to point out at [113]–[114] that following the collapse of a number of the operators of these types of funds during the global financial crisis of 2007–8, only a small number (143) remain operational.

[18] Broadly, for investment-related transactions, a person is treated as a retail client unless they invest more than $500,000; they are a large business; they are a high net worth individual; they are considered (and certified) by the financial services firm to be an experienced investor; or they are a professional investor (such as an AFS licensee or APRA regulated entity): see Corporations Act sections 761G and 761GA and Corporations Regulations 7.1.11–7.1.28 and 7.6.02AB–7.6.02AF discussed in R. Baxt, A. Black, and P. Hanrahan, *Securities and Financial Services Law* (9th ed, 2017) [6.17]–[6.25].

[19] Section 601ED of the Corporations Act. This is so unless the particular scheme was exempted from the requirement to produce a Product Disclosure Statement (which is the equivalent of a registration statement or prospectus) in connection with the initial sale of interests in the fund on other grounds, for example because it was a small-scale private offering: see section 1012E of the Corporations Act.

As explained in Section 3, to qualify for registration a fund must have a responsible entity that is an Australian public company and that is appropriately licensed by ASIC. Currently there are about 470 licensed responsible entities in Australia, and 3,600 separate registered managed investment schemes.[20] An individual responsible entity may operate only one scheme, or up to several hundred separate schemes. There is no requirement for each fund to have its own board separate from that of the responsible entity, and none do. Instead, responsibility for the operation of the fund rests ultimately with the board of the responsible entity. Most of the funds operated by the large banks and insurance companies do not have an outside custodian or trustee; instead, the assets are held in-house.

2.3 The Australian Mutual Fund Market

The Australian retail mutual funds market is fairly concentrated. The 20 largest responsible entities (of the 470 in total) between them control about 70 percent of total funds under management. Of the top ten, four are affiliated with large vertically integrated financial institutions in Australia; the others are mostly the largest global funds management firms.[21]

Most investors in these funds are middle income households (often described in the Australian market as "mum and dad" investors) who hold their investments directly or through their self-managed superannuation funds (SMSF).[22] Investors usually invest following a consultation with a financial planner or financial adviser (although not, typically, a stockbroker, who in the Australian market is more likely to be concerned with the sale of listed securities).[23] Until 2013, that planner or adviser was probably

---

[20] ASIC, *Annual Report 2016–17*, p. 19.
[21] See www.morningstar.com.au. This includes BlackRock, Vanguard, UBS, State Street, and Fidelity, all of which have Australian subsidiaries licensed to offer retail mutual funds in Australia. See also Theodore Golat, 'Banks' Wealth Management Activities in Australia' *Reserve Bank of Australia Bulletin—September Quarter 2016* 53. The Royal Commission into Misconduct in the Banking, Superannuation and Financial Services Industry, called by the Australian government in December 2017, has coincided with the announcement by a number of Australian banks to dispose of their wealth management businesses.
[22] About one third of retirement savings in Australia are held in SMSF, which are individual trusts established to hold investment products selected and managed by a trustee who is, or is a company controlled by, the SMSF member or members. SMSF may have up to five members and so they are often family rather than individual structures. They are mostly used by older and wealthier Australians. Younger people or people with lower retirement savings account balances usually hold their money in one or more APRA-regulated superannuation entities, which are large, professionally managed investment pools. For an overview of the Australian retirement savings sector, see Commonwealth of Australia, *Financial System Inquiry—Final Report*, November 2014, Chapter 2.
[23] Financial advisers and planners are licensed to give personal financial advice to retail clients. This is a process that usually involves a full review of the client's financial position and objectives, followed by the adviser recommending a range of financial products that may include retirement savings products, investment products, and personal insurances. Sales of mutual fund products in Australia typically occur either through this 'advised' channel or by the client sourcing the product directly, including over the internet. Most individual financial advisers or

420 *Research handbook on the regulation of mutual funds*

entitled to receive a commission from the operator (that is, responsible entity) of the relevant fund for the sale of its products, but the payment of commissions in relation to investment products has since been proscribed.[24] Some investors access the market directly through the internet or other channels, but this is less common.

3 THE LEGAL AND REGULATORY FRAMEWORK

This section explains in greater detail the legal and regulatory framework within which retail mutual funds are constituted and operate under Australian law. The current arrangements comprise a network of interlocking restrictions and requirements, built on three pillars. The first is the AFS licensing requirement, which controls who can operate a mutual fund in Australia. The second is the scheme registration requirement, which shapes the legal structure (but not portfolio composition) of, and imposes a governance regime on, mutual funds. The third is the mandatory presale and ongoing reporting and disclosure requirements, including those imposed by the Product Disclosure Statement (PDS) regime.

3.1 Development of the Australian Regime

The unique "single responsible entity" structure described in the previous section dates back only 20 years. Prior to that, Australian law and regulation had followed a more typical path.

The first recognizable mutual funds in Australia were established back in the 1930s,[25] but an organized regulatory response to the particular issues arising from the mutual fund structure did not emerge until the mid-1950s. At that time, the Parliament of the State of Victoria broke new ground by enacting legislation that applied generally accepted securities law principles (with their particular emphasis on mandatory presale disclosure to potential investors by way of a prospectus)[26] to collective investment

---

planners are either employed by a major bank or insurance company, or work in small principal-owned firms that are "authorized representatives" of licensed companies owned by a bank or insurer.

[24] The payment of commissions in connection with the sale of certain financial products, including mutual funds and other investment products, to retail investors was mostly banned in Australia in 2012, through the enactment of the *Corporations Amendment (Future of Financial Advice) Act 2012* (Cth) and the *Corporations Amendment (Further Future of Financial Advice Measures) Act 2012* (Cth). The relevant restrictions are now contained in Part 7.7A of the Corporations Act. For an explanation of the law governing the sale of financial products to Australian households see Pamela Hanrahan, *Background Paper No 7 for the Royal Commission into Misconduct in the Banking, Superannuation and Financial Services Industry—Legal Framework for the Provision of Financial Advice and Sale of Financial Products to Australian Households* (April 2018).

[25] *Australian Fixed Trusts Pty Ltd v Clyde Industries Limited and Ors* [1959] SR (NSW) 33.

[26] Australia is a federation, comprising six states and two territories. Until 2001, when legislative power was referred to the federal government, corporations and securities law was a matter for individual states. The Victorian parliament had been at the forefront of developments in this area since the nineteenth century.

schemes (CIS) for the first time. The 1955 legislation went further, requiring that the operator of the scheme itself be a public company, that an independent trustee be appointed to protect the interests of investors, and that the scheme be constituted pursuant to a deed that contained certain prescribed covenants and that was approved by the relevant regulatory agency.[27]

As the Australian mutual fund market grew over the rest of the century, this model was adopted in all states and various layers and refinements were applied to it. Coinciding with the development of the substantive law was a staged transfer of responsibility for corporations, securities, and financial services regulation from the individual Australian states and territories to the federal government, including through the establishment of the Australia Securities Commission (now ASIC) in 1991 and, eventually, the full referral of legislative power covering these areas by the states to the federal government in 2001.

The interests acquired by investors in schemes constituted and operated under these early regulatory arrangements were known as "prescribed interests." Prescribed interest schemes were trust-based vehicles, not corporations. The interests (at least in the case of prescribed interest schemes that operated as mutual funds) were an undivided but proportionate beneficial interest in the assets held by the fund; they were not shares in a company and therefore the holders of the interests did not have the ordinary rights and entitlements of shareholders. The trustee was usually a specialist fiduciary company established and approved for that purpose, which was independent of the promoter and operator of the scheme, known as the management company. Each of the trustee and the management company had separate roles and responsibilities under the approved deed. However, the statutory regime did not operate as a code. Instead, the legislative requirements operated alongside and through the prism of the underlying law of the form—in the case of mutual funds, the law of trusts.

The prescribed interest regime came under significant stress in the early 1990s, from an unexpected quarter. Mutual funds were not the only type of prescribed interest scheme that operated in Australia; there was also a significant number of unlisted property and mortgage funds that used this vehicle to accept investor contributions, to be invested directly in real property or lent against the security of real property. A reversal in the Australian commercial property market in 1990 precipitated a run on these funds, causing widespread investor losses and structural dislocation in the sector.[28] Urgent legislative intervention in 1991 froze investors' rights to redeem their interests, a move that was intended to allow the orderly winding down or conversion of

---

[27] Pamela F. Hanrahan, *Managed Investments Law and Practice* (CCH Australia, Loose-leaf 1998, 2018) ¶2–200.

[28] These problems recur from time to time in "shadow banking," in entities that borrow short and lend long and are not subject to adequate prudential regulation. The events in 1991 were triggered by the collapse of the Estate Mortgage group, discussed in B. Mees, M. Wehner, and P. Hanrahan, *Fifty Years of Managed Funds in Australia* (2005). Unfortunately, many Australian unlisted property and mortgage funds faced the same problem in 2008, and froze redemptions. Several years later, many fund members were still trying to recover their investments. See ASIC, *Information Sheet 111—Information for Investors in Frozen Funds* (November 2011).

these schemes to closed-end, listed vehicles. The collapse also prompted a more wideranging review of the prescribed interest regime, conducted jointly by the Australian Law Reform Commission (ALRC) and the Company and Securities Advisory Committee (CASAC).

The ALRC and CASAC reported in 1993; the report recommended the repeal of the prescribed interest regime.[29] Following a protracted process, new legislation replacing that regime was enacted by the Managed Investments Act 1998 (Cth).

3.2 Features of the Current Regime

The new regime imposed a raft of requirements on operators of mutual funds that are required to be, and are, registered with ASIC.[30] These include that the fund must have an appropriately licensed responsible entity as its operator; must have a constitution in approved form; and must have a "compliance plan" and, unless the majority of the directors of the responsible entity are external directors,[31] a compliance committee to monitor compliance with the plan. Interests in the fund may only be offered by way of a complying PDS containing prescribed information. The responsible entity must report periodically to members, and the financial reports and its compliance with the compliance plan must be audited. Both the responsible entity and the directors of the responsible entity must comply with a range of statutory duties, including duties of care and fiduciary duties of honesty and loyalty. The statutory duties are described below.[32]

---

[29] Australian Law Reform Commission and Companies and Securities Advisory Committee, *Report No 65: Collective Investments—Other People's Money* (2 vols and summary) (1993). The report prepared by ALRC and CASAC contains a detailed analysis of the nature of collective investment schemes and options for their regulation.

[30] In broad terms, a mutual fund must be registered with ASIC if it has (or is part of a group of schemes determined by ASIC to be closely related that has) more than 20 members or it was promoted by a person, or an associate of a person, who was, when the scheme was promoted, in the business of promoting managed investment schemes, and interests in the scheme have been or will be offered to investors in circumstances requiring the offeree to prepare and provide a Product Disclosure Statement (PDS) under Part 7.9 of the Corporations Act. A PDS is usually required unless the offer is restricted to certain categories of sophisticated or wholesale investors, including those investing over $500,000 in the fund.

[31] A person is external if he or she is not, and has not been in the previous two years, an employee of the responsible entity or a related body corporate or a senior manager of a related body corporate; is not, and has not been in the previous two years, substantially involved in business dealings, or in a professional capacity, with the responsible entity or a related body corporate; is not a member of a partnership that is, and has been in the previous two years, substantially involved in business dealings, or in a professional capacity, with the responsible entity or a related body corporate; does not have a material interest in the responsible entity or a related body corporate; and is not a relative of a person who has a material interest in the responsible entity or a related body corporate.

[32] The elements of the new regime were summarized by Justice (later Chief Justice) Marilyn Warren in *Australian Securities and Investments Commission v ABC Fund Managers Ltd & Ors (No 2)* (2002) 20 ACLC 120 at 126–7 in the following terms: (1) A prescribed interest was replaced with the concept of an interest in a "managed investment scheme." (2) Managed investment schemes were required to be registered with ASIC if [they had] more than 20 members or [were] promoted by a person in the business of promoting such schemes. (3) Each

Under this regime, a responsible entity is permitted to offer interests on the basis that they can be redeemed on request if the majority of the fund's investments are liquid, but is not required to do so. Many managed investment schemes, particularly those that hold physical rather than financial assets, are offered as closed-end funds from the outset. However, if a fund has been offered as open-end and its underlying investments become, in the opinion of the responsible entity, illiquid at any time, the responsible entity is required to suspend any redemption rights the investors might otherwise have. This occurred in a small number of funds that held unlisted investments during the global financial crisis of 2007–8, including hedge funds and other alternative investments.

3.3 Sources of Law

The structure and governance requirements for retail mutual funds are contained in Chapter 5C of the Corporations Act. The AFS licensing system was introduced by the Financial Services Reform Act 2001 (Cth), replacing the licensing regime for securities dealers in the earlier law, and is now contained in Part 7.6 of the Corporations Act. At the same time, a new mandatory presale disclosure regime replaced earlier prospectus requirements; it is the PDS regime now contained in Part 7.9 of the Corporations Act.

These parts of the Corporations Act are, along with the general law of trusts and some subordinate legislation contained in the Corporations Regulations 2001 (Cth), the principal sources of law governing the operation of Australian mutual funds (and other noncorporate CIS) that are open to retail investors. ASIC does not have the power to make binding rules with respect to mutual funds, but it does have certain discretionary powers in the administration of the registration and licensing regimes that it uses to impose particular requirements on schemes and their operators.[33] These include the

---

managed investment scheme was required to be operated by a single responsible entity, rather than a trustee and a separate manager. (4) The responsible entity was required to be a public company and to hold a securities dealer's licence authorizing that entity to operate the managed investment scheme. (5) As part of the registration process, the responsible entity was required to submit to ASIC a compliance plan containing measures to ensure compliance with the requirements of the law and the law and the constitution of the particular managed investment scheme and also to set out the custodial arrangements to be provided for scheme property and, further, stating the arrangements for monitoring compliance with the individual compliance plan. (6) Performance of the compliance plan was required to be audited annually. (7) Penalties were imposed for failure to register a managed investment scheme. (8) Fund raising by managed investment schemes was to be regulated under the prospectus provisions of [the *Corporations Law 1991*]. (9) Special provisions were imposed with respect to financial statements, audit and annual returns of managed investment schemes.

[33] Australian fund operators and their advisers frequently refer to two types of regulatory documents published by ASIC: ASIC Regulatory Guides and ASIC Instruments. Both are available at www.asic.gov.au/publications. The Regulatory Guides explain how ASIC interprets and applies the law in particular circumstances and how it exercises its statutory powers to modify or grant exemptions from the law in particular or general cases. When ASIC exercises these powers in cases of general application, it usually does so by way of Instrument, which has the practical effect of amending the law in the situations and for the purposes described in the instrument.

power to modify the law or grant exemptions from it in specified circumstances. The exercise by ASIC of its discretions in administering in the law, and the AFS licensing regime in particular, is important. For example, a financial firm that seeks to be licensed to act as a responsible entity must meet strict eligibility criteria imposed by ASIC and is subject to ongoing operating conditions relating to, among other things, its financial and nonfinancial resources.[34]

3.4 Three Key Aspects

In thinking about how the Australian regime addresses the consequences of the separation of funds and managers at the heart of the mutual fund structure, it seems to us that three particular aspects of the regime repay closer examination.

The first is the fiduciary-type duties imposed by Australian law on responsible entities and their officers, discussed in Section 4 of this chapter. These duties are one of the main mechanisms adopted by the regime to overcome the principal–agent divide that results from the separation of funds and managers. The second is the extent to which external monitoring (for example, by an independent trustee or depository) of a responsible entity's management of the fund plays a role in the Australian framework, as discussed in Section 5 of this chapter. The third is the rights conferred on investors, including withdrawal rights, voting rights (including a right to remove and replace the responsible entity), enforcement rights, and information rights, discussed in Section 6 of this chapter.

4 DUTIES OF RESPONSIBLE ENTITIES AND THEIR OFFICERS

Because most mutual funds in Australia are constituted as unit trusts, each fund's constitution is a deed of trust under which the responsible entity is appointed as trustee to hold the fund for the benefit of the investors, who are referred to in the Corporations Act as the fund's "members." The conditions attaching to the AFS license held by a

---

[34] The responsible entity must be a public company that holds an AFS license: section 601FA of the Corporations Act. Under section 913B(1) of the Corporations Act, ASIC must grant an applicant an AFS licence if (and must not grant such a license unless) certain criteria are met. These include that "ASIC has no reason to believe that the applicant is likely to contravene the obligations that will apply under section 912A if the licence is granted." As part of the licensing process, ASIC obtains information from the applicant to enable it to make an assessment as to whether there is any reason to believe that the applicant will not comply with these obligations. This information includes the "core proofs" explained in section E of Regulatory Guide 2 of ASIC's AFS Licensing Kit, and any additional proofs requested by ASIC under Regulatory Guide 3. The C2 proof, described in Regulatory Guide 3 of the Kit, is generally required for all responsible entities. It includes information about the applicant's scheme operating capacity. Another criterion is that ASIC must be satisfied that there is no reason to believe that any of the applicant's responsible officers are not of good fame and character, or if ASIC is not so satisfied, that the applicant's ability to provide the financial services covered by the license would nevertheless not be significantly impaired. "Responsible officer" is defined for this purpose in section 9 of the Act as an officer who would perform duties in connection with the holding of the licence.

particular responsible entity may require it to appoint a separate custodian to hold legal title to those assets,[35] but where it does so the custodian does not have any oversight function and is essentially the delegate of the responsible entity. This reflects the policy underpinning of the Australian regime, that there be "a single party responsible for all activities and functions of the scheme."[36] This structure means that the responsible entity is a trustee for members, with all the usual obligations in equity that this entails.

In addition, the responsible entity and its officers are subject to statutory obligations designed to address the agency problem inherent in the mutual fund structure. The statutory framework purports to privilege the interests of the fund members over those of the responsible entity itself in its management of the fund.

Because an Australian mutual fund is constituted as a unit trust rather than as a corporation, the fund itself is not a legal person. Rather than owing duties to the fund as a corporate entity, the responsible entity and its officers owe their duties directly to the members of the fund. Whether those duties are owed to each member individually or to the members collectively—one of the more interesting legal issues that arises from the mutual fund structure—is discussed below. For now it is sufficient to note that the better view is that the duties are owed to each member individually, subject to the (perhaps strange) qualification that members acting collectively (through the exercise of their statutory voting rights) can affect each other's position in a manner that impacts on their individual relationship with the responsible entity.

The statutory obligations imposed on the responsible entity mostly mirror and reinforce its general law duties as a trustee (and therefore, under Australian law, a fiduciary). The imposition of fiduciary-type duties directly on the officers of the responsible entity is, on the other hand, a more significant departure from ordinary trust principles, because ordinarily an officer of a corporation that is a trustee does not owe fiduciary duties directly to beneficiaries of the trust.

4.1 The Responsible Entity's Duties at General Law

The responsible entity is, first and foremost, a trustee.[37] As a trustee, it is subject to the default rules of Australian trust law that still contain the vestiges of the old notion of the trustee as a selfless volunteer.[38] However, many of these rules (with the exception

---

[35] See ASIC, *Regulatory Guide 133: Managed Investments and Custodial and Depository Services: Holding Assets* (November 2013).

[36] Parliamentary Joint Committee on Corporations and Securities, *Report on the Managed Investments Bill 1997* (April 1998) [1.37].

[37] Generally an express trust arises under the terms of the constitution. In any event, section 601FC(2) of the Corporations Act provides that "The responsible entity holds scheme property on trust for scheme members." See generally Pamela F. Hanrahan, "The responsible entity as trustee" in I. Ramsay (ed.), *Key Developments in Corporate Law and Trusts Law: Essays in Honour of Professor Harold Ford* (2002) 227.

[38] In J.D. Heydon and M.J. Leeming, *Jacob's Law of Trusts in Australia* (7th ed., 2006), the authors describe the duties of a trustee in the following terms: to become acquainted with the terms of the trust; to get in trust property; not to impeach the validity of the trust instrument or the title of the beneficiary; to adhere to and carry out the terms of the trust; to act impartially between the beneficiaries; properly to invest the trust funds; to keep and render proper accounts

of the requirement that the trustee act in the administration of the trust in the interests of the beneficiary, which is at the heart of the trust relationship) can be, and are, modified by agreement between the parties in commercial trusts, including mutual funds.

While the Australian mutual fund is constituted as a trust, it is not a donative trust in the traditional sense. In a donative trust, a settlor settles property on a trustee to be held for the benefit of another person, the beneficiary. In a mutual fund, there is no separate settlor because the members themselves transfer their contribution to the responsible entity to be managed collectively for their joint benefit. As one Australian commentator observed in 1997, these structures are essentially contractual arrangements and (within the confines of the statutory regime) it is open to the parties to agree their terms:

> To sum up, a unit trust deed is a contract that establishes an investment scheme. It makes provision for rights and obligations on a consensual basis. As part of the contract, it employs the trust as a holding device. With the trust, its trust incidents follow. Inevitably, some of those incidents may not be compatible with the mutual intention of the parties. In this respect, therefore, the trust deed makes provisions for the alteration of those trust incidents, in addition to its scheme provisions.[39]

Trust law allows for considerable flexibility in the terms on which the trust will operate. However, even without the constraints imposed by the statutory requirements on the freedom of the parties to agree the terms on which a mutual fund is to operate, some things cannot be negotiated away. As Lord Justice Millet in the English Court of Appeal has observed, there is "an irreducible core of obligations owed by the trustees to the beneficiaries and enforceable by them which is fundamental to the concept of a trust," that is, the duty of the trustees "to perform the trust honestly and in good faith for the benefit of the beneficiaries."[40]

The responsible entity also owes to members of the scheme a duty of care, arising under contract, at common law, and in equity. Because the responsible entity is a professional financial firm that holds itself out as having special or particular knowledge, skill, and experience and invites members to rely on its expertise, the standard of care required is that of a professional person exercising investment functions.[41]

---

and to give full information when required; to exercise reasonable care; not to delegate duties or powers; to pay and transfer the trust property and the income thereof to the right persons; and to act gratuitously.

[39] Kam Fan Sin, *The Legal Nature of the Unit Trust* (1997) 105–6. See also Michael Bryan, "Reflections on some commercial applications of the trust" in I. Ramsay (ed.), *Key Developments in Corporate Law and Trusts Law: Essays in Honour of Professor Harold Ford* (2002) 205.

[40] *Armitage v Nurse* [1997] 2 All ER 705 at 713.

[41] See e.g. *Australian Securities Commission v AS Nominees Ltd* (1995) 13 ACLC 1822 at 1832 per Finn J.; *Australian Securities and Investments Commission v Australian Property Custodian Holdings Ltd (rec & man apt) (in liq)* (2014) 332 ALR 45; *Trilogy Funds Management Ltd v Sullivan (No 2)* (2015) 331 ALR 185; *Australian Securities and Investments Commission v Managed Investments Ltd (No 9)* (2016) 308 FLR 216; *Australian Securities and Investments Commission v Avestra Asset Management Ltd (in liq)* (2017) 348 ALR 525.

Finally, because the relationship between a trustee and a beneficiary is recognized as fiduciary in character under Australian law,[42] the responsible entity owes to the members of the fund the interlocking proscriptive duties of a fiduciary. They are, "unless the fiduciary has the informed consent of the person to whom they are owed, first, not to obtain any unauthorised benefit from the relationship and, secondly, not to be in a position where the interests or duties of the fiduciary conflict, or there is a real or substantial possibility they may conflict, with the interest of the person to whom the duty is owed."[43] The prescriptive duties that the responsible entity owes to members as a function of its office—including the duty to act with care, skill, and diligence and the duty to act in good faith in the interests of members in the exercise of its powers and discretions in relation to the fund—arise in equity but are not necessarily described as "fiduciary" duties by Australian lawyers.[44]

4.2 The Responsible Entity's Statutory Duties to Members

Chapter 5C of the Corporations Act imposes duties on the responsible entity that, in many cases, reinforce and are informed by the content of the general law duties. They include duties of honesty, care and diligence, and loyalty, as well as express duties to comply with law and documents.[45]

---

[42] The recognized categories include trustee and beneficiary, agent and principal, solicitor and client, director and company, and partners: *Hospital Products Ltd v United States Surgical Corporation* (1984) 156 CLR 41; [1984] HCA 64 at CLR 68 (Gibbs CJ) and CLR 96 (per Mason J).

[43] *Wingecarribee Shire Council v Lehman Bros Australia Ltd (in liq)* (2012) 301 ALR 1 at [732]. This important decision of the Federal Court of Australia held an investment bank liable for the sale of complex financial products to local municipal councils prior to the global financial crisis, in part because it breached the bank's fiduciary duties to its (wholesale) client not to advise the client in circumstances where it had a conflict between its duty (to act in the client's interest in giving the advice) and its personal interest (in selling the products).

[44] There has for a while been a slightly sterile debate in Australian law about whether these positive duties are properly described as fiduciary. It follows from observations made by two judges of the High Court of Australia in *Breen v Williams* (1996) 186 CLR 71 at 113 that "Australian courts only recognise proscriptive fiduciary duties ... not to obtain any unauthorised benefit from the relationship and not to be in a position of conflict." As to the current state of the law, see *Westpac Banking Corporation v Bell Group Ltd (in liq) (No 3)* (2012) 44 WAR 1 and *Hasler v Singtel Optus Pty Ltd* (2014) 311 ALR 494. See also Hon H Gummow, 'Knowing assistance' (2013) 87 *Australian Law Journal* 311; Chief Justice T F Bathurst and S Merope, "It tolls for thee: Accessorial liability after Bell v Westpac" (2013) 87 *Australian Law Journal* 831; Justice K M Hayne, "Directors' duties and a company's creditors" (2014) 38 *Melbourne University Law Review* 795.

[45] Section 601FC(1) of the Corporations Act provides that: "In exercising its powers and carrying out its duties, the responsible entity of a registered scheme must: (a) act honestly; (b) exercise the degree of care and diligence that a reasonable person would exercise if they were in the responsible entity's position; (c) act in the best interests of the members and, if there is a conflict between the members' interests and its own interests, give priority to the members' interests; (d) treat the members who hold interests of the same class equally and members who hold interests of different classes fairly; (e) not make use of information acquired through being the responsible entity in order to gain an improper advantage for itself or another person, or

The duties control the manner in which the responsible entity must act in exercising its powers and carrying out its duties (that is, functions) in relation to the fund. The parallels with the responsible entity's obligations at general law are obvious. Importantly, section 601FC(3) of the Corporations Act goes on to say that "a duty of the responsible entity under subsection (1) or (2) overrides any conflicting duty an officer or employee of the responsible entity has under Part 2D.1." Part 2D.1 of the Corporations Act sets out the duties owed by an officer of a company to that company.

The statutory duties set out above include, crucially, an obligation on the responsible entity to "give priority to the members' interests" if there is "a conflict between the members' interests and its own interests."[46] This rule is different from the fiduciary obligation, which prevents the responsible entity from being in a situation where its personal interest potentially conflicts with its duties to the members (although the members' informed consent is a defense to a claim against the responsible entity for breach of fiduciary duty in these circumstances). The statutory obligation related to interested dealings is supplemented by specific and separate requirements that apply where the responsible entity or its controllers or officers have an interest in a transaction affecting the fund. Under Part 5C.7 of the Corporations Act, fund members are given a veto power over certain dealings. The purpose of the part is to "protect the interests of the scheme's members as a whole, by requiring member approval for giving financial benefits to the responsible entity or its related parties that come out of scheme property or that could endanger those interests": see section 601LB. Member approval is discussed in Section 6 of this chapter.

In addition to its specific duties as a responsible entity imposed by Chapter 5C of the Corporations Act and the general law, the responsible entity is also subject to a range of statutory obligations that attach to it as the holder of an AFS license. The operation of a registered managed investment schemes is one of the defined "financial services" to which the obligations relate. These include obligations to do all things necessary to conduct their business efficiently, honestly, and fairly, and to manage conflicts of interest.[47]

---

cause detriment to the members of the scheme; (f) ensure that the scheme's constitution meets the requirements of sections 601GA and 601GB; (g) ensure that the scheme's compliance plan meets the requirements of section 601HA; (h) comply with the scheme's compliance plan; (i) ensure that scheme property is clearly identified as scheme property and held separately from property of the responsible entity and property of any other scheme; (j) ensure that the scheme property is valued at regular intervals appropriate to the nature of the property; (k) ensure that all payments out of the scheme property are made in accordance with the scheme's constitution and this Act; (l) report to ASIC any breach of this Act that relates to the scheme and has had, or is likely to have, a materially adverse effect on the interests of members as soon as practicable after it becomes aware of the breach; and (m) carry out or comply with any other duty, not inconsistent with this Act, that is conferred on the responsible entity by the scheme's constitution."

[46] Section 601FC(1)(c) of the Corporations Act.
[47] Section 912A of the Corporations Act provides that: "A financial services licensee must: (a) do all things necessary to ensure that the financial services covered by the licence are provided efficiently, honestly and fairly; (aa) have in place adequate arrangements for the management of conflicts of interest that may arise wholly, or partially, in relation to activities undertaken by the licensee or a representative of the licensee in the provision of financial

The imposition of duties by way of statute is significant for two reasons. First, it constrains the parties' ability to negotiate away the relevant duties. As the foregoing discussion about the responsible entity's general law duties makes clear, trust law generally allows the parties to negotiate the terms on which the arrangement will proceed (so long as they do not purport to negotiate away the irreducible core of the trust relationship—the obligation to perform the trust honestly and in good faith for the benefit of the beneficiaries). The statutory obligations cannot be excluded by agreement and prevail over any inconsistent contractual provisions.

Second, it provides the regulator and members with access to statutory sanctions and remedies in the event of breach. The sanctions and remedies available to ASIC and members for breach by a responsible entity of one of these statutory obligations are of particular interest because they include sanctions and remedies under Australia's civil penalty regime.

A breach of section 912A(1) may provide a basis for ASIC to exercise its administrative powers under the AFS licensing regime, and impose conditions on the responsible entity's license or suspend or cancel its license.[48] Because Chapter 5C comes within the definition of "financial services laws" for the purposes of section 912A(1)(c) and (ca), this includes a breach of section 601FC(1).

Also, section 601FC is a "civil penalty provision" for the purposes of the Corporations Act. This means that, under Part 9.4B of the Corporations Act, ASIC can take enforcement action for breach of that provision in civil, rather than criminal, court. If ASIC can establish, on the balance of probabilities, that a responsible entity contravened the provision, the court will make a declaration of contravention and ASIC can extract a "pecuniary penalty" (like a fine) of up to AUD 200,000—the equivalent of about USD150,000—if the contravention materially prejudices the interests of the fund or its members or is otherwise "serious."[49] Orders can be made against the responsible

---

services as part of the financial services business of the licensee or the representative; (b) comply with the conditions on the licence; (c) comply with the financial services laws; (ca) take reasonable steps to ensure that its representatives comply with the financial services laws; (d) ... have available adequate resources (including financial, technological and human resources) to provide the financial services covered by the licence and to carry out supervisory arrangements; (e) maintain the competence to provide those financial services; (f) ensure that its representatives are adequately trained, and are competent, to provide those financial services; (g) if those financial services are provided to persons as retail clients have a dispute resolution system complying with [statutory requirements]; (h) ... have adequate risk management systems; and (j) comply with any other obligations that are prescribed by regulations made for the purposes of this paragraph'. For a discussion of "efficiently, honestly and fairly," see *Australian Securities and Investments Commission v Cassimatis (No 8)* (2016) 336 ALR 209.

[48] ASIC's powers are contained in Subdivision C, Division 4 of Part 7.6 of the Corporations Act, and explained in ASIC, *Regulatory Guide 98: Licensing: Administrative Action against Financial Services Providers* (July 2013). In 2018, the Australian government foreshadowed changes to the law to provide for other civil sanctions for breach of the licensing requirements, as part of the ASIC Enforcement Review conducted at the request of the relevant minister in 2016–17.

[49] Section 1317G of the Corporations Act. The maximum civil penalty that can be imposed will likely be increased very soon, following the recommendations of the ASIC Enforcement Review referred to in the preceding note.

entity itself or against any person "involved in the contravention."[50] Since the global financial crisis, ASIC has successfully prosecuted several responsible entities under these provisions, including one of the largest domestic managers in respect of a hedge fund negligently operated by it.[51]

Independently of ASIC's exercise of its enforcement powers, a court may order the responsible entity to compensate members by transferring an amount ordered to the fund or, if the entity responsible for the wrongdoing has been replaced, to the new responsible entity to be held as an accretion to the fund. The amount to be paid represents the damage that resulted from the responsible entity's contravention: for this purpose, the legislation provides that the damage suffered includes "any profit made by any person resulting from the contravention" and "any diminution in the value of the property of" the fund.[52]

Finally, a fund member who suffers loss or damage because of a contravention of Chapter 5C has standing to bring civil proceedings under section 1325 of the Corporations Act for recovery against the responsible entity and anyone involved in the contravention. The collective action problems that arise from the trust-based (as distinct from corporate) structure of Australian mutual funds for members seeking to pursue their rights to recovery are discussed below.[53]

4.3 The Officers' Duty to Members

The governance regime established for mutual funds under Chapter 5C of the Corporations Act goes further than the general law of trusts, by imposing specific statutory obligations on the officers and employees of a responsible entity, owed both to the members and (because they are also civil penalty provisions) to the state.[54] In the ordinary course, the officers of a corporate trustee are not in a fiduciary relationship with the beneficiaries of the trust, and do not themselves owe duties directly to the beneficiaries. Instead they owe duties to the company itself, which may result in

---

[50] "Involved" has a particular meaning under section 79 of the Corporations Act, and extends to any person who "has been, in any way, by act or omission, directly or indirectly, knowingly concerned in, or party to, the contravention."

[51] *Re Macquarie Investment Management Ltd* [2016] NSWSC 1184. The responsible entity was subjected to civil penalties for "unwarranted reliance on van Eyk in the selection of investments and failure to bring adequate independent judgment to bear … allowing withdrawals when the fund was not liquid … [and] failure to monitor investments and the activities of van Eyk such that the liquidity issue arose": at [4].

[52] Section 1317H of the Corporations Act.

[53] ASIC does have the ability to cause proceedings to be brought in a member's name when it is in the public interest for that to occur, under section 50 of the *Australian Securities and Investments Commission Act 2001* (Cth) (ASIC Act); however, this power has been used sparingly, particularly since the Federal Court of Australia introduced reform to facilitate "class actions" which can now be funded by third party litigation firms.

[54] The responsible entity's officers include, by definition, its directors, company secretary, and any other person "who makes, or participates in making, decisions that affect the whole or a substantial part of the business of the [entity]; or who has the capacity to affect significantly the [entity's] financial standing, or in accordance with whose instructions or wishes the directors … are accustomed to act" (excluding professional advisers).

liability to the company if their actions as officers cause the company to incur liability to beneficiaries for breach of trust.

This position is altered, for officers of responsible entities, by section 601FD(1) of the Corporations Act. It imposes duties directly on the responsible entity's officers that, among other things, require the officers to prioritize the interests of the fund members over the corporate interests of the responsible entity.[55]

Section 601FE(1) extends the statutory duties not to make improper use of their position or of information obtained through it to all employees of the responsible entity.

As with the obligations on responsible entities, the obligations imposed on officers and employees are expressed to override any conflicting duties the person owes to the responsible entity itself. They are both civil penalty provisions, with the consequences explained above for the relevant officer or employee and for anyone involved in the contravention. A contravention may be the basis for a claim for damages; intentional or reckless contravention by an individual of these sections is a criminal offense, and can attract a significant penalty.[56]

Wrongdoing on the part of an individual in connection with a mutual fund may also result in a person being disqualified from acting as a company director or being banned or disqualified from providing financial services in future.[57] These orders have both a punitive and a protective function. They protect the public interest by excluding undesirable people from the mutual fund industry.

---

[55] Section 601FD(1) provides that: "An officer of the responsible entity of a registered scheme must: (a) act honestly; (b) exercise the degree of care and diligence that a reasonable person would exercise if they were in the officer's position; (c) act in the best interests of the members and, if there is a conflict between the members' interests and the interests of the responsible entity, give priority to the members' interests; and (d) not make use of information acquired through being an officer of the responsible entity in order to gain an improper advantage for the officer or another person or cause detriment to the members of the scheme; (e) not make improper use of their position as an officer to gain, directly or indirectly, an advantage for themselves or for any other person or to cause detriment to the members of the scheme; and (f) take all steps that a reasonable person would take, if they were in the officer's position, to ensure that the responsible entity complies with the Act, any conditions imposed on the responsible entity's Australian financial services licence, the scheme's constitution, and the scheme's compliance plan."

[56] The penalty can be a fine of up to AUD 340,000 or imprisonment for five years, or both. Unlike civil penalty proceedings instigated by ASIC, prosecutions are commenced by the Commonwealth Director of Public Prosecutions in criminal court, using a criminal burden of proof and criminal rules of evidence and procedure.

[57] Division 8 of Part 7.6 of the Corporations Act allows for banning orders and disqualification orders to be made against individuals, either by ASIC or by Courts (depending on the circumstances). Banning orders prohibit a person from providing financial services. Disqualification orders, which can be made by a court on the application of ASIC, exclude people from the financial services sector. Section 206C allows a court to make an order disqualifying a person from managing corporations either for a period of time or indefinitely, where the person has contravened a civil penalty provision such as section 601FD.

5 INDEPENDENT OVERSIGHT

The fiduciary-type duties imposed on responsible entities and their officers and employees, outlined in Section 4 of this chapter, are the main mechanism adopted by Australian law to address the agency problem that arises from the separation of funds and managers in mutual funds. The Australian duties are onerous by world standards. It is particularly important to note that these duties, including the duty of care, can be and are enforced by ASIC in civil court—that is, the enforcement activities of the state are not confined to criminal prosecutions.

While it is notable that the duties are onerous, what matters ultimately is how effectively the system works to ensure those involved comply with these duties. Different legal systems use different mechanisms to achieve this. Some use real-time oversight, by an independent person, to prevent noncompliance. Some use the threat of *ex post* enforcement to deter wrongdoing. The latter approach depends on there being a high level of vigilance and capacity on the part of members,[58] and also the regulator, to take timely and effective action in enforcing the duties against the responsible entity and those who control it.

Globally, mutual funds are often thought to give rise to particularly acute collective action problems that might impact on the efficacy of members' private enforcement of the fund operator's performance obligations. For example, mutual funds typically do not have institutional investors holding large blocks of stock. A regulator's continuous real-time monitoring of the conduct of a fund operator (in the nature of prudential supervision) is rarely an option. For this reason, many jurisdictions impose some form of structural requirement on mutual funds to require the appointment of an independent third party to monitor the operation of the fund on behalf of investors.

In its examination of governance for CIS conducted in 2005, IOSCO placed significant emphasis on independent oversight mechanisms. IOSCO defined CIS governance as "a framework for the organization and operation of CIS that seeks to ensure that CIS are organized and operated in the interests of CIS investors, and not in the interest of CIS insiders." The examination concluded that member jurisdictions "agree that as a primary principle, CIS Governance must provide for independent review and oversight of the organization and operation of the CIS." The examination identifies the "independent entity" as the primary source of independent oversight and its main objective should be "ensuring that CIS Operators respect the applicable rules, their contractual obligations and their duties, from 'an outside perspective', and therefore protect CIS investors from divergent behaviours of the CIS Operator."[59] The examination concludes that "in order to ensure that CIS Operators do not deviate from their duties it is fundamental that their activity be properly monitored." The nature of the independent entity depends on the structural model for CIS adopted in the relevant jurisdictions—in corporate models it is often the fund's board of directors, and independent directors in particular, that serve this function. In contract and trust-based

---

[58] Or those with an incentive to monitor the actions of fund operators on their behalf, such as law firms. The extent to which private class actions encourage or incentivize others to perform this function in the Australian market is discussed in section 6.

[59] IOSCO, above n 10, 10.

models, that function is performed by a depository, trustee or other entity that is "desirably ... legally and commercially independent from the CIS Operator."[60]

As explained in Section 3 of this chapter, mutual fund regulation in Australia before 1998 required that a prescribed interest scheme have both a management company (that promoted and operated the fund) and an approved trustee. The trustee was required to be independent of the management company: it was obliged to "exercise all due diligence and vigilance in carrying out its functions and duties and in protecting the rights and interests of" the holders of the relevant prescribed interests.[61] However, in 1993, the ALRC and CASAC identified what they characterized as two fundamental flaws in this two-party structure. These flaws were described in the following terms:

- **Displacement of responsibility**. The Review was told, particularly by trustee companies, that some managers tend to regard a proposal as acceptable if they can "get it past" the trustee. This attitude is a direct result of the two-party structure that the law imposes, which does little to encourage scheme managers to take responsibility themselves for seeing that the law and the scheme's constitution are adhered to.
- **An inefficient structure to promote compliance**. What will best promote a scheme operator's compliance with the law and the scheme's constitution will depend, among other things, on how the operator is structured, what is involved in running the scheme and how restrictive and complicated the constitution of the scheme is. But the present law, with minor exceptions, recognises only one way to promote compliance. In practice, at least for significant trusts, a statutory trustee company is employed as 'trustee or representative'. It is inefficient to limit schemes in this way. This inefficiency is compounded by the trustee companies' fee structure. The fee for each scheme is generally worked out as a small percentage (often no more than 0.1%) of the value of the scheme's assets no matter what the work load. Many participants in the collective investments industry agree that this fee structure does not produce enough revenue for trustee companies to carry out even their present role effectively.[62]

Largely because of this finding, the requirement to have a separate trustee was abolished in Australia in 1998. Notably, unlike in other jurisdictions without the requirement for an independent trustee or depository, it was not replaced with a requirement that the fund itself have its own board, separate from that of the fund sponsor or adviser.

The regulatory regime adopted in 1998 instead placed significant emphasis on creating what was referred to as a "culture of compliance" within the responsible entity

---

[60] Ibid, 11–12.
[61] The prescribed interest laws were intricate. They included lengthy and detailed prescribed covenants that had to be included in an approved deed, including a covenant by the management company that it would strive to carry on and conduct its business in a proper and efficient manner and to ensure that any relevant undertaking, scheme or enterprise was carried on and conducted in a proper and efficient manner; a covenant by the trustee or representative that it would exercise all due diligence and vigilance in carrying out its functions and duties and in protecting the rights and interests of the holders of the relevant prescribed interests; a covenant by both to perform their functions and exercise their powers under the deed in the best interests of all interest holders and not their own, and to treat holders of the same class equally and different classes fairly.
[62] ALRC and CASAC, above n 29, Summary [10].

itself. Consistent with the regulatory fashion of the day, reliance was placed on requiring the responsible entity to formulate a "compliance plan" that set out the measures it would take to ensure that the scheme's operations comply with the legislation and the scheme's constitution. The responsible entity is expected to monitor and ensure its own compliance with that plan. The adequacy of the plan, and the responsible entity's compliance with it, is audited annually by a registered company auditor. Also, if fewer than half of the directors of the responsible entity itself are external (that is, independent) directors, the responsible entity is also required to establish a "compliance committee" for each fund it operates. The compliance committee has a limited role in monitoring the responsible entity's compliance with the plan.

So, is there an "independent entity" in the Australian structure that is responsible for monitoring the activities of the responsible entity, in the sense envisaged by IOSCO? The fund itself does not have its own board. There is no independent trustee or other fiduciary with an oversight function.

The answer, probably, is "not really". As the regulator, ASIC certainly has a role to play, although, as we will see, it is not a supervisor in the true sense. There is a level of independent oversight of the scheme's compliance arrangements by an independent auditor and, in some cases, a compliance committee. But the following discussion indicates that, as oversight mechanisms, they have significant limitations. Neither ASIC oversight nor audit of the compliance plan provide real-time monitoring of fund transactions. A compliance committee is not required at all if the board of the responsible entity (that is, the fund's operator—not the fund itself, which does not have its own board) has a majority of external directors. Where it is required, it is appointed, resourced, and remunerated by the responsible entity. It is difficult to judge whether these committees have provided the "outside perspective" recommended by IOSCO.[63] Arguably, the emphasis placed on formal internal processes for compliance has been more successful in creating an industry rather than a culture of compliance.

5.1 Oversight by ASIC

ASIC has extensive statutory powers that would enable it to supervise the operation of mutual funds on an ongoing basis, were it minded and resourced to do so. Responsible entities are required to self-report breaches to ASIC, and ASIC has extensive powers to request information and conduct what are referred to as "surveillance checks" under section 601FF of the Corporations Act on the operation of a fund at any time. However ASIC does not see its role as inspecting the ongoing operations of responsible entities; instead, it uses a "risk-based" approach to allocating its regulatory resources that is largely reactive to complaints and breach reports, and trend data that identifies higher risk parts of the CIS sector overall.[64]

---

[63] In several of the failed mortgage funds, it was clear that compliance plans were not followed: see for example *Trilogy Funds Management Ltd v Sullivan (No 2)* [2015] FCA 1452.

[64] ASIC's *Annual Report 2016–17* explains (at p. 22) the level of surveillance activities undertaken by its 23 staff employed in this area. The 20 largest responsible entities, which between them hold 70 percent of funds under management, are the subject of routine

In this respect, the regulatory oversight of responsible entities is different from that applied to the trustees of regulated public offer superannuation (that is, pension) funds. Superannuation trustees are prudentially supervised by the Australian Prudential Regulation Authority (APRA), which also regulates Australian banks and insurance companies. This is not the case for responsible entities.

The tools available to ASIC as a regulator were described by the then Chairman of ASIC in 1998 as including:

> the ability to conduct surveillance checks; to direct changes to the compliance plan; to accept enforceable undertakings; to remove the licence; to appoint ... temporary responsible entities; to wind up a scheme; to deregister a scheme; to enforce the civil penalty provisions; to seek injunctions; and to take civil action under section 50 of the [ASIC Act].[65]

The regulatory regime introduced in 1998 removed the requirement for an independent trustee. At the time, the ASIC chairman emphasized that the new regime was "not just about a one-off replacement of a whole lot of trustees with one government based regulator. It is not that at all. It is about an entirely new approach to regulating the offering of managed investments." The requirement for a formal written compliance plan, adherence to which was to be monitored by external parties, was seen as central to this model.[66]

Because ASIC is not a supervisory agency, its enforcement actions tend to be after the event, rather than preventative.[67] It is important to note that ASIC is not able to regulate the commercial features of a fund and that fund failures may result from a

---

surveillance every two years. The examination of the 60 responsible entities identified as most at risk of noncompliance and 18 responsible entities identified as at risk or of concern was said to vary from year to year. The remaining 368 were potentially subject to "reactive surveillances"— that is, they are not examined unless there is a complaint. ASIC says that its surveillance activity "includes onsite visits and desk-based reviews and can vary in intensity. A high-intensity surveillance generally takes more than two days of effort to complete."

[65] Parliamentary Joint Committee on Corporations and Securities, Report on the Managed Investments Bill 1997 (March 1998) CS 58–9. Enforceable undertakings are settlements agreed between ASIC and an entity or individual that has contravened the law, under section 93A or 93AA of the ASIC Act. For a recent review of the use by ASIC of enforceable undertakings, see Helen Bird, George Gilligan, and Ian Ramsay "The who, why and what of enforceable undertakings accepted by the Australian Securities and Investments Commission" (2016) 34 *Company and Securities Law Journal* 493.

[66] Chairman Cameron said in evidence: "My approach to the compliance plan is that it is very much real-time, continuous regulation. It is not about the government regulator, the Securities Commission, being the regulator. It is about self-control and self-disciplines that are imposed within the scheme itself, but it is also about those things happening on a real-time, continuous basis. It is not after the event regulation, and it is certainly not regulation at a primary level by the regulatory [agency]": ibid, CS 58.

[67] ASIC's regulatory performance was subject to searching parliamentary review in 2014. See Commonwealth of Australia Senate Economic References Committee, *Performance of the Australian Securities and Investments Commission* (June 2014). Chapter 4 of the inquiry report provides an explanation of ASIC's regulatory philosophy and approach, and Chapter 17 comments on ASIC's enforcement decisions.

flawed investment strategy or business model, rather than from misconduct or mismanagement. That said, there is evidence of poor practice in the sector.[68]

5.2 Compliance Committees

Another regulatory arrangement that might potentially provide some independent monitoring of the responsible entity's activities is the compliance committee.[69]

A responsible entity is required by section 601JA(1) of the Corporations Act to establish a compliance committee if "less than half of the directors of the responsible entity are external directors" as defined.[70] Remember, the fund itself does not have its own board—the requirement arises if the board of the responsible entity itself does not include the relevant number of external members. If it is required, then a compliance committee must have at least three members, and the majority of them must be external.[71]

The functions of the compliance committee are set out in the legislation. They are fourfold. The committee is required to monitor the extent to which the responsible entity complies with the scheme's compliance plan and to report on its findings to the responsible entity; to report to the responsible entity any breach of the Corporations Act or the scheme's constitution of which it becomes aware or that it suspects; to report to ASIC if it is of the view that the responsible entity has not taken, or does not propose to take, appropriate action to deal with a matter so reported; and to assess at regular intervals the adequacy of the compliance plan and report to the responsible entity on that assessment and make recommendations for improvements.[72]

---

[68] This appears to be particularly so in parts of the mortgage fund sector. In the mutual fund space, smaller alternative investment funds seem to exhibit higher compliance risk. The most high-profile example of fraudulent practice in the mutual funds area in recent years was the collapse of Trio Capital Ltd: see Parliamentary Joint Committee on Corporations and Financial Service, *Inquiry into the Collapse of Trio Capital* (May 2012).

[69] See generally, Grant Moodie and Ian Ramsay, "Compliance committees under the Managed Investments Act 1998 (Cth)" (2005) 33 *Australian Business Law Review* 167.

[70] See n 31.

[71] Section 601JB of the Corporations Act provides that a member of the committee is an external member if that person: is not, and has not been in the previous two years, a nonexternal director, an executive officer or an employee of the responsible entity or a related body corporate; is not, and has not been in the previous two years, substantially involved in business dealings, or in a professional capacity, with the responsible entity or a related body corporate; is not a member of a partnership that is, and has been in the previous two years, substantially involved in business dealings, or in a professional capacity, with the responsible entity or a related body corporate; does not have a material interest in the responsible entity or a related body corporate, and is not a relative or a de facto spouse of a person who has a material interest in the responsible entity or a related body corporate.

[72] Section 601JC of the Corporations Act. The manner in which the committee performs its functions must be set out in the compliance plan itself, which must include provisions "ensuring that the compliance committee functions properly, including adequate arrangements relating to" the membership of the committee, how often it meets, its reports and recommendations and its access to accounting records and other information, and to the auditor. Subject to those arrangements, the committee may regulate its proceedings as it thinks appropriate. It is required to keep minutes of meetings and records of its reports and recommendations: s 601JH. The

The compliance committee members are chosen and remunerated by the responsible entity. In carrying out their functions they are subject to statutory duties of honesty, care, and loyalty.[73] A compliance committee member's contravention of his or her statutory duties carries similar consequences to those for breach of duty by an officer as explained in Section 4 of this chapter.

5.3 Compliance Plan Audit

A further potential oversight mechanism is the compliance plan audit. Regardless of whether there is a compliance committee appointed in relation to a fund, the responsible entity's compliance with the compliance plan must be audited annually by a registered company auditor. The auditor's responsibilities are: to examine the compliance plan; to audit the responsible entity's compliance with the compliance plan; and to report to the responsible entity on whether the responsible entity has complied with the plan, and whether the plan meets the requirements of Part 5C.4 of the Corporations Act.[74]

The auditor is under a separate statutory obligation to notify ASIC in writing if it becomes aware of (among other things) circumstances that the auditor has reasonable grounds to suspect amount to a contravention of the Corporations Act.[75] ASIC has said of this reporting obligation that "while we do not expect auditors to engage in a systemic search for all possible contraventions of the Corporations Act, auditors should be alert to matters that come to their attention that may indicate such contraventions."[76]

6 INVESTOR RIGHTS

The third part of the Australian framework that is important in understanding the way the regime purports to resolve the issues arising from the mutual fund structure can be described as "investor rights." These are rights that determine the extent to which members can monitor and take self-help action, either individually or jointly, in respect

---

responsible entity, its officers, any agents and any agents' officers must allow the compliance committee access to the books of the scheme, provide information and explanations about the scheme when requested by the committee to do so, and otherwise assist the committee in the performance of its functions, reg 5C.5.01 of the Corporations Regulations 2001.

[73] Section 601JD(1) of the Corporations Act provides that a committee member must: (a) act honestly; (b) exercise the degree of care and diligence that a reasonable person would exercise if they were in the member's position; (c) not make use of information acquired through being a member of the committee in order to gain an improper advantage for the member or another person or cause detriment to the fund members; and (d) not make improper use of their position as a member of the committee to gain, directly or indirectly, an advantage for themselves or for any other person or to cause detriment to the fund members.

[74] Section 601HG of the Corporations Act. The reporting obligation applies if the contravention is either significant, or is not significant but is one which the auditor believes has not been or will not be adequately dealt with by commenting on it in the auditor's report or bringing it to the attention of the responsible entity's directors.

[75] Section 601HG(4), (4A), or (4B) of the Corporations Act.

[76] ASIC, *Regulatory Guide 34 Auditors' obligations: reporting to ASIC* (May 2013) [34.14].

of conduct on the part of the responsible entity or its officers or affiliates that advantages those insiders (whether or not at the expense of the members) or improperly reduces the value of the fund.

Those rights fall into four broad categories: information rights, voting rights, enforcement rights, and exit rights. As we will see, by international standards Australian fund members have strong information rights and voting rights, relatively strong enforcement rights, and weaker exit rights.

6.1 Information Rights

The Australian regime places a heavy emphasis on disclosure as an investor protection mechanism.

First, the responsible entity of the fund is required to produce and provide a PDS to potential investors before they acquire an initial interest in the fund.[77] The content requirements for a PDS have changed over time, and in recent years the law has been amended to include a simplified PDS requirement for most managed funds.[78] For "simple" schemes as defined, the PDS must not exceed eight pages in length and must deal with certain prescribed matters under prescribed headings. The headings require information about the responsible entity, the fund, the approach to investment taken by the fund, and the fees and costs payable.

Second, both the responsible entity and the fund are subject to ongoing periodic reporting obligations. The responsible entity, as an Australian public company, must produce and publish a financial report as to its own corporate position and a directors' report (incorporating audited financial statements) at least annually.[79] Separate financial reports and directors' reports must be produced and provided for each registered fund, generally half-yearly.[80]

Third, the responsible entity must provide each fund member with a personalized statement for each reporting period, containing prescribed information about the member's transactions over the period as well as about the performance of the fund, and the fees and expenses incurred.[81]

Fourth, most widely held mutual funds are subject to a continuous disclosure obligation. This obligation requires the responsible entity, if it becomes aware of information that is not generally available and that a reasonable person would expect—if it were generally available—to have a material effect on the price or value of interests in the fund, to disclose that information as soon as practicable.[82]

---

[77] Part 7.9 of the Corporations Act as modified by Part 7.9, Division 4, Subdivision 4.2A of the Corporations Regulations.
[78] See Schedule 10E to the Corporations Regulations. This shorter-form disclosure is not available in respect of more complex funds, such as alternative investments.
[79] Chapter 2M of the Corporations Act.
[80] Chapter 2M of the Corporations Act.
[81] Section 1017D of the Corporations Act, as modified by the Corporations Regulations.
[82] The continuous disclosure obligation is contained in Chapter 6CA of the Corporations Act, as modified by Chapter 6CA of the Corporations Regulations. The information is usually disclosed by way of notice to ASIC or on the responsible entity's website: see ASIC, *Regulatory Guide 198 Unlisted Disclosing Entities: Continuous Disclosure Obligation* (June 2009).

Fifth, a member may apply to a court for an order allowing for inspection of the mutual fund's books.[83] "Books" is broadly defined. These applications are usually made as a precursor to some kind of enforcement action, as they can provide the member with information about the management of the fund.

Sixth, a person may apply to inspect the register of members of a registered mutual fund, a right that can be important in soliciting proxy votes where members are seeking to exercise their power to remove and replace the responsible entity.[84]

These information rights are significant secondary investor protection mechanisms. The obligation to disclose is thought to impose a natural discipline on responsible entities in their operation of funds—a "disinfectant of sunlight" against, among other things, the excessive consumption of perquisites by the responsible entity. Also, the information provided informs members' exercise of their voting and enforcement rights in respect of the fund.

6.2 Voting Rights

Chapter 5C confers on members the right to vote on certain key questions relating to the constitution and administration of the mutual fund. While these do not extend to a right to instruct the responsible entity as to the operation of the fund, they nevertheless potentially empower members in important ways. The main voting rights conferred on members are to:

- amend the scheme's constitution (although the responsible entity can amend the constitution without member consent if it reasonably considers the proposed change will not adversely affect members' rights);[85]
- remove the responsible entity;[86]
- approve the appointment of a new responsible entity following the retirement of the incumbent;[87]
- veto certain related party transactions;[88] and
- initiate a winding up of the fund.[89]

---

[83] Section 247A of the Corporations Act.
[84] Section 173 of the Corporations Act.
[85] Section 601GC of the Corporations Act. The dividing line between constitutional amendments that can and cannot be made without member approval is one of the most frequently litigated issued in Australian mutual funds. This was particularly the case after the global financial crisis in 2007–8, when a number of responsible entities sought to restructure funds by constitutional amendments made without member approval. Australian courts now take a wide view of what adversely affects members' rights: see *360 Capital RE Ltd v Watts* (2012) 91 ACSR 328.
[86] Section 601FM of the Corporations Act.
[87] Section 601FL of the Corporations Act.
[88] Part 5C.7 of the Corporations Act. Member approval is required if a responsible entity seeks to transact with a related party other than on arm's length terms.
[89] Section 601NB of the Corporations Act.

In funds that are functioning as expected, it is rare for members to be called upon or to seek to exercise their voting rights. However, after the global financial crisis of 2007–8, a small number of funds either suspended members' rights to redeem their interests (because the underlying fund investments became illiquid) or failed outright.[90] In some cases this resulted in attempts to restructure funds or replace incumbent responsible entities by member resolution, as an alternative to handing control of the fund to an insolvency practitioner for winding up.

Mutual funds, unlike Australian public companies, are not required to hold an annual general meeting of members. Members' meetings occur ad hoc. A responsible entity may call a meeting of fund members at any time.[91] Members holding at least 5 percent of the voting rights or numbering at least 100 may request the responsible entity to call a meeting for a permissible purpose,[92] and, if it fails to do so, convene the meeting themselves.[93] Members have one vote each on a show of hands, and on a poll have one vote for each dollar of the value of their individual interest in the fund.[94] Generally speaking, a responsible entity and its associates cannot vote on a resolution if they have an interest in the resolution or matter other than as a member.[95]

Constitutional amendments may be proposed by the responsible entity or by the members themselves,[96] and require a special resolution to pass.[97] Removing and replacing the responsible entity requires an extraordinary resolution,[98] as does a resolution requiring the responsible entity to wind up the fund.

The right to veto certain related party transactions is given to fund members by Part 5C.7 of the Corporations Act. It requires that, before certain financial benefits that come out of scheme property or could endanger the interests of the members can be given to the responsible entity or its related parties, they must be approved by members. This is subject to various exceptions, including for benefits given on arm's length terms.

The fact that a majority of members, through the exercise of their voting rights, can affect the operation of the scheme in a manner that binds all members gives rise to a

---

[90] At this time, most diversified mutual funds in Australia experienced a decline in net asset value that reflected the overall fall in global markets, but did not fail. However, in some other types of managed investment scheme—particularly alternative investments and specialist schemes invested in infrastructure assets (such as toll roads), forestry plantations, and commercial property loans (referred to as mortgage funds)—there were significant failures.

[91] Section 252A of the Corporations Act.

[92] Section 252B of the Corporations Act.

[93] Section 252C of the Corporations Act.

[94] Section 253C of the Corporations Act.

[95] Section 253E of the Corporations Act. This means that, in an unlisted fund, members of the same financial group as the responsible entity cannot vote their interests in, for example, a contest to remove and replace the responsible entity. See *AMP Life Ltd v AMP Capital Funds Management Ltd* [2016] NSWCA 176.

[96] The members' right to propose resolutions is contained in Division 3 of Part 2G.4 of the Corporations Act.

[97] That is, a resolution passed by at least 75 percent of votes held by members who are entitled to vote, and do vote, at the meeting.

[98] That is, a resolution passed by at least 50 percent of the total votes that may be cast by members entitled to vote on the resolution.

range of complexities and considerations that are not well resolved in Australian law. Members do not owe each other any fiduciary or other duty in relation to the exercise of their rights and, in the absence of a statutory remedy for oppression, are not constrained by the general interest in the exercise of their rights.

6.3 Enforcement Rights

Fund members have various remedies available to them in the event of maladministration of a mutual fund by its responsible entity or misconduct by the responsible entity's officers and others involved in the operation of the fund. Generally speaking, the statutory remedies extend the right to recover beyond the principal wrongdoer to any person involved in the contravention giving rise to the right of action.[99]

Each member is entitled to recover under ordinary equitable principles against a responsible entity that acts in breach of trust. Further, a member has standing to bring civil proceedings to recover loss or damage caused by a contravention of Chapter 5C of the Corporations Act, under sections 601MA (in respect of a contravention by a responsible entity) or section 1325 (in respect of a contravention by any person) of the Corporations Act. Also, a range of statutory remedies is available in respect of incorrect or inadequate disclosure, including statutory rights to recover loss or damage caused by failure to comply with the responsible entity's mandatory disclosure requirements or any misleading or deceptive conduct on the part of the responsible entity or others.[100]

That said, it is rare for a retail member of a mutual fund, on his or her own, to have the resources or the incentive to pursue recovery through the courts. Two legal mechanisms might go part of the way to overcoming this collective action problem: class actions, and proceedings commenced for the benefit of members by the responsible entity.[101]

First, the rules of both the Federal Court of Australia and most of the state superior courts allow for cases to be brought as representative proceedings or "class actions." These actions may, under Australian law, be funded by third party litigation funders.[102] Where fund members as a whole have suffered loss or damage as a result of an actionable breach of trust or breach of statutory duty, it is possible for proceedings to

---

[99] "Involved" is defined in section 79 of the Corporations Act; see n 50.

[100] These arise under Chapter 2M, Chapter 6CA, and Parts 7.9 and 7.10 of the Corporations Act. Australian law contains a general prohibition on engaging in misleading or deceptive conduct. Where such conduct causes loss, a person may make a claim without having to establish any kind of blameworthiness (such as intention, recklessness, or negligence) on the part of the defendant. In the securities area, most class actions involve claims of misleading or deceptive conduct in respect of disclosures made (or not made) under the continuous disclosure laws in Chapter 6CA of the Corporations Act: see R. Baxt, A. Black, and P. Hanrahan, *Securities and Financial Services Law* (9th ed., 2017) Chapter 9.

[101] If ASIC has brought proceedings against a responsible entity or its officers for contravening a civil penalty provision, the court may make compensation orders for recovery by the scheme under section 1317H. It may do so with or without the responsible entity joining the proceedings.

[102] The largest litigation funder in the Australian market is IMF Bentham Ltd, a company listed on the Australian Securities Exchange. Slightly under half of class actions would have third-party funding on commencement.

be commenced in this way. However, it is worth noting that to date there have been no successful class actions maintained against responsible entities or their officers in respect of the operation of a managed investment scheme. This is despite the fact that several managed investment schemes have failed, and those failures have resulted in successful enforcement action against responsible entities and their officers in a number of cases. A range of factors explain this. The economics of class actions in Australia—in particular, the facts that the losing party is exposed to the risk of adverse cost orders and that lawyers are not permitted to charge contingency-based fees—have not encouraged the development of an entrepreneurial plaintiff bar. Further, actions maintained by members or former members of schemes face a technical problem to do with the idea of "reflective loss"—that members cannot separately sue for a loss that is recoverable on behalf of all beneficiaries by the trustee.[103] Those class actions that have been commenced in respect of managed investment schemes have generally been based on allegations that there was inadequate or incorrect disclosure, rather than mismanagement.[104]

The second way in which the law addresses the collective action problems is under the law of trusts. Because Australian mutual funds are constituted as trusts, there are various circumstances in which a responsible entity is permitted or required to bring proceedings for the benefit of fund members against former responsible entities or others whose actions have harmed the interests of fund members. For example, a responsible entity has standing to pursue a remedy for breach of the civil penalty provisions discussed above.[105] Amounts recovered are held by the responsible entity as trustee for the members at the time of recovery. Again, these actions are rare, but there are examples.[106] Technically this is the most straightforward way to proceed, but it requires the responsible entity to initiate proceedings and it is not clear that they can be compelled to do so by a resolution of members.[107] Responsible entities are assisted in this regard by the fact that they are trustees, which means that under Australian law they can approach the court for judicial advice relating to the administration of a trust. So, for example, a responsible entity could ask a court to rule on whether it is

---

[103] See *Hodges v Waters (No 7)* (2015) 232 FCR 27. This action was commenced by some members and former members of a mortgage fund against the fund's compliance plan auditor, KPMG.

[104] For a useful annual overview of the Australian class action landscape, see King & Wood Mallesons *The Review: Class Actions in Australia 2015/16*. In total 35 class actions were commenced in Australia during 2015/16, of which 11 related to failed financial or investment products.

[105] These include sections 601FC and 601FD, discussed in section 3 of this chapter. Recovery is provided for in section 1317J(2) and section 1317H of the Corporations Act.

[106] In *Trilogy Funds Management Ltd v Sullivan (No 2)* [2015] FCA 1452, a case involving a mortgage fund, a new responsible entity brought proceedings against the directors of the former responsible entity.

[107] Under general principles of trust law, a beneficiary can make an application to a court for an order compelling the trustee to commence proceedings, as part of its duty to get in trust property.

appropriate for it to expend trust funds on litigation, or whether it ought to accept an offer of settlement.[108]

Unlike members of companies, individual members of mutual funds do not have a general statutory remedy in respect of conduct that is oppressive, unfairly discriminatory, unfairly prejudicial, or contrary to the interests of members as a whole.[109]

6.4 Exit Rights

In most jurisdictions the unqualified right of mutual fund investors to withdraw from the fund on demand, at a price linked to the underlying value of the fund's investments, is seen as an important discipline on fund advisers, and a key investor protection mechanism. That right does not exist in the Australian regime. Instead, members have only those withdrawal rights (if any) that are specified in the fund's constitution. Further, Chapter 5C of the Corporations Act requires that the redemption of interests in funds be suspended in conditions of illiquidity.

The constitutions of most mutual funds in Australia do confer a right on members to redeem their investments on demand. The use of a trust rather than a corporation as the legal structure for the mutual fund overcomes the procedural difficulties that Australian companies face in buying back their shares or otherwise reducing their capital.[110] Under Chapter 5C of the Corporations Act a mutual fund constitution may make provision for a member to withdraw from the scheme, wholly or partly, at any time while the fund is liquid.[111] A fund is liquid if "liquid assets" account for at least 80 percent of the value of its investments. A "liquid asset" includes money in an account or on deposit with a bank, bank accepted bills, marketable securities, and "any other property ... [that] the responsible entity reasonably expects ... can be realized for its market value within the period specified in the constitution for satisfying withdrawal requests."[112]

However, despite what is in the constitution, a responsible entity of an Australian mutual fund must suspend redemptions if the fund ceases to be "liquid." This occurred with a number of alternate investment funds and other managed investment schemes (including mortgage funds) during the global financial crisis in 2007 and 2008. For the most part, these schemes have been "managed out," with assets progressively sold down over several years and moneys returned to investors. In one case, a large Australian fund manager was held accountable for its negligent management of the fund that had resulted in its illiquidity.[113] However, experiences with these funds does not appear to have altered the trajectory of the mutual funds market in Australia.

---

[108] *Hodges v Waters (No 7)* (2015) 232 FCR 27 is an example of an application for judicial advice by a responsible entity.
[109] This type of conduct can be the basis of a claim for relief by a shareholder in a company, under section 232 of the Corporations Act.
[110] See Chapter 2J of the Corporations Act.
[111] Section 601KA(1) of the Corporations Act.
[112] Section 601KA(6) of the Corporations Act.
[113] *Re Macquarie Investment Management Ltd* [2016] NSWSC 1184.

7 CONCLUSION

This chapter identifies a number of features of Australian mutual funds and their regulation that are unique. We have focused on three: the fiduciary duties of fund operators and their officers; the (lack of) an independent entity such as a trustee or depository or fund-specific board to oversee the operator's conduct of the fund; and the investor self-help mechanisms that are available under the Australian regime.

The duties imposed on responsible entities and their officers by the Australian statute are onerous by global standards. But there is no ongoing monitoring of the responsible entity's management of the fund by an "independent entity" of the kind recommended by IOSCO. ASIC is not a prudential supervisor—while it has extensive enforcement powers (particularly through its licensing and registration powers, its use of enforceable undertakings, and what is provided under the civil penalty regime), its actions tend to be after the event. Australian investors have significant rights "on the books" but collective action problems have meant that these rights are often exercised only when a rival responsible entity seeks to take, or has taken, control of a fund.

In 2018, the current regulatory arrangements for mutual funds in Australia will have been in place for 20 years. It is proposed that Australia will introduce a new form of collective investment vehicle that is a corporation rather than a trust as an alternative to the registered managed investment scheme This new product, known as a CCIV, has been developed in response to Australia's participation in the Asia Region Funds Passport.[114] It may be that in future Australian mutual funds will gravitate towards this new legal form.

Also, the Australian government is considering strengthening the regulatory net at the public funds level, by giving ASIC power to prevent particular products from being offered to the retail market and by imposing an obligation on product issuers to consider the needs and risk tolerance of the target market in the design of new products. This may affect how the sector develops in future.[115]

---

[114] The Asia Region Funds Passport Memorandum of Co-Operation was signed by Australia, Japan, Korea and New Zealand in April 2016. The Passport is intended to facilitate the cross-border offering of eligible collective investment schemes while ensuring investor protection in economies participating in the Passport. The Corporations Amendment (Asia Region Funds Passport) Bill 2018 was introduced into Parliament in March 2018. The Treasury Laws Amendment (Corporate Collective Investment Vehicle) Bill 2017 was still in exposure draft form at the time of writing. Key aspects of the proposed CCIV regime are that: (1) a CCIV will be a public company that is limited by shares and structured as an umbrella fund with sub-funds, each of which may hold different assets and have different investment strategies; (2) the CCIV will be operated by a corporate director that is an Australian public company and holds an Australian financial services (AFS) licence authorizing it to operate a CCIV; (3) a retail CCIV will have a depositary that is either an Australian public company or a foreign company registered under Part 5B.2 of the Corporations Act, and holds an AFS licence authorizing it to act as a depositary of a CCIV; and (4) the depositary will be responsible for holding the assets of the CCIV on trust and oversight of the operation of the CCIV.

[115] Commonwealth of Australia, *Financial System Inquiry—Final Report* (December 2014) Chapter 4.

This handbook opens up a discussion of how differences in law and regulation in different jurisdictions might be explained and evaluated in the context of an increasingly globalized mutual fund market. How different regimes seek to resolve the issues that result from the separation of funds and managers in mutual funds provides, we think, fertile ground for further study in comparative governance scholarship.

BIBLIOGRAPHY

Austin, Robert and Ian Ramsay, 2018, *Ford, Austin and Ramsay's Principles of Corporations Law*, 17th ed.
Australian Law Reform Commission and Companies and Securities Advisory Committee, 1993, *Report No 65—Collective Investments: Other People's Money*.
Australian Prudential Regulation Authority, 2018, *Statistics—Annul Superannuation Bulletin 2017*.
Australian Securities and Investments Commission, 2011, *Information Sheet 111—Information for Investors in Frozen Funds*.
Australian Securities and Investments Commission, 2013, *Regulation Impact Statement: Holding Scheme Property and Other Assets—Update to Regulatory Guide 133*.
Australian Securities and Investments Commission, 2017, *Annual Report 2016/17*.
Baxt, Robert, Ashley Black, and Pamela Hanrahan, 2017, *Securities and Financial Services Law*, 9th ed.
Commonwealth of Australia, 1997, *Financial System Inquiry—Final Report* (Wallis Committee).
Commonwealth of Australia, 2014, *Financial System Inquiry—Final Report* (Murray Committee).
Commonwealth of Australia—Australian Trade and Investment Commission, 2017, *Australia's Managed Funds 2017 Update—Trade and Investment Note*.
Commonwealth of Australia—Parliamentary Joint Committee on Corporations and Securities, 1998, *Report on the Managed Investments Bill 1997*.
Commonwealth of Australia—Parliamentary Joint Committee on Corporations and Financial Services, 2009, *Inquiry into Financial Products and Services in Australia*.
Commonwealth of Australia—Parliamentary Joint Committee on Corporations and Financial Services, 2012, *Inquiry into the Collapse of Trio Capital*.
Commonwealth of Australia—Senate Economic References Committee, 2014, *Performance of the Australian Securities and Investments Commission*.
Commonwealth of Australia—Senate Economic References Committee, 2016, *Agribusiness Managed Investment Schemes: Bitter Harvest*.
Grave, Damian, Ken Adams, and Jason Betts, 2012, *Class Actions in Australia*.
Hanrahan, Pamela, loose-leaf 1998–, *Managed Investments Law and Practice*.
Hanrahan, Pamela, 2007, *Funds Management in Australia: Officers' Duties and Liabilities*.
Hanrahan, Pamela, 2011, 'ASIC and managed investments' 29 *Company and Securities Law Journal* 287.
Hanrahan, Pamela, 2016, 'Revisiting responsible entity directors' liability to scheme members' 34 *Company and Securities Law Journal* 321.
Hanrahan, Pamela, 2018, *Background Paper No 7 for the Royal Commission into Misconduct in the Banking, Superannuation and Financial Services Industry—Legal Framework for the Provision of Financial Advice and Sale of Financial Products to Australian Households*.
King & Wood Mallesons, 2016, *The Review: Class Actions in Australia 2015/16*.
Mees, Bernard, Monica Wehner, and Pamela Hanrahan, 2005, *Fifty Years of Managed Funds in Australia*.
von Nessen, Paul, Sean Robertson, and Paul Wiedman, 2008, *A Practical Guide to Managed Investments*.

Index

Abner, D. 409
Abromeit-Kremser, B. 345
accounting rules addressing misconduct (GAAP Rules) 102
Ackerman, A. 240
Ackert, L. 411
active management debate 132–3, 257, 258–60, 407–9
see also management headings
Adler, J. 320
adverse incentives 192, 193, 195–6, 200
advertising 40, 127–8, 289–90
advisors see investment advisors
affecting conduct standard 214–15
affiliated directors 193–4
see also directors
agency capture, and public choice theory 52–3
agency enforcement actions and Investment Advisors Act 80, 86, 92, 94–6, 97, 98–9, 103
aggregate portfolios and high costs of active management 120
Aguilar, L. 202, 215, 216
Ahmed, A. 67
Aiken, A. 65, 68, 69
Akinbami, F. 391
Alden, W. 67
Allen, F. 400
Allen, K. 292
alpha funds, absence of, and irrational investors 119–20
alternative investment funds (AIFs)
 Australia 418, 423, 436
 EU see European investment fund law, Alternative Investment Fund Managers Directive (AIFMD)
 Ireland see Ireland, mutual fund governance, alternative investment funds (AIFs)
Andenas, M. 391
Anderson, B. 278, 280, 281, 287, 296
Angel, J. 238
arm's-length fees 166, 171, 173, 175, 178, 181
Arnott, R. 253

Asia Region Funds Passport 444
Athanassiou, P. 341
Augenblick, R. 168, 169, 174
Austin, D. 292
Australia, cases
 AMP Life Ltd v. AMP Capital Funds Management Ltd 440
 Australian Fixed Trusts Pty Ltd v. Clyde Industries Limited 420
 Australian Securities Commission v. AS Nominees 426
 Australian Securities and Investments Commission v. ABC Fund Managers 422–3
 Australian Securities and Investments Commission v. Australian Property Custodian Holdings 426
 Australian Securities and Investments Commission v. Avestra Asset Management 426
 Australian Securities and Investments Commission v. Managed Investments Ltd 426
 Breen v. Williams 427
 Hasler v. Singtel Optus Pty Ltd 427
 Hodges v. Waters (No 7) 442, 443
 Hospital Products Ltd v. United States Surgical Corporation 427
 Re Macquarie Investment Management Ltd 430, 443
 Trilogy Funds Management Ltd v. Sullivan 426, 442
 Westpac Banking Corporation v. Bell Group 427
 Wingecarribee Shire Council v. Lehman Bros Australia 427
Australia, regulation of mutual funds 414–45
 alternative investment funds 418, 423, 436
 Australian Financial Services (AFS) licensing regime 416, 423, 424–5, 428
 Australian Prudential Regulation Authority (APRA) 433
 Australian Securities and Investments Commission (ASIC) 416, 418, 421, 422, 423–4, 432, 434–6, 444
 closed-end funds 423

447

Corporations Act 416, 417, 418, 423–4, 427–8, 430, 431, 434, 436, 437, 441, 443
financial planner/advisor 419–20
Financial Services Reform Act 423
managed investment schemes 417–18, 422, 423
registerable schemes 418–19
self-managed superannuation funds (SMSF) 419
unit trusts 416–17, 425
Australia, regulation of mutual funds, independent oversight 432–7
class actions 441–2
collective investment schemes (CIS) 432–3, 444
compliance committees 436–7
compliance plan audit 437
enforcement rights 441–3
exit rights 443
inefficiency concerns 433
recovery rights 441, 442–3
responsibility displacement concerns 433
Australia, regulation of mutual funds, investor rights 424, 437–43
continuous disclosure obligation 438
information rights 438–9
inspection orders 439
Product Disclosure Statement (PDS) 438
reporting obligations 438
veto rights 428, 440
voting rights 439–41
Australia, regulation of mutual funds, legal and regulatory framework 420–24
commercial property market reversal effects 421–2
external monitoring 424
fiduciary duties 424, 427, 428
prescribed interest schemes 421–2
Product Disclosure Statement (PDS) regime 420, 422
state to federal government transfer 421
Australia, regulation of mutual funds, responsible entities 417, 419, 420, 422–31
access to statutory sanctions 429
civil penalty provision 429–30
compensation provision to members in event of wrongdoing 430
conflicts of interest and priority to members' interests 428
duties 424–31, 433
duty of care 426

flexibility 426
officers' duties to members 430–31
statutory obligations 425, 427–30
veto powers over interested dealings 428
Authers, J. 405, 408, 409

backtesting, exchange-traded funds (ETFs) 253
Baert, R. 28
Baghai, P. 280, 292
Baily, M. 389
Bair, S. 234, 235
Bals, W. 345
Baltzer, C. 312
Balzer, P. 344
Barbash, B. 94
Barber, B. 117
Bassler, M. 318, 345
Bathurst, T. 427
Baxt, R. 441
Baxter, J. 231
Beckett, J. 359
Belsky, E. 391
Bencivenga, V. 316
Bender, D. 237
Benedict, J. 165, 167, 170
Bengtsson, E. 387, 405
Benoit, D. 153
Bent, B. 229
Berghuis, W. 327
Bergstresser, D. 125
Berk, J. 120
Berkowitz, J. 237
Bernanke, B. 43, 233–4
Bieber, S. 74
Bines, H. 84, 85, 336
Birdthistle, W. 1–7, 51, 60, 143, 144, 148, 192–3, 258, 267–77, 318
Blake, C. 160
blind pools or black boxes investment 343–4
boards of directors
advisor-primacy over board-primacy 157
advisors, officers and employees on 145
affiliated 193–4
board-centred investor protection 146–9
fiduciary duties 67, 178–9
governance 61–2, 188–90
independent 199, 292–3
Ireland see Ireland, mutual fund governance, boards of directors

obligations and securities law, mutual fund governance improvements 185–6
percentage affiliated with investment advisor 147–9
Bogle, J. 116, 122, 132, 186, 204
Bok, S. 85
Booth, R. 97
Bootle, R. 402
Bowden, A. 66
brand evolution *see* mutual fund brand evolution
Bressler, G. 32
Brexit effects 358–9, 380, 382–3, 396, 405
broker-dealers 46–7, 104–5, 208–9, 212, 250–51, 255, 256, 257, 258
brokerage commissions 270, 271, 272
Broome, L. 221
Brown, H. 229
Brown, S. 160, 161–2
Browning, L. 283
Bruner, C. 85
Brunnermeier, M. 259
Bullard, M. 4–5, 22–56, 81, 99, 103, 104, 105
Bullman, T. 341, 346
Burne, K. 240
Burnham, K. 48
Busch, D. 341
Bush, E. 231
business continuity plans 93
business judgment rule 85, 151, 166
Buttgieg, C. 390

Caccase, M. 158
Cadigan, L. 202
Câmara, P. 308, 318, 326, 331
Cannon, J. 68
Capon, N. 119, 124, 128
Carhart, M. 119
Carney, J. 241, 242
Carns, A. 276
Cavoli, J. 155
Chalmers, J. 125, 126
Champ, N. 63, 71–2, 295
Chen, L. and F. 288
Cheng, S. 411
Cherry, J. 254
chief compliance officer (CCO) administration duties 211–13, 214
Chiu, I. 7, 382–413
Choi, J. 118, 121
Christie, R. 292
Chung, J. 77

Cici, G. 288
Clarke, B. 7, 360–81
class actions 177, 441–2
Clerc, C. 325
closed-end funds 16, 35–7, 60, 262–3, 342, 423
closet 'index huggers' 408–9
Coates, J. 159–60, 162, 174, 191, 192
Collective Asset-Management Vehicles (ICAVs), Ireland 365, 366, 368, 372, 377
collective investment schemes (CIS) 28–30
Australia 432–3, 444
UK *see* UK, collective retail investment funds regulation
Collins, S. 44
common good services, UK 407
competition
EU distribution countries and equivalence standards 323–4, 325–6
and fee litigation under ICA section 36(b) 167–8, 171–2, 174–5
and investor protection 159–62
unfair, and shadow banking 235
compliance
chief compliance officer (CCO) administration duties 211–13, 214
committees, Australia 436–7
developments *see* mutual fund compliance developments
programs, and fiduciary structure of investment management regulation 92–3
Condon, C. 187
conduct-based rules 99–102, 395–8
conflicts of interest
avoidance, fiduciary duties 71
boards of directors, Ireland 370–71, 378
broker-dealer compensation 46–7
broker-dealer investments 104–5
collective retail investment funds regulation, UK 396–7
investor protection, SEC regulation 159
mutual fund governance improvements 190, 199–201
priority to members' interests, Australia 428
Cooper, M. 116, 119
Cooter, R. 82
Copeland, R. 77
corporate governance code 377–9, 388–9
corporate personality effects 149–50
Courvoisier, M. 336

Cox, G. 403
Cox, J. 80, 96
Cristoffersen, S. 125
Crockett, A. 400
Crook, M. 408
Cross, F. 53
Crotty, J. 403
Crowe, S. 37
Cumming, D. 386
Cunningham, L. 61
Curtis, Q. 5, 20, 143, 144, 145, 149, 152, 154, 162, 164–84, 186, 192, 293

Dallas, L. 402
damages assessment 155, 156–7, 169, 431
Davidoff, S. 286
Davis, G. 181
Deidda, L. 317
Del Guercio, D. 116, 119, 125
Delbeque, B. 387
DeMott, D. 5, 57–78, 82, 156
depositary regulation
    European investment fund law *see* European investment fund law, Undertakings for Collective Investments in Transferable Securities (UCITS) Directives, depositary and manager regulations
    Ireland 369–70
    UK 398–400
Dichev, I. 122
directors *see* boards of directors
disclosure requirements
    Australia 420, 422, 438
    European investment fund law 334
    fiduciary obligations 87–90, 95–6, 101
    hedge funds confluence 289
    limited portfolio disclosure, exchange-traded funds (ETFs) 258–9
    money market funds and shadow banking 233, 237
    revenue sharing arrangements 45–6
    sales regulation and disclosure to investors, European investment fund law 333–4
    UK 388, 393–5
    see also information access
Dolan, K. 233
Donohue, A. 214, 220
Dornseifer, F. 318, 346
Driebusch, C. 197
dualism, investor dualism and market protection 316–19

Easterbrook, F. 84, 173–4, 185
Eckhold, T. 344
Eckner, D. 326, 330, 331, 332, 340
Eisenberg, M. 194
Elias, B. 292
Elser, T. 343
enforcement powers
    Australia 441–3
    fiduciary structure of investment management regulation 93–9
    investor protection, SEC regulation 158–9
Engler, H. 219
equivalence standards, EU 323–4, 325–6
European Court of Justice (ECJ)
    Emerging Markets Series of DFA Investment Trust Company v. Dyrektor Izby Skarbowej w Bydgoszczy 355
    Santander Asset Management 355
European investment fund law 302–59
    Brexit impact 358–9
    Capital Market Union (CMU) 309
    Capital Requirements Directives 308–9, 333
    cashflow control and financial intermediaries 316–17
    European Regulation on Long-Term Investment Funds (ELTIFR) 304, 309, 310, 314, 330, 345
    European Regulation on Social Entrepreneurship Funds (EuSEFR) 304, 309, 310, 314, 315, 330, 332–3
    European Regulation on Venture Capital Funds (EuVeCaR) 304, 309, 310, 314, 315, 330, 332–3
    European Securities & Markets Authority (ESMA) 306, 307, 308, 311, 312, 313, 323, 331, 334, 335, 341, 356, 359, 380
    and fee reduction 357–8
    financial crisis effects 307–9, 313, 317–18, 326
    future of 356–9
    harmonization 309–13, 320–21, 355–6, 359
    historical development 305–9
    Investment Services Directive 317
    investment triangle 327–9, 354
    investor dualism and market protection 316–19
    investor protection vs. systemic risk 356–7
    investor type 313–14
    leverage limits and margin requirements 318–19
    long-term finance viability concerns 401–2

ManCo control 305, 306, 321–2, 327, 347, 348–50, 351, 352, 353, 354, 357
market protection and systemic risk 317–18
Markets in Financial Instruments Directive (MiFID) 302–3, 304, 317, 332, 333, 336, 364, 365, 369, 380, 389, 397
Markets in Financial Instruments Directive (MiFID), third country passports and equivalence standards 323, 324, 325–6
Member States' fund legislation fragmentation 307
Money Market Fund Regulation (MMFR) 314–15, 330, 334, 356
moral hazard 319
National Competent Authorities (NCAs) 312–13, 322, 331, 336, 350
pension funds 303, 304, 317
product regulation for retail funds 334
Prospectus Directive 307
public or private law dimension 315
regulatory objectives 314–26
risk and liquidity management 331–2
sales regulation and disclosure to investors 333–4
Securitization Transactions Regulation (STR) 332
Shareholder Rights Directive 326
stakeholder protection and public interest 325–6
transaction costs 357
European investment fund law, Alternative Investment Fund Managers Directive (AIFMD) 303–4, 307–9, 310, 340–46
blind pools or black boxes investment 343–4
disclosure to investors 334
European passports 321–2
hedge funds 345–6
high net worth individuals (HNWi) funds 344
insolvency cases 337
investment in accordance with defined investment policy 343–4
investment vs. operating company 336
investor numbers 342–3
investor type 313–14
Know Your Customer requirements 315
and Lamfalussy process 311–12
private equity funds 325, 345
product regulation for retail funds 334
qualified investor funds (QIF) 344
real estate and infrastructure funds 345
and systemic risk 309, 319, 332, 356–7

technical standards implementation 311–12
third country passports and equivalence standards 323–4, 325–6
European investment fund law, Single Capital Market 319–24
competitiveness of distribution countries and equivalence standards 323–4, 325–6
cooperation agreements 324
national private placement regimes (NPPR) 323
tax information exchange 325–6
third countries 323–4
European investment fund law, Single Capital Market, European passports 319–22, 355
crossborder access and regulatory arbitrage risk 320
fund management company licenses 322
supply and demand imbalance issues 320
European investment fund law, Undertakings for Collective Investments in Transferable Securities (UCITS) Directives 302, 303, 304, 305–7, 310, 313, 317, 335–40
capital raised from the public 338, 341
disclosure to investors 334
and European passports 321–2, 355
fee reduction 357–8
investment flexibility 305–6, 354
investment triangle 327–9, 354
investment vs. operating company 336
investor type 313–14
Key Investor Document 306–7
liquid financial assets 339
open-ended funds and redemption rights 339
pooling of assets 336–7
product regulation 340, 351–4
risk-spreading principle 338–9
success secret 354–6
third party investment management 337–8
transferable securities 339
European investment fund law, Undertakings for Collective Investments in Transferable Securities (UCITS) Directives, depositary and manager regulations 314–15, 330–33, 347–51, 350–51
cash custody function 349
eligible entities 349–50
harm caused to investors beyond lost assets 350–51

investors' standing in relation to legal
    recourse 351
reuse of assets 348
safekeeping of assets 347–8, 350
strict liability for lost assets 350
third party custody of funds 350
European investment fund law, Undertakings
    for Collective Investments in
    Transferable Securities (UCITS)
    Directives, product regulation 306,
    351–4
  eligible assets 351–2
  investment limits 352–3
  investment limits violation 354
  management control ban 353–4
  retail funds 334
  trash quota 352, 353–4
European passports *see* European investment
    fund law, Single Capital Market,
    European passports
Evans, D. 391
Evans, R. 117
exchange-traded funds (ETFs) 3–4, 247–66
  active management and investment
    discretion 257, 258–60
  backtesting and smart beta index-tracking
    253
  broker-dealers as Authorized Participants
    250–51, 255, 256, 257, 258
  closed-end funds comparison 262–3
  Financial Stability Oversight Council 263–4
  free rider concerns 259, 263
  futures trading jurisdiction 249
  hedging investments 251, 254, 286
  index participations 248–9
  index-tracking types 252, 254, 256–8
  investment advisor, absence of 256–7
  Ireland 361
  limited portfolio disclosure 258–9
  market volatility susceptibility 264–5
  mutual fund brand evolution 48–50
  mutual fund comparisons 254, 255, 257,
    264
  portfolio transparency concerns 256, 258,
    260–63
  redemption rights 261–2, 264
  regulatory framework and exemptive relief
    255–65
  rise and growth 252–4
  SEC denials of exemptive relief 261–3
  SEC rulemaking 260–61
  SEC rulemaking, Rule 6c-11 and
    transparency conditions 261

second generation index exemption 257–8
securities' liquidity concerns 264
shadow Investment Company Act 35–8,
    39–40
shares and shareholders 249–52, 256,
    259–60, 261–2, 263
smart beta index-tracking 253, 258
systemic risk 263–5
traditional management 253–4
unit investment trust (UIT) 257
exchange-traded funds, UK 409–11
exemptive relief, exchange-traded funds
    (ETFs) 255–65
exit rights 19, 20, 68, 70, 142, 145, 153–4,
    156, 157, 159–60, 401, 443
external investment advisors, investor
    protection 143–5, 150

Fahlenbrach, R. 117
Fama, E. 119, 120, 268
Fanto, J. 6, 205–26
Farlow, A. 390
Fattouh, B. 317
Fausti, K. 103
Fayvilevich, G. 241
fee levels
  directors and fee negotiations 152–7
  and European investment fund law 357–8
  fee-based advisors 127
  and fiduciary duties 74–5
  funds that shared upfront marketing fees
    with advisors 125
  reductions in public interest 267–9, 275
fee litigation under ICA section 36(b) 164–84
  BlackRock Global Allocation Fund 180,
    181, 182–3
  competition 167–8, 171–2, 174–5
  corporate law standards 166
  fiduciary duties 169–70, 173–4, 178–9
  fund fees concerns 165–8
  fund size focus 177–8
  Investment Company Amendments Act
    adoption 168–70
  management fees 177, 178, 180
  private, non-fund clients 167
  real-world operation 176–9
  reasonableness standard 168–9, 170
  recovery of fees, limits to 170
  settlement options 176–7
  shareholder derivative suits and state
    corporate law 166
  shareholders' right of action 169

size of the fund industry, concerns over 166–7
subadvisory suits 179–83
Wharton study 166–7
fee litigation under ICA section 36(b), judicial approach 171–6
arm's length fees 166, 171, 173, 175, 178, 181
Gartenberg decision 155, 156, 164, 171–3, 175, 176, 178, 179, 182
intra-fund fee comparison 175
Jones case 144, 155, 156, 164, 173–6, 179, 180, 182, 183, 191, 193
liability determination 172–3
money market fund and pension fund comparisons 175
reasonableness standard 171–2, 173
Ferran, E. 391
Fetzer, P. 159
fiduciaries 2, 57–78
branding of mutual funds 61
closed-end mutual funds 60
conflicts of interest avoidance 71
contrast between Advisors Act and ICA 71–2, 73–5, 76
exculpatory provisions 76
fees 74–5
governance and board of directors 61–2
individualized investment management 69–70
internal compliance 72
investment advisor 59–60, 61–2, 64–6, 67, 76
investment company definition 59, 60
open-end mutual funds and net asset value (NAV) 60
public offering of shares 60–61, 62
scalping practice as fraud or deceit 71
self-dealing prohibitions 72–3
unit investment trust (UIT) 60
fiduciaries, private funds 62–9
definition 62–3
issuer exclusions 63–4
legacy funds 66
limited partnership agreements 66, 67
liquidation event 63, 67
private equity funds 63, 64
qualified purchasers 64
venture capital funds 63
fiduciaries, private funds, hedge funds 63, 67
Aberrational Performance Inquiry 66
conflict committees 73–4
directors 67

redemption rights and manager's discretionary power 67–9
self-report information 65
fiduciary duties
Australia 424, 427, 428
breaches 154–5
fee litigation 169–70, 173–4, 178–9
Ireland 372
SEC regulation 158
vigilance concerns 191, 195–6
fiduciary structure of investment management regulation 79–110
agency enforcement actions and Advisors Act 80, 86, 92, 94–6, 97, 98–9, 103
fiduciary relationship definition 81
Investment Company Act and rulemaking 80, 90–91, 99–100
investment management industry size 79
SEC statements 80
fiduciary structure of investment management regulation, codifying fiduciary norms 99–105
accounting rules addressing misconduct (GAAP Rules) 102
broker-dealer investments and conflicts of interest disclosure (*Press v. Quick & Reilly*) 104–5
conduct-based rules as alternative to fiduciary obligation 99–100
conduct-based rules and generalized standards, relationship between 100–102
laddering and spinning sales practices 102
partner's duty (*Meinhard v. Salmon*) 102–4
securities industry and disclosure rules 101
fiduciary structure of investment management regulation, fiduciary obligations 86–99
advisor's trading as a principal with advisory clients 89–90
business continuity plans 93
compliance programs 92–3
disclosure duties 87–90, 95–6, 101
enforcement cases 93–9
enforcement cases, settled actions 96–9
industry rules 86–93
market timing actions 96–8
proxy voting 90–92
fiduciary structure of investment management regulation, loyalty and care duties 81–6
agent liabilities and 'reasonable efforts' 84–6
deception temptations 83–4
differentiating loyalty from care 82–3

discretionary authority of trustees 84
proxy voting 91–2
Prudent Investor Rule 82, 83
financial crisis effects
   European investment fund law 307–9, 313, 317–18, 326
   money market funds and shadow banking 231–3
   UK *see* UK, collective retail investment funds regulation, financial crisis effects
financial intermediaries
   and cashflow control 316–17
   and investors' identity *see* investors' identity, financial intermediaries' role
financial press and investor education 134–6
financial regulation reform, UK 390–92
Financial Stability Oversight Council (FSOC) 53, 234, 235–6, 263–4, 290–91
Fink, M. 165, 166
Firippis, I. 213
Fisch, J. 6, 144, 150, 174, 186, 228–46
Fischel, D. 84, 185
Fishman, D. 240
Flannery, A. 96
Fleischer, V. 292
Flynn, A. 240
Foley, S. 236
Franco, J. 102
Frank, M. 259
Frankel, T. 63, 64, 74, 84, 346
fraud, scalping practice as 71
free funds and retirement savings as public infrastructure 267–77
   brokerage commissions 270, 271, 272
   fee reductions in public interest 267–9, 275
   free publicity capitalization 272
   free services comparison 275
   fund manager reputation and fund value issues 274–5
   fund size 271
   index funds 269–70
   inexpensive funds as starting point 269–71
   institutional involvement 275–6
   lowering expenses 271–2
   management fee paid to investment advisor 272
   operating costs 270
   press coverage and public interest 274
   revenue generation 272–3
   revenue generation, soft dollars 273
   short selling and securities lending 272–3
free rider concerns, exchange-traded funds (ETFs) 259, 263

Freedman, B. 82
Freeman, K. 160, 165, 166, 168
French, K. 119, 120, 268
Friesen, G. 122, 126
futures trading jurisdiction, exchange-traded funds (ETFs) 249

GAAP Rules (accounting rules addressing misconduct) 102
Gabrysch, N. 345
Gale, D. 400
Gallagher, D. 216, 235
Garten, H. 235
Gastineau, G. 254, 409, 410
Geithner, T. 233, 234
Germany, manager regulation and open-ended funds 307
Getmansky, M. 63, 65, 67
Glazer, M. 283
Glushkov, D. 253
Golat, T. 419
Goldberg, J. 32
Goldfarb, L. 68
Goldsmith, R. 316
government brand, mutual fund as 23–5
Graas, R. 399
Graber, S. 149
Greenwood, J. 316
Greer, A. 66, 69
Grind, K. 153, 161, 284
Gruber, M. 119
Guedj, I. 410
Gullapalli, D. 43, 229, 233
Gummow, H. 427

Hackethal, A. 122, 126
Hamilton, J. 236
Hanrahan, P. 7, 414–45
Hansmann, H. 20
Hanson, S. 231, 232
harmonization
   European investment fund law 309–13, 320–21, 355–6, 359
   UK *see* UK, collective retail investment funds regulation, UCITS regulation and harmonization impact
Hasanhodzic, J. 287
Hayne, K. 427
Hazen, T. 102
Healy, R. 66, 69
hedge funds 4–5, 28–30
   European investment fund law 345–6

exchange-traded funds (ETFs) 251, 254, 286
fiduciaries *see* fiduciaries, private funds, hedge funds
and public advertising 40
hedge funds confluence 278–300
  advertising restrictions removal 289–90
  bank investment limitations 294
  derivative trading and short selling, efforts to curtail 295
  disclosure requirements 289
  distribution-in-guise payments by mutual fund advisors 284
  Dodd–Frank Act 279–80, 288–9, 290, 292, 293–4
  exchange traded funds (ETFs) 286
  federal securities regulation 295–6
  Financial Stability Oversight Council (FSOC) 290–91
  interest rates 279, 287, 292
  investment advisor registration provisions 293–4
  Investment Advisors Act 284–5
  Investment Company Act 286, 288, 293
  investor preferences 286–7
  JOBS Act 279–80, 288–90, 292, 294
  litigation measures 283–4
  and market forces 279
  multimanager series trusts 287–8
  mutual fund governance effect 292–3
  private fund industry evolution 291–2
  private and mutual funds confluence 285–91
  private and retail alternative funds, proliferation of 280–82
  regulation 288–91, 292
  retail alternative funds 286–8, 293–5
  retail investors 287–8
  risk-taking concerns 292
  SEC Rule 18f-4, proposed 296–7
  side by side management of mutual and hedge funds 288
  systemically important financial institution (SIFI) designation 280, 289, 290–91
  verification procedures and contractual requirements 282–3
Heinemann, F. 387
Hemel, D. 267, 275
Heydon, J. 425–6
high cost, actively managed funds, decline in 132–3
high net worth individuals (HNWi) funds 344
Hill, C. 190

Hojat, S. 410
Holden, S. 124
Hooghiemstra, S. 308, 322
Hooker, J. 241
Huang, J. 410
Huang, V. 267
Hubbard, G. 159–60, 162, 174, 191, 192
Hudson, A. 337
Hudson, M. 403
Huff, A. 214
Hughes, A. 86, 88
Hunnicutt, T. 38, 240

independent directors and fee negotiations 152–7
independent oversight, Australia *see* Australia, regulation of mutual funds, independent oversight
index funds
  exchange-traded funds (ETFs) 248–9
  and irrational investors 117–18
  low cost, growth of 133
index huggers, closet, UK 408–9
index-tracking 249–50, 252, 253, 254, 256–8
individualized investment management 69–70
industry rules, fiduciary structure of investment management regulation 86–93
information access 88–9, 157–8, 274, 316–17, 438–9
see also disclosure requirements
innovation 3–4, 39–47, 48, 356, 359
insolvency cases, European investment fund law 337
interest rates 33, 229, 231, 237, 239–40, 241, 279, 287, 292, 358, 389–90
International Organization of Securities Commissions (IOSCO) 367, 432, 434
investment advisors
  absence of, and exchange-traded funds (ETFs) 256–7
  Australia *see* Australia, regulation of mutual funds, trustee and fund advisor and sponsor as responsible entity
  fees 160, 161
  fiduciaries 59–60, 61–2, 64–6, 67, 76
  limited numbers of 145–6
  primacy over board-primacy 137
  registration provisions 293–4
  trading as a principal with advisory clients 89–90
Investment Advisors Act

agency enforcement actions 80, 86, 92, 94–6, 97, 98–9, 103
fiduciary duties 71–2, 73–5, 76
hedge funds confluence 284–5
investor protection 158
mutual fund compliance developments 208, 209
investment advisory firm connections, and traditional governance model *see* mutual fund governance improvements, traditional model and investment advisory firm connections
investment companies
  definition 59, 60
  Ireland 365–6, 368, 369, 370–71, 372, 374–5
Investment Company Act (ICA) 10, 12, 13–14, 15, 16, 19–20
  contrast between Advisors Act and ICA, fiduciaries, fiduciary duties 71–2, 73–5, 76
  exemptions, mutual fund brand evolution 24
  hedge funds confluence 286, 288, 293
  investor protection 143–8, 151, 157
  money market funds and shadow banking 229
  mutual fund brand evolution 22, 23–4, 47, 49
  mutual fund compliance developments 209
  and mutual fund governance improvements 189
  mutual fund governance improvements, traditional model and investment advisory firm connections 193
  and rulemaking, fiduciary structure of investment management regulation 80, 90–91, 99–100
  section 36(b) fee litigation *see* fee litigation under ICA section 36(b)
  shadow *see* mutual fund brand evolution, shadow Investment Company Act
Investment Company Amendments Act adoption 168–70
investment fund law, Europe *see* European investment fund law
investment fund management company licenses, EU 322
investment fund manager reputation 274–5
investment fund organizational structure effects 143–4
investment fund size focus 177–8
investment limits, EU 352–3

investment, long-term, EU 304, 309, 310, 314, 330, 345
investment management regulation, fiduciary structure *see* fiduciary structure of investment management regulation
investment protection measures, Ireland UCITS 363
investment triangle, European investment fund law 327–9, 354
investor protection 141–63
  advisors, limited numbers of 145–6
  advisory fees 160, 161
  board-centred 146–9
  competition debate 159–62
  damages assessment 155, 156–7
  director percentage affiliated with investment advisor 147–9
  exit rights 142, 145, 153–4, 156, 157, 159–60
  external investment advisors 143–5, 150
  fiduciary duty breaches 154–5
  fund organizational structure effects 143–4
  independent directors and fee negotiations 152–7
  Investment Advisor Act 158
  Investment Company Act 143–8, 151, 157
  investor-focused efforts 153–4
  investors and advisors, conflicts between 145
  litigation 154–7
  litigation, reform 156–7
  profit margins 161–2
  redemption rights 153
  sanctions 156, 159
  UK 388–9
  unitary boards 146
  voting and exit 153–4, 156
investor protection, misconceived board, reconceiving 149–53
  board as investor governance representative 151–3
  corporate personality effects 149–50
  investments as products, misconception of 150
  mutual fund as legally distinct entity 150
  mutual funds as collective action mechanisms 149–50
investor protection, SEC regulation
  advisor conflicts of interest 159
  advisor-primacy over board-primacy 157
  disclosure requirements 158
  enforcement powers 158–9
  ex ante guidance 158

ex post enforcement 158–9
fiduciary duty standard 158
market intelligence gathering 157–8
monthly reporting requirements 158
Rule 12b-1 exemption 157
investor protection vs. systemic risk, EU 356–7
investor rights, Australia *see* Australia, regulation of mutual funds, investor rights
investor-chosen advisory committees 67
investors' identity 112–40
   fundholding households 113–14
   and low costs funds 112, 117, 120, 123, 132–3, 136
   portraits of fund investors 128–31
   portraits of fund investors, industry's portrait 129–30
   portraits of fund investors, SEC portrait 130–31
   and retirement savings 114
   twin funds 117
   US Internal Revenue Code 401(k) plans 112, 114, 123–4, 127, 133–4
investors' identity, financial intermediaries' role 123–8
   conflicted advice 125–7
   conflicted payments 124–5
   fee-based advisors 127
   fund advertising 127–8
   fund's past performance emphasis 125
   and marketing fees 125
   misguided market timing 126
investors' identity, irrational investors 115–23
   aggregate portfolios and high costs of active management 120
   alpha funds, absence of 119–20
   chasing past performance 119
   choice of asset classes 121
   fund loads (including 12b-1 fees) 118
   ignorance of fund characteristics 115–16
   inattention to fund expenses 116–18
   index mutual funds 117–18
   investor returns vs market performance 122–3
   investors continue to chase past returns 120–21
   market timing (buy high and sell low) 121–2
   name changes 119
   retail and institutional investors comparison 117
   return persistence studies 120
   risk and asset diversification 116
investors' identity, retail fund market, recent shifts 132–6
   active management doubts 136
   fees focus 135
   financial press and investor education 134–6
   high cost, actively managed funds, decline in 132–3
   low cost index funds, growth of 133
   market timing 136
   past performance, futility of chasing 135
   target date/lifecycle funds, growth of 133–4
Ireland, Dublin as major UCITS originating jurisdiction 386–7
Ireland, mutual fund governance 360–81
   Brexit referendum issues 380
   Central Bank authorization requirements 365, 366, 367, 368, 369, 372–6
   Collective Asset-Management Vehicles (ICAVs) 365, 366, 368, 372, 377
   common law system 361–2
   Companies Act 2014 371–2
   conflicts of interest management 370–71, 378
   corporate governance code 377–9
   depositary requirements 369–70
   directors' fiduciary duties 372
   EU regulatory changes pending 380
   Euronext Dublin stock exchange 361
   exchange traded funds (ETFs) driver 361
   Fitness & Probity Standards 374, 375, 379
   fund administrator 370
   fund investors 367
   Fund Management Companies–Guidance 375–6
   International Financial Services Centre 360–61
   International Organization of Securities Commissions (IOSCO) 367, 370, 371
   investment companies 365–6, 368, 369, 370–71, 372, 374–5
   Irish Funds Industry Association (IFIA) 377–9
   limited companies regulation 371
   management companies 368–9, 371, 372, 373, 374–5, 376
   private companies limited by shares 371
   product-only qualified investor funds 307
   shareholders 367, 373
   tax regime 364, 366, 377
   umbrella funds 366–7
   variable capital investment company 365

Ireland, mutual fund governance, alternative investment funds (AIFs) 363–5
  management passport 364–5, 369, 380
  qualifying investor alternative fund (QAIF) 364, 374–5
  regulations 372–3, 374–5
  retail investor alternative funds (RIAIF) 364
Ireland, mutual fund governance, boards of directors 368, 372, 375
  Central Bank's Fitness & Probity Standards 374, 375, 379
  corporate governance code 377–9
  location requirement 376
  organizational effectiveness role 376
  time commitment 376, 379
Ireland, mutual fund governance, UCITS 361, 362–3
  investment protection measures 363
  management passport 362, 368–9, 380
  regulations 372–3, 374–5
Ireland, P. 403
irrational investors *see* investors' identity, irrational investors

Jackson, J. 215
Jain, P. 128
James, K. 407
Janofsky, A. 242
Jensen, M. 151–2
Jickling, M. 292
Johnson, E. 193–4
Johnson, L. 5, 141–63, 186, 191
Johnson, S. 238
Jones, E. 185–6
Jones, M. 125
Jones, R. 408
Jovanovic, B. 316
judicial approach, fee litigation *see* fee litigation under ICA section 36(b), judicial approach

Kaal, W. 7, 75, 278–300
Kacperczyk, M. 233, 404
Kahan, M. 345
Kam, F. 426
Kämmerer, J. 312
Kaplow, L. 87
Katz, I. 236, 292, 295
Kay, J. 411
Keen, S. 234, 235
Kennedy, D. 87

Kerwin, T. 193
Key Investor Information Document (KIID) 306–7, 394–5
Kirsch, C. 60
Knickle, H. 175, 179
Know Your Customer requirements, EU 315
Knowles, D. 292
Kong, S. 146
Kostovetsky, L. 61
Kraakman, R. 86, 87
Kraskin, M. 218
Krouse, S. 136, 161
Krug, A. 6, 144, 148, 185–204

Laby, A. 5, 65, 66, 69, 73, 74, 76, 79–110
laddering and spinning sales practices 102
Lamfalussy process, and European investment fund law 311–12
Langbein, J. 84
Langenbucher, K. 312
Langevoort, D. 83, 144, 148, 160, 186, 192, 283, 295
Larrabee, D. 231
Lattman, P. 75
Layette, S. 218, 223
Lee, C. 292
Leeming, M. 425–6
Lehmann, M. 312
Lemke, T. 96
Leonard, R. 285
Leslie, M. 85
Levine, R. 317
Lhabitant, F.-S. 292
Li, S. 400
licensing, manager regulation 330–31
lifecycle funds 133–4
limited companies regulation, Ireland 371
limited partnership agreements 66, 67
Lin, L. 187
liquidity 11
  European investment fund law 331–2, 339
  investor preference for 400–405, 409, 411
  rule, opting out of 30, 36
  securities' liquidity concerns 264
Lo, A. 287
location requirement, Ireland 376
Lofchie, S. 219
long-term finance viability concerns, EU 401–2
Longo, J. 341
Longo, T. 194
Loritz, K. 337
Loss, L. 94

Index   459

low cost funds 112, 117, 120, 123, 132–3, 136, 269–70, 405–11
Lowenstein, R. 292
loyalty and care duties, fiduciary *see* fiduciary structure of investment management regulation, loyalty and care duties
Lund, D. 268
Lutton, L. 35
Luxembourg
  as major UCITS originating jurisdiction 386–7
  manager and product regulation 307
Lybecker, M. 12
Lynch, S. 236

Mahoney, P. 159–60
Maiello, M. 194–5
Malito, A. 219
Malkiel, B. 408
Mallaby, S. 292
Mamudi, S. 190, 232
management companies 17–21
  active management debate 132–3, 257, 258–60, 407–9
  Ireland 368–9, 371, 372, 373, 374–5, 376
  traditional management, exchange-traded funds (ETFs) 253–4
  UK, collective retail investment funds 388–9, 395–9
management control ban, EU 353–4
management discretion, and redemption rights 67–9
management fees 74–5, 116, 118, 133, 177, 178, 180, 272, 406–9
manager regulation, European investment fund law *see* European investment fund law, Undertakings for Collective Investments in Transferable Securities (UCITS) Directives, depositary and manager regulations
Mann, A. 343
Marcus, K. 68
market distortions, UK *see* UK, collective retail investment funds regulation, market distortions
market failure protection 24–5
market timing 41, 49, 96–8, 121–2, 136
market volatility susceptibility, exchange-traded funds (ETFs) 264–5
market-based comparisons and competition, fee litigation 171–2, 174–5

Markets in Financial Instruments Directive (MiFID), EU 302–3, 304, 317, 323, 324, 325–6, 332, 333, 336, 364, 365, 369, 380
Markham, J. 33, 148, 221, 229, 231
Marriage, M. 295
Marte, T. 321, 323, 324, 325, 342
Martin, C. 289
Martin, T. 64
Massari, J. 94
master-feeder funds 34–5, 306, 314, 358
Maxey, D. 239, 240
McCabe, P. 229
McCarthy, D. 287
McCrary, S. 282
McDonald, D. 237, 242
McDonnell, B. 190
McKee, B. 400
McNamara, J. 240
Meckling, W. 151–2
Mees, B. 421
Mendales, R. 390
Mercer, M. 124, 128
Merope, S. 427
Metz, R. 36
Michaels, D. 236
Michel, N. 233
Miller, G. 235
Miller, R. 118
Millon, D. 152
Mills, D. 292
mini-accounts 26–8
misconceived board *see* investor protection, misconceived board, reconceiving
Moloney, N. 305, 306, 307, 312, 346, 391
money market funds 33–4, 42–4, 52, 53
  Money Market Fund Regulation (MMFR), EU 314–15, 330, 334, 356
  pension fund comparisons 175
money market funds and shadow banking 3, 228–46
  "breaking the buck" adjustment 230, 232
  cash management services 231
  financial crisis effects 231–3
  floating NAV investment concerns 239, 240
  fund sponsors 229–30
  fund's net asset value (NAV) 229–30
  future of 239–42
  interest rates 33, 229, 231, 237, 239–40, 241
  Investment Company Act 229
  lower yield investment consideration 239–40

moral hazard problem and excessive
    risk-taking 232
municipal securities purchases 231
penny rounding 230
portfolio management 230–31
Regulation Q and capped interest rates 33,
    229
risk-taking concerns 241
SEC Rule 2a-7 and securities valuation 230
share redemptions and money market fund
    run 232
short-term financing and need for
    alternative sourcing 242
sponsor support 230–31
stress testing 233, 237
unregistered investment options 240–41
money market funds and shadow banking,
    Reserve Primary Fund (RPF), political
    response 231–6
banking regulation concerns 235–6
Financial Stability Oversight Council
    (FSOC) proposals 234, 235–6
SEC Rule 2a-7 amendment 233
shift from fixed to floating NAV 233, 234,
    236, 237
systemically important financial institutions
    (SIFIs) designation 234–5, 236
unfair competition and shadow banking 235
money market funds and shadow banking,
    SEC Rules (2014) 236–8
disclosure requirements 237
floating NAV concerns 238
institutional funds 237
retail funds 237, 238, 241
monitoring 158, 210–11, 218–20, 312–13,
    424, 438, 439
Moodie, G. 436
moral hazard 232, 319
    see also risk management
Morey, M. 160
Morgenson, G. 64
Morley, J. 1–7, 9–21, 23, 51, 58, 62, 63, 67,
    142–54*passim*, 157, 162, 164, 167, 177,
    186, 192, 282, 293, 415
Mraović, B. 402
Mullainathan, S. 126, 161
multiclass funds 32
multimanager funds 35, 40, 287–8
mutual fund brand evolution 14–16, 22–56
    exchange-traded funds regulation 48–50
    fiduciaries 61
    free market policies exception 23–4
    government brand 23–5

hedge funds and public advertising 40
Investment Company Act (ICA) regulation
    22, 23–4, 47, 49
liquidity rule, opting out of 30, 36
market approval concept 25
market failure protection 24–5
market timing abuses 49
SEC's abandonment of mutual fund brand
    50–53
securities rules 25
stagnating industry growth 47–50
substitutes, degree of acceptance of 25–6
substitutes, hedge funds, separate accounts
    and collective investment trusts 28–30
substitutes, mini-accounts and penalties
    26–8
unit investment trust (UIT) 36, 37
mutual fund brand evolution, regulation and
    growth 39–47
broker-dealer compensation 46–7
conflicts of interest in broker-dealer
    compensation 46–7
disclosure of revenue sharing arrangements
    45–6
FINRA inspection program 47
fixed pricing under Section 22(d) 4
market timing scandal 41
money market funds 42–4, 52, 53
money market funds, bailout management
    43–4
pricing arbitrage problem 41
revenue sharing arrangements 44–6
SEC 12b-1 fees and revenue sharing 44–6
stagnating regulatory innovation 39–47, 48
mutual fund brand evolution, shadow
    Investment Company Act 22, 31–9
closed-end fund 35–7
exchange-traded funds 35–8, 39–40
joint liability policies 39
master-feeder funds 34–5, 306, 314, 358
money market funds 33–4
multiclass funds and 12b-1 fees 32
multimanager funds 35, 40
transactional exemptions 38–9
mutual fund compliance developments
    205–26
annual review and assessment requirement
    210–11
broker-dealers comparison 208–9, 212
chief compliance officer (CCO)
    administration duties 211–13, 214
compliance program rules 207–13
Investment Advisors Act 208, 209

Index 461

Investment Company Act 209
  liability for failure to supervise 208–9
  oversight by service providers 210
  "reasonably designed" criterion 210
  risk management 210, 221–3
  scandals, effects of 209
  Securities Exchange Act 208
  self-regulatory organizations (SROs) 208, 209, 211, 212
  statutory supervisory liability 207–8, 213–17
  statutory supervisory liability, and "affecting conduct" 214–15
  statutory supervisory liability, compliance officer inclusion concerns 214–16, 217
  statutory supervisory liability, compliance officer overlap 213–14
  technology and compliance 216, 217–20
  technology and compliance, surveillance role 218–19
mutual fund governance improvements 185–204
  adverse incentives 192, 193, 195–6, 200
  board appointments and independence 199
  board governance 188–90
  board obligations and securities law 185–6
  conflicts of interest 190, 199–201
  fund administrator 187, 196–9
  fund adminstrator, administration firm 196–7
  and Investment Company Act 189
  multiple advisors 196–7, 201
  new model analysis 199–203
  smaller advisory firms and risk factors 202–3
  time saving benefits and operational efficiencies 198
mutual fund governance improvements, traditional model and investment advisory firm connections 186–7, 190–96
  advisor influence 192–3
  affiliated directors 193–4
  candidates to serve on the fund's board 191–2
  fiduciary vigilance concerns 191, 195–6
  Investment Company Act 193
  unitary boards 191–2, 194–6, 201

Nagy, D. 209
name changes, and irrational investors 119
Natarajan, S. 242

National Competent Authorities (NCAs), EU 312–13, 322, 331, 336, 350
national private placement regimes (NPPR), EU 323
Naveaux, V. 399
net asset value (NAV) 60, 229–30, 233, 234, 236–40*passim*, 251–2, 259–60, 261, 262
no-fee funds 267–8
Nohel, T. 279, 288
non-UCITS retail schemes (NURs), UK 384, 385, 395, 396, 399–400, 401, 403, 405
  see also Undertakings for Collective Investments in Transferable Securities (UCITS) Directives
Nutt, W. 200

O'Brien, J. 149
Opdyke, J. 145
organizational structure and separation of funds and managers 17–21
Osterman, E. 100

Palmiter, A. 5, 112–40, 148, 160, 185
Papagiannis, N. 278
Paredes, T. 388
Park, J. 97, 101
passports
  European investment fund law 321–2, 323–4, 325–6
  Ireland 362, 368–9, 380
Pastor, L. 408, 409
Paul, G. 316
Pedersen, L. 259
Pender, K. 36
penny rounding, money market funds and shadow banking 230
pension funds 13, 19, 175, 303, 304, 317
  see also retirement savings
performance focus 119, 120–21, 122–3, 125, 135
Petruno, T. 36
Phelps, J. 230
Phillips, R. 194, 200
Plaze, R. 86, 87
Polkovnichenko, V. 408–9
Porter, G. 120
Pozen, Richard 239, 240
Pozen, Robert 403
Preiner, C. 336, 337, 341, 342
Prentice, R. 405
prescribed interest schemes, Australia 421–2
press coverage and public interest 274

see also information access
Price, L. 74
private funds
   European investment fund law 325, 345
   fiduciaries *see* fiduciaries, private funds
   and hedge funds 280–82, 285–92
Product Disclosure Statement (PDS), Australia 420, 422, 438
product-only qualified investor funds, Ireland 307
Protess, B. 75
proxy voting, fiduciary obligations 90–92
   see also voting
Prudent Investor Rule 82, 83
public choice theory, and agency capture 52–3
Pugliese, D. 410

qualified investor funds (QIF), European investment fund law, Alternative Investment Fund Managers Directive (AIFMD) 344
qualifying investor alternative fund (QAIF), Ireland 364, 374–5

Ramsay, I. 7, 414–45
Raymond, N. 232
reasonableness standard, fee litigation 168–9, 170, 171–2, 173
"reasonably designed" criterion 210
recovery of fees 156, 170
redemption rights 67–9, 153, 261–2, 264, 339, 441, 442–3
Regulation Q and capped interest rates 33, 229
Reid, B. 239
Reklaitis, V. 271
Relly, D. 241
Rendón, V. 66
Reserve Primary Fund (RPF) 3, 42, 44
   shadow banking *see* money market funds and shadow banking, Reserve Primary Fund (RPF), political response
responsibility displacement concerns, Australia 433
retail alternative funds, hedge funds confluence 286–8
retail and institutional investors comparison 117
retail investment funds
   European investment fund law 334
   hedge funds confluence 287–8
   money market funds and shadow banking 237
   product regulation for retail funds, European investment fund law 334
   UK *see* UK, collective retail investment funds regulation
retail investor alternative funds (RIAIF), Ireland 364
retirement savings 114
   and free funds *see* free funds and retirement savings as public infrastructure
   see also pension funds
return persistence studies 120
reuse of assets, European investment fund law 348
Reuter, J. 116, 125, 126, 128
revenue sharing arrangements 45–6
Riassetto, I. 306, 329
Ribstein, L. 81, 83
Richards, L. 96
Rickmers, B. 337
Riewe, J. 159
Riggs, D. 90, 185, 188, 288
Ripken, S. 88
risk management 16–17, 18–19
   and asset diversification 116
   European investment fund law 331–2, 338–9, 356–7
   and hedge funds 292
   and moral hazard 232, 319
   mutual fund compliance developments 210, 221–3
   smaller advisory firms 202–3
   systemic risk 263–5, 309, 317–18, 319, 332, 356–7
   UK 396
Roche, D. 400
Rock, E. 345
Rogers, W. 165, 167, 170
Roiter, E. 6, 58, 60, 61, 70, 74, 75, 143, 147, 148, 151, 186, 229, 230, 231, 247–66, 293, 367
Rosella, M. 410
Rosen, K. 103
Rowland, C. 229, 233, 236
Roy, S. 404
Rubin, B. 213

Sale, H. 295
sanctions 156, 159, 320–21, 429
Sanders, B. 292
Sanders, W. 103

Sapp, T. 122, 126
scalping practice as fraud 71
Schapiro, M. 234
Schiffman, H. 168
Schmitz, R. 336
Schnabl, P. 233, 404
Schonfeld, V. 193
Schrass, D. 124
Schubauer, D. 305
Schulmeister, S. 402
Schumpeter, J. 317
Schwarcz, S. 309
securities 10–13
  and board obligations 185–6
  and disclosure rules 101
  European Securities & Markets Authority (ESMA) 306, 307, 308, 311, 312, 313, 323, 331, 334, 335, 341, 356, 359, 380
  liquidity concerns, exchange-traded funds (ETFs) 264
  money market funds and shadow banking 231
  Securities and Exchange Commission (SEC) *see* US Securities and Exchange Commission (SEC)
  Securitization Transactions Regulation (STR), EU 332
  special securities regulation *see* investment funds and special securities regulation
self-dealing practices 72–3, 83, 87, 151
self-managed funds 337–8, 419
self-regulatory organizations (SROs) 208, 209, 211, 212
self-report information, hedge funds 65
separate accounts 28–30
Seretakis, A. 292
shadow banking *see* money market funds and shadow banking
shadow Investment Company Act *see* mutual fund brand evolution, shadow Investment Company Act
shares and shareholders
  EU Shareholder Rights Directive 326
  exchange-traded funds (ETFs) 249–52, 256, 259–60, 261–2, 263
  and fee litigation 166, 169
  fiduciaries and public offering of shares 60–61, 62
  Ireland 367, 373
  money market funds and shadow banking 232
  see also voting rights
Sharifzadeh, M. 410

Shecter, P. 159
Shiller, R. 390
Shilling, G. 292
Shilling, H. 230
short selling 251, 272–3, 295
Siena, J. 308, 328
Silverblatt, R. 149, 161
Single Capital Market *see* European investment fund law, Single Capital Market
size of fund industry, concerns over 166–7
Sjostrom, W. 283
Slaughter, S. 188
small investors 13–14, 19–20
smaller advisory firms and risk factors 202–3
smart beta index-tracking 253, 258
Smith, B. 316
Smith, D. 82
social entrepreneurship, European Regulation on Social Entrepreneurship Funds (EuSEFR) 304, 309, 310, 314, 315, 330, 332–3
Solin, D. 133, 136
Sommer, J. 135, 161
Sonder, N. 312
Spence, D. 53
Spillane, T. 218
sponsors
  Australia *see* Australia, regulation of mutual funds, trustee and fund advisor and sponsor as responsible entity
  money market funds and shadow banking 230–31
Stadler, R. 343
Stecklow, S. 43, 229, 233
Stein, K. 238, 295
Stevens, P. 228, 264
Stevenson, A. 75, 292
Steverman, B. 32
Storck, M. 306, 329
Stork, V. 222
Strachman, D. 282
Strauts, T. 122
stress testing, money market funds and shadow banking 233, 237
Stulz, R. 280, 287
subadvisory suits, fee litigation 179–83
substitutes 25–6, 26–30
Sunstein, C. 25
supervision and monitoring 158, 210–11, 218–20, 312–13, 424, 438, 439
supply and demand imbalance issues, EU 320
Swagel, P. 232

Swedroe, L. 407–8
Sylla, R. 317
systemic risk 16–17, 263–5, 309, 317–18, 319, 332, 356–7
  see also risk management
systemically important financial institutions (SIFIs) 17, 234–5, 236, 280, 289, 290–91
Szylar, C. 388

Taha, A. 118, 120, 129
Tang, D. 146
target date funds 35, 112, 126, 133–4
taxation 27, 47, 114, 127, 167, 275, 325–6, 344, 355–6, 364, 366, 377
Team, T. 239
technical standards implementation, European investment fund law 311–12
technology and compliance 216, 217–20
Temple-West, P. 46
Tergesen, A. 28
Thaler, R. 25
Thel, S. 84, 85, 336
third countries, European investment fund law *see* European investment fund law, Single Capital Market, third countries
third country passports and equivalence standards, European investment fund law 323–4, 325–6
third party custody of funds, European investment fund law 350
third party inducements prohibition, UK 406–7
third party investment management, European investment fund law 337–8
Thomas, L. 268
Thompson, R. 295
Tian, Y. 411
time commitment, Ireland, boards of directors 376, 379
time saving benefits and operational efficiencies 198
timing, market timing 41, 49, 96–8, 121–2, 136
Timmons, H. 286
Tkac, P. 119
Tower, E. 408
transferable securities *see* European investment fund law, Undertakings for Collective Investments in Transferable Securities (UCITS) Directives
transparency concerns 256, 258, 260–63, 406–9

trash quota 352, 353–4
triangle, investment triangle law 327–9
Trifts, J. 120
trustees, Australia *see* Australia, regulation of mutual funds, trustee and fund advisor and sponsor as responsible entity
trusts, law of trusts, Australia 442–3
Turner, A. 410
twin funds 117

UCITS *see* Undertakings for Collective Investments in Transferable Securities (UCITS) Directives
UK
  Armitage v. Nurse 426
  Brown v. Innovator One 385
  FCA v. Capital Alternatives 385
  Financial Services Authority v. Fradley 385
  FSA v. Asset LI 385
  Raymond Bieber v. Teathers Ltd (in liquidation) 385
  rules displacing fiduciary standards 100
  In re Sky Land Consultants 385
UK, collective retail investment funds regulation 382–413
  borderline arrangements 385
  Brexit effects 358–9, 380, 382–3, 396, 405
  EU legislation role 385
  EU Markets in Financial Instruments Directive 389, 397, 406–7
  Financial Conduct Authority (FCA) 384–5, 401
  management companies 388–9, 395–9
  non-UCITS retail schemes (NURs) 384, 385, 395, 396, 399–400, 401, 403, 405
UK, collective retail investment funds regulation, financial crisis effects 389–400, 404
  conduct of business regulation 395–8
  De Larosière Report to European Commission recommendations 392–3
  depositary regulation 398–400
  and financial regulation reform 390–92
  investor disclosure document 393–5
  Key Investor Information Document (KIID) 394–5
  prudential management concerns 390
UK, collective retail investment funds regulation, market distortions 400–411
  active or passive management debate 407–9
  asset allocation by funds and asset managers 401
  closet 'index huggers' 408–9

Index 465

and common good services 407
destabilizing consequences 404–5
exchange-traded funds, market growth of 409–11
investor preference for low cost 405–11
money market funds 403–4
third party inducements prohibition 406–7
transparency and moderation in management retirement fees and charges, targetting 406–9
UK, collective retail investment funds regulation, UCITS regulation and harmonization impact 384–5, 386–9, 395–8, 400–405, 409, 411
asset growth 387
conflicts of interest 396–7
corporate governance mechanisms 388–9
depositary regulation 399
derivative products 388
disclosure provisions 388
internal control mechanisms 396
investor protection regime 388–9
portfolio diversification 387–8
risk management policies 396
safety appeal 386, 388
umbrella funds, Ireland 366–7
Undertakings for Collective Investments in Transferable Securities (UCITS) Directives
European Investment Fund law *see* European investment fund law, Undertakings for Collective Investments in Transferable Securities (UCITS) Directives
Ireland *see* Ireland, mutual fund governance, UCITS
UK *see* UK, collective retail investment funds regulation, UCITS regulation and harmonization impact
unit investment trusts (UITs) 36, 37, 60, 257, 416–17, 425
unitary boards 146, 191–2, 194–6, 201
unregistered investment options 240–41
US
Crowdfunding Act 295
Dodd–Frank Act 29, 46, 64, 66, 115, 130, 220, 221, 234, 263, 279–80, 288–9, 290, 292, 293–4
Employee Retirement Income Security Act (ERISA) 13, 28–9
Financial Industry Regulatory Authority (FINRA) 46, 47, 206

Internal Revenue Code 401(k) 13, 15, 112, 114, 123–4, 127, 133–4, 274, 276
Internal Revenue Code, Section 401(k) 1, 13, 14, 15
Investment Advisors Act 40, 59–60, 64–5, 66, 69, 70, 71, 73, 74, 75
Investment Company Act 2, 10, 12, 13–14, 15, 16, 19–20, 73, 74–5, 286, 288
JOBS Act 29, 279–80, 288–90, 292, 294
liquidity mimicking concerns 404
Pension Protection Act 134
Securities Act 14, 157, 189
Securities Exchange Act 9, 14, 46, 101, 105, 157, 189
Thrift Savings Plan 3
Truth in Lending Act 100
US, cases
Air Line Pilots Ass'n Int'l v. O'Neill 82
In re Banc of America Capital Management 97–8
Barnes v. Andrews 85
Bd. of Trs. of AFTRA Ret. Fund v. JPMorgan Chase Bank 87
Belmont v. MB Inv. Partners 94
In re Blackrock Mut. Funds Advisory Fee Litig. 159, 180, 181, 182–3, 214, 220
Brown v. Calamos 194, 195
Brown Shoe Co. v. U.S. 28
Burks v. Lasker 143, 144, 148
Burwell v. Hobby Lobby Stores 149
Campbell Harrison & Dagley L.L.P. v. Lisa Blue/Baron and Blue 85
Capital Research and Mgmt. Co. v. Brown 45
In re Caremark Int'l 85
Chamber of Commerce v. U.S. Department of Labor 158
Chevron U.S.A. v. NRDC 96
Chicago Mercantile Exchange v. Securities and Exchange Commission 248–9
In re Citigroup Global Markets 220
In re Columbia Mgt. Advisors and Columbia Funds Distributor 98
Daily Income Fund v. Fox 144, 155
Ernst & Ernst v. Hochfelder 101
Financial Planning Ass'n v. SEC 94
In re First Boston S'holders Litig. 148
Gartenberg v. Merrill Lynch Asset Management 155, 156, 164, 171–3, 175, 176, 178, 179, 182
Geman v. SEC 95–6
In re Goelzer Investment Management & Gregory W. Goelzer 218

In re Gutfreund 214, 215
Harvard College v. Amory 83
Herman & MacLean v. Huddleston 96
Hollingsworth v. Perry 69
Howard v. Shay 85
Hughes v. SEC 86
Janus Capital Group v. First Derivative Traders 149–50
Jones v. Harris Assoc. 144, 155, 156, 164, 173–6, 179, 180, 182, 183, 191, 193
Kahn v. M&F Worldwide Corp 151
Kahn v. Tremont 148
In re Kohlberg Kravis Roberts & Co. 75
Kornman v. SEC 96
Krinsk v. Fund Asset Management 155, 172
Meinhard v. Salmon 102–4
Metro Commun. Corp. BVI v. Advanced Mobilecomm Tech. 87
In re Moody's Corp. Sec. Litig. 88
Morris v. Wachovia Sec. 86
Northstar Financial Advisors v. Schwab Investments 62, 157, 284
In re Paradigm Capital Management 73–4
Press v. Quick & Reilly 104–5
Reading v. Regum 84
Redus-Tarchis v. New York Life Inv. Mgmt. 284
In re Reserve Fund Sec. & Derivative Litig. 43
In re Ruffle 73
R.W. Grand Lodge of F. & A.M. of Penn. v. Salomon Bros. All Cap Value Fund 284
Santa Fe Industries v. Green 94
Saxe v. Brady 166, 167, 169, 173, 175
SEC v. Blavin 82
SEC v. Capital Gains Research Bureau 71, 80, 81, 83, 88, 94, 98, 99
SEC v. Chenery Corp. 57, 83, 84
SEC v. Moran 95
SEC v. Ralston Purina Co. 284
SEC v. Slocum, Gordon, & Co. 95
SEC v. Steadman 80
SEC v. Strebinger 150
SEC v. Treadway 95
Sivolella v. AXA Equitable Insurance Co. 155
Sullivan v. Chase Inv. Serv. of Boston 88
Sullivan v. Harnisch 72
Tannenbaum v. Zeller 193
Tibble v. Edison Int'l 57
Transamerica Mortg. Advisors (TAMA) v. Lewis 72, 80, 93
TSC Indus. v. Northway 88
In re Urban 215
US v. E.I. du Pont de Nemours 28
US v. National Ass'n of Sec. Dealers 47
US v. O'Brien 85
In re Western Asset Management Company 220
US Securities and Exchange Commission (SEC)
  abandonment of mutual fund brand 50–53
  exchange-traded funds (ETFs) 260–61, 261–3
  fiduciary structure of investment management regulation 80
  investor protection *see* investor protection, SEC regulation
  and money market funds *see* money market funds and shadow banking, SEC Rules (2014)
  Rule 2a-7 33, 230, 233
  Rule 6c-11 39, 261
  Rule 12b-1 32, 44–6, 74–5, 118, 147, 157, 177
  Rule 18f-4, proposed 296–7

Van Binsbergen, J. 120
Van Setten, L. 341, 407
variable capital investment company, Ireland 365
Velasco, J. 82, 84, 85, 87
venture capital funds 63, 304, 309, 310, 314, 315, 330, 332–3
veto powers 67, 337, 428, 440
Volcker, P. 235
voting rights
  Australia 439–41
  and exit 153–4, 156
  proxy voting, fiduciary obligations 90–92
  see also shares and shareholders

Wachter, S. 391
Waggoner, J. 136, 194
Wallace, K. 270
Walsh, J. 205, 209, 210, 211, 217
Walsh, L. 75
Wang, W. 188
Waters, D. 83
Watson, M. 401
Weber-Rey, D. 312
Weinrib, E. 152
White, Mark 7, 360–81

White, Mary Jo 40, 46, 158, 215, 236, 279, 289, 292
Wiersema, M. 61
Wiese, K. 45
Wigglesworth, R. 240
Wilcox, R. 116, 119
Wilhelmi, R. 318, 345
Williams, A. 240
Williams, C. 400
Williamson, C. 197, 198
Williamson, O. 20
Wilmarth, J. 229
Wilmer, S. 240
Wilstein, S. 36

Wu, J. 128
Wyatt, M. 66
Wymeersch, E. 312, 410

Yang, J. 35
Yeung, A. 165, 166, 168
Youngdahl, J. 103

Zask, E. 284
Zetzsche, D. 7, 302–59
Zhang, J. 37
Zingales, L. 58, 77
Zitzewitz, E. 128
Zweig, J. 70, 127, 136